Southern Biography Series
WILLIAM J. COOPER, JR., EDITOR

JOHN A. QUITMAN

JOHN A. QUITMAN

Old South Crusader

Robert E. May

Louisiana State University Press

Baton Rouge and London

Library of Congress Cataloging in Publication Data

May, Robert E.
John A. Quitman: Old South crusader.

(Southern biography series)
Bibliography: p.
Includes index.
1. Quitman, John Anthony.   2. Mississippi—Politics and government—To
1865.   3. Mississippi—Governors—Biography.   4. Legislators—United
States—Biography.   5. United States. Congress. House—Biography.
6. Lawyers—Mississippi—Biography.   7. Secession.   I. Title.   II. Series.
F341.Q84M39   1984   976.2'03'0924 [B]   84-10019
ISBN 0-8071-1188-0
ISBN 0-8071-1207-0 (pbk.)

The author gratefully acknowledges permission to reprint the following: Excerpts
from the letter of John A. Quitman to Mansfield Lovell, March 15, 1850, in ML
364, by permission of the Huntington Library, San Marino, California; excerpts
from the John A. Quitman manuscripts, Monmouth, Natchez, Mississippi, by permission of Ronald Riches; excerpts from the John A. Quitman Papers, by permission of the Houghton Library, Harvard University, Cambridge, Massachusetts;
Chapter 11 herein, which appeared, in somewhat different form, as "John A.
Quitman and His Slaves: Reconciling Slave Resistance with the Proslavery Defense," in *Journal of Southern History*, XLVI (November, 1980).

Publication of this book has been assisted by a grant from the
Andrew W. Mellon Foundation.

Frontispiece: John A. Quitman at mid-life. Courtesy Monmouth, Natchez,
Mississippi, and Ronald Riches

For Beth and Heather

Contents

Contents

Illustrations

Maps

Preface

It is surprising how little has been written about the southern secession leaders. Though historians have long displayed an inordinate fascination with the Civil War, there are only a handful of thorough, book-length studies of the men who stoked the coals of secession and made possible the transformation of the Old South from region to nation.

Such neglect is particularly striking in the case of John Anthony Quitman, not only the premier secessionist of antebellum Mississippi—the second state to secede from the Union—but also one of the half dozen or so most prominent radicals and the most strident slavery imperialist in the entire South. Though Quitman—who achieved fame in the Mexican War, served in the U.S. House of Representatives at the climax of the Kansas crisis, and held highest rank in all three branches of Mississippi government— was hardly an obscure, behind-the-scenes manipulator, he has been the subject of only one published biography, J. F. H. Claiborne's two-volume *Life and Correspondence of John A. Quitman*, a work written before the Civil War which is neither comprehensive nor critical.

The following study of Quitman will, it is hoped, redress an important omission in southern political biography and facilitate a more subtle understanding of secessionist motivation and ideology. Quitman's career sheds light on many facets of the Old South's politics, economy, and mores, such as social mobility, political culture, family custom, martial propensities, master-slave relations, and the regional assimilation of transplanted Yankees. Study of his attitudes and behavior addresses such contemporary historiographical issues as whether the South's essence was bourgeois-capitalist or premodern and antibourgeois; Quitman crossed definition boundaries— he was too entrepreneurial to be a prebourgeois patriarch, yet too paternalistic to be an unmitigated capitalist. Still, Quitman deserves attention primarily because he was so instrumental in legitimizing and fomenting states' rights, and later secession, in Mississippi. Explaining his radicalization and describing his contribution to southern secessionism, therefore, are the primary concerns of this book.

Quitman's life, I feel, warns us against reducing secessionist motivation to facile formula or stereotype. A lot of recent research has proposed that the Old South's radicals were misfits or societal outsiders. Quitman, however, became an insider among Mississippi's elite society *prior* to his emergence as a radical politician, and his strong physique and martial air should bury presumptions that all radicals suffered from traumas of physiological inadequacies. Similarly, Quitman's career mocks traditional portrayals of secessionists as "fire-eaters" who trounced unionist rivals into submission through oratorical mastery—he was a terrible public speaker. What Quitman's history *does* illuminate is the truth of David M. Potter's essay of some twenty years ago, "The Historian's Use of Nationalism and Vice Versa," which attacked scholars so consumed with finding the roots of the Confederacy in Old South cultural uniqueness that they ignored shared values linking all Americans and which warned against categorization of antebellum northerners as unadulterated Americans and antebellum southerners as sectional deviates. Potter urged that we remember that the Old South's inhabitants conceived of themselves as both Americans *and* southerners with no sense of hypocrisy or reason to feel hypocritical. Quitman's life speaks to this observation. Although scholars have taken him as a pure radical, the "high priest of the secession cult in Mississippi," analysis of Quitman's thought and behavior teaches us that he only advocated secession for a few, separated years during a public career which spanned some three decades, that he approached disunion with a Calhounian sense of deep despair rather than with an exuberant southern nationalism (in fact, he never articulated a convincing case for the prospects of a new nation), and that his radicalism derived primarily from the rather specific mandates of a southwestern slave expansionist mentality and being a slaveowner under siege rather than from the conviction that southerners had lost all cultural commonality with the North. If Quitman, one of the South's most vocal and persistent radicals, pursued a halting course, we must ponder anew how agonized was the overall southern road to secession.

*

This biography has benefited so much from the assistance of a great many people that I am most reluctant to resort to the cliché that it would have been impossible without the help of others. I feel a deep sense of gratitude to those who far exceeded the requirements of professional duty or friendship to provide me with aid.

Space limitations preclude my listing the scores of librarians and archivists who have assisted me. Mention must be made, however, of several who provided special access to documents, alerted me to materials which would have otherwise passed unnoticed, or went beyond the call of duty in responding to my research requests: Michelle Hudson, Caroline Allen Killens, and Ronald E. Tomlin, Mississippi Department of Archives and History; Michael P. Musick, National Archives; Carolyn Wolf, Hartwick College Library; Jeanne Wilson, Barker Texas History Center Archives. Dr. Don E. Carleton, director of that repository, went out of his way to help me while I was there.

Lynda L. Crist, associate editor of *The Papers of Jefferson Davis*, alerted me, without any prompting on my part, to materials pertaining to Quitman which she discovered in the course of her work on those volumes. Ronald W. Miller, now Executive Director of the Historic Natchez Foundation, gave unstintingly of his time when I visited Natchez. He showed me around sites, such as Jefferson College, which had been touched by Quitman's career; he also shared with me his expertise about the structure and architectural style of Monmouth, Quitman's mansion. Mr. and Mrs. Thomas H. Gandy of Natchez provided access to their private collections of books from the Quitman family library and Natchez photographs and maps. Mrs. June McLendon, whose husband, the late James H. McLendon, wrote a fine dissertation about Quitman (University of Texas, 1949), generously shared with me some of his research materials. Frank E. Everett, Jr., author of *Brierfield: Plantation Home of Jefferson Davis* (1979), provided maps which enabled me to better understand Quitman's Palmyra plantation on the Mississippi River.

A Grant-in-Aid from the American Council of Learned Societies facilitated my research trip to Texas. Purdue University has supported the project with a summer "XL" (research) grant and a semester's appointment to the university's Center for Humanistic Studies. Purdue colleagues Oakah L. Jones and Walter O. Forster of the Department of History critiqued parts of the manuscript relating to their particular areas of scholarship. Ingeborg Maria Hinderschiedt of Purdue's Department of Foreign Languages and Literature and Gordon R. Mork of the Department of History translated German-language materials about Quitman's father.

I owe an incalculable debt to Ron Riches, owner of Monmouth. Ron's generosity in providing gratis copies of hundreds of privately owned manuscripts, printed documents, and photographs was overwhelming. Just as important, his enthusiasm for a published work on Quitman was infectious and helped me through some of the more difficult phases of research and writing. Similarly, there is no way to measure how much the support of my department head, Dr. Donald J. Berthrong, has meant. Don understood the need for a biography of Quitman, and alleviated my academic responsibilities whenever possible so that I could pursue that end. He also provided unlimited typing help. Finally, my wife Jill discovered Ron Riches for me and did some important editing. Much of this biography, in intangible as well as tangible ways, has her imprint upon it.

Abbreviations

DU	William R. Perkins Library, Duke University
HSP	Historical Society of Pennsylvania
HU	Houghton Library, Harvard University
LC	Library of Congress
LSU	Department of Archives and Manuscripts, Louisiana State University
MDA	Mississippi Department of Archives and History
M-N	Monmouth-Natchez (Private collection in the possession of Ronald Riches, owner of Monmouth)
NA	National Archives
NYHS	New-York Historical Society
SHC	Southern Historical Collection, University of North Carolina
UnS	Jessie Ball duPont Library, University of the South
UT	Barker Texas History Center Archives, University of Texas
UV	University of Virginia Library
JAQ	John Anthony Quitman
JMH	*Journal of Mississippi History*
PMHS	*Publications of the Mississippi Historical Society*
RG	Record Group

JOHN A. QUITMAN

1

Yankee Roots

S URELY John Anthony Quitman played Davy Crockett's charade as well as any politician of the day. Crockett, directing some healthy barbs at stump politicians, once observed how office seekers courted votes with "long-winded speeches" which denounced incumbents and hypocritically proclaimed their own disinterestedness in personal advancement.[1] Quitman fit the mold. He had a fetish for protracted speeches of up to three hours, and he constantly preached to audiences, political connections, friends, and relations that only a burning sense of duty to the public weal induced him to sacrifice the comforts of home and the demands of his private affairs for the tribulations of campaigning and the responsibility of position.

There is a marvelous—though probably apocryphal—tale, in fact, that Quitman was once rudely put down at a mass rally for taking this tactic just a bit too far. The story goes that Quitman had been telling his listeners how much he owed to the people of Mississippi for befriending him even though he had arrived in their midst an indigent newcomer, when a mountaineer wearing a coonskin cap and a patchwork coat approached the speaker's stand and stirred Quitman on to greater oratorical effusions by yelling, "Gin'ral! you're punkins!" Whereupon Quitman recalled his recent service as a general in the Mexican War, saying that when the "tocsin of war" sounded he had tried, to the best of his "humble" abilities, to prove himself worthy of his state's confidence: "It is always an invidious task to speak of self, but I think I may safely say that the flag of Mississippi under my guidance, was ever among the foremost in danger and in victory!" Coonskin exclaimed, "Gin'ral! you're *some* punkins!" When Quitman then said that although he had "toiled . . . unremitingly [*sic*]" for Mississippi in the past, he was ready to toil for her again, the mountaineer, tears flowing from his eyes, hurled his cap to the ground and stunned the crowd by saying, "Gin'ral! I'm goll

I

darned ef you ain't all punkins! an we've kept you workin' for us all yer life, an' it's a dam shame, so it is! I go in fur lettin' you rest a little bit now; an' so *I'll jest vote for the other man!*" [2]

Whether or not this particular incident actually occurred, Quitman did give many of his contemporaries the impression that he lusted for office more than was becoming. William Gwin even believed Quitman "one of the most bigotted egotists I have ever met, and all of his life eaten up with ambition." This may have been an unfair judgment coming from Gwin, a man who frankly admitted that his own migration to California was prompted solely by his anxiety for a U.S. Senate seat; certainly Gwin's assessment ignored the many times Quitman sacrificed political advancement to stand on principle. Still, too many of Quitman's other acquaintances volunteered commentary on Quitman's ambition for Gwin's calumny to be lightly dismissed. Truly, a craving for recognition and, more important, lasting fame underlay Quitman's emergence within the upper echelons of military and political life in both his region and nation. Quitman's ambition drove him beyond wealth to become a classic expression of what before the Civil War they called the "public man." [3]

For this ambition, Quitman could thank the circumstances of his upbringing. Quitman's father, the Reverend Frederick Henry Quitman, expected Quitman to follow his example and be a Lutheran minister, and saw to it that John was trained for the cloth. Had John capitulated to his father's will, he would never have become a southerner, much less one of the region's foremost defenders. To no small degree, Quitman's life constituted a renunciation of this paternal design.

*

Far more than geography separated the circumstances of John Quitman's childhood from the elitist southern mansion society he would represent and champion as an adult. There was nothing glamorous about the Hudson River valley town of Rhinebeck, New York, where he spent his first years. The vista was pleasant enough, with the lush Catskill Mountains nearby. But a "plain, homely set" of Palatine and Dutch farmers constituted the bulk of the local population, and the Quitman family lived what John's elder sister Louisa would later describe as the "plain country life." [4]

The Reverend Frederick Henry Quitman and his wife Anna were immigrants, recently come to Rhinebeck. Reverend Quitman, a Rhenish German born in 1760 in the duchy of Cleves near The Netherlands, had been educated at the University of Halle. He tutored for a while following his graduation, before receiving ordination from the Lutheran Consistory of the United Provinces of Amsterdam, which assigned him to a congregation on the Dutch West Indies island of Curaçao. Frederick arrived in approximately 1783, and it was there that he met John's mother, the daughter of the island's governor. They married, started a family, and battled the tropical heat and diseases for over a decade. William Frederick, Frederica, and Louisa were born before Frederick and Anna departed from the Indies.[5]

In 1795, Frederick and Anna sailed for the United States, where Frederick was welcomed with open arms by the Lutheran church hierarchy. With his Halle background, he was a boon to the new republic's Lutheran community. Lacking in theological seminaries, the American Lutheran church depended upon trained Europeans for leadership. Quitman quickly procured a dual assignment to congregations in Schoharie and Kobles Kill (Cobleskill), villages west of Albany, New York. Sometime prior to February, 1798, Quitman moved on to assume ministerial duties at Rhinebeck.[6]

Rhinebeck proved a taxing assignment for the immigrant pastor. Though based at St. Peter's Church—or the "Old Stone Church"—there, he had in his charge three additional congregations in the vicinity. His contract committed him to preach a set number of Sundays and festival days at each locale, and he also had to handle marriages, baptisms, and other church procedures. The one weekend a year for which he was unscheduled enabled him to attend the New York Ministerium synod, the ruling body of the Lutheran hierarchy in the state. For his work he received use of the ten-room Rhinebeck parsonage, situated atop a hill a short distance from the church, as living quarters for his family, as well as a modest monetary income, bushels of wheat, and firewood. Frederick was also entitled to use church lands for personal purposes, and his family kept a garden where they raised asparagus and other vegetables.[7]

Later, Frederick shouldered even heavier burdens, accepting a call to the congregation in Pine Plains (a settlement well to the east) and serving as president of the board of trustees of a Lutheran seminary from 1816 to 1828. Since public education belonged to the future and pedagogy was expected of ministers at that time, Frederick dispensed sacred and classical literature to the youth of his congregations. In 1807, the Ministerium designated him "Theological Professor" to prepare ministerial aspirants for ordination.[8]

A "brief, practical, biblical and impressive" preacher by reputation, Frederick experienced a meteoric rise within his state's Ministerium. Competent in English, German, and Dutch, he overwhelmed his colleagues with his language proficiency and theological erudition. Elected secretary as early as 1797, he had to wait only ten years to advance to president. Frederick retained the presidency for nearly two decades, and molded the Ministerium to his theological bent. His training at Halle had stressed rationalism, scientific research, and intellectual freedom, and he infused such values into the church. Thus he coaxed against the Calvinist doctrine of predestination and its insistence that a cruel God "sports with the Misery of his Creatures" by bestowing his blessing on a chosen few; and he wrote a rationalist catechism in English which sanctioned the use of "reason" to achieve understanding of an abstract, impersonal deity.[9]

Meanwhile, Frederick's family grew rapidly. Stephen Henry was born in Schoharie. John, born September 1, 1799, and baptized Johan Anton (the Germanic spelling was soon dropped), was the first of Anna's children in Rhinebeck. Ike Albert followed on September 1, 1800. On July 26, 1802, there was another girl, Anna Eliza. Possibly constant childbirth undermined the health of John's mother. She passed away in February, 1805, when John was only six years old. Family legend, however, has it that she had never adjusted to the Rhinebeck winters, and that her homesickness for Curaçao caused her death.[10]

Of John's growing up in a drafty, overcrowded parsonage, we know relatively little. Surviving family correspondence maintains silence on his childhood, and he was not prone to discuss it in any depth when he was an adult. On a rare occasion when he did refer to his early years, he portrayed them in disarmingly pastoral terms. What remained with him were images of the "old winter apple-tree," the village's "tranquil shades," and the "delights of cakes, apples and nuts" on Christmas Eve. Other glimpses of Quitman's youth reveal him romping with his brothers in nearby woods and finding playmates among the families whose residences were near the parsonage. A childhood friend remembered that John spent some of his time making violins and a set of chessmen, and playing chess and sports. It was a very modest, unpretentious life, one that he would strive to escape.[11]

What the record neglects is how John was raised and evidence of his early character formation and values. Nothing, for instance, survives about Anna's personality, much less what influence she might have exerted upon John. We also lack insight as to whether John was affected significantly by her premature death. In the absence of substantive material, one can only insert a few intriguing questions. Why, of the many Quitman children, were John and his sister Frederica the only ones to eventually marry? Was there something about the Quitman upbringing that produced social maladjustment? Did Quitman's brother William, who practiced medicine in both Rhinebeck and New York City as an adult, for instance, have manic-depressive tendencies? William admitted his own "unfortunate bias," his "always looking forward to a miserable futurity of anticipating the most gloomy consequences of every action. I have always been much given to despondency, have often not acted because I feared evil would result instead of good." Should significance be attached to a single description of John's being temperamental, prone to challenge authority, and subject to extended bouts of "gloom and melancholy" during his childhood?[12]

One aspect of John's upbringing, however, is apparent. His father designed his education to prepare him for the ministry. Reverend Quitman, in fact, may have intended a religious dynasty. He prodded John's brother William, who was appointed a vicar in 1807 and was presented as a candidate for the ministry in 1809. He also remarried about a year after Anna's death into a strategically connected Lutheran family. Mary Mayer had two sons who were Lutheran ministers: Philip F. Mayer of St. John's Church in Philadelphia, and Frederick G. Mayer of Ebenezer Lutheran Church in Albany. Both attended Ministerium synods, as did Mary's son-in-law, Dr. Augustus Wackerhagen, who had become minister at St. Paul's Church back in Schoharie. Wackerhagen, moreover, served as secretary during much of Reverend Quitman's presidency. Since there were generally fewer than twenty delegates at Ministerium gatherings, the Quitman family constituted a virtual caucus.[13] Had John accepted the cloth, Reverend Quitman's hand would have been further strengthened.

Frederick personally supervised John's early education, and then sent him when about ten to live with Wackerhagen and his wife in the Schoharie parsonage. Frederick anticipated that Wackerhagen—a skilled linguist and a graduate of the University of Göttingen—would broaden John's training, and left his son under his stepson-in-law's tutelage at least until the onset of the War of 1812. Wackerhagen found John a conscientious, courteous student already "well posted in Greek and Latin," and witnessed John's athletic prowess and interest in hobbies. Still engaged in making violins, John had also begun collecting birds, insects, and reptiles.

Sometime during the war, John returned to Rhinebeck, and Reverend Quitman again assumed responsibility for his education. John now hunted during his spare time; he trapped muskrats, and sold their skins to help pay for his clothing. A friend recalled that John was a better shot than his peers, and that he learned the lessons that his "venerable Father gave us sooner than all of us." The characteristics of leadership that John demonstrated as an adolescent would become much more apparent later on.[14]

In the fall of 1816, John was sent off again, this time to the relative wilderness of Otsego County, so that he could study theology and earn some money teaching at a Lutheran school which had opened in the little town of Hartwick. Hartwick Academy, though technically an academy of the classics when it opened in December, 1815, was the product of a two-decade-long struggle by the Ministerium to establish an institution to train Lutheran ministers, and it became a seminary by charter of the Regents of the University of the State of New York the following summer. John's father, a member

5

John A. Quitman

(as were Frederick Mayer and Augustus Wackerhagen) of the board of trustees, may have seen Hartwick as a way to train a cadre of family ministers; its principal, Ernest L. Hazelius, was an erudite Lutheran pastor whose Bible instruction classes were a major part of the curriculum. When John boarded the stage for Otsego at Albany that fall, his sandy-haired younger and closest brother Albert accompanied him. By 1817, a nephew, Frederick W. Quackenboss, had paid tuition at Hartwick.

A recently completed two-story brick building on the east side of the town, Hartwick Seminary was located near the point where the upper Susquehanna River almost flows into Otsego Lake. Though only nineteen students attended the school's opening, enrollments often went much higher—there were sixty-six by April, 1817. Attendance proved highly erratic. Students would appear in the middle of terms, and courses had to be quickly arranged on an *ad hoc* basis to accommodate them. All students (with the exception of theological students, who received training free) paid moderate fees for their tuition, ranging, as of October of the next year, from $3 to $6 per quarter, depending upon an individual's course of study. An employee who made winter fires and cleaned rooms was supported by a surcharge.[15]

As assistant to Dr. Hazelius, John played the Renaissance scholar, offering a range of courses that would stagger most modern educators. He taught in both the elementary and secondary divisions, handling assignments in Latin, Greek, arithmetic, English grammar, composition, and geography. John had to rise early in the morning and study until classes commenced at nine; it was the only way he could keep ahead of his charges. John's students were older than he and, conscious of his vulnerability, they sought to embarrass him with perplexing questions. Eventually he gained confidence, found the students less demanding, and even disparaged them as lacking sufficient academic motivation.[16]

There was, however, time for the lighter pleasures, and John gave increasing attention to the opposite sex. A surviving letter to an unidentified female, written in February, 1818, reveals John's borrowing her copy of *Paradise Lost*, daydreaming about her, and developing a rather flowery writing style. The "icy hand" of winter had dispersed the birds whose "melodious notes, warbled on Crumhorn hill, tickled the ear of the wandering lover, and melted his heart into a sweet melancholy." John's vulnerability to "Cupid's dart"—as he put it, in a playful verse mocking the romantic inclinations of a Hartwick companion—apparently troubled his father, for Reverend Quitman warned that John should avoid "passions" which would undermine his "health and peace of mind" and his "future prospects." But John continued to put aside his books for rounds of parties, picnics, sleighing, and ice-skating. There was also time to go rowing with Albert on Otsego Lake, and to cement a friendship with Henry Pohlman, who had journeyed from Albany with them for the 1816 fall session. Initially Pohlman was one of John's students; following his advancement from the common school to the academy the two became boon companions. John, Albert, and Pohlman all participated in the seminary's debating club, the Philophronean Society. For about two and a half years, few outside concerns impinged upon John's protected Hartwick existence, and, for a brief interlude, time seemed to stand still. "Mountains—before, behind and on each side—fence us in from the inquisitive world," John reflected.[17]

Time, of course, could wait only so long. Decisions about a career loomed, and John sensed that he lacked his father's devout nature and commitment to Lutheranism. He had already given some signs that he wanted something more active than the ministry. During the martial excitement of the War of 1812, a United States Army recruiter had arrived in Schoharie's vicinity, and the village became a mobilization center for volunteers. Young John had formed a company of his friends to imitate the soldiers' drills, and so ingratiated himself with the troops and the recruiter that his mock company was presented with a drum, fife, and a pair of colors. John, while at Hartwick, did not know exactly what occupation he would choose. But he did sense that he craved prestige and material success in the temporal world, and this realization probably triggered the occasional bouts of depression which punctuated the latter part of his stay at Hartwick. Frederick hoped that John could conquer such doubts with an increased exertion of will power. "What reason can a young man have for melancholy," he wrote, "unless they be of his own creation? Occasional propensity to gloom seems to be a family complaint; but this ought to be counteracted as early as possible." But the problem was not solved so easily.[18]

By early 1818, John was planning to leave Hartwick. An immediate break, however, would have left the school shorthanded, so John postponed his departure until summer. (Pohlman noted on February 1, "Our school here goes on bravely. We have in the common school between twenty and thirty and in the Academy about thirty, therefore Mr. Quitman will not go as yet a while.") Finally, armed with a recommendation from Principal Hazelius, John made his way to Philadelphia in August and, after his arrival, arranged to join the staff of Mount Airy College, a Catholic academy some eight miles outside the city. Here John would be adjunct professor of English, at a salary of $350 a year plus board, lodging, washing, and fuel. Even before his teaching duties commenced, however, John expressed reservations that life at the institution would prove too restricted, and resolved that he would limit his stay to a year.[19]

Founded in 1807 by the immigrant priest Francis Xavier Brosius, Mount

7

Airy, when John arrived, was under its third principal, a Strasbourg-born and Paris-educated bachelor named P. F. Blondin Constant. A single stone building, the academy was so close to the heavily traveled Germantown Road that pedestrians walked under its second-story balcony. Surrounding the structure were the school water pump, stables, barns, hog pens, and a walled latrine. Academy curriculum emphasized languages, history, geography, and mathematics.[20]

From the beginning, John was restless at Mount Airy. It was partly that he had wearied of teaching; he lacked the motivation to spend six hours a day in the classroom. But the responsibilities of guardianship particularly sapped his enthusiasm. Whether or not legends are true about chaotic night-time pillow fights, these were students who bore surveillance. John's schedule included supervision of study hall for an hour every morning and an hour every evening. Since his father expected him to continue his own education simultaneously, he also threw himself into study of the Spanish language, benefiting from the presence of a recently naturalized Spaniard who was on the staff. This language facility would one day be a boon, but John had no way of knowing this and spent much of his time remembering with pangs the "charming female society" he had enjoyed at Hartwick and worrying about passing all his spare moments with his fellow teachers. John liked the other instructors and found some of them amusing, describing one as "a poor sheepish Yankee, afraid of a fly, and the butt of all the others," but fretted that he could not escape into Philadelphia. Reassurances from his father that social deprivations might "perhaps be remedied in time" proved an insufficient salve.[21]

Besides, John aspired to "something more than a mere support" for himself. A mere support had been all that Reverend Quitman, for all his influence and publications, had ever managed for his family. There was no "paternal inheritance"—as Louisa put it some years later—for the Quitman children to anticipate. This, for some reason, grated especially on John, who wanted at least to live "genteelly."[22]

John thought back upon an experience he had at Hartwick. While taking a mail stage one day, he had conversed with Platt Brush, a Dutchess County native who had established a law practice with his brother (and soon-to-be congressman) Henry in Chillicothe, Ohio. Brush encouraged John to take up preliminary studies toward a legal career, apparently made some very enthusiastic comments about opportunities to the west, and may have extended a tentative offer that John become an apprentice in his firm. Whatever the case, John now saw Brush as a means to an alternative career. He wrote home in March, 1819, that he was planning to write to Brush, and that he definitely would leave the Philadelphia environs, which were "dull" and offered no chance for adventures. The Panic of 1819 had brought distress to town, and John, noting the failure of countinghouses, concluded naïvely that prosperity could be found in the "wide fields open South and West, where much can be done with little money." Brush responded that John would indeed be welcome in Chillicothe, and could tutor his sons for a subsistence until he was ready to tackle the bar. Quickly John made plans and, by June, broke the news to his father that he would be the first in the household to leave the East.[23]

Frederick accepted John's decision as gracefully as might be expected, for his dream of a family dynasty controlling the Lutheran church was fast fading away. William had decided to become a physician, necessitating Reverend Quitman's announcement at the 1813 synod of the Ministerium that his son had renounced the ministry and was returning his license to preach. At about the same time that John turned his eyes toward the bar, Albert had joined in the merchant marine. Nor could Dominie Quitman, now double-chinned and whitened with age, hope to carry on much longer, for by 1819 he was racked by infirmities apparently brought on by obesity. Legend has it that Reverend Quitman's 330 pounds necessitated a rope specially rigged from an iron ring so that he could raise himself from bed. His last years in the ministry were marked by physical indignities such as having to be carried to his pulpits, and by intellectual disappointment as pietistic emotions released by the Second Great Awakening reversed the rationalistic course he had set for the New York Ministerium. Although Frederick lingered until 1832, he resigned all ministerial duties in 1825 and the family remained at the parsonage only on the charity of an increasingly evangelical Rhinebeck congregation.[24]

Reverend Quitman thus allowed only a hint of disapprobation to creep into a reluctant endorsement of John's intentions. Letting John know that the break from the ministry did not catch him unawares, he spoke of his dislike for the way lawyers had to flatter people to get ahead. However, he also declared that John had reached the age of "discretion" and that he would never compel his children "to enter upon any occupation against their own inclination." The complaint was far too feeble to affect John's outlook in any way, and John not only forged ahead with his own plans but also did what he could to smooth Albert's break from home. John's feelings came out most vividly, in fact, in a letter endorsing Albert's course, when he exclaimed, "Why should any human being be tortured by an occupation in which he can find no happiness?"[25]

One can only wonder whether in the end Reverend Quitman's faith and ministry were too abstract and scholarly, too rational, for successful transmission to his children. One son, Henry, may have found evangelicalism more appealing; Henry's tombstone was inscribed "I will arise" because of a childhood confession of faith during a discussion of death.[26] John, on the other hand, seems to have relegated religion to a subsidiary position in his life. John would discard his Lutheranism as inconvenient soon after leaving Pennsylvania, and apparently experienced conversion only on his deathbed, when his confession may have been more an easing of his family's anguish than an expression of his own salvation. This minister's son had determined, by the end of adolescence, to make his mark in the temporal world.

*

In the early morning of October 21, 1819, young John Anthony, accompanied by a traveling companion named Whiting, boarded a Pittsburgh-bound stage out of Philadelphia and cast his lot, like thousands of other countrymen after the War of 1812, with America's West. The recent fighting had greatly diminished Indian power across the mountains, and throngs of easterners, enticed by laudatory travelers' accounts and promotional literature from town newspapers in Ohio and other parts of today's Midwest, took up "squatting" there and capitalized on recently liberalized terms for purchasing land at government land offices. Pittsburgh, with its strategic location, had become a gateway to the region.[27]

The trip to Pittsburgh consumed an unnecessary thirteen days. John and Whiting, irritated by what they considered an exorbitant stage fee, made part of the journey on foot. From Pittsburgh, which struck John as dingy because of the coal dust emitted by its factories, the two took cabin passage aboard a Kentucky keelboat for their trip down the Ohio River. Always gregarious, John wasted little time making the acquaintance of his fellow cabin passengers. A journal which he maintained during the trip downriver records rounds of whist and a good share of drinking with the males aboard. His cloistered Mount Airy experience, however, had left John especially starved for female companionship, and when the boat put in to shore the first night, he persuaded Mary Griffith, the daughter of New Jersey state legislator William Griffith, to join him for a walk on the riverbank. Mary, traveling with her mother, was on her way to visit brothers in Natchez. Thereafter John gave Mary quite a bit of attention. He played his flute to her while they sat under a tree, carved her initials on a Virginia oak, discussed the merits of Sir Walter Scott's *Lady of the Lake*, and mused about certain "sentiments" which she had expressed about him. Mary, in turn, teased him about his breaking the Sabbath by shooting ducks. On November 14 he exulted, "This evening I was presented, for my gallantry with a beautiful lock of Miss

Griffith's hair, in spite of my breaking the 4 commandment." Romance helped suffuse the whole voyage with a rosy light, and John came to appreciate the river which carried him along. "I[t] seemed," he wrote, "as if we were gliding down a stream of fairy land." [28]

The journey passed so pleasantly that John found it painful, when the boat arrived at Portsmouth, due south of Chillicothe, to take leave of his new companions. Watching the keelboat with all "familiar faces" fade into the distance, John fought a momentary bout of depression as he became aware that his travels had suddenly left him "alone in the world." Fortuitously, he did not have to linger in this state very long. Encountering a man who needed a horse delivered to Chillicothe, John accepted the responsibility and was able to make his way quickly to his destination. Late in the afternoon of November 22, after two days of hard riding, he dismounted at a Chillicothe inn, exclaiming to a startled innkeeper, "Hic labor extremis, hic meta longarum viarum." [29]

John's new hometown was one of Ohio's more established communities. Located on a bend in the Scioto River (which joined the Ohio at Portsmouth), Chillicothe was surrounded by some of Ohio's best farmland. Thomas Hulme, who traveled there a few months prior to John's arrival, observed "very rich lands on passing Paint Creek, and on approaching the Scioto River"; and local newspapers contained notices that delinquent subscribers could pay their bills in wheat, rye, corn, pork, potatoes, butter, and other farm products, advertisements for a steam flour mill and the "Farmer's Hotel," columns about how flaxseed could be used for cattle feed and why crops adjacent to woods did not grow well, and statements, which reassured local husbandmen, that agriculture was the "noblest of all the arts, because it is the most useful." [30]

Chillicothe had been carved out of the Virginia Military District, land set aside for Virginia veterans of the American Revolution; most of the early settlers, therefore, came from Virginia and its offspring Kentucky. Once Chillicothe had been the most important town in Ohio, serving as both territorial and state capital. In its heyday, it had displayed some of Ohio's most fashionable society, with parties, dances, and elaborate meals prepared by free black servants who preserved traditions cultivated in Virginia mansions. Amid the town's log cabins, there were many large Georgian-style homes with state dining rooms patterned after Virginia plantation residences. Although Columbus became the capital in 1816, Chillicothe when John arrived was still a dynamic community, with a courthouse, copper and tin producers, several inns and taverns, churches, banks, a theater, a brewery, and a textile mill. It had, as one traveler put it that year, "considerable business for its size." But there was no sewage system, and Hulme noted disapprovingly that the town gave off a stench because of water stagnating on its very level streets.[31]

Soon after arriving, John ironed out the final terms of his situation with Platt Brush. It was agreed that he would study law in Brush's office, room at Brush's house, eat at that residence, and have his clothes washed there. In return, John would instruct Brush's sons in the classics and teach Brush the Spanish language.[32]

John plunged into his studies immediately and engrossed himself in the standard legal text of the day, Sir William Blackstone's *Commentaries on the Laws of England*. He spent months on the *Commentaries*, at some sacrifice to his social life. But ambition John had aplenty—he was, after all, bound to live "genteelly." He boasted in a letter to his sister, "I traveled one thousand miles, sometimes on foot, but as a gentleman." Thus, the sacrifices would prove their worth, and he explained, "Blackstone occupies all my thoughts; and transferring property engages my mind. . . . I have . . . a profession to study, a fortune to accumulate, then perhaps I may again think of amusement." He also aided Platt Brush with legal correspondence and the preparation of cases; invested in a copy of the various state constitutions at a book auction; attended circuit court in Chillicothe; and by March had graduated from Blackstone to George Cooper's volume on English equity law. He progressed satisfactorily, for although Brush chided him "how frequently we overrate our abilities," he noted on May 13, 1820, that "Mr. Brush in the evening gave me great hopes, of doing well in my profession."[33]

Just as significant were the contacts John developed with other young aspirants to the bar, as Chillicothe supported a large legal community because of the frequency of court sessions held there. John would stay up until all hours, arguing Blackstone or playing chess with fellow students, and he also joined a legal debating society called the Gougers, which argued the merits of trials in local courts. One of John's peers was John T. McMurran, who would later follow him to Natchez and become his law partner.

Such contacts expanded when John attended the Ohio legal circuit as Brush's assistant. Ohio lawyers at that time represented an extremely tight-knit community, as they were thrown together on circuit in abominable accommodations, sometimes lodging eight or ten to a room. The beds frequently were vermin-infested, and John found inn fare on the circuit unpleasantly coarse.[34]

John's preoccupations, however, were not solely legal. Unscholarly by instinct, he retained an adventurous streak—if disappointed in his expectations of legal success, he anticipated, he would become a "good soldier, or a fur trader in the Rocky Mountains." So he sought out fellow huntsmen, and continued those outdoor activities which had been so important during his New York boyhood. "After dinner I went gunning accompanied by Hinckston," John recorded. "We crossed Paint Creek and had hardly got in the hills before I decried an immense flock of turkies feeding on the ground. Immediately crawled within about 200 yards of them and let go . . . wounded several but got none. They flew a little way, we followed up. . . . I continued following them till night." He was proud of his shooting abilities, boasting in his diary that he won matches and writing home that "they consider me here a crack shot with a rifle." He had so much pride in his physical prowess that after he suffered a couple of black eyes in a fracas on the streets he avoided public view until his eyes healed.[35]

John had less success in his initial Chillicothe social endeavors. He found the town dull at first, and wondered whether he would be able to say at the end of his life "Vixi—I have lived." Rather than despair, however, he sought out social opportunities, attending a musical society, going to a Thespian performance, and virtually mapping a campaign to meet the town's eligible women. He seems to have attended the Episcopal church primarily as a scouting expedition. He wrote on December 4, 1819, "In the morning I went to the Episcopal church, was much disappointed in not seeing any pretty girls. The scarcity of this precious commodity . . . is . . . astonishing." Next week he tried the Presbyterian church, apparently without any better luck, and later switched back to Episcopal attendance.[36]

Once John gained entrée into Chillicothe society—apparently through the parties and gatherings at the Brush residence—he found an almost confusing array of young belles. He was charmed by Alice Claypoole and her sister, Sarah, visited their residence regularly, and escorted them around town. He wrote on Washington's birthday, 1820, "At night we had a ball numerously attended by beaux and belles. Miss Alice Claypoole shone foremost. . . . I did not return before two o'clock." However, a "Miss Taylor" improved "upon acquaintance" and became "more intimate with me." And yet another female companion "almost gave me a fever" by her charms and smiles at a ball at the Brush residence. John offered mock protest in his diary about how easy a victim he was for "powerful Cupid": "Alas! What an unhappy person am I. As soon as I see a pretty face that is new to me, as soon as I receive a kind word or even a look from a pretty girl; my heart is gone." But he cherished every minute of being one of Chillicothe's gay blades, and often stayed up partying until two or three in the morning.[37]

John soon, however, had to put Chillicothe society behind him. His mentor, Platt Brush, in the spring of 1820 received a political plum—the position of register at the federal land office in Delaware, a town north of Columbus. Ohio land sales had been booming. Between 1812 and 1821, Ohio land offices disposed of more acres of public land than did federal land offices anywhere else in the nation. Times were getting worse, and a new act to take effect on July 1 would eliminate the credit purchases of federal land which had led to considerable defaulting in recent years. Nevertheless, the same legislation reduced the minimum acreage purchase to eighty and the minimum price to $1.25 an acre. Brush could expect substantial business; thus he asked John to accompany him to Delaware and assist him as clerk, promising that John would have ample time to continue his legal studies.[38]

John accepted the offer, but found it hard to sever ties with his Chillicothe circle. He engaged in a last round of dancing with the belles and drinking with his legal friends—noting that his mood of melancholy led him to "dissipation"—and made his last social calls. Ever the sentimentalist regarding women at this stage of his life, he wrote on July 13, "Loaded some waggons with furniture. I called upon the Misses Claypooles. . . . Sarah was not at home. Oh fortune do not force one away without seeing her." But he rationalized the separation on the grounds that he was too vulnerable to "sirens" and that he had been distracted from his books. On July 14, he copied forms at the Chillicothe land office so that he would have working documents at his new job, and "rolled off in a gig towards Delaware." About two in the afternoon of July 16, he arrived at his newest residence.[39]

Although Delaware boasted such signs of civilization as a newspaper, gristmills, tanneries, and stagecoach service in 1820, it provided a far more provincial setting for John's apprenticeship than had Chillicothe. Delaware—and Delaware County—had been settled recently, and the whole township included just 797 people in 1820. Deer, turkey, and other wildlife were abundant, the town found it necessary to offer bounties on wolves, and roads became impassable during the wet season. John described Delaware as sitting "on the very edge of white population," and he encountered Seneca Indian towns on travels in the neighboring area. Possibly such experiences kindled his later fervent imperialism. If, as has been suggested by some authorities, attitudes developed initially toward Indian tribes underlay America's nineteenth-century philosophy of territorial expansion at the expense of other peoples, then John may have demonstrated this evolution. Listening to tales of Indian wars and atrocities, he could little help but internalize the prevailing dislike of "red sons of the forest." Thus, after visiting some Indian mounds, he reflected that on a mound top "perhaps the victim of war has been tied to the stake and sacrificed to barbarous ferocity."[40]

John worked hard in Delaware as Brush's clerk. Land sales required a lot of paper work, as far more was involved than a one-step transaction; following auction sales, receipts had to be sent to the General Land Office in Washington, and when signed patents were returned they had to be delivered to the purchaser. Lands not purchased at auction were subsequently available at the minimum $1.25 price, "the finest opening for colossal fortunes in the world," in John's words. Sales proved brisk, and John spent countless hours poring over tract books. In August, 1821, a month when Brush's office offered forty-five townships at auction, John observed that the transactions kept him occupied "day and night." [41]

But these were hours well spent. John was accumulating a knowledge of land law which would prove invaluable in his later Mississippi speculations, and he was continuing to progress in his legal studies. Brush encouraged John to believe that a partnership was in the offing, and John hurried through William Cruise's *A Digest of the Laws of England Respecting Real Property*. He also handled at least one case for Brush in everything but name, and attended court sessions, learning the ins and outs of practical application. [42]

Meanwhile, he continued tutoring Brush's children, [43] and, despite an intriguing claim in a letter home that he found keeping close to his office and out of "public concerns" the "best method of acquiring and retaining popularity," John was hardly a recluse. He joined the local debating society—which considered such questions as "Is the form of the government of the U.S. preferable to that of Great Britain?"—and dabbled in journalism, submitting pieces to the Delaware *Gazette*. He also attended teas and the formal Christmas ball, where he refused to dance when it was decided that partners would be chosen by lot—John had an eye for beauty, and had no intention of taking his chances on the field. More significantly for his later career, he commenced serious involvement in military affairs. He volunteered for militia duty, which meant a considerable amount of drilling. On Independence Day, 1821, John's volunteer unit, the "Independent Rifle Corps" of Delaware, elected him first lieutenant. When the captain fell sick the next month, John assumed command of the company. [44]

John's legal studies reached fruition in late July, 1821, when the supreme court was sitting in Delaware. Platt Brush felt that John's abilities merited application to the Ohio bar, and John followed his advice. On the evening of the twenty-seventh, after a day of fretting whether he would ever be summoned, John underwent an examination of "several hours" rendered by two supreme court judges and three practicing lawyers. The next day, Brush told him that he had passed, and John took his oath before the day was out. [45]

John, however, had no intention of establishing an Ohio practice. During his keelboat trip, Mrs. Griffith had urged him to consider Mississippi as a destination. Since her sons had built up lucrative law practices at Natchez, he might do the same. John could not forget what she had said, and within half a year of his arrival at Chillicothe, he apparently made at least a few inquiries about prospects in the South. "No country town I perceive is free from gossip," he wrote. "The ladies brought a story from Cincinnati that I was hurrying to complete my studies in order to move down the Mississippi."

By the following winter, John had decided to try his fortunes in either Natchez or St. Stephens, Alabama, and had taken up French in earnest so that he would be able to adjust more rapidly to the culture of the lower Mississippi River valley, which had been under the dominion of France and Spain during the eighteenth century. He may, at this point, have written Mrs. Griffith for more specific information; in April, prior to returning to New Jersey from Natchez, she sent him a letter reinforcing her earlier suggestions. Natchez, she reiterated, offered an "excellent place to make money." The Natchez bar would prove less competitive than in the North, since most young men in the community fell prey to "profligacy and idleness." Natchez also boasted a "gay and fashionable" society. She promised that if John came to Natchez—warning that he would have to put up with heat and mosquitoes in the summer—she would provide him a letter of introduction to her sons which would open the gates to Natchez society. And she reassured him that transferring into the Natchez bar could be effected with ease; a practicing attorney in another state need merely ask for an examination. No additional study was required. Because of her persuasiveness, John dropped all thought of moving to Alabama and planned on going to Natchez.[46]

It was the condition of Ohio's legal profession which caused John to abandon the state. John moved to Delaware in 1820 fully expecting to join Brush as a partner. In August, 1820, he borrowed $137.78 from Brush to buy some 110 acres of land in the Delaware District, and that same month he suggested that one of his brothers effect a permanent move to Ohio; the next month he wrote an eastern acquaintance that he would "stake every thing on the rapid progress of this region," and hoped that with luck the time would come when he would "reap the reward of my labor." But, gradually, John concluded that the prospects for the Ohio bar were dim.[47]

Events had simply not fulfilled John's expectation that he could escape bad times in Philadelphia by moving west. Ohio, prior to John's arrival, saw a proliferation of banks designed around the need for bank credit to finance land purchases during a specie shortage. The notes which then flooded the state had no metallic backing, for stock in banks could be purchased upon a mere promise to pay money later. All went well for a while, so long as the Second Bank of the United States branches at Cincinnati and Chillicothe accepted the state bank notes. But in 1818 those branches had refused to extend further credit, which led to failures of state banks and foreclosures upon many Ohio citizens. Hard times undercut farm prices: wheat dropped from $1.45 a bushel in 1818 to $.72 a bushel in 1820. Since money and credit were scarce, Ohio citizens could ill afford to pay lawyers' fees, and they often offered depreciated lands or personal goods as substitutions. Relief laws, moreover, made it difficult for lawyers to recover debts.[48]

The more John reflected on these conditions, the more determined he was to move south. He complained in February, 1821, that Ohio farmers did not have "money enough . . . to give their babies to cut their first teeth with." But in Mississippi and Alabama and the greater South, cotton, sugar, tobacco, and rice commanded cash, and fees were high. Ohio might provide excellent prospects in fifteen or twenty years, he wrote his father, but he lacked that kind of patience and was convinced that it was a "great advantage to a young man to make a good choice first, and then settle down permanently." Several of John's friends, moreover, had died, and he believed that Ohio's climate was the cause. The death of a law student who succumbed to fever in October, 1820, after John had nursed him for a week, had a depressing effect upon him. It seemed that consumption in Ohio killed more people than did "all the various diseases at the South." Disregarding yellow fever and malaria epidemics which ravaged the South almost yearly, he believed that most deaths there resulted from "Dissipation," a trap to which his moral habits and hard work would never allow him to fall victim. John also looked forward to escaping the harsh Ohio winters. John assured his family that he had the perseverance to move again and that he would find "Happiness" and "friends" everywhere. In fact, they would not see him at Rhinebeck again until he had first achieved "Independence and fame." [49]

It took John about three months after his admission to the bar to make preparations for his move south, and this period merely convinced him that he was making a wise decision. He observed Ohio being "scourged" by "Intermittent and bilious fevers," and reflected that his new status meant only that he could now add "esquire" after his name. His fees for drawing up deeds and handling minor legal cases brought in enough funds for clothes and pocket money, but not enough to travel and to set himself up independently in Natchez. John eventually collected $20 due from Hartwick, apparently received a bonus from Brush for faithful and competent service, and left Delaware on November 5.[50]

That morning, as he reached the height outside town, John paused and turned Nancy Dawson, his horse, around to face Delaware for a last reflective glance. Once again a "lonely sojourner on the world's wide waste," [51] he could not know what his future had in store. Probably he thought a bit about his past, and what he had become.

He had, in fact, become quite a high-spirited young man. Physically strong and over six feet tall, he was a man's man. He relished physical sports, loved to hunt and go tramping through the woods, and formed fast friendships with male peers. He smoked Havana cigars, played chess, whist, and backgammon for hours on end, and enjoyed drinking with his friends. Others acknowledged his leadership, demonstrating their confidence in him by pushing him into such positions as captain of a ball team and president of a debating society. He liked lusty literature such as *Tom Jones*, which presented a "fine sample of human nature." [52]

Yet there was another side to John, the nineteenth-century romantic. He cut a Byronesque figure, with his curly hair, delicate nose, thin lips, and small gray eyes, which gave the impression that he could conquer the world. His reading tastes included Sir Walter Scott, and he might have fancied himself a reflection of Scott since he copied Scott's poetry down and sent off rhymes to female acquaintances. He wrote paeans to nature, appreciated music, and played the flute. Foppish in dress, John preferred being the most stylish young man in town. He pined over the "*many* girls I have loved," and could occasionally lose himself in the depths of melancholic reverie. [53]

An exuberant young man, John could sometimes appear trite. He seems to have adopted a remarkably nonchalant attitude toward religion for the son of a distinguished Lutheran minister. References to church and God occupy little space in his Ohio diary. In Chillicothe he sampled the Episcopal and Presbyterian churches, primarily for their social utility. In Delaware he went to a Methodist meeting, and he seems to have been totally impervious to the initiation of Lutheran worship there in January, 1821. He liked to make quips, and took pride in his wit. "I invented a new comparison today," he wrote on one occasion. "A farce is to the mind what a dessert is to the body." Yet, he cared deeply about others. A generous man, he gave to charity and loaned money despite his own limited means. In Chillicothe, he turned out at three in the morning to help extinguish a fire. He would do almost anything for his family. He wrote one of his brothers in December, 1820, "We should not all desert papa in his old age," and tried to help his brothers and sisters as best he could. He followed Albert's career on a whaler in the Pacific with both pride and concern, and he supported William's efforts to get a position in the navy by pulling strings with Platt Brush's congressman brother. In June, 1821, he wrote that if he was successful in Mississippi, he hoped to see some of his immediate family join him there. [54]

This, then, was John Anthony Quitman as he coaxed his horse around, left Delaware behind him, and set off for the Ohio River and a career in the Cotton Kingdom. Ohio had left an imprint upon his character and had allowed him to sow his wild oats, but he would become an expression of his destination.

2

Mecca

AS his Mississippi River steamer drew near the lights of Natchez after
dusk on December 3, 1821, John Quitman could not help but ru-
minate about the pending change in his prospects. He had been
struck, as the *Car of Commerce* made its way downriver, by the
character of the landscape. Viewing plantations, cotton gins, cypress trees,
and Spanish moss for the first time, he sensed the fresh start and opportunity
before him. "My heart began to throb at the hopes and fears that alternately
ran thro' my bosom," he confided to his diary later that evening. Perhaps in
the South his "ambition" would finally be satiated and his "peregrinations"
could cease.[1]

Disembarking at the "landing," John first encountered that oldest and
most infamous part of Natchez known as "Under-the-Hill." Below the high
bluff which Natchez occupied, there was a symbiotic community around the
boat docks on a strip of fairly level land. Here one found a "village of ragged
buildings" providing boardinghouses for riverboatmen and several shops.
Inhabited by a coarse, polyglot population, Under-the-Hill spawned vice and
violence. John discovered over the next several days that gamblers, bullies,
and harlots, as he put it, held sway even over Sabbaths there.[2]

Crossing this strip from the wharf, John found a road which led up to the
city proper. Mosquitoes—a novelty for that time of year to a young man
bred on northern winters—welcomed him. Surveying the scene, John saw a
public square with a jail, city hall, public cistern, firehouse, and market-
house, and sensed the town's history. Variously occupied by the Natchez Indians, the French, and the British, Natchez came under Spanish dominion
during the American Revolution. The Spanish imprint lingered well after the
United States gained sovereignty over the Natchez District in the late 1790s
by treaty. John wrote Ernest Hazelius that the houses had been "generally
built in the Spanish fashion, with a piazza around them."[3]

Natchez, by John's arrival, had developed a cultural life, especially when compared to the general lack of refined society in most of the Southwest at the time. The town had hosted the first known theatrical performance in English given west of the Allegheny Mountains back in 1806, and in 1821 maintained a three-story brick hospital, a coffeehouse, a reading room, and other symbols of cultural and social progress. Politically important, Natchez served as state capital, though its glory was waning. The state legislature, the next year, would transfer the capital to the newly laid out village of Jackson some one hundred miles to the northeast.[4]

Holding social and economic—if not political—sway over the community was the metropolitan and outlying Adams County aristocracy. The "nabobs," a group of families intertwined in a bewildering maze of marriage ties, had fashioned an elitist mansion society from the profits of their business interests and extensive landholdings in the county and in nearby locales such as Concordia Parish, Louisiana, across the river. Late in the Spanish period, neighborhood planters had begun making fortunes from the region's rich soil, the newly invented cotton gin, and the labor of black slaves (who constituted 40 percent of the area population by 1796). Adam L. Bingaman, for instance, known for his enthusiasm for horse racing and the thoroughbreds he entered at the Fleetwood (later St. Catherine's, then Pharsalia) track, started his rise as a planter before the United States gained title to the area. His wealth multiplied with passing years, and the 1830 census would show that he had accumulated 171 slaves within Adams County. Similarly, William Dunbar, a scientific oriented planter noted for introducing the iron cotton press and square baling into the region and for his membership in the erudite American Philosophical Society, established his holdings during the Spanish years; though Dunbar had passed away before John's arrival, his family maintained his splendid country mansion—The Forest—in fine style.[5]

Though he came to Natchez with only fifteen dollars in his pockets,[6] John set his sights from the start upon rising into this elite society, and his success at accomplishing this feat quickly, while hardly unique, surely ranks among the classic examples of social mobility in early-nineteenth-century America. Within just weeks, John discovered that virtually everything Mrs. Griffith had promised about opportunity in Mississippi was true.

On his first day in town, John, carrying his letter of introduction from Mrs. Griffith, made separate calls on her sons, and both gave him a warm welcome. A visit to court that same day confirmed Mrs. Griffith's summary of the Natchez bar; John noted a legal establishment graced with "high fees" and ample business, yet "not overstocked with eminent lawyers." The next day William Griffith offered to pay some of John's expenses and allow him use of his office and books in return for John's aid with his case preparations.

Just two days after arrival, therefore, John could exult in his "good prospects." His biggest challenge now would be to play the role of gentleman for a while, and hide his financial condition, so that the somewhat snobbish town gentry would accept him. William Griffith wore foppish attire, and extravagance seemed to be the mode among those who aspired to social acceptance; John discovered that young Natchez "beaux" typically ordered one-hundred-dollar suits, about ten a year, from Philadelphia, as well as shoes from the North and boots from Paris, and he caught on quickly. "I must appear as a gentleman, or I can not expect to be treated as such," he wrote home. So, no sooner had he made his arrangements with Griffith than he purchased a plaid coat for appearances. Two years later he would write that he had "caught the habit" of ordering stylish Philadelphia suits, but for the time being he rented a relatively economical—yet "respectable"—hotel room for forty-five dollars a month (including meals) and wrote his letters on soiled papers to save money. For a while, he would be a "tavern waif." [7]

A month later, John began earning income. On January 8, he easily passed his supreme court examination and could then practice law in the state courts. So, in combination with William Griffith and other attorneys, John began collecting fees for cases on the Mississippi circuit at places like Port Gibson and Warrenton, and at supreme court sessions in Natchez. On February 22, John gave his first speech to a jury and helped clear a client of a murder charge. By May, he was winning judgments regularly. Griffith was impressed; when he left for New Jersey in June he put his entire legal practice in John's hands. Partnership was only a matter of time, and in January, 1823, the local *Mississippi Republican* announced that Griffith and Quitman had "formed a connection in the practice of the Law," and would handle circuit court cases in six counties, as well as cases in the state supreme and chancery courts, and in the United States District Court. Meanwhile, Griffith and John agreed that they would split expenses such as office rent and stationery, but that Griffith, by virtue of his established reputation, would receive two-thirds of all fees earned. As for the size of those fees, Griffith believed that the nabobs, whose "whole idea is wealth and its importance," would not appreciate their attorneys without paying "heavily." [8]

John found Mississippi a virtual attorney's paradise. How fortunate that the town attracted the scum of the Mississippi River; adventurers "from many lands" brought with them "vice and infamy," and the court wheels kept turning. John was so enthusiastic that his letters even encouraged Platt Brush to think of visiting Natchez to look things over. Brush wanted to know whether the judges were "deep or shallow, fast or slow," and whether the "niggers" were really "branded and cropped, and fed on salted cotton-seed," and if every master maintained a "mulatto concubine" and a "harem of darkies." Other Ohio lawyers did make the move, one of them being John's old crony, John T. McMurran, who by February, 1823, had located in Port Gibson, where he taught school at the Beach Hill Academy.[9]

Meanwhile, John's relationship with the Griffiths quickly ripened into far more than a business partnership. John's winning personality made him a welcome visitor at the Griffith residence. He turned up there for breakfast, whist games, and chats, and joined the Griffiths in goose-hunting escapades. And, for both social and business reasons, the Griffiths fulfilled their mother's promise and saw to John's entrée into elite Natchez society. John passed New Year's day at The Forest with the Dunbars, and soon other invitations arrived. By January, 1822, he had joined the local Masonic lodge, and February found him attending the track.[10]

John identified immediately with the nabobs. Awed by cotton plantations which took in thirty to fifty thousand dollars a year, John realized that he had reached the kind of society which he had craved in more middle-class Ohio but had not found. He found the mansion residences "delightful," lauding The Forest's magnificent oaks, park, and fields, where peach and plum trees blossomed and birds sang in the honeysuckle. Here, in the big houses, could be found a graceful people, a people who dispensed "costly Port, Madeira, and sherry," a people who provided hospitality naturally and made ostentation into an endearing way of life. He wrote about one aristocratic residence in which he had stayed: "Your coffee in the morning before sunrise; little stews and sudorifics at night, and warm foot-baths, if you have a cold; bouquets of fresh flowers and mint-juleps sent to your apartment; a horse and saddle at your disposal; every thing free and easy, and cheerful and cordial."

When yellow fever struck Natchez in the summer of 1823, John found that he and other town lawyers were welcome at the planters' country residences, away from the river's mosquito concentration (although no one knew at the time that mosquitoes caused the fever). One residence put up ten to twelve transient guests a day, serving them mint juleps in the morning before breakfast on the veranda, and then opening the grounds for riding, hunting, fishing, and other activities. Yet, the planters displayed a social conscience, and John noted that during the epidemic they sent wagons loaded with fowl and vegetables to the edge of Natchez for free distribution to the poor. It was an "indolent, yet charming life," he summarized, "and one quits thinking and takes to dreaming."[11] He had found his mecca.

Acceptance of the aristocratic way of life necessitated acceptance of slavery, the South's "peculiar institution." Because of black labor, plantation society flourished, and the "well-dressed and aristocratic servants" (as John

22

put it) made possible the comfortable life he thought so enticing. John did not find this ideological adjustment particularly taxing. Initially he expressed some surprise that slaves could seem happy, writing after a visit to the Griffith place just before Christmas: "The manifestations of joy of the slaves on the plantation at the approach of the holidays, was a novel scene to me. They repeatedly came from their quarters to the house and maneuvered round it with the music of horns, cow jaws, and singing. Poor creatures!— Yet they appear to be happy!!" Later John noted that unfortunately some slaves had to be sold off when their owners died insolvent. But John had an instinctive affinity for the southern white upper class, and he found it easy to internalize their justification for their way of life.[12]

Not only did John fail to note any evidence of slave discontent or planter brutality toward slaves, he indignantly refuted Platt Brush's insinuations about the slave system and the gentry. "[T]hese 'niggers,' as you call them," he informed Brush, "are the happiest people I have ever seen. . . . So far from being fed on 'salted cotton-seed,' as we used to believe in Ohio, they are oily, sleek, bountifully fed, well-clothed, well taken care of, and one hears them at all times whistling and singing cheerily at their work." He wrote of one plantation where the annual Christmas festival lasted seven to ten days, where servants were provided religious instruction by visiting ministers and shared in family prayers and afternoon siestas, and where formal marriage ceremonies were conducted by black clergymen. John found slaves childishly ceremonious, observing that they addressed each other as general, judge, doctor, and other titles in imitation of their masters and dressed up on occasions such as weddings with canes, parasols, huge cigars, and other paraphernalia inappropriate to their station. Already John expressed what would, years later, become a staple in the proslavery defense that blacks were naturally inferior and without white control would "degenerate into drones or brutes."[13]

John's almost precipitate adoption of the southern gentry's world view is less mysterious than one might presume. Though the northern states had begun abolishing slavery during the American Revolution, the process was nowhere near complete when John was growing up, particularly in his own state of New York. Colonial New York, with its relatively thriving slave system (as compared to New England), had suffered slave revolts and conspiracy scares, and this heritage survived well after the Revolution. As late as 1788, in an act contradictory to a trend elsewhere in the North, New York had passed a comprehensive slave code. In 1799, the year John was born, emancipation proponents finally steered a bill through the state legislature, but it only freed children born after July 4, 1799, and these children would not be liberated until the age of twenty-five (women) and twenty-eight (men). Legislative provision for the voluntary emancipation of adult slaves, moreover, offered a rationale for ousting old and crippled blacks. Technically, slavery persisted in New York until July 4, 1827, a date established in an 1817 act. John's native county, Dutchess, and the Schoharie of his stay with the Wackerhagens, in fact, resisted emancipation well after it became established state policy. Schoharie had some 125 slaves during the War of 1812. Rhinebeck town records and area newspapers attest to slavery's continuing presence. Had John read the Poughkeepsie *Journal and Constitutional Republican* in June of 1807, for instance, he would have found a county slaveowner offering a fifty-dollar reward for a runaway slave with a scar on one side of his head who spoke Dutch and broken English. How similar would be fugitive slave advertisements in the Natchez of his adulthood.[14]

But John did not require secondhand familiarity with the institution before moving south, for his own upbringing had been touched by the vestiges of northern slavery. There is some indication that his parents, who may have owned slaves in Curaçao, migrated to the United States from the island because they feared racial insurrection.[15] Once in the United States, moreover, the Quitmans always maintained at least one black servant. John was raised, in part, by a black nurse named Eme, who had a child—Jack—in November, 1801. When John and Albert left for Hartwick years later, they were attended by a black servant. John's father believed in Nordic superiority and undoubtedly passed his attitudes on to his children.[16]

Even in Ohio, where slavery had been banned since the Northwest Ordinance (1787), John encountered traces of the peculiar institution. It was only natural that the people of Chillicothe, because of the community's settlement patterns and proximity to Kentucky, empathize with slaveowners' interests; and local newspapers not only printed fugitive slave announcements but also defended slaveholding as constitutional. Although the town of Delaware had less of a southern influence, Platt Brush's household included one of the town's four blacks—who almost certainly functioned as a family servant.[17]

John's acceptance of the southern way of life, therefore, represented no sharp departure from his own upbringing; he does not seem to have been exposed to the liberal philosophy underlying the emancipation movement in the North. His easy transformation from northerner to southerner, moreover, was typical of his generation. His fellow countrymen were a mobile people, and thousands of young men and women, despite all the attention historians have given the "westward movement," journeyed across the Mason-Dixon Line rather than across the Mississippi River. The census of 1860 enumerated a good 360,000 northerners living in the South. Most transplanted Yankees, like John, made a gradual peace with the institution of slavery—economic opportunity created unlikely candidates for ideological alienation. How similar to John was Joseph Farnsworth, who wrote home to Vermont from Natchez some seven years after John's arrival, "I think this is a good place to make money if a body had a little capital to begin with . . . the Planters . . . will make a crop of 3 or 400 Bales of Cotton . . . they will employ from 50 to 200 Negroes they are all the time a bringing them down the River for sale." John would later encounter fellow Yankees constantly as he pursued his planting interests and political career. In Louisiana, his sugar estate would be neighbor to a plantation owned by John M. Pelton, formerly a New York attorney. John would form a partnership for land speculation with Robert J. Walker, a Pennsylvanian, husband of a great-granddaughter of Benjamin Franklin, and graduate of the University of Pennsylvania. John would have close political ties with Seargent S. Prentiss, a remarkable political orator who owned slaves, excelled in the supposedly southern ritual of dueling, and hailed initially from Maine. John would have been an anomaly within southern society only had he taken a moral stance against slavery and jeopardized his hopes for social and material advancement; there were no limits on the potential success of Yankees who avoided condemning the South's ways. Prentiss would serve eventually in the House and Walker in the Senate.[18]

John had far more difficulty enduring what he lamented as a "want of female society" than adjusting to slavery. After almost two months in town, John grew rather despondent. How long would he have to keep his passions in check? he wondered. Frustration drove him to reminisce about past romances and beyond into erotic fantasy. "I dream about them [women]," he confided to his diary, "sometimes I fancy myself devoted to some fair nymph all beauty, all perfection, all love. . . . I woo her and hear her utter the heart thrilling accents of consent, enraptured I print my eager kisses on her burning cheek and taste the nectar of her dewey [*sic*] lips." [19]

Fortunately John's partnership with William Griffith seems to have been advantageous socially as well as professionally. By August, 1822, John had paid a visit to Edward Turner's residence, and since Griffith would marry Turner's daughter Theodosia less than a year later it is likely that John's entrée was smoothed by his partner's ties to the family. Turner, born and trained in law in Kentucky, had been a power in territorial—and then state—politics following his removal to Mississippi in 1802, and had become quite wealthy. The six-foot-two-inch attorney owned $22,000 worth of property and fourteen slaves and six carriages locally, and he had purchased a plantation upriver on Palmyra, a peninsula at what became known as Davis Bend. Most important for John Quitman's social requirements, Turner had a stunning brunette niece, not yet fifteen years old, the daughter of his recently deceased brother Henry. Henry, a Natchez merchant, had purchased land in the Palmyra settlement and established a country seat near Natchez known as Woodlands.[20]

Eliza Turner, though markedly younger than John, dazzled him. He was an ambitious, love-starved young man, and she was a beautiful daughter of one of Mississippi's most prestigious families. Subconsciously he must have known that matrimony would provide a means to cross the southern aristocracy's class line in one bold stroke; it had served this function in the South ever since colonial times. As for Eliza, now fatherless, it was not difficult for her to fall for the dapper, virile, and self-assured newcomer. The Turners do not seem to have had significant reservations about Eliza's being courted by someone below her class. Perhaps John's educational accomplishments impressed Eliza's cultured relatives—despite his love of the outdoors, John continued to read, and had just finished *Hamlet*.[21]

Sometime between February 1, 1823—when John mentioned in a letter home that he had no serious interest in marrying because his heart had yet to be "thoroughly touched"—and the summer of 1824, John found himself in love with Turner's niece. He took her for walks in the woods at her mother's estate and along the banks of the Mississippi near Palmyra. John and Eliza soon confessed their feelings for each other, and spoke of marriage. John agonized when his legal duties took him on the road, fretted that she was sick when her letters were delayed (reassuring himself that the "heart that had recently beat with emotion for me could never be changed. I know my Eliza too well"), exulted in her reaffirmations of affection for him, and pined for their reunions when, "If I am not disappointed you may expect to fold to my bosom, my lovely girl. . . . My impatience is almost intolerable, nothing but Hope could keep up my spirits."[22]

So he wrote Eliza's mother, Sarah, in September, 1824, asking to marry Eliza that December. Permission was granted, though John found it difficult to get through the remaining months. He daydreamed constantly about Eliza's looks and what she had said, and felt "the burning kiss of Love upon my lips." Incurably romantic and chivalrous toward this girl, he assured her that their "happy life" together in the "stream of time" would give him strength. He would use the power her love gave his arms to protect her. Their marriage would bind them "forever," for if their ties were broken, he would "cease to exist." He felt that his "intercourse with the world" would never repress his romantic nature.[23]

Finally, on December 24, John surrendered what had become—to this former gay blade—an unsatisfactory bachelor's existence. John now stood a member of the plantation gentry which he had so admired. But, to protect

the family interests, Eliza's mother had John sign a contract a few days before the ceremony, making herself, Edward Turner, and William Griffith
trustees for Eliza's share of her father's still-undivided estate of slaves and
landholdings in Mississippi, Kentucky, Louisiana, and elsewhere. This estate was to be divided among Eliza and her brothers George, Henry, and
Fielding. John and Eliza's children, according to the contract, would eventually gain title to Eliza's share. But if Eliza should die without lawful issue
the land and slaves would go to Eliza's "personal representatives" rather
than to any children John might have by a second marriage.[24]

Despite the restricted nature of John's admittance into the Turner family
circle, he had clearly come a long way since those penniless first days in
Natchez. Now a respectable community member by virtue of his legal practice and his marriage, John had fulfilled his own criterion for a return visit
east. Thus when his father, racked by rheumatic pain, wrote that the Rhinebeck relations were anxious to meet Eliza, John finally agreed to a homecoming.[25]

More a northern tour than a family reunion, John and Eliza's travels consumed the whole summer of 1825. They departed from the landing on May
20, journeyed east by the rivers to Wheeling and then by stage to Baltimore,
and remained in and around Rhinebeck and other parts of the Middle Atlantic states from June until September. They spent some $1,492 financing their
travel and side trips, which included a stop at the Saratoga Springs resort
(where John won eight volumes of British poetry in a raffle), a chance to
view the grandeur of Lake George, and a considerable stay in Philadelphia.
Perhaps the extended fling was a reflection, in part, of an awareness on John
and Eliza's part that new responsibilities would make such a journey less
feasible in the foreseeable future. During the river part of their trip eastward, Eliza told him that she was pregnant. Happy about the prospect of
fatherhood, John also found himself "anxious and full of solicitude."[26]

At Woodlands the following January 28, in the early morning, with a mid-
wife's aid, Eliza gave birth to a large, "round-faced" baby girl. In a sensitive
gesture, she named the girl after John's sister Louisa. John proved a proud
father, and allowed himself to be convinced by several callers that the baby
bore a striking resemblance to him.[27]

January, 1826, also brought John an awareness that the appropriate time
for moving into a permanent residence had arrived. He needed room for his
wife, baby girl, and any children to follow, required ample space to accommodate visits from his brothers and sisters which he hoped would commence
soon, and sensed that—if he made his choice wisely—it would legitimize
his place amid the local gentry. He selected an estate a little more than a
quarter mile from Woodlands. This was Monmouth, a two-story Federal

brick mansion presiding over some thirty-one acres of land. The house conformed to the symmetry then common to southern town mansions: four rooms per floor with broad, central hallways bisecting each story, and a curved stairway connecting the two floors. The main building stood in front of a cluster of smaller structures including a two-story brick west wing holding a kitchen and servants' quarters, a garden house, and "convenient out houses in good repair." A cistern stood by the door, a cellar underlay half the house, and the grounds featured a developed garden. Distinguishing the whole property was the graceful front vista. One approached Monmouth by taking a drive up a moderately inclined hill dotted with large oaks festooned with Spanish moss. John deemed the $12,000 asking price well below Monmouth's real value, and purchased it in March.

In later years, under John's direction, Monmouth would undergo significant remodeling, and would become an expression of the predominant masculine strain within John's personality. Four massive square columns—round columns were more usual in Greek Revival architecture—would become Monmouth's most noteworthy trademark. Other exterior attributes, including cornices, balustrades, and porches (all bereft of ornamentation) and a plastering of the front façade, which gave an appearance of stone, together projected an aura of weight and volume. Monmouth came to represent a stark, plain interpretation of the classic architectural style. It exuded, and still exudes, permanence. John and Eliza would plant their roots deep, and never move.[28]

Monmouth became John's gateway to the outside world. This was a town residence, not an isolated fiefdom. The garden and orchards would produce vegetables and fruits for the table, but never staple crops for market. It was a fitting residence for a lawyer with commercial and political ambitions. Crops and slaves would soon become an important part of John's life, but he never would have been satisfied residing permanently on a plantation in the hinterland. Monmouth stood near the Natchez-to-Washington road, and Natchez's business district beckoned from less than a mile away. So close was Monmouth to the hum of commerce that in later years John's children were able to listen from their windows to the tunes of steamboat calliopes on the Mississippi.[29] Monmouth provided a suitable home base for an aspiring public man.

3

Public Man

H AD I your gifts," John Quitman quipped in a letter to his brother William in 1820, "I would engage that, in two years, you would have a governor for your brother, and most probably in twenty years a supreme judge or a president." [1] While the remark seems flippant since he had not even passed the Ohio bar at that point, it nonetheless suggests that Quitman may have anticipated political prominence for himself from a very young age.

Ambition, in fact, best explains Quitman's political baptism, since there is no evidence that any particular issue or ideology mandated his becoming a politician. [2] Certainly his private affairs could have been enough to consume his energies had he not harbored political intentions. His law practice with William Griffith was highly lucrative, he trained legal apprentices, and he also helped Eliza manage her share of her father's estate, particularly the plantations at Palmyra and at Point Pleasant, a nearby river bend. His memoranda book reveals that he visited the plantations and purchased such items as rope and bagging in their behalf; surviving bills of sale show that Quitman bought slaves—at least a half dozen in 1828 alone. [3]

Quitman saw America as a land of boundless opportunity, and he felt indebted to his nation's founders for bequeathing a "fee simple of liberty" which left "ambition uncontrolled." [4] He conceptualized self-fulfillment, to no small degree, in terms of public reputation, and he never considered resting content with mere material success and social acceptance. Rather he set out methodically to achieve political rank.

Quitman's first step was to get his name before the people. Even before his marriage, he parlayed his Ohio militia credentials into an officer's appointment in the Mississippi militia system, and he used militia functions as a springboard to recognition as a responsible public servant. He explained in February, 1823, "I have recently visited what are called 'the Pearl River

29

counties,' on a tour of duty, having been appointed brigade inspector, with the rank of major. The place affords me some gratification, and occasions but little expense. Its duties are performed during vacation, and it will give me an extended acquaintance." [5]

It did not take long for Mississippi's new brigade inspector to become aware of serious deficiencies within the militia. The problem was that many Mississippians had come to regard it as dispensable. Requirements that young white men arm, attend musters, and drill seemed outmoded at a time when the threats of Indian attack and foreign assault, the original rationale for the militia system, had largely disappeared. By the time of Quitman's emigration to the South, wars both intertribal and against Europeans, white diseases like smallpox and measles, and the decimation of the fur trade had long since taken a tremendous toll upon the Indian peoples of the Mississippi River valley. Mississippi's two surviving tribes, the Choctaws and the Chickasaws, faced bleak times. Although the Indians still controlled about two-thirds of the state's thirty million acres when Mississippi reached statehood in 1817, they had ceded millions of acres to federal negotiators in a sequence of treaties beginning in 1801. A Choctaw domain across the Mississippi River in the Indian Territory awaited Choctaws willing to emigrate westward voluntarily, and Mississippi whites were already demanding that the federal government complete the treaty process and extinguish *all* Indian title to land within the state. [6]

Quitman felt that the relaxation of militia standards in Natchez, where young men no longer drilled, had gone much too far. Acute threats to public order, especially from "vagrant adventurers" who traveled on the river, still endangered the town, yet Natchez lacked even an effective police system. Quitman found that there were other young males who similarly disparaged the militia's decline. Since the state government would not enforce mandatory training, these young men would see to the town's defense themselves!

In April, 1824, Quitman and some forty men organized the Natchez Fencibles, a volunteer militia unit. They adopted a constitution and motto ("Try Us"), and elected officers. Quitman was selected as company leader, or "captain." The men donned blue uniforms and commenced regular drills. In their first nine months, Quitman put them through twenty-three parades and drills, and twenty-six company meetings and courts-martial. By fall, the local newspaper was compelled to notice the "rapid advancement" that these "young men totally inexperienced in military tactics" had made. When the Marquis de Lafayette reached Natchez during his triumphant return to the United States the next year, the Fencibles awaited his formal inspection. Gradually the Fencibles worked their way into other community affairs, particularly public dinners and Fourth of July celebrations. [7]

The Fencibles provided Quitman with public exposure. Their activities were talked about and reported, and Quitman's leadership was acknowledged. Thus the newspaper covered a Saturday drill and observed that company members had "presented to Captain Quitman a superb belt, as a token of their esteem." The press even reported "toasts" at public dinners; Natchez citizens in July, 1826, read Captain Quitman's innocuous cheer to "The Candidates for Congress. Fair Play ! ! ! and no Hobby riding."[8]

Quitman's efforts to establish community credentials as a concerned and reliable public servant were not restricted to militia drills. Apparently upset by the death of a close friend, state attorney general Richard Stockton, in a New Orleans duel, Quitman helped organize an Adams County antidueling association. Members pledged that they would henceforth settle their personal differences by resorting to a "Court of Honor." Quitman found a more lasting outlet in the local "Harmony" Masonic lodge. He had joined the Masons in Delaware, Ohio, and resumed his affiliation soon after arriving in Natchez. He rose swiftly in the order's complex hierarchy, achieving its highest statewide rank, Grand Master, at the January, 1826, meeting in Natchez. Quitman also served on the standing committee of the Natchez-dominated Mississippi State Bar Association (perhaps the first voluntary and selective state bar association in the United States) and was active in Trinity Episcopal Church—the church of the town's elite.

Quitman earned a stream of press comment for such contributions, but the value of these endeavors to his subsequent political career went beyond merely keeping his name before the public. He was constantly finding important contacts, such as John I. Guion, Fencibles second lieutenant. Guion, who eventually moved to Vicksburg, became president of the state senate and a circuit court judge, and ultimately one of Quitman's most fervent allies when Quitman took up radical states' rights politics. Similarly, it did not hurt Quitman to meet Masonic "Grand Orator" William L. Sharkey, who later became speaker of the Mississippi lower house and judge of the state High Court of Errors and Appeals.[9]

Given the comprehensive nature of Quitman's entrance into community life and his success at breaking into Natchez society, it is somewhat surprising to find one historian's hypothesis that Quitman's political radicalism was the product of his northern antecedents and his need to prove himself to his adopted state.[10] This does not take into account how completely Quitman had become a Mississippian by the mid-1820s, well before his emergence as a southern sectionalist. His later political opponents, even in a day when slander ran rampant, were wary of trying to make his origins an issue; they found safer grounds for their case against Quitman. There simply is no evidence that Quitman's political options and strategy were ever structured by a sensitivity to inadequate roots. If he had ever been insecure—and lack of confidence was rarely a John Quitman trait—his uneasiness had dissipated within a few years. Quitman became an insider very quickly.

Politically, Quitman bided his time while he consolidated his position in Natchez. He initially identified with John Quincy Adams' wing of the only viable national party—the Republicans (which would later splinter into the pro-Adams "National Republicans" and the pro–Andrew Jackson "Democrats")—a move which made sense since Adams had a considerable following locally. Quitman even handled secretarial chores at the Adams County meeting which nominated the former secretary of state for president in 1824. Whether Quitman fully approved of the centralizing tendencies of the subsequent Adams administration cannot be determined. No records have survived of his opinion on such Adams programs as federal internal improvements, an invigorated national militia system, and federal observatories or "light-houses of the skies." However, Quitman did petition the Bank of the United States for a branch in Natchez in 1827.[11] Perhaps what Quitman did not stand for bears more import than his actual political principles. By not embracing states' rights early on, he provided ammunition for later political enemies who took delight in reminding voters of his endorsement of Adams and suggesting that his radicalism was suspect. That Adams eventually became one of the country's antislavery leaders did not help matters.

In 1827 Quitman made his bid for political office by announcing his candidacy for the January, 1828, session of the state house of representatives. He chose an opportune time to run—Adams County would have two seats in that body (with election being determined by the two highest vote totals rather than by separate contests), and only two competitors, Adam Bingaman and Natchez attorney Charles B. Green, emerged to challenge Quitman— and for a political novice, conducted a shrewd campaign. By lining up pledges of support and announcing for office early, he apparently preempted Bingaman. "Col. Bingaman consented to become a candidate," reported an observer in Natchez, "but it was (however) after Capt. Q. was out, and it was thought that he had come out to injure Q——s election which made his [Quitman's] friends anxious to keep Bingaman out, and more anxious to elect Green & Quitman." J. F. H. Claiborne, moreover, tells us that Quitman won many voters over by beating the county's crack shot in a mid-campaign shooting match. Through such politics of personality, hardly unusual when the state had not yet fostered a mature two-party system and still tolerated what has been described as an "antiparty," "pre-partisan political culture," Quitman garnered 589 votes—almost double Bingaman's count and enough to edge out Green.[12]

Before Quitman could assume his position, he suffered a serious setback.

That October, bilious fever struck down William Griffith. Quitman had just returned to Monmouth one morning from a trip to the Claiborne County court when he saw Griffith's servants hurrying to town with the news that their master was critically ill. Quitman rushed to his partner's side only to find him already in convulsions. He and Edward Turner nursed Griffith through the day, but the convulsions continued until the agony ended the next morning. "I closed his dying eyes," Quitman reported to his brother.

Griffith's death had a depressing effect on Quitman. Quitman formed close male relationships, and he felt, as he told his brother, that he had lost his "best friend." He wrote in his journal that Griffith was "one of the best of men" and that the "blow is severely felt." He felt some responsibility, too, for Griffith's wife and two children. But Quitman rebounded well from adversity, and did have a replacement for Griffith standing by. John McMurran had been working in the Griffith-Quitman office for about a year. Now Quitman promoted him to partner. It proved a fortunate decision. Quitman and McMurran developed an effective and intimate business and social relationship, a relationship which became an indirect family connection when McMurran in 1831 followed Griffith's path and married a daughter of Edward Turner.[13]

Having surmounted his partner's death, Quitman was prepared two months later to travel to Jackson, where he would assume the responsibilities of being a state legislator. Quitman used the family carriage to cart his belongings, and took along Robert, a servant whom he had bought about a year earlier. He arrived in Jackson on the evening of January 6 after a difficult journey along primitive roads, and quickly developed an instinctive distaste for the rustic capital. Quitman's friend John I. Guion spoke for both of them a few years later when he called the fledgling Pearl River town "detestable." Jackson offered few amenities suitable for an upcoming member of Mississippi's gentry, and Quitman dismissed it as a "poor miserable" place which lacked polite company and provided such inferior water that he was forced to drink cider. A week after his arrival Quitman griped, "I have not since I have been in this place seen a single white woman but an old witch who pours out our coffee & tea." He told Eliza on January 12 that he was already "heartily tired" of Jackson.[14]

His antipathies to capital life probably reflected, in part, an insecurity over abandoning his family for an indefinite period. Thoughts of Eliza still aroused his ardor, and now she was pregnant again. He worried about her health and sent her quasi-medical advice instructing her to tend the garden and walk for exercise. He wondered, too, whether she would be able to keep the servants in line. "Please to set Robert actively to work as soon as he returns and keep him busy," Quitman advised. Sensitive to the responsibilities which he was placing on Eliza, he reassured her of the intensity of his affections. "[A]s long as I breathe," he wrote, "I live for you and dear little puss [his baby daughter Louisa]." But his need for public recognition overrode his qualms: "It is as you truly observe a long separation for us. . . . But these things are incident to Life. . . . Were I always with you, our child would never be able to point out to her co[n]temporaries that her father had done any good in this world." [15]

Thus on January 7, 1828, an aspiring John Quitman took his seat. He found several acquaintances, including William Sharkey, among his fellow representatives, and soon realized that Mississippi politics were in ferment and transition. There was substantial geopolitical tension within the state. By 1828, Mississippi had progressed midway through a transformation which ultimately transferred control of the state from the lower Mississippi River counties to other regions. Initially, the old French-defined Natchez District, which included later Adams, Jefferson, Claiborne, Wilkinson, Warren, and parts of Amite and Franklin counties, had dominated the political scene. Natchez District delegates controlled the 1817 state constitutional convention and drafted provisions which reflected the objectives of the planting and commercial elite. According to one provision, to be eligible for the house of representatives, one had to own 150 acres of real estate. Popular democracy was carefully circumscribed; the legislature, rather than the voters, had the obligation of choosing all state officials other than the governor and the lieutenant governor. Early state legislatures reflected the river elite's control of the political process. Indicative of this dominance was the legislature's selection in 1818 of Natchez as the site of a chartered monopoly, the Bank of the State of Mississippi. Although the institution did not provide enough credit to suit many planters, its existence stood testimony to Natchez's statewide influence. [16]

Other parts of the state, such as the "Piney Woods" and the "New Purchase," objected to the disproportionate power of the river counties. These areas, generally, were poorer than the Natchez District. Herdsmen, subsistence farmers, and lumbermen inhabited the nutrient-deficient land in the Mississippi counties north of the Gulf Coast and west of the southern Mississippi-Alabama border known as the Piney Woods. The New Purchase lands, along the Big Black, Yazoo, and Pearl rivers, included 30 percent of all white Mississippians and 18 percent of the state's slaves (in 1830), but had less than 14 percent of the assessed property value in Mississippi.

In the future, the non-District regions would dominate. As new counties from these areas achieved representation in Jackson in the 1820s and 1830s, their legislators found it increasingly possible to chip away at the privileges of the river elite. Not only did the legislature transfer the capital from

Natchez, but in 1826 it changed the site of the Mississippi Supreme Court from Natchez to Monticello in Lawrence County. In 1827, Powhatan Ellis became Mississippi's first U.S. senator from the Piney Woods, defeating Thomas B. Reed of Natchez in a geographically determined vote in the state legislature. Natchez and the other lower-river counties gradually became politically beleaguered. Office seekers from east Mississippi discovered that a superb campaign strategy entailed attacking the river nabobs and their perceived manipulation of state politics. This method, for instance, benefited Franklin E. Plummer, of Westville in Simpson County, during his campaign for election to Congress in 1830. "Six weeks before the election Mr. Plummer was hardly spoken of," explained one of Quitman's correspondents, "and I am certain if the election had come at that time he would not of got 50 votes in the countys [*sic*] adjoining Perry, but he came round . . . making stump speeches saying that he was the peoples man, that he had fought the battle . . . in the State legislature in their behalf that he was opposed in every point by the members from the Mississippi, that their interest and ours were quite different." [17] With such intrastate friction on the rise, Quitman's legislative mission in 1828 centered upon defending Natchez against a further erosion of power, and perhaps regenerating some of its lost glory.

Regional friction within Mississippi, however, constituted only part of the political ferment of 1828. A presidential election loomed in the fall, and Quitman, who had supported John Quincy Adams, now witnessed a tide of Jacksonian fervor sweep over the state. Andrew Jackson had defeated Adams statewide even in 1824. In the 1828 rematch, he would capture a whopping 7,088 of 8,690 votes cast. Some of Quitman's closest Natchez acquaintances, including Robert J. Walker and his brother Duncan, campaigned in Old Hickory's behalf. [18]

Mississippi Jacksonians distrusted the incumbent Adams administration's inclinations toward increasing the authority of the federal government. Robert J. Walker, for instance, believed that "the central power" posed the greatest threat to the nation. "If ever the golden chain of our union be broken," he warned, "it will be, when the centripetal, altogether overcomes the centrifugal attraction & our 24 political planets [states], torn from their spheres, shall exist only as spots on the disk of the sun—or as spots scarcely discernible from the President's 'lighthouses of the skies.'" Adams had argued that the federal government's moral commitment to promote agriculture, commerce, manufacturing, the arts, literature, and science should override popular opposition to federal programs; Secretary of the Treasury Richard Rush endorsed protective tariffs for industry while Secretary of State Henry Clay was renowned for his "American System" of federally financed internal improvements, protective tariffs, and a national bank. In the

summer of 1827, a Harrisburg, Pennsylvania, convention attended by delegates from thirteen states, an event viewed as an Adams maneuver, had endorsed protective tariff schedules on such items as raw wool, manufactured
woolens, iron, glass, and flax. Mississippi Jacksonians feared that this meeting indicated the direction of a second Adams administration, a direction
which would cost Mississippians money because they would have to pay
higher prices for goods which they imported from the North.[19]

The 1828 Jacksonian whirlwind in Mississippi, however, transcended
ideological reservations about John Quincy Adams' program. Jackson himself in 1828 had avoided assuming a stance exactly antithetical to the Adams
position. Regarding the protective tariff, Jackson apparently stood on his
ambiguous call four years earlier for "judicious" duties. Very few Mississippians, moreover, shared the profound and growing conviction of many
South Carolinians that centralized federal power portended an ultimate assault by Washington on the southern slave system. William Haile, a Mississippi congressman who had been born in South Carolina, did harbor such
apprehensions. He named his boy after (and corresponded with) the increasingly states' rights–oriented vice president John C. Calhoun of South Carolina, and warned that "*the Yankees*" and their tariff would drive the southern
states into starvation through extortionate prices for northern goods. Haile
accepted the possibility of eventual war with the North (and allegiance with
England) to prevent the degradation of the southern states. But he was an
exception in 1828: few Mississippians then embraced his apocalyptic vision.[20]

Probably Indian affairs had the most to do with Jackson's lopsided margin
in Mississippi in 1828. Mississippians had reached a point of acute impatience: they wanted the Choctaws and the Chickasaws moved westward beyond state borders, but the tribes seemed determined to adopt white customs
as a means of retaining their lands. Choctaws had reorganized their government, enabling them to present a united front against land cessions, and for
the past decade they had been moving into the Yazoo River valley to farm.
Missionaries dispatched by the American Board of Commissioners for
Foreign Missions succeeded in establishing schools for Choctaws on the
Yalobusha River, in the Tombigbee River valley region, and in other areas.
Chickasaws, moreover, set up schools and churches, planted cotton, and
raised cattle and hogs. Meanwhile the federal government, bound by the
Constitution to regulate "commerce" with the Indians, had vacillated be-
tween aiding this kind of assimilation and pressuring the tribes to remove
westward. The Adams administration did assign commissioners to propose
to the Chickasaws that half-bloods would receive specific land allotments in
Mississippi if the tribe would cede its total holdings; but these commissioners met with a sharp rebuff. Adams not only failed to dislodge the Mis-

sissippi tribes, he also took a seemingly pro-Creek stance in the Georgia Indian crisis, even threatening to use federal force to impede efforts by Georgia whites to survey Indian holdings. By 1828, Mississippians desperately wanted to claim Indian lands for cotton, slavery, and speculation, and correctly perceived in renowned Indian fighter Andrew Jackson a man who would cooperate more willingly in seeking Indian removal. Not only did that winter's legislature petition Congress to expedite the removal of Choctaws and Chickasaws to a region "more congenial to their nature," but the House passed bills restricting tribal hunting rights and extending civilian court jurisdiction over whites residing on Indian lands—measures which Quitman supported.[21]

Mississippi politics, therefore, were in considerable flux as John Quitman's first legislative session began. Determined to make an immediate mark, he quickly established himself as a workhorse. House records show him constantly making motions, presenting petitions, and suggesting legislation. He served on the judiciary and enrolled-bills standing committees, and procured assignment to a number of select committees such as the body assigned to consider a recommendation in Governor Gerard Brandon's opening message that there be an increase in the state militia. Sensitive to the attention his parliamentary activism attracted, he exulted to Eliza on January 17, "I am excessively engaged on committees & believe I have much influence in the House. This experience will be of great benefit to me & I hope will hereafter be the source of happiness to us all."[22]

Much of Quitman's frenetic activity benefited his Natchez constituents. Responding to a request for the incorporation of a "Natchez Theatre," he successfully steered an appropriate bill through the house. When his own Trinity Church petitioned for the right to sell lottery tickets, he saw to it that the petition was referred to committee for consideration.[23] Quitman did so much for his town, he was taken aback when his inability to get Duncan Walker elected judge of the Adams County Criminal Court elicited criticism from home. "Our county of Adams has injured my feelings . . . in her protests about Walker's defeat," he rejoined to McMurran. "I feel injured because no exertion on my part to procure the election of Walker was wanting."[24]

Service in the 1828 legislature provided Quitman with superb training in defending minority interests, for he and Natchez District cohorts absorbed several disappointments in efforts to restore some of their constituents' lost power. River interests, for instance, committed a blatant act of geopolitical aggression in February when they tried to make Port Gibson (a Mississippi River town south of Natchez) the state capital. After a tie vote stymied this attempt, they tried unsuccessfully to rally a majority behind Clinton, an interior town west of Jackson. Quitman's votes supported these maneuvers, as well as a bill which would have banned further importation of slaves into the state. This was prompted by fears that there were too many blacks in the lower valley's population and by a realization that new slaves reduced the monetary value of blacks already owned by river planters. Despite Governor Brandon's plea that importations "excited uneasiness" among whites and risked class unrest because slaves undermined the economic independence of white workers, the house voted 20 to 9 to continue augmenting the pool of black labor. However, the session also taught Quitman how coalitions could be manipulated to advance minority interests, as the state's interior had not yet achieved such an iron grip on the legislature as to preclude such log-rolling. Although the details of his behind-the-scenes bargaining remain unclear, he did manage to secure a rather significant boon for Natchez by gaining passage of a bill which provided that the state supreme court, which then met exclusively in Monticello, should hold its winter session at Natchez. This success compensated Quitman for his defeat in the matter of Walker's candidacy, and he let McMurran know it: "You lawyers ought to give me much credit for procuring one term of the Supreme Court at Natchez. It was so hard a task that it is now here generally said that I have great influence over many eastern members." [25]

Through such bargaining, as well as his committee work and floor participation, Quitman gained recognition as a stalwart defender of his constituents and as a talented politician. Even more significant for his immediate future, he earned acknowledgment as an expert on the state judicial system from his work on the committee on the judiciary. His prized accomplishment was a bill, which eventually passed both houses, establishing an extra judicial circuit for the state's superior court system. To carry the legislation, Quitman resorted to the logic of mass democracy. When serving on a joint house-senate conference committee to iron out technical differences on the bill, Quitman, in response to an objection that the house bill would force one of the state's district judges to change his residence if he wanted to retain his position, asserted that the "private convenience of the judge must be subservient to the public good" and that the people needed and demanded the bill's passage. [26]

By the time the legislature adjourned on February 16, Quitman had been absent from home some six weeks. His letters to Eliza expressed hopes of a short session, conveying the impression that he abhorred the long absence from her which his position necessitated. Anxious to again fold his "sweet & affectionate wife and my dear little child to my heart," Quitman complained about Jackson and implied that the legislative process was usually dull and that he had a nonexistent social life ("Last night there was a ball at Clinton. . . . I was not present having and feeling no desire for amusement"). Once his legislative duties ended, Quitman resumed his normal legal practice and started following the circuit. Nevertheless, politics was now in his blood. On July 24, shortly after Eliza gave birth to a son (bearing the name John Anthony despite Quitman's earlier intention to name his first son after his father), Quitman announced his candidacy for reelection to his seat. But it proved one of the shortest candidacies on Mississippi record. Two days later, without explaining his motives, he announced—to the disappointment of the pro-Adams Natchez *Ariel*—his withdrawal from the race.[27]

Quitman's withdrawal proved but a preliminary to his assuming a more significant, and onerous, public duty—one which would confer on him the appellation of "judge" to replace his "captain" standing in the title-conscious Southwest. In the fall, Governor Brandon, cognizant of Quitman's legal experience and recent contributions on the judiciary committee, offered Quitman the prestigious appointment of chancellor of the state of Mississippi. Quitman accepted the position, which committed him to running the four-district system of equity courts which state law had established. In all, Quitman was responsible for holding up to eighteen weeks of court each year—provided business required full terms—at Clinton, Natchez, and the Lawrence County and Perry County courthouses.[28]

Quitman began his duties at Clinton on December 1, 1828. Many of the cases under his jurisdiction, as might be expected in a land-hungry state, revolved around real estate matters. But chancery cases ranged over a wide variety of other subjects, such as a plantation owner's attempt to recover what he deemed an overpayment to an overseer but which had been ordered by the Claiborne County circuit court, a landowner's efforts to reduce a mechanic's charges for repairing a cotton gin and mill, a doctor's contention that he had been illegally made liable for medicines purchased without permission by a partner, and a man's attempt to annul his marriage on the grounds that his wife already had two husbands on the day that they had been married. Quitman's duty was not so much to decide law in these cases; often there was no applicable legislation. Instead, he had to determine what constituted fair settlement. Quitman, for all his later military adventurism, thrived on the bench. Not only did he do his job well, he found his work fulfilling. When Franklin Plummer wrote him that he was seriously considering trying to get the state legislature to abolish the chancery system, Quitman answered that he regretted Plummer's intention and would speak more bluntly against the idea were he not vulnerable to conflict-of-interest charges. The chancellorship earned for Quitman a statewide reputation for

integrity and responsibility which he would never forfeit. Even his later political rival Henry Stuart Foote conceded his competency and popularity as
state chancellor.[29]

Quitman's judicial status removed him, perhaps to his advantage, from
the increasingly partisan whirligig of Mississippi politics. These were not
good times for Adams supporters, given the Jackson landslide in Mississippi
in the fall of 1828. Wealthy Adams County planter Stephen Duncan could
lament that Jackson lacked a "solitary qualification for the [presidential] station," but even in Natchez, where one report attributed a "Matrimonial Hurricane" to euphoria over Jackson's election, the new president and his
Democrats prevailed. Jackson's Indian policies only enhanced this stature.
He upheld the concept of state sovereignty over Indian holdings in his December, 1829, message to Congress and, reinforced by a congressional appropriation, used the resources of the executive department to initiate new
tribal emigrations from the Southeast to the trans-Mississippi public domain. Administration negotiations with the Chickasaws foundered for a
while, after an abortive attempt to arrange a cession at Franklin, Ten-
nesssee, in August, 1830. But in a gathering with some five to six thousand
Choctaws at Dancing Rabbit Creek, Noxubee County, in mid-September,
1830, Secretary of War John Eaton and General John Coffee pressured the
Choctaws into a treaty terminating tribal holdings in Mississippi. In the late
1820s and into the 1830s an anti-Jackson identity constituted virtual political
suicide in most parts of Mississippi—as John I. Guion found to his dismay
in 1830 when rumors "telling the people that I was an Adams man" proved
enough to sabotage a campaign for office.[30]

Chancellor Quitman, as virulently anti-Indian as most Mississippi voters,
had been hoping for just such progress in Indian removal. In January, 1829,
while the legislators pondered extending state authority over the Choctaw
and Chickasaw nations, he had provided Franklin Plummer with his own
blueprint for pressuring the tribes out of Mississippi. The legislators should
"extend process into the Indian territory, and impose taxes on white persons
residing therein," he believed. "Drive off the Northern missionaries and the
lawless whites in the Indian nation, and we shall have no trouble in removing them." Quitman had to hand it to Jackson for supporting state jurisdiction over tribal holdings, and he praised the president for the Dancing Rabbit
Creek Treaty at a public dinner in October, 1830.[31]

Quitman's enthusiasm for Jacksonian Indian policy, however, was not
enough to induce him to convert to the president's Democratic party. Quitman
apparently advised Edward Turner that Adams supporters should dissolve
their impotent party organization and back the most appealing Jacksonian
candidates, but he never announced himself a Democrat. Rather, he main-

tained his judicial immunity, hosted Jackson's rival Henry Clay at Monmouth in early 1830, and bided his time. When former law student J. F. H. Claiborne suggested a run for the United States Senate, Quitman discouraged such thoughts, explaining that establishing his credentials as chancellor took priority over political aspirations.[32] But he did not rule out the possibility in the future. Lacking a party identity, Quitman stood at a political crossroads as the new decade began.

4

The Making of a Nullifier

EXPERIENCE taught southerners to trust northerners who settled permanently in Dixie. Few transplanted northerners entertained antislavery perspectives once they became acclimated. Many ultimately became slaveowners themselves. One Mississippi newspaper explained, "You may take a Yankee . . . accustomed all his life to denounce slavery as a God-abhorred institution, and ten to one if he does not become a harder negro driver than an overseer on a Louisiana sugar plantation. Whoever knew a Yankee, after coming South, to hesitate about owning slaves, if he found them a profitable investment."[1] John Quitman, though never a vicious disciplinarian, became a conspicuous example of this process. He joined the slaveholding ranks and then went on to surpass most native Mississippians in his willingness to justify slavery as an institution. He came to defend it, in fact, with the kind of zeal characteristic of the religious convert turned proselytizer.

Quitman's emergence as a states' rights radical underlined his own deepening identification with the southern planter class. By the late 1820s, Quitman was in the enviable position of having funds to spare, as he was reminded by John Guion, who, eyeing some Concordia Parish property, wrote to find out if the offer of "the credit of your name in Bank if I should wish it" was still available. Lending money to associates provided one means for Quitman to utilize his surplus, and he also joined the ranks of the land speculators more directly. In 1829, for instance, he and an associate purchased a house and lot at a sheriff's sale in Natchez for $1,340, which they sold just a few months later for $2,500. Later he joined a syndicate involving William Gwin, Robert J. Walker, and others which speculated in Choctaw lands ceded in the Dancing Rabbit Creek Treaty.[2]

Between 1828 and 1834, Quitman acquired two plantations. The first began from lands he and a Dr. John Bell bought in 1828 and 1829 in Terrebonne

42

Parish, Louisiana. These purchases, located in mosquito-infested country on the west bank of Grand Caillou Bayou about twenty miles due north of the Gulf of Mexico, became the nucleus of Live Oaks, Quitman's sugar and molasses plantation. Quitman was in the vanguard of Anglo developers of this "singular looking" land dominated by inhabitants of French descent. S. S. Prentiss, who visited the region about the same time as Quitman made his investments, left this description of its inhabitants and unusual terrain:

> They [the French-speaking inhabitants] are the poorest, most igno-
> rant, set of beings you ever saw—without the least enterprise or indus-
> try. They raise only a little corn and a few sweet potatoes. . . .
> The lands here lie in a very curious manner. There are a great
> number of creeks, or bayous, as they are called, running up from the
> ocean, parallel to each other. Upon each of these is a strip of high
> land, from one to ten acres in depth, on either side, after which it falls
> into a swamp, and so continues till you come to another bayou; thus,
> between every two bayous there is an extensive swamp.

Civilization kept its distance from the Grand Caillou area; there was no mail service, and it was a difficult half-day's trip to Houma, the nearest town. The isolation, Spanish moss, orange groves, alligators, crab, oysters, and swamps gave the place an exotic vista unlike any terrain which Quitman had known. Years later, his son, wrapped in Grand Caillou's mystique, described the "myr[i]ads of brilliant wild flowers" clothing its banks in the midst of winter, and how the "gigantic Live oaks" bent "their crooked trunks toward the glassy surface of the beautiful stream."[3]

Soon after purchasing the land, Quitman and Bell visited their holdings. Inured to the hardships of travel by his circuit practice, Quitman found the journey—by steamer to Donaldsonville, skiff on Bayou Lafourche into the parish, and then on land—bearable, and promised Eliza that the day would come when she too would "delight" in taking his "tour." He was completely satisfied, moreover, with what he found. "I am delighted with the country and particularly our place," he wrote home. "The Doctor & I have amused ourselves with examining the plantation, or rather the place. I write from a cabin with a ground floor—but very comfortable."[4]

Quitman and Bell used an overseer to operate the place initially, though Bell took up residence in the parish. However, Bell's death soon afterward temporarily took the property out of Quitman's hands. Put up at a probate sale in April, 1831, Live Oaks, now totaling some 1,770 arpents, fetched an $8,000 bid. Quitman had to spend $12,000 to repossess the property a couple of years later, and increased his stake in the place by purchasing equipment on credit. Needing a new manager, he looked to his brother Al-

43

bert, whose career in the merchant marine had been nearing its end, what with a leg injury, attacks of dysentery and cholera, and his not securing a desired ship command. Despite doubts about his ability, Albert succumbed to his elder brother's letters and traveled to the plantation in the fall of 1833. Less than a year later, Quitman enlarged Albert's responsibilities by purchasing an adjacent piece of land and in 1837 Quitman gained Robert J. Walker's 1,200-arpent tract about two miles farther up the bayou.[5]

On New Year's Day, 1834, Quitman, for $66,500 in cash and credit, purchased a functioning cotton plantation called Springfield, in Natchez's immediate vicinity. A nine-mile horseback ride from Monmouth, Springfield fronted the Mississippi River. Although the fifteen slaves and the gins and other equipment were included in the agreement, Quitman had to make additional major outlays to bring this place up to his expectations. Even before he took possession, he spent $104 for two yoke of oxen, and in February he bought three sorrel horses for $250. He also had seventeen plows, a barrel of pork, a keg of nails, and other items brought out. Since Springfield did not have enough slaves to suit him, he purchased "4 negroes to wit—James[,] Joice, Grace & Elizabeth from Mr. Tabor for $2050." His overseer drew a $600 annual salary, and, as with Live Oaks, Quitman quickly bought adjacent tracts. In 1835, he purchased an additional forty slaves "to aid Albert and to improve my own means."[6]

These investments put Quitman in a serious financial hole, but his hopes were high. Planting during a period of economic boom, he assumed that profits would roll in before his obligations came due. "Land, negroes, and every description of property has become very valuable here," he explained to his brother Henry. "The country is in the most prosperous condition. Cotton at 20 cents and sugar at 10 cts. Albert and myself will I hope next year make 150 hhds."[7] He found far more cause for concern, in fact, in the growth of antislavery feeling in the North. For a man who had craved wealth and respectability since adolescence, it was intolerable that the morality of his past accomplishments and his means of becoming prosperous were suddenly being called into question.

There had always been some antislavery agitation in the North since the early days of the Republic; indeed, some of the slave states had even demonstrated an occasional interest in emancipating the slaves. But the northern abolition movement of the early 1830s was something else entirely. There was a stridency to the demand for emancipation that had been lacking earlier—an insistence that an immediate start be made. The movement, though it never represented more than a small minority of the northern people, still had a wider base of mass support than emancipationists had been able to summon in the past. Thousands of committed northern men and women were joining antislavery societies, and antislavery presses were churning out thousands of pages of tracts. The new movement had the fervor and perfectionist philosophy of the day's religious revivals; abolition speakers utilized evangelistic methods to persuade audiences of the righteousness of the cause. The abolitionists, moreover, drew inspiration from the English Parliament, which had enacted a program of emancipation in the British West Indies.

Southerners feared that the abolitionists might ultimately gain the political strength to eradicate slavery either by congressional fiat or constitutional amendment. They also perceived that abolitionists might be able to destroy the institution if they managed to secure legislation banning the domestic slave trade, ending slavery in the national capital, and crippling slavery in other indirect ways. Even if abolitionists refrained from blatant political assault, or lacked the political muscle to enact such programs, there remained a possibility that they could export their message to the slaves and undermine the institution. On January 1, 1831, William Lloyd Garrison released the first issue of his militant antislavery newspaper, the *Liberator*. When Nat Turner, just months after the *Liberator* first appeared, organized a slave revolt during which some sixty white men, women and children were killed, many southerners assumed that the newspaper had provided Turner's inspiration. Though there was no evidence that the Virginia slave preacher had read Garrison's words, North Carolina put a price of $5,000 on Garrison's head and Georgia offered the same reward for Garrison's extradition to Georgia for trial.[8]

Few white southerners enjoyed total immunity from apprehensions of servile revolt, but uneasiness naturally waxed strongest in those regions which had the most at stake economically in slave labor and which had the highest demographic ratio of blacks to whites. Mississippians, living in a state where 48.1 percent of the population was black, certainly had cause for concern. To J. F. H. Claiborne, the "servile population" was increasing with such "alarming rapidity" that the state stood over a "volcano . . . ready to belch up its lava." He could foresee a "scene so dark and gory" that the mother would "shudder and hug her infant more closely to her bosom." Few Mississippians were unaware of the "fate of St. Domingo"—the triumph of black revolution just a few decades earlier—and the press kept a vigil over incidents of slave unrest both in the United States and in other countries. Thus, subscribers to the *Mississippi Democrat* (Woodville) in 1831 could follow Nat Turner's actions and also learn that authorities in Rio de Janeiro had uncovered a plot "amongst the blacks and mulattoes to murder all the white population of the country."[9]

Sensing their own vulnerability, some Mississippi whites favored deporting free blacks to Africa, as a means of defusing the potential for black uprising. Free blacks were feared as a subversive group capable of revolutionary acts themselves or of inciting or inspiring slaves to dangerous behavior.[10] But other Mississippians, including Chancellor Quitman, found South Carolina's nullification movement a far more effective response to demographic realities and the challenge of abolition.

Nullification, a doctrine commonly identified with John C. Calhoun, Andrew Jackson's first-term vice president, sought to restrain federal power by giving individual states the right to deem federal laws unconstitutional and unenforceable within their borders if they did so through state conventions; according to the South Carolinian's logic, since state conventions had initially ratified the United States Constitution, they therefore had the right to determine when federal power had exceeded its authorized limits.

Ostensibly, nullification derived from South Carolina's outrage over the 1828 federal tariff—legislation which gave considerable protection to northern pig-iron, hemp, flax, and wool producers, and wool manufacturers. Protective tariffs caused southerners to pay more for such goods, and also risked foreign retaliation against the flourishing southern export trade in cotton and other staple crops. When South Carolinians actually availed themselves of Calhoun's theory in a November, 1832, convention, they declared the 1828 and 1832 tariffs null and void. However, many nullifiers were prosperous rice planters and economically optimistic Sea Island cotton growers troubled far more by South Carolina's racial imbalance and the possibility of slave revolt than by rising prices for imported goods. Coastal areas had as much as an eight-to-one black/white ratio, and in Charleston in the early 1820s there had been an abortive slave revolt and repeated instances of arson by slaves. What South Carolinians really intended through nullification was to establish a *precedent* of state power which could later be applied to any federal interference with slavery. The tariff issue had the advantage of making the desired point without bringing the actual legitimacy of holding slaves even into debate.[11]

Unfortunately, we lack hard evidence as to why John Quitman, in particular, became a nullifier—a southern radical—in the early 1830s. He left no documents explaining his process of conversion, if, indeed, he experienced a single moment of political revelation. However, it is clear that he harbored no affection for protective tariffs. His memoranda book reveals that he read newspaper arguments on both sides and that he concluded that the protective tariff was injurious to his own economic welfare. "In Aug 1827," he wrote, "I purchased 1300 yds bagging for use at 30 cts. [A]t this time Scotch bag. was selling at Jamaica for 10 1/2 cts, we therefore paid on this article upwards of $200 tax to tariff."

It is even more apparent that Quitman had some doubts about the long-term security of the slave regime, and that he was troubled by abolitionism. Quitman's plantations and home were all located in areas of high black population density. Blacks outnumbered whites in the Natchez region; in the Live Oaks vicinity, the median number of slaves held per plantation reached a whopping eighty-one. Quitman never panicked about the danger of race revolt. But during the late 1820s and early 1830s, the period when his adult ideology became fixed, Quitman was concerned that the black labor force might overstep the bounds of control. Quitman advocated a tighter militia system, for instance, partly because of the "slave population around our firesides." He also envisioned a potential northern threat to slavery if states' rights principles were not soon established at the national level. Writing to Claiborne in January, 1830, he warned how northern *"friends"* had taken southern "Indians and negroes under their special care," and predicted that ultimately the North would try to "regulate all our domestic legislation" unless the state resisted.[12] Circumstantial evidence, thus, indicates that timing—a matter of chronology—lay at the heart of Quitman's radicalization. Quitman could not cope with the challenge that abolitionists seemed to present *at the very moment* when he had joined the planter ranks.

Quitman had come to identify with his adopted section and its institutions so completely that when he returned to Rhinebeck for a visit in the summer of 1831 (including a two-week sojourn in New England), he felt alienated from what he saw happening there. Given the religious attitudes he inherited from his father, he could not help but find week-long revival meetings offensive. He also noted the connection between the rise of religious evangelicalism and the abolition movement. He was repulsed by evangelical preachers who begged for contributions for Indians, slaves, and other causes such as temperance societies and foreign missions, and concluded, after seeing the "splendid edifices" housing the American Tract Society and other New York City philanthropies, that corruption lay at the root of reform. In one of the most bitter comments he would ever make about northern society, he denounced the philanthropic "clerks . . . salaried liberally out of contributions wrung from pious and frugal persons in the South; and these officials, like the majority of their theologians and divines, are inimical to our institutions, and use our money to defame and damage us! . . . I am heartily tired of the North, and, except parting from my relations, shall feel happy when I set my face homeward."[13]

As Quitman began speaking of his anxieties to acquaintances, he found himself striking a responsive chord. Congressman Ellis, for instance, wrote Quitman that national power might extend so far that federal authorities might prevent Mississippi River slaveowners from punishing slaves "if they attempt to rise to insurrection against their Masters." Some advisors pressed him to go public with his opinions since state legislators had begun considering him as a possible candidate for the Senate and they wanted to know his views in more depth. Claiborne informed him that while he could stay aloof from issues as chancellor, he had to declare his principles openly if he had any political aspirations. "[I]t will be expedient and proper to take bold ground on the leading questions of the day," Claiborne urged. "You are not regarded strictly as a party man, but your sentiments are believed to be in harmony with the great body of the people." [14]

Ready, indeed, to return from the political shadows, Quitman only puzzled over how to direct his emerging strict constructionist logic into appropriate political channels. Could he support Andrew Jackson, who had frozen Vice President Calhoun out of his administration and made clear that he would not tolerate any effort to implement nullification in South Carolina? In addition, it seemed that Martin Van Buren, who had been instrumental in steering the 1828 tariff through Congress, might displace Calhoun as vice president in a second Jackson administration. Yet Henry Clay, the National Republican alternative to Jackson, seemed unappealing. Too much distance had come between Quitman's ideology and Clay's American System; Quitman simplified Clay's constituency, stigmatizing the Kentuckian as drawing his support from Anti-Masons, religious fanatics opposed to Sunday mail deliveries, manufacturers, laborers, and philanthropists. This would not do for Mississippi's leading Mason, a man who had rejected evangelism and its theological and social thrust. Perceiving both parties as ideologically tainted, Quitman turned to the idea of an independent, third-party movement. Perhaps southern Republicans could unite behind an antitariff ticket headed by Calhoun, or run an unpledged ticket of electors who could make concessions to the South the price of their votes. [15]

Quitman was influenced toward the latter course after encountering George Poindexter, a U.S. senator from Mississippi, in Charlottesville, Virginia, during his return from Rhinebeck in 1831. Poindexter may have been one of the most "dissipated" politicians Mississippi had ever produced—he was often intoxicated during congressional sessions; his personal affairs had been marred by a divorce, the death of his second wife, gambling, and many feuds. Nevertheless, he had an extended public career, was renowned for his codification of state law, and provided Quitman a model for independent political behavior. Technically a Jacksonian when appointed senator, Poindexter harbored little love for the president and had seized upon the tariff and patronage matters to break openly with the administration. Sensing local discontent over Jackson's tendency to select out-of-staters for Mississippi's patronage plums, Poindexter had influenced the Senate to obstruct several presidential appointments. Mississippi Jacksonians were furious at Poindexter's course, particularly when he was instrumental in the Senate's refusal in January, 1832, to confirm Jackson's choice of Van Buren as minister to England. "Judge Poindexter is Dead . . . he is not Worth a whores Curse," sneered one administration booster.[16]

Quitman found Poindexter a man of "extraordinary intellectual powers" who was far more moral than his opponents would acknowledge, and marveled at the similarity between Poindexter's "political opinions" and his own. Apparently Poindexter tutored Quitman in nullification principles during their talk, for it was in the months following their meeting that Quitman announced his radical beliefs. Spurning an opportunity to serve as elector in 1832 for Henry Clay's pro-Bank ticket, Quitman asserted that the tariff issue should supersede other public questions. He began giving speeches endorsing state resistance to the protective principle. "[R]ode to Natchez and from thence to the old court house to [hear] Judge Quitman on subject nullification supposed they were nullifying doctrines," noted a former client of Quitman's, Natchez planter John Nevitt, that July.[17]

Concern over the security of the Mississippi plantation regime, which he had so recently joined, shaped John Quitman's transformation from transplanted northerner to southern sectionalist. Though he never expressed fear of harm at the hands of his own servants and field hands, Quitman did believe that the whole slave system might be undermined by outside pressure. This explains his promising a Texan acquaintance in 1842, for instance, that southerners would "never permit an Indian and negro colony to be planted on the frontier. Come what will, that must not happen." Slave revolt remained the unspoken fear of many Mississippi whites, a subject, as Claiborne put it, on which "the curtain must remain undrawn."[18] Quitman never rid himself of anxieties that the slave labor system might prove vulnerable to attack; this explains why he insisted so vocally upon its inviolability.

5

Everything Has Gone Against Us

THOUGH he could tolerate a lot of discomfort, John Quitman never did adjust to Jackson, Mississippi. Back in town again for six weeks in September and October of 1832, a delegate to his state's second constitutional convention, he found that the town had just not grown up enough. His shared room at T. B. J. Hadley's tavern was passable; but the fare was poor and the weather miserable. The nights in September were so sultry that he found sleeping difficult, and after the heat wave broke, the sun rarely appeared. Constant brawling among the town's common sort repulsed him, and he wrote home that an innkeeper was near death after being shot by a carpenter.

Quitman's perspective on the town might have been cheerier had things been going his way during the convention's deliberations; but that meeting was bent on what its majority faction considered reform, which to him meant endorsing "lawless force and violence." He found himself battling for the losing side on most important issues. Six weeks in Jackson cost Quitman twenty pounds in weight and brought an unhealthy yellow tint to his complexion. It is ironic that he would later be remembered as the "father" of Mississippi's constitution, because as he prepared to vote on it during the convention's last day, he could only calculate the extent of his failure.[1]

By the early 1830s, a new Mississippi constitution had become but a matter of timing, as strident calls for alterations in the 1817 document could no longer be suppressed. Prevailing opinion held that public funds could be saved if the state legislature held only biennial rather than annual sessions; legal experts promoted reforms such as limitations on judicial tenure; demands circulated for revised court districts and legislative apportionment. Even Quitman's Natchez District acknowledged the necessity of a convention. Given the inevitability of a new constitution, and since convention apportionment would be based upon apportionment in the state legislature, the

Natchez area stood to gain if the meeting occurred before thirty new counties in the Choctaw cession could formally organize. In December, 1830, the legislature called for a referendum on a convention, and the next August the people endorsed the call by a 4-to-1 majority. The legislature then decided that delegates would be selected at the next general election—set for August, 1832—and that the convention would meet that September.[2]

John Quitman worked earnestly for a seat in that convention perhaps, in part, as an outlet from domestic problems. Louisa had almost died of scarlet fever during the family's return trip from the North, and the child remained weak for some time thereafter. In June, death finally rescued Quitman's father from debilitating pain and discomfort. While Reverend Quitman's death was somewhat of a relief to his son, his passing nonetheless brought problems. As the most successful male in the Quitman line, John felt responsibility for his Rhinebeck relations. He learned by mail that his stepmother and sister Frederica were in the process of moving to Albany, but he did not know what the rest of the family would do when they had to vacate the parsonage the next spring. John pondered their future and began to assume a somewhat supervisory role toward his New York relations. He directed the preparation of an appropriate marble slab for his father's tomb, the first of many obligations. Meanwhile, the Quitman brood at Monmouth was ever multiplying; Eliza and John had had a child every even-numbered year. Frederick Henry had been born in September, 1830. The most recent arrival had been Edward Turner, born in April, 1832.[3]

Although Quitman managed to win the endorsement of an Adams County meeting in May for election to a convention seat, his strident nullification views, which by now were circulating among public officials, jeopardized his candidacy. Already Quitman, like Calhoun, had to confront a charge—which would echo again and again throughout his career—that his states' rights views masked his real objective, southern secession. Withdrawal from the Union, to much of the Adams County gentry and town citizenry, portended dislocations and social disorder. It seemed to make little sense to chart such an uncertain course during good times, with a southern slaveholder as president. So "MANY CITIZENS" issued a call for a public meeting on July 19 at the Natchez courthouse to reconsider Quitman's nomination. According to the summons, Quitman's views paralleled Calhoun's and intended "anarchy," "*disunion*," and a "Southern league."

Quitman could not afford to ignore this challenge. So he released his own statement which maintained that his private political opinions were irrelevant to his convention service, but nonetheless obliquely considered the secession charge. Calling for the public to attend a separate meeting at the courthouse on the twentieth to hear his side of the controversy, he traced his philosophy to Thomas Jefferson's resolutions against the Alien and Sedition Acts of 1798. It was a prudent move. Jefferson, as one of the most hallowed of the founding fathers (particularly among Jacksonians), provided a far more reputable ideological fountainhead than did the controversial Calhoun.[4]

Quitman soon found that he had to attend the meeting on the nineteenth. Too many people, from all parts of the county, were appearing in Natchez for it, and he heard that he might get dumped as a candidate. So he went, and may well have bored the crowd into agreeing that he could continue his candidacy because the meeting's report described him as speaking "at considerable length" about federal-state governmental relations. Apparently Quitman managed to muddle the secession issue, because the meeting issued an ambiguous explanation of its decision:

> *Resolved,* As to the sense of this meeting, that we are opposed to the doctrine of nullification, and believe that its propagation would endanger our dearest and best interests; that John A. Quitman having at this meeting made a distinct exposition of his views upon the subject of the relation which the state and federal government bear to each other, said views do not amount to nullification, *according to the usual acceptation of the term* [italics mine], and that said John A. Quitman ought to be supported for the convention on the ticket as originally selected.[5]

Quitman, however, remained insecure about his election prospects. A few days later, he issued a 4,144-word position paper entitled "To the Electors of Adams County" in a further effort to harmonize his views with those of his constituency. The statement shrewdly diverted attention from the volatile nullification question (Quitman said that he had already, and publicly, met the charge of "entertaining obnoxious political principles") to new issues which had been brewing since the legislature's convention call. Although he noted his opposition to taxing citizens' riverfront lands at rates higher than for the same quality of land elsewhere, he focused almost exclusively upon a growing demand that the convention establish an elective judiciary. Quitman, disputing the fashionable view of the masses as "saints" in all things, contended that that would cause the judiciary to forfeit its independence and integrity—particularly its already-demonstrated willingness to preserve private contracts against such majoritarian attacks as debtor relief laws. The courts would have no motive to fulfill their mission of protecting the weak against the strong, the infirm and poor against the rich and powerful. Rather, judges would render decisions pleasing to voters, regardless of the weight of evidence. They could hardly be impartial, he argued, if they assumed the bench just after a "hot electioneering canvass" when they had benefited from political favors and developed enmities toward opponents. Even if they did strive for impartiality, they would never win the trust of former rivals. In the end, the entire judiciary establishment would be lowered in public esteem. Judicial selection, Quitman urged, should be entrusted to the governor. Let some other state initiate the "new-fangled" experiment of electing judges before Mississippi took the plunge into legal disorder.

A conservative had spoken, but it was a reasonable conservative rather than a reactionary. Quitman conceded that there should be limits on judicial tenure and affirmed support for universal manhood suffrage. He repudiated rumors that he had claimed that mechanics should stay out of politics and that he favored a property requirement for voting and officeholding. Restrictions on suffrage, he warned, would inevitably produce "discontent and revolution."

Thanks to Quitman's speech and statement, he led a field of six candidates in the county balloting that August, and naturally concluded that the people had given him a mandate to take his brand of conservatism to the convention, where he might brake the popular, and apparently victory-bound, democratic forces. Finishing up some duties on the judicial circuit, he wrote Eliza, "Wherever I have been hundreds have expressed their gratification at my election to the convention. The people have I fear gone wild throughout the state." Quitman observed how his friend John Guion had been denied election by the democratic tide. The chancellor would have his work cut out if he was to make a serious effort in restraining Mississippi's rush to reform.[6]

On Monday, September 10, Quitman and forty-seven other delegates filed into the state capitol to commence deliberations on the constitution. The convention decided that separate committees should consider the main divisions of the constitution, which included the bill of rights, executive department, judicial department, legislative department, and general provisions. Quitman was appointed to preside over the fifteen members of the judicial committee. He was a natural for this assignment, given his status as chancellor and his outspokenness on the judiciary question during his recent campaign.

When he accepted the committee duty, Quitman wondered if it might prove meaningless. The delegates listened to him with "the greatest attention and respect," and he had willing allies such as his friend Judge John Black of the Mississippi Supreme Court. But he felt that most of his colleagues were too young and inexperienced, and he worried that intrigues might subvert his efforts. Within a few days he believed his apprehensions realized. On the twenty-third he wrote Eliza that he expected to be outvoted by the "judge electing men" who had "prejudged the cause" and were not really prepared to give his viewpoint genuine consideration.[7]

It turned out that Quitman could not even control his committee, much less the convention floor. He had to dissent from his committee's report, presented to the convention on the nineteenth. The committee went "whole hog" in rallying to the elective principle: now the people would decide the composition of the supreme court (to be renamed the High Court of Errors and Appeals) and would elect court clerks and justices of the peace. On the twentieth, supported by Thomas Falconer (a Wayne County nullifier), he submitted a minority report offering striking alternatives to the majority's proposals. The minority report conceded that circuit court clerks might be elected, but proposed that the governor appoint judges and that the higher state courts, which under Quitman's scheme would continue the chancery court instead of combining it with the supreme court, could select their own clerks.[8]

Quitman carried his crusade to the convention floor, and the judiciary became the meeting's most hotly contested issue. He almost relished the role of playing Quixote for a losing cause, writing Eliza on October 2, "Several days ago I made a long speech on . . . the Judiciary. All the ladies from Clinton 40 or 50 in number were here and besides them a large audience. We have however no hope of success[.] The *people's* doctrine will undoubtedly prevail. We may succeed in making some modifications which will make the pill less bitter and more palatable." But the pill remained potent, despite his efforts and the efforts of others sympathetic to his logic. That very day the convention crushed an attempt to amend the majority report by striking out the election of the three judges of the High Court of Errors and Appeals in a 26-18 vote. The next day brought an even more ignominious defeat, when Quitman, trying to underline his warning that campaigning for office would politicize the judiciary, moved that judges elected to the high court be ineligible for any state office for five years after their election, and found only two other delegates willing to join him in the balloting. However, Quitman did win a few concessions. He persuaded the convention to require a two-thirds—rather than one-half—vote of both legislative houses in impeachment proceedings against supreme and circuit court judges; the delegates also agreed to perpetuate the chancery court system. Nevertheless, it was evident that mass democracy would define the Mississippi court system, and the final document left the choice of chancellor, judges of the high court, justices of the peace, circuit, probate and other court clerks, boards of police, district attorneys, and the state attorney general to the people's wisdom.[9]

To Quitman's chagrin, moreover, democratization was carried well beyond the judiciary. State officials such as treasurer, secretary of state, auditor of public accounts, and militia officers would be elected, despite the preference of Quitman and other conservatives for legislative selection. For Quitman, many of the convention ballots were little more than an exercise in futility; thus, when he supported an attempt to moderate rotation in office by allowing sheriffs and coroners to hold office for four of every six years rather than four of every eight years, he found himself in a minuscule eleven-man minority (out of fifty-two votes). When yet another effort to move the state capital came to nought, Quitman despaired to Eliza, "A vote was taken yesterday on the seat of Gov't. Jackson succeeded. I am . . . sorry. . . . I voted for Vicksburg." Mississippi's convention was producing, despite John Quitman and other determined conservatives, the most democratic constitution (for whites, of course) in the whole country.[10]

Still, Quitman stayed until the end, taking solace in newspaper notices of his speeches and resolutions; the articles, he wrote Eliza, proved that he had "not taken an inferior station in this body." Because he persisted, he left his personal imprint on the final document—not only in the bill of rights but in one clause which did promise some restraint on democracy run amok. Article VIII, Section 9, carefully circumscribed procedures for future commitments of state credit. This provision, making it difficult for the state to back corporation bonds, later had such an impact upon Quitman's public career and the course of antebellum Mississippi politics, it bears quotation:

> No law shall ever be passed to raise a loan of money upon the credit of the State, or to pledge the faith of the State for the payment of any loan or debt, unless such law be proposed in the Senate or House of Representatives, and be agreed to by a majority of the members of each House . . . and be referred to the next succeeding Legislature, and published for three months previous to the next regular election, in three newspapers of this State, and unless a majority of each branch of the Legislature so elected, after such publication, shall agree to, and pass such law.

Thus pledges of state credit would have to pass two successive legislatures before becoming law.[11]

Such victories, however, came nowhere near compensating for the string of defeats which Quitman experienced. When in late October it came time for the final vote on the entire constitution, Quitman tried to obstruct its implementation by moving its submission to the people in a referendum to be held on the second Monday in January, 1833. This one he lost, 26 to 19. Given his opposition to popular democracy throughout the convention, his motion might be chalked up to hypocrisy, but he seems to have genuinely believed that it was fraudulent to force a constitution upon a people without their consent. "Everything has gone against us," he exclaimed to Eliza. "The Convention has just refused to submit the amended constitution to the people. This I consider one of the greatest outrages ever committed on a free people." His ideology, it seems, made a sharp differentiation between republican government and democracy run rampant. Then on October 16, he registered his alienation from the prevailing political culture by voting, with nine other dissidents, against the adoption of the document upon which he had labored so diligently. Following a farewell address by convention president P. Rutilius R. Pray congratulating the delegates for having "pushed forward the bounds of legitimate democracy," the historic meeting adjourned.[12]

Quitman discovered, however, that he could not put the convention behind him. He had, after all, more than an abstract interest in the elective judiciary principle. The convention's decisions meant that he would have to run for office if he wanted to retain his chancellorship. That he would choose to do so was not at all an automatic decision. Becoming a supplicant for votes held little appeal for him; besides, he hazarded the charge of hypocrisy if he participated in the very election process which he had denunciated so fervently. Perhaps he would surrender his position without a fight.

Members of the Mississippi bar attending chancery court in Clinton that December were appalled to learn of Quitman's irresolution. They petitioned him to run in the 1833 spring election, praising his integrity and assuring him that the state's voters would not want to do without his services. Their flattery and the encouragement of correspondents like John Black (who was now filling a partial term as U.S. senator) persuaded Quitman to give it a try. Ironically, as things turned out, no one rose to challenge him. People from all over the state who had never even met him, as Quitman's nephew Frederick Quackenboss explained from Yazoo County, felt comfortable about having him on the bench. Quitman had established an enviable reputation.[13]

Upstaging Quitman's personal vindication, moreover, was the general trend indicated in the first balloting under the new constitution, which not only failed to bring an earthquake to the state's judicial structure but hardly even produced a slight tremor. The new elective process elevated familiar faces to office. Two of the three elected judges of the High Court of Errors and Appeals, William Sharkey and Cotesworth P. Smith, had served on the former supreme court. High court judges were more likely to be nullifiers than Jacksonian Democrats. One had to use a political magnifying glass to find evidence for Quitman's dire predictions that an elective judiciary would bring the degradation of the entire judicial framework. Mass democracy was demonstrating surprising restraint.

Quitman's anguished crusade for an appointive judiciary had been proven irrelevant. Coming years would do little to vindicate Quitman's jeremiads.

Quitman himself eventually came to realize his folly. In 1845 he wrote that his fears had not been well founded, and that experience had established the Mississippi system as "the best mode of selecting judicial officers." [14]

Actually, it is somewhat ironic that Quitman put such emphasis in the first place on keeping the judiciary apolitical since he had no intention of staying aloof from politics, even when reelected chancellor. Soon John Quitman, the southern politician, would find himself quite involved in the partisan fray.

6

Calhoun's Protégé

OR a man who considered himself an expert marksman, it must have been humiliating. Early in March, 1833, Quitman had set out to visit his Terrebonne Parish interests. After stopping in New Orleans, where he picked up some toys for the children and a variety of items for Eliza including a breastpin and ornaments for the mantel, he proceeded to Grand Caillou. His mishap occurred when he decided to take a boat journey down the bayou to the Gulf. Standing on a bench of the boat, he drew his loaded pistol from his pocket—apparently to shoot at wildlife—and it accidentally discharged, the bullet going through his calf and settling in his instep. He had to be hauled forty-five miles by boat and cart to a plantation physician, and when neither that doctor nor a surgeon in New Orleans could extract the bullet, he had to return, lame, to Monmouth. Hoping that the ball would eventually pass totally through his foot, he confined himself to bed, occasionally making his way around the house on crutches. He was still using crutches in May and, as late as August, needed a cane to get around.[1]

Misfortune stalked Quitman that spring. In May, while he was recuperating, a cholera epidemic claimed the lives of his sons Edward and John, who died within a day of each other. Quitman had them buried together beneath a tree near his garden. He poured out his anguish in a letter to his sister: "The hand of Providence has fallen heavily upon me in these last three days. Our beloved little Edward . . . was for about a week affected with derangement of the bowels, which at length resulted in cholera, and his pure spirit left this world. . . . Oh! this was a severe blow to his fond parents, but a heavier blow yet was in store. On the night before last, my beloved, my beautiful, noble, and affectionate little John was seized with the fatal scourge, without any premonitory symptoms, and in six hours the little angel left this world." That his eldest son had borne the affliction with incredible resignation only wrenched Quitman's heart all the more. John had calmly predicted his own death, just two hours after he first fell ill.

The tragedy seems to have sapped some of the vitality from Quitman's marriage. Eliza fell "inconsolable" with grief, and Quitman found it very hard getting over his loss even though Eliza would give birth again within the year (Sarah Elizabeth, on March 14, 1834). He had desperately wanted sons to follow in his footsteps; but now all he had left was Henry, a youth who seemed to him more a Turner than a Quitman. John Anthony, especially, had reminded him of his own father. "High hopes" and "expectations" had all been shattered. Consolatory letters arrived from family and friends; fellow Natchez attorney Felix Huston wrote that he was still shedding tears on his own "midnight pillow" for a departed son. But words of sympathy could only go so far. In August, Quitman and Eliza were still constantly dwelling on "the time when we were surrounded by our dear little boys." Much of their hearts were buried, he wrote, in their sons' graves.[2]

Consumed by sorrow, Quitman found an outlet in resumed political advocacy and public service. During the very months he was laid up at Monmouth, South Carolina's confrontation with federal power over the tariff entered its final stage. That state threatened secession if President Jackson and Congress did not accede to its unilateral abrogation of the 1828 and 1832 tariffs. Jackson showed a willingness to compromise on tariff schedules, but also denounced nullification as "treason" and took steps to quash South Carolina's resistance, including a request to Congress for authorization to employ the army and navy in the crisis. The specter of war hung in the air until Congress passed Senator Henry Clay's bill which lowered the tariff gradually over a ten-year period. In response, South Carolina's convention met again on March 11, 1833, and repealed its tariff nullification. Although no other state had officially joined the Palmetto State in its resistance, the issue of whether an individual state could defy federal law lay unresolved. South Carolina had intentionally left this issue dangling, by coupling a nullification of Congress' "Force Act" (legislation granting the president authorization to use military power against South Carolina) with its repeal of the nullification of the tariff. Already Mississippi's legislature and congressional delegation had spoken out, with the legislature endorsing Jackson's position and Senators Poindexter and Black and Representative Plummer rallying to South Carolina. Quitman, who—as Jefferson Davis later put it—had made John Calhoun's principles his "light and guide," could remain aloof from politics no longer.[3]

During an unusually severe cold wave in January, 1834, which sent temperatures plunging to zero, Quitman took up South Carolina's right to nullify the tariff. He had traveled to Jackson, accompanied by a body servant named Harry Nichols, to conduct a chancery court session. Since the weather delayed the arrival of some of the lawyers, court business sputtered, providing Quitman ample time to mingle with acquaintances and exchange views about federal power. Judges William Sharkey and Cotesworth P. Smith of the High Court of Errors and Appeals, then also in session, and quite a few members of the bar concurred that Mississippi should support South Carolina. So a "spur of the occasion" meeting of twenty-two men was held in the senate chamber on the night of January 11.

Quitman opened the meeting by calling Chief Justice Sharkey to the chair, who announced that the gathering's purpose was to organize a "State Rights" political party. Then Sharkey turned the proceedings over to Quitman, who introduced resolutions—which were unanimously approved—calling for a general convention in Jackson on the third Monday in May. Supporters were asked to hold meetings in their respective counties to select convention delegates. Quitman, Natchez acquaintance and former supreme court judge George Winchester, and one other participant were to draft an address for statewide circulation; then the meeting adjourned. Reconvening on January 20, the States' Righters approved the address. Quitman's name headed this radical document, which called for the preservation of the states against the "Force Bill" principles; said that the people had the right to judge how much power they had ceded to the federal government in the U.S. Constitution; and argued that federal laws not pursuant to the Constitution were "null and void" and could bind neither a state's government nor its people. The document warned that the president might assume dictatorial powers if not restrained, and pronounced it the "duty of every good citizen who loves his country and cherishes the sacred institutions of his fathers, never to suffer an invasion of our political constitution . . . without a determined persevering resistance."

George Poindexter's law partner, former state supreme court judge Isaac Caldwell, left the January meetings hopeful that within two years the "Nullies" would capture their state by persuading people to "throw off the despotic yoke . . . and espouse the true doctrines of republicanism." By February, four papers circulated in the state upholding the cause, but it proved difficult to translate a party apparatus into a mass movement. Democrats immediately counterattacked, and their followers rallied. The Democratic organ, the *Mississippian*, lambasted Quitman and the other judges for infringing on the traditions that the bench should be apolitical, and revived the bugaboo that nullification portended secession. According to *Mississippian* gossip, one of the January nullifiers had even been overheard saying privately, "*Oh! what a snug little Republic we could have South of the Poto-*

mac.'' The paper warned that the nullifier program would "terminate in civil commotion and bloodshed.'' How foolhardy it would be for Mississippians to desert a president who had provided the nation peace and a full treasury.[4]

Undaunted, the States' Righters forged ahead with their May convention. Thirty delegates appeared for the opening session on the nineteenth, and others filtered in later. Most hailed from the old Natchez District, but some came from Hinds, Madison, Rankin, and Tallahatchie counties. After a day devoted to organizational proceedings, the convention adopted a constitution for a state party with affiliated county associations and selected John I. Guion as "President of the State Rights Association of Mississippi.'' On the twenty-first, the delegates approved resolutions which maintained that the legislature's support for President Jackson had been unrepresentative of public opinion in Mississippi, and contended that Mississippians would have rushed to South Carolina's rescue had Jackson dared use force to "butcher'' her citizenry.

The "*leading spirit*'' of the convention (according to a hostile reporter), Quitman served on the steering committee, helped draft the resolutions, and made floor addresses. Speaking on the twentieth in support of the proposed party constitution, he contended that the states were separate political entities joined in a league rather than a consolidated government. Ungenerously, he attributed his opponents' inspiration to the lure of federal patronage, striking a theme to which he would too often revert later in his political career. He even dared to label the Jacksonians as "Federalists'' in his effort to taint them with centralist doctrines. How proud States' Righters should be, he suggested, that they, unlike Democrats, were not motivated by ambition for public office. The delegates justified his exaggerations by wildly cheering his remarks. The next day, in response to reports that his speech had already been "severely criticized out of doors,'' Quitman denied the nullification-secession equation, arguing that the party's goal was to perpetuate the Union by keeping the lines between the states and federal authority distinct.[5]

The May meeting was fated, however, to be the apex of Mississippi nullification. The States' Rights party, had it been able to muster all disaffected Democrats and other anti-Jacksonians, might have evolved into a truly competitive political movement. But this was not to be. At the national level, nullifier John C. Calhoun was cooperating with the leadership of a new anti-Jackson political coalition, the Whig party, and by the spring of 1834 the new organization was gaining ground in Mississippi.

Whiggery made for a fragile coalition, as its national leaders, such as Calhoun and Henry Clay, did not agree on what constituted legitimate exercise of federal power (though Clay edged a bit toward Calhoun's strict constructionism in the mid-1830s). However, Whigs found unity in the belief that President Jackson had abused his prerogatives of office, particularly regarding the Bank of the United States. The president had vetoed recharter of the institution in 1832 and, in the early fall of 1833, had tried to hasten the Bank's expiration date by transferring government deposits to other banks— "pet banks," in the jargon of Jackson's opponents. Nicholas Biddle, president of the Bank, in an effort to pressure Jackson to reverse direction, ordered his branch bank executives to curtail loans. This forced state banks to call in loans to meet obligations to the Bank at a time when they had overextended themselves. An economic panic resulted. Whigs thought the president had gone much too far. The party, in fact, took its name from British parliamentary opposition to King George III during the American Revolution.

Mississippi proved fertile ground for Whig organizers, for panic struck the state in 1834. The Natchez branch of the Bank (which had finally been chartered in 1831) reduced its discounts in response to Biddle's policies, and the Planters' Bank of Natchez, the new depository for federal funds in Mississippi, was forced to call in loans after receiving notification that $500,000 had to be transferred to the Union Bank of Louisiana. When rumors soon circulated that the Planters' Bank might lack the specie to redeem the notes it had issued, cotton prices plummeted and credit dried up.[6]

The sudden emergence of Mississippi Whiggery posed quite a dilemma for Quitman. The new party could hardly be ignored; in fact it soon absorbed many in his nullifier faction. In Congress, George Poindexter assumed so vigorous a pro-Bank position that Whig senators rewarded him with the position of president *pro tempore*, and John Black demanded that federal deposits be returned to the Bank. Black, moreover, pressured Quitman to join the Whigs, arguing that if the States' Righters persisted in running candidates for office, they would only split the anti-Jacksonian ranks and ensure Democratic victory. Could not Quitman sacrifice his "own particular notion of State remedies" for the "broad *Whig* principles of opposition to assumed power"? But Quitman hesitated to sell out the States' Rights party. He was not as certain as Black that the Whigs would prove an effective instrument for ensuring strict constructionist principles.[7]

Ultimately, Quitman proved realist enough to acknowledge that his dream of a potent states' rights party had become a will-o'-the-wisp. Rather than continue a futile crusade, he effected a marriage of convenience with the Adams County Whigs. He would become a states' rights Whig. On June 18, he participated in a local Whig gathering which formulated party policy. The meeting censured the president, endorsed rechartering the Bank, and recommended that a state convention of the new party be held in December.[8]

The Jacksonians had a field day attacking the Whig party, because it amalgamated so many disparate ideologies. Whiggery, from their perspective, seemed a "many headed monster," an alliance of "heterogeneous political materials" as abominable as an "African naming his child George Washington." Special barbs were hurled at Quitman for betraying his own principles by supporting a political cause which, through banking, would enhance federal power. "Curtius," in the *Mississippian* observed, "It will be perceived by the Resolutions adopted at the late Natchez meeting, that the Federalists and the Nullifiers have openly united, and come out in favor of the Bank. I confess that I am astonished . . . that the Nullifiers would so far abandon their ground . . . to sanction and support the United States' Bank, in the very teeth of their *constitutional scruples*. . . . And yet, Chancellor Quitman and Mr. (by courtesy, *Judge*) Winchester, who assume to be the leaders of the Nullifiers in this State, have publickly [*sic*] pledged themselves to the Bank." But, on second thought, what could one expect from a man who had always been, deep down, a John Quincy Adams supporter? The *Mississippian* virtually dared Quitman to resign his chancellorship and seek nonjudicial office.[9]

The attack stung Quitman. Recoiling from the charge of hypocrisy, he denied that participating in the Natchez gathering made him a Whig. He claimed that he had actually voted against the Bank resolution at the meeting. In fact, contradicting his own public statement of just two years earlier that the Bank was a "valuable institution, well calculated to promote the general good by its tendency to lessen the price of exchange . . . and to preserve a uniform and sound paper currency," he now opined that the Bank was unconstitutional. He had attended the meeting for ideological purposes; he wanted to sustain the United States Senate in its battle against "Executive encroachments" (the Senate had censured Jackson earlier in the year for his deposit-removal policies). He remained a "pure nullifier" who opposed affiliation with the "nationals." Intelligent nullifiers would not be manipulated into elevating the Whig party to power.[10]

But did Quitman have qualms about Whig votes promoting nullifiers to office? By now, his chancellor's duties were wearing thin. His stage to the Jackson court session that July encountered swollen streams, and passengers had to be evacuated in heavy downpours. There was no time for rest, and Quitman came down with diarrhea. Eventually the stage broke down completely, necessitating transfer to a hired wagon for the final miles into town. When Eliza, hearing of his plight, suggested resignation, Quitman responded emotionally, "The labour is too severe. To do my business here would take three months. I will no longer make myself the slave of the public." On September 27, he informed the governor that he wished to be relieved of his duties as of October 1.[11]

Eliza's idea was that Quitman would spend most of his time, now, at home. But, despite advice from his brother to stay clear of partisan politics, Quitman wrote his resignation so that he would be free to run for other offices. He had a duty to raise his voice against "misrule and corruption." Prominent men, he told his brother, could hardly avoid politics when "party feeling runs high." So he declared for a fortuitous vacancy in the state senate. District Whigs, anxious to build a majority coalition, took him "with all his odious [nullification] doctrines," as an onlooker put it, and he rode their votes to a 272-to-215 victory over Thomas G. Ellis, a former legislative colleague.[12]

Quitman should have been able to enjoy at least a respite from public duties before starting his legislative stint, since the legislature, which only convened biennially, was not due to meet again until January, 1836. However, George Poindexter's U.S. Senate term was to expire in March, 1835, and Democrats were determined to replace Poindexter—who had been such a thorn in President Jackson's side—with Robert J. Walker. To do this, they needed a special legislative session, since U.S. senators were elected by a joint ballot of the state senate and house of representatives. Democratic governor Hiram G. Runnels, therefore, announced that session for January, 1835, and, to ensure Walker's success, granted writs of election to new heavily Democratic Choctaw cession counties entitling them to legislative representation.[13]

Finding himself in his senate seat a year earlier than anticipated, Quitman was not at all happy about the tactics behind Runnels' summons. To Quitman and other nullifier and Whig lawmakers from the Natchez-Vicksburg area, the Democratic gambit appeared but a further harbinger of the ongoing shift of political power to the state's interior. Considerable animus toward river nabobs with "dainty fingers and beaver gloves" who lived in "palaces" still colored Mississippi politics. "Watchman" in the *Mississippian* assured readers that the "spanking days when Natchez . . . told the members of the legislature what they had to do . . . will never return."[14] Quitman and his allies appreciated neither the advent of Choctaw cession representation nor being put in the position of strengthening President Jackson's hand in Washington.

Quitman and his friends quickly made their displeasure felt. The session opened on January 19. Governor Runnels' message, which included praise of President Jackson for halting Bank "oppressions" and a shopping list for state legislation, was submitted two days later. Then the river nabobs, who still controlled the state senate, went to work. On the same day as the governor's report, Whig senator John Henderson of Wilkinson County called for an inquiry about the legal status of the Choctaw cession representatives, who had been seated by the house of representatives. On January 22, the senate voted 9 to 3 to establish a three-man investigatory committee. On January 26, Henderson, committee chair, reported the committee's belief that, according to the state constitution, elections for those new members should not have been held until November, 1835; that the proportion of senators to representatives had to be fixed by enumeration and that seating the new members would create a temporary disproportion favoring the house; and that the state constitution limited the house to 100 members, but theoretically 109 representatives might claim seats if as many new counties as possible were created. The committee's conclusion was that since the house was improperly constituted, legislative business could not be legally conducted.

The governor, seeing that he had been finessed by the senate, had no choice but to abort the session and send the lawmakers home. On January 31, the legislature disbanded, to the consternation of Democrats from the affected counties, who protested that their "natural rights" had been violated.[15]

Quitman returned to Monmouth satisfied with the outcome. He had voted for the creation of the select committee, endorsed the Henderson report, and taken a "prominent stand" in debate, and by doing so had helped postpone the nabobs' day of political reckoning. Democrats' complaints found him impassive. Acknowledging that he and his allies had "raised a hornet's nest" and unwilling to admit the partisan purpose behind Henderson's stratagem, Quitman took refuge behind the logic that his sole intent had been to defend the state constitution.[16]

Reprieved from senate duties, Quitman devoted his spring and summer to legal matters, plantation management (he rode out to Springfield every week to look things over),[17] and other pursuits. Although popular myth often portrays planters as sovereigns of feudal estates who passed their time supervising crops and relaxing on porticoes, many planters also made a mark in business,[18] and Quitman proved no exception. In the 1830s, he was open to new forms of investment and diverse entrepreneurial projects.

Quitman served as one of thirteen directors of the Natchez parent branch of the Planters' Bank, helping to formulate loan policy, and he was also caught up in a railroad enterprise. Natchez, by 1835, stood in risk of forfeiting the rich trade it had built up with the state's interior. In the past, planters in the Pearl River valley had shipped their cotton to New Orleans via Natchez—even though roads from the capital to Natchez were rough, and virtual quagmires in the winter. There was no easy route from Jackson to New Orleans. Large rivercraft were unsuited to the Pearl between Jackson and the Gulf, and the river was not even navigable north of the capital. But in January, 1835, the Louisiana legislature chartered the New Orleans and Nashville Railroad Company, with the intention of connecting New Orleans with the Jackson area and, ultimately, with Nashville. Since this direct connection would have bypassed the Mississippi River and Natchez merchants entirely, Natchez civic leaders rallied to forestall this potential economic disaster by developing their own line to Jackson.

Quitman did not stand to benefit directly from a railroad linking Natchez and the capital. Rivercraft could dock at his Springfield plantation to pick up produce, and he had no difficulty shipping his own cotton to New Orleans. But a decline in Natchez's overall prosperity would threaten his legal practice and political ambitions, and would mean problems for associates and friends. So he became one of Mississippi's pioneer railroad developers. In October, 1834, he attended a meeting at the Natchez courthouse to consider a Natchez-Jackson connection. Two months later he traveled to Gallatin, a town in Copiah County, for a convention on the railroad project. This now extinct community expected to sit astride the proposed line, and its convention formed committees to apply to the legislature for an act of incorporation and to Congress for a grant of contiguous land. Some kind of outside funding would be required, since much of the land between Natchez and the Pearl was pine forest, and business during the construction period would be minimal. The next month during the abortive senate session, Quitman announced his intention of introducing a bill for a "Mississippi and Pearl River Rail Road Company."[19]

Quitman's concept of public service, however, transcended mere commercial projects, as it had since his first arrival in Natchez. His commitment to Jefferson College, a struggling institution in the nearby town of Washington, especially, was longstanding. He not only supported the school's financial prospects by purchasing lots which it owned in Natchez (and providing security for J. F. H. Claiborne's purchase of college lots) but also participated on the school's board of visitors. Quitman seems to have been sensitive to the South's deficiency—as compared to the North—in education, and boosted Jefferson College as a step toward closing that gap. When giving the school's commencement address, on one occasion, he asserted that student proficiency there demonstrated how "our Southern clime is no enemy to severe application."

That June of 1835, Quitman also joined the board of trustees. He would attend five board meetings before state business summoned him again to Jackson in December. Over the following seven years, he attended an additional twenty-one board sessions. His role was hardly honorific, though he did feel compelled to share in ceremonial functions like the inauguration of the college's new president. He received a variety of assignments, such as investigating funds due the college from the state treasury.[20]

More than ever a pillar of Adams County society, Quitman took pride in how well he fulfilled all requirements of noblesse oblige. "To show you that I am not wasting the prime of life in ignoble ease," he wrote his brother, "I may mention that I am a senator in the Legislature, President of the State Rights Association, President of the Anti-abolition Society, of the Anti-gambling Society, of the Anti-dueling Society, of the Mississippi Cotton Company, of the Railroad Company, Director of the Planters' Bank, Grand Master Mason, Captain of the Natchez Fencibles, Trustee of Jefferson College and of the Natchez Academy." Given his exemplary record of public service, moreover, it is hardly surprising that Joseph Holt Ingraham, a Maine native, dedicated to Quitman a two-volume work about his southwestern travels.[21]

By the summer of 1835, therefore, through politics and civic work, Quitman had been able to put family tragedy behind him. But the very intensity of his commitment to local welfare made him more sensitive than ever to threats to community stability, and Quitman received a jarring reminder that southern slave society rested on a very insecure base.

That same summer and fall, rumors of a massive slave uprising rocked Mississippi society to its foundations. Purportedly John A. Murrell, a white scoundrel interned in the Tennessee state prison, had masterminded a servile rebellion to be touched off on Christmas Day. His outlaw network of over one thousand men, known as the "Mystic Clan of the Confederacy," would ply blacks with money and alcohol and lure them into revolt with abolitionist propaganda and tales of how West Indies slaves had seized their freedom by slaughtering whites. Then, during the turmoil, Murrell's band would turn on banks and paralyzed cities in an orgy of plunder and murder. The outlaws selected Christmas since whites would naturally have their guard down and blacks customarily were given more freedom of movement on that occasion.

Actually, Murrell was a counterfeiter and slave thief at worst, and there was no "Mystic Clan." But rumors alone were sufficient to panic a society mindful of what Nat Turner had done in Virginia. Rather than take chances, whites, particularly in Madison County where blacks in some areas outnumbered them fifty to one, launched preemptive strikes. Regular committees of safety, patrols, and mobs tortured and intimidated white and black suspects into confessions, and carried out floggings, banishments, and executions in a wave of repression that spilled over into other states. Committees of safety alone executed seven whites. No one kept count of how many blacks felt the full wrath of Mississippi's aroused white populace, but as many as fifty may have died.[22]

Although Quitman—who in a letter to his brother discounted all danger of massive uprisings and only conceded a potential for "partial insurrectionary movements"—may be credited with reacting to the Murrell rumors in a more measured way than did many other Mississippians, he nonetheless took part in the purge. Vicksburg hanged five gamblers suspected of links to Murrell and banished others from town, and some of the expelled gamblers transferred their operations to Natchez. Quitman responded by using the Adams County Anti-Gambling Society's vigilance committee and the Fencibles to round up gamblers, whip them, and expel them from town. He also took his militia company to Vicksburg, where it conducted a public drill in demonstration of white solidarity. One observer was unimpressed, noting that "the Fencibles paraded for drill, and marched to the court house yard. Commanded by Capt. Quitman, a lawyer of high standing. . . . Appears to be a man of firmness, and a gentleman, but not a good drill officer." However, this skeptic did concede that the Fencibles' presence had produced "a relaxation among many of the citizens." Even as the repression ran its course, Quitman remained apprehensive. Hearing from Eliza while he was out of town that a series of fires had destroyed Natchez's City Hotel, cotton stores, and other property and that gamblers were suspected, he alerted the Fencibles and he urged his wife to be cautious.[23]

The events of summer and fall served, if anything, to confirm Quitman in his already strong commitment to nullification. He was sure that slaves would never even consider revolt, were it not for the "agrarian and fanatical doctrines" foisted on them by northern abolitionists.[24] It seemed more necessary than ever that a barrier be established between northern power and southern slavery, and he took this mission with him back to the legislature.

A quirk in Mississippi's constitutional structure gave Quitman, after he returned to the legislature, more power than he anticipated to advance nullification principles. The state, in late 1835, found itself without a chief executive. Governor Runnels' term ended November 21, yet his Whig replacement, Charles Lynch, was not to assume official duties until January. The constitution of 1832 designated the president of the state senate to serve as interim governor, but the old senate's term had expired, and the new senate would not meet until January. Thus, there was no presiding officer of the senate. To rectify matters, Secretary of State David Dickson on November 21 (despite the fact that his own term had expired along with Governor Runnels' term) called upon the incoming senate—to which Quitman had been reelected that month—to come together briefly in December and select a president.[25]

Quitman complied, apparently intending to pass a few days in Jackson, cast his ballot, and return home. At least this is the way he explained the trip to Eliza, who was now in the last weeks of one of her biennial pregnancies.

But the power-hungry, anti-Jacksonian coalition controlling the senate had other plans for him. They could serve notice upon the Democratic house of their intention to elect a Whig U.S. senator in January if they elected their candidate governor. Quitman found himself "the only one of the Anti Caucus party having sufficient strength" to gain election. He led from the start, and after the seventh ballot on December 3 found himself the new president of the senate and de facto governor. Ever modest in his public references to his attitudes about holding office, Quitman reminded his colleagues that he had not sought the position and accepted the "arduous" trust from his "sense of duty . . . and a just respect for your opinions." Having fulfilled its mission, the one-day session then adjourned, leaving Quitman behind in the capital to manage state business.[26]

In the past, Quitman may have complained about living conditions in Jackson. Now, however, the town seemed to be growing up. Quitman found it suddenly more "respectable" in its society. He attended Governor-elect Lynch's inaugural ball, and marveled that there was now "a spacious ball room, and it was well filled with really *handsome* ladies." Yet Quitman seemed destined for uncomfortable residences in that central Mississippi town. This time his problems stemmed from his wife's reaction to his staying on after the legislature adjourned. Back in Natchez, expecting her baby momentarily, Eliza began to wonder what was important to him. Quitman could only respond by asking her to take pride in his growing reputation and to realize how burdened he was with the "business occasioned by the absolute confusion of the Executive Department." She should, he affirmed, "try and make yourself happy at the idea that you are a governor's wife," and be patient for just a few more days.

Quitman presumably made it back to Natchez in time for the birth of his child—a girl—on December 18. A later letter seems to indicate that he spent some time at home before the legislature convened in January. But the stay must have been abbreviated: by January 6, he was back in the capital "engaged here night & day . . . [and] completely exhausted by fatigue." Before the winter ended, his extended absence would put more than a slight strain on his marriage.[27]

Quitman simply felt that he could ill afford to shirk the opportunity and responsibility before him. He was, after all, governor—albeit a temporary one—of his state. His states' rights faction expected him to utilize his position for the cause. "My friends here properly insist that I should set an example to the country of what a *Nullifier* can do," he told Eliza. "You have no idea of the enthusiasm with which my election has animated our party." So he spent those early January days laboriously drafting a message to the legislature, even though his term would expire on the seventh. A message would get the nullifier credo rare statewide circulation because gubernatorial addresses were customarily reprinted in the press—he could issue a clarion call about the abolitionist threat. Finally, on the fifth, he sent his product to the house and senate, and achieved relief from what had become his "most pressing cares."[28]

Quitman pulled few punches in his moment in the public spotlight. Reserving state business for later in his message, he began with a nullification diatribe. The states, he warned, grew ever weaker before the accruing power of "centralism" in Washington. Things would get worse rather than better: federal treasury surpluses for the foreseeable future meant that any "ambitious aspirant who may happen to fill the Executive chair or a victorious party, eager for the spoils of conquest" would have a ready fund to buy support and undermine the "liberties of the people of these States." Yet it was a dangerous time, he stressed, for the southern states to surrender their power, for northern abolition societies had tried to stir up black rebellion. Reiterating his "partial insurrection" theory, he reminded the legislators that although slave-master relations were far too congenial for a massive black uprising to occur, there was always the possibility of "partial scenes of violence and bloodshed." After all, the northern antislavery movement was gaining momentum: "For some years past, the citizens of the planting States have seen . . . a disposition evinced in other sections of the Union, officiously to agitate the subject of domestic slavery, as it exists among us. Reviews, orations, tracts, and even school books, emanating from the nonslave holding States, have been found to contain insidious attempts to array public sentiment against our domestic institutions, from which they, as well as ourselves, have reaped so rich a harvest of wealth and prosperity." Quitman suggested that, ironically, the slaves, not the masters, had been the primary losers in the abolitionists' onslaught. Forcing southern whites to vigilance against revolt had necessitated a curtailment of the slaves' social life for purposes of control.

The solution? Quitman proposed that the legislature clamp down upon abolitionists in Mississippi and issue a resolution requesting northern states to enact penal laws to put down all "incendiary attempts" to foment servile rebellion. But Quitman went on to all but state that secession from the Union might provide the only workable escape from the morass. Should the northern states not cooperate, then "I suggest for your consideration, a concert of action with our brethren of the slave holding States, to devise measures for the full and ample protection of our rights, our domestic happiness, and repose." [29]

His nullification venom expended, Quitman hardly proved mute on state topics. As befitted the corporation executive, railroad promoter, and education booster that he had become he found it incumbent upon himself to share his vision of Mississippi's progress. He wanted the state to continue its past liberal practices in incorporating private internal improvements companies, mentioning his own Natchez-Jackson project at some length (a "noble undertaking"). Sounding like a modern laissez-faire capitalist, he insisted that private enterprise would work much better than public sponsorship, because it was "unwise policy to force trade into unnatural channels, or build up markets by Legislative compulsion." He also hoped that the state would charter new private banks to expand capital, and advocated a broad system of common schools:

> In monarchical governments, the heir to the throne is educated at the public expense. Why should not the same care be taken in republics to communicate at least the elements of knowledge to those who are to become the rulers of their destinies?
>
> I would not be understood as conveying the utopian idea, of conferring a complete scientific education upon every member of the community; but it is my deliberate opinion, that the means of a plain practical education should be extended to every free child in the country, cost what it may.

Thomas Jefferson could not have put it better.

Other portions of Quitman's message touched on a variety of topics. He called for a state penitentiary, militia reform, constitutional revision so that the state could avoid the interregnum which had elevated him to the governorship, and the state's collecting its 5 percent of net proceeds due on federal sales of Chickasaw lands in Mississippi. Several of his proposals were borrowed from Governor Runnels' message of the previous January. Nonetheless, the message was thorough and incisive, and Quitman had every reason to be content with the results of his labors. [30]

Two days later, Governor-elect Lynch took the oath of office and Quitman's stint as state chief executive was over. Rather than simply take up his duties as president of the senate, Quitman, acknowledging that he had not really been selected for that purpose, sent a message to the senate resigning as presiding officer. He explained that he wanted to provide an "opportunity for a full expression of the opinion of the Senators." Perhaps he saw it as a vote of confidence on his recent message. If so, he achieved vindication.

Despite a "determined disposition" by the "Van Buren party" to dump him, he survived the challenge and triumphed on January 8 on the thirty-ninth ballot.[31]

But this victory was more than counterbalanced the very next day by his disappointment when the legislature in a close vote chose Democrat Robert J. Walker as Mississippi's new United States senator. "We are thus chained to the car of Van Buren for six years," Quitman complained. He had supported George Poindexter for reelection, switching to James Wilkins, a Whig from Natchez, after Poindexter lost support on the second ballot. Fearful that the election signified Democratic control of the remainder of the session, Quitman was appalled when his nullifier ally, Isaac Caldwell, was killed in a duel with Jacksonian Samuel Gwin just days later. No matter that Caldwell had issued the challenge; Quitman blamed the tragedy on the Democrats. "A corrupt political party is seeking to destroy the independence of this state," he remarked bitterly. Federal patronage would carry "every thing" for the Van Buren "dynasty." Quitman's disillusionment found other ears, and rumors (apparently unfounded) circulated that he intended to duel with former governor Runnels.[32]

"Tired" and "disgusted," Quitman nonetheless plunged into his legislative responsibilities. After all, he still anticipated that the session might aid Natchez's railroad ambitions. "The measures now before the legislature are very important," he wrote Eliza. "In a week we shall I hope be able to act definitely upon our Rail Road charter." But he knew he would have to overcome the "great prejudice against Natchez."

Quitman lobbied as best he could, and by the time the big debate came in the first week of February he had successfully mustered his forces. His supporters beat back efforts to modify the charter, and the railroad bill cleared the legislature, winning endorsement in the senate by a resounding 18-to-1 vote on February 5. The final act created the "Mississippi Rail-Road Company," a corporation to be capitalized at three million dollars, with stock being either paid for in cash or secured by mortgages on real estate. Shares pegged at one hundred dollars were to be sold by nine specified commissioners and once 2,500 such shares were sold, the company's president and directors could purchase, lease, and sell real estate, as well as issue notes or bonds in return for money loans based upon lands mortgaged for company stock. Funds raised were to be applied to building a Natchez-Jackson line, which was to extend to the town of Canton, north of Jackson. The directors could subcontract work on any section of the road. Optimistically, the legislators set a ceiling of 15 percent net profit per year upon the project.[33]

Then Quitman had to ensure that the chartering of his pet project would not prove a Pyrrhic victory. The proposal to link New Orleans and Nashville by rail also made the legislative agenda. Quitman's response was that the lawmakers should divert the railroad over the Pearl south of Jackson, which would reserve the upper Pearl trade for Natchez since Jackson was on the west bank of the river. He wrote Eliza that he considered "the prosperity of Natchez gone" without such provision for the New Orleans line, and supported the restriction in debate and vote. He also supported other amendments to limit the company's potential, such as an automatic cancelation of its charter in seven years if the Louisiana legislature did not reciprocate by granting any Mississippi railroad company which applied within three years similar privileges in Louisiana. The senate passed the New Orleans and Nashville Railroad Bill by a convincing 14-to-6 margin, but with an amendment, which the house agreed to, requiring the line to cross the Pearl at Georgetown, a town on the west bank some thirty-five miles south of the capital. Since the conference committee could not agree on several other provisions, however, the bill was held over until the next legislative session. Natchez had won at least a temporary respite from Crescent City competition.[34]

Meanwhile, the legislature had not ignored Quitman's other gubernatorial recommendations. The 1836 session, for instance, appropriated $75,000 so that a state penitentiary could be erected in the Jackson vicinity. Quitman also had the satisfaction of seeing the senate judiciary committee, after considering his warnings about abolitionism, report that there was already a "pervading spirit of partial disaffection among our slaves" and call upon the legislature to request other states to interdict abolitionist publications and speeches. The committee suggested that the South might have to show the North that it would use force to get its way.[35]

Yet, Quitman's overall mood was pessimistic. Democratic party predominance rested at the core of his pessimism, but an increasing strain with Eliza undoubtedly contributed to his malaise. He had left a formidable burden on his wife. Not only did she have to care for a newborn baby and the other children, she also had to direct the daily functions of household domestics while keeping an eye on the hired overseer at Springfield. Immersed in the details of legislation, John virtually abdicated responsibility on the home front. He instructed Eliza to make any decisions that she thought proper, for he was in no position to provide "any directions about plantation affairs."[36] Yet he sent these instructions during a time of master-class tension, since the slave insurrection scare was only just tapering off.

Eliza did not hold up well under pressure. Her physical and psychological recovery from childbirth proved agonizingly slow, and she fell into a state which modern physicians would probably diagnose as postpartum depression. She confided to a friend that she had been suffering a "most miserable, lonely time of it," and told John in early January that she and the children were ailing and wished that he could come home. Later she reassured him that she had improved physically, but continued to urge his return. Her apprehensions seem to have been exacerbated by a loss of control over the household servants. She complained in a classic expression of managerial exasperation: "Alfred and Fred have become perfectly lawless—they go off whenever and wherever they please, get drunk and of course do no work, but Alfred particularly has behaved with so much insolence, perfectly regardless of the most simple orders. . . . We I should say I could not go to church because he, Alfred, took himself away upon his own amusement, tho' he had been told expressly that the carriage would be wanted." A man was needed at Monmouth to put things in order. She said that she did not know what she might do if he did not return home soon.[37]

John was not insensitive to his wife's plight. He pleaded with her not to panic about the arson in Natchez. He also expressed solicitude about her health and hinted he might rush home should her condition become serious. He spoke cautiously, moreover, about his rather well defined ideas for their new child's name. He wanted the girl named Antonia, as a reminder of their "Heaven gone" son John Anthony. But Eliza should be the ultimate arbiter—"Choose for yourself, you have borne the labor & still have the trouble, & should have the satisfaction of giving the name." She should remember, furthermore, that he endured loneliness too. At midnight, he consoled, he liked to sit alone in his room and "look into my little fire and think of you & the little ones."[38]

Yet Quitman's solicitude never quite reached to the depths of his wife's despair. His letters barely skimmed his own deepest thoughts, despite his wife's dependence upon them for emotional sustenance (though they seem to have achieved an almost mystical communication about the naming of their daughter; Eliza said that she too had been thinking of "Antonia," but had been reluctant to bring it up). Politics had become Quitman's preoccupation, yet he declined to "annoy" Eliza with legislative matters in which she could not take a "very deep interest." Nor would he consider abandoning Jackson ahead of schedule to please her. Other legislators might leave town early, but Quitman's "station" required *him* to stay until the "last moment of the session." His solutions to her emotional problems—exercise and a better cultivation of "female friends"—were trite. When he made the mistake of providing Eliza an opening by complaining that the times were so "corrupt" that politics had become "peculiarly unpleasant," his distraught wife exploded. "I hope you may never again be tempted to become a candidate for any political office whatever," she wrote, adding that political life brought no "honour" and sacrificed a lot of time. "I am sick and tired of living alone."[39]

74

Eliza ultimately got her wish at least partially fulfilled, as Quitman would drop out of politics for a while. But she was deluded in hoping that she might tie this restless, ambitious man to Monmouth. Ironically, he would no sooner return home than display again the wanderlust that was part of his masculine independence.

7

"Cincinnatus" in Texas

A LITTLE-REMEMBERED Mississippi secessionist may have explained John Quitman as well as anyone when he characterized Quitman as a model of the "United States Citizen Soldier." Quitman, according to Henry Hughes, was a "Cincinnatus of America" who demonstrated that the country's "bold yeomanry" were "born soldiers" and that "busy home-spun citizens" could match the "drilled and spangled myrmidons" of another power.[1] Despite all his political and social ambition, John Quitman was rarely more at peace with himself than when on a military campaign. Had he followed Thomas Jefferson's precedent and written his own epitaph, he surely would have put his military accomplishments at or near the top of his tombstone.

Given the paucity of information about Quitman's upbringing, it is impossible to isolate the roots of the later soldier. Although Quitman's fascination with guns and uniforms might be represented as a latent rejection of his father's preoccupation with books and learning, there is no evidence for the supposition. All that is clear is that Quitman demonstrated martial tendencies from adolescence on. "When a boy . . . of eleven years of age," he later recalled, "I was a Captain of a company of Cadets, armed with wooden guns, and have a distinct recollection of some skirmishes with a half-gipsy, half-Indian race of vagabonds living in the hills." Hunting was one of his most satisfying social outlets as a youth. In Ohio, he gained some distinction in the militia. By the time Quitman headed south, martial tendencies infused his very language. He observed geese and duck on Ohio River sandbars forming what appeared to be "regimental muster," and compared the crackling of cane on a fire to the "discharge of musketry."[2]

Nurtured by his northern childhood and adolescence, Quitman's martial spirit reached full flower in the South. Hunting continued to occupy much of his spare time. His sustained commitment to the Natchez Fencibles served as testimony to his militaristic strain and attracted public attention to his expertise in militia matters. In 1829, the state legislature chose "Captain" Quitman to devise a program to upgrade the militia. The substance of Quitman's suggestions, including a more reliable method of collecting fines from individuals evading musters and state treasury funding of key militia officers, appeared in the resultant thirty-four-page act. Quitman was in character at the 1832 constitutional convention when he joined the majority in a close vote which repealed Mississippi's practice of allowing conscientious objectors to buy their way out of militia service.[3]

Quitman, by mid-life, had developed a warrior's physique. His "large muscular frame" and "commanding air" marked him for leadership. Rarely sick, he maintained confidence that his "iron" constitution would enable him to endure campaigning, and his martial proclivities only awaited a war for true fulfillment. Success in life rendered him optimistic.[4]

Soon after the Mississippi legislature disbanded in 1836, events across America's boundary with Mexico provided Quitman with his opportunity. Texas, part of the former state of Texas-Coahuila, had been settled primarily by Americans. Mexico had permitted this settlement in the hope of establishing a buffer to contain an expansionist American republic, but the experiment had not worked out well. Many of the colonists insisted on owning slaves, in defiance of Mexican law. In addition the settlements were plagued by ethnocultural conflict, as the Americans, who were mainly Protestant, chafed at Mexican efforts to impose Catholicism upon them, could not adjust to Mexican legal customs which, among other things, excluded trial by jury, and found it difficult to get along with neighbors of Spanish extraction. Mexican tariffs only compounded the tension, and when Mexican dictator Antonio López de Santa Anna in 1835 tightened the government's grip on its outlying regions as part of a plan to fashion a more centralized Mexican state, Texas unrest exploded in revolution. On March 2, 1836, a convention of dissident Americans assembled at Washington-on-the-Brazos drafted the Declaration of Independence for the Republic of Texas. Then, while Santa Anna's forces held the Alamo under siege, the convention chose former Tennessee governor Sam Houston as commander of Texan armed forces and began to draft a constitution. After news arrived late on March 16 that the Alamo had fallen, the convention hastened to finish the constitution and to establish an interim government.

Back in the United States, people followed the unfolding drama closely. Expansionists coveted Texas' domains, speculators saw Texas' vast expanses as a potential land bonanza, and many Americans concurred that the struggle represented a case of U.S.-style republicanism in mortal combat with tyranny. Southerners, because of Mexico's antislavery policies, fearing that Texas if subdued might become a base for English subversion of American slavery or a refuge for fugitive slaves, took a special interest in the revolt.

Quitman was one such southerner who watched the rising storm in Texas with apprehension. Could he stay aloof from a struggle wherein a free people were "struggling for their violated rights"? In October, 1835, he confessed to his brother that only his family responsibilities held him back. Even while in the legislature, he could not get Texas off his mind. The more he observed what he considered the plague of corruption and patronage sweeping his own state, the more his thoughts drifted westward. He would go, with a "few friends," to the "wild woods of Texas, where at least Honor & honesty may be appreciated." So he sent a Polish dagger by messenger to Sam Houston with a note urging Houston on in his battle for freedom. Houston responded on February 12, virtually begging Quitman to come and lend a hand. Quitman should drop all matters at home and bring "auxiliary aid." Quitman's "presence" and "force of . . . character and example" would contribute decisively to Texas' future prosperity.[5]

Returning from Jackson, Quitman found Natchez, which had long been a focal point of pro-Texas ferment, burning with war fever. Well-founded reports circulated of Santa Anna's intention to free slaves, and people expressed outrage that some former local residents had been among the victims at the Alamo. By the time Quitman reached town, Felix Huston was already planning to lead a five-hundred-man force to rescue Texas. John Ross, Huston's law partner, even sent his brother Reuben $200 to enable Reuben to drop plans for legal practice back in Virginia and to hurry to Natchez to take part in the expedition. Quitman was caught up in this war spirit. If Santa Anna were not stopped soon, Mexican forces might sweep all the way to Louisiana and liberate the slaves.[6]

By the time Texas recruiting agent Thomas J. Green arrived in early April, Quitman had committed himself. "Capt. Quitman a gentleman of high standing . . . visits our bleeding country . . . a soldier," Green wrote in a letter of introduction for Quitman's use in Texas. Quitman cooperated with Huston in preparing the expedition. He chaired a public meeting to collect subscriptions and supplies for the cause, and on April 2 he and Huston issued an announcement that an expedition for Texas would leave within days and that volunteers were desired. Quitman wrapped up his financial affairs by stating in the press that McMurran would handle his business for the next two months.[7]

April 5 was the appointed departure date. Ceremonies at the courthouse appropriate for the occasion—including a rendition of the Natchez Fencibles' banner song—let Quitman know that the townsfolk wished him well.

The hoopla over, Quitman and some seventeen volunteers, and his servant Harry, boarded the steamer *Swiss Boy*. The ship was bound for the mouth of the Red River below Natchez.[8] Huston remained in Natchez with the assignment of organizing a mounted force.[9]

Quitman left without fully consulting his wife. Having invested fifteen hundred dollars in Texas land at the end of March, he led her to believe that this trip was little more than another land speculation. The result of his deception was that while the local Democratic paper praised Quitman's courage in forsaking "wealth" and "renown" at home for the cause of "liberty and his species" elsewhere, Eliza only felt distress when she learned the truth. When she came across the April 2 call for troops and realized that her husband commanded a military company that was going to war, she was astounded. Again, she found herself entreating him to return home, this time with an air of desperation. "Are you tired of your wife and little children that you should fly from them?" she wrote. "I am nearly crazy. My beloved husband if you do indeed Love your Eliza and her children return to them immediately. . . . O John how is it possible that you could make such arrangements, and not inform your wife of them?" She appealed to his conscience by remarking that their infant daughter Sarah suffered from a bowel affliction and suggested that Felix Huston, a *"snake in the grass,"* must have hoodwinked him into his dereliction. But Eliza was destined for a long time of anguish. Quitman paid no heed to her protests, merely instructing her to disregard reports that he was in danger and realize that he would avoid "exposure."[10]

Green had advised Quitman to proceed to Sam Houston's aid by a flank movement via Natchitoches, Louisiana, a point up the Red River. So the *Swiss Boy* ascended the Red, following its northwesterly direction ever closer to the Sabine and Texas. At Alexandria, the citizens turned out to encourage the men. But confusion greeted Quitman's force at Natchitoches. Although some residents there expressed optimism about Houston's chances, rumor had it that Houston, reportedly east of the Colorado, had only five hundred men to challenge Santa Anna's forces. David Kaufman, a former legal apprentice under Quitman who now had a local practice, warned that Houston's prospects were dim and that the leaders of the Texas rebellion had fallen to disputing land claims among themselves rather than preparing to meet the enemy.[11]

After a short layover at Natchitoches, Quitman and his band forsook the Red and struck out westward toward the Sabine. They passed through a gently rolling area of pine forest and sandy soil, taking care to skirt a U.S. Army post, Fort Jesup. Technically, since the United States remained at peace with Mexico, Quitman and his men had no right to invade Mexican territory, and their interference in the Texas uprising rendered them liable to arrest. Secretary of War Lewis Cass, in fact, had ordered General Edmund P. Gaines to use the Sixth Infantry Regiment at Fort Jesup to prevent any crossing of the Sabine by hostiles on either side. Quitman, therefore, discreetly avoided "bearding the lion in his den," and waited until he was beyond Fort Jesup before taking the rough wagon road which led from the post to the Texas boundary. On April 9, Quitman and his force arrived at Gaines's Ferry. Joined by some dozen Virginians heading the same way, they crossed the river immediately.[12]

From the west bank, they set off on horseback for Nacogdoches, about fifty miles distant. Each man was an armed camp unto himself, fitted out with a rifle, holster and belt pistols, and bowie knife. They traveled light, hoping to forage and make good time; tin cups, some blankets, coffee and sugar, borne by two mules, were the only supplies they brought along. On April 10, Quitman halted his men at San Augustine, a new town amid some woods, to rest for the evening. Quitman came close to not leaving the town alive. By an unlikely coincidence, the town had been taken over by gamblers, among whom were the very group expelled from Natchez by Fencibles' vigilante action the previous summer. The gamblers recognized Quitman and decided to even the score. No sooner had Quitman taken off his coat, preparing to bed down, than one of the gamblers burst in upon him with dueling pistol drawn and bowie knife at his side. Quitman reacted instantly, drawing his own pistol. They faced each other, five feet apart. Some tense moments followed. Finally Quitman defused the situation, making clear that he no longer had anything against the gamblers, and that he would not be intimidated. The gambler, realizing that revenge might mean his own death ("my intention was to shoot him down upon the slightest motion of his pistol," Quitman later entered in his journal), decided to make the best of it. "Captain," said the gambler, "you are a brave man, and I will be your friend." Then he left. Only slightly unnerved, Quitman went on toward Nacogdoches the next morning.[13]

While Quitman's small company hastened westward to reinforce Sam Houston, Houston made its task easier by his own route of campaign. He had assumed command of a 374-man garrison at Gonzales in south central Texas on March 11. Judging that Santa Anna's superiority in numbers, morale, and equipment precluded an immediate stand, Houston guided his force eastward. He crossed the Colorado in March and the Brazos on April 12–13, hoping for time to assemble more troops and train his army. By crossing the Brazos, he was within 150 miles southwest of Quitman.

Houston's retreat had far-reaching implications. The Texan government, fearing capture without Houston's shield, moved eastward from Washington to Harrisburg on Buffalo Bayou and eventually to Galveston Island. The combined army-government retreat sparked a mass panic among civilians. Massacres of Texan troops at the Alamo and at Goliad, when some 350 had been slaughtered after their surrender, had conferred the stigma of butcher upon Santa Anna. Civilians lost all perspective when reports started circulating that the invading Mexicans had struck an alliance with Indian tribes in the area and intended to unleash the tribes upon Texan settlements. Anglo settlers abandoned home and belongings, and fled eastward toward the Sabine and comparative safety.

Meanwhile, Santa Anna determined to achieve a decisive victory. Although he had divided his forces for various operations, with the intention of reuniting them before fighting Houston, Santa Anna could not resist when he learned that the president, cabinet, and other governing officials were all at Harrisburg. They appeared sitting ducks. With forced marches, he might carry the day in dramatic style. But by the time Santa Anna arrived at Harrisburg, the Texan leaders had already fled.[14]

Quitman learned of the civilian panic even as he first entered Texas. At Gaines's Ferry, he witnessed Texan families fleeing into Louisiana. At San Augustine he heard that thousands of Mexican cavalrymen had crossed the Brazos and then linked up with fifteen hundred Indians; supposedly this force, now at the forks of the Trinity River, was poised to launch its attack. Leaving San Augustine, Quitman found the Texas exodus virtually sweeping by him. "Advancing into the country," he wrote to Felix Huston, "we found the roads literally lined with flying families, and, instead of the men turning their faces to the enemy, we met at least 300 men, with arms in their hands, going east." Abandoned wagons, furniture, and provisions cluttered the road to Nacogdoches.[15]

Little fazed, Quitman pushed on. Crossing an area of sandy soil and pine growth broken by patches of red and black soil, he and his men approached within eight miles of Nacogdoches by nightfall on April 11. But now they found it necessary to deal with the civilian panic before they could continue on to Houston's aid. Information arrived in camp that a Mexican-Cherokee force of two to three thousand had actually begun marching on Nacogdoches. Families from town were streaming eastward, and town authorities considered firing the community rather than permitting it to fall into Mexican hands. Quitman could not simply abandon these people to their fate. If he did not do something, the Mexicans might go on to slaughter defenseless refugees on the road. Rather than have such a tragedy on his conscience, he decided to lend a hand to those Texans remaining in the area.[16]

On the morning of the twelfth, Quitman brought his men up just outside the town and sent off a messenger to contact municipal officials and offer the aid of his volunteers. The offer was accepted, but by the time Quitman arrived the town seemed deserted. Most women and children had fled, while the men waited in camp outside the town. Contact was again established; after receiving a firm request to stay and help defend the town, Quitman and his men galloped again into Nacogdoches. They would set themselves in the path of the enemy to buy time for the women and children trying to escape. "Each of my Natchez boys swears he is good for ten Mexicans; the Texans say they will not be outdone. If I must die early, let me die with these brave fellows and for such a cause," Quitman proclaimed gallantly in his journal.[17]

Quitman and his men took up posts, and the town simmered. Anglo townspeople feared a Mexican-Indian attack, and the distrust between remaining American and Spanish-speaking residents was mutual. With the Mexican army making its way eastward through Texas, the Americans saw Spanish residents as a potential fifth column; Spanish residents questioned the intentions of their American neighbors. Rumors that the Americans planned to exterminate all Spanish residents led the Spanish to arm and withdraw from town. By the time of Quitman's arrival, two hundred Spanish horsemen joined by some "straggling" Indians threatened Nacogdoches from an encampment in some nearby woods.

Anglo townspeople were anxious to disarm their Spanish neighbors before the Mexican troops arrived. So, on April 14, Quitman, as their agent, rode out to the Spanish camp for negotiations. Learning that the encampment had only defensive objectives (although the men there said that they would not oppose a Mexican attack on Nacogdoches), Quitman returned with his news. Then the Nacogdoches Committee of Vigilance and Safety contacted the Spanish and persuaded them to return to the town in peace. Quitman, on April 15, drew his men together on the square as part of an Anglo show of force to confront the Spanish as they reentered town.[18]

Reconciliation within Nacogdoches provided Quitman and his men the leeway to reconnoiter against the expected assault from without. Quitman, who had found Indians in the area friendly, already suspected that the crisis was a sham. On the fourteenth, he concluded that any Mexicans east of the Trinity numbered no more than 250 and were still seventy-five miles away, as heavy rains had impeded their progress. Meanwhile, General Gaines, sympathetic to the Texas cause, had sent letters to the governors of Alabama, Tennessee, Mississippi, and Louisiana requesting volunteer troops to help prevent Indian tribes from crossing the border into Texas. Already an agent from the Nacogdoches vigilance committee was on his way to solicit

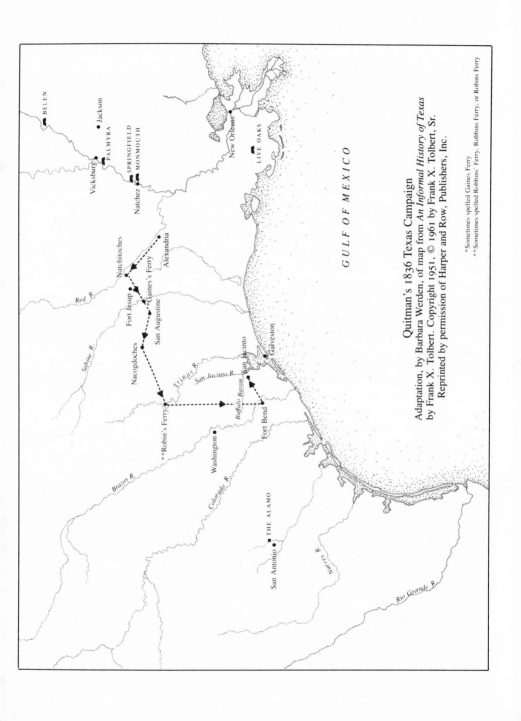

Quitman's 1836 Texas Campaign

Adaptation, by Barbara Werden, of map from *An Informal History of Texas*
by Frank X. Tolbert. Copyright 1951, © 1961 by Frank X. Tolbert, Sr.
Reprinted by permission of Harper and Row, Publishers, Inc.

*Sometimes spelled Gaines Ferry
**Sometimes spelled Robbins' Ferry, Robbins Ferry, or Robins Ferry

GULF OF MEXICO

BELEN
Jackson
Vicksburg • PALMYRA
SPRINGFIELD
Natchez • MONMOUTH
New Orleans
LIVE OAKS

Natchitoches
Alexandria
*Gaines's Ferry
Red R.
Fort Jesup
Sabine R.
San Augustine
Nacogdoches
Trinity R.
San Jacinto R.
San Jacinto
Galveston
Buffalo Bayou
**Robin's Ferry
Fort Bend
Washington
Brazos R.
Colorado R.
THE ALAMO
San Antonio
Nueces R.
Rio Grande R.

direct military help from Gaines. Later in April, Gaines would direct thirteen regular infantry companies to the Sabine.[19]

While in Nacogdoches, Quitman managed to send a couple of letters to his wife. He reassured her that he had never been in better health despite sleeping in the woods and depending on a pork and cornbread diet, and rationalized that he never would have proceeded so far had he not encountered so many settlers begging for protection. "It made my heart bleed," he related, "to see the little children not larger than our little lovely Sarah traveling through mud nearly knee deep . . . & crying to their mothers." Now since the Mexican threat had receded, he could push on even farther, to the Brazos, in his quest for profitable land speculations. Others might proceed to Sam Houston's army, but he would capitalize on "the greatest opportunity for purchasing lands cheaply." In fact, if he could be assured that the United States would eventually annex Texas, he would "not stop at any sum." Meanwhile, he explained, she should disregard any reports by cowardly men who were deluded into believing he was in danger—"Some men would run from Natchez if it was reported that ten thousand Chinese were on their march from Woodville." [20]

Quitman simply could not muster the nerve to confess his true intent. Undoubtedly he believed that the lie saved Eliza anxiety over a situation beyond her control. The very day (April 15) that Quitman professed to be after more land, word came that Sam Houston's army was in difficulty. Houston, reportedly, had arrived at Groce's Ferry on the east bank of the Brazos, while some nine hundred Mexican troops were readying to cross the Brazos farther south. Aware that Nacogdoches no longer risked annihilation, Quitman prepared his men to resume their campaign. Before leaving he wrote to Felix Huston, asserting that it was virtually now or never if Huston and the follow-up Natchez troops hoped to have any impact on the fighting.[21]

So Quitman and his men, now totaling thirty in number, pushed off again. Making their way through some heavy rainstorms, relying almost exclusively on beef roasted on sticks for food (they simply shot cattle they came across), the party hurried westward. By April 17, they had reached and crossed the three-mile-wide Trinity River at Robin's Ferry. There they saw more refugees fleeing with loaded wagons and learned that Houston was preparing to make a stand on the lower Brazos at Fort Bend to prevent Santa Anna's advance column from crossing the river. So Quitman changed direction and rushed his force southward. By the time they reached Fort Bend, however, Houston was reported east on the road to Harrisburg. It proved to be a wild-goose chase. On April 21, on a stretch of broken prairie along the San Jacinto River not far from the Gulf of Mexico, Houston attacked Santa

St. Peter's Lutheran Parsonage
Reprinted by permission of the Mississippi Department of Archives and History

Eliza Turner Quitman at the time of her marriage
Reprinted by permission of the Mississippi Department of Archives and
History

John A. Quitman at the time of his marriage
Reprinted by permission of the Mississippi Department of Archives and
History

Monmouth
Courtesy Monmouth, Natchez, Mississippi, and Ronald Riches

F. Henry Quitman
Courtesy Mrs. Earl B. Shaw, Jr.

Monterrey

Lithograph from Daniel P. Whiting, *Army Portfolio No. 1* (New York: G. & W. Endicott, 1847). Reprinted by permission of the Manuscript Department, William R. Perkins Library, Duke University.

Sword awarded Quitman for heroism at
Monterrey
Reprinted by permission of the Mississippi
Department of Archives and History

Quitman during his last years
Reprinted by permission of the Jessie Ball du Pont Library, University of the
South

Anna's encamped army and completely crushed it. Houston's men killed 630 Mexicans; the day after the battle, Santa Anna himself was taken prisoner. Amazingly, only 9 Texans were killed in the battle.

Quitman arrived at Houston's headquarters at the junction of Buffalo Bayou and the San Jacinto two days too late. Instead of finding a Texan army desperate for assistance, he found that the action had passed him by. Touring the battlefield, he witnessed ground "literally strewed with dead Mexicans." To some of his men, it was a bittersweet sight. They had hoped for glory in battle, and perhaps officers' commissions in the Texas army as a reward for valor. But they had to content themselves instead with reflecting on might-have-beens. "Suffice it to say," despaired Reuben Ross, "that six days of anxiety of false alarms and the fatigues of watching Nacogdoches against an imaginary foe . . . terminated our prospects of more useful service to Texas or Advantage to ourselves." Quitman was less disappointed, because he had conceived the expedition only as a rescue mission and sought no long-term commitment. In fact, when Houston, who had received an ankle injury in the battle, gave him a hearty welcome and offered him the rank of second-in-command in the Texas service, Quitman turned the commission down. Nonetheless that night, as he put his head in his saddle pillow and thought about the "carnage" and the Texan triumph, he could not escape a nagging wish that he had been there.[22]

Over the next few days, Quitman became one of Houston's confidants. Houston consulted him about what course he should adopt toward Santa Anna. Quitman talked with the infamous prisoner several times. Initially he found the Mexican "disposed to cringe—and cower," but with time Quitman came to appreciate Santa Anna as a "man of genius, fertile in his resources, and of great energy." Quitman reacted negatively when Houston, responding to a Texan desire for vengeance, suggested that Santa Anna be put before a court-martial with Quitman sitting as judge advocate. Despite the flattering allusion to his judicial experience, Quitman wanted Houston to resist calls for revenge. Eventually the Texan came around to this position, after Santa Anna's conciliatory intentions became more pronounced.

Quitman and his men passed about two weeks in camp. They could not rule out a resumption of hostilities, because thousands of Mexican troops under Santa Anna's second-ranking officer, Vicente Filisola, might yet attack. With a possible role in the Texas drama still in the offing, the volunteers from Natchez could hardly tear themselves away. Quitman accompanied both Houston and Santa Anna on a Buffalo Bayou flatboat on May 1 when it was decided to shift the camp up the bayou to escape the repulsive odor of battlefield corpses. During their trip, Santa Anna not only praised Texan bravery but even said that it would be politic for Mexico to acknowledge Texan independence because an independent Texas would serve as a buffer between the "grasping" United States and his own country. He pledged that he would work to that end if released.[23]

Things broke on May 4–5. Houston, who had never recovered satisfactorily from his wound, surrendered his command to Texas Secretary of War Thomas J. Rusk, who had joined the army prior to the battle. The next day Houston and Santa Anna boarded the steamer *Yellowstone*, the former to be taken to Galveston (and ultimately New Orleans) for recuperation, the latter to Velasco—the newest seat of the ever mobile Texan government—where negotiations over Texas' future could take place. Rusk marched his men westward toward the Brazos, and Quitman, fearing a collision with Filisola's force, accompanied them. However, Rusk soon informed Quitman that an armistice had been negotiated with Santa Anna back in camp. Santa Anna had ordered Filisola and other Mexican commanders in Texas to retreat and avoid hostilities, and Rusk's instructions only encompassed observing the Mexican retreat. Quitman, now convinced that an *immediate* resumption of hostilities was unlikely, prepared to return to the United States. He turned over the Natchez troops to his first lieutenant (now captain) William J. Strickland, and arranged for those of his men who did not want to stay to take passage home by sea via Galveston.[24]

Taking his own leave on May 6, Quitman set out via Galveston Bay for the east bank of the Trinity, where the Thompsons, some family acquaintances, lived. He departed the army optimistic, if not euphoric, convinced that the new republic would soon become part of the United States. He liked the Galveston Bay region (thinking that it appeared much like New York City harbor) and wrote Eliza from the Thompsons' that he hoped that some day she would get to see the bay's scenery herself.[25]

Accompanied by his "faithful Harry," Quitman then returned to American soil, by a trail which passed through Opelousas, Louisiana. Ironically, as on his trip into Texas, Quitman had a brush with death that had nothing to do with the enemy. Traveling with but a servant, he appeared easy prey to some of the lower American elements filtering into Texas to capitalize on the anarchy caused by the revolution: three robbers blocked Quitman's path through some dense underbrush near the Sabine with felled trees. Quitman prepared to shoot it out with them, using his horse as a shield, when, incredibly, the same gambler whom he had faced down at San Augustine came to the rescue and chased off the bandits. It was a small world. "Well, Captain, I am glad I have had a chance to serve you," said the gambler, who was on his way to join the Texan army. Quitman thanked him profusely, and resumed his trip. That May 27, William Johnson, a black barber from Natchez, recorded how "Governor Quitman" had returned to town "in fine Health."[26]

Quitman, in fact, returned to Natchez with much more than his health. He also had a stake in Texas' future. Enraptured by the expanses of the eastern part of the republic (which he described as "extensive rolling plains covered with beautiful green sod & enlivened with herds of thousands of fat cattle . . . interspersed with beautiful groves & clumps of trees . . . [giving] it the appearance of park scenery"), he tried his hand at land speculation before returning east. His turning down the commission from Houston eliminated his eligibility for 4,605 free acres under Texas' headright system; nevertheless, he had little difficulty acquiring land from Spanish settlers who were fleeing the revolution and willing to sell cheaply. How could he pass up fertile land at fifteen cents an acre? So he bought twenty thousand acres. Once the United States annexed Texas, which he felt would occur within eighteen months, the value of his holdings would surely leap to twenty dollars an acre.[27]

Landholdings—though he dismissed them as "small"—gave Quitman a proprietary interest in Texas' future. He had not entirely rejected the thought of someday removing permanently to Texas; by summer, he had even managed to reconcile Eliza to the idea despite her earlier outrage over his expedition. He encouraged Rusk to support a policy permitting Americans to hold lands in Texas without migrating; although he would never present a claim upon Texas for the $3,000 he had spent to buy arms and provisions for his men, he would "consider it a hard case to be deprived of . . . holding lands which I purchased at a fair pr[ice]." Of course, nothing would be more pleasing than annexation. If Texas became a "component part of the Confederacy," American land titles would surely be valid. As time passed, and northern opposition to slavery expansion complicated attempts to annex Texas, Quitman despaired. He bristled at reports that Texans were uncivilized, and concluded that people were being misled by "Northern prints . . . hostile to the extension of Southern territory."[28]

Nothing, however, jeopardized Quitman's speculations or commitment to slavery expansion more than the possibility that Mexico might yet renew her sovereignty over Texas. Santa Anna, true to the sentiments he had pronounced while aboard the Buffalo Bayou boat, signed agreements at Velasco which called for Mexican troop evacuation across the Rio Grande and provided for a treaty of commerce, amity, and limits which would recognize Texas and establish the Texan-Mexican boundary no farther west than the Rio Grande. The Mexican legislature, however, repudiated the agreements. Mexico was hardly ready to acknowledge Texan independence, much less recognize the Rio Grande as the republic's legitimate boundary. Texas, under Mexican rule, had not extended so far westward. On May 20 the Mexican legislature decided to resume efforts to pacify Texas, and on June 6,

General José Urrea was ordered to accomplish this. Although Urrea's campaign ultimately fizzled out, and although the United States formally recognized the Republic of Texas in March, 1837, the specter of war arose intermittently during the next several years. Periodically, reports reached the United States that Mexican troops were again marching to trounce Texas into submission.

Quitman kept tabs on the evolving situation through the press and his correspondence with Rusk. No sooner did he return to Natchez than he began sending additional "volunteers" out to General Rusk. He would do his part, yet, to keep Texas' soil from being "trod by the foot of an enemy." Rusk need only signal that the situation was desperate, and he would again "spare [no] exertions to be serviceable to your country." Furthermore, the United States should see to it that Mexico never again conducted the "murderous and savage system of warfare" that characterized the spring campaigns of 1836. Gradually, Quitman came to agree with his friend Felix Huston—who had risen to high command in the Texas army—that the best way to achieve stability in Texas would be for the Texans to take the war south of the Rio Grande and crush the Mexican army.[29]

When in early 1842 it appeared that the long-awaited moment of decision might finally be at hand, Quitman favored bold action on behalf of the Lone Star. Mexico, provoked by an impotent Texan effort to seize New Mexico the previous year, unleashed several incursions into Texas. The raids galvanized Texas authorities into mobilizing troops for a major campaign, and Quitman was electrified that Texans might settle the issue once and for all. "You must conquer the invaders, or be exterminated," he instructed an acquaintance at Galveston. Quitman outlined what he believed a foolproof campaign strategy: half the Mexican army should be drawn into Texas and across the Colorado River by offering only token resistance; then a force of all available men sixteen to forty-five should be mustered secretly on the Colorado behind the Mexican advance. Trapped in an envelopment, the Mexicans would succumb: "[L]et your deadly rifles do their part, and then rush to the attack sword in hand, firmly resolved to conquer or die. No Mexican army can stand the shock of your charge. . . . Your victory will be easy and complete. Follow it up without delay. Carry the war at once into the heart of Mexico, and, before the end of summer, the banner of the single star will float proudly over the walls of the city of Montezuma [Mexico City]." While the Texans could not expect much help from a cautious United States government, the South, still wary of the danger of Mexico's planting an "Indian and negro colony" on its frontier, would provide aid and moral support. His town pulsing again with martial fervor, Quitman addressed a meeting at the courthouse called "in favor of Texian emigrants."

Quitman, apparently, had no intention of *personally* retracing his tracks, for the captainship of the 1842 volunteers devolved upon an Irishman named Walter Hickey. But when Sam Houston, now president of Texas, sent an agent to Natchez, the agent found Quitman thoroughly aroused for the Lone Star. Quitman "spoke in the most enthusiastic manner of the bravery and patriotism of yourself and the Texas people." He offered to arm and equip ten men for the Texas army at his own expense. Quitman subsequently provided funds for Hickey's "emigrants," and sent Houston best wishes in the "glorious enterprise to force the recognition of the Independence of your country from Mexico at the point of the bayonet." [30]

In the end, full-scale war between Mexico and Texas failed to materialize (though there were several skirmishes, including an unsuccessful raid on the Mexican border town of Mier on Christmas Night which resulted in the imprisonment of most of the invaders in Mexico's Perote fortress), and Quitman backed off from his involvement with Texas. For Quitman, however, the 1836 escapade had brought laurels to complement his already long list of achievements. Although too late for San Jacinto, his courage in forsaking home and rushing to Texas had been reported as far away as Poughkeepsie, in his native New York county. Quitman marveled at how he almost seemed to attract fame like a magnet. "When I saw the newspapers I could not but remark that I belong to the fortunate class of men," he wrote to his brother Henry. "Whatever I undertake prospers—and while some are labouring & toiling for reputation & fame without success, I obtain it without seeking or meriting it." [31] Texas left Quitman's ardor for battle unfulfilled, but it helped soften the sting of prior disappointments and put him in a positive frame of mind. His psyche was ready for new challenges.

8

Entrepreneur

WHEN John Quitman returned from Texas in the late spring of 1836, he found his state basking in the fading rays of what later earned the appellation "flush times." Gripped by a state of mind which equated land and cotton with wealth and progress, Mississippians had surrendered to one of the signal instances of mass speculative mania in the country's history. "The people here are run mad with speculation," concluded a traveler in Vicksburg. "They do business in . . . a kind of phrenzy." Columbus, Mississippi, won honors as the busiest land office in the nation in 1834 and 1835.

The "*cotton making* fever" and land craze sweeping the state derived from the Choctaw and Chickasaw cessions. These agreements dumped vast amounts of fertile, inexpensive land upon the market. Unfortunately, the manner by which Mississippians responded to the land bonus boded ill for the future. Far too much land was purchased with paper-money loans supplied by institutions which lacked adequate specie. The Planters' Bank, for instance, became so overextended that it even lent out money in its sinking fund which had been earmarked to cover interest due on its state-endorsed bonds. Railroad companies chartered with banking privileges on the side also fed the boom. Several, in fact, gave themselves almost totally over to banking, forgetting that their primary function should have been the laying of track.

Optimism prevailed. State auditor John Mallory had reported to the legislature that state "coffers" were so full and state finances so sound, there should be a reduction of the poll tax. Mallory expressed particular satisfaction with the "prosperous condition" of the Planters' Bank, which he attributed to expert management. When one newly chartered bank put its limited amounts of stock up for sale that year, auctions had to be held to determine which avid potential investors would win the right to commit their

90

money. The euphoria was infectious: "Tell Teachers in your part of the Country," a Natchez newcomer wrote to a North Carolina acquaintance, "that this is the country to make money in." He had just turned down a teaching contract for ten months which would have given him a far higher salary than he had ever been paid elsewhere.[1]

These were Mississippi's last halcyon days before the crash, and they were occurring during the first post-Jackson presidential campaign. Martin Van Buren hoped to inherit Jackson's office, but Whigs were plotting to destroy Van Buren's aspirations by nominating different candidates to run in different parts of the country. None of those candidates could be expected to win outright; Whig electoral strength would be too diluted for that to happen. But because the Whig candidates could capitalize on their own popularity in specific locales, the Whigs hoped that their cumulative total of electoral votes might throw the contest into the House of Representatives. In Mississippi and much of the South the name of slaveholder Hugh Lawson White of Tennessee headed the Whig ticket. Since White had been a Jacksonian opposed to nullification, southern Whig newspapers sought Democratic votes on the grounds that a vote for White was a vote for Jackson and misrepresented Van Buren as an antisouthern conniver with abolitionist connections. It was a cruel distortion of the Little Magician's record; though a New Yorker, he had worked to keep the Democratic party faithful to strict constructionist constitutional principles. He supported passage of the gag rule in the House of Representatives which suppressed debate on abolitionist petitions, and in March, 1836, publicly denounced the idea of abolishing slavery in the national capital.[2]

At first, Quitman paid little attention to the political ferment. He was genuinely weary of political infighting and had more personal concerns on his mind, particularly his dwindling Rhinebeck family. Death had taken William in December, 1834, and Henry, Eliza, and Louisa skimped along on a farm, depending in part upon Quitman's subsidies. Quitman had dreamed, on migrating to Natchez, that all his relations might one day join him. The warm days of 1836 seemed the moment. For all his skepticism about Mississippi's prevailing political ethic, Quitman had few reservations about economic prospects. Land deeds in several counties in 1835 and 1836 bore his name as purchaser; in the fall of 1835 he had even contributed six thousand dollars to a land-speculation consortium. Sell the farm, he advised Henry that spring, and hurry to Monmouth. Provisions for a new residence could be made after the move.

Quitman almost pulled it off. Before the summer ended, Henry sold the farm with payment and change of possession scheduled for April 1, 1837. But Henry worried that he might prove inadequate in the society Quitman had become accustomed to. He and the sisters, Henry explained, were merely "middle class" and would be ill at ease. Besides, Henry hesitated to surrender what little remained of his self-sufficiency for further dependence upon his brother's generosity. In the end, the three postponed moving when their purchaser ran into difficulty arranging mortgage financing. Their move southward was delayed until 1841, and then their destination would be a sixty-acre farm about six miles from Baltimore.[3]

Unexpected opportunity, however, seduced Quitman back into partisan politics. On July 31, Mississippi congressman David Dickson died at Hot Springs, Arkansas. Whigs and nullifiers alike wanted Quitman to announce for the remainder of Dickson's term in the Twenty-fourth Congress. Despite misgivings, Quitman resigned his legislative seat and consented to run. He should have followed his intuition, because he had made too many enemies in recent years to win a statewide race. Mississippi had not yet established congressional districts; thus, elections proceeded on an at-large basis. Quitman had earned the reputation of sectionalist within statewide politics. He would have a difficult time winning votes in the northern part of the state, given his opposition to Choctaw cession representation in the 1835 legislature. His opponent, Monroe County Democrat Samuel J. Gholson, moreover, had endorsed representation in that same legislative session. The contrast was too stark.

The Democratic party hammered away at Quitman's inconsistencies and anti–popular politics stance. How dare he ask for the people's trust when he had passed through such an exotic political metamorphosis? Quitman had supported Adams, the tariff, and internal improvements, yet switched to Calhoun and nullification. Now he had suppressed his own radical rhetoric and was running for Congress on a ticket headed by a Whig presidential candidate who had opposed nullification. Even where Quitman was consistent, the Democrats railed, he had hardly earned confidence. From the 1832 constitutional convention, where he had opposed the election of the judiciary, to the recent legislatures where he had opposed representation, railroads, and banking charters to benefit the state's interior, he had always resisted the popular impulse. Why did not Quitman reaffirm what the Democrats knew to be true: that he was still at heart the nabob nullifier? Voters should be on their guard. "Judas was the noisiest of his Savior's disciples in declarations of devotion, his subsequent conduct however proved the insincerity of his heart."[4]

Quitman would have preferred that his candidacy rest on his career as chancellor, legislator, and constitution drafter. Gholson, though a better speaker, had far less prestigious a reputation. However, Quitman could suffer the Democratic critique in silence for only so long, and in October he belatedly took to the stump. On the eleventh, he addressed a crowd at Liberty in Amite County. Then, piqued by some handbills being distributed in the northern part of the state, he set out to court the voters in Holmes, Yalobusha, and some of the other Choctaw and Chickasaw counties. He gave speeches, collected copies of the hostile handbills and circulars, and found the people somewhat warmer than he had expected. He also marveled at how the land had been transformed since he and Eliza had passed through it on their northern jaunt in 1825. The country had spawned plantations, homes, and villages; the land teemed, he noted, "white with cotton fields."

Yet, acknowledging that Gholson had traversed almost the entire state and he had not, Quitman sensed that his efforts were too little too late. He found no respite from the Democratic rhetoric. He was now "John Adams Quitman," a Federalist in disguise who would surely vindicate the Alien and Sedition Acts. The Democrats could hardly have concocted a more farfetched accusation. Of course, they also restated the now standard refrain that Quitman favored secession. The *Mississippi Free Trader* raised this bugaboo again just a couple of weeks before the election.[5]

Quitman arrived back in Natchez on November 5, and two days later he turned up in town for a last ditch "Anti-Van Buren meeting" at the courthouse for the purpose of swaying votes and policing the polls. According to one Democratic account, the Whigs, always strong in Natchez, exceeded their stated intentions and actually tried to prevent Democrats from voting, and the sheriff had to intervene. Meanwhile, Quitman climbed on a box right outside the polling building and delivered a last desperate diatribe in the hope of fashioning a Whig majority. He attacked Martin Van Buren's popular credentials by asserting that Van Buren had favored a property qualification for voting in the New York constitutional convention of 1821 (distorting the fact that Van Buren had actually supported a property restriction on free blacks only) and claiming that Van Buren had unpatriotically opposed the War of 1812. It was not one of Quitman's finer moments, and a visitor listening to him "harranguing the people" concluded that it was to little avail anyway. "The Election for President takes place here today," the visitor wrote, "but there is no excitement. The Southerners are too much occupied [with] cotton and money to think about politics."[6]

Quitman lost to Gholson by 779 votes, a greater margin than that by which Van Buren—the national victor, with 170 to 24 electoral votes—took the state from White. Professing little concern over the defeat ("I was most unwillingly brought out and am privately glad I am not elected"), he took satisfaction nonetheless that he had run a close race. His nabob consciousness encouraged presumptions that nineteen-twentieths of the "intelligence of the state" must have supported him.

Still, the results indicated a lingering stigma attached to Quitman's recent espousal of nullification. Mississippi politicos and voters could forgive Quitman's Yankee antecedents; even the Jackson *Mississippian*, which had opposed his campaign, conceded that Quitman had been a resident of the state for "many years," filled "several of its highest offices," and gained a wide recognition. But the state's citizenry, which had been indifferent to states' rights advocacy at the height of the tariff controversy, was hardly prepared to support a candidate identified with disunion and radical political change at a time when the cotton economy was booming and the future appeared bright. If Quitman harbored any doubts on this point, he should have been disabused of them eleven days after the election, in William Johnson's barbershop. "I cut Jud[g]e Quitmans hair this Evening—there came in a Drunking man from Franklin County and he was cursing the Nulifyers[.] He gave them some or made pretty I[n]solent Remarks to the Jud[g]e Respecting his party," Johnson recorded in his diary.[7]

*

A few weeks later, Johnson saw the former chancellor in a quite different context. "Today about Dinner," he noted on December 8, "they had a learg quantity of Gentlemen . . . on the Bluff to see the car Start, They had put down about 40 feet of Rails and had put on a Car, and they were a Running it Backwards on the Small Road that they had constructed, There were present Gov. Quitman . . . and a greate many more." Johnson had more than a passing interest in this christening of the Mississippi Railroad Company; he had purchased twenty shares of company stock. Quitman, being company president, had even more reason to attend. Neither man suspected that despite this auspicious occasion the company's days were numbered. Financial hardship would plague the railroad, and its president, in the years ahead.[8]

The Mississippi Railroad Company had the misfortune of beginning operations just as Mississippi plunged from "flush times" into hard times. The Panic of 1837 was caused as much by international and national economic dislocations as by anything within Mississippi. In the state, however, the primary cause was the sudden drying up of easy credit. The president and Congress both had their hands in this development. By insisting in his Specie Circular (1836) that federal land offices would accept only specie in payment, Jackson instantly undermined the value of notes issued by most of the banks in Mississippi. Congress, the same year, passed the Distribution Act, which called for the states to share an abnormal $5 million federal surplus.

Each state's share was to be allocated in proportion to congressional representation, with pet banks holding federal deposits being responsible for making the payments to state officials. Since the two pet banks in Mississippi, the Planters' and the Agricultural, were overextended, they had to call in outstanding loans to collect specie to cover the payments.[9]

Suddenly, there was not enough credit to go around. Borrowers, particularly land speculators counting on eventual sale of their purchases to cover their loans and assuming that they could get their notes extended if necessary, were caught short. Lenders were forced as a result to turn to note endorsers for satisfaction. Many endorsers, never expecting to be called upon, were unprepared to meet these demands. As people rushed to the banks to collect specie those institutions revealed their own inadequacies. The pet banks both suspended specie payment by May 11, 1837, other banks followed, and Mississippi's economy became a shambles. Debtor-creditor litigation filled court dockets, businesses suffered for lack of a paying clientele, and cotton prices plummeted in reaction to the credit constriction and overproduction. When commission merchants in New Orleans and elsewhere, pressed themselves by banks in New York and England, insisted that planters make good on outstanding accounts, they only compounded Mississippi's misery.

Politicians collided over what should be done to ease the distress. Democrats, blaming the depression upon merchants and bankers, demanded lower tariffs, an end to imprisonment for debt, revision of trade and finance patterns, and banking reform. Democrats attributed much of the responsibility for the economic collapse to the Bank of the United States and paper money, and contended that a specie economy would provide greater stability. Party spokesmen urged that bank notes be gradually phased out, and rallied to President Van Buren's Independent Treasury program which, if passed, was expected to curtail the ability of banks to issue paper notes. Whigs, on the other hand, generally attributed the depression to the hard-money policy initiated by Jackson and continued by Van Buren that the Democrats wanted to extend. Many Whigs argued that a national bank, by providing a stable paper currency again, would prove the most effective way to resuscitate the economy. From their perspective, the country did not have enough specie to support an efficiently functioning hard-money system.[10]

Despite this contraction—surely an inauspicious time to launch a major construction effort dependent on credit—Quitman and the nine other directors of the Mississippi Railroad Company worked to get the project under way. The company hired slaves at about $20 a year each as well as white laborers to do the construction. Builders received contracts to oversee the work on different parts of the proposed route. In December, 1836, the chief engineer reported that six hundred laborers and seventy teams were under his direction, and that forty-six miles (thirty-six east from Natchez and ten west from Jackson) had been put under contract.[11]

For several years, Quitman made the railroad company his principal civic concern, though he continued to participate in a wide spectrum of Natchez public affairs.[12] In February, 1837, hoping to attract new investment capital, he wrote to Nicholas Biddle, now president of the United States Bank of Pennsylvania (the former national bank operating under state charter), and asked if Biddle's institution might purchase $500,000 of Mississippi Railroad Company bonds. Quitman stressed the security of the bonds— the railroad's stock was backed by money and by mortgages "of lands generally of three times the value of the actual appraisement, and of course of six times the value of the stocks they secure." That summer Quitman had to pursue slave laborers fleeing the construction sites; rancid food, floggings, yellow fever and diarrhea epidemics, unendurable heat, and inadequate shelter produced more than a little discontent among the laborers. The next year he successfully petitioned the trustees of the town of Washington to set lenient grading requirements so that building costs there could be kept down. Visiting Natchez in June, 1838, Vicksburg *Sentinel* editor James Hagan attributed almost all the progress the railroad had made to Quitman's diligence: "He visits the work, examines all the estimates, and superintends every thing that calls for expenditures, from the purchase of the iron in Europe to that of a team at the landing."[13]

Sensitive to the threat which currency contraction posed to his railroad, land, banking, and planting interests, Quitman drew close to Whig economic doctrine. On April 25, 1838, he attended a Natchez public meeting which petitioned the legislature to establish a branch of Biddle's United States Bank of Pennsylvania in Natchez. At the gathering, Quitman offered resolutions (adopted unanimously) castigating the Specie Circular as "unwise" and "deleterious in its effects" while calling for its repeal and blocked an effort by the local Democratic newspaper editor to have the meeting denounce the Distribution Act, which had been a Whig measure in Congress. In June, Quitman appeared at a public meeting in Jackson and again helped draft resolutions attacking the Specie Circular (this time on the grounds that Andrew Jackson had assumed powers which rightly belonged to Congress) and criticizing Democratic Postmaster General Amos Kendall for demanding that specie be paid, in advance, for postage. Kendall, it was argued, should understand that since banks were no longer paying specie, bank notes were the only currency available. The meeting decided that, pending a change of policy, people should suspend all subscriptions to all non-Natchez newspapers and deny patronage to steamboats and merchants not accepting the notes of Natchez banks. On August 17, Quitman, back in Natchez, attended a Whig meeting where he blamed Van Buren's administration for ruining the country.[14]

It was hardly surprising, therefore, that when Quitman that August announced his candidacy for major general of the Second Division of the Mississippi militia, the local Democratic newspaper fell on him with a vengeance. The *Free Trader* endorsed his main competitor, Democratic wheelhorse William Gwin, and attacked Quitman as a "noted political demagogue" who had advocated "*mob Law*" in the matter of Post Office policies. On election day, September 9, the paper ridiculed claims in pro-Quitman handbills that his fifteen years of conducting Fencibles' drills prepared him for a state office in the militia. "If it has taken him fifteen years to learn infantry *company exercises* merely, (for he is notoriously an awkward swordsman) how long will it take him to 'maneuvre' a division?" the paper mocked.[15]

Quitman fumed. The personal attacks were an affront to his honor, sure justification for a duel challenge. But Quitman resisted this impulse, perhaps because he had established himself as an opponent of the custom, perhaps because he did not consider editor Lorenzo A. Besançon enough of a gentleman to justify an affair of honor. There were other ways. Quitman dallied at the polls, waiting for Besançon to cast his ballot. At about one in the afternoon, Quitman, emerging from the courthouse, spotted Besançon entering the yard. Confronting the editor, Quitman asked whether he had indeed called him a demagogue. When Besançon answered affirmatively and simultaneously started drawing his sword, Quitman exclaimed that Besançon was a "contemptible puppy and liar" and attacked Besançon on the head and shoulders with a thin iron cane he was carrying. When the cane bent, Quitman put his fists to work ("the weapon with which the God of Nature has armed every man"). Besançon, meanwhile, tried unsuccessfully to plunge his sword into Quitman. William Johnson later claimed that Quitman was saved by a piece of silver in his pocket which stopped the sword. A few observers finally pulled them apart.[16]

Quitman won the militia election, but tempers continued hot. Recriminations filled the press. Quitman implied that he would have beaten Besançon to a pulp, had others not intervened. Besançon called Quitman a bully, said that if Quitman had not been carrying a purse in his breeches pocket he would have had "such a breach made in his carcase about the groin" that he would now be "feasting with Pluto somewhere near the river styx," and sneered that Quitman had not fought at San Jacinto. He even accused Quitman of voting for himself to gain election as president of the state senate the year before. This was too much for Quitman, who rebutted with a card in the local Whig paper which claimed that every member of the senate knew that he had not voted for himself, and that Besançon had either "recklessly penned a calumny" or stood "a convicted liar." [17]

Soon thereafter, Quitman found a means of resolving disputes with local Democrats far preferable to physical and verbal brawling: he joined them. Democratic strict construction theory had always been more appropriate to the defense of slavery than was Henry Clay's American System. Jackson's indictment of nullification had merely obscured this for a while. When in October, 1837, Calhoun subordinated his rivalry with President Van Buren and rejoined the Democrats on the grounds that Van Buren's Sub-Treasury, if passed by Congress, would lessen the control of northern capitalists over the federal government, Quitman found himself isolated from his ideological mentor. Not until December, 1838, did he announce his own conversion, in a public letter printed in the Vicksburg Democratic organ. He proclaimed himself a Jefferson-Calhoun strict constructionist, a states' rights advocate, and a "true Democrat" all in one. He denounced federal internal improvements as unconstitutional, "corrupting" schemes which gratified "private and sectional avarice." The tariff contradicted the letter and spirit of the Constitution, as well as the "great principles of free trade, that constitute so important a part of the new and noble science of political economy." The Sub-Treasury plan would help check government extravagance and retard "excessive issues of paper currency" by private banking institutions. Denouncing Whig presidential aspirants Clay, Daniel Webster, and William Henry Harrison as "Federalists of the old school," Quitman called on other "state rights men" to open their eyes to political truth.

Whigs naturally were upset over Quitman's defection. The Vicksburg *Whig* stigmatized Quitman and other converted nullifiers as hypocrites who should pause and recall how Democrats just a few years earlier had been talking of hanging them for treason. Democrats, on the other hand, welcomed the new members in their ranks. Within months the Vicksburg *Sentinel* was boosting Quitman for the state legislature as a man of "purity, honor and patriotism." In Dixieland, old times *could* be forgotten![18]

Despite his revived political prospects, Quitman's focus remained the railroad (his new militia duties demanded little more than conducting occasional inspections of units within the Second Division), though a yellow fever epidemic which struck Natchez in the fall of 1837 occupied him for a time. Quitman insisted on nursing fellow Fencibles and helping provide military honors at the funerals of those who succumbed, despite the warnings of Edward Turner that he should avoid town lest he risk his own well-being. December brought the birth of another daughter, Mary Geraldine. But after that event, railroad affairs were again primary.[19]

Construction had been proceeding apace on the Natchez-Jackson line.

William Johnson in December was able to ride out to the Pharsalia Race Course near St. Catherine's Creek some six miles from the bluff. The fare was seventy-five cents each way. The next month, a train tested a company-built bridge which spanned the creek. By June, cars were skirting a corner of the Jefferson College campus in Washington, and the bed had been graded almost twenty miles beyond that town. Revenues averaged one hundred to two hundred dollars a day. Local residents were proud of the accomplishment. Surely the St. Catherine's bridge with its brick piers, wood superstructure, and solid railing constituted "the greatest work of the kind in the Southern States." By April the next year, the railroad extended some fourteen miles from Natchez. Loads of cotton, carried from the depot in Washington to Natchez at forty cents per bale, seemed indicative that the railroad would fulfill its promoters' dream and capture the staple trade of the state's interior.[20]

Yet the prevailing credit stringency threatened the line. Continued funding of contractors depended on investors paying cash installments due on their stock subscriptions. While Quitman seems to have met payments due on his personal account with the railroad, other investors ignored notices of payment deadlines which the company posted in the press.[21]

Quitman tried to offset the deficiency with new sources of credit. In February, 1838, the company stockholders' meeting was able to thank him for winning from the legislature amendments to the company charter that permitted the company to engage directly in banking functions as a means of producing revenues for further construction. The bank opened in July with Quitman serving as president and, as of August 1, began offering interest of one cent per day for every hundred dollars deposited for a month. Later that year he unsuccessfully petitioned the Union Bank for a loan. In February, 1839, he lobbied again in Jackson, this time influencing the lawmakers into what became known as the Transfer Act, which required the governor to transfer twenty thousand state-owned shares of the Planters' Bank capital stock to the Mississippi Railroad Company. The government of Mississippi, in return, received twenty thousand shares of company stock, secured by a lien on the company's assets. The company was to assume the responsibility for paying interest on Planters' Bank bonds and for redeeming them as they came due. The *Free Trader* lauded Quitman's coup: with the infusion of new funds, the railroad could be completed; a "new era in the prosperity of Natchez" was on the horizon.[22]

While in Jackson lobbying for the Transfer Act, Quitman had the opportunity to exchange thoughts with one of South Carolina's leading nullifiers, Robert Hayne. Hayne arrived in town to promote his own scheme of a railroad linking Charleston and the Mississippi River valley in combination with a

99

direct shipping line to Europe from Charleston. Quitman organized and presided at Hayne's speech in Representative Hall. Later in the month, Quitman handled most of the arrangements for Hayne's appearance in Natchez. Hayne's oration at a dinner for two hundred guests at Natchez's Southern Exchange on the twenty-fifth became a major public event. With Quitman sitting directly to his right, Hayne gave an obvious sectional slant to the whole argument for railroad growth. Lauding Quitman's work on the Natchez-Jackson line, Hayne predicted that eventually a rail system would unite Natchez with Charleston and other eastern cities. Interior farmers would be tied more firmly to plantation interests by this commercial outlet for their surpluses. Moreover, railroads would enhance the South's war-making potential in wintertime, so abolitionists would learn to temper their offensive. Of course, war should be unnecessary: by also uniting North and South, railroads would ultimately dispel unfounded sectional stereotypes. Quitman's townspeople appreciated Hayne's vision. That night there were fireworks and a general illumination. A large crowd boarded the cars in a symbolic progression to Washington. "The Rail Road forever," trumpeted the *Free Trader*.

Quitman found Hayne's ideology appealing. He had long since concluded that the involvement of Yankee merchants in the marketing of southern crops forced the "staple states" to pay "Northern Monopolists" commercial tribute; and that cotton profits would rise if southerners could establish their own shipping lines to Europe which would bypass northern ports, northern shipping lines, and New Orleans factors (many of whom were agents of northern houses) and thus eliminate the cut of middlemen. Back in November, 1836, Quitman had become a charter stockholder in the Natchez Steam Packet Company. Incorporated in 1838 by the state legislature, the company's ship hauled over 40,000 bales of cotton in 1839 from Natchez direct to Europe. Hayne's visit seems to have prompted Quitman to increased exertions for direct trade, perhaps in the knowledge that an upturn in the economy could only redound to his railroad's advantage. That same February, he became a commissioner handling stock subscriptions for a newly chartered statewide direct-trade concern, the Mississippi Importing Company. The following month, he accepted appointment as one of several Mississippi delegates to a southern commercial convention to meet in Charleston on the third Monday in April, which was expected to take up direct-trade and railroad matters.[23]

However, Quitman's career as economic reformer was soon cut short by his railroad's precarious finances. Quitman's direction of the company's bank won encomiums in the press, for he applied bank profit to railroad construction while many other railroad bank executives in Mississippi squandered income by extending loans to their own boards of directors. But all this would be for nought if the company could not market the securities of Planters' Bank stock it had acquired in the Transfer Act. Quitman decided that he could not afford the luxury of attending the Charleston convention, and instead planned a trip—on company account—to London, where he hoped to market the bonds.[24]

To prepare for the journey, Quitman resigned as vice president of the Jefferson College Board of Trustees and arranged that Eliza would spend the summer vacationing in the North. She agreed only reluctantly, as she would have preferred going along with him. (Even after he left, she found herself "tempted to take passage and come to you," but afraid that he would not approve; and he had to reassure her that only a "robust man" could have endured his stage trip east through the Piney Woods and that sea voyages were not for women and children.)[25]

On May 25, 1839, accompanied by Joseph S. B. Thacher, a fellow director of the Mississippi Railroad Bank, Quitman took passage from New York on the sail packet *Sheridan* bound for Liverpool. The Atlantic voyage was swift, until they ran into head winds off the southwestern Irish coast. Around June 10, Quitman and Thacher transferred to a fishing hooker which delivered them to nearby Kinsale, from which point they could travel overland to Dublin. They believed that by traveling quickly to Dublin and taking a ship across St. George's Channel, they would beat the *Sheridan* to Liverpool.

Coincidence brought Quitman and Thacher into Dublin at the very time the city was celebrating the anniversary of Napoleon's defeat at Waterloo. Dublin went all out for the occasion; thousands of British and Irish troops under commanders who had actually participated in the battle reenacted the event before spectators in Phoenix Park. Quitman, who had barely missed his chance for martial glory in Texas, took it all in. "You may imagine my enthusiasm," he wrote Eliza. "When the infantry *charged bayonet*, I wept with deep interest. Oh! how I should like to have seen & been in the reality!!!" Quitman remarked in a similar vein to his brother that it was "the most glorious sight" he had ever witnessed.[26]

Quitman and Thacher crossed the water to Liverpool, and then set out by post for London via Birmingham, Warwick, Stratford-on-Avon, and Oxford. Quitman played the tourist. Everywhere he went, he sought out Mother England's rich historic and cultural legacy: "I have seen the glorious ruins of Kenilworth Castle, the old Warwick Castle, the room in which Shakespeare was born, his tomb, the antiquities of Oxford—Westminster Abbey with the tombs of all the old kings of England, The tower &c &c. I have been in the room where poor Anne Boleyn was imprissoned [*sic*] seen her marks on the wall, stood on the spot where she was executed, & sighed over her obscure grave. I have been in the dungeon where the young princes were suffo-cated by Richard IIIrd [and] the bloody tower I passed." Perhaps England overpowered this sojourner from a state just removed from the frontier and only beginning to fashion a culture and sense of history.[27]

Historic grandeur, however, was one thing, and English banking practices another. Quitman arrived in London on June 25, already aware of what had been obscure to him in Mississippi—that the Panic of 1837 had been part of an international economic downturn. Money in England was scarce; interest rates were high. English merchants were in such need of funds that they were selling their cotton cheaply and flooding the market, which drove down prices. Quitman wrote business letters—one day for six hours—and made contacts, but could not borrow on the securities of the company.

England no longer seemed so glamorous. Only the "antiquities of the country," it turned out, had met his expectations. Writing from the St. James Royal Hotel, within fifty steps of St. James's Palace, Quitman released his disillusionment in critiques of London society and manners. Residents of this "Babylon of people" took advantage of travelers. Strangers were "fleeced" by high prices and inadequate fare. Roast beef, no better than cuts available in Natchez, cost more. Invited by the Marquis of Lansdowne to attend the House of Lords, Quitman concluded that politics in the United States had more to offer. Finding it as easy to disdain English nobles as to disparage hack politicians back home, he summarized his impressions of parliamentary debate with a strikingly nationalistic comment: "Lord Well-ington & some of their first orators spoke and . . . they are not equal to *our* first men. I shall return to the United States, better satisfied with our coun-try. In a moral & intellectual point of view, I doubt much whether any nation of Europe is our equal." Obviously Quitman, at this stage of his life, though a radical southerner, also perceived himself a proud American.[28]

Unsuccessful in England, Quitman responded to an invitation from an old acquaintance, William Brune, to visit Prussia. Brune, a German, had made his fortune in a hardware business in Natchez and then returned to West-phalia. Brune encouraged Quitman to visit him and offered to write on Quitman's behalf to banking connections in Paris, Amsterdam, Frankfort, and Hamburg. Quitman took Brune up on the offer, seeing the trip as hold-ing out not only financial hope but also a once-in-a-lifetime opportunity to track down surviving European relations and find out something about his ancestry. Leaving London on July 15, Quitman and Thacher crossed to Rot-terdam and then sailed up the Rhine to Düsseldorf. En route, Quitman man-aged to locate some of his mother's relatives in Holland. From Düsseldorf they traveled eastward by land. At Iserlohn, Quitman found his family name engraved in iron at an entrance to an old zinc mine, and discovered two daughters of a "Mr. Quitman." Though they could tell him little about the family, Quitman did locate a family descendant at the zinc operation and learned to his satisfaction that the Quitmans had become "one of the richest and most respectable" families in Westphalia. After looking over some of the family tombs and church pews, he continued on to Brune's home, which was in the town of Soest. Brune gave the two travelers a hearty welcome, and even gave a dinner in their honor. Knowing Quitman's interests, he invited several military figures. When the company burst into singing after the meal, Quitman gave a rendition of the Fencibles' banner song.

Accompanied by Brune, who generously offered to guide them to the banking house of the Rothschilds at Frankfort, Quitman and Thacher returned to the Rhine at Cologne. After taking time to view the mammoth Gothic cathedral there, they resumed their upriver trip. Between Cologne and Mainz, Quitman had the opportunity to see many castles and ruins. From Mainz, the travelers proceeded to Frankfort. Quitman appreciated Germany much more than England, describing its inhabitants as "the finest race of people" he had encountered in Europe. However, his negotiations went no better in Frankfort than in London. Failing to dispose of company bonds with the Rothschilds, he and Thacher set off anew. Perhaps aid might be forthcoming at Brussels or Paris.

Brussels brought an opportunity to visit the real Waterloo battlefield. Again, Quitman was in his element: "There I spent a day full of enthusiasm . . . stood on the spot where Napoleon stood when he ordered his last charge & almost fancied that the British & Prussian legions were before me." (Claiborne claims that Quitman awed the guide and some visiting British officers with his knowledge of the battle, and told them that he had carried a chart of the battlefield around in his head for years.) Paris and its environs offered strolls through the palace of Versailles and the art collections of the Louvre. Quitman also took in the famous Notre Dame cathedral. Yet Quitman, seeing through the splendor of the city, perceived some troubling undertones: "Paris is truly a city of Palaces. . . . Yet with all this splendor, the King is a slave. He dares not show himself. The city is crowded with soldiers & when the King rides out, he drives at full gallop with a regiment of dragoons around him. In almost all of Europe there is a constant contrast between splendor & the most abject misery." Coming from a southern aristocrat, the observation is most intriguing. Quitman's implicit American nationalism is, in itself, intrinsically fascinating. But he had also internalized the values of Jacksonian democracy enough to catch a glimpse of some of the forces which would make Europe explode in revolution a decade later.[29]

Quitman had converted his company errand into the classic "grand tour," but had nothing concrete to show for his travels. European banking houses, already overextended in unsteady American state bonds, had little interest in digging their hole deeper. By August 19, Quitman was back in London. "Ruinous consequences," he predicted, lay ahead for the railroad and Natchez.[30]

Returning on the *British Queen*, an immense steam packet, Quitman joined Eliza and the children in September in Philadelphia—they had passed their summer at Philadelphia, New York, and Cape May—and took them home by way of Wheeling and the river route. On November 11, he arrived at Monmouth and two days later was welcomed home "in true military style" by the Fencibles and Natchez Guards (another volunteer unit), who came out to his estate.[31]

Unfortunately, despite the uncertain prospects for Quitman's European negotiations, the railroad company had expanded operations in his absence. By late July, it had contracted for thirteen sections of road for $325,000, a depot for $35,000, a machine shop for $20,000, and apparently a track down the bluff to the landing. Yet Quitman and the other company officials had been unable to meet payments due even before his departure. Contractor Joseph Hicks, for instance, had called at the banking house the previous January and been persuaded to extend his bill of $18,000:

> Upon calling for payment Genl Quitman requested an interview with me . . . and . . . called at my room at the City Hotel and gave me a statement . . . of the Bank and requested a continuance of the money by paying interest on it untill [*sic*] the following November by which time the stockholders would have an opportunity of selling their cotton & paying in their stock due—& the bank would also be enable[d] to get into more successful operation—giving me assurance that the money should be paid in specie funds punctually—pleased with the open and frank . . . manner of Genl Quitman I determined to permit the money to remain on deposit.

Continued extensions depended upon faith that the bank's operations were sound, but the bank had taken to issuing twelve-month post notes at 5 percent interest (meaning that they would be redeemed in specie plus 5 percent interest twelve months after issue) as its circulating medium. Because of widespread disbelief that the bank would redeem all these notes in specie on maturity, they already circulated at a 25 percent discount.

Once Quitman revealed that his quest had failed, the game was up. It became obvious that the company could never meet the 25 percent of capital due on the bank bonds by January 25, 1840. By early 1840, the wolves smelled blood. Natchez merchants made the rounds of local stores, collecting signatures on an agreement that all establishments would refuse the bank notes. In mid-February, the run on the bank finally came. Hicks was one of the many calling at the bank for payment. The cashier turned him down.[32]

Almost overnight, Quitman was transformed from hero to goat. The *Free Trader* charged that the bank directors had speculated in cotton rather than investing funds in track, and that this had caused the disintegration. Quitman admitted that the directors had, in discharge of their "thankless labors," occasionally bought cotton, but asserted that when they did so they had merely acted to pay off liabilities abroad for iron and other necessary construction materials. Bank notes fluctuated so wildly, he explained, that cotton proved a more reliable medium of exchange. The Vicksburg *Sentinel*, which had always lauded Quitman's conduct of the bank, charged that the failure would force the state's taxpayers to pay off the Planters' Bank bonds. Further, Mississippians would flee the state rather than accept exorbitant taxes to pay off the bonds. "The state is now . . . rapidly undergoing . . . depopulation," the *Sentinel* warned. "They are running off in droves daily, from every landing point on the Mississippi river, and before twelve months, we really believe one third the population of Hinds, Madison, Yazoo, Carroll and Lowndes Counties, will have sought a resting place in Texas, or the wilderness of Louisiana."[33]

Quitman could not take the heat. His personal finances were not all that stable, and he did not want to subject himself any longer to public criticism for what he perceived as community service. On February 26, after being unanimously reelected president of the railroad company, he announced his resignation. Quitman got out in time to escape the worst. On June 13, Governor Alexander McNutt revoked the railroad's banking privileges on the grounds that all banks, by a new law of February 21, had been required to pay specie for all notes of five dollars and under, and the railroad bank had not complied. Later in the month, the company tried to sell eleven of its slave workers to raise cash, but two claimants on the company persuaded the blacks to go with them rather than suffer sale at New Orleans.[34]

Trains kept running for a while. In October, 1841, the company announced that people could catch a train to Franklin at eight o'clock in the morning every day but Sunday. But the Mississippi Railroad Company lived on borrowed time, and Natchez never became the giant market center that its promoters had envisioned. Perhaps town denizens should have attached symbolic importance to a devastating tornado which struck the bluff on May 7, 1840. Quitman did. Hearing of the disaster while in Jackson, he lamented, "Our poor devoted city, seems to be doomed." Amid the rubble, he later found out, was the railroad company's own brick depot. Begun during unpropitious times, the Mississippi Railroad Company wound up in liquidation. Natchez would have to wait until the 1880s for its railroad connection with Jackson.[35]

9

Hard Times

Early on the morning of January 15, 1840, cannon fire on the Natchez bluff alerted the citizenry that Andrew Jackson, straight from an anniversary celebration in the Crescent City of the Battle of New Orleans, had arrived at the landing. The town buzzed with excitement. The Committee of Arrangements and the members of the militia hurried to escort Jackson up the bluff and then through the streets to the Mercer House. People cheered the former president all along the way. That evening, the hospitality included a big dinner, toasts, a rendition of *The Hunters of Kentucky*, and a ball at the Southern Exchange.

Prominent among the Natchez dignitaries participating in the festivities was John A. Quitman. In advance of the Old Hero's visit, Quitman served on the town's arrangements committee and financed band music (apparently out of his own pocket) to be played in Jackson's honor. On the actual day of Jackson's arrival, Quitman served as town marshal. He directed the military parade and presented the students of Jefferson College to the former president. Quitman also paid twenty dollars for a ticket to attend the dinner and ball.[1]

Quitman's involvement, though prompted more by patriotic respect for an American hero than by partisanship, nonetheless attested to his new Democratic affiliation, as Jackson had once inspired Quitman's enmity. Jackson represented the Democratic party as much as did any living American, and Quitman continued certain that nullifiers were best off in the Democracy, even though Democrats were unlikely ever to turn to his choice for president, John C. Calhoun—a man much too "philosophical" to give the necessary "gingerbread and beer" to the voters. Quitman had no doubt in this presidential election year that the incumbent Martin Van Buren and "sound Democratic principles" were far preferable to Whig William Henry Harrison and "monarchy."[2]

When Democratic party leaders tried to convert Quitman's support for Van Buren into some active work for the ticket, however, they ran into resistance. On February 14, a meeting of Democratic state legislators "and other citizens" at the hall of the house of representatives in Jackson selected Quitman as one of Mississippi's four Democratic presidential electors, but Quitman had no interest in taking on the assignment. Presidential electors were expected to stump vigorously for their candidates, and Quitman could ill afford the time. He announced that "circumstances of a private nature" necessitated his turning the position down.[3]

These "circumstances of a private nature"—which also contributed to his resignation as railroad president and his not accepting an interim appointment to the Mississippi High Court of Errors and Appeals—were Quitman's discreet way of confessing that he was in debt and could no longer afford public service at minimal pay.[4] Quitman's problems derived from several sources, but particularly from endorsing the notes of acquaintances so that they could get loans. He was being sued to make good as half security on an 1836 loan of $6,000 which fellow nullifier (and then state treasurer) Charles C. Mayson procured from Mississippi's sinking fund. Similarly, Quitman had been one of three co-endorsers of the notes to the Planters' Bank of a couple of Natchez merchants who had purchased town property. The merchants had paid back only a fraction of the loan before failing, one of the co-endorsers was "considered irresponsible in property," and Quitman and William Gwin were left holding a $13,495.38 liability. Quitman found himself in the unenviable position of being driven to "distress and ruin" for merely being an endorser at no profit to himself.[5]

Quitman had never been tight with his money. He and Eliza lived well, and he had taken the aristocratic code of noblesse oblige seriously. His daybook shows such contributions as $5 for a carpet for the Natchez courthouse, $10 to another county's volunteer militia, $10 to a local library, and $25 for a Masonic school. A theological liberal, he even made $50 donations to the Catholic and Baptist churches.[6] Thus, when Quitman became liable for the debts of others, he had little to fall back on. By January, 1840, he was appalled to find himself some $95,000 in debt. He poured out his frustrations to J. F. H. Claiborne: "I can not build a greenhouse for my wife or buy a new piano for my daughter; and when I meet . . . the trader, or . . . the Christian Shylock, I am compelled to acknowledge the superiority which the look of '*you owe me and can't pay*,' gives them. I have never avoided a friend or an enemy, but I confess, when I see these men approaching on the street, and the supercilious smirk on their faces, and know that my pockets are empty, if I can conveniently dodge them I do." Quitman still owned extensive property and about 160 slaves, but these holdings did not represent ready cash. It is not surprising, therefore, that Quitman gave priority to private financial affairs in 1840—despite believing that he had reached a point in his life "when the effort for fame should be made, if made at all."[7]

Resolved "never [to] be a slave" to debt again, Quitman set out to erase his obligations. Rejoining McMurran in the practice of law, and operating from a shared office on Natchez's Pearl Street, he pursued business in a kind of frenzy. In May, while attending court in Jackson, he reported home, "There are more than 2000 suits on the docket, involving an immense amount of property. I begin to feel quite at home in my old profession & shall have no desire to leave it until I am entirely relieved from difficulty." Letters from Jackson during similar court sessions over the next several years reveal a man often staying up through the night poring over briefs, as he prepared for cases dealing with such disparate matters as creditor-debtor litigation, federal pension requests, colonization, banking, and the legal expiration date of the terms of interim circuit court judges. Claiborne, observing Quitman's arguments in the last case (before the High Court of Errors and Appeals), applauded Quitman for dissecting "with a master's hand several great constitutional points." One of the more prominent cases which Quitman shouldered was the defense of the state treasurer Richard S. Graves, who was arrested in March, 1843, and charged with embezzling state funds. Quitman's defense was sharply abbreviated when Graves escaped from confinement by donning women's clothing and blacking his face, so that he would appear a black servant.[8]

Frequent trips to Jackson court sessions put renewed strain on Quitman's marriage. During one sojourn in the capital, his eldest daughter Louisa was reduced to pleading with him to return to Monmouth because her mother had been depressed since his departure, was scarcely eating, and was "continually sighing as if some heavy grief lay upon her heart." Eliza then complained that he had kept her ill informed about his activities. Quitman, predictably, rejected this indirect effort to rein him in. He exploded in self-righteous indignation that his time had been "almost exclusively taken up in the severe pursuits of the profession," that he was as "closely chained" as a "galley slave," and that he worked longer hours than did "factory wretches." Eliza made meek effort at protest, explaining that she had been particularly troubled by a remark of his before leaving home that it would not be of "much consequence" whether or not he wrote her. However, she bowed to his indomitable will. She deserved all his criticism, she admitted, was "truly repentant," and would try to be more devoted in the future. "Your letter has pierced my heart with a thousand arrows," she soothed.[9]

Eliza may have suspected her husband of infidelity. A social animal since adolescence, Quitman had lost none of his personal charm, and in letters home, he bragged about his accomplishments in society. In January, 1844, he informed Eliza, "Not to be out of the world or behind the times, I attended both Govr. [Tilghman M.] Tucker & [Albert G.] Brown's parties. Mrs. Brown is really a well bred charming lady. . . . At the parties I did not lose my reputation for gallantry." On another occasion he related that ladies had sent him bouquets of flowers.[10] Eliza, who was never secure about her own social abilities and often felt slighted by relatives, neighbors, and acquaintances,[11] could not deal with her husband's adroitness in polite society. She teased him, writing uneasily that "if you do not tell me all the Jackson news take care or perhaps I will not trust you so much and so long up there by yourself"; she also complained about women at parties Quitman attended letting themselves be written up in the press. On one occasion, she may have denied him her bed for doubts about his behavior in Jackson. He wrote in February, 1846, from the capital:

> When I parted from you, Eliza, having made two efforts to have a reconciliation between us, I determined never again to attempt what had been so scornfully rejected: but pitying the delusion under which you seem to labour, and reflecting over the heart rending consequences which might arise to our good & innocent children, I am fixed by the overflowings of a fond & afflicted father's heart, again to ask you, for the sake of our early love . . . to abandon your unjust suspicions and to consent to an unqualified reconciliation. . . .
> I have ever been, until you have rejected my affection
> your devoted J A Quitman[12]

It is difficult to judge, from letters written when the two were separated, the day-to-day flow of the Quitman marriage. Undoubtedly considerable affection linked John and Eliza most of the time. Quitman often made profuse and flowery expressions of devotion, as when he wrote how "dearly how intimately are entwined all the affections of my heart with you & our beloved children." Eliza's insecurities, in good part, were a projection of her continuing intense affection for her husband. When she heard in February, 1845, that he had fallen sick in Jackson, she prepared to rush to his side despite flooded rivers in the interior and possible danger to herself. Time, moreover, seems to have healed most of the differences, even the 1846 rift.[13]

Undoubtedly Eliza's overwhelming maternal responsibilities contributed to her difficulties. Children still came with regularity. Annie Rosalie was born on July 25, 1840; Eliza Theodosia was born on May 30, 1842; and Mary Fredericka was born on May 30, 1844. John was often unavailable when they fell sick, putting the burden on his wife. Two daughters died during this period: Mary Geraldine in April, 1845, and Sarah Elizabeth in May,

1846. It is not surprising, in this context, that Eliza suffered bouts of depression. Had Quitman encouraged his wife to join him occasionally on his out-of-town trips, there might have been less tension between them; but he believed that Eliza's place was at Monmouth, where she and her daughters could practice what Quitman called the "good sense and domestic virtues" appropriate for a woman's role and earn praise in "quiet circles." The wives of other lawyers and politicians showed up at Jackson, but Mrs. Quitman stayed at home.[14]

Quitman, moreover, did not restrict his out-of-town trips to legal affairs. He also spent more time on plantation visits, because he had made a new investment as a long-range solution to his financial problems. Back in December, 1836, he and Eliza had ceded Eliza's one-fourth share of Palmyra to Eliza's brothers Henry and Fielding Turner for $40,000. Henry had dropped out of medical school in Philadelphia because of eye problems, and perhaps the sale represented generosity on Eliza's part. Eliza's other brother, George, had subsequently bought out Fielding's share. On March 2, 1842, Quitman and Henry Turner bought George out for $200,000. In one swoop, Quitman gained a half interest in some 5,710 acres (divided into the Palmyra plantation and two islands known as "upper Palmyra Island" and "lower Palmyra Island"), 230 slaves, and some 60 head of cattle.[15]

Palmyra was a gamble. To get title, Quitman assumed debts incurred by Fielding and Henry Turner, who had not operated the estate efficiently. Many of the obligations were for small sums, but Henry Turner had been sued in the U.S. Circuit Court in Jackson by slave trader Rice C. Ballard for reimbursement for slaves provided Turner. Turner had refused to pay, asserting that the slaves were not in good health as Ballard had claimed, and that some were older than their stated age. The dispute became so bitter at one point Turner contended that Ballard had been planning to assassinate him. Quitman and McMurran handled the litigation, completing an out-of-court settlement in November, 1842: Turner was to return the slaves and their increase, provide a "reasonable hire" sum for their use during the years that Turner and Ballard had been bickering, and compensate Ballard for several slaves who had died while under Turner's care; Ballard, for his part, was to subtract from the sum due amounts for defects in the slaves. Quitman, in taking over the debt, was committing himself to a $75,000 obligation which he would make payment on until it was erased in 1857.[16]

Quitman, however, believed that Palmyra had great potential. "I hope," he wrote Eliza, "that in a few years by close attention to the disordered state of the affairs, and by rigid economy we shall be enabled to wipe out the debts and then we shall have one of the finest estates on the river." To procure operating capital and loans so that he could pay off debts and meet installments due Ballard, he arranged for the New Orleans factorage house of A. & J. Dennistoun to take a mortgage on Palmyra. He also put Springfield up for sale, but had no luck. Meanwhile he transferred slaves from Springfield to Palmyra, and took other steps to get Palmyra moving. Henry Turner stayed on the place and, with the help of overseers, supervised operations on a day-to-day basis. But Quitman visited Palmyra frequently, advised Turner by mail, and handled many of the marketing and purchasing arrangements. Fortunately, 1842 proved a good year. Turner reported in January, 1843, that 1,253 bales of cotton had been picked, ginned, and pressed.[17]

Quitman needed little incentive to regenerate his economic optimism. As soon as he heard from Turner that the 1842 crop looked good, he started exulting to Eliza that "plantation income and professional proceeds" would allow him within a few years to "throw into your lap enough to gratify all your wishes." By the time the 1842 crop was marketed, he felt that belt-tightening could end. He should try some speculations again. In June, 1843, he invested $10,288.33 for 961 acres of land in Holmes County and a half interest in 640 acres in Yalobusha County and 1,760 acres in Lafayette County. The next year he picked up some land in Rankin County. He also acceded to new requests to serve as security for the notes of others; now, however, he carefully arranged mortgages so that he would not be left empty-handed if his borrowers failed. Thus when Quitman became security for John W. Grant's bond for an appearance at the Adams County Circuit Court on a charge of selling liquor without a license, he received a mortgage on land Grant owned which bordered on part of Monmouth.[18]

Improved prospects meant that Quitman could once again participate in civic affairs. In late 1843 he gave a dinner for the Fencibles at Monmouth, showed up at a courthouse meeting to petition Congress for a naval depot and armory in Natchez, and joined in the eighth anniversary dinner for the Natchez Guards. In 1844 he accepted appointment to the first board of trustees of the University of Mississippi. The next year his fellow Masons honored him with a new term as Grand Master of the state lodge.[19]

Before long, Quitman was even thinking of giving up the law again. His sister Louisa wrote on May 8, 1844, "I was so glad to learn from your last that you think seriously of retiring from the practice of the law." But there was little comfort for Eliza in this. Louisa knew her brother well enough to suspect his next move: "You do not, I presume . . . intend to engage in political life? Alas, what would become of your leisure and your recreations then!"[20] Actually, Louisa's words of caution came far too late. John Quitman had terminated his political retirement within two years of its announcement. He had too much ambition to remain on the sidelines for long.

10

Repudiation

B Y middle age, John Anthony Quitman had accomplished a great
deal. Among the members of Mississippi's most fashionable urban
society, he had one of the finer homes. Plantations, slaves, and servants awaited his command. His large family seemed testimony to
his bounty, and even political antagonists conceded his right to the appellation "gentleman." Having weathered his hard times, Quitman could imagine
his children building on the aristocratic foundation he had established at
Monmouth.

Education for the Quitman children was charted so that they would acquire the proper attributes for acceptance in Natchez polite society. They
began lessons as early as four years of age, and received instruction in spelling, reading, penmanship, drawing, music, dancing, mathematics, Latin
and French, and other subjects deemed appropriate for a gentleman's son
and daughters. For schools, Quitman relied upon the private establishments
available in and around town. When Louisa wrote him, for instance, that she
wished to attend a school being opened by a Thomas Brown and three
Frenchwomen in the "old Montgomery house out by Mr. Dahlgren's Place"
and described the promised instruction as "music, drawing & painting,
french, and all the branches which constitute an english education," Quitman
consented.[1]

Unfortunately, Quitman had little control over the quality of such classes.
There were no set standards or certification procedures, so instruction
proved erratic and unreliable. Eliza apparently shocked him when she wrote
in January, 1842, about just what was transpiring at the Brown establishment. Brown, she explained, had "thrown aside the higher branches of
study such as Astronomy & c. and his vulgarity is extremely disgusting, one
thing he teaches the young ladies whilst lying down across a table at full
length." Quitman transferred Louisa temporarily to "Miss E. Marcilly's

Academy for Young Ladies" just outside town while he searched for a more lasting solution to the problem. Sometime in late 1842, he joined neighbors John McMurran and John Ker in opening a school in a garden house at Monmouth. Now, through the little "school in the woods," he could exert more direct control over educational content and methodology. Other nabob pupils were accepted on a fee basis.[2]

For a year or two, Quitman experienced difficulty in maintaining consistent instruction at his own school. He employed several preceptors (including a future Louisiana legislator) before settling on O. H. Waldo, a long-limbed, black-haired New Yorker who made an unforgettable physical impression because of a distinctive facial mole. Waldo maintained rigid standards, which led to some grumbling by the children. (Henry found himself "reciting every day at least two hours on a dead streak & sometimes longer without a single moment of intermission.") But Waldo also had a knack for making even the dryest subject interesting, stimulated intellectual curiosity, and held the students enthralled with his discourses on literature. Hired sometime prior to March, 1845, Waldo remained the family tutor until 1849; many relations and neighbors confirmed his competency by entrusting their children to his instruction. As Waldo put it, if the school did "not make as much noise as the great school in town," it nonetheless had the reputation of having "more of books and a good deal less of Deviltry." The Quitmans came to regard Waldo as an extension of the family and seem to have taken him along on at least some social visits and to have left Monmouth occasionally in his trust.[3]

As was customary at the time, the girls' formal education ceased upon graduation from the private school. However, Quitman did not end the learning process at this stage; indeed, his correspondence indicates just the opposite. "Now my dear daughter," he instructed Louisa in 1850, "I am not much given to sermonizing, but allow me again to urge upon you some regular study. It matters less what it is than that it should be something of a task—Spanish, German[,] drawing, history, chemistry, mineralogy, geology." The point was that the essence of their education was oriented toward social acceptance. Mastery of any one field of learning or artistic expression was deemed subordinate to some accomplishment in many. Graduation certified that a girl could function with poise in the best circles, become a debutante, and aspire to marry a gentleman. How well Quitman's sister Louisa understood this concept. When she heard in 1843 that his eldest daughter— her namesake—had graduated from Monmouth's school, she wrote her niece: "And so you have really arrived at the termination of your school-going life, and as a matter of course will now take your place in society, or 'come out' as the phrase is. . . . Blest as you are with indulgent Parents, and pleasant connexions, and moving in a circle of refined and polished acquaintances, who can say that your privileges are not great." Very few women of any social class or geographical region of pre–Civil War America attended college. Quitman provided his daughters about as much education as they could rationally hope to achieve.[4]

A son's training, however, was entirely another matter. Too much was at stake for anything less than a college education. Quitman constantly reminded Henry that he was "the only male representative" and that the Quitman family name would be judged by his accomplishments. Although Quitman expected Henry to cultivate integrity, a level temper, moderate habits, and filial loyalty, he stressed Henry's duty to accumulate "knowledge and information." "The Latin and Greek languages," Quitman advised, "must be well acquired by every man who expects to get a liberal education." Quitman subjected Henry to a barrage of somewhat overbearing advice about devoting his "whole soul" to his studies without depriving himself of the "plays and amusements for boys," and occasionally specified books which he expected Henry to read. Cognizant of the pitfalls which threatened young men at Henry's "time of life," Quitman worried that his son might lapse into "dissipation" if he did not pass enough hours at intellectual pursuits. Thus, articulating a concern about unrestrained passion characteristic of many planters, Quitman queried: "Do you eat & drink temperately? Do you rise early? Do you hold your passions in subjection?" Henry also received reminders that letter-writing style helped define an aristocrat, and that he should work on punctuation and other technical matters. After graduation from Waldo's school, Henry could expect to proceed to college and receive the final educational polish of an aristocrat's son.[5]

The Quitman children won the welcome in elite circles which their father sought for them. Exchanging visits with children of other leading Natchez families signified their acceptability. "Henry and I were invited to a party at Mr Robert Dunbars which we attended," Louisa reported to her father in January, 1843. She explained that it had been a "delightful" affair, and that the dancing had lasted until two in the morning. Reciprocal gatherings with the Turners and McMurrans filled their social calendar.[6]

Confident of his social circumstances, Quitman nonetheless felt a certain lack of fulfillment. Though he had served in all three branches of Mississippi's government, he could not enjoy his self-imposed political retirement. Ambition and ideology again compelled him to speak out on the issues. Once more, however, as in the cases of nullification and legislative representation, he demonstrated a knack for joining the unpopular side of a significant public question. This time, when he dared challenge a popular mandate that the state government renounce responsibility for the payment of state-endorsed bank bonds, he almost created his own political oblivion.

The bond dispute derived from two ill-advised measures which the Mississippi legislature enacted in 1838. In order to expand the amount of credit available to Mississippians, the lawmakers had chartered the Union Bank, headquartered in Jackson, capitalized at $15.5 million. Since the bank could never assemble anything like that amount through private investment, the incorporation act provided a state loan in the form of 7,500 $2,000 state bonds (bearing 5 percent interest and maturing in periods ranging from twelve to twenty years) which the bank could then sell. The bank was to guarantee the loan with mortgages on the property of its stock subscribers. Several days later, the legislature passed a supplementary act providing that the state government would also invest directly in the bank by purchasing 50,000—or $5 million worth—of its $100 shares. The shares were to be paid for through the sale of state bonds. Following passage of the act, the bonds were delivered to the bank in exchange for stock, and the bank then appointed commissioners to negotiate their sale. On August 18, 1838, the commissioners sold the entire series to Nicholas Biddle at less than par value (because Biddle received interest on the bonds before the bank received Biddle's payment). The Philadelphia banker subsequently sold the bonds to European investors.[7]

Unfortunately, mismanagement defeated the institution's purpose and soon threatened to bankrupt the state. Bank officials played middleman in cotton transactions, advancing to insolvent planters more money per bale than cotton could bring on the market. Other specie was expended on a variety of insufficiently secured loans. When word leaked out that the Union Bank was incapable of collecting the specie to redeem its "shin plasters" (a derogatory term for bank post notes), the notes fell sharply below par value. Hovering on the verge of failure, the bank threatened to pull the state government, which had guaranteed millions of dollars of bonds in its support, down with it.

The plight of the Union Bank, which had passed the legislature because of Whig support, confirmed many Democrats in their conviction that improper banking procedures had caused Mississippi's depression and that economic recovery required the dismantling of the state's banking establishment. Leading the Democratic assault was two-term governor Alexander McNutt, a Warren County planter and onetime Vicksburg attorney, who vetoed the chartering of several new banks. When McNutt (in his January, 1840, inaugural) suggested that the time had come to assess whether a banking system "destructive to the morals and injurious to the trade of the country" should be "abandoned altogether," the legislature responded by revoking its 1837 act allowing Mississippi banks to issue post notes and specified that banks doing so in the future were to forfeit their charters. In July, 1840, McNutt declared the Union Bank charter forfeit.

The Democratic offensive encompassed repudiation of the state bonds. There being no possibility that the state treasury could find funds to meet even interest payments on the bonds, Democrats inevitably questioned why taxpayers should be liable for a debt which should have been redeemed by the Union Bank. Looking for loopholes to absolve the state of responsibility, they found several. For one thing, bank commissioners had violated a provision that they should negotiate the sale of the bonds at par value. For another, although the charter of the Union Bank had passed two consecutive sessions of the Mississippi legislature, as required by Quitman's constitutional provision regarding the state's pledges of faith, the supplementary act had passed only one legislature. Thus Governor McNutt, despite his having signed both bank bills years earlier, formally called on the January, 1841, legislature to repudiate the bonds. When the legislature instead called on Mississippi to "preserve her faith" and redeem the bonds, a political showdown became inevitable.[8]

For the next two years, repudiation dominated Mississippi's political scene—tearing the state apart and revealing politicians at their worst. Democrats aroused latent anti-Semitism, insisting that Mississippians had no obligation to pay homage to the "Jews" of European banking houses. Overpaid Union Bank managers, they contended, moreover, had cheated the people by diverting the bank's assets to their own benefit. Whigs countered with their own mudslinging, charging Democratic repudiators in the legislature with conflict of interest because they had defaulted on their own payments for Union Bank stock and saw extermination of the bank as a means of escaping such obligations. And when the stakes were high, state politics reached a new low: bank president (and former governor) Hiram Runnels caned McNutt and fought a duel over press charges that bank directors were swindlers.[9]

Supposedly without either "time or inclination to embark in a political cause however good,"[10] Quitman could not stay aloof from the bond battles. Since he had written the crucial 1832 constitutional provision, his authority was frequently invoked in the debate. As one of the now despised class of bank directors, his honor was at stake. As a considerable property holder, he shrank from the confiscatory implications of a cancelation of bondholders' property rights.

It was at a rally in the Natchez courthouse for John D. Freeman, a candidate for state attorney general, in October, 1841, that Quitman first spoke

out. Freeman, a repudiationist, implied that Quitman's clause in the constitution had given the state legislature the very authority to pledge its faith for
bank stock which had caused so much trouble. Quitman, who had viewed
his clause as a restraint upon legislative excess, pressed Freeman on the
point before the crowd. Before sitting down, Quitman was asked for his own
opinion on the Union Bank bonds. Quitman responded that the state was
liable to innocent bondholders who had made their purchases in good faith.
He later wrote the editors of the *Free Trader* a letter about the incident which
predicted naïvely that "nine-tenths of the people of this state of all parties"
would come around to his position after dispassionately considering the
subject.[11]

In Jackson that winter on legal business, Quitman discovered that other
prominent Democrats shared his disagreement with their party's antibond
doctrine. Rather than join the Whigs, they determined to convert the Democracy to funding the bonds. On the night of January 29 the dissenters
convened a meeting of "Democratic Bond Payers," at which Quitman gave
an hour's speech about Mississippi's legal and moral responsibility to pay the
bonds. Responding to a suggestion that the bond payers might be drummed
out of the party for their views, he defied the Democratic leadership to try:
"Sir, standing where we have always stood, in defense of the great principles of Democracy and Equal Rights, we defy the power of any party to
drive us from our position. We cannot be read out of the party, or dragooned
into the Anti-Bond ranks. Here, in the face of the world, we renounce them
and their measures, we repudiate the repudiators." Following the meeting,
Quitman braced for the attack. Party leaders, he blustered to Robert J.
Walker, would be wise not to provoke him. They would never "kill" him off,
and once aroused he might become "dangerous."[12] It was as if Quitman realized that his political credibility could not withstand another change of party.

New developments, however, sorely tested his resolve. Repudiation candidates had triumphed in the 1841 legislative elections, and both branches of
the legislature fell into antibond hands. In February, 1842, the lawmakers
resolved, by convincing majorities, that the state had no "legal or moral obligation" to make good on the $5 million of Union Bank bonds. On February
26, Governor Tilghman M. Tucker, McNutt's Democratic successor, approved the legislature's decision. With repudiators going on to question the
validity of the earlier Planters' Bank bonds (which *had* passed the legislature in regular form) and to consider dismantling the entire banking structure of the state,[13] Quitman found himself being edged more and more into
the Whig camp, where most of the resistance to repudiation was centered. In
May, 1842, he even served as intermediary on behalf of S. S. Prentiss when
Prentiss challenged Governor Tucker to a duel over some articles in re-

pudiator James Hagan's Vicksburg *Sentinel* which Tucker had reportedly endorsed. His earlier reservations about affairs of honor being eroded by the heat of political argument, Quitman shed few tears when a son of one of his close friends gunned Hagan down the next year in a duel.[14]

Still, Quitman fought tenaciously to remain a bond payer and a Democrat. In February, 1843, he turned up at the Democratic state convention in Jackson, where, determined that Alexander McNutt should not be rewarded for his repudiationism with a nomination for U.S. senator, he helped influence the convention to defer the nomination until the Democratic caucus in the next legislature. Although he resisted suggestions that he make his bond views the basis for a gubernatorial bid, he did spend much of the year crusading for payment and thereby aiding a partial state ticket fielded by the probond Democrats. On May 29 he addressed a Natchez public meeting which adopted resolutions staking out a bond payers' credo. In July, Quitman delivered a probond speech to another Democratic state convention, where his remarks fell on deaf ears—the meeting chose a repudiationist ticket. In the early fall, Quitman mailed a public letter to an "Anti-Repudiating Club" in Lowndes County reiterating his belief that repudiation would tarnish the state's honor. He contended that since the people of Mississippi had previously reelected Governor McNutt and most of the legislators responsible for the original state guarantee of the Union Bank bonds, the voters had given prima facie evidence that they recognized the validity of the bonds. November brought Quitman upriver to Vicksburg to address the "Anti-Repudiating Club" of that city.[15]

All this put Quitman in even better stead with Whigs. He won encomiums —a "volunteer in the cause of justice," a "gallant soldier," an "upright gentleman"—from a party in flagrant ecstasy over what the issue was doing to Democratic unity. The Yazoo *Whig* even bandied Quitman's name about as a possible Whig candidate for governor. Some Whigs, encouraged by the conservative thrust of the antirepudiation Democrats, actually considered sacrificing their party identity in the bond cause; they would coalesce behind the Democratic bond-paying ticket. Such talk appalled Henry Clay, who happened to visit Vicksburg at the time of this ferment; Clay exhorted his Mississippi Whig brethren to maintain their party identity.[16]

Whig sanction, however, only made Quitman's effort to convert the Democracy more difficult and jeopardized his political future. Rejecting his contention that party structure could tolerate dissent over the bank bonds, many Democrats concluded that he was unreliable and that his campaign might do the party irreparable damage. Ferdinand L. Claiborne, a close associate, warned Quitman to desist, lest by dividing Democrats he deliver the state to Henry Clay, the Whigs, and the protective tariff in 1844: "The truth is General Quitman you never had a friend that wished to be more *devoted* to you than myself. . . . You think right—your principles are right, but your actions & association with partys [*sic*] I do condemn. I don't care two straws about any statesmen or politicians on earth except Mr Calhoun and *your-self*. . . . You won't place it in my power to show my zeal." After gubernatorial nominee Albert Gallatin Brown and the rest of the Democratic repudiationist ticket swept the fall 1843 elections, Quitman could only wonder whether the state would "be fit to live in." The Adams County Democracy expressed its displeasure with him the next month by excluding his name from its list of forty-five delegates to the next party state convention. When John Nevitt made a special effort to add Quitman to the list, a resolution carried which specifically rejected him.[17]

Finally seeing that the issue could completely destroy his political career, Quitman decided to drop his bond campaign. Ignoring the whole matter as best he could, he shifted his advocacy to a cause far removed from banking and state politics—the annexation of Texas. By so doing, he managed to recoup his political fortunes in remarkably short order. For once, Quitman's ideology—in this case his fervent expansionism—meshed with the public will.

The Texas question exploded at just the time to rescue Quitman. Although there had been a lot of interest in Texas' joining the Union back at the time of the revolution, the matter had been in abeyance. Fears that Mexico (which had never recognized Texas' independence) would go to war over annexation and that annexation might stir up sectional and intraparty strife over slavery expansion kept American policy makers wary of Texas. Quitman was fortunate that the president of the United States, John Tyler, foundered in a kind of political limbo not unlike his own. The first vice president in American history to succeed to the presidency, Tyler desperately needed a popular issue if he was to be nominated for a second term. In October, 1843, his administration offered Texas an annexation treaty. On April 12, 1844, John C. Calhoun, now secretary of state, signed a treaty of annexation.

Had the Senate merely approved the measure, there would have been little capital in it for Quitman. However, that august body—partly because Calhoun had converted Texas into a seemingly southern cause, having written the British minister in Washington, in a well-publicized note, that Texas was needed to protect slaveholding interests from reputed British abolitionist intentions—voted against the treaty on June 8. Tyler never got his nomination, but the Texas question infused the 1844 presidential campaign. Democratic candidate James K. Polk committed himself enthusiastically to annexation. Whig nominee Henry Clay took a cautious stance, opposing immediate annexation.

Quitman jumped on the bandwagon eagerly, giving major addresses for Texas at Jackson public meetings on January 9 and May 10, 1844. At the latter affair, Quitman offered resolutions that Texas belonged to the United States by virtue of the 1803 Louisiana Purchase Treaty, that England would exploit an American refusal to annex Texas (a possibility "inconsistent with the safety and even existence of the south-western states"), that the annexation advocates were "devoted to the permanency of the federal Union, the prosperity of our whole country, and the extension of constitutional government and free institutions," and that the United States had a duty to "interpose in the dissensions and wars of their neighbors" if such unsettled conditions threatened the American frontier. The resolutions fused nationalism and sectionalism, "manifest destiny" and southern destiny, in a strange blend—perhaps indicative of Quitman's own bifurcated commitment to his country at this point in life—but made sense to his audience, which endorsed them unanimously. Then, in July, Quitman reviewed the Texas question for the Adams County Democratic Association, explaining the U.S. Senate vote and predicting that the year's election would provide a mandate for annexation.[18]

Hoping that outspokenness on Texas would erase memories of his Union Bank bond crusade, Quitman labored to make Texas the state Democracy's preeminent issue. At one local party meeting, he even demanded that "no candidate for any office at the hands of the democracy should receive their suffrage unless he was in favor of annexation." Quitman did expound on other issues. He ridiculed Whig protective-tariff doctrine, suggesting that if Americans were restricted to buying from home manufacturers, Europeans would not have the specie to afford southern cotton. Soon the ships of the American merchant marine would rot from disuse, and Americans would "relapse into the condition of the South Sea Islanders before the great humanizer—commerce—was known to them." But again and again he declaimed upon Texas.[19]

That summer and fall, Quitman stumped conspicuously for the James K. Polk (and George M. Dallas) Democratic ticket. In August he not only helped organize a mass Democratic barbecue at neighboring Washington, he even roped Eliza and daughter Louisa into serving on a committee to plan decorations. When the big day arrived, Quitman served as marshal and led a procession of Democratic carriages and horsemen from Natchez to the affair. At the barbecue, Quitman delivered the welcoming remarks, and introduced repudiationist governor Albert G. Brown—the main speaker—to the crowd. When a teen-age auxiliary of the local Democratic association, the "Juvenile Association," held a noisy torchlight parade for Polk and Dallas in September, Quitman was on the scene to address the "fine little fellows" and invite them out to Monmouth for a barbecue. In late October, the press reported political appearances by Quitman at Grand Gulf and Port Gibson, and even at a barbecue in Tensas Parish, Louisiana.[20]

Quitman also worked behind the scenes for the Democratic cause. Hearing that his close friend and family doctor Samuel A. Cartwright (an influential medical theorist, proslavery ideologue, and Democratic politician) might go public with protectionist views, which was bound to help the Whigs, Quitman penned a note urging Cartwright to refrain from public comment—even if he favored a high tariff—if he cared at all about Democratic victory.[21]

By giving of himself without stint to the Texas cause and the Polk campaign, Quitman won his redemption. The *Free Trader* relegitimized his Democratic status as early as April, when reporting on one of his orations: "The meeting was . . . ably addressed by Gen. John A. Quitman, who showed the true line of demarcation between the two parties, and proved conclusively that the Whigs were, with some honorable exceptions, the federalists and national republicans of old; and that the democrats of 1840 and 1844 advocate the doctrines of 1798." When the time came that November for the Adams County Democratic Association to celebrate Polk's triumph, Quitman seemed a natural choice to chair the committee drafting resolutions to hallow the event.[22]

Winter brought a short respite from politics. Around the first of February, Quitman traveled to Vicksburg, where he met with William Wood and William Mylne, agent and factor, respectively, of A. & J. Dennistoun and Company. Wood, a Scotchman, found Quitman a "very intelligent, pleasant man" and agreed to reduce the interest rate on the Palmyra debt. Quitman then boarded the train to Jackson, where he planned to attend the high court and chancery court sessions. The trip was rough, however, and he contracted a severe case of chills, which confined him to his Jackson room for several days and left him with headaches a week later.[23]

Still, he kept posted on the Texas question and, in March, again in good health, picked up where he had left off in the fall. Back in Natchez, Quitman persuaded the Democratic association to take the unusual step of celebrating Andrew Jackson's upcoming birthday on the fifteenth. Although it was not customary to observe the birthdays of living illustrious men, Quitman insisted that Jackson, in the "decline of life with the frosts of nearly four score winters upon his head," merited recognition. Quitman joined a large committee to plan a dinner celebration, and on the appointed day Quitman again played a conspicuous part. Prior to the dinner, he gave a speech for Texas at a Hickory pole, and at the dinner offered a toast which implicitly integrated the Monroe Doctrine into the argument for Texas annexation: "True American Policy. Not to permit European interference in the political concerns of North America." [24]

Quitman's persistence began to bring dividends. The January, 1846, legislature was expected to choose two U.S. senators (one for a full term; one to replace Robert J. Walker, Polk's choice for secretary of the treasury). J. F. H. Claiborne, who had favored Quitman for the Senate back in 1830, decided the moment propitious to promote Quitman for the full term. Following Quitman's Hickory pole address, Claiborne successfully persuaded the Adams County Democratic Association to endorse Quitman, on the grounds that Quitman had done more than any Mississippian for Polk's election. Support, too, mounted in other parts of the state. Up in Yalobusha County, a Coffeeville paper, while not specifically mentioning the Senate seat, urged that Democrats not pass over Quitman in selecting their state ticket. Quitman, the paper argued, lacked "spot or blemish" and had given Polk "widely-felt help." [25]

By the late spring of 1845, Quitman was pinning his hopes on the Senate seat. Cognizant that his selection required at least some eastern Mississippi support, he inquired of Jasper County acquaintance John J. McRae, a newspaperman and former Union Bank director, whether the "people" were ready for him. He also consulted Volney Howard, a prominent Democrat in Jackson, about his chances. Both were encouraging. McRae wrote that he rode "high" on Texas, carried more "moral weight" with "our people" than anyone else, and would founder only in the event of a revitalized bond debate. Howard, also optimistic, contacted associates throughout the state on Quitman's behalf. Unsolicited support in the mail further buoyed Quitman's spirits. [26]

Following custom, Quitman refrained from open stumping. Active pursuit of votes was deemed inappropriate in U.S. Senate campaigns, since the legislature rather than the voting public made the actual selection. However, Quitman, who appeared in Jackson for court sessions, kept his name before the people. Newspapers noted his role in memorial proceedings in June for Andrew Jackson and his appearance in July at yet another Texas meeting at the capital. [27]

Meanwhile, other contenders emerged. Former governor McNutt minced no words about his interest; he even ignored precedent and gave speeches in his own behalf. Newspapers and county meetings responded with quick endorsements. Jackson attorney Henry Stuart Foote was another who sought the legislature's nod. Foote had helped found the *Mississippian*, and certainly had a claim on the party. William Gwin wanted the job, but had to live down charges about his being involved in Choctaw land frauds. Roger Barton, a Holly Springs lawyer and politician, had a core of support in northern Mississippi. Congressman Jacob Thompson coveted the office. And Governor Brown himself was reported anxious to trade his Jackson residence for a stay on the Potomac.[28]

Quitman had nothing against Gwin or Foote. He had been associated with the former in several financial matters, and had worked with the latter in the Polk campaign. Foote, an unusually articulate, hot-tempered, small man with a disproportionately large head, had even called Quitman distinguished, chivalrous, and accomplished, in a volume he had written about the Texas Revolution. Governor Brown had won Quitman's appreciation by going out of his way to call on Quitman earlier in the year when Quitman had been sick in Jackson. But Quitman had little respect for McNutt, the "great repudiator," and McNutt was quickly emerging the front-runner in the race.[29]

McNutt had one obvious weak spot: he had not taken an advanced position on Texas. By playing up McNutt's lack of expansionist vigor, Quitman's supporters could at once tarnish their opponent's image and heighten their own candidate's strength. In March, and possibly with Quitman's connivance, the Jackson *Southern Reformer* began a running attack on McNutt. The paper accused McNutt of predicting that acquisition of Texas would drive down Mississippi land values, denouncing Calhoun's treaty of annexation, and promoting U.S. Senator Thomas Hart Benton's efforts to renegotiate annexation in such a manner that Mexico would not be offended. Quitman, Foote, and those other "gentlemen" who had "gallantly entered the field in favor of annexation, ere the smoke of the first gun of the enemy had cleared away" showed far better judgment, according to the paper.[30]

McNutt fought back stubbornly. "I am now and ever have been in favor of the immediate re-annexation of Texas to this Union," he declared. "I never advocated Mr. Benton's bill—never considered the assent of Mexico necessary to effect the re-annexation of Texas." In the 1844 campaign, he asserted, he had actually lambasted the Whigs for their anti-expansionism. McNutt's hometown Vicksburg *Sentinel*, moreover, suggested that McNutt's accusers were on personal vendettas: reports of McNutt's hostility to Texas came from a state senator defeated for reelection because he had challenged McNutt's position on the Union Bank bonds and from a man who had a grudge to settle against one of McNutt's relatives.[31]

Then McNutt turned the tables on Quitman. On June 20, the *Sentinel*, in an extra, published a copy of a devastating anonymous letter; the letter, possibly written by McNutt himself, had been sent to Benjamin F. Dill, editor of the Oxford *Organizer* (a newspaper which had been supporting Quitman and denouncing McNutt). Professing to have only the "warmest" personal regard for Quitman, the anonymous correspondent asserted that he was writing because most voters in the state were unfamiliar with Quitman's political history and needed to learn about it, since the "General" was "too modest to proclaim his own political acts."

Much of the letter argued that Quitman should not be considered a reliable Democrat—he had supported a national bank, John Quincy Adams, the Whig ticket in 1836, and Whig congressional candidates in 1838, and had shown an independent strain even when technically a Democrat. Had not Quitman supported Philip Barbour for vice president in 1832, a move calculated to divide the Democratic vote? Certainly Quitman had opposed causes popular with the state's Democratic masses, such as the election of judges and the seating of the Choctaw cession representatives. The diatribe blended in a few falsehoods too, such as saying Quitman had opposed representation of the Chickasaw counties in the 1837 legislature, when he was not even a member.

The letter also implied that his nomination by the Adams County Democracy had been a fluke. The particular association meeting which chose him, according to the document, was actually an afterthought to a celebration of Jackson's birthday, and only one-tenth of the local party membership had attended. McNutt supporters present had permitted the resolution endorsing Quitman to pass merely as a compliment to his speech that day.

Whoever wrote the letter apparently had inside information on Quitman and knew him fairly well. The writer asserted, for instance, that Quitman had refused to pledge in 1844 that he would support Van Buren if the New Yorker garnered the Democratic nomination. This, in turn, made the implications of corruption against Quitman all the more damaging. Quitman's "Natchez Rail Road Bank" had been the "vilest shin-plaster shop in the land." Quitman had tried to "draw the wool" over the eyes of the "Jew Brokers" in Europe by peddling his company's worthless stock. When this scheme collapsed, he returned home and resigned as president so that he could get "some pickings out of the rotten concern" as its attorney before it went under.[32]

Signed "HUME" (for the famous eighteenth-century Scottish writer David Hume), the letter threw the Senate race and the Democratic party into an uproar. Papers throughout the state took sides. Naturally the *Reformer* blasted the article, saying that "demagogues" were sporting with Quitman's character and subjecting him to a blatantly "ungenerous" calumny, given his reluctance to campaign. The *Free Trader*, though not endorsing Quitman, defended Quitman's judgment and Democratic credentials in a point-by-point defense. Even the *Mississippian* expressed qualms about the piece, and the editors of a Hernando paper, which carried McNutt's name for senator on its masthead, nonetheless praised Quitman as a gentleman and pledged that nothing derogatory about Quitman would tarnish its columns.[33]

Amid forebodings that Democratic infighting might unnecessarily throw the race to the Whigs, matters degenerated further. On July 2 the *Sentinel* bluntly accused Quitman of acknowledging privately that he had never heard McNutt say anything against Texas but refusing to go public with the admission. Quitman's plan, the *Sentinel* explained, was to ride Whig votes to election by the legislature.

Quitman found out about this piece during a trip to Vicksburg later in the month. Knowing that he could not afford insinuations of Whiggery, he wrote to *Sentinel* editor John Jenkins, demanding to know Jenkins' source. Jenkins answered that his information derived from a conversation with McNutt and some of McNutt's friends, but that McNutt had since said that Quitman had specifically told him (McNutt) that his (Quitman's) hopes rested on the votes of Democrats in revolt against the legislative caucus nomination system. Quitman, according to McNutt's account, had also said that while he would not "court" the Whigs in the legislature, he would "certainly not object to Whig votes." Quitman responded on July 30, writing Jenkins that it was absurd to think that he might confide a "political intrigue" to a "political enemy." It was "utterly untrue," Quitman insisted, that he relied on disaffected Democrats or a Whig-Democratic coalition for election. Quitman then gave his version of the disputed conversation with McNutt, which he said occurred on a Vicksburg street: "I observed . . . that I had seen indications that some democratic members of the Legislature would be instructed against him [McNutt] and if so that they would not go into caucus, without excepting [i.e., rejecting] him, or disregarding the will of their constituents. In the same conversation in reply to a remark of his that some whigs would support him, I said in substance that while as a democrat, I would not court whig votes, I certainly would not quarrel with a whig for voting for me." Jenkins plastered the petty dispute all over the August 8 *Sentinel*, and other newspapers took note of the new controversy. Honor was at stake.[34]

By this time, in fact, "honor" had taken to the stump. Although Quitman had gained some commendations for following tradition and not actively campaigning, McNutt had no such inhibitions. In his speeches, McNutt would mock the "Sleepies"—like Quitman, Brown, Thompson, and Gwin —who refused to meet him before the people. Some of his speeches amplified the newspaper attacks on Quitman. Reluctant to tackle a clearly superior speaker head-on or to forfeit the credit he had earned for not puffing himself, Quitman nonetheless realized that something had to be done. So while in Jackson that July, apparently after consulting with fellow aspirant William Gwin, Quitman took the unconventional step of persuading Henry Foote to "travel McNutt's campaign trail & rebut his speeches." What Quitman promised in return is unclear. But Foote did take after McNutt, usually speaking for thirty minutes following McNutt's customary three-hour harangues. Foote charged the former governor with authorship of the Hume letter. From Panola, Foote wrote Quitman, "According to my agreement with you, I have every where presented your claims to a seat in the United States Senate in terms of respectful and cordial commendation, and defended you with zeal and such energy as I possessed against all that Gov. McNutt has either directly charged or darkly insinuated." Foote tried to divert public attention to Quitman's persistent defense of the slave system. "I carried the war into Africa in all cases," he wrote.[35]

Disturbed by information from Foote that McNutt had been attacking him as a "bond-paying champion in 1843," Quitman decided, as he had in his earlier congressional race, that he could not afford to wait passively for the verdict. So he used his militia position as a pretext for speaking to the people. He announced his retirement as major general of the state militia so that his availability for the Senate could not be questioned. His term, however, did not expire until November 5, and he put his waning authority to political use. Military reviews that September of units in the eastern counties of Covington, Jones, Wayne, Clark, Lauderdale, and Jasper provided a setting for campaign harangues and denials of the "Hume" charges. "Quitman is *vexing* himself to find out the author of 'Hume,'" observed the hardly disinterested Governor Brown.[36]

If we are to believe Reuben Davis, the sharp-tongued McNutt did not flinch: "In a speech at Aberdeen, McNutt said, 'Fellow-citizens, I understand that General Quitman is now in the eastern counties reviewing his militia, and that he says when he meets me he intends to whip me. Now, I tell him, at this far-off distance, if he whips me it will be because he can outrun me, for I have a great horror for the barbarous practice of personal violence.'" Davis claimed that McNutt's unconventional profession of cowardice won applause and laughs, because of his uncanny ability to turn popular prejudices to his own advantage. Nevertheless, Quitman's campaign appeared to be gaining momentum. The Port Gibson *Correspondent* published a lengthy defense of Quitman's politics, and ultimately an endorsement, while even the *Sentinel* muted its attacks and conceded that he was an "honorable" man worthy of selection as senator if McNutt should falter. Benjamin Dill, meanwhile, became an unofficial campaign manager. He boosted Quitman in his paper, sent on strategic tips, and wrote other politicians and editors in Quitman's behalf. Dill even gave away pro-Quitman issues of his paper in northern Mississippi towns prior to appearances by McNutt. By mid-September, Quitman felt better about his chances.[37]

From October until the convening of the legislature in January, Quitman's movements are obscure. Since there are few surviving documents, it is difficult to determine the extent of his campaigning. On October 25, Quitman attended an Adams County–Concordia Parish meeting to formulate a local response to a call for a "Southern and Western [Commercial] Convention," which had been scheduled for Memphis in mid-November. A few days later, Quitman wrote an answer to a public letter in the *Mississippian* which had charged that the Transfer Act of 1839 had been detrimental to the state's taxpayers and suggested that defaulting subscribers to the Mississippi Railroad Company stock should be made liable for the state's losses on the Planters' Bank bonds. Quitman, realizing that continued concern about his bond position undermined his candidacy, argued that the state had actually gained from the transfer, because the legislation had given Mississippi a claim to the assets of the railroad company, and, prior to its collapse, the company had made good on interest payments on the state bonds. In November, Quitman chaired a Natchez meeting organizing a town welcome for John C. Calhoun, who was traveling downriver after presiding over the Memphis gathering. December brought Quitman back to Grand Caillou. Albert had died on November 26. Upon hearing the news, Quitman traveled to Live Oaks, disinterred the body, and brought it to Monmouth, where a formal burial was held on December 30.[38]

The Senate contest was still open-ended when Quitman arrived in Jackson in the first week of January. F. L. Claiborne was predicting that Governor Brown was the man to beat, but no one knew anything for sure. How could they, when only a few legislators had declared their preferences during the fall legislative races? Intrigues were in the air; deals were there for the asking. But Quitman resisted the temptation, or so he told Eliza. With their daughter Sarah seriously sick at the time, Eliza only half wanted him to win and congratulated him on maintaining his integrity. Perhaps even McNutt offered a trade. Since Eliza wrote that Quitman was right in refusing to "yield to men who have abused and misrepresented you in all things," it is possible that McNutt promised to support Quitman for the short Senate term if Quitman went along with McNutt for the longer term. Quitman, however, would be the stoic.[39]

On January 7, nineteen Democratic senators and sixty-four representatives gathered in the senate chamber to end the speculation. On their initial ballot, Quitman came in third, with sixteen votes. McNutt led with twenty-one, but the big surprise was Foote, who won eighteen votes (Thompson had fifteen votes, Brown a surprisingly low nine, and Barton five). McNutt held strong for five more ballots, but support for Quitman and the others eroded in favor of Foote, who became the consensus stop-McNutt candidate. On the seventh ballot, several McNutt supporters switched to Foote and it was all over. The actual election by the full legislature three days later was only a formality.[40]

The defeat staggered Quitman. Although his friend John Guion saw nothing remarkable in Foote's victory ("A seat in the Senate of the US has been the goal of Footes ambition for many years"), Quitman recoiled in disappointment. Yet, he had contributed to his own defeat by giving Foote carte blanche the previous summer to campaign as his stand-in. By so doing, Quitman had provided Foote a rationale for putting himself before voters and legislative candidates all across the state as a valiant defender of another candidate's integrity rather than as a mere aspirant for office. Whether Foote, as he later claimed in his memoirs, warned Quitman that the strategy could backfire is immaterial. The 1846 loss was continuing testimony to Quitman's ineptitude as a Jacksonian Era politician. He found it difficult to combine his ambition for political power with his unwillingness to compromise old-fashioned principles of proper political behavior.[41]

11

Patriarch of a Plantation World

FOR a brief moment in July, 1847, Springfield transcended its mundane role as one of John A. Quitman's three plantations. A Pennsylvania physician who had for years searched the Mississippi River valley for fossils and Indian relics, Montroville W. Dickeson, made an astonishing discovery while digging under the Springfield bluffs. There he found a large Indian mound which contained immense quantities of skulls and bones of natives who he estimated had inhabited the area a thousand years earlier. The skulls were remarkable to observe. Quitman's son Henry, who visited the site, described them as "flattened in a very peculiar manner" with the "frontest bone and the back" compressed and the sides just above the ear "pressed out in great bunches." The heads had been so compressed that in some cases the forehead was two and a half inches above the lower jaw. Hypothesizing that he had happened upon remains of the extinct Natchez Indian tribe, Dickeson rushed off a score or so of the skulls to the Academy of Sciences in Philadelphia.

News of the archeological find at the "plantation of Gen. John A. Quitman" soon appeared in several newspapers, one as far away as Houston, Texas. But the plantation was not identified by name, nor was it located for the readers' enlightenment. Such specifics would have rent the curtain which veiled Mississippi's plantation world from the general public. In the paradoxical environment of antebellum Mississippi, though plantation ownership underlay the politics and ideology of important public figures such as Quitman, the plantations themselves were generally considered unworthy of news attention. This held true even when newspapers provided biographical sketches of leading men. Newspaper readers occasionally caught glimpses of the mansions of prominent individuals. The *Mississippian* in one article explained Monmouth's location and described its "flowery bowers," "shadowy lawns," and "honey-suckle retreats." [1] The life and labor on Quitman's plantations which supported this existence, meanwhile, stood removed from view. Only close acquaintances and business contacts comprehended that Quitman presided as patriarch of a virtual plantation world, a world whose components functioned in a complex, organic relationship. Palmyra, Springfield, and Live Oaks transcended their role as suppliers of cotton and sugar to world markets. They affected each other, and also were connected with the economy of Monmouth.

Palmyra had diverse purposes within the Quitman plantation web. Located adjacent to the plantations and residences of future Confederate president Jefferson Davis and his brother Joseph (who owned Brierfield and Hurricane, respectively), Palmyra was a large operation. Spreading over 2,500 acres of land, the plantation was divided for managerial reasons: Upper Palmyra, Lower Palmyra, and Palmyra Island. Plowing alone necessitated the use of some 50 two-mule teams a year. Palmyra had its own cotton gin and cotton press, and marketed cotton in bulk. Hazards such as flooding, worms, and late frost took a considerable toll of a crop that ranged anywhere from about 400 bales in poor years to as much as 2,200 bales under optimal conditions.[2]

Palmyra also provided direct and indirect revenue from other sources. "With this I send you a coop containing Two dozen chickens—Eggs are so scarce at This time, I cannot make up a box for you," wrote Henry Turner on one occasion. Quitman kept considerable stock on the Warren County place (130 head of cattle, according to one tax compilation) and encouraged his slaves to raise poultry. Quitman purchased fowl for the Monmouth dinner table directly from his Palmyra slaves, and the plantation was a source of dairy products for his family. The island had a good stand of timber, which Quitman also used. Outfitted with a sawmill, Palmyra sold cords of wood to river steamers which put in at its landing, and supplied lumber for construction at Monmouth. In 1842, for instance, Quitman had lumber shipped for a greenhouse he was building.[3]

Sugar and molasses production constituted, of course, Live Oaks' *raison d'être*. The place on Grand Caillou was, like Palmyra, a large-scale operation. As was customary throughout the Louisiana sugar region, the cane stalks were not only raised and cut, but were also processed—in a sugarhouse on the premises (which had its own landing on the bayou)—into brown sugar and its by-product molasses. Processing required engine-run rolling machines to extract the juice from crushed cane and boiling machines to evaporate water from the juice. The steam engines consumed immense amounts of wood: rolling alone, one year, required 1,700 cords of wood. Machine maintenance often delayed production. "[W]hen I last wrote," Albert noted during the 1844 processing season, "we had commenced at the

131

boilers and the engineer thought it would require four days to repair them but upon close examination we found them very much corroded with the salt so that it took nearly seven plates of Iron to repair both thoroughly . . . the machinery has not worked . . . well since the first season." Sugar was a far more precarious crop than cotton. Premature frosts, especially, took a serious toll. But hurricanes and storms also played havoc with the crops and the machinery. Three hundred hogsheads of sugar—large barrels weighing about one thousand pounds when packed—made a normal crop; 2 hogsheads per cultivated acre was considered a satisfactory season. In good years Live Oaks produced 400 hogsheads; unfavorable conditions could mean as few as 80. Annual molasses production was about 150 hogsheads. Barrels for storage and shipping were generally constructed on the premises, and Live Oaks had a kiln to fire its own construction brick.[4]

Live Oaks, however, like Palmyra, had secondary functions within the Quitman plantation economy, as Quitman revealed when he wrote Eliza that Albert had "shipped some sugar, molasses and a barrel of pickled oysters for us. When they arrive, have a barrel of molasses sent to Springfield." Quitman also supplied Palmyra with Live Oaks sugar, and apparently received occasional shipments of oranges from the Caillou groves.[5]

A churn rather than a cotton boll might have symbolized Quitman's Adams County place. In December, 1842, Quitman consciously converted Springfield into a dairy farm by purchasing 63 additional head of cattle for the plantation. Although Springfield continued to produce cotton for market, Quitman came to depend on the farm for Monmouth's butter and meat, as well as meal ground from its corn crop. His daughter Antonia remembered, "My Father owned . . . a plantation called Springfield . . . a kind of farm place where he received weekly or semi-weekly supplies of butter, eggs[,] meat, corn, oats, fowls or anything else that the home place did not furnish in sufficient quantity. . . . Twice in every week a cart came down with all these supplies." Springfield's dairy operations can be traced in a surviving account book. Selected slaves received special assignment to the dairy and stock operations: "Ben Plow driver and general supt of the feeding of the stock[.] Nelly milks and attends to makeing [sic] Butter." Quitman increased the dairy and stock functions over time: his 1850 Adams County tax receipt credits him with 108 head of cattle. He also kept some 220 hogs and 70 sheep. Dairy, meat, and meal deliveries to Monmouth were considerable. Quitman's mansion received, for instance, a total of fifty-one pounds of butter—in three deliveries—for the week of June 3–9, 1846. Antonia never forgot Guinea Moses, the "one-armed negro" who made many of the Springfield-to-Monmouth deliveries. Springfield also supplied cotton for mattress making at Monmouth.[6]

Springfield generated an extra $20 or so a month by its ferriage operation. Flatboat conveyance across the Mississippi from the Springfield landing cost $.25 per person—whether black or white—one way; charges for horses and mules were set at $.50 each. Freight was assessed by weight; twenty-three bags of cottonseed, for instance, cost $2.40. Further income came from selling wood, at $2 a cord, to passing steamboats.[7]

Because Quitman conceived his plantation empire as an interlocking system, slaves as well as produce moved from locale to locale depending upon where they were most needed. Although he seems to have provided his labor force with a fairly stable existence, he did uproot workers if necessary. Thus Henry Turner wrote Quitman during one planting season at Palmyra: "We are now in *much need* of the negroes who were sent to the Caillou—will you be good enough to have them sent up as soon as convenient—we have much hard and heavy work to do at this time as is always the case in preparing for another crop." Similarly, while visiting Albert at Live Oaks, Quitman's brother Henry noted that "your 4 boys will be of great service to him [Albert] and seem to take hold with spirit, tho' they were very tired when we arrived." House servants were also moved around, and black artisans switched locations. Occasionally Quitman provided slaves on loan to Eliza's mother and stepfather.[8]

As extensive and complex as Quitman's plantation network was, he sought its expansion to the very end of his life. The late 1840s brought regular spring flooding to both Springfield and Palmyra. An April, 1847, overflow, for instance, flooded the slave quarters at Springfield and reached the yard fence of the overseer's dwelling. During an inundation of Palmyra in the spring of 1850, Quitman decided that he had tolerated partial crops long enough and set out upriver on the Yazoo with Henry Turner to locate higher ground. In Holmes County he found what he was looking for. Amid a healthy stand of cypress trees, he established his last cotton plantation. Set back from the Yazoo a half mile at its closest point, Belen extended over 1,640 acres along a body of water shaped vaguely like the letter *B* and named, appropriately, Bee Lake. Quitman expected Belen to produce consistently, and he allotted it some thirty of his Palmyra slaves.[9]

Quitman also occasionally assumed managerial authority over the Turners' land and slaves. Eliza's mother, Sarah, and her second husband, Jared Fyler, traveled a lot in the North and often expected Quitman to keep an eye on their business matters and their home. "[I]f Mr. Quitman will give a look occasionally at the affairs at Woodlands we will be much obliged to him, to prevent the servants straying too widely if possible," instructed Sarah from the Union Hotel at Saratoga Springs in August 1838. While Eliza's taciturn brother George and his wife Annie lived in the North (from the fall of 1852

until early 1854), Quitman accepted the chore of running their Point Pleasant plantation in Concordia Parish. Not only did Quitman have to handle
slave matters—"the yellow girl Hetty at the Woodlands ought at once to be
sent up to the Point where her family is," wrote George from New York City
on one occasion—but Quitman had to hire the overseer and see that he was
supplied with such items as molasses and shoes for the labor force.[10]

Although Quitman ran his plantation network efficiently, distributing manpower and production according to need, he never achieved—or really sought
—self-sufficiency. The ideal, rather, was to *approximate* self-sufficiency.
Cotton and sugar were the money crops which financed the aristocratic life
at Monmouth. It was preferable to supplement corn and meat production on
his places with outside purchases and not risk overproduction of food at the
sacrifice of extra bales and hogsheads. Thus in 1850, when the Davis plantations on Palmyra Bend yielded about sixty-four bushels of corn per slave,
Quitman and Turner's workers produced less than thirty-nine bushels apiece.
Frequently food reserves were inadequate, and Quitman bought from outside sources so the hands would not go hungry. Returning from Live Oaks,
Quitman reported, "The crop will exceed 300 hhds, but I shall be a considerable expense in the purchase of corn, which I found quite deficient."
Quitman's factor billed him $246.13 on another occasion for a purchase of
pork.[11]

Quitman looked beyond plantation limits for such necessities as bagging,
rope, nails, cartwheels, shoes, lime, and machine parts. Some items could
be acquired from John Knight, W. A. Britton and Company, and other
Natchez merchants and shopkeepers. Quitman owed Britton and Company
thousands of dollars at his death. But most items were channeled through the
same New Orleans factors who marketed his crops: the Dennistoun firm for
years after the Palmyra acquisition; Hill, McLean in the early 1850s until
H. R. W. Hill—Quitman's contact in that firm—died of yellow fever in
1853; and finally Estlin, Lee and Company. While most correspondence between Quitman and his factors revolved around New Orleans and European
market conditions, the quality of Quitman's cotton, and the best time to sell,
the factors also acquired many items on Quitman's behalf which were not
available locally. This included, of course, a wide spectrum of household
goods. Quitman's daughter, for instance, informed Eliza in 1857 that Estlin
had sent a sewing machine to Live Oaks. Quitman's running account with
Estlin on May 12, 1856, showed an indebtedness of $28,631.75. Large defi-
cits were common prior to the sale of the crop, because factors supplied
credit (usually at 8 percent) for purchases and paid bills in Quitman's name
and in the name of his agents. Thus Quitman told his son, who was in New

York City in late 1853, to "draw upon me at twenty days sight payable at the counting house of Estlin Lee & Co. New Orleans" if he ran short of funds.[12]

From time to time, Quitman utilized Yankee suppliers. "I visited Cincinnati with a view of procuring some materials for Live Oaks," he explained on one occasion. Little concerned with whatever irony attached to his patronizing the merchants and strengthening the economy of a section he had come to regard with considerable disdain, Quitman even purchased non-essentials in the North: "My intention is to see the family to Philadelphia where your mother wishes to procure some dresses & c," he could report to his son with no sense of shame or hypocrisy. In this, he only mirrored his generation; it was characteristic for upper-class southerners to fall victim to the magnetic appeal of northern shops and goods. When, however, in 1850–1851, Quitman kept his son in a northern college while advocating southern secession, at least some eyebrows were raised.[13]

Quitman coordinated his plantation empire from Monmouth, but he visited his holdings occasionally[14] and understood all facets of his crop operations. Thus, when as a personal favor, he sent two sacks of his cottonseed to an acquaintance using different strains in northern Mississippi, he provided detailed planting instructions: "I recommend that in planting you roll the seed. It goes further and makes a more certain stand. The process is to dampen a pile of the seed on a smooth piece of ground, by sprinkling it with water & then sack it in loose dry earth, until the seed is coated with the earth. This should be done immediately before planting. It may then be scattered very thinly . . . & slightly covered."[15]

Day-to-day supervision, however, depended on the decisions of others. Management of Palmyra rested with Henry Turner and subordinate overseers, and Turner, not Quitman, was the true lord of Palmyra. "At last we got to Palmyra House, and were received by Mr. Turner," wrote William Wood to his wife about his February, 1845, visit. "There was a fine, rousing wood fire in a large comfortable parlor, and two famous easy rocking-chairs, which were given to Mylne and me. . . . We then had supper; capital preserves, beautiful cream, and had coffee. At nine we retired to bed. Each had a fine, large room, beautiful white sheets, large four-posted beds, and rousing wood fires. . . . I only wished you had been with me. After the dirt and discomfort of Vicksburg the contrast was charming." Wood then told how William, a "respectable negro servant," lit the fire in his bedroom the next morning, and how after a breakfast of venison, sausages, rolls, corn bread, and other delights, he and Mylne had been provided horses for a hunt. Similarly, although Quitman ran Springfield briefly in 1842, overseers customarily managed that place. Live Oaks was in the hands of his brother Albert until Albert's death in 1845. Then Quitman employed overseers until his son Henry was old enough to assume management. Henry apparently took up residence there in early 1856, and ran the place in conjunction with overseers.[16]

Misunderstandings and high personnel turnover marred Quitman's dealings with his hired managers. Most applicants were semiliterates well below Quitman's social class; once hired, they were accorded little respect. Thus Quitman complained about Samuel P. Crow, chief overseer at Palmyra for the whole tenure of Quitman's ownership, "It is entirely impossible from Crowe's [*sic*] letters, to say what is the state of the crop or what is going on. It seems to me that any man of sense, even if illiterate [*sic*] could describe these things." Quitman was appalled when N. D. Fuqua, his Live Oaks overseer, dared aspire for public office in 1855 and announced his candidacy for sheriff of Terrebonne Parish.[17]

Quitman never overpaid his overseers. Salaries ranged from the $240 paid Thomas F. Rees for running Springfield in 1842 to the $700 W. R. Smither received for managing the Upper Palmyra place in 1852. Moreover, accommodations for overseers apparently ran to the primitive. William Wood described Crow's dwelling as a meager two-room affair fronting on the Mississippi with no glass in the windows.[18]

It is hardly surprising, therefore, that Quitman recruited mediocre overseers and that they often failed to measure up to his standards. Quitman's relations with his Live Oaks overseer illustrate well the kinds of problems encountered. N. D. Fuqua never did things right, despite his efforts to conciliate the Quitmans by such gestures as inviting Quitman to his daughter's marriage. In a February, 1852, letter, Quitman lambasted Fuqua on several accounts. Why had Fuqua failed to keep Monmouth informed of the seasonal end of schooner service from New Orleans to Grand Caillou? Fuqua's negligence left the place short of pork, and Quitman would have to incur extra expense to send in a special shipment. And why had the overseer been so inconsistent in his packing of sugar hogsheads? Quitman's factor in New Orleans had written that none of the hogsheads weighed the expected one thousand pounds. A few were too heavy; many did not weigh enough. "This has never happened before with the same sised [*sic*] hhds, and shows something wrong. . . . The fact is the crop will fall 25 hhds short of ordinary weight, and consequently the expenses that much increased, besides injuring the sale of the sugar." Quitman regarded Fuqua as a "fool" who was so unreliable in his predictions of crop sizes—he always anticipated the worst—that Quitman could give "no weight to his opinions even when candidly given." When Quitman's son assumed control of Live Oaks, he discovered that Fuqua, to save effort, had been gradually taking land out of cultivation and allowed the drainage ditches to fill with water.

Quitman fired Fuqua in late 1856, but could do no better for a replacement than Robert O. Love, a former Springfield overseer who had been dismissed for incompetency after transferring to Belen. Quitman found him only slightly more acceptable at Live Oaks. When Love requested a leave of absence during the 1857 rolling season, Quitman concluded that the overseer was weak and displayed "capriciousness of character." Quitman attributed Love's not keeping him informed of plantation happenings to lingering resentment over his firing from Belen.[19]

Quitman gave more regular supervision to the orchards, vegetable gardens, and greenhouse at his Natchez estate than he did to his plantations. They were far more to him than a source of food for the family table; they were his hobby, his way of renewing that communion with nature which he had enjoyed as a young man. If absent from home, he would send a stream of instructions for his head gardeners, who were hired whites until 1850, when he gave the assignment to a black servant named James. When on hand, Quitman saw personally to his trees and plants. "Father has returned to his old habits and occupation of gardening and pruning trees—he in fact lives in the garden," remarked Eliza to their son on one occasion. Quitman would even tend his plants in inclement weather. Eliza reported in another instance that Quitman "as is his wont" was busy "in the garden in the rain setting out Cellery [*sic*] plants, cabbage Lettuce & c." Quitman cultivated numerous fruits at Monmouth, including apples, peaches, pears, strawberries, blackberries, nectarines, melons, figs, grapes, and plums. Vegetable production included celery, cabbage, lettuce, potatoes, peas, eggplant, cucumbers, tomatoes, asparagus, and turnips. Quitman was experimental in his approach to orchards and gardening. His records note ten different strains of pear and seven types of peach tree on the place.[20]

Monmouth grew along with the stature of the man, acquiring somewhat palatial—though by no means ornate—dimensions by Quitman's old age. A poultry yard and brick stable were added in 1849. In 1854 the mansion itself underwent significant improvement when a two-story wing was added. Since the new wing roughly paralleled the detached two-story kitchen building which extended back from Monmouth's left, the structure had become something of a massive two-story square *U* in shape. With acres of gardens, servants' quarters, and scattered outbuildings to its rear, Monmouth generated increasing awe from its visitors. While William Wood could only use the adjective "fine" to describe the place in 1845, former minister to Spain Daniel Barringer was far more effusive a decade later during a steamboat stopover in Natchez: "[M]y friend who is an acquaintance of *Genl. Quitman* proposed a ride to visit him. . . . The Genl.'s place is very striking—very much improved, yet left so as to give the most natural effect & the beautiful ground & splendid oaks, with long hanging moss, to their branches. . . . He lives in princely style—in a . . . castle of a house—plain & rich—old fashioned . . . with very plain but rich furniture. He is immensely rich." [21] Monmouth anchored Quitman to the life of the elite and constituted his expression to outsiders of that same life.

Behind the curtain functioned John Quitman, slaveowner. Quitman merits classification as a large slaveowner, though the number of slaves he owned varied by year. Palmyra was his largest operation: there he kept some 311 slaves (under sixty years of age) in 1848. His other holdings were smaller: Springfield had 39 slaves in 1842; Live Oaks included 45 slaves in 1840 and 85 in 1850; Belen had 29 slaves under sixty in 1855 and 32 slaves under sixty three years later. Quitman also maintained a substantial staff of household servants at Monmouth, and on occasion supplemented his work force with hired bondsmen. [22]

Although Quitman never met the famous paternalistic standards of his Palmyra neighbors, Joseph and Jefferson Davis, he clearly approached more the paternalistic than the tyrannical model of southern planter. "Harshness makes the negro stubborn," he contended; "praise, and even flattery, and, more than all, kindness, make them pliable and obedient." Quitman shared this perspective with Henry Turner and his overseers. Exceptions, however, did occur, as in 1844 when an overseer killed a black youth. More in keeping with Quitman's philosophy was the Live Oaks overseer who followed Albert. A neighboring planter praised him for being "kind to the people at the same time that he requires them to perform their duty." Punishment on Quitman's holdings was calculated to be commensurate with the specific infringement of routine involved. Sometimes, when there were extenuating circumstances, punishment was suspended. Henry Turner, for instance, did not discipline a runaway because "he seemed penitent and is usually a good boy." [23]

The shadow of the whip hung over labor. The lash was employed for breaches of discipline and for such offenses as picking insufficient or "trashy" cotton. Turner noted on one occasion that a slave discovered in the Palmyra kitchen without permission was given "a few cuts." Quitman and Turner were convinced that firmness was a necessary complement to kindness for achieving efficiency. But they also preferred those overseers who tended toward the lenient, to those who were too free with the whip. They took slave complaints about mistreatment seriously. Thus Turner prepared Quitman for the probable dismissal of W. R. Smither from Palmyra in 1853:

"Smither does not please me . . . and I think he will have to be discharged unless he changes much for the better. He is getting to be, too severe with the negroes—Too fond of his whip and the use of the 'stocks'—The latter should not be used except in extreme cases. The negroes complain almost every day and many would have been runaway, were I not at home." [24]

Some of Quitman's overseers were apparently too relaxed about discipline. Eliza felt compelled to fire Thomas Rees from Springfield during one of Quitman's absences after learning that the slaves had gained free run of the place. "Mr. Kent . . . reported that the overseer was in a constant state of intoxication, that the negroes were idle doing nothing whatever, that no cotton had been weighed for some time and that he had shot some of the cattle for mere sport," she explained. What is striking about this incident is that Quitman rebuked her. "I fear you have done wrong in discharging Rees," he answered. "These reports are generally exaggerated. . . . I would rather trust to him even if he drinks, than to a stranger who knows nothing of my plans for the place." Obviously Quitman preferred permissiveness to repression, and did not construe permissiveness as conducive to servile rebellion. Quitman always trusted that he could maintain authority. Thus when Turner informed him in September, 1843, that "religious fanaticism" had broken out among the force at Upper Palmyra, Quitman told Eliza that he would "soon settle that matter & will stop [there] to see it all quiet." Some years later Quitman simply dismissed out of hand a suggestion from Fuqua that dissatisfied white workmen at Live Oaks might incite the slaves to rebellion. [25]

In addition to showing restraint in disciplinary matters, Quitman permitted an incentive system to operate within his labor economy. Slave and master made reciprocal concessions, so that this system could function. Slaves requested and won pay (which they usually spent on extra shoes and calicoes) for chopping wood on Sundays, their rest day. Slaves also sold chickens to Monmouth and demanded prompt payment: "Harry takes down some chickens which the negroes have furnished. I have given him a bill of same—can you sent me the money by letter. They are very troublesome in the way of asking for their dues when not paid." Quitman allowed his slaves to visit other plantations at night and sanctioned parties at designated times. Mid-winter at Live Oaks after the rolling of cane was completed, for example, brought a time of marriages, dances, and other celebrations. In their quarters, Quitman's slaves could develop their own community life. [26]

Quitman apparently provided respectable housing for his slaves, at least in comparison to some slave dwellings in the South. "The Negro quarters are good and comfortable," noted an observer at Palmyra, "and being arranged in rows each house separate, all whitewashed had a very neat appearance forming a street with houses uniform on either side." Quitman's paternalism encompassed medical treatment. Outbreaks of yellow fever, malaria, pneumonia, measles, tuberculosis, and a variety of other illnesses and ailments made health care a constant preoccupation on Quitman's holdings. The 1849 cholera epidemic took the lives of at least eighteen of Quitman's Palmyra slaves alone. Although the frost and wintertime brought relief from mosquitoes and the diseases they carried, the change of season also ushered in an onslaught of throat ailments and related problems as slaves labored frequently in damp, cold conditions. Quitman's son, for instance, reported during a visit to Live Oaks in January, 1852, that there was an epidemic of "putrid sore throat" and that three deaths had already occurred.

Quitman responded to these illnesses in a variety of ways. Sometimes he administered his own cures. He answered Henry's letter, for example, with instructions that his son tell Fuqua to spurn medicines and rely on gargles and "cold bathing of the neck" and administer a spoonful of mustard seed before bed every night as a preventative. Frequently, however, Quitman employed physicians. Thus a Doctor C. T. Leggett billed Quitman $25 for treating a tumor on a "black child" and for providing medicines for the same patient. In 1847, Quitman's Live Oaks overseer arranged for a physician to visit twice a week year-round for a $200 annual fee.[27]

Obviously Quitman intended to do the best he could to preserve his investment. When household servants fell ill, he became particularly alarmed because he knew them on a much more personal level than he did his field hands. "For a week past since my return from the North," he wrote at the height of the 1853 yellow fever epidemic, "I have been so occupied in nursing and prescribing for sick negroes, as to be unable to advise you of my safe return and the health of the white family. . . . I am sorry to inform you . . . that I found Flora, Joe & Dick quite ill. The two latter have recovered but two days since we consigned to the grave the remains of poor Flora."

Yet there are indications that Quitman might have been a bit slack in some areas. Quitman's instructions to Fuqua in 1852 to reduce the Live Oaks pork allowance and "make it up in molasses or sugar" because of a sharp rise in the market price of pork might be evidence that he would skimp on nutrition under certain circumstances. Likewise, when Henry Turner the next year alerted Quitman that at least fifty pairs of blankets were needed at Palmyra because it had been "several years" since any had been distributed among the hands and many were "very much in want of the article," it may have been an indirect admission that at least some of Quitman's blacks had passed previous winters uncomfortably. Quitman's slaves did not run around naked; correspondence and surviving records indicate that clothing and shoes were distributed twice a year. If William Wood's opinion is to be credited, slaves appeared content with their condition. Wood thought that blacks returning to their quarters from work in the Palmyra cotton fields appeared as "happy as English farm servants or cotton-mill spinners." However, just as Quitman underpaid overseers, he may have cut some corners on slave care.[28]

Paternalism defined relations between Quitman and his household servants; he had less direct contact with his field hands. Family members never called Monmouth's domestics slaves, but referred to them as servants, Negroes, or, occasionally, "darkeys," and Quitman perceived his servants as distinct, but nevertheless real, extensions of his own family. How intimate an extension he seems never fully to have determined. In one letter he apparently intended to instruct his daughter to extend his "love" to the servants but had second thoughts and rewrote the sentence, substituting "regards." [29]

The Quitmans regarded their house servants with affection. Some members of the Monmouth staff had been with the family for decades. Aunt Dicey, mammy and nurse, is mentioned in family correspondence as early as 1833, and was still around at Quitman's death. To the children, she was as much companion as slave; they thought of her singing African songs, participating in doll weddings, helping care for their pet dog, and dressing up on Christmas Day. Harry Nichols, the servant whom Quitman had taken to the Texas wars, had a similar status with the Quitmans. It was only natural, when hearing of the death of a servant in a neighboring house, that Quitman's eldest daughter should reflect "how hard it would be for us if Aunt Dicey or Harry should die." [30]

The Quitmans extended special privileges to house servants in recognition of this personal relationship. When Harry Nichols in 1848 decided to marry Flora Withers, a maid, Quitman summoned an Episcopal minister from Natchez to conduct the wedding ceremony. When a servant traveling with Quitman's son Henry in New Orleans pleaded for an opportunity to attend a Negro ball in the city, Henry capitulated to his wishes even though it necessitated a delay in the servant's return to Monmouth. Presents—some hand-me-downs, some purchased—were distributed by the Quitmans to the servants every Christmas to affirm both obligations and emotional ties linking the two segments of the household together. House servants, moreover, maintained initiative in such personal matters as naming their own children.[31]

Household domestics reciprocated the affection and concern demonstrated by the Quitman family. Mary McMurran, caring for the Quitman children during Quitman and Eliza's absence in January, 1848, was taken somewhat aback when she encountered Aunt Dicey during a visit to Monmouth: "Old Dicey seemed quite brisk and wanted to know when all her children were coming home." Dicey was particularly protective of the health of the Quitmans. Other family servants demonstrated similar loyalty. When a fire broke out in the Monmouth kitchen, for instance, servants came running to extinguish it. Family servants rallied with consistency during crises.[32]

Given such manifestations of the harmonious master-slave relations on his own plantations and in his own household, Quitman concluded that human bondage offered a superior system of regulating labor. There was nothing hypocritical when he issued public statements in defense of the southern way of life, which he did do from time to time, particularly in his later years. Thus he could claim that "negro slavery, as it exists in the South" was good for the nation's economy and was "an element of moral and military strength" as well. Surely slavery had more positive attributes than the northern free labor system, where "factory wretches" worked eleven-hour days in "fetid" conditions while their intellects were destroyed "watching the interminable whirling of the spinning-jenny." Privately, Quitman told J. F. H. Claiborne that his slaves were "faithful, obedient, and affectionate."[33]

Yet, Quitman's household and plantations won no immunity from the antimaster patterns of black behavior which plagued slaveowners throughout the South. Slaves were much less content with their conditions than their masters liked to believe, and manifested their displeasure in both overt and covert ways. While Quitman, his family, and his overseers never had to contend with outright servile rebellion, they did find that black resistance interrupted the flow of plantation life and household affairs.

Particularly irksome was the frequency with which slaves ran away. Henry Turner reported on one occasion, "Last Evening George and Abram ran away and I presume will go to Natchez. William Smith the boy who ran away from me is in jail at Port Gibson and Crow will go after him in the morning—as fast as we get one set in others appear to take their place." But slave resistance took other forms too. Slaves staged work slowdowns, and may have sabotaged equipment. Overseer Robert Love's entry in his Springfield journal that "Saml broke one of the new plows" may or may not have reflected deliberate misconduct on the slave's part. Slaves at Palmyra in 1843 used the religious awakening there as an excuse for general misbehavior.[34]

Prescribed medical care also seems to have provoked some resistance. Quitman alerted Albert in 1839 about how slaves feigned health while sick because of their dislike of hospitals and special diets, and cited the cases of slaves who had died because they put off treatment until they were past help. Turner recounted the instance of a Palmyra slave who hid cholera symptoms for three days, until he finally collapsed while working. The slave died within hours. Although such behavior may have indicated suicidal tendencies among Quitman's chattels, it more likely reflected skepticism about the efficacy of Quitman's cures. The slaves seem to have particularly objected when quarantines separated them from the rest of the slave community. They would "slip off at night to the quarter, which invariably makes them [the healthy slaves] sick." [35]

Pampered house servants, likewise, registered displeasure, despite the privileges they were accorded. Sloppy work, infringement of household rules, and sullenness became trademarks of servants' subversion of the system. Thus, Quitman felt compelled to apologize to Henry Clay when his "trusty servt." failed to locate magnolia trees during the Kentuckian's visit to Monmouth. "From some mistake, he was unable to find those to which I had directed him, and did not inform me of his failure until it was too late to make another attempt." Another servant injured family members when he ran a carriage over a three-foot embankment on the way to a neighborhood wedding. The Quitmans described the servants as "lazy" and the cause of "trouble and vexation." They were prone to "take advantage" when white supervision became lax. Even Aunt Dicey had her moments. In 1842, Eliza banished her to Springfield. When Quitman visited the place in July, Eliza warned him that Dicey might try to persuade him to allow her to return to Monmouth. If this occurred, he was to "tell her that if she thinks she can behave herself and never give me any more trouble . . . she must come and see me about it." [36]

Quitman, though aware of instances of black misbehavior, chose to overlook them when he evaluated the merits of the southern labor system. There were compelling reasons for him to avoid dwelling on the deficiencies in his slave regime. His economic well-being, for one thing, was a product of the free labor provided by his plantation blacks. In addition, constant attendance by house servants, despite occasional lapses, was one of the most important luxuries which defined membership in the southern upper class and made the aristocracy's life appealing. Servants looked after the Quitmans at Monmouth and when they were away from home. Quitman took servants on political jaunts and into war; family members had slaves accompany them on social calls and during visits to resorts. Quitman's daughter wrote, "Polly is very attentive & gives me not the slightest trouble, I could not have got along . . . without a maid," when she visited New Orleans in 1849. Family domestics made beds, cooked, chased bats from the mansion, escorted the children back from school, fetched ice cream, carried bedtime snacks, and performed many other tasks which molded the day-to-day routine at Monmouth. [37]

However, to attribute Quitman's ideology to greed is to miss the point. Other influences operated to blind, or at least shield, him from the fundamental wrong that slavery was. Quitman did not understand what his slaves were signaling by their resistance, in part, because of his racial perspective.

Quitman and his family lived in the presence of blacks, slave and occasionally free, both at home and away. Natchez's free black barber, William Johnson, cut Quitman's hair. The family constantly encountered black domestics in other homes, because the Quitmans only circulated in polite society. A May party at a neighbor's, for instance, included "an old negro" as musician who "scratched away the same tune over and over again." Constant proximity mellowed incipient prejudice within the family. Certainly Johnson seems to have felt that Quitman accorded him respect. The barber wrote, "Gen. Quitman handed me a Letter to day that was given Him at Jackson for me. He did me proud, He did me proud." Although daughter Rosalie once complained about the "characteristic odor" of Monmouth's cook, which she derided as a "native gift," most family members refrained from such hostile characterizations of blacks as a race.[38]

Nonetheless, the Quitmans could not help but absorb the racial stereotypes prevailing in their society—that Negroes were simple, naturally lazy, childlike, and careless. Such notions, hardly calculated to instill a curiosity among masters about black culture, black thought, or black behavior patterns, help explain why Quitman felt little need to ponder the implications of his slaves' misbehavior. Does one really analyze the simplistic misdeeds of children? These misconceptions allowed the Quitmans to operate from an assumption that their blacks felt it a privilege to be a Quitman slave. Family members found confirmation of their preconceptions when they gave attention to the black personality. Thus they observed their servants as sad and tearful when they departed Monmouth on trips, and found the same servants exultant when they returned home. The Quitmans sought no complexity of emotion behind their domestics' response to them. Quitman seems to have viewed his field hands through a similarly restricted lens. When some of his family visited Live Oaks for the Christmas holidays in 1856, he suggested that the "poor negroes" there would have "a new life opened to them by seeing among them my whole family."[39]

With such a myopic perception of the black personality, the Quitmans could not even address intellectually *blatant* instances of black resistance. The Quitmans could attribute slave misbehavior to anything other than anger toward their bondage. An aura of illusion suffuses their response to acts of rebellion. Quitman found it surprising that his servant John could prove so "ungrateful" as to run away from a rooming house while the family was in Boston on the way to a Newport vacation. Eliza and their son Henry hypothesized that John must have been drugged and kidnapped unwillingly; they expected him to return if the opportunity ever arose. "He has allway[s] been as kind, attentive & faithful as any one could be towards his master's family. . . . I myself have heard him say, that if it were in the power of these abolitionists to give him a *thousand freedoms he would not desert us & his wife at home*," Henry reflected. When the servant Sandy spilled the family carriage, the Quitmans simply assumed that he had been intoxicated, not that he had done it intentionally. Difficulties with field hands could be attributed to poor management by overseers. The Quitmans never considered that slavery itself was the problem.[40]

Economically, psychologically, and socially predisposed to believe in slavery, the Quitmans found reinforcement for their convictions in demonstrations of loyalty by house servants. The case of Isaac illustrates this tendency. Isaac, apparently, did not adjust well to being a Quitman servant; Eliza requested his sale for laziness and for being unavailable when needed in 1850. But in 1855, after accompanying Quitman to Washington, D.C., Isaac complained about the cold weather there. Quitman provided him a pass to return to Monmouth, and Isaac, traveling alone, made it home as promised. Since Isaac could have used the occasion to escape, Quitman's family was impressed by his fealty. Louisa wrote that Isaac had been done "much injustice" and that he was "a very kind hearted, well intentioned fellow."[41]

Servants such as Harry Nichols, who gave unflagging service to the Quitmans over extended periods of time, also buffered Quitman from the implications of resistance by other slaves. Harry's role helped confirm Quitman's conviction that his labor system functioned well. Quitman never hesitated to trust Harry with a variety of tasks, which ranged from caring for tomato plants to escorting the children's horseback rides and going to town on errands to procure items such as plank for fences or medicine. In 1850, he seems to have carried a letter from Eliza at Monmouth to Quitman in Jackson.[42] Harry, moreover, had a special bond with his master; they had shared experiences, such as the Texas escapade, which even Quitman's white family knew little about.

Harry's significance far transcended his reliability. His most important function may have been to confirm the Quitmans in their stereotype of thankful, happy slaves. Family correspondence mentions Harry's smiling visage so frequently that one cannot escape the conclusion that he appeared— whatever his private feelings may have been—happy. Harry seems to have known how to say what the Quitmans liked to hear. Daughter Rosalie recorded, "Papa left us about a week ago for the sea shore two or three days before he left He & Harry were bringing to light some past events 'No one knows all we have been through Harry do they?' Said Papa Harry fairly splitting with a smile replied with his usual 'That's a fact sir.'" Because Harry seemed so unthreatening, the Quitmans dealt with him in a very relaxed manner. Thus Quitman had Harry's daguerreotype taken when they were in Mexico in 1847, and sent the picture back home so that the kitchen help could have a "laugh." Louisa then sent word to Harry through her father, kidding Harry about the weight he had put on. Such casual banter must have alleviated somewhat the tension intrinsic to the master-slave relationship. When Louisa told Quitman to tell Harry "we all miss him very much," she was subconsciously attesting to Harry's role in substantiating the family's convictions about the benevolence of its hegemony.[43]

There were, therefore, reasons why Quitman could believe in the efficacy of the slave system despite good evidence that his own slaves resented their bondage. To overcome the restricted vision which societal pressures and racial beliefs created, Quitman would have had to have been an extraordinarily sensitive individual. But his life, economic welfare, and mental peace depended on his repressing any doubts which arose. There is little evidence, moreover, that Quitman harbored even subconscious reservations about slavery. Perhaps he was gone too much. Rarely around Monmouth, he was even more a stranger to his cotton and sugar plantations. Public affairs and entrepreneurial matters constantly drew him away from his holdings and liberated him from the necessity of dealing with slave disciplinary matters on a day-to-day basis. Henry Turner, Albert Quitman, overseers, and, often, Eliza bore the brunt of the regular rhythm of black resistance.

Once, Quitman absented himself from home and plantation for a whole year and a half. This occurred in 1846 and 1847, when war exploded between the United States and Mexico, bringing to Quitman the opportunity for martial glory and national fame which he had so long coveted. John Quitman, part-time planter, quickly became John Quitman, full-time soldier.

12

We Came for Action

JOHN QUITMAN possessed a more acute instinct for war than for politics. He demonstrated this vividly in 1845–1846, when he manipulated his own emergence as a military figure of national prominence at the very time that his campaign for a U.S. Senate seat sputtered to its disappointing conclusion. Sensing that American annexation of Texas had to eventuate in conflict with Mexico, he pressured Governor Brown to "remember" him when the fighting started, and assured the governor that his militia division could fill any federal requisition on the state for troops. Being Mississippi's "oldest major general," Quitman asserted, he had earned the right to muster and command such requisitioned troops.

Though Brown responded that he had learned from Secretary of War William Marcy that the federal government viewed war as unlikely, Quitman continued to believe otherwise. Encouraged by Brown's promise that his wishes would be respected if war did occur, Quitman read the report of John C. Frémont of the U.S. Army's Corps of Topographical Engineers about his recent experiences leading a party of men on an exploration of the Far West. Frémont's account must have provided marvelous intellectual tonic for Quitman's martial ardor—not to mention his longstanding conviction that American expansion should come at Mexican expense—because the expedition had taken a howitzer and violated Mexican territory in California and New Mexico.[1]

Events on the Mexican border made Quitman a prophet. President Polk had sent Brevet General Zachary Taylor and an "Army of Occupation" into disputed territory between the Nueces River and the Rio Grande, provoking a Mexican attack in April, 1846, on American dragoons. When Congress voted for war on May 11–13, the stage was set for Quitman's next move.

Despite the fact that his twelve-year-old daughter Sarah—who had fallen critically ill—died less than a week after Congress' declaration of war,

Quitman, just two days after her death, wrote directly to the president telling Polk that he should count on Mississippi's raising a volunteer brigade and that given his own "long and successful service" in the state militia he would be a good choice to command it as brigadier general. The following day, Quitman solicited Mississippi's congressional delegation to lobby in his behalf on the basis of his "more than twenty years" experience as an active militia officer. Mississippians, he reported, wanted to participate. They needed an opportunity to show that they accepted responsibility for the an-nexation of Texas, as well as to win honor for their state and "laurels" for themselves. Quitman's letter revealed that he shared the current fervor for *manifest destiny*—a term coined by New York journalist John L. O'Sullivan connoting America's God-given mission to spread its sovereignty over the continent. Like President Polk, Quitman saw the war as a means of acquir-ing California, still part of Mexico, invoking America's ability to carry its "eagle" to the Pacific Ocean. But his letter also betrayed a trace of the old nullification spirit. Quitman suggested that if Mississippians demonstrated their might in fighting, their antislavery antagonists might back off in the future. "The Northern States question our strength in war. Then let this be the test. . . . We are near the theatre of war. We are inured to the sum-mer sun." [2]

When Quitman told Eliza of his pursuit of a commission, it was Texas all over again. She knew her husband well enough to suspect that he would put his life in danger if an opportunity for heroism beckoned, and she told him that he had no right to leave her again. Still Quitman forged ahead. Within days of his own letter to the president, friends and associates were swamp-ing Polk with recommendations on his behalf. Henry Foote, who certainly owed Quitman a favor, lobbied for Quitman, a "chivalrous & noble re-spected American," as the preference of Mississippians for commander of state volunteer troops. John Nevitt and J. M. Thacher told Polk how Quitman had supported Texas and the 1844 Democratic ticket, and cited Quitman's militia record. Governor Brown came through on his earlier promise and pressed Polk on appointing Quitman brigadier general, and the entire Mississippi congressional delegation united with several congressmen from Louisiana, Texas, and Florida in urging Quitman's claims to a general-ship on the basis of his "position in society" and past "military services." Appended to the latter petition was a statement by Quitman's old friend, and now congressman, David Kaufman, recalling how Quitman in 1836 had gal-lantly rushed to Texas to prevent the "savages" from harming women and children. Finally, on June 29, the Mississippi delegation went in person to the president. [3]

Meanwhile, Quitman arrived on the scene. He and Eliza had been planning a summer trip north even before the war began; his hopes for an army commission led him to include Washington in his schedule. Leaving Monmouth to the family tutor and the servants, Quitman and his family departed Natchez in late May, and spent most of June in the national capital.[4]

Ultimately events played into Quitman's hands. Polk's ambitious military objectives required far more troops than the U.S. Army could provide. Secretary Marcy, therefore, called on the western and southern states near the front to provide 17,133 volunteers—divided into twenty-two regiments—for twelve months' service. Polk had to find the general officers to command these new troops in the militia services of the states called upon: the army had only three officers above the rank of colonel, and Congress refused to authorize more than one new major general and two new brigadier generals through promotion within the regular officer corps. When Congress in late May abolished a standing restriction upon the use of militia generals in the federal service for more than three months, the way was paved for Quitman's appointment. Polk, in fact, almost had to select Quitman as one of his new brigadiers. Mississippi was in a war fever, and volunteer units all over the state were mobilizing and drilling; yet Marcy had only requisitioned a single regiment. Mississippians were outraged over what they perceived as a slight. Polk could mollify public opinion there by appointing Mississippi's favored candidate for high command.[5]

Quitman had moved on to Baltimore when word came of the brigadiership. He took Eliza and the children to Philadelphia, completed financial arrangements so that they could pass the summer comfortably at the Long Beach and Saratoga resorts in New York, and returned, alone, to Washington. On the morning of July 7 he called on Adjutant General Roger Jones to take his oath and receive his commission. He was assigned to report to Zachary Taylor's force on the border. In the afternoon, Quitman called on the president. He found Polk—who appeared rather "haggard and careworn"—polite but somewhat distant, and learned to his disappointment that the relative ranking of the six volunteer brigadier generals had already been determined by lot and that he had drawn the second-lowest ranking. Disturbed, Quitman tried to stake a claim to as much seniority and authority as he could, suggesting to Jones that since his written acceptance of commission had been received in the War Department on July 3, his name should be enrolled as of that date rather than the date on which he took his oath.[6]

Then it was time to be off, so that he could tie up his affairs at home before reporting to General Taylor. Quitman caught the cars for Cumberland, Maryland, on July 9, and from that point proceeded to Pittsburgh. Arriving there when the temperature was 102°, Quitman found himself ruminating about his first visit to the city and how much had changed in the interim in his pursuit of wealth and fame. Once he had traveled through Pittsburgh with all his worldly goods packed in a single trunk. "Today," he mused, "I can draw on my merchants in New Orleans, New York, and Liverpool, and the attentive landlord at the noble hotel where I put up secures for me a state-room in a splendid steamer."

From Pittsburgh, Quitman took a steamer to Louisville, where he hired a free black named Albert to accompany him to the war as a servant. Then Quitman proceeded downriver, paying a surprise visit en route to his brother-in-law George Turner and his wife Annie. Somewhat startled by Quitman's sudden appearance in the middle of their afternoon nap, the Turners saw before them a truly transformed relation. Sparkling in military "coat, buttons & . . . gallant trim," Quitman impressed Annie as much "younger & handsomer" in military dress than in civilian apparel.

Finding the servants at Monmouth well and obedient, Quitman kept his stay brief, departing on July 30 aboard the *Cora* for New Orleans and, then, the seat of war. He took two horses along; one of them, Messenger, had been a gift from Joseph Dunbar. At Quitman's side, in addition to Albert, was his old campaign servant and companion, Harry Nichols.[7]

By the night of July 31, Quitman was ensconced with several other generals at the St. Charles Hotel in New Orleans, waiting for conveyance to Zachary Taylor's army. Taylor, now a major general, had gained instant fame in May by winning a couple of battles north of the Rio Grande and then had crossed the river. During July, Taylor had been shuttling troops upriver to the Mexican town of Camargo, which seemed to offer a suitable staging point for a campaign against Monterrey. The capital of Nuevo León was a vital strategic target because of its proximity to the Rinconada Pass, the main route through the Eastern Sierra Madre to Saltillo, the capital of Coahuila, and points farther south. The Polk administration's hastily improvised war plans envisioned the conquering of Mexico's northern reaches as a means of inducing Mexican officials to cede desired territory. By the time Quitman arrived in New Orleans, Colonel Stephen Kearny was already moving on Santa Fe, New Mexico. Soon, American armies would penetrate Chihuahua and California. Should Taylor take Monterrey, Polk's strategy would be well on its way to fruition.[8]

While awaiting transportation, Quitman busied himself in the Crescent City. Anticipating the need of a cook, he purchased a new slave, named Caesar. Perhaps feeling a pang of remorse over leaving his family, he had several daguerreotypes taken and arranged to have them distributed among his family, his sisters, and the McMurrans. McMurran, in fact, was vacationing at nearby Pass Christian; hearing that Quitman was in New Orleans, he came over with his son John, Jr., to spend a day. It should have been a

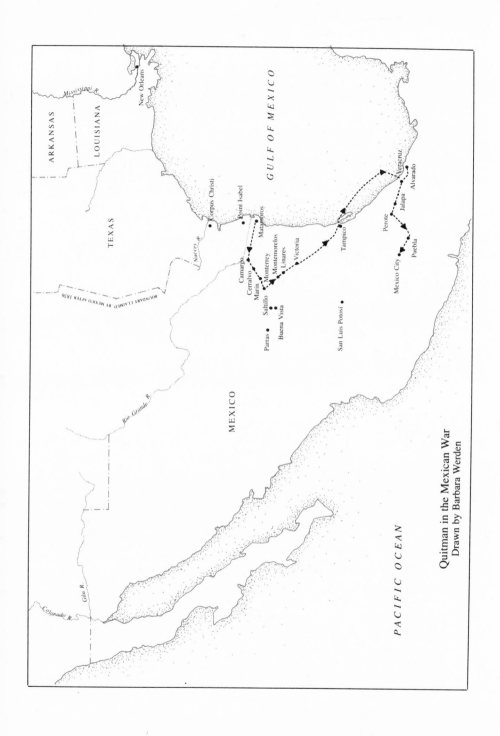

Quitman in the Mexican War
Drawn by Barbara Werden

pleasant interval, but Quitman was impatient to reach the army. Was the "imperturbably civil" army quartermaster in the city, Lieutenant Colonel Thomas Hunt, deliberately holding him back because of his volunteer status? Quitman thought so. Prejudice upon the part of regular officers and enlisted men against the volunteer troops ran rampant. After dull years in a stagnant peacetime army, the regulars looked forward to winning glory and promotions in war and resented having to share the limelight with upstart volunteers. Many regulars believed that volunteer enlisted men—being unused to army discipline—would attack Mexican civilians, inciting unnecessary reprisals, and that they would never hold up under the duress of campaigning. General Winfield Scott, commanding general of the whole army, elaborated:

> A regiment of regulars, in 15 minutes from the evening halt, will have tents pitched & trenched around, besides straw leaves or bushes for dry sleeping;—arms & ammunition well secured & in order for any night attack; fires made; kettles boiling. . . . This is the result of discipline, order, methods. . . . Volunteers neglect all these points;— eat their *salt* meat raw (if they have saved any at all) or, worse than raw, *fried*—death to any Christian man the fifth day;—lose or waste their clothing; wet or on wet ground . . . leave arms & ammunition exposed to rain, mud & dews;—hence both generally useless & soon lost. . . . In a short time the ranks are thinned, the baggage wagons & hospitals filled with the sick, & acres of ground with the graves of the dead!

Prejudice extended to volunteer commanders, who were perceived as political hacks who procured their commissions through the Democratic patronage mill and had no understanding of tactics or strategy.[9]

Since Hunt only detained Quitman in New Orleans a few days, Quitman's suspicions at this point were probably overdrawn. That Quitman detected the prejudice at such an early stage, however, signified that he, like most other volunteers, had no intention of taking a back seat to the more experienced regulars in the war effort.

On August 4, Quitman boarded the steamer *New York*. Four days later the vessel deposited him at Brazos Santiago, a four-mile barrier sandspit in the Gulf across a bay from Point Isabel, General Taylor's supply port. Noting, as he disembarked, that the bay was crowded with American vessels, Quitman began to comprehend the magnitude of national war.

At twilight, leaving Harry to bring his baggage by ship, Quitman rode down the beach to the encampment of Mississippi's lone regiment on a ridge of sandhills near the mouth of the Rio Grande. Here he was warmly received by the regiment's elected colonel and his Palmyra neighbor, Jefferson Davis. Quitman spent that night and the day following with Davis and his troops, noticing with sorrow how many of the men suffered from acute diarrhea—in fact, one soldier died during his stay in camp.

After being rejoined by Harry, Quitman crossed the Rio Grande to Matamoros, which Taylor had occupied in May. The sight here stirred Quitman's nationalism, which his sectional consciousness still had not entirely displaced. "This town," he observed, "is filled with soldiers, and all along the river from the mouth up to that place the shores are covered with the American tents. Our glorious stripes and stars float over every town on the Rio Grande for 500 miles from its mouth." Then, Quitman and his retinue of servants boarded a river steamer for Camargo, where they arrived on August 17. Quitman found General Taylor's tents just above the town, which had been badly damaged in recent storms. Taylor seemed glad to see Quitman, and invited him to dine as well as to attend a troop review. Quitman immediately took to the sixty-two-year-old, gray-haired, stocky commander, describing Taylor, who was known for his informality and lack of pretentiousness, as remarkably "farmer-like" and friendly. Quitman pitched his own shelter some fifty yards from the general. "I wish you could take a peep into my tent—dirt floor—two mess chests . . . 3 camp stools without backs, and what is quite a luxury a camp cot with two blankets on it," he wrote his children. For the time being, Quitman was assigned command of a brigade consisting of Mississippi, Alabama, and Georgia regiments and a battalion from Maryland and the District of Columbia.[10]

Quitman would have liked to have seen action immediately, as he had been preparing himself psychologically to fight the Mexicans. He had studied the country's populace on the trip upriver and in Camargo, and concluded that they were an inferior lot deserving to be conquered. Mexicans had slovenly habits, he felt, and they failed to adequately cultivate the rich lands they possessed. They looked and acted, to Quitman, very much like a part of his own country's population which he had written off many years ago: "With a tropical climate and excellent soil, they have no fruits & scarcely any vegetables except those which grow wild. The whole population bathes every evening—but still they are very filthy & resemble much our Indians."[11]

However, Quitman learned, to his disappointment, that he would have to endure another delay before any hope of meeting the Mexicans in battle. On the nineteenth, he passively witnessed General William Worth lead Taylor's Second Division out of Camargo as the vanguard of the long-awaited thrust into Mexico's interior. Taylor confided to Quitman that he would send Brigadier General David E. Twiggs's First Division next, followed by a force of four thousand volunteers. Since Taylor did not clarify which troops would be left garrisoning Camargo, Quitman feared that the volunteers might be so assigned. He hoped Taylor would know better than to provoke the volunteer "discontent" which would follow such a decision. "We came for action," Quitman proclaimed, "and must have it." [12]

While waiting, Quitman learned some of the tribulations which went along with rank. He had to make decisions about discharges, police, and camp sanitation, and he got his first dose of the mounds of paper work attached to high command. In fact, military returns proved such a headache that he chose, despite his own predilection for volunteers, a lieutenant in the regular army—William A. Nichols—as his aide. Nichols knew the ropes. Supply problems proved even more worrisome, as Quitman encountered incompetence in both the quartermaster and medical departments. Some of his soldiers were succumbing to disease, as Camargo crawled with bugs and vermin and had stagnant air and temperatures in the hundreds. And his men were being armed with "refuse muskets" and other inadequate paraphernalia. "There are here," he complained to Felix Huston, "no horse-shoes or nails, no iron to make them; and, though we have 6000 men, there are no medicines." Compared to his little campaign through eastern Texas a decade before, the command problems were awesome.

Finally, Taylor made good his promise to get the volunteers into action. A "Field Division" of volunteers, consisting of one regiment each from Kentucky, Ohio, Tennessee, and Mississippi, was put under Major General William Butler to participate in the Monterrey campaign. Quitman was thrilled to learn that he would command Butler's Second Volunteer Brigade, made up of the Tennessee and Mississippi regiments; thousands of bitterly disappointed volunteers were to be left behind at Camargo under volunteer Major General Robert Patterson of Pennsylvania. Quitman studied Spanish, and shared his exuberance with Claiborne. "I know what my friends expect of me," he wrote, "and if opportunities offer, they shall not be disappointed. A major general's baton, fairly won on the field of battle, or a Mexican grave!" [13]

Quitman's immediate orders were to take his brigade to the town of Cerralvo, roughly halfway between Camargo and Monterrey, where Taylor's advance troops had already established a supply depot. Uncertain whether Mexican troops would contest Monterrey, Taylor concentrated on Cerralvo preparatory to deciding on a final plan of campaign. Quitman scheduled his leaving Camargo at 5:00 A.M. on September 7, but this proved impossible because there were not enough pack mules to carry his food, hospital stores, and other camp equipment. Quitman waited for several hours and only departed when quartermaster agent Henry L. Kinney promised to bring up supplies later that day. Kinney could not do that early enough to suit

Quitman. Stalled eight miles from town on September 8, Quitman sent back an angry protest. Finally he was able to push on, and reached Cerralvo on the thirteenth after a difficult march which left many of his men sick.[14]

Within sight of the Sierra Madre, Cerralvo offered welcome relief from the grime and heat of Camargo. Bracing air, a cold mountain stream, tall shade trees, and tidy stone houses made the town a paradise to the exhausted volunteers. But there was little time to enjoy its comforts, as Twiggs's First Division had already set out along the road to Monterrey by the time the volunteers arrived. Bearing two days' rations in their haversacks, the volunteer division—minus a detachment left to continue the occupation—departed on the fifteenth. Two days later, at Marín, Quitman and his men caught up with Taylor's regulars.[15]

The next morning, Taylor's united forces departed Marín in closed columns on the final leg of the march to Monterrey. Fields of sugarcane, corn in silk, and melons, groves of pecan, oak, mesquite, ebony, and brazilwood, all made an indelible impression upon the soldiers as they passed. The column stretched out for three miles, presenting a majestic sight to observers. Few men straggled, for many of the soldiers sensed that battle was imminent: enemy pickets had been observed on the march to Marín, and there had even been some skirmishing. A reporter traveling with the column noted that knapsacks and arms were being looked after with much more care than earlier in the campaign.

It was at about nine in the morning on the nineteenth that Taylor and his advance guard arrived on the plain before Monterrey. Approaching the Citadel, part of a formidable complex of defensive bastions ringing the city, they attracted a burst of enemy artillery fire. Rather than attempt an immediate assault, Taylor established a sheltered encampment in a watered grove of oak and pecan trees about three miles northeast of the city (called the Santo Domingo wood or the "Walnut Springs"), sent off some of his engineer officers on a reconnaissance of the Mexican positions, and contemplated his next move.[16]

While Taylor mapped strategy Quitman composed a proclamation to inspire his brigade for the fight ahead. He urged his troops to remember that they were part of a unit which needed to act in a coordinated fashion. Although the American way of life which structured their peacetime existence emphasized individuality, they should now remember to preserve their ranks, "confide" in their officers, and "never act alone." If they followed his instructions, he promised, they could impress those "veteran" regular officers who were skeptical about the efficacy of a volunteer service. "[S]how to them—to your country & to the world, that American volunteers are not only brave, but can be cool—steady & well-disciplined." Quitman knew that his own military reputation would be vindicated or tarnished by how well his men functioned over the next few days.[17]

Had Quitman consciously sought the setting best calculated to test his own courage and the mettle of his volunteers, he scarcely could have improved upon Monterrey. Situated on the north bank of the Santa Catarina River, a natural defensive advantage, the city was flanked on its southern and western sides by mountains. This terrain rendered military maneuver difficult, and, making matters worse, forts and other defensive works stood on top of the steep hills which overlooked the only practicable way through the mountains, the road from Saltillo which ran east from the pass into the city. Fewer natural hazards blocked access to Monterrey from the north and east. The terrain, a mix of chaparral and fields of cane and corn, sloped gently down toward the city and river. However, formidable defensive works menaced any military force attacking from those directions. Standing about a quarter of a mile from the city near the juncture of the roads from Marín and Monclova, the Citadel (called the "Black Fort" by unappreciative American soldiers)—an uncompleted cathedral now walled and manned by four hundred veterans—could train its cannon on attackers approaching from the north. South of the Citadel was a three-gun earthwork called La Tenería, so named because it stood just thirty steps or so from a tannery. The stone tannery had a flat roof where sharpshooters could fire from behind sandbags at advancing troops. Just several hundred yards away, across a small stream which fed into the Santa Catarina, was yet another fortification known as Fort Diablo.

Breaching such imposing outer defenses, however, posed only part of the mission. Once beyond them, the invaders would face the bleak prospect of subjugating a city where limestone houses had iron- and wooden-grated windows and flat roofs with parapets—dwellings virtually tailormade for directing a raking fire against exposed troops advancing through the streets. Mexican commander General Pedro de Ampudia, with over seven thousand troops to distribute among his multiple defense works, could be expected to make any attack on Monterrey a costly endeavor.[18]

Recognizing that the defensive obstacles would be even more formidable if Ampudia received reinforcements, General Taylor, after studying the reconnaissance reports, decided to take the Saltillo road preparatory to assaulting the city. To this end, he sent General Worth and some two thousand troops on September 20 off on a wide flanking movement to the west. Once Worth's troops captured the road and adjacent works, Taylor could attack the city from two directions at once. By nightfall, Worth had pulled to within three miles of the road. Meanwhile, Taylor used the balance of his army— including Quitman's brigade—to threaten Monterrey on the north and east so that Ampudia could not capitalize on his interior lines and rush reinforcements to the western heights. Quitman's brigade saw no action that day, though Taylor ordered some feints made toward the city. But on September 21, Quitman and his men were in the thick of the fighting.

Early that morning, drums called Butler's volunteer division to arms and regimental formation. While Worth was breaking through to the Saltillo road and then attacking the redoubt on Federacíon Hill, Taylor marched his remaining regulars and the volunteers to what Quitman called "somewhat depressed" ground (other soldiers termed it a "ravine" or "hollow") about a mile from the city where an American battery had already been established. In their protected position, with Mexican round shot ricocheting over their ranks, Quitman's brigade waited in reserve while some of General Twiggs's regulars and the Baltimore volunteer battalion attacked the city's eastern and northeast defenses.

Quitman's patience must have been sorely pressed by this one last wait for battle. But by mid-morning, General Taylor felt compelled to commit reserves. Although some of his regulars under Captain Electus Backus had managed to take the tannery near La Tenería, intense Mexican fire from the Citadel, La Tenería, roofs in the city, and other defensive works had proved too much for the American columns. Most of the attacking units either found themselves pinned down in the city's streets or fled. So Taylor sent in Quitman's brigade at about nine in the morning. Quitman marched his troops obliquely toward the fighting around La Tenería, the Tennesseans on the left, the Mississippi Rifles to their right, all the while under fire from the Citadel. Marching double-time, the men ascended a slight elevation and came in full view of La Tenería, about a half mile off. Now La Tenería's artillery opened up on them. Casualties mounted. One Mexican round hit seven Tennesseans at once, killing four. But on they pressed. Quitman, the only general in the vicinity, rode right up with his men and, just as Eliza had anticipated, made no effort to shield himself from enemy fire during the hour or more of their advance. Rather he went up and down the column, urging the men on and barking out orders. One horse was shot out from under him, he took a shell fragment in the thigh, but he kept on going.

The volunteers held their fire until within effective shoulder-arms range of La Tenería, about two to three hundred yards out. Then they re-formed their lines and commenced a slow march upon the fort—the Mississippians toward an open embrasure on the fort's northwest side, the Tennessee regiment against La Tenería's north side—shooting determinedly as they advanced and drawing support from the regulars under Backus who had a direct line of fire into La Tenería from the building they had taken.

What happened next defies precise reconstruction. There was so much noise and confusion that battle participants gave muddled and contradictory accounts, and subsequent efforts to sort things out engendered controversy that lasted literally for years. We know that the volunteers' firing took its toll on La Tenería's defenders; that the Mexican rate of return fire seemed to dwindle as parts of the brigade approached the fort's walls (Backus later claimed that his regulars' musketry had already defeated the Mexicans by the time the volunteers neared the fort); that both the Mississippians and Tennesseans were anxious for the glory of taking La Tenería and seized the relative lull as an advantageous time to charge; and that the Mexicans were put to rout and were soon observed fleeing from La Tenería's rear sally port. But who ordered this most successful charge? Tennessee regimental colonel William Campbell, separated from Quitman, ordered the Tennessee thrust. However, Mississippi regimental commander Jefferson Davis, his second-in-command Lieutenant Colonel Alexander K. McClung, and Quitman himself all claimed credit for the charge of the Rifles. Probably orders were issued virtually simultaneously; at least one postbattle account indicated as much. But such logic had little influence on the later debate. Heated controversy also surfaced between Quitman's Tennesseans and Mississippians over which state's troops started to charge first, and which made the initial entry into the fort.[19]

Whether Quitman maintained overall direction of his brigade as he implied in his postbattle report, he certainly failed to maintain his grip in the moments following La Tenería's fall. Everything happened too fast. The fort's defenders scattered, about twenty of them seeking refuge at the tannery while the balance fled to Fort Diablo. Smelling victory, Davis, McClung, and some of the Rifles set off after those fleeing to the tannery. Though McClung fell with a serious wound, the Mississippians managed to force their way into the stone building before its gate could be closed on them. The Mexicans immediately surrendered. Then Davis crossed the creek with some of his men and put Diablo under fire. Discovering that he lacked the manpower to try another charge, Davis returned to the creek to try to bring up more of his regiment.

Quitman said little in his official report about the period after La Tenería's fall, and other accounts of the fighting on September 21 do little to illuminate his role. We do know that he joined some other officers at La Tenería in restraining overanxious brigade members from firing on the retreating Mexicans, for fear that they might hit units of the brigade in pursuit. Otherwise, obeying a directive from Taylor, who was concerned about the heavy casualties in the eastern part of the city, Quitman made his most noticeable appearance when he rode into the Diablo sector and personally ordered the Rifles to withdraw. Davis, then in the process of rallying his men for an at-

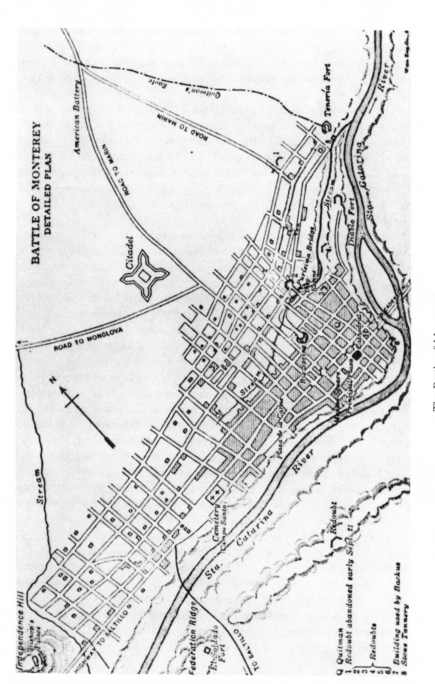

The Battle of Monterrey
Adaptation of map from Justin H. Smith, *The War with Mexico*. Reprinted by permission of the United Board for Homeland Ministries.

tack, disliked the command; he later contended that Diablo could have been taken with "very little loss." However, he did withdraw. Those Tennesseans and Mississippians still at La Tenería and the tannery also returned to camp (following their relief by a regiment of regulars) where they passed a cold, rainy night.

The volunteers had persevered through a day of gruesome battle; with 9 Mississippians and 27 Tennesseans killed, and an aggregate of 131 wounded, Quitman's brigade had taken the most casualties in Zachary Taylor's whole army. One of the Texas Rangers concluded that the "Tenn—and Mi. Boys" had "distinguished themselves" during one of the most "noble charges ever know[n] in the histories [*sic*] of Battles." Hyperbole aside, Quitman's troops had certainly endured their baptism in blood and proved that volunteers could fight.[20]

Taylor could not afford to give the volunteers much time for recuperation. Around nine the next morning, he sent them back to La Tenería to relieve the regulars. Again passing within range of the Citadel, the volunteers took further casualties before reaching their objective. Although engaged in no combat that day, the men nonetheless were subject to constant rounds of enemy grape, round shot, and shell until nine at night. Quitman considered moving upon the nearby Mexican works, but ultimately ruled out an offensive after his reconnaissance noted some 1,500 Mexican infantry, almost three times the size of his command, guarding the enemy positions.[21]

Starting around midnight, Quitman and his men heard enemy troop movements, but could not tell what the Mexicans were up to. Actually, Ampudia had decided to concentrate his troops in Monterrey proper behind its barricades, and had ordered withdrawals from all the outer works save the Citadel, something that became apparent to the Americans only with daylight. Once apprised of what had transpired, Quitman detached troops to occupy Diablo and sent word of his improved position to Taylor. The general responded with permission for the volunteers to make a guarded entry into the city. Following Taylor's instructions, Quitman sent a company of Rifles forward to test the enemy reaction. At first, all went well. Mexican soldiers fled from their outer breastworks at the American approach. However, enemy sharpshooters assumed a tactically advantageous position atop a hospital building, threatening the American advance. Quitman committed more troops. Rounds of enemy fire burst upon his ranks. What commenced as a cautious advance erupted in all-out battle. By ten o'clock Quitman had to call forward the troops he had left at Diablo. Then General Taylor arrived in the battle zone and summoned a detachment of Texas Rangers as well as the Third Infantry Regiment and an artillery battery. But with the Mexicans pouring heavy fire onto the American troops from the city's flat roofs, progress was difficult. Quitman's men had to take the houses one by one, to provide sufficient cover for the advance through the streets. The men would force their way into the courtyards and gardens, through homes, and up to the roofs. Quitman followed the advance troops, instructing artillery officers how to maneuver their weapons through the brisk enemy fire.

Less than a mile to the west, General Worth's command also began advancing. Worth had taken all remaining fortifications to the west of the city on the day before. But Taylor, inexplicably, had sent no orders as to what should be done next. Hearing the roar of battle, Worth now began moving into the city proper toward the plaza, which put the Mexican defenders in the middle of a pincers. By three in the afternoon, Quitman's troops had fought to within less than two squares of the Grand Plaza of the city. However, the Mexicans had erected another group of street barricades, and they met the American rush with withering fire from behind these obstructions. Unable to storm this last obstacle, Quitman's men seized pack saddles and baggage found in the houses and began putting up their own defensive wall.

Thus matters stood when Taylor made an unfortunate tactical misjudgment. Because his artillery seemed unable to penetrate the barricades, and since the troops were hungry and running low on ammunition, Taylor decided to withdraw, regroup, and coordinate plans with Worth rather than fight things to a conclusion and risk a nighttime counterattack. Quitman's brigade received orders to return all the way to camp, though other units occupied already-captured enemy works. Had Taylor been in better contact with Worth, he probably would have maintained the pressure and the plaza might have fallen; but he had no way of knowing how successful Worth had been. Taylor's withdrawal allowed Ampudia to shuttle forces to his western side and keep Worth at bay. Worth progressed to within a block of the plaza, but had to call a halt for the night.

The fighting on September 23, nevertheless, ended the struggle. Worth's artillery, by evening, was dropping shells into the Mexican positions. Ampudia could not risk the battle going on much longer, partly because he had his ammunition stored in a cathedral on the plaza. One well-placed American artillery round would have spelled disaster. That night, Ampudia requested negotiations. The next day Taylor appointed three officers to meet with the Mexicans, and these commissioners arranged an armistice by which Ampudia's army would evacuate Monterrey and retire southward below a line embracing the Rinconada Pass and the towns of Linares and Parras. For their part, Taylor's negotiators agreed that the Mexicans could keep their personal arms and 1 six-gun field battery, and that Taylor would not cross the armistice line for eight weeks or until one of the governments disavowed the agreement. The Mexican army evacuated Monterrey over September 26–28.[22]

The armistice effectively sentenced Quitman to occupation duty and camp life for the indefinite future, and he did not like it. Since Taylor had not included him in the negotiations or consulted him about the merits of an armistice, Quitman felt no particular loyalty to its generous terms, which had been extended partly to facilitate a diplomatic resolution of the whole war. Although Quitman wrote his son that he hoped that the agreement would produce a peace "with honor" for the United States, he was skeptical and may have wished the fighting to resume. The battle had not fully sated his martial ardor. Bloodshed, rather than unnerve him, had merely confirmed the grandeur of combat. He boasted in letters home about the honor his troops had won, the shell fragment he had taken, how three horses in all had been shot from under him (only Messenger had survived unscathed), how an enemy ball had passed through his hat, and how his brigade had attracted some 3,000 enemy cannon shots during its advance (one had cut down seven men positioned very close to him). He even explained how Harry, who had stayed to the rear of the brigade, had been forced to dodge cannonballs. Other officers such as Jefferson Davis sought furloughs after the battle and returned to the United States; he would not do so unless it became clear that the war was over.

Ultimately Quitman's uneasiness about the armistice ripened into vehement dissent. Were he mapping strategy, he wrote eldest daughter Louisa, he would already have troops marching on Mexico City. Chain-of-command formalities did not keep Quitman from going public with his qualms. On the same day (November 10) he sent off his letter to Louisa, Eliza was writing him that Felix Huston was saying that everyone knew Quitman "disapproved of the Capitulation that you had the City without it," and that such reports were creeping into the press. Eliza apparently felt that Huston was indiscreet—she called him a "blustering fool"—but Quitman showed that the revelations were no accident. On November 12 he protested to Treasury Secretary Walker that Taylor's terms had converted "a brilliant and decisive victory into a drawn battle." Although some high-ranking officers favored the conservative strategy of simply holding areas already conquered until Mexico sued for peace, he told Walker, he knew that the way to beat Mexico was to deal it "hard blows." Without a new offensive, the army would become a sitting duck for Mexican attacks.[23]

The more time passed, the greater became Quitman's stake in a resumption of the fighting, because he learned that reports were circulating in the States that he had not demonstrated sufficient personal courage at Monterrey. Quitman was appalled by such fictions—which he attributed to the jealousy of regulars toward volunteers—as they affronted his honor and threatened his ambition for a major generalship. But he could hardly trumpet his own cause in letters to the press as other officers were doing, because he did not believe that the way of a gentleman. To quell the rumors permanently, he would have to demonstrate his bravery even more conspicuously in battle.[24]

Meanwhile, Quitman performed the duties of an occupation commander. Nights were cold at "Camp Allen," Quitman's brigade station within the Santo Domingo wood, and, because of a shortage of blankets, the men suffered. Quitman eventually paid what he considered almost extortionate prices for extra blankets so that he could stay warm. Droves of wolves, scenting decaying corpses, penetrated camp bounds for a week after the battle, and their howling was a depressing interruption of the clear stillness of Monterrey's nights for the rest of the occupation. Food supplies were insufficient. Quitman wrote in one letter that the men subsisted on meat and green corn, and, as late as October 7, he observed that the whole diet consisted of "corn soup, beef coffee & sugar." Dysentery and chills took a heavy toll.[25]

Fortunately conditions improved with time. Quitman set up a market near the spring in his camp, and Mexican vendors began bringing bread, cakes, chickens, vegetables, fruit, and other items for sale. Quitman, of course, also benefited from servants, who rubbed his horse down, cooked, and did many of the disagreeable chores of camp life. "Harry manages to get my clothes neatly washed & put up by soldiers' wives—some few of whom have followed the army," he reported with satisfaction. Boredom became more of a nemesis than deprivation. The evenings, in particular, passed "long & tedious." "Sitting in my tent by the glare of a poor Mexican candle, I can neither read nor write and unless some officers call, I must spend them in meditation, or in watching the sentinel who walks before my quarters all night, or listening to the wolves." Quitman went into the city once a week and dined with General Butler (who had been wounded in the battle) or General Worth. On one such occasion he joined Worth in attending high mass at the cathedral. Quitman even joined a party of other officers and climbed a mountain to break the monotony. He boasted to Louisa that the peak had been considered "impracticable to a man of my age."[26]

Quitman also had to cope with the restlessness of his men. The city offered few social diversions, because many of the upper-class residents had abandoned their homes. Military manuals were often the only reading material; it took weeks for newspapers and mail to reach camp. Homesickness inevitably plagued men affected by the natural letdown after the battle. Summing up the mood in camp one day, a Mississippi captain noted that there was "no social intercourse" going on, and that everybody was "dull and gloomy." Soldiers took refuge in cheap pulque and rowdyism, and sometimes vented their frustrations by attacking the persons and property of Mexican civilians, despite General Taylor's desire that soldiers show restraint and pay for all items so that the army would not provoke guerrilla resistance or destruction of crops.

Quitman supported Taylor's policy. When some of his Mississippians observed men from General Thomas Hamer's brigade murder a "penniless Mexican" leaving the camp market, Quitman sent a lengthy report on the incident to General Taylor. Quitman, moreover, paid for goods which he personally acquired during the occupation, such as a silk shawl for Louisa, and he expected similar restraint from his men. Realizing that boredom lay at the root of the difficulty, Quitman instituted an elaborate camp routine starting October 15 to keep the men occupied. From reveille to taps, his soldiers were put through rounds of company drill, battalion drill, regimental drill, dress parade, and roll call. Infractions of routine brought penalties ranging from confinement to camp to cleanup details to being tied to trees.[27]

Helping Quitman administer Camp Allen was Mansfield Lovell, a second lieutenant in the regular artillery. Lovell became aide-de-camp on October 7 after William Nichols was promoted to the adjutancy of his regular regiment. Lovell and Quitman established a close intellectual and personal relationship. Years after the war, *two* of Lovell's brothers would marry daughters of Quitman.[28]

However much Quitman succeeded as a manager of inactive troops, though, he still pined for battle, and things began to go his way toward the end of the year. Taylor had assumed that the enemy verged on seriously considering American peace terms, not knowing that Mexico was actually mobilizing for extended war. The U.S. Navy, acting under instructions from Washington, had permitted Santa Anna—then in exile in Cuba—to pass through the blockade of Veracruz. President Polk, perhaps, should not be censured for crediting reports that Santa Anna favored accepting American terms; things might have worked out. But the result was that he had facilitated the return to power of "the one man," as a biographer puts it, "who could rally the [Mexican] nation to prosecute the war against the United States." Santa Anna proceeded to Mexico City, assumed overall command of Mexican military forces, and began assembling reinforcements for Ampudia. On October 8, Santa Anna arrived in San Luis Potosí with the first detachments of these reinforcements. If he could mobilize the area, he might be able to march on Taylor's army and crush it.[29]

Polk and his advisors responded by increasing the pressure on Mexico. On September 22, Marcy drafted instructions to Taylor to move upon both San Luis Potosí and Tampico. This contravened Taylor's Monterrey armistice, and the administration had no choice but to negate the agreement. On October 13, Marcy so informed Taylor and alerted General Robert Patterson at Matamoros to mobilize for a penetration of Tamaulipas.

With no guarantee that even these moves would bring Mexico to terms, the administration also began mapping long-range strategy. Perhaps American armies would have to penetrate the very heart of the country and, like Hernando Cortez in 1519, take Mexico City. Polk increasingly contemplated a plan current in Washington: the port of Veracruz offered the key to Mexico City; once the strongly defended harbor was taken, American armies could then march along the National Highway to the capital. Marcy's October 13 dispatch to Taylor alerted the general that this strategy was under consideration, and brought up the possibility that Taylor might have to contribute some of his own forces to its execution.[30]

Marcy's orders of October 13 arrived in camp on November 2. Taylor did not respond graciously to the repudiation of his armistice, but he complied and informed Santa Anna of its abridgment. Subsequently he resumed offensive operations in northern Mexico. On November 13 he accompanied General Worth and some one thousand men on an expedition to capture Saltillo, which had considerable strategic significance for any extended defense of Monterrey. Taylor also hoped to use Saltillo as an access to Mexican food resources. On November 16, the troops entered the city.

After the fact, Taylor learned that the administration would have preferred his staying at Monterrey! Marcy suggested in an October 22 letter that the new government in Mexico, which had recently declared for a decentralized system of administration, would be likely to win civilian support, and Taylor's move south might incite resistance in a previously apathetic populace. Rather, Taylor should hold Monterrey and prepare to shift four thousand of his troops to the Veracruz operation which would be conducted by another commander and given priority. The general, already a possibility for an 1848 presidential nomination, was unwilling to play a purely passive role and objected to giving up troops. So, despite his instructions, Taylor maintained control over Saltillo and pushed ahead with the War Department's earlier suggestions that he consider operations against Tampico. When the U.S. Navy took the port on November 14, Taylor shifted focus to Victoria, a town on the road *toward* Tampico. Taylor contended that the northern theater of war, rather than a campaign against Mexico City, should continue to be the strategic focal point. He intended to drive Mexico to peace negotiations by conquering a defensive line including Tampico, Victoria, Saltillo, and Parras.[31]

Taylor's intention to occupy Victoria liberated Quitman from the Camp Allen doldrums. Taylor decided to leave General Butler as commander in Monterrey, with responsibility for keeping open communication with the Rio Grande, and to use General David Twiggs's regular division and Quitman's brigade—now strengthened by the addition of the regiment of Georgia volunteers and the battalion from Baltimore and the District of Columbia—for the new offensive.

Before leaving for Victoria, Quitman sent a last letter to Eliza, informing her of his new destination and predicting that the Mexicans would "run" rather than contest the town. Since the barber had just clipped his hair, he enclosed several locks in the envelope for daughters Antonia and Rosalie. The hair was of the "least grey," he said, that he could find. Whether it had been the tribulations of campaigning or creeping old age, the war experience had greatly transformed his appearance. That he had grown a curly gray beard and moustache only accentuated the change.[32]

Yet if Quitman looked different, his state of mind showed remarkable consistency. His quest was still glory. He had almost found it in September; he would have to win it in the months ahead. He sensed that it could not elude him indefinitely. He had too much persistence.

13

Conquest Without Glory

O N the night of November 20, 1846, Major General Winfield Scott, general in chief of the United States Army, called on President Polk at the White House in response to a summons to discuss war strategy. An American military giant since the War of 1812, Scott had so far played a relatively inconspicuous part in the Mexican War. While Zachary Taylor had been gaining laurels for military conquest, Scott had spent many hours mapping strategy in Washington. But his time had come. Polk, the day before, had selected him to command the pending Veracruz expedition. Now consultation was necessary to resolve several problems, such as how the move might be executed without the Mexicans' learning of it prematurely, and which volunteer generals should be transferred to Scott from Taylor's command.

One of the men discussed that night as a possibility for transfer was John Quitman. Scott informed Polk that he would require four of the volunteer brigadier generals, and asked Polk for his evaluation of the eligible candidates. Though Polk professed only a "slight" acquaintance with Quitman and said a lot more about some of the other volunteer brigadiers he had appointed, he evidently said nothing to rule Quitman out. By early January, Scott had concluded that he would "embrace" Quitman in the Veracruz operation.[1]

Thus Quitman's fate was being determined in Washington as he set out for Victoria on December 14 on his last march for General Taylor. Ten days of the Victoria campaign would pass before Taylor even received Scott's November 25 letter announcing his intention to "take from you most of your gallant officers & men . . . whom you have so long & so nobly commanded." And it would be some time longer before Taylor learned exactly what Scott intended. The November 25 communication, because of strictures on secrecy, did not mention Veracruz as the specific military objective behind the realignment of forces.[2]

Quitman's Mississippians and Tennesseans were still bickering over regimental bravery in the September battle as they made their departure from Monterrey. Little enemy resistance materialized at first, and Mexican civilians continued tolerant of their Yankee conquerors. Village women would offer the soldiers corn bread and sweet bread for sale; men approached with donkeys laden with sugarcane and oranges. One alcalde provided Quitman with a local guide. As the Americans passed between two mountain ranges, young John S. Holt of the Mississippi Rifles, who had become Quitman's secretary, noted that the men could see the light from enemy campfires on the peaks during their night encampments. But there were no engagements. Progressing rapidly, Quitman's men made about fifteen miles a day.[3]

However, the tenor of the campaign transformed at Montemorelos. Taylor had joined the advance and was organizing the next phase of the Victoria operation, when on December 17 he received a call of distress from General Worth at Saltillo. Worth had learned that Santa Anna intended to capitalize on the division of the American army by marching from San Luis Potosí on Saltillo. Taylor, rather than forfeit Worth's position, decided to reinforce it. So he took Twiggs's division on a forced march, leaving Quitman's brigade, supplemented by a second Tennessee volunteer regiment and a battery of artillery, to continue to Victoria as best it could. Suddenly Quitman had his first independent command, albeit a temporary one. At Victoria he would be superseded by General Patterson, who was supposed to march from Matamoros and join him there. But should Patterson fail to make it, Quitman was to act on his own. Taylor believed he had troops sufficient to anchor the Victoria sector of the proposed defensive line, and ordered him to watch the nearby Sierra Madre and their passes for signs of enemy troop movements.[4]

Quitman left Montemorelos on December 19, after rearranging his command into a field division of two brigades and assigning volunteer captain Theodore O'Hara, a Kentuckian, to direct his supply train. For a day, the men enjoyed the same relaxed conditions to which they had become accustomed. But then word arrived of enemy forces in the immediate vicinity. Quitman tightened his two-and-a-half-mile-long baggage train and kept his men under strict discipline to avoid provoking Mexican civilians, who remained outwardly friendly. At the end of every day's march he remained in his saddle until the whole division and baggage train had safely arrived in camp, which he customarily located in thickets of chaparral—sites uncomfortable for his men but too dense for easy penetration by enemy horsemen. Mexican cavalry waited in vain for an opportunity to isolate part of

Quitman's command or strike at his baggage train. Quitman managed to approach Victoria without waging battle or losing a man, winning grudging admiration from his soldiers, who would have preferred less discipline. Proud of his feat, he boasted how his men had refrained from rape and plunder and proven themselves the best behaved in the volunteer service.

Not only did Quitman's march through the countryside pass with little drama, Quitman also found that neither the Mexican cavalry which had been observing him nor the citizens of Victoria intended contesting his occupation of the town. Arriving about three miles out on December 29, he was met by a deputation of officials bearing an offer of surrender. Quitman assured the Mexicans that his troops would respect property and Catholic customs, and marched his men to the town's central plaza, where the American flag was raised above government buildings and the alcalde handed over the city keys to Quitman. The ceremony broke up anticlimactically when some donkeys' braying drowned out the proceedings. Quitman then encamped his men about a mile west of town, so that he could intercept any Mexican forces breaking through the nearby mountain pass from Tula. The next day he assigned five companies to garrison duty around the plaza, and established his own headquarters at the one-story stone home of the governor of Tamaulipas. This choice won applause from Harry, who expressed delight that his master was again ensconced in a legitimate dwelling.[5]

Mission accomplished, Quitman awaited General Patterson. With just 2,200 men and no cavalry, Quitman could not hope to challenge, and had no orders to challenge, a reported concentration of 4,000 to 7,000 enemy at Tula. So he only sent Lieutenant George C. Meade of the Topographical Corps and some 20 men "mounted on sorry ponies" on a scouting expedition toward Las Minas on the road to Tula. Taylor had detached Meade for service with Quitman for the specific purpose of finding out how easily his defensive line could be penetrated by attack through the mountain passes around Victoria. Meade reported back that wagons and artillery would not be able to use the Tula road.[6]

Situated on a clear rivulet from the mountains, Victoria had, nonetheless, a tropical climate. Sugarcane abounded in the vicinity, and green parrots flew around the town, to the soldiers' astonishment. Quitman's troops feasted on oranges, bananas, dates, and other tropical fruits as they awaited their orders. Two vicious "northers" struck Victoria, however, while Quitman was there. The second sent temperatures plunging to near freezing. Soldiers suffered from the cold because local homes lacked fireplaces and glassed-in windows. Shivering along with his men, Quitman hovered near a pan of coals in an effort to keep warm.[7]

On January 4, 1847, the garrison suddenly more than doubled in size.

First arrived was none other than General Taylor himself, accompanying Twiggs's division. The troops had never gotten to Saltillo. Just a few miles along the Monterrey-Saltillo road, they had learned from a messenger that Generals John Wool and Butler had both reinforced Worth.[8] No longer needed, the troops countermarched to Victoria. An hour after Taylor's arrival, General Patterson's column from Matamoros marched into town. The reinforcements increased American troops at Victoria to more than five thousand.

Though supplanted in chief command, Quitman gave his superiors a gracious welcome, inviting Patterson and other officers to his headquarters for fruit and wine. Soon he ascertained the plans to transfer most of Taylor's highest-ranking volunteer officers to Scott's command, and that Veracruz was the probable destination of the pending new offensive. Quitman relished being close to naval support again, which would mean improved supply and better communication with home. Believing that an attack on Veracruz presented a sounder strategy for ending the war quickly than Taylor's operations in northern Mexico, Quitman hoped that he would be one of the brigadiers selected. Yet he also disliked leaving the command of "Old Rough and Ready," with whom he had "served with so much satisfaction."[9]

By this time Scott had arrived. He had reached Brazos Santiago on December 27 and, within a week, decided on his basic troop dispositions. On January 3, he issued orders assigning all the troops of Patterson, Twiggs, and Quitman to Tampico in preparation for the Veracruz assault. Taylor could deduct from these a garrison for Victoria as well as an escort for his return to Monterrey, Scott leaving it up to Taylor's discretion whether Victoria should be held but cautioning him to adopt a "strict defensive" policy.[10]

It was near sunset on January 14 when a wagon train from Matamoros arrived at Victoria, bringing Scott's January 3 orders. Though forewarned, Taylor was furious at how much of his army he was being asked to give up. He was convinced that Scott had made it impossible for him to retain control over northern Mexico. But he had little option other than to comply, at least insofar as troop dispositions were concerned. So that evening, while the camp buzzed over the exciting news, Taylor and his generals deliberated their course of action, deciding to abandon Victoria. Taylor chose Jefferson Davis and the Mississippi Rifles as part of his escort back to Monterrey.[11]

Though naturally saddened by being separated from his state's troops, Quitman had no qualms about parting with Colonel Davis, with whom he had just experienced quite a falling out. The tall, thin regimental commander, back from his furlough, had arrived in Victoria on January 4, bearing letters and a scarf for Quitman from Eliza. Davis' manner when delivering these items, however, seemed unfriendly, and Quitman became further upset during subsequent days when Davis neglected to pay him expected social calls. Davis, in turn, chafed over Quitman's unwillingness to issue a formal statement in what had become a very public debate over whether Mississippians or Tennesseans had been first into La Tenería. Casual friendship degenerated into petty spite, with Quitman attributing Davis' behavior to jealousy and wondering how he had ever considered Davis "generous and noble hearted," and Davis concluding that Quitman was evading his responsibility to reveal the truth about Monterrey with "paltry excuses and petty complaints."

Perhaps political ambition was the unspoken root of their mutual disaffection. Both men were up-and-coming expansionist Democratic politicos hoping to gain in reputation from the war (Davis, in fact, had been elected to Congress and served a partial term before going off to fight). Monterrey had made each a hero, fashioning a competitive tension which was only enhanced after they went separate ways. A little over a month after Victoria's evacuation, Taylor met Santa Anna south of Saltillo in the Battle of Buena Vista, a fray in which Davis suffered a heel wound and demonstrated great heroism leading a charge of the Mississippi Rifles. The wound gave cause for Davis' return to the States with his regiment, and that August his services were rewarded by gubernatorial appointment to a vacant U.S. Senate seat. Though it would have been ungentlemanly for Quitman to acknowledge his burgeoning rivalry with Davis, he must have perceived Davis as an obstacle to his own advancement.[12]

On January 16, at 4:00 A.M., reveille awakened Quitman's brigade for the march to Tampico. Patterson's volunteers and Twiggs's regulars had already departed. Quitman's assignment was to bring up the rear, and he had his hands full. Most of the route traversed dry, mountainous terrain, and thirst proved a serious problem for several days. Mexican lancers and musket-armed cavalry, moreover, harassed the column, occasionally cutting off stragglers. If Quitman attempted ambushes in retaliation, the enemy always managed to flee into the chaparral. Finally, sandy soils, contorted-appearing banyan trees, palms, thorny vegetation, and the Pánuco River meant that his troops had reached the coastal plain. But Quitman's problems were not ended. When his command arrived in Tampico's vicinity on January 25, Patterson assigned the brigade a campsite on swampy land beside a lagoon with such low vegetation that the troops were fully at the sun's mercy. With the men in misery from the heat, wet bedding, mosquitoes, and scorpions, Quitman's brigade surgeon and regimental commanders began protesting that the health of the men was at stake, leaving Quitman little choice but to remonstrate with Patterson.

Quitman rode into Tampico the next day. He found the city already in the midst of the buildup for Veracruz: troops were drilling on the outskirts; soldiers crisscrossed the streets in search of amusement and bargains; a "theatrical corps" offered drama such as "The Siege of Monterrey." In what seemed to resemble an American town for the first time in a while, Quitman liked what he witnessed. And his mission went well. Patterson granted permission for the brigade to move to higher ground some three miles outside the city.[13]

On January 28, Quitman moved his troops to their new encampment, pitched his tent atop a bluff, and began the wait for orders. Little could be learned about the Veracruz plans for some time, as delays in the acquisition of ordnance and surfboats necessary for the investment of Veracruz and other logistical problems were interfering with General Scott's projected mid-February attack. Quitman worried in characteristic fashion that the higher-ups were not being aggressive enough. Perhaps the assault would never come off. If the government wanted to avoid becoming the "scorn" of Europe, it had better prosecute the war "more vigorously." Contemplating indefinite inactivity, he considered resigning.

Meanwhile Quitman found diversions. He boned up on his Spanish and sought out Tampico's upper class. "Yesterday . . . I dined . . . at the house of an old Spanish Don. The house is fitted up with much splendor and cost. Sofas pianos & pictures graced the drawing room." It was too bad that, in contrast, most Mexicans were impoverished. "So far as I have seen there is no middle class in Mexico. The fashionable grandees on the one hand and the dirty, miserable and poor peons on the other." That stark contrast rendered further proof of the superiority of American institutions.[14]

He continued to sulk about Jefferson Davis. When Eliza urged a reconciliation, he answered that Davis had become "fiercely ambitious" and "impatient" of his being superior in rank. Moreover, he had learned that Davis, in a speech at Vicksburg during his leave after Monterrey, had not even mentioned his name or his role in making important troop dispositions during the battle. Quitman also took umbrage at Whig newspaper criticism of himself and other Democratic brigadiers. But far be it from him to hire editors to "puff" his record.[15]

Finally, on February 19, Scott put in a brief appearance at Tampico. Acting on advice from Commodore David Conner, the American fleet commander in the Gulf, he had selected the protected anchorage at Lobos, a small island southeast of Tampico, as his preliminary troop rendezvous. There he hoped to fuse the Tampico troops, regulars under William Worth at Brazos Santiago and new volunteers into a cohesive army of invasion. Thousands of troops were already training on the island and waiting aboard ships off the island. Scott, therefore, stayed at Tampico for only twenty-four hours. However, he found occasion to inspect Quitman's brigade. Pleased to find it "quite efficient from tactical instruction and habits of subordination," he determined to include it in the Veracruz assault. Scott so praised Quitman's abilities that Quitman felt himself blushing in embarrassment. The timely flattery helped offset Quitman's festering resentment of the Davis business.[16]

Quitman, however, almost missed the "fandango" (as his brigade quartermaster put it) at Veracruz. General Patterson embarked for Lobos at the end of February, leaving Quitman in temporary command of Tampico. Quitman moved into the city and pressured Scott's quartermaster general to get his troops off. But it was not until March 7 that Quitman and about a thousand of his troops boarded the steamer *New Orleans*; by then, Scott, anxious to start the invasion before the onset of the yellow fever season, had already transferred his troops from Lobos to Antón Lizardo, the protected anchorage twelve miles below Veracruz in the Gulf which had been selected as the launching spot for the actual landings. Stormy weather made for a miserable voyage down the coast, and Quitman suffered terribly from seasickness. Finally at 9:00 A.M. on March 9, the *New Orleans* caught up with the invasion force. It was none too soon. Scott, hailing the vessel from his own flagship, yelled that the landing was just about to commence and that Quitman's troops should assume their place in his second invading line.[17]

That bright, balmy day, Quitman had the good fortune to take part in one of the most successful amphibious landings in the history of warfare. Scott could not attack Veracruz directly from the sea, because the harbor was protected by the fort on San Juan de Ulúa, one of the strongest fortifications in North America. Yet he could not bypass the city and hope to maintain supply lines. So he decided to land his troops at Collado Beach less than three miles to the southeast and challenge Veracruz by land.

Quitman's brigade, functioning as part of General Patterson's volunteer division, participated in the second of three waves of men going ashore in surfboats during the late afternoon and early evening. To Quitman's astonishment, enemy cavalry fled rather than contest the landing. "They might have fired upon us from behind the sand hills with entire impunity," he noted, "and occasioned great loss." By eleven o'clock that evening, some 8,600 soldiers had landed, without the loss of a single man. Quitman bivouacked his men on the beach. Lying on wet sand with their feet toward the Gulf, the exhausted soldiers fell asleep, wondering whether the Mexicans would yet attack. Around midnight the stillness was broken by some enemy musket fire. Soldiers jumped to their feet expecting an onslaught. But things soon quieted down again.[18]

There would be, in fact, no head-on battle with the enemy for Quitman

173

and his brigade at Veracruz. General Scott believed that one conquered by strategic finesse (if possible), and he intended to take Veracruz by siege. On March 10, Scott landed more soldiers and ordered his troops to begin encircling the city.

Late that afternoon, Quitman's brigade advanced across the sandy plain beyond the beach toward the sandhills which loomed about two miles from the sea, skirmishing with some Mexican cavalry before halting for the night. The next morning, Quitman led his troops against Mexican positions on some of the sandhills, driving off what he believed to be a thousand enemy; only three of his men were killed and eight wounded. This success brought the brigade under bombardment from artillery in the city; Quitman later estimated that one hundred "tons of iron" had been hurled at his troops that day. However, the barrage proved ineffective—Quitman's men found that they could usually dodge approaching shells. By midday, March 13, American troops had fanned out in a seven-mile semicircular line around the city from Collado Beach to Vergana on the Gulf to Veracruz's north. In addition, the troops had cut off the city's water source as well as the road to Alvarado to the south. Scott now needed to land heavy batteries and push siege lines close enough to the city for effective bombardment. Unfortunately, on March 12 a norther blew in, preventing for several days the landing of either heavy artillery or sufficient supplies.

Quitman put his brigade on a half ration of bread, and suffered through the inclement weather with his men. A newspaper correspondent who caught up with him on March 16 noted both his unrelenting martial spirit and the deprivation he was enduring: "I yesterday rode out to Gen. Quitman's headquarters; they were throwing shot all around him, but he seemed as composed as if 'twas sweet music to his ears. To tell you the truth, I do really think he delights in such sounds for his countenance seemed to become pleasantly animated every time a shot would pass. He is quite well, but seemed a little fatigued from his marches across sand banks, exposures to night air and rains for five or six days past. He has had but one blanket and no tent."

Though many of Quitman's men, by now aware how other volunteers had recently achieved glory under Taylor at Buena Vista, hoped that Scott would yet choose to storm the city, it was not to be. After the landing of a powerful naval battery on March 22, Scott was able to direct devastating artillery fire at the city's garrison and civilians. On March 26, surrender negotiations commenced, and three days later the city capitulated. Under a parole agreement, the Mexican garrison stacked its arms and filed from the city, pledged not to fight again unless regularly exchanged for captured American troops.[19]

Scott had now secured a base. However, supply deficiencies threatened his projected march on Mexico City. Without sufficient food and pack animals, he could not hope to provision his army for an expedition deep into enemy terrain. Since the rainy season on the coast would begin in April, bringing with it mosquitoes and the dread "vomito" or yellow fever, there attached an urgency to Scott's predicament.

To alleviate his shortages, Scott ordered Quitman just one day after the fall of Veracruz to undertake what developed into one of Quitman's most fatiguing wartime ordeals. Scott decided that Quitman's brigade, reinforced by part of the Third Artillery Regiment and a squadron of dragoons, should conquer Alvarado. Located about a mile from the Gulf of Mexico on the coastal river Papaloápan, Alvarado stood in the midst of a large ranching area; if Quitman could take the town, he might be able to provide the beef cattle, horses, and mules for the campaign. Protected by a fort which overlooked the bar to the river, Alvarado had withstood two attacks by United States naval vessels. But Scott thought that Quitman, if he coordinated his attack with the navy, would not only take the town but also trap its garrison, the fort's garrison, artillery and military stores, and the remnants of the Mexican navy which had sought refuge there. Before leaving Veracruz, Quitman boarded the frigate *Mississippi*, flagship of Commodore Matthew C. Perry (who had replaced Conner as commander of the American "Home Squadron" in the Gulf), for consultations. They agreed upon a simultaneous assault, so that the Mexicans could neither escape nor destroy their stores. Perry dispatched Lieutenant Charles G. Hunter, commanding a converted iron-screw steamer called the *Scourge*, to proceed to Alvarado and establish a blockade off the Alvarado bar prior to the arrival of other naval vessels and Quitman's land movement.[20]

Quitman's brigade assumed its line of march at about 3:00 P.M. on March 30, setting off southward along the beach. There was little indication, at first, of the difficulties ahead. Moonlight permitted Quitman to keep his troops going until the early evening hours, when he halted at the mouth of the Madellin River about eight miles south of Veracruz. The next morning, Perry's naval forces were on the scene to create a pontoon bridge for Quitman's infantry while the artillery and wagons crossed at a nearby ford.

Then things fell apart. After traveling along the beach for several more miles, the road led inland across a parched prairie. Under a beating sun, the men marched, drained their canteens, yet found no new water. Scores dropped out; the main body of troops stumbled on until 9:00 P.M., when they finally reached a muddy pond. They quenched their thirst, ate a hasty meal of salt pork and crackers, and bedded down for the night. The next day was even worse. Again they found no water; suffering from bleeding and blistered feet, the men would break ranks to chase mirages. When the troops finally found a pool, its waters proved so foul that the men vomited almost immediately after drinking. Quitman tried to encourage his soldiers by telling them that he had "lived for several weeks at a time on worse waters," but he was unconvincing. "I scarcely believed it," recalled one soldier later, "for I saw a dead alligator in the pond where the men were drinking." By the time the brigade reached Alvarado on April 2, the men had been ravaged by diarrhea and exhaustion.[21]

And all the suffering was for nought. About fifteen miles from Alvarado, Quitman received word from a naval midshipman that the town had already fallen to the navy. Lieutenant Hunter, a hotheaded officer who had once killed a Philadelphia lawyer in a duel, had defied orders, crossing the Alvarado bar and firing at the Mexican fort in advance of the army's arrival. This alerted the Mexican garrison and civilian authorities. Knowing about the events at Veracruz, they decided against resistance—the garrison evacuated the area, and the town then surrendered to Hunter. Hunter had assigned a few men to occupy the fort and town until Quitman arrived, and proceeded up the river and forced the surrender of Tlacotalpan.

It was one of those rare occasions when a battle would have been far preferable to an enemy surrender. Hunter's impetuosity not only gave the Mexican soldiers ample time to evacuate the town but also allowed them to burn craft in the river, drive away herds of horses desperately needed by Scott, and bury arms in the sand. Thus Hunter made unnecessary Quitman's miserable march. As one wit put it back home,

> Five sailors sat within the fort,
> In leading of a lad, oh!
> And thus was spoiled the pretty sport
> Of taking Alvarado.

All that Quitman could recoup from the situation was a herd of five hundred horses provided by Tlacotalpan authorities in return for restraint by navy and army forces after Hunter took the town.

Under the circumstances, Quitman accepted with remarkable grace what had happened. He laughed about the naval faux pas when the midshipman in charge transferred Alvarado to his jurisdiction, and assumed a subdued tone about the incident in his official report. Perry was far more outraged than Quitman by the breach of orders, and had Hunter arrested and court-martialed. When the court judged Hunter guilty, Perry relieved the lieutenant of his command and sent him home.[22]

Quitman, most likely, would have been less conciliatory had he realized that the detour would preclude his participation in the next major battle of the campaign. Determined to avoid the vomito, Scott hastened to leave

Veracruz, despite his supply difficulties. He had already sent an advance into the interior when Quitman arrived back at the city by forced march at noon on April 6. When General Patterson led the volunteer division from the city's walls on April 9, Quitman's "reduced" brigade, still debilitated by diarrhea, had to remain. Though authorized on April 11 to bring his troops forward as "fast as the means of transportation" could be procured, Quitman had to wait still longer while his men recuperated, deferring his departure until April 18. That morning, at 7:00 A.M., he marched his brigade—which had been reorganized to include the Georgia, South Carolina ("Palmetto"), and Alabama regiments, two regiments of Tennessee troops, some 250 mounted Tennessee riflemen, and three companies of Pennsylvania volunteers (left at Lobos because of a smallpox outbreak)—out from Veracruz in pursuit of Scott's columns.

It was at evening encampment on his second day's march from Veracruz that Quitman learned how events at Alvarado had deprived him of a chance to fight Santa Anna. The wily general had returned to Mexico City and then hastened to block the American advance at a defile in the National Highway about fifty miles from the coast near the village of Cerro Gordo. Scott had turned the Mexican position and won a stunning victory on April 18. Many of Quitman's men cheered loudly when the news reached camp that night, but Quitman acted disappointed about missing another chance to fight, an emotion which remained unaltered after his brigade came upon the battlefield two days later. Evidences of the recent carnage appalled some of Quitman's soldiers, especially his newer recruits. But Quitman, who had witnessed what happened at San Jacinto many years earlier, seems to have been unmoved. More disturbing was his discovery of General James Shields, a fellow Democratic brigadier whom he had gotten to know quite well at Tampico, lying in a hut, near death from a wound in his right lung. Taking his friend by the hand, Quitman vowed that he would personally see to it that Shields's "reputation" would be given "full justice" if he died. To Quitman, honor in war had come to transcend almost all human aspirations. Seeing Shields, in fact, seems to have stiffened his will to fight. Ten days later, after his brigade finally caught up with Scott's army at Jalapa, Quitman wrote home that he intended to let his beard grow until Mexico City was conquered. Only the conquest of the enemy capital, he felt, would end the war and do good "both to our country & to the poor enslaved Mexicans." [23]

Quitman remained at Jalapa for better than a week, long enough to become entranced with the community, as did virtually every American soldier stationed there who left a recorded impression. With attractive homes, beautiful flowers, a variety of fruit, salubrious air, and a vista of snow-capped Orizaba, Jalapa seemed perfect. Perhaps in future summers, after his troops helped bless Mexico with a "good government," he could pass time there with Eliza and the girls. However, Quitman's stay was blemished by insinuations that he could not keep his troops under adequate control. While in Veracruz, some of his men had drawn the ire of Spanish officials by stoning the Spanish consulate. Now charges were raised that his brigade had killed over one hundred head of cattle and done other damage at Santa Anna's hacienda at Encero on the way up from Cerro Gordo. Since Quitman had not stayed at the Encero encampment, but had preceded his brigade into Jalapa, he was forced to inquire of his regimental commanders and others whether the charges had any validity. The result was a report generally denying the accusation, yet including an admission by Quitman that his men had slaughtered a few sheep.[24]

General Scott initially scheduled Quitman's brigade and the rest of Patterson's volunteers to leave Jalapa on May 4. The next important objective was Puebla, a metropolis of some eighty thousand inhabitants, and, although guerrillas were now seriously harassing his supply line back to the coast, Scott had sent General Worth's division on toward Puebla prior to Quitman's arrival. However, the bulk of Patterson's men, including Quitman's brigade, were twelve months' volunteers serving enlistments due to expire within the next month and a half. Nine-tenths of these men made clear their determination to go home, despite bonuses proffered for their reenlistment. Rather than commit these soldiers to advancing into the interior, which would make their evacuation more difficult, Scott did the humane thing and released them prematurely. Scott also detached Patterson, now without a legitimate division, to accompany the seven regiments back to the United States, and assigned Quitman to the command of the four volunteer regiments remaining at Jalapa. These regiments—the Palmettos, two from Pennsylvania, and one from New York—had joined the army later than the relieved units, and their terms of enlistment called for service for the duration of the war.[25]

Leaving the second regiment of Pennsylvania volunteers at Jalapa for garrison duty, Quitman departed for Puebla early on the morning of May 7. Anxious to close the gap with Worth, who had taken Perote on April 22, Quitman drove his troops at a brutal pace. Making about twenty miles his first day over broken, mountainous terrain, he quickly wore out teams and equipment. Fifteen of his mules died that day, according to a quartermaster's report; numerous upset wagons testified to his insistence on speed.

After an uncomfortably cold night, Quitman marched his men the remaining few miles into Perote. By their arrival in the afternoon, the soldiers were exhausted. "I pitied some of Gen. Quitman's men," noted one of Worth's soldiers, "for they seemed . . . worn out and fatigued. They hardly could keep on the last day's march, on account of sore feet and diarrhea, and being unaccustomed to marching." While his soldiers rested Quitman in-spected Perote's fortress of San Carlos, where Texans captured during invasions of Mexico had formerly been imprisoned. Seeing the "vast and horrible dungeon" and imagining what the prisoners must have endured, Quitman could only further despise the enemy.[26]

Quitman's arrival freed Worth's division, already under orders to con-tinue to Puebla, to pull out on May 9. The next day, after further depleting his brigade by assigning its other Pennsylvania regiment to garrison duty at the Perote fortress, Quitman followed.

For most of the march to Puebla, about twenty-five miles separated Quitman from Worth's column. The gap almost brought disaster when Santa Anna arrived in Puebla and found out what was happening. Hoping to strike the Americans while they were divided, he sent three thousand cavalrymen against Quitman's one-thousand-man brigade. Unfortunately for the Mexi-can leader, however, the gap narrowed just as the assault was getting under way on May 14. Worth, reaching Amozoc—a town some ten miles from Puebla—halted on May 13 rather than push into Puebla. Learning of Santa Anna's presence, Worth sent word that Quitman should hurry. Receiving the message at 4:00 A.M., Quitman had his men on a forced march by dawn. Further, when Worth was informed that enemy cavalry was trying to turn his position and attack Quitman, he ordered artillery to be directed against the Mexicans. Not only did the battery rounds kill some of the enemy, lead to the capture of others, and disrupt cohesion, but the noise was audible to Quitman, who then urged his men toward the fighting at "double-quick time." Although some of the attackers regrouped beyond the range of Worth's guns, all chance of success had passed. By the time they came upon Quitman, their supposedly unsuspecting target had pulled his entire brigade—even hospital cases—into battle formation and had drawn within easy distance of re-inforcement from Worth. Prudently, the cavalry withdrew into the hills. The next day Quitman and Worth made a negotiated, unopposed entry into Puebla. Santa Anna, faced by a lack of enthusiasm among the citizens for mobilization, had forfeited the city. Affected by the enemy evacuation, Quitman began to ponder whether even Mexico City would be contested. "They are said to be all in confusion in the sacred city," he reported to Eliza.[27]

Puebla became Quitman's headquarters until the first week of August. It took Scott, who arrived on May 28, that long to put together enough troops for the final advance on Mexico City. Scott brought up units from Veracruz, summoned his garrisons from Jalapa and Perote (sacrificing reliable lines to the coast), and waited for the arrival of additional troops from Zachary Taylor's zone which the administration now shifted to his own campaign.[28]

Despite occasional bouts of diarrhea (which he assured McMurran were less severe than cases among his soldiers), Quitman enjoyed his days in Puebla; his letters refer to Harry's hunting down bargains at the local market, the joy of eating ice cream packed in snow from Popocatépetl, horseback rides in the park, and a sightseeing trip to the ruins of the pyramid at nearby Cholula. From the top of that structure, Quitman commanded a breathtaking view of the surrounding countryside.

The more he saw of Mexico, the more Quitman was confounded by its exotic climate and topography, and how the terrain could be blighted by a people so undeserving of its beauty and riches: "It is almost impossible to conceive that here in the torrid zone I am sitting comfortably with my great coat on, and that within a few miles of us on one side ice and snow is procured for our shops, and on the other side within the same distance, grow all the tropical fruits—bananas, pineapples, cocoa nuts. . . . It is truly a strange country, beautiful beyond description, where every thing save man, is found in perfection." Since such a "poor" "miserable race" plagued by "bad Government" did so little with the land's bounty, it was up to the United States to make something of Mexico by means of arms. Quitman wrote Robert Walker that the administration should demand transit concessions from Mexico in any peace negotiations, particularly permission for any future southern transcontinental railroad to cross northern Mexico and a guarantee that American citizens could construct a railroad or canal across the Isthmus of Tehuantepec to link the Gulf of Mexico with the Pacific.[29]

Unlike many fellow soldiers, however, Quitman neglected to attribute Mexican backwardness to the intense religiosity of the country. It was not that he was oblivious to the centrality of Catholic institutions to Mexican life; Puebla, he observed, "contains an immense number of churches & monasteries. Sometimes you may hear 500 bells ringing at the same time." Rather, he resisted making the common ideological jump from noticing such religious manifestations to attributing them to the grip of the priests. Although other Americans saw a relationship between the poverty of the masses and the wealth of the church, Quitman, ever a seeker of the good life, tended rather to admire that wealth. "The churches are splendid beyond description," he informed Eliza. "I wish that you . . . could but see the cathedral[.] The balustrade around the altar is of silver & gold, said to be worth several millions." Quitman's own religious permissiveness, surely tested by this Mexican passage, was destined to remain impervious to the undertones of majoritarian intolerance.[30]

Occupation duty also turned Quitman's thoughts to matters of status and recognition again. On March 2, Congress had voted him a sword for his role at Monterrey. In April, President Polk, acting on authorization from Congress to appoint two new major generals in the regular army—with the important stipulation that they were to be "immediately discharged" when the war ended—chose Quitman for one of the promotions.[31]

Quitman's appointment gave official sanction to the honor that the volunteers had won in the war, and it met with approbation among the rank and file at Puebla. Quitman had been far more than a courageous battle commander and competent leader in march and occupation. He evoked genuine affection from his men by demonstrating consistent concern that they be well supplied, by sharing personally in their hardships, and by attending to his sick and wounded. Even regulars now accorded Quitman due respect, viewing him as a "gentleman" and possibly the "best of the [volunteer] appointments." U.S. naval officer Raphael Semmes, encountering Quitman at some of Scott's levees at Puebla, noted that regular army officers respected Quitman's zeal: he approached soldiering with an enthusiasm akin to that of a lover for his mistress.[32]

Quitman could scarcely contain his euphoria over the promotion. Here was that "baton" he had coveted. Only Lieutenant General George Washington had ever achieved a higher rank in the U.S. Army. And the new appointment was as a regular—a *much* higher status than his volunteer brigadiership. Since the other division commanders at Puebla—Worth and Twiggs—were only brigadiers, Quitman assumed that by rank he had jumped to second-in-command of Scott's army. So carried away was he by the prospects before him that in an exuberant but hardly chivalrous moment he hypothesized how he might reach the very top, should the "casualties of war" remove Scott.[33]

How disillusioning it was to find out after Scott's arrival at Puebla that not only did General Worth outrank him by virtue of a "brevet" (honorary) appointment as major general, but his appointment in the regular service did not guarantee him command of regular troops. Rather than deplete Worth's or Twiggs's divisions to provide Quitman with a command commensurate with his new rank, Scott instead told Quitman that he would have to continue as volunteer commander until new regular units arrived from the States.

Quitman was appalled. He did want to command regulars, and he was sensitive that his volunteer command, which came to include the New York, South Carolina, and Second Pennsylvania regiments, and six companies of the First Pennsylvania Regiment, fell far short numerically of a legitimate division. Major generals were supposed to command divisions, and Quitman chafed under the "humiliating" circumstances in which he found himself.

Risking a serious falling out with Scott, who had a notorious proclivity for personal feuds, Quitman vented his disappointment. On May 30, he complained how "juniors in rank" had superior commands; on June 3 he reminded Scott that he was a "Major General in the Service of the United States" and that congressional legislation in February mandated that divisions have ten regiments. Scott, giving little, answered that Quitman's protests were highly inappropriate at a time when the "high duties of the campaign" provided "no leisure for a laborious correspondence," and suggested that Quitman "cheerfully bend to the circumstances."

In the end, Quitman took his medicine. Concluding that he would get further working with Scott than against him, Quitman decided to postpone confrontation until Mexico City fell. In fact, over the following weeks, Quitman went out of his way to conciliate his superior. Semmes noted that Quitman listened attentively to Scott's tedious discourses on military affairs while other officers made scant effort to conceal their boredom. When General Worth called for a court of inquiry regarding a dispute he was having with Scott, Quitman, sitting on the court, sided with Scott.[34]

By the waning days of the occupation, chess engagements were cementing a Quitman-Scott friendship. Quitman preserved this relationship with care. When Scott called an officer's conference to consider whether a $10,000 "douceur" (bribe) should be passed to Santa Anna to foster negotiations, Quitman voiced opposition. But he also refrained from going public with his dissent when the attempt was made and the money lost. Months later, when War Secretary Marcy inquired about the conference, Quitman refused to break the confidentiality of the meeting, and only released details when ordered to do so, explaining that his reservations had derived from convictions that national dealing with other countries should be "high-toned and above board," and from fears that if news of the bribe got out it might influence American public opinion against any treaty. That Quitman and Scott joined in attaching personal recommendations to a petition from the regular officers at Puebla, requesting congressional pensions for widows and orphans of officers killed in the remaining course of the war, further testifies to their alliance.[35]

By early August, Scott had troops at Puebla sufficient for the final thrust to Mexico City. Commanding a force which would soon exceed ten thousand men (including sick), Scott on August 5 ordered an advance. His army, now divided into four divisions plus a Puebla occupation force, would move out commencing August 7, the divisions marching a day apart.

As military bands blared out "Hail Columbia," "Yankee Doodle," and "The Star-Spangled Banner," and as cheers for the "Halls of the Montezumas" rent the air, Quitman's Fourth—still "Volunteer"—Division, now supplemented with a battalion of marines, paraded out of Puebla on August 8. They took up the second position in the initial line of march, following General Twiggs's Second Division, and General Scott himself joined their column for this stage of the advance. The men gave a smart appearance, since Quitman had subjected them to five-hour drills during the final weeks of the occupation. Quitman savored the moment, gallantly dashing up and down the column to the cheers of the men.[36]

Over the next few days, Quitman led his division across the mountain range between Puebla and the Valley of Mexico, despite interference from enemy cavalry which picked off a dragoon in his rear guard. Though the men suffered from a very cold rain as they crossed terrain some ten thousand feet above sea level, they looked in superb condition when they linked up with Twiggs's division near Lake Chalco, southeast of the capital city, on August 15. "The Volunteer Division came up this morning. . . . It is about 2200 strong and is looking remarkably well *considering the material*," acknowledged one of Twiggs's West Point graduates with reluctance.[37]

But the ensuing days proved most frustrating for Quitman. Scott, because of some superb reconnaissance, had determined that a southern approach to the capital—though less direct than an advance from the east—offered a means to bypass many of the enemy's outer defensive works, and, on August 15, ordered the army to take a road which skirted the southern shores of Lake Chalco and Lake Xochimilco and led to San Agustín, some nine miles south of the city. Worth's division reached the latter point on August 18. The other divisions followed, with Quitman's arriving the next day.

Scott would have preferred, at this point, moving on the city by way of a road which led northward from San Agustín. But reconnaissance revealed formidable Mexican defenses at the hacienda of San Antonio, an important objective ahead. So Scott adopted the engineers' recommendation that he turn the San Antonio defenses. Though an apparently impassable lava bed known as the Pedregal seemed to prevent a westerly march around San Antonio (wet ground and enemy guns blocked passage to the east), the engineers had discovered a path across the southwestern edge of the Pedregal which intersected the road approaching the capital from the west via Contreras and San Angel. The only major difficulty was that a road would have to be constructed along the path so that the siege train could pass. Thus, on August 19 Scott directed Worth's division to threaten San Antonio and divert enemy attention from the Pedregal, and assigned engineer captain Robert E. Lee and some five hundred men from volunteer major general Gideon Pillow's division to build the road. Twiggs's units were to reinforce the road builders, should enemy resistance materialize.[38]

Quitman's troops received the support job of guarding the depot, the sick, and the teams and wagons at San Agustín. When a Mexican force under Gabriel Valencia appeared to contest the American advance across the Pedregal with artillery fire upon the workers, Quitman's disappointment at what appeared a secondary assignment became mortification. How frustrating it was to passively watch from the roof of San Agustín's highest building, a hotel, as fighting unfolded with a roar of cannon and musketry "more fierce than at Monterrey."

Quitman reacted in character. Calling at Scott's headquarters, he complained that the defensive assignment had "cast a gloom" over his battle-hungry division. He almost went too far. Scott told him that his protests were "unmilitary." When Quitman countered, with Cerro Gordo in mind, that the volunteers had been prevented from gaining "any credit" during the march from Veracruz, Scott neared his explosion point. "He showed considerable excitement, and I left him after I had said that he must pardon my sensibility respecting orders which left me and my division no means of distinction," Quitman recounted.

However, the point had been made. An hour later he received orders to send out two regiments to assist the advance. Quitman committed General Shields's brigade (Shields had made an incredible recovery from his wound) and it played a significant role in the fighting—the battles of Contreras and Churubusco—which continued until late afternoon on August 20 and resulted in Valencia's rout, an enemy withdrawal from San Antonio, and Santa Anna's pullback to Mexico City's inner defenses. Shields's brigade took some 240 casualties, including the death of Colonel Pierce Butler, Palmetto commander. Now Quitman had some cause for pride. His official report praised the "good conduct" of "the portion of my division which had the good fortune to be actively engaged." [39]

After Churubusco, Quitman's division remained posted at San Agustín. Scott might have attempted an immediate assault on the capital; he had taken far fewer casualties than Santa Anna, who had suffered the loss of some 10,000 men (or about a third of his total force). In the waning moments of the fighting, American dragoons had pursued Mexican forces virtually to the walls of the city and taken a battery just beyond the San Antonio Garita at one of the southern entrances. Santa Anna himself expected the city to fall, and American soldiers at the time and some scholars since have argued that Scott should have kept the pressure on. But Scott, as at Puebla, responded to enemy peace feelers, in the hope of avoiding unnecessary bloody battles. Thus he stationed his various divisions in holding positions at the villages around the Pedregal and north of the Churubusco River, while the negotiations resumed. [40]

On August 22, Scott appointed Quitman to a three-man commission to arrange armistice terms so that serious treaty negotiations could commence. Scott presented Quitman and Brigadier Generals Persifor Smith and Franklin

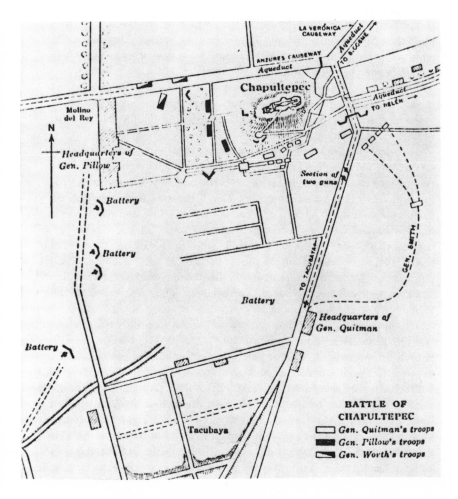

The Battle of Chapultepec
Adaptation of map from Justin H. Smith, *The War with Mexico*. Reprinted
by permission of the United Board for Homeland Ministries.

Pierce with a ten-article armistice *projet*, which they were to press on the Mexicans. Scott's terms included provisions that neither side could attempt reinforcements while talks were in progress; that the American army would remain beyond city guns and refrain from reconnaissance within such range; that Mexican forces west and southwest of the city—including the garrison at the castle of Chapultepec—were to be pulled back to within musket shot of the city; and that messengers on either side would enjoy unhampered passage on the highway to Veracruz.

Skeptical that Mexican officials would negotiate in good faith and convinced that the conquest of Mexico City would facilitate greater territorial concessions than if the capital remained in enemy hands, Quitman served on the commission only with reluctance. That night and into the next morning, he and his colleagues labored over terms with their Mexican counterparts at the British consul's house at Tacubaya, about three miles southwest of the capital. He became increasingly dubious when the Mexicans proved intransigent about some of Scott's proposals, such as the forfeiture of Chapultepec, and added new stipulations of their own. Nonetheless, when Smith and Pierce proved amenable to the revisions, Quitman suppressed his reservations and signed the document.

By this time, Quitman had reconciled himself to Scott's belief that the war might conclude without another battle. "All here believe it will end in a peace," he wrote home on August 23. Even if fighting resumed, he did not expect it to amount to much. "Mexico is now so crippled that she can make but feeble resistance[.] We could enter the city in a few hours without much loss." But prospects of inactivity while the war wound down did not please him. It had been almost a year since Monterrey, and he *had* wanted one last chance at glory. "Lt. Judd . . . informs me that Genl. Quitman intends returning to the United States," reported an artillery officer at Tacubaya. "He came out not to make political capital, but to fight, and is, I presume, disheartened at not being engaged in the last battles."[41] Quitman's war experience verged on ending on a very sour and anticlimactic note.

14

Old Chapultepec

ONLY a few weeks after John Quitman was reported mired in self-pity over the Tacubaya armistice, he was serving as temporary ruler of Mexico's capital and in an exuberant mood. "I am really Governor of Mexico & you my modest blushing daughter, are no less than a Governor's daughter," he boasted in a letter to Louisa.[1] Quitman had every reason for pride. In the fighting which had just culminated in the surrender of Mexico City, he had finally given incontrovertible proof of both his bravery and his capacity for generalship. His appointment as "Civil and Military Governor" represented General Scott's acknowledgment of his achievement.

Quitman, in a way, had Santa Anna to thank for the striking change in his fortunes. Too insecure politically to accede to concessions demanded by President Polk's negotiator, Nicholas P. Trist, the Mexican leader had utilized time provided by the armistice to strengthen the capital's defenses rather than reach a peace settlement. Since American troops could plainly see enemy soldiers improving the Chapultepec works and defenses on the road beyond Tacubaya, Scott had little choice but to cancel the agreement (which he did on September 6). By evening of the next day, Scott had selected a new military objective, the Molino del Rey (King's Mill). A group of heavily walled, parapeted red sandstone buildings, the Molino housed a flour mill and a foundry for bronze cannon. Believing that the Mexicans were using the structures to melt down church bells and convert the metal into cannon, Scott determined to attack. In bloody fighting on September 8, Worth's division carried the works, only to discover that no cannon production was actually in progress. The troops destroyed the buildings and withdrew, having sustained heavy casualties in an endeavor which did little to improve Scott's hopes of taking the city.[2]

Quitman, meanwhile, brought his division up to Coyoacán, a town north of the Pedregal. His troops were now close to the fighting and within seven miles of the city itself, but Quitman still brooded over being denied "an active part in the victories of Contreras & Churubusco."[3]

Finally, on September 11, Quitman was accorded a significant role in Scott's battle plans. Scott called Quitman, as well as other general officers and engineer officers and staff, to a war council that morning at General Pillow's headquarters in Piedad (a village east of Tacubaya and south of the Belén Gate), to help him resolve how to move on the city. Given his positions, Scott had to attack from the south or west. But access to the capital from these directions was limited to five stone causeways, the only means for his army and artillery to traverse the marshy terrain before them. Three of these causeways ran to the city from the south, each leading to enemy-held, fortified garitas (gates) which barred final entrance to the city proper. Two causeways approached from the southwest and west, respectively, but they also led to garitas. Considerable risk attended whatever selection of route Scott made. If he moved on the city from the southwest or west, he first had to deal with Chapultepec, which loomed on the road from Tacubaya that led from his positions to the causeways. This castle, built as a palace at enormous expense by a Spanish viceroy back in the late 1700s, now housed Mexico's national military academy. It seemed awesome, being situated—as a regular infantry lieutenant noted—atop a "steep and rockey [*sic*]" bluff which "lifts itself from the valley to the altitude of 150 feet perpendicularly" about two miles west of the capital. However, an approach from the south posed conceivably greater difficulty. Reconnaissance had determined that the Mexicans, expecting the American attack to come from that direction, had used the armistice to construct fieldworks and entrenchments; Scott, moreover, had just learned that canal water had been released to flood the fields flanking the southern causeways. Given these considerations, it is hardly surprising that Scott wanted consultations.[4]

When Scott opened the meeting, he stacked the deck for a Chapultepec attack by announcing that his ordnance officers felt that bombardment and cannonade could reduce the fortress in a day, and that he believed that its fall would induce a peaceful capitulation by the city. But he said that he could be swayed, and asked for other opinions. Pillow then argued for the southern gates. Quitman, in an uncharacteristic moment of indecision, announced that he had not gained enough familiarity with enemy defenses to render an informed opinion. Rather, his own "superficial" understanding of the art of war induced him to reserve his judgment until more was heard from the engineers. When several of the engineers then gave reasons for an assault on the southern San Antonio Garita, Quitman as well as Generals Shields, Pierce, and George Cadwalader expressed disagreement with the general in chief. But General Twiggs concurred with Scott, and testimony by Lieutenant P. G. T. Beauregard which differed diametrically from the other engineers' converted Pierce to Scott's plan. Scott announced for the western gates, and dissolved the conference.[5]

Quitman learned later in the day that he would participate in the Chapultepec assault. At five in the afternoon Scott ordered Quitman and Pillow's divisions to make a demonstration at Piedad on the causeway toward the San Antonio Garita. Beauregard had stressed the need for surprise, and these maneuvers were intended to reinforce enemy presumptions that the attack would come from the south. Around midnight, Quitman and Pillow, following further instructions, transferred their commands to Tacubaya, where Scott maintained headquarters with Worth's division. Scott summoned Quitman and told him that, barring an enemy surrender because of artillery bombardment, his troops would attack Chapultepec.[6]

During the night, Captain Robert E. Lee and the engineers erected batteries at strategic points near the castle. At daylight, bombardment commenced, drawing a swift answer of enemy round shot, shells, and grape. Quitman held his division in and around Condesa, a hacienda near the Tacubaya road, in support of two of the American batteries. His men were now within about eight hundred yards of the fortress itself.

That afternoon, Quitman and Lovell reconnoitered the enemy batteries which had been firing on the division. They drew brisk fire, but discovered two batteries: one, a work mounting four guns on the road ahead; the other, a flanking emplacement of one gun which could sweep the low ground to the left of the road and the ground between the road and the base of the Chapultepec hill. Quitman felt that this information justified the wounds seven men suffered in supporting the reconnaissance. Meanwhile the American artillery continued to pound enemy positions. "A $10\frac{1}{2}$-inch mortar was opened upon the place during the afternoon," reported a newspaperman, "and as several shells have been seen to fall and explode directly within the enemy's works it is certain that great damage has been caused." But there was no capitulation, so Scott completed assault plans. At dusk, scaling ladders were brought forward to the advance American positions.[7]

During the evening of September 12, Quitman joined Scott and General Pillow for yet another strategy session. Scott had suspended the cannonade until daylight, when it would be resumed preparatory to the main assault. Scott instructed Quitman and Pillow in a two-pronged assault plan. At eight in the morning, he would temporarily silence the batteries. Then Pillow's division, from the Molino del Rey, would assault the fortress' western front, where the slope of the hill was the most gradual, while Quitman's command would move northward from the Tacubaya road against the steeper south-eastern incline. Each division was to be reinforced by a special 250-man storming party (plus officers) of regulars who volunteered for the assignment. Quitman drew his group, led by Captain Silas Casey of the Second Infantry, from Twiggs's division; Twiggs was also instructed to keep a brigade within support distance of Quitman's column and to effect a diversion during the battle on the Niño Perdido road to the east. The volunteer stormers dubbed themselves "the forlorn hope" in anticipation of the heavy casualties they were bound to take.[8]

Despite Quitman's confidence that his men were equal to nearly any task, he must have had some concern about what lay ahead. Even to reach the hill to Chapultepec castle, his men would have to contend with the two enemy batteries ahead as well as soldiers manning a nearby ditch. These positions guarded the critical junction southeast of the castle where the Tacubaya road met the causeway to the Belén Garita (the gate and customs post at the southwest corner of the capital) and a parallel aqueduct which supplied springwater from Chapultepec to the city. Somehow the troops would have to silence these batteries or pass through their fire, yet a fifteen-foot-high wall ran along the whole south side of the Chapultepec mound, broken only by an opening at about midpoint which was secured by a sandbag redan. Troops moving on the wall from the Tacubaya road would be restricted in their approach, moreover, because intersecting ditches cutting through adjacent meadows made maneuvers off the road problematic. Should Santa Anna send a flanking attack from the capital against the column as it marched, things would be even worse. Then, even if the troops managed to pass the wall, there would be a second wall to contend with about halfway up the hill, followed by the castle itself. Santa Anna had left the Chapultepec works seriously undermanned; commanding officer General Nicolás Bravo had far less than the two thousand men he required. However, Quitman had no way of knowing this as the battle neared.[9]

Shelling of the castle resumed at about 5:30 in the morning. As planned, 8:00 brought a temporary cessation of the firing, signaling Quitman and Pillow to launch their assaults. Quitman sent a brigade of regulars under General Persifor F. Smith, which had been attached to his command, off to the right to shield his column from any enemy attack from the capital and to possibly turn the enemy batteries. He ordered his other brigade, under General Shields, toward the castle on the Tacubaya road at a "double quick" pace. Led by the special storming party, forty pioneers chosen from the volunteers and armed with ladders, pickaxes, and crows—they were under the command of marine captain John G. Reynolds—and yet another special force of 120 men under Major Levi Twiggs of the marines, Quitman's column advanced some six hundred yards under raking fire from the castle and enemy batteries. Reaching within about two hundred yards of the batteries, they were stopped cold by a withering fire of musketry and grape from the ditch and batteries. Twiggs fell, and while some of the marines took cover in ditches to their left, deploying to answer the enemy batteries and to fire against the lower wall, others of the advance fell back about fifty yards to a bend in the road. Some, including Quitman, sought shelter in nearby adobe huts.

Quickly recovering, Quitman ordered Shields to march his brigade obliquely to the left, hoping that the troops could penetrate a partial opening in the wall caused by artillery fire, and then commanded the marines to capture the batteries. Shields's South Carolinians waded across ditches and meadows to the wall, and used their bayonets to loosen the stones in the wall and cross at the opening; soldiers from the Second Pennsylvania and the New York regiments broke through at the redan (their way paved by some regular voltigeurs who had cleared the work) and linked with Pillow's command on the western slope. Shields took a severe arm wound, but pushed on, and soon the soldiers were at the second wall. Up came the scaling ladders. Over the troops went, and then into the castle and up to its very parapet. The carnage at some points became terrible, and as one of the "forlorn hope" admitted: "The havoc among the Mexicans was now horrible in the extreme. Pent up between two fires they had but one way to escape and all crowded toward it like a flock of sheep. I saw dozens hanging from the walls and creeping through holes made for the passage of water and whilst in this position were shot down. . . . Our men were shouting 'give no quarter to the treacherous scoundrels' and as far as I could observe none was asked by the Mexicans." However, at other points in the castle, the troops showed restraint, and accepted surrenders, including that of General Bravo. By 9:30, it was all over. Ascending to the parapet, Quitman could see escaping Mexicans beating a hasty retreat to the Belén Garita.

Quitman's military instincts seized the moment. Scott, unsure how the battle would unfold, had watched the action through field glasses from a Tacubaya housetop and deferred issuing orders for following up the conquest of Chapultepec. Quitman, after gaining the castle, could have awaited instructions, but he was anxious for glory and reluctant to provide the enemy time to regroup. Even before mounting the parapet, he had taken the precaution of having his own troops reassembled in the road below. Now he located General Pillow, who had been wounded, and persuaded the Tennessean to release his division for a joint pursuit of the enemy along the Belén causeway. When a marine adjutant warned that storming the Belén Garita might prove costly because it was close to the Ciudadela, a converted tobacco factory about three hundred yards northeast of the gate which served as barracks for the city's garrison, Quitman snapped, "I am aware of it Sir." Determined to carry things through, he descended the parapet.[10]

Advancing along the causeway with almost the entire Chapultepec attack force, Quitman encountered a barrage of enemy grape, canister, and musketry. Fortunately, the eight-foot-wide stone aqueduct to the capital ran right down the middle of the causeway, and its heavy masonry pillars provided partial cover. Arch by arch, moving during the intervals between bursts from enemy guns, the troops pushed forward.

Meanwhile, General Scott had hastened to the castle. Viewing Quitman's advance, as well as the arrival of General Worth's division (which had been making a demonstration toward the castle's north side) at the northeast corner of the Chapultepec grounds, Scott began channeling reinforcements forward. To Quitman, he sent Franklin Pierce's brigade and Captain Simon H. Drum's artillery. But, sensitive to the strong Mexican position at the citadel beyond the Belén Garita, he hoped to limit Quitman to a feint and carry the capital with Worth's forces. So he sent word to Quitman to proceed cautiously, and put most of his punch behind Worth. Worth was to follow the Verónica causeway north from the castle until he intersected a road about a mile to Quitman's left which led east to the San Cosmé Garita on the capital's northeast side.[11]

Quitman however, continued his "hot pursuit," oblivious to all signals from Scott for restraint. A two-gun enemy battery and field redan about halfway along the causeway stalled progress for a while, but the Mexicans were routed. Quitman pressed on, helped by Persifor Smith's brigade which worked at filling in ditches in the causeway so that artillery could be brought forward. When enemy forces threatened Quitman's flank by the Piedad road, the artillery was turned in that direction and dispersed the threat.

A little past noon, Quitman and his men drew before the Belén Garita. Now the enemy fire grew hotter. Engineer P.G.T. Beauregard thought it the "most terrific" instance of "ball, grape canister & musketry I ever witnessed." Smoke covered the causeway. But Quitman's eight-inch howitzer, operated by Captain Drum, answered. Shell fragments and masonry splinters wreaked havoc upon the garita's defenders. When, around 1:00, the Mexicans, who were short anyway on manpower and ammunition, panicked at rumors that their position was being turned and began pulling back from the garita toward the Ciudadela, Quitman sensed that the time had come to charge. Grabbing a rifle from the wounded Major William W. Loring of the regular Mounted Rifle Regiment, Quitman fired his last cartridge, tied his red silk handkerchief to the weapon's muzzle, and waved it in signal for the Rifles and the Palmettos, who had been in his advance, to follow him over the breastwork. With loud cheers they charged the garita, taking it by about

1:20. John Quitman witnessed his soldiers enter the city and plant their various standards, knowing he had just experienced that ultimate moment of battle ecstasy of which he had been so long in quest.[12]

Glory, however, came at a steep price. By disregarding several messages from Scott to hold back so that the attack would support—rather than precede—Worth's assault on the San Cosmé Gate, Quitman exposed his men to the brunt of enemy resistance. Success did not come, as Scott later put it in a gentle rebuke, "without proportionate loss."[13]

Had the storming of the garita precipitated an immediate enemy surrender, it might be argued that events legitimized Quitman's impetuosity. However, in the hours afterward Quitman was unable even to widen the breach, much less force a capitulation. Santa Anna naturally rushed to the Ciudadela with ordnance and reinforcements. Soon he had guns on the *paseo* (a promenade which ran north from the garita), in houses east of the paseo, and in the citadel itself, all concentrating their fire on Quitman's men. The Palmettos and Rifles penetrated the city by following farther the arches of the aqueduct, but were stopped one hundred yards short of the Ciudadela. Artillery was brought up, but soon all available shot was expended, and Quitman's troops had to retreat to the garita and to sandbag walls being raised nearby.

Quitman sent to Scott for more artillery support, which was later provided, but found it barely possible to hold on as an "iron shower" of enemy shot crashed through the walls of the garita. Casualties mounted. By nightfall, every member of his staff, Beauregard, and all his artillery officers had been either killed or wounded. In all, Quitman's troops that day had had at least 8 officers and 69 noncommissioned officers and privates killed, and 454 officers and men wounded. His command had borne the brunt of the heavy fighting, as Scott's entire army had only suffered 130 killed and 703 wounded.

Nighttime helped. Firing ceased, and Quitman used the cover of darkness to bring up artillery. He also set out with the wounded Beauregard, early in the evening, on a reconnaissance to determine optimal positions for battery emplacements. Perhaps artillery fire could soften the Ciudadela enough for an assault. They fell into a canal, which cost Quitman one of his shoes, but completed the mission. By nine o'clock, the engineers were working on battery construction. As dawn broke, Captain Edward J. Steptoe had cannon and siege howitzers ready to blast away.[14]

Perhaps Quitman faced the new day with trepidation. He had, after all, seen men literally killed at his side and could only attribute the sparing of his own life to "Providence," which "seemed to turn the bullets from me." On the other hand, as Beauregard noted, he had consistently demonstrated "coolness & gallantry" throughout the battle, and given no outward sign of faltering. Fortunately, there was no need to put his fortitude to another test. Worth's forces had also entered the city by nightfall, not only taking the San Cosmé Garita but also lobbing ten-inch mortar shells near the National Palace. This proved enough for the citizens of the city. City magistrates had no stomach for a fight to the end, and persuaded Santa Anna, who still had some ten to twelve thousand troops available, to abandon their defense. By 1:00 A.M. on the morning of September 14, Mexican forces had withdrawn. At 4:00, just about the time Quitman's batteries were nearing completion, a city delegation approached Scott's headquarters near Chapultepec to announce the surrender. A couple of hours later, a white flag appeared on the Ciudadela. Quitman immediately sent Lovell, Beauregard and some troops to see to its occupation.

Scott allowed Quitman's troops the honor of officially occupying the Grand Plaza and raising the U.S. flag atop the National Palace. Around 7:00, covered with dust and lime, missing one shoe and part of the other, Quitman proudly marched three regiments before the "Palace of the Montezumas." Though momentarily vexed when a couple of overenthusiastic soldiers broke ranks, rushed to the palace, and waved their regimental colors from a second-story building before the flag was raised, Quitman nonetheless took great satisfaction from the recognition Scott had bestowed on his command. The general in chief, moreover, doubled the honor, by coming personally to the palace later in the morning and naming Quitman "Civil and Military Governor" of the city. Whatever misgivings Scott harbored about the rash methods Quitman had employed, he readily conceded that Quitman's volunteers had abetted Worth's advance and had demonstrated bravery equivalent to anything he could have expected from regulars. This recognition was quite a tribute to the volunteers, because it came from a great soldier who had once disparaged the whole volunteer service.[15]

Quitman learned quickly that Scott had conveyed far more than an honorific plum in his imposing new title. Scott assumed responsibility for establishing overall occupation policy, but delegated to Quitman the administrative responsibility for implementing policy. Scott's September 18 orders announcing that the capital's civilian officials could continue collecting customs at city gates until procedures were "modified by the Civil and Military Governor . . . according to the view of the Gen. in Chief" effectively stated the division of authority he intended. Similarly, when Scott decided that captured tobacco should be distributed to the army "rank and file," he left up to "the consideration of the Civil & Military Governor" the "manner of rendering" the allotment. Though without any real sleep for the last three days of fighting, Quitman would have to push himself just a bit longer.[16]

Establishing law and order in the city took primacy over other policy objectives at first. Within hours of the raising of the American flag, sniper fire announced that the conquest did not sit well with the entire enemy populace. Quitman instinctively attributed the outbreak to the lower classes—the "leperos"—whom he dismissed as "ragged beggarly, dirty Mexicans with blankets on," the most "infamous population with which any gr[e]at city was ever cursed." Three days were required to eliminate the sniper fire, an accomplishment effected only by sending troops into some homes, training artillery on others, and Scott's threatening the ayuntamiento (city council) that he might unleash his soldiers and let them sack the city if resistance did not subside.[17]

However, the diminution of sniper fire by no means relieved Quitman of efforts at pacification, as enemy resistance clothed itself in more subtle apparel. Churches closed their doors on September 19 to protest the occupation. Civilians took to enticing soldiers into drinking-houses, plying them with liquor, and then stabbing them to death. Meanwhile, American soldiers, prone to disorderliness after their hard campaign, risked inciting further opposition by committing unwarranted offenses against civilians.

Quitman counteracted the pressure toward confrontation in various ways. Not above heavy-handedness, he threatened the clergymen that if the churches remained closed, the American flag would be removed from church towers. It was unnecessary for him to elaborate that the soldiers would interpret this as a signal that churches were no longer under army protection, and that the troops might proceed to plunder the gold, silver, and other valuables. The ploy worked; the churches reopened.[18]

Generally, however, Quitman preferred carrot to stick. To soften impressions of the totality of American rule, he worked through the ayuntamiento: rather than strip it of authority, he permitted it to continue functioning, in the hope of achieving a cooperative approach to city government. When reports reached him that American soldiers were baiting local police, he issued stern orders that officers "suppress all cause of complaint" and punish such soldiers as "serious offenders." To deemphasize the physical presence of the military, he ordered army wagons off the Alameda. When he heard that the family of an imprisoned Mexican general was in ill health and destitute, he had the general paroled and gave the general's wife 3 ten-dollar gold pieces out of his own pocket. Yet Quitman always took care that his reconciliation efforts did not encourage a collapse of vigilance. Thus he issued orders that all unauthorized Mexican army officers in the city report to Inspector General Ethan Allen Hitchcock or risk punishment as spies, and warned American officers and men to wear their side arms while in the city streets.[19]

In time, the city settled down. Stores began opening their doors as early as September 17, and by October 1, Beauregard could describe as "quiet" the general atmosphere in the capital. Gradually, the Americanizing process, which Quitman had witnessed at Matamoros, Tampico, and other locales across the path of the American army, took hold. Mexico City teemed with "hotels, taverns, billiard rooms, *cafes*, and theatres—all advertized in the 'American style.'" Soldiers could have their daguerreotypes taken, attend performances of an American theatrical company at "El Nacional," where an orchestra belted out "Yankee Doodle" and "Hail Columbia" evey night to bring down the house, or take in the "Ethiopian extravaganza singer" at a nearby theater who filled the intermissions with renditions of "Lucy Neal," "Old Dan Tucker," and other familiar tunes from the States. Merchants appeared, to hawk such American culinary delights as mince pies and eggnog. Quitman entered a subscription to the *North American*, one of two American sheets now running presses in the city.[20]

Faced with a reduced enemy threat, Quitman could concentrate on administrative tasks. Burial procedures, prison security, replacing window glass in the palace, setting exchange rates for U.S. coins, processing restaurant applications, and handling leave-of-absence requests were his daily routine. He also reviewed legal disputes, such as a case of horse theft and an objection filed by a British resident over the confiscation of chewing tobacco he had purchased from a Spanish merchant. Complaints about Quitman's decisions seem to have been few, and there is no reason to doubt the *Daily American Star*'s assertion that Quitman won respect from natives—though "firm in his decisions, he is courteous and gentlemanly in his language and conduct towards all who have business with him." At the least, Quitman took his responsibilities conscientiously.

Though immersed in administrative detail, Quitman found time to address the future direction of American policy in Mexico. Despite the hope of the army high command that the Mexicans would now come to terms, the war dragged on. Thousands of enemy troops besieged the American garrison at Puebla at the very time American forces were entering Mexico City, and the siege persisted into early October. Reinforcements from Veracruz came under attack from organized enemy army units and guerrilla bands. American land and naval operations, on the other hand, also continued throughout Mexico. Santa Anna's resignation as president in late September and his subsequent surrender of the command of the Mexican army indicated that a better climate for negotiations might lie ahead, but for the time being, there were no Mexican peace initiatives.[21]

Mexico's resiliency perplexed Quitman. He volunteered to Scott to lead two thousand men and clear the National Highway to the coast, and gave further vent to his own imperialistic emotions. If the Mexicans refused a peace, he wrote Eliza, then perhaps the only alternative would be to "make this beautiful & rich country a portion of the United States." Again inviting public attention to his views, he sent Henry Foote an exuberant burst of manifest destiny: "I speak to you boldly, as *we* spoke when the Texas question arose, hold on to this country. It is destiny, it is ours." Quitman advocated annexation for both economic and geopolitical reasons. "Take the mines, & the sugar & coffee plantations, the olive groves, the vineyards, the bellowing herds & bleating flocks that slake their thirst in the snows of Orizaba and Popocatepetl, and lie down at night beneath the cocoa groves of the vallies [*sic*]." If the United States did not seize the moment, anarchy would make Mexico a "waif" vulnerable to seizure by England, which had considerable mining interests in the land. Could the United States afford, moreover, to concede to other nations control of transit between the Atlantic and Pacific oceans across Mexico's Isthmus of Tehuantepec? Such transit would one day provide "the power to tax the commerce of the world." Significantly, Quitman avoided mention of Mexico's meaning for slavery expansion, and argued that Foote need not worry that annexation would pose a danger to the Union. The war, thus, had pushed Quitman to an increasingly nationalistic orientation.

Patience, Quitman seems to have believed, was the most promising means to accomplish annexation. He ruled out military conquest of the whole country, saying that it would take fifty thousand men to garrison every state capital and take every important city, a requirement that was too costly and that would demoralize the army as a "war of details always does." Nor could he accept the policy being promoted by John C. Calhoun and others back in the States that the army should give up the capital, retire to a defensive line in northern Mexico, and wait things out. Quitman, rather, recommended that the government commit ten thousand men to the continued occupation of the capital and Veracruz and maintenance of communication between them. Tariff revenues, he believed, could cover the costs. Sooner or later the Mexicans, frustrated by their inability to break the American hold, would concede defeat.[22]

Although Quitman's policy orientation leaned toward a long-term American presence in the capital, he had little predilection to play much part in it. His quarters at the National Palace were pleasant enough. He liked to watch from his suite of rooms as fine carriages crossed the plaza, and he enjoyed the benefits of a richly furnished private parlor and the use of the presidential study for his bedroom. His request for a lieutenant governor to lighten his burden (submitted to Scott's headquarters) had been honored; he also directed a considerable staff. Yet, there were few social outlets. He joined other officers in an "Aztec Club" for the purpose of "friendly intercourse" and became its president. He also attended theater. But he was preoccupied with administrative chores, and, other than the earthquake which rocked the city on the morning of October 2, there was little to break the undramatic day-to-day routine. Though General Scott had announced that he would need all his officers and that none would be relieved except for severe cases of disability or ill health, Quitman sought alternative assignment. Ultimately, of course, he still hoped to achieve something in national politics; he wrote somewhat wistfully to Foote that he would "openly & boldly advocate" his strategic concepts were he by Foote's "side in the Senate." But his most realistic possibility for the time being seemed appointment to a more active army command. On October 25, in a letter to Scott's headquarters, Quitman renewed the issue which he had raised at Puebla of his need for "a command *in this army* suited to my rank." With an "inactive" force in quiet possession of the capital, there was no longer reason for him to remain "without an adequate command." Since the government might find it incumbent to undertake "partial reorganizations of the forces in the field" to subdue the continuing Mexican resistance, he wanted permission to report personally to the secretary of war "for some permanent assignment to duty." [23]

Scott not only came through with permission to report to Washington, but also endorsed Quitman's request with a note to Marcy verifying that Quitman had never received the regular division command which he merited by rank. Had it not previously required over a thousand men to escort Quitman safely, Scott intimated, he would have dispatched Quitman long since to the Rio Grande frontier to take over the new regular forces being assembled. [24]

Suddenly, after a year and a half in a foreign country, John Quitman was going home. Quickly he made plans. Fully intending to visit Monmouth before reporting to the War Department, he alerted Eliza to expect him. Eliza, who now fondly called him her "*Blue Beard*," had finally reconciled herself to his irrepressible militarism. "I have arrived at the conclusion and think that you did right in going to the Army," she had written earlier in the year. "I believe . . . that you never would have been satisfied with yourself had you not gone. . . . So my dear husband I have long since forgiven you, and am resigned to my fate." Anxious to see her, he anticipated again embracing the "beloved one of my youth and my mature years." Yet, he still suffered some pangs of conscience about leaving behind his fellow soldiers. On the same day he wrote Eliza, the officers of the volunteer division called on him at the National Palace. In an emotionally charged farewell ceremony, he found himself apologizing for leaving them and saying that he would stay were not a permanent field command at stake. [25]

Travel home waited upon the departure of a wagon train to the coast. It would have been far too dangerous for Quitman to attempt a solo trip down the guerrilla-infested National Highway. Scott had not sent a train eastward since the Puebla occupation. But he had a lot of wounded men who needed transfer from the poor quarters in the capital, and was now only waiting for the road to dry. Finally, on November 1, conditions were favorable and Quitman accompanied a train of four hundred wagons bound for the coast. Seventeen days later, he boarded the steamer *Alabama* at Veracruz. Since General Taylor had already asked for a leave, many newspapers assumed that Quitman would inherit Taylor's post as American commander in northern Mexico.[26]

In a sense, however, it mattered little whether Quitman's quest for a new field command was successful. The Mexican War, whatever its frustrations and tribulations, had already fulfilled the emotional needs which had initially brought Quitman to put his name forward for army service, and for the rest of his life, he would cling tenaciously to the associations he had formed during his campaigns. Following the war, he traveled to soldiers' reunions and put up many a wartime comrade at Monmouth. Eventually he would join the "Montezuma Society," a successor to the Aztec Club, which held at least a couple of annual meetings in New York City. "Com. Perry was here this morning to see us," reported Quitman's daughter Antonia during the 1856 reunion. "He with fifty or sixty officers of the Army and Navy will dine together tomorrow to commemorate the taking of Mexico. Father of course will be one of them. Capt Lovell almost lives in our parlor." Already, she noted, the officers were busy rehashing "the old times in the war."[27]

Certain calendar days, in particular, brought Quitman's thoughts back to the glory in Mexico. "This day five years ago was also Sunday," he wrote his son on September 13, 1852, "& spent by myself in bombarding Chapultepec. Tomorrow will be the anniversary of my entrance into the city of Mexico by the Belen gate." To have a visual reference, he spent $160 for a painting of Mexico City's Grand Plaza. Because he wanted others to similarly recall the war, he found himself promoting its memory. Thus he advanced funds for the production of lithographed lists of the Mississippi regiments and presided over a meeting to raise money for a monument to commemorate those Mississippians who died in the Mexican War. Quitman donated $100 to the latter cause, and was noted in the press as one of the first contributors.[28]

When newspapers and acquaintances began calling him "Old Chapultepec," Quitman must have been in his glory.[29] Though not encouraged by Quitman, the sobriquet aptly summed up the image of a weathered war hero which he hoped to project. After all, even after Mexico City fell, he kept his beard. It, too, commemorated his service at the Halls of Montezuma.

15

War Hero

IT was the fourth estate which ensured that John Quitman's return to the United States would prove anything but subdued. Naturally the hometown papers carried accounts of his exploits in the battle for Mexico City: "You should have seen our son Henry," Eliza had written on October 17, "it being Saturday he was in town, he got an extra courier [Natchez *Courier*] containing all the details of the battle, he came rapidly to me holding it extended in his hand, exclaiming with tears in his eyes . . . Oh Mama glorious news from Mexico! Papa has greatly distinguished himself." But all over the nation the press paid homage to what Robert W. Johannsen has aptly designated a "new set of heroes" ready to enter "the American pantheon," and Quitman was at the center of the celebration. Thus Philip Hone, former mayor of New York City, found his Saturday paper full of the "astonishing achievements of Scott, Worth, Quitman, Persifor Smith, Pillow, Twiggs, and the whole band of heroes." Even before Quitman boarded ship for home, the call was out in the press to give the "gallant old Southron" a "welcome, such as language cannot portray." [1]

Quitman could scarcely have anticipated how exuberant that welcome would be as he, Shields, and Colonel William S. Harney debarked the *Alabama* at New Orleans late at night on November 23, 1847. But the next day he undoubtedly began to comprehend what lay ahead. The Crescent City seemed to throw itself at his feet. Salutes in honor of the soldiers were fired from the Place d'Armes (today's Jackson Square) and Lafayette Square; tickets were offered for boxes at the theater; and all day long a stream of visitors poured in and out of their rooms at the St. Charles. "I am . . . almost pressed out of my apartments by the crowd of my countrymen—who are lionizing me," Quitman marveled. When the three officers arrived at the theater in the evening, a band heralded their entrance. After the performance, a crowd followed them back to the hotel, where "loud huzzas" summoned

Quitman and Shields to their balcony. Quitman was in his element, and, with due humility, thanked the crowd "in the name of his companions and of the army in Mexico." [2]

More hoopla attended Quitman's Natchez homecoming. An Adams County meeting had signaled local pride in Quitman by commissioning an ornate sword to be crafted in his honor and, though the sword remained unfinished when Quitman's steamer arrived at the landing on Saturday, November 27, the community more than amply demonstrated its appreciation. Quitman brought with him a couple of brass eighteen-pound Mexican cannon captured at Alvarado which Commodore Perry had presented him in atonement for the navy's blunder; that night the pieces were hoisted to the bluff and fired in Quitman's honor. Monday brought more cannon rounds and some formal festivities. Accompanied by an escort of Masons and War of 1812 veterans, Quitman paraded from Monmouth to the City Hall for a feast in his honor. Orators waxed eloquent, of course, and Quitman graciously accepted the congratulations of "an immense crowd of ladies." Though hoarse from speechmaking and conversation, Quitman made further public appearances in the days following the celebration. [3]

In mid-December, still assuming he would receive appointment to an active command, Quitman departed for Washington with Eliza and his eldest and youngest daughters in tow. Wherever his travels took him, he met people anxious to show their gratitude for his contribution to the war. News of his advent in Montgomery, Alabama, triggered a suspension of regular business in the Alabama legislature. A select legislative committee called on Quitman at his quarters and escorted him to the capitol for speeches of welcome. Charleston, South Carolina, outdid Montgomery. By the time Quitman arrived on December 22, the city was already in a frenzy over General Shields, who had preceded him by two days. Military honors greeted Quitman's arrival, and later in the day the Hibernian Society gave a dinner for the two generals. The next day the Masons followed suit. Even their exit on December 24 had to be done in style, as one diarist noted: "This day the [military] Companies were out to escort Generals Quitman and Shields to the Wilmington Boat on their way to the city of Washington. The Boat not arriveing [*sic*]—Genl. Quitman reviewed the troops on Horseback in front of the Charleston Hotel and were then dismissed. . . . Subsequently the Boat arrived late in the afternoon and both the Heroes left about 1/2 past 7 PM[.] Health Prosperity and Long Life attend them." [4]

Perhaps the most significant testimonials occurred in Washington. The Quitmans and General Shields arrived on December 27, giving national politicos occasion to express their veneration. At a sold-out dinner four nights later attended by Vice President George M. Dallas, Secretary of State

Buchanan, Senators Stephen A. Douglas of Illinois and Reverdy Johnson of Maryland, the mayor of the city W. W. Seaton, financier W. W. Corcoran, and other congressmen and nationally prominent individuals, the two heroes learned that the city on the Potomac loved them too.[5] The sight of distinguished American statesmen fawning over uniformed officers proved unsettling to the city's antiwar, antislavery newspaper, the *National Era*: "Heroes abound on every side. The citizen's garb is disdained. The drawing-room, the public walk, the Senate Chamber, are startled with the glare of military array. Is it of vital importance to the public, does the safety of the country demand that these men of the army should be assailing our eyes every day with their multitudinous and gilded finery?" The *Era* believed that homage to Quitman and Shields undermined the nation's traditional, healthy distrust of military institutions. What the paper did not recognize, however, was that Quitman and Shields were revered, in part, precisely because they were civilians who had *temporarily* donned military garb. To thousands of Americans, the two generals' successful records vindicated the *anti-militaristic* American tradition that the country did not need a massed soldiery to protect its boundaries. In an emergency, the militia and volunteers could do the job. Quitman dwelt on that very point at the dinner when he contended that the willingness of "free American citizens" to volunteer during the war justified the faith of the nation's "fathers" that America would not require "large standing armies" to preserve its independence.[6]

If Washington acted swiftly to fete Quitman, President Polk reacted cautiously to his petition for an active division command. "Your Father has gone this morning to see the President and Secretary of War," Eliza informed Henry in one letter. "I hope he may hear of what nature his appointment may be." Quitman, however, learned nothing conclusive. Although Polk lamented Scott's inability to provide Quitman a full division in Mexico, he would not guarantee that amends lay ahead. Polk queried Quitman as to what command he would prefer. Quitman designated General Taylor's former district, provided that he could establish headquarters at San Luis Potosí. Polk agreed in principle, but said that he would only confer the appointment if Congress passed the pending ten-regiment bill; this would allow him to add a brigade to the northern Mexico occupation force.[7] Thus Quitman remained in limbo.

With time to spare, Quitman continued to accept invitations to receptions (though he claimed to have "declined over one hundred invitations to public dinners and ceremonies"). He saw his share of railroad trains, taking the cars to Richmond in January and Albany in February. Both trips, which included invited addresses before state legislatures, evoked the fanfare that he by now had grown accustomed to: cheering throngs in holiday dress,

welcomes by governors and mayors, dinners, Masonic and military ceremonies, levees, gratis theater tickets, and balls. When he arrived at the
Hudson River at New York City en route to Albany, he was met by crowds
and reception committees on both sides of the river. "A splendid band
of music is pouring forth its harmonies; the steamboats are decorated with
many-colored bunting, and New York is ready to give him a glorious
welcome," observed one reporter.[8]

If the December trip to Washington had demonstrated what Americans
thought of Quitman, the January and February jaunts—though they certainly reflected his continuing popularity—perhaps were most significant
for what they revealed of Quitman's convictions about his country. Two
years before Quitman would recommend the secession of Mississippi from
the Union, he stood before the American people as an unabashed patriot and
nationalist. A Richmond *Enquirer* reporter at the Virginia legislature felt
that although people had so jammed every nook and cranny of the house
that he could not take notes during Quitman's speech, he simply had to
make mention of "one point touched upon eloquently and forcibly by
Gen. Quitman":

> Looking around at the interesting audience, he remarked that *here* was
> the great secret of the success of the American arms—that the officers
> and soldiers were but carrying out into practice the *American senti-
> ment*, which animated all ages and sexes—and that the approbation of
> a grateful country, and of a great and noble people, were . . . the
> brightest reward which a soldier could ask.

When Quitman arrived at the Hudson, his remarks focused on New York as
his "native home" and his "brothers" from the New York regiment. To the
legislature in Albany, he affirmed that as Americans with "one common
country and feelings enlisted in one common cause," they should all celebrate the national achievement in the war. Only by witnessing the tyranny
everywhere in Mexico did he achieve a full comprehension of the meaning
of free American institutions. In the U.S., he observed, there was no need
for "bolts and bars and bayonets to protect property":

> When I look . . . upon the facilities of intercourse through our ex-
> tended country—when I see our iron roads unprotected, and needing
> no protection from a standing guard—when I see the wires that com-
> municate intelligence with electric rapidity from one portion of our
> country to the other . . . I am filled with gratitude towards our fore-
> fathers and our countrymen who still preserve and adhere to our
> glorious institutions.

Thus republicanism guaranteed progress. Quitman revealed that he had experienced an "overpowering emotion" upon returning to the United States, where the "self-ruled" masses moved together "in harmony," after residing in a land torn by "misgovernment" and autocracy.[9]

Quitman also made a trip to Baltimore that winter. Consumption had taken his last brother, Henry, in November, leaving his sisters with bleak financial prospects. Henry had never managed to pay off the mortgage on their Maryland cottage, and they now depended on Quitman's arranging regular support payments. Exactly what transpired during this visit is unclear, but Quitman may have advised Eliza and Louisa to give up the property, as they auctioned their carriage, horses, and other valuable items the following March and moved to Philadelphia.[10]

Quitman kept his family with him on most of his trips, a pace which wearied Eliza, who became homesick for Monmouth. Louisa, on the other hand, took everything in stride, and emerged one of the bright lights of the Washington social season. "Miss Quitman is much admired," remarked one observer. "Her intercourse is as sweet as her fine form and features are surprisingly winning."

By all accounts a strikingly attractive young woman (now twenty-two), Louisa was accomplished in drawing, oil painting, and other decorative arts. More significantly, she possessed, as Edward Turner put it, a "cultivated mind." Whatever the prevailing mores about excluding politics from the women's sphere, Louisa maintained political convictions. Though she bowed to convention by sometimes prefacing opinions with disavowals of expertise—as, for example, "though I know or understand nothing about politics"—she nonetheless forged ahead and expressed her views. Quitman tolerated her outspokenness, even when she controverted his own convictions. During the war, she had rejected his imperialism. Reasoning from a nativist perspective, Louisa contended that annexing Mexico would damage the United States by incorporating a Catholic people who were both "ignorant" and "disorderly." She also followed current affairs enough to be able to praise Calhoun's "dignified" defensive line policy and note that Whigs would make political capital from Calhoun's falling out with the Polk administration. There was much to recommend Louisa, and it is little wonder that she captivated some of Washington's eligible bachelors.[11]

Unfortunately, Louisa preferred the wrong suitor. She fell in love with her father's traveling companion, James Shields. The bachelor general led her to believe that he had matrimonial intentions. When she discovered that Shields intended only a flirtation and was pursuing other women, she became disconsolate. Quitman reassured Louisa: sudden fame, he believed, had turned Shields's head; he had been spoiled by "too many attentions from

Quitman on horseback
From Chappel's original painting, in Gratz Collection, Historical Society of
Pennsylvania. Reprinted by permission of the Historical Society of
Pennsylvania.

George Poindexter
Reprinted by permission of the Mississippi Department of Archives and
History

A. G. McNutt
Reprinted by permission of the Mississippi Department of Archives and History

Albert G. Brown
Reprinted by permission of the Mississippi Department of Archives and
History

Henry S. Foote
Reprinted by permission of the Mississippi Department of Archives and
History

General Winfield Scott
Engraving by T. Doney. Reprinted by permission of the Library of Congress.

General Zachary Taylor
Reprinted by permission of the Library of Congress

Felix Huston
From Dudley G. Wooten, *A Comprehensive History of Texas, 1865 to 1897*
(2 vols.; Dallas: William G. Scarff, 1898).

ladies." Whether Quitman would have favored his daughter's betrothal to his friend, who was twenty years her senior, is unclear. But once it became evident that Shields did not want marriage, Quitman advised that Louisa and Eliza discontinue corresponding with him.[12]

While Quitman awaited action on his command application, he came in for some political speculation. This, 1848, was a presidential year, and the incumbent, Polk, had expressed no interest in a second term. The Democratic presidential and vice-presidential nominations seemed up for grabs. A visible symbol of the successful aspects of the war, and temporarily resident in the nation's capital to boot, Quitman inevitably drew a lot of attention.

Mississippi Democrats naturally led the way. The Vicksburg *Sentinel* endorsed him for either of the offices. In January the state party convention passed a resolution declaring its "abiding confidence" that Quitman was "equal to any station, and deserving the highest honor." The legislature further enhanced Quitman's prestige by incorporating a town in his honor in Clark County.[13]

Quitman did nothing to orchestrate the Mississippi boosterism. State pride responded spontaneously to his achievements; the state Democratic party naturally sought to promote its interests and the welfare of Mississippi through his candidacy. If Quitman abetted his chances in any significant way, it was by virtue of his October letter to Henry Foote about Mexican occupation policy. This statement helped elevate his candidacy from a case of state self-indulgence to a legitimate national movement. Foote released the letter in December, and it spread quickly to the nation through press reprintings. This was the first time that Quitman had ever addressed a national constituency on a policy matter. Overnight he transcended his presence as soldier-hero and rose to that of statesman, particularly with the expansionist wing of the Democracy. Many Democrats by 1848 believed that the United States should annex all of Mexico, and they found Quitman's sentiments very appealing. His bombastic nationalism on tour, moreover, enhanced his acceptability, as did the politic stance he adopted on the controversial issue of whether the United States should rely on regular soldiers or volunteers for its defense. Although Quitman praised the volunteer soldiery in his remarks to the New York legislature, he added circumspectly that West Point and regular troops had provided the "necessary nucleus" for citizen soldiers to rally around. How could anyone take offense?[14]

Rumors swept through the southern states that Quitman would receive the nod for either the Democratic presidential or vice-presidential nomination. A New Orleans *Daily Picayune* reporter in Washington, for instance, believed that Quitman was emerging the *pis aller* for the supporters of several presidential hopefuls who feared that the Democratic nomination would fall to General Worth. Another report intimated that supporters of Senator Lewis Cass of Michigan regarded Quitman as the best prospect for balancing the Democratic ticket. President Polk heard that the Tennessee State Democratic Convention, though refraining from formal nominations, preferred Quitman for vice president. Nullifiers in Charleston, South Carolina, looked to Quitman to carry their standard as president. By late January, one anti-imperialistic Whig U.S. senator had pessimistically conceded that Quitman's selection on an expansionist platform was a foregone conclusion. Willie P. Mangum of North Carolina predicted that "the bold, broad & unprincipled issue of the entire Conquest of Mexico, & the perpetual holding of the conquered Country" would be presented by "the friends of Cass & Quitman." Mangum was so concerned about the strength that the popular Quitman would bring to the Democratic ticket, he felt it might be incumbent upon the Whigs to turn to a military man like Scott or Taylor to neutralize Quitman's appeal.[15]

Amid all this speculation, Quitman and his family left Washington. After dusk on February 19, a New Orleans *Delta* correspondent had arrived from the seat of war bearing a peace treaty which Nicholas Trist had finally worked out with Mexican commissioners. According to the treaty, initialed at Guadalupe Hidalgo on February 2, the United States received Texas to the Rio Grande, New Mexico, and California for $15 million and American disavowal of claims against Mexico. Although the treaty did not cede Baja California or control of transit across Tehuantepec to the United States, and certainly fell far short of the ambitions of some "All-Mexico" proponents, it conformed enough to Polk's initial war design to gain the administration's acceptance. Polk submitted the instrument to the Senate, which ratified it formally on March 10. Any need for new regiments—and a command for Quitman—seemed to vanish with Senate passage of the treaty. The Quitmans, with little reason to remain in Washington, set off for Mississippi on March 13.[16]

By month's end, Quitman was back at Monmouth.[17] Even though almost half a year had passed since his return from Mexico, his state had still not had its fill of feting its hero. After all, his Adams County neighbors had not yet found occasion to present him their sword, the citizenry of Jackson had extended an invitation way back in December, and now Vicksburg wanted in on the show. So it was time for one final round of welcoming speeches, torchlit parades, Masonic receptions, feasts, and the other trappings that accompanied fame. Quitman fulfilled his Natchez commitment on April 11. Early in May, he visited both Jackson and Vicksburg for receptions and ceremonies.

If nationalism proved the mark of Quitman's eastern progression, chivalry carried the day in Mississippi. In Natchez, Quitman praised the "fair ladies." At Jackson, female academy students threw flowers into his carriage, leading Quitman to congratulate the "rainbow arch of beauty" gracing the community. Everywhere Quitman impressed onlookers as properly modest in speech. Everywhere Quitman demonstrated magnanimity of spirit, even applying the adjective "gallant" to his rival, Jefferson Davis. Riding on the crest of his popularity, Quitman was in a mellow mood.[18]

Quitman alluded in his Natchez speech to the possibility that he might have to brandish his new sword in war. However, he was staking his hopes on his political prospects. He had eyed national office, without result, for years. Now things seemed to be coming his way. As he put it to Lovell, the "gales of popular favor" were blowing with sufficient force to propel him into "the tempestuous ocean of politics." By April, Quitman was actively promoting his own candidacy. Before leaving Washington, he had released a summary of his political views in reply to the "very complimentary remarks in relation to myself and the presidency" made by a Virginia correspondent. Now he helped edit a ghostwritten biography of himself to enhance his national visibility. Carefully he manipulated the words to preserve his image as a consensus candidate:

> To avoid misconstruction and the jealous criticism of my friends in the regular army, I submit to your judgment the following—
> In 8th line from bottom of page 14 after the word "resource" insert: *with a comparatively small regular establishment*—maybe—or some words to indicate that I wish not to dispense entirely with a regular army nor underrate their services.

He seemed to be succeeding. A supporter wrote that his name was "spoken of frequently in connection with the Vice Presidency, particularly in Washington," and that it had become almost a "settled *thing*" that he would be nominated for the second slot to balance the ticket if a northerner were the Democratic presidential candidate. Quitman looked ahead to the May gathering of the Democrats in Baltimore with optimism.[19]

Quitman learned the convention's decision while on a trip back east. Technically still a general in the army, he remained subject to military orders. Upon returning from his Vicksburg appearance, Quitman found instructions waiting for him. He was to report to Frederick, Maryland, where his testimony was desired in a court of inquiry on May 29 or soon thereafter.[20]

At issue was a messy quarrel between General Scott and some of his subordinate commanders. The dispute derived from Scott's dissatisfaction with Gideon Pillow's official reports about the battles before Mexico City, as well as Scott's exasperation over anonymous letters appearing in the press. These documents inflated Pillow's role, while minimizing Scott's contribution, during the late stages of the campaign. Pillow emerged a leader virtually directing grand strategy. Supposedly, for instance, Scott was so demoralized by the "disaster" at Molino del Rey that he would never have ordered the Chapultepec assault had he not been persuaded by Pillow's strategic insight. Pillow's bravery also received unearned plaudits: it was suggested that he had been wounded in the charge on the castle and had had himself carried in the forefront of the assault while in that condition; actually Pillow had been wounded by a ricocheting shot when under cover and was brought to the castle behind his troops.

The feud involved General Worth, who took offense at Scott's General Orders 349 of November 12, which attempted to suppress the release of accounts to the press; it also brought Brevet Lieutenant Colonel James Duncan, who professed authorship of one of the controversial letters, into the lists on Pillow's side. Scott arrested all three under a variety of charges, permitting them the freedom of Mexico City while they awaited court proceedings. President Polk, never inordinately enamored of Scott anyway and upset over breaking reports about Scott's Puebla bribe attempt, had the three officers released, and also had Worth assigned to command at his highest brevet rank and Scott replaced by William O. Butler as occupation commander. Secretary of War Marcy initiated the court of inquiry supposedly to investigate Scott's complaints as well as charges lodged against Scott by Worth and Pillow. Quitman, having been deeply involved in the disputed incidents, was expected to have information bearing on the case.[21]

Complying promptly with the summons, Quitman, on May 14, boarded an upriver steamer. On May 22, about the time he passed through Cincinnati, the Democratic convention convened in Baltimore. Reports continued to reach Quitman that he would win the vice-presidential nod, but the party did not oblige. The delegates chose Lewis Cass as their presidential candidate, and, conforming to press speculation, turned to the South for Cass's running mate. Quitman was one of six southerners put up for the position. He ran strong on the first ballot, drawing a lot of support from the lower South, Old Northwest, and Middle Atlantic states. He even got 5 votes from the hotbed of abolitionism, Massachusetts. His 74 votes trailed only the front-runner, General William O. Butler, whose 114 fell well short of the necessary two-thirds margin. William Yancey of Alabama, an outspoken states' rights proponent whom Quitman had met in Montgomery in December, abandoned his state's favorite son for Quitman on the next ballot; but large numbers of New England, lower Northwest, upper South, and

Pennsylvania delegates united behind Butler. The Kentuckian, a sectional moderate, easily captured the nomination.[22]

When Quitman received the news, he made valiant effort to mask his disappointment. Thus he professed to Eliza indifference about his defeat, and graciously suggested to John Nevitt that Butler better deserved the nomination. Yet he could betray his own emotions only to a point. Irked by reports from informants that old nemesis Alexander McNutt—one of the convention delegates—had poisoned his chances by telling other delegates about his onetime support for John Quincy Adams and alleging that he had waited until 1844 to become a Democrat, and bothered by intimations that Jefferson Davis had opposed his candidacy, Quitman convinced himself that a majority of the delegates had gone to Baltimore inclined to his nomination but had changed their minds because of the "old falsehood" of his supposed Whiggery and some political deals.[23]

Quitman met delays in his scheduled testimony in the Pillow case. He reached Washington on Friday, May 25, spent the weekend at his lodgings, and set out for Frederick on Monday according to his summons, only to discover that testimony had been postponed because General Pillow had not arrived. Returning to the capital, Quitman utilized his time to pressure the War Department into awarding him a brevet major generalship for his Monterrey exploits. Polk had hesitated in conferring the brevet, on the grounds that it would not be appropriate for a volunteer officer. But Quitman countered this logic, informing Marcy that other volunteer officers had since been breveted and that Polk had confessed Quitman's claim to the award in a conversation in Robert J. Walker's presence. Without the recognition, Quitman contended, there would be "an implied censure" of his "conduct at Monterrey" which would jeopardize his reputation.[24]

Quitman, however, did not curry favor with the administration in the Pillow case. The Tennessee general had finally appeared at Frederick on June 5, and Quitman attended the court the next two days to give his evidence. Despite ties to Worth and Duncan, Quitman in his testimony generally corroborated Scott's argument. Quitman denied that Pillow had taken a forward position on the need to attack Chapultepec; rather, Pillow had favored an attack from the south against the San Antonio Gate and been relatively reserved about expressing any opinion at all. Quitman also could not substantiate reports that Pillow had opposed the unfortunate armistice with Santa Anna. On the other hand, Quitman did confirm that in Mexico City, Pillow had initiated several efforts to smooth over differences with Scott. The court instructed Quitman to hold himself available for ten days—further testimony might be required. But there was no recall, and on July 1 the decision was rendered. Finding no conclusive evidence linking Pillow to the newspaper articles, and deciding that Pillow's battle reports were within legitimate bounds, the court determined that the specifications against Pillow should be dismissed.[25]

Though now technically free to return home, Quitman lingered in and around Washington. Polk acceded to his request for a brevet, but Quitman remained unsatisfied with his official army status and wanted to straighten matters out before departing. The Senate, not in session in April, 1847, when he had been promoted to major general of regulars, had never confirmed the appointment. Honor demanded that his selection receive official endorsement. Quitman, therefore, urged President Polk to see the matter through.

Polk looked upon the omission as innocuous, since the pending dismissal of the volunteers would render academic any need for the appointment. But Quitman was persistent, lobbied with other army officers and congressmen to induce the president to act, and Polk soon felt the heat enough to complain that Quitman was working the hotels and putting "out of doors" pressure to bear on him. Reputedly, Quitman had even threatened to "make an issue" of it if the president failed to act. Polk resented the pressure and was inclined to let the matter rest. However, Jacob Thompson soothed the president with assurances that Quitman had not voiced any threats, and Marcy and other advisors recommended putting the nomination through. Polk sent the matter to the Senate for action on July 7.

Quitman's case then faltered in the Senate Committee on Military Affairs, where Jefferson Davis, to Quitman's ill fortune, was sitting as temporary chair. Days passed without action, and July 20—the day Polk set for the discharge of the volunteer forces—rapidly approached. In desperation, Quitman called on Senator Foote at his Georgetown Heights house, and persuaded him to intervene. Foote demanded an executive session of the Senate, a device which enabled him to pry the report out of committee. Though Davis advised inaction, Foote and Stephen Douglas took strong exception. Foote apparently threatened Davis that if he did not relent, he would expose the whole matter to Mississippi's voters, who would hardly be appreciative that Davis had prevented a state hero from receiving his due. The nomination carried. When Quitman officially became a private citizen again on July 20, he could do so with a sense that the nation had fully met its responsibility to him.[26]

While still in the East, Quitman also arranged the final steps in his son's education. Waldo had certified Henry as ready for collegiate study, and the school Quitman had his eye on was easily accessible from Washington. Ever since colonial times, Princeton had been a mecca for the sons of the southern upper class. Among Quitman's social circle in Natchez, it was particularly fashionable. John B. Nevitt and plantation magnate William J. Minor had both entrusted their sons to the New Jersey institution, and one of Eliza's cousins had attended. In 1840, the school's Cliosophic Society had extended Quitman an honorary membership. Quitman never considered an alternative: Princeton would put the finishing touches on the gentleman's education he was providing his son. Thus, after testifying in the Pillow case, Quitman visited the school, where he not only enrolled Henry for the next winter's term and arranged his board but also scouted the college and community. Quitman, ever the director of his son's upbringing, was concerned that Henry fall into the right "social intercourse" and join the right organizations. Such preparations, he assured Eliza, would prove beneficial for Henry's "conduct & future happiness." Eight years tardy, Quitman underwent formal initiation into the Cliosophic Society, so that he could investigate whether it matched his perceptions of Henry's needs. (It passed the test; Henry joined shortly after his arrival at Princeton.)[27]

Taking the northern river route for the third time in the last five months, Quitman made his way homeward in late July, returning to a wife who still harbored illusions that he would one day retire from public life. Weeks earlier, upon hearing of her husband's disappointment about the vice presidency, Eliza had urged him once more to forfeit political ambition and become a "domestic man." Eliza contended that he would have found high political office "hollow and empty" had he achieved it, and expressed a conviction that true personal satisfaction derived from the happiness which she and the children could provide.[28]

Quitman, however, had no more interest than he had had before in settling down and managing his home and plantations. There would be future campaigns. If he had not yet demonstrated sufficient reliability as a party man, and if such deficiencies had spoiled his chances at Baltimore, then he would just have to try harder. Thus in June he had written John Nevitt that Mississippi Democrats should rally behind the Cass-Butler ticket, and he sent a ringing endorsement of the national Democracy in a letter declining attendance at an Independence Day rally in Philadelphia. He praised the "great Democratic party" for its traditional adherence to the principles which had brought the country "happiness, prosperity and power." He lauded the party's choice of "distinguished citizens" with "long and honorable career[s] in the public service" as nominees. The Whigs, however, had deserted their traditional principles and leadership and nominated Zachary Taylor, a "military chieftain," whose opinions on such issues as internal improvements, the tariff, and banking were not even public knowledge. As he passed through Louisville in late July on his journey home he gave an oration to the city's Democratic faithful.[29]

Using Monmouth as his base, Quitman labored diligently for the party cause from his arrival home straight up to the November election. "I am doing all I can for Cass and Butler," he wrote Shields on September 9, and indeed he was. That very day he had contributed $20 to the local Democratic club and had given a major address at the courthouse. In that speech he took extreme liberties with history when he told the people why circumstances mandated a Democratic vote. Democratic presidents and their policies, he contended, deserved sole credit for America's progress in "population, commerce, navigation, arts, science and husbandry." Whigs, in contrast, had been shown to be poor prophets in their statements that destruction of the Bank of the United States and passage of a low tariff would ruin the country. In early October, he issued a public letter to a Democratic committee in Franklin County, claiming that almost all Taylor supporters in the North countenanced abolitionism, but the "sterling Democracy" in that section could be counted on. Quitman urged that southerners demonstrate by their votes that they appreciated the "noble band of Northern and Western Democrats, who with Gen. Cass at their head, are defending our Thermopylae." Fighting off a bad cold, Quitman traveled down to Clinton, Louisiana, later in the month to join Felix Huston in addressing a Democratic barbecue. On November 6, Quitman appeared at the Pharsalia Race Course by day and the city market by night to rally last-minute support for Cass. Calling Cass a mild but firm man, Quitman said that he had grown to "love" the Democratic nominee and that voters should beware General Taylor's running mate, Millard Fillmore of New York. Fillmore, he warned, harbored anti-slavery convictions.[30]

Before it was all over, Quitman even wound up being one of Cass's Mississippi electors. When Alexander McNutt, who was serving in that capacity, died shortly before the election, the state Democratic Central Committee hurriedly chose Quitman as a replacement and altered the Democratic tickets at the last minute. Despite fears that the resulting confusion would damage Cass's chances, the Michigan senator carried the state by a few hundred ballots. Quitman traveled to Jackson in December to cast his electoral vote, but it was in a losing cause; though Taylor and Cass evenly split the thirty states in the Union, Taylor emerged with the most electoral votes and the presidency.[31] Nonetheless, Quitman had given convincing proof of his Democratic regularity in consecutive presidential contests. His loyalty put him in good stead for another bid for high national office.

Unfortunately for Quitman's ambition, a political storm brewing over the future of slavery in the United States already threatened to neutralize all the good will in Democratic circles which Quitman had established. In August, 1846, a Pennsylvania Democrat named David Wilmot had attached an amendment to an appropriations bill before the United States House of Representatives which would have prohibited slavery in any territory acquired from Mexico. This stipulation, or Wilmot Proviso, passed consecutive sessions of the House but failed to gain Senate approval, and thus was never enacted into law. Nevertheless, it stirred up a hornet's nest which ultimately had a profound influence upon Quitman's career.

The Wilmot Proviso brought the issue of slavery expansion squarely before the American people, since most Americans assumed that the United States would acquire at least some Mexican territory as the fruit of war. Northern advocates of the containment of slavery, who became known as Free-Soilers, crusaded for passage of the proviso, and managed to steer endorsement of it through several state legislatures; southerners, meanwhile, grew apprehensive about the social, political, and economic consequences if Free-Soilers succeeded in excluding their way of life from the territories. Some southern leaders responded to the threat with remedial proposals. Calhoun, for instance, put a series of resolutions before the Senate in February, 1847, which contended that the states owned the territories as common property, and that citizens of the various states, therefore, had a constitutional right to go to those territories with their own property, including, of course, slaves. Congress would be infringing upon the Constitution, he asserted, were it to impair that right. A year later, William Yancey's "Alabama Platform"—which maintained that Congress had a *duty* to protect slavery in the territories—passed the Alabama Democratic state convention.

Nothing had been decided when the 1848 presidential campaign got under way. In fact, the issue became more divisive because the Trist treaty, which added over 500,000 square miles to the national domain, meant that Americans were no longer dealing with a hypothetical problem, and much of the campaign revolved around the issue. The Whigs, hoping to alienate neither North nor South, avoided drafting a national platform; Taylor, moreover, avoided clear position statements on the issue. Cass, on the other hand, tried to fashion a compromise which would appeal to both sections. In December, 1847, he had written a letter to A. O. P. Nicholson of Nashville, Tennessee, suggesting what later became known in American political jargon as "popular sovereignty." Cass contended that Congress should refrain from taking *any* position on slavery in the territories and, in true democratic-majoritarian fashion, leave the whole matter up to the people actually living in the territories. The Free-Soilers, meanwhile, merged with dissident elements in both major political parties and formed a third party. Former president Martin Van Buren ran for president in 1848 as the Free-Soiler candidate; though he failed to take any states, he did poll some 291,000 votes and altered the political balance of power in several states.

Free-Soil agitation impaled Quitman on the horns of an ambition-ideology dilemma. For all his talk about the glories of American republican institutions and the reliability of the northern Democracy, he was profoundly troubled by the implications of the Wilmot Proviso, and this jeopardized his commitment to party. Wilmot and Van Buren, after all, were both Democrats. Their defection, and the abandonment of the regular party structure by thousands of other party members in the North over the slavery issue, portended ill. The Democratic party in the past had usually worked to repress sectional debate over slavery; perhaps the party, to maintain its northern backing, would be far less solicitous of southern needs in the years to come.

Quitman had championed Cass partly on the grounds that leaving slavery up to territorial inhabitants seemed an equitable answer to the imbroglio and might ensure some expansion of the institution. In February, long before Cass's nomination, a newspaper correspondent reported Quitman as believing that "the condition of a territory is a mere ordinance of congress, and that great political rights in the hands of the people, are not touched by it. If there is the climate, the products and market for southern staples in Mexico, the people will avail themselves of the cheapest labor, and if it is necessary, establish without hesitancy, the institution of slavery." In his September speech at Natchez, Quitman had explicitly endorsed Cass on the basis of the Nicholson letter.[32]

Yet, Quitman's seemingly confident endorsements of Cass and the Democracy veiled doubts about their reliability. Though it had been a long time since Quitman had been able to provide his plantations close personal attention, he identified with the southern slaveholding class more than ever. Having years earlier divested himself of bank and railroad interests, Quitman was far less the entrepreneur than he had been in the 1830s, when Mississippians had first expressed serious apprehensions about the perils of abolitionism. He was not at all sure that moderates such as Cass would forever be able to control the northern Democracy and see to it that southern institutions were protected. He had observed in his letter to the Philadelphia Democracy that "discontented and misguided men" were attempting to "introduce into the Democratic creed new and inadmissable tests of faith." He was hardly certain that they would not ultimately succeed. As he told the Clinton Democratic barbecue, the time was not distant when southerners would have to abandon political party identifications and rally around the southern rights cause if they wanted to preserve their way of life.

Following the election, Quitman would wrestle anew with the tension existing between his slaveowner's identity and his political aspirations. His resolution would not only risk a forfeiture of whatever hopes for the presidency or the vice presidency he still cherished, but would push him to ideologies diametrically opposed to his recent nationalistic rhetoric. During the campaign, though he avoided talk of secession as a counter to antislavery agitation, he undoubtedly was already considering that option when he told the Clinton Democracy that they could not submit to invasions of southern rights.[33] Soon after Cass's defeat, Quitman would, for the second time in his life, assume a position on the radical fringe of southern politics.

16

Civilizing the "Rosin-heels"

QUITMAN had every reason for concern as he waited at the Natchez landing on a day late in January, 1849, for the steamship which would take his son off to college. Henry, to be sure, had fine academic preparation. Waldo's training was so thorough that Henry would be entering Princeton at the sophomore level. However, Henry's pending departure signified a release from parental control, and Quitman feared that he might cultivate bad habits or make undesirable acquaintances. Then, too, the dread cholera had reappeared in the United States for the first time since the epidemic which had taken Edward and young John Anthony. Quitman worried that his sole surviving son would contract the disease during his trip.[1]

Quitman's forebodings persisted after Henry's safe arrival at Princeton in February. He not only asked several Mexican War officer acquaintances from Philadelphia and Princeton to keep a benevolent watch over his son's activities but also tried to shape the general context of Henry's collegiate experience. Perceiving the function of college to be as much the molding of a "gentleman" as the conveying of knowledge, Quitman sent a stream of advice touching virtually all aspects of Henry's affairs from academics to finances to morals. Henry was told to become "well acquainted with the elements of science" and to "pursue every branch of knowledge" as if his reputation depended on mastery; Henry was asked to keep detailed financial ledgers and avoid borrowing money when possible; Henry was urged to maintain a diary where he could record his "tastes, feelings and opinions" as well as events. Many of Quitman's admonitions, with their practical emphasis on the work ethic, could have been pirated from Ben Franklin. Quitman told his son to exercise, sleep no more than seven hours a night and waste no more than a half hour a day on personal grooming, and avoid deferring "to the morrow what you can do today." When it came time for Henry to plan his summer vacation, Quitman knew precisely where his son should go, whom he should see, and how he should behave:

I . . . propose that you first spend a day or two in the city of New York, calling merely on your mother's uncle Love Baker. Thence to Rhinebeck for a day or two. You will there find your aunts, who have taken board for a part of the summer in the parsonage house where I spent my infancy. Thence to Clermont to salute Dr. Wackerhagen & family. Thence a short visit to the Catskill mountain house. Spend a couple of days in Albany & call upon your aunt & cousins. Thence to Niagara where you will not be satisfied in less than 3 or 4 days. . . . Return by Lake George and Saratoga and before you settle down at College visit Philadelphia. . . . When in Rhinebeck visit the tomb of your Grandfather & mother. Wherever you go . . . take your quarters independently at a Hotel. Do not extend your calls or visits so as to interfere with the business of any one. . . . Move from place to place leisurely, without haste or hurry but without waste of time. . . . Form acquaintances but do it with caution. From every point write to one of us.

Quitman even sought to guide Henry's ideological maturation, fearing that centralist political doctrines current in some circles in the North might undermine what Henry had learned at home about states' rights. Beware, Quitman wrote, of the "high federal heresies of Kent's and Story's Commentaries on the Constitution." [2]

Unfortunately, Henry could not fully measure up to his father's standards. His most serious derelictions occurred over the summer, when he fell in with some West Point cadets and neither conformed to his father's itinerary nor kept his parents posted on his whereabouts. After waiting for two months for news, Quitman exploded that he was "mortified" over Henry's silence and that he had assumed that "a family feeling if not a respect for my wishes would have induced you to visit my native place and shown yourself to my relations, or at least that you would have given me the reasons for a departure from the tour which I had planned for you." Were his "high hopes" for Henry on the verge of ruin? Quitman complained that Henry's failing made it painful to be a parent, and threatened a correspondence with the Princeton faculty, however humiliating, to learn about Henry's performance. Quitman also queried whether Henry had been late in joining the junior class after the vacation. When Henry finally responded to his father's remonstrances, he did so in such a "chilly" manner that he threw Quitman into even more emotional turmoil. Quitman reassured Henry that he only extended advice for his own good, and did not mean to impugn Henry's honor. After all, he could hardly be blamed for "anxiously watching over" his son's education and desiring to share his son's joy and sorrows. It took several exchanges of letters before a reconciliation could be fully effected.[3]

Part of the generational strain derived from concern about finances. Like countless modern parents, Quitman was chagrined to discover that the cost of higher education could greatly exceed one's anticipations. Quitman complained about exorbitance in Henry's accounts throughout his son's time at college, but was particularly distressed about it this first year. "To pay the bills which you report to me, the tailor's bill & your pocket money," Quitman lamented in one letter, "will require nearly $400 in addition to the $500 you have received. This will be $900 in eight months, a sum considerably greater than I supposed all your expenses could possibly amount to."[4]

Quitman, of course, believed it necessary to foster moderation and prudence as character traits in his son. But significant financial reverses in 1849 made Quitman particularly intolerant of Henry's excesses. Quitman had never paid the judgment rendered against himself as security for Charles Mayson in the Adams County Circuit Court in 1840, but rather had appealed to the High Court of Errors and Appeals. However, the high court affirmed the circuit court's decision in a February, 1849, ruling. Quitman also discovered that he still owed money to Robert J. Walker on a note which he thought his agents had paid during the war. In addition, the cotton crops were deficient, and he lost a good number of slaves to cholera. Quitman, by no means, faced bankruptcy: "I will not say that I am not able to afford such expenditures," he conceded to Henry. The strain of meeting obligations, however, necessitated a careful watch over Henry's money.[5]

Until the fall of 1849, Quitman spent most of the year at Monmouth, though he still left for weeks at a stretch. He proceeded to Jackson immediately after Henry's departure to see to the high court litigation; in March, accompanied by Louisa, he visited New Orleans on a business trip. But in a relative sense, he was around home far more than he had been in many years. Eliza's letters to Henry portray her husband in an uncharacteristically domestic context—there are glimpses of him sallying out to shoot at robins in his vegetable garden, constructing a chicken yard, and immersed in the demolition of his old stable and barn so that a new brick structure could be raised. In one letter, Eliza wrote in a moment of obvious affection how funny Quitman looked with "a venerable gobbler in his arms," trying to teach the turkey to climb a ladder so that it would roost in a pine tree.[6]

Quitman's letters to his wife in the years after the war are replete with expressions of affection. He called Eliza the "best friend I have on earth," and liked to shower her with presents. "Take them with all my heart," he urged from New Orleans on one occasion. "You know I do not feel rich enough *now* to make them more costly." Yet, whether Quitman's fault or not—and his residency at home soon proved short-lived—Eliza suffered recurrent bouts of depression. She complained about frequent headaches, disinterest in the "excitements of the world," and reluctance to "mix in what the world calls society." She found her fulfillment in countless hours alone on Monmouth's gallery or sitting beside a walk contemplating her home's "melancholy charm" and attached memories. No one else, she believed, could comprehend how many "afflictions and trials" she had endured during her "lonely and solitary life at Monmouth." Neighbors and other acquaintances found her disagreeable company, and ceased returning social calls. Antonia related in one letter how her mother had come to rationalize that rainy weather was keeping people away when actually the days were "delightful." Eliza could not admit, Antonia remarked, that people lacked "interest" in her.

What relief Eliza found from her melancholy came primarily from religion, something that Quitman could not share with her. She had become increasingly devout over the last several years, and it appears that an otherworldliness sheltered her from whatever she found lacking in her relationship with others. She wrote her stepmother that, with good works and faith, they could soon arrive "at that blessed rest which remaineth for the good people of God" where they would discover "exquisite happiness." Mention of Providence now permeated her written expression, and her reading interests tended toward such volumes as Henry Blunt's *Lectures Upon the History of Our Lord and Saviour Jesus Christ.* Whereas Quitman, for instance, urged good behavior on Henry for utilitarian reasons, Eliza insisted on morality for spiritual fulfillment. Henry should cultivate his intellect at Princeton, and he should always employ it in the service of "God our Father and Saviour Jesus." "If God has given you wealth," she instructed, "if you expend it not to the nourishment of pride and luxury, not only to gratify your own pleasure of humor, but to the furtherance of God's honor . . . you do honor to your Creator." [7]

Perhaps the church represented Eliza's answer to Quitman's preoccupation with political affairs. If so, the Mississippi diocese of the Episcopal church surely benefited from her anxiety. Church documents record her pledging $200 for the bishop's salary, and becoming a life member of the "Protestant Episcopal Society for the Diffusion of Christian Knowledge in the Diocese of Mississippi," which was established to send out missionaries and disseminate Bibles, prayer books, and religious tracts. She put up ministers and bishops at Monmouth and summarized their sermons in her letters. Of course church attendance was very important to Eliza; she considered it the only meaningful activity she engaged in beyond the confines of

Monmouth. It became a source of considerable satisfaction to her when Quitman attended church with her during the convention of the Mississippi Episcopal diocese in May, 1849, and seemed "charmed and deeply impressed" by the sermons.[8]

Quitman attended church, that May, a front-runner for the Democratic gubernatorial nomination. For two months, county conventions and party organs had been busy promoting his selection. Democratic politicos recognized the advantage of having a war hero head their ticket, and anticipated that Quitman would draw a modicum of Whig support and ease into office. Quitman remained a Democratic partisan; after attending Vicksburg receptions for Whig president-elect Zachary Taylor, he denounced his former commander as an "uncouth," incessant talker who was so trite that local Whigs were "ashamed." Nonetheless, the hopes of Democratic leaders that Quitman would draw some opposition support were not unrealistic. Many Whigs did remember Quitman as a former ally who had affiliated with the probond camp, the "best man" the Democrats could offer.[9]

By the time the Democratic state convention assembled in Jackson on June 18, Quitman's nomination was only a formality. Apparently Quitman expected success, as he was in town though not a delegate. His nomination, in fact, passed uncontested at the opening session. He accepted the call that afternoon.

The convention took place amid a buzz of rumors that former president Polk had died, and that night, after the reports had been verified, Quitman gave a eulogy in support of a resolution of sorrow introduced by Jefferson Davis (word subsequently leaked out that Quitman and Davis had mended fences). Quitman praised Polk as "master-spirit of the Texas movement" and fountainhead of the "progressive policy" of the Democrats—presumably a reference to Polk's engineering of tariff reductions and an independent treasury. He also claimed that nationalistic revolutions which had erupted against European monarchs in 1848 took inspiration from American prosperity and success in the Mexican War: obviously, the American democratic experiment worked, and other peoples wanted to assume its benefits. However smug and narrow-minded Quitman may have been in suggesting American inspiration of the protests and uprisings which had swept across France, Austria, Hungary, Italy, and other countries on the Continent, the bombastic content of his remarks serves notice that, as late as mid-1849, this Mississippi planter-aristocrat retained some faith that the American Republic had bright prospects.[10]

Quitman almost ran uncontested. Mississippi's Whig party had been falling off in popularity; there was considerable thought in party circles that it would be futile politically as well as counterproductive to challenge

Quitman, given his quasi-Whig ideology. Whigs gave striking evidence of their indecision when their belatedly summoned state convention met in July and nominated Thomas G. Polk, a political unknown who had never held state office, yet simultaneously *passed* a resolution virtually endorsing Quitman:

> *Resolved*, That in Gen. John A. Quitman, the nominee of the Democratic convention . . . we recognize the gallant soldier, the upright gentleman, and an early and unflinching advocate of the payment of the Union and Planters' Bank Bonds; and that, next to our own nominee, we will hail his election as the best evidence of a reform, both in taste and principle, in the Democratic party of Mississippi.

Given these circumstances, Polk can surely be pardoned for declining his party's nomination.[11]

The Whigs finally mounted a concerted campaign against Quitman in August, when Luke Lea, a one-legged Jackson attorney and former state legislator, was persuaded to accept their now tainted nomination. Whigs dredged up the old repudiation issue, and tried to undermine Democratic confidence in Quitman by reminding voters of Quitman's previous heresy. Should Democrats really support a trimmer who shaped his politics "to the popular breeze for the sake of gratifying an unworthy ambition"? Lea took to the stump, hammering away at Quitman's unreliability on the bond issue. In a speech at Canton, Lea asserted that Quitman's Transfer Act had cost the people three million dollars and had set the stage for the failure of the Planters' Bank bonds. It was a shrewd tactic: by diverting public attention from Quitman's war record to mundane facets of economic policy, Lea and the Whig organs hoped to reduce their opponent from demigod to common politician.[12]

Despite the Whig offensive, Quitman entertained illusions that he could win office without a campaign. Duty, rather than desire, had elicited his candidacy, he told Henry. Although willing to submit to his nomination as a "link in the chain of my destiny," Quitman saw little reason to solicit votes when he was doing the people a favor by even running.[13] Relying on his past laurels, Quitman avoided speechmaking through the summer.

As usual, Quitman found that he could ill afford "to revel in luxurious ease" (as a Whig editor satirized his silence). By fall, Quitman had decided that he had better answer the Whig charges. Although he would have liked to have stayed at Monmouth to superintend the completion of his new stable roof, he set out on September 30 to canvass his Achilles' heel—Mississippi's northern and eastern counties.[14]

Quitman traveled north via Jackson, apparently timing his arrival to coincide with a "Southern State Convention" called for October 1. Sectional relations had gone from bad to worse, in the perspective of many Mississippians, and the assembly had been summoned to determine a course of action for the state.

Part of the ferment reflected Democratic partisan unrest regarding the installation of a Whig administration in Washington. To get Democratic votes in 1848, Whigs had presented Taylor as a man above party, and the general himself had emphasized that he was not an "ultra-Whig." Taylor, indeed, made genuine efforts to rise above party during his early administration, in both patronage and policy. His cabinet appointments shunned longstanding Whig stalwarts like Henry Clay and Daniel Webster, and his paper in Washington emphasized that the party should not press for such traditional Whig demands as high protective tariffs. Nevertheless, Mississippi Democrats had no intention of forfeiting their majoritarian status to fall in behind the Whigs, and, seizing on any evidence available that Taylor was firing Democrats or intending to promote Whig tariff and banking policies, accused Taylor of a virtual double-cross.[15]

But Democratic partisans would have made little headway against Taylor, had not Mississippians of all political persuasions shared profound fears that the antislavery movement had been gaining important ground and that Taylor, despite personal slaveholdings, was becoming an abolitionists' tool. Most of this anxiety reflected western territorial developments. Oregon had been given territorial status by Congress in 1848, with a ban on slavery within its limits. Now, in 1849, it seemed that slavery might be denied any share in the Mexican cession, and that Taylor was a good deal at fault. Confronted with Congress' inability to organize *any* of the new acquisitions into territories because of sectional disagreement over whether slavery should be permitted, Taylor had hit on the stratagem of sending an agent to California to suggest that inhabitants simply apply for statehood and skip the territorial stage. Taylor hoped, thus, to circumvent the whole problem of the Wilmot Proviso, which was intended to apply only to territories. Most Americans, with the exception of northern abolitionists, concurred that new states—being equal in privileges with previously admitted states under the American system of government—had the right to make their own decisions regarding slavery. Although Taylor's scheme was designed to avoid insult to southern institutions and Calhoun's resolutions since there would have been no outright congressional prohibition on slavery expansion, it nonetheless promised to bring California into the Union as a free state and strengthen antislavery power in Congress because most settlers on the Pacific were from the North. Even worse, Mississippians perceived that Free-Soil efforts to apply the Wilmot Proviso to the West were but a part of a general antislavery resurgence. Back in December, 1848, the House of Representatives had adopted a resolution prohibiting the slave trade in the District of Columbia. Northerners were also proving increasingly refractory about returning fugitive slaves or protecting slave property in transit in northern states.[16]

These trends ignited a grassroots sectional consciousness in Mississippi. Through the spring and summer, meetings—often bipartisan—demanded remedial action. Many gatherings threatened secession if concessions were not immediately forthcoming from the North. Symptomatic of this consciousness were calls for economic and intellectual self-sufficiency and an end to what was perceived as crippling dependence on the North: Mississippians should build railroads and factories, educate children at their own institutions instead of northern colleges and academies, patronize their own resorts rather than Yankee watering spots. Although not all proponents of progress were secessionists, some did promote development to strengthen the state if secession proved necessary. Thus Hinds County slaveholder and agricultural reformer Colin S. Tarpley told a county meeting that a New Orleans–Jackson railroad would enable Mississippi and Louisiana to "rely upon each other for preservation" should a "dissolution of the Union" and war occur.[17]

By 1849, Mississippians were far more receptive to calls for southern unity than they had been in the past. John C. Calhoun, for years, had contended that the best—and perhaps only—way for southerners to preserve their institutions was to forgo their Whig and Democratic parties and coalesce in a united southern movement which would make sectional demands on the North the price of maintaining the Union. Hoping to fashion a southern party, he had joined four members of the southern congressional caucus in January, 1849, and drafted the *Address of the Southern Delegates in Congress to Their Constituents*, which attempted to undermine the party structure in favor of a general southern movement. Although no Mississippi Whigs in Congress had been included in the forty-eight southern congressmen who signed the address, state Whigs, vulnerable to Democratic charges that Taylor's policies amounted to indirect implementation of the Wilmot Proviso, needed to prove their reliability on slavery to retain political status and were receptive to calls for a nonparty coalition to chart a course of state resistance.[18]

The "Southern State Convention" established Mississippi's primacy in the southern resistance movement. South Carolina would have taken the lead, but politicians there hesitated because of recollections of the 1830s, when the state's advanced position had led to embarrassing isolation. Rather, a statewide meeting at Columbia in May had announced that South Carolina would join *other* southern states willing to take action. Mississippi's convention seemed an answer to South Carolina's bid. Congressman Daniel H. Wallace of South Carolina, an agent of that state's radical governor, White-marsh B. Seabrook, was on hand to observe the proceedings.[19]

Quitman took more than passing interest in the Jackson assemblage. Intermittent cooperation with the major parties had never fully erased his suspicion of the corrupting aspects of spoils politics, and it would have been shocking had he remained aloof from a movement molded in Calhoun's image and a virtual reincarnation of his own 1834 State Rights party. Despite his oft-expressed nationalistic sentiments, he was increasingly irked by antislavery efforts to consecrate the empire he had helped conquer—at the risk of his life—to free soil. He had also been touched personally by the fugitive slave controversy since his servant John had run away from Eliza in Boston during the war. And he had learned recently, to his dismay, that he lacked influence on presidential patronage despite his wartime relationship with Taylor. When he tried to advance the army careers of deserving wartime associates, the president proved indifferent to his counsel. Like other Mississippi Democrats, Quitman construed Taylor's patronage rebuffs as a harbinger of worse to follow: "You have better hopes of Gen. Taylor than I have," he pessimistically concluded to a correspondent. "In my opinion, his leading measures will be Whig, ultra-Whig. The old fogies of that party will not readily break with him if he consents to rob the South by a high and partial tariff, and to squander the public treasure by a brilliant system of internal improvements."[20]

Quitman readily accepted an honorary seat at the convention, which had all the trappings of a nullifier reunion. George Winchester served as president *pro tem*; William Sharkey acted as permanent chair; John I. Guion participated in the proceedings. The delegates agreed on resolutions which maintained that Congress lacked constitutional authority to prohibit slavery in the territories or the District of Columbia, or to interdict the interstate slave trade, and warned that such legislation would force southerners to regard the nonslaveholding states as enemies. The convention also established a state association at Jackson to promote action, called on the legislature to convene a state convention if Congress imposed the Wilmot Proviso or attacked slavery in the District of Columbia, and took a major step in the Calhounian direction of southern unity by summoning a slaveholding states' convention for Nashville, Tennessee, for the first Monday in June to fashion a strategy of southern resistance to northern aggression.[21]

Encouraged by the proceedings, Quitman resolved to implement the convention's will if his gubernatorial campaign succeeded. "We must maintain our equality in the Union, & our constitutional rights, at any & every haz-

224

ard," he informed South Carolina agent Wallace. However, sensitive that his strength lay in his wartime laurels and that his secessionist reputation had long been vulnerable to attack by political enemies, Quitman neither participated actively in the convention nor used his subsequent campaign to rally public opinion behind the convention's work. "[He] is engaged in a heated canvass, and is compelled to use much caution . . . as he is charged by the Whigs with being ultra on all questions of Federal policy, as it is well known, that he is a *Calhoun man, a nullifier of 1832*," Wallace reported to Seabrook. The best Quitman could manage was a promise that if he was elected, Wallace would "know where to find me," and that Mississippi would make "common cause with the slave states who go for resistance." But Wallace worried that however much Quitman might be with South Carolina in spirit, he would only promote secession if his state could be mobilized for that cause with ease. Wallace warned Seabrook that the "prejudice" in Mississippi against South Carolina might ultimately induce Quitman to back down, especially if Quitman, as seemed likely, entertained aspirations for "other personal honors." [22]

Leaving Jackson immediately after the convention, Quitman spent the whole month of October stumping in northern and eastern Mississippi. Although he might have won without the effort, given Whig ineptitude, his campaigning undoubtedly contributed to a comfortable margin of victory. He swept all the northern and eastern counties except Panola and Wayne, and wound up with 46 of 58 counties, 70 percent of the ballots, and an advantage of more than 10,000 votes. In some of the counties where he had canvassed, such as Attala and Monroe, Quitman almost doubled Lea's total. It was a most satisfying triumph: he had prevailed, he told Henry, despite "a very bitter political opposition from the Whigs . . . supported by much falsehood." [23]

Quitman benefited from the two months' grace period between his election and inauguration. The incumbent governor, Joseph W. Matthews, would hold the position until the legislature convened on January 7 and certified Quitman's election. This gave Quitman the opportunity to make a trip to New Orleans and Grand Caillou to straighten out his financial and plantation affairs. It also gave him time to make plans for his family, as being governor was a year-round proposition. The governor was expected to inhabit the Executive Mansion, a square Greek Revival structure three blocks down Capitol Street from the capitol.

Quitman expected his family to join him at his new residence, and, although prospects of mixing in a new social set delighted Louisa, Eliza was resistant. However much she might have complained in the past about forced separations, Eliza had no desire to forfeit Natchez for the still frontierlike atmosphere of the capital. Perhaps because of her family lineage, perhaps because she was far less traveled than her cosmopolitan husband, she internalized too well the stereotypical elitism of the nabobs. She passed these undemocratic standards, moreover, to her children. Henry, for instance, had arrogantly "rid" himself of a roommate earlier that year because the student, though a fellow Mississippian, was a *"rough illnatured Pine Woods man."* Quitman was fortunate that his political enemies could only *guess* the elitist context of Quitman family conversation.[24]

After considerable pressure, Eliza finally relented—she would become "Lady Governor" and try to "civilize" the "Rosin-heels & Backwoods society" in the capital. Quitman and Henry—the latter now fully repentant and thankful to be home for Christmas vacation—took the Vicksburg-Jackson train shortly after the holiday to scout the Governor's Mansion and tell Eliza what would have to be supplied from Monmouth so that the family could enjoy its customary amenities. They looked over the mansion during a visit with the governor and his wife on January 5, and what they saw was disconcerting. The structure was impressive enough: the front portico was supported by four fluted Corinthian columns; the interior displayed handcrafted lintels, ceiling friezes, and cornices; there was a fine carpet in the drawing room. However, the legislature had erred in specifying a roof of zinc. It may have been fireproof, but it leaked during heavy rains. Interior walls had suffered considerable damage. Although Quitman received intimations that the legislators intended mansion-improvement appropriations during their upcoming session, the short-run prospects left a bit to be desired. He alerted Eliza that she should expect to live at first in a cottage behind the mansion that he would fix up before she arrived, and warned her to count on nothing when it came to supply: "If you doubt about any thing bring it along," he instructed. She certainly would require bed linen, towels, napkins, and a set of china from home. However, he beckoned her to come "immediately," stressing that it was "very important" to him that she be in Jackson "as early as possible."[25]

Quitman, however, had far more on his mind than living conditions as he prepared to become governor of Mississippi for the second time in his life. The passing of his fiftieth birthday in September had left him self-conscious over advancing years and sensitive that "decline" lay in the not-too-distant future. He aspired to do something more of importance while still vigorous, and found his mission in the continuing North-South crisis. Surely the voters' approval of his candidacy in November indicated their "rebuke" to President Taylor's "antisouthern" administration: he had *far* outpolled

Cass's effort of the year before in Mississippi.[26] Construing his own election as a mandate for action against federal aggression, Quitman drafted an inaugural address which would take Mississippi a step toward secession from the Union. On January 10, he would make good on his promise to Congressman Wallace.

17

Secessionist

WRITING about her father years after the Civil War, Rosalie Quitman Duncan rejected rigid classification of John Quitman as a disunionist. Rather, she remembered him as a man who embraced secession resignedly, seeing it as a necessary tactic to counter the "aggressive policy of the North" which was being "forced on the South." His discussions with her about the crisis of the Union, she recalled, left her feeling "disquieted" and "anxious." [1]

It is hardly surprising that Rosalie would try to differentiate her father from the extreme "southern nationalists" of his day—men so convinced that the "shared interests" of the people of the slaveholding states were "incompatible" with those of northerners, [2] and that southern independence would bring glory, that they approached secession without remorse; secession, after all, had been thoroughly discredited by the northern victory in the Civil War. Nonetheless, her comments reflect considerable truth. When Quitman threw his influence as Mississippi's governor in 1850 behind the secession cause, he did so as a defensive Calhounian American rather than as an exuberant disunionist pining for separate nationhood. Thus he spoke in terms of his "fear" and "regret" that the Union might be nearing its end, and pronounced it a "gloomy prospect." He would have preferred the North's receding "from her positions" to enduring an ultimate sectional showdown. [3] Quitman's radicalism was insistent, yet qualified. He never fully donned the raiment of the pure southern nationalist.

Quitman delivered his gubernatorial inaugural a little over a month after President Zachary Taylor had sent his annual message to Congress, and its radical content was in part a response to policies expounded in Taylor's document. Taylor had recommended that Congress not only admit California as a free state but also refrain from organizing the balance of the Mexican cession—New Mexico—as a territory, because that region would soon follow California's precedent and seek direct admission to the Union as a state. Many southerners found cause for concern in Taylor's suggestions, because it was generally expected that New Mexico, like California, would apply for admittance as a free state. Rather than tolerate further decline in the relative political power of the slave states, discontented southerners rallied behind Texas, which held an outstanding claim to much of eastern New Mexico, including the important trading center of Santa Fe. At the least, such an addition to Texas would supplement the land available for the extension of slavery. However, since Texas had joined the Union under a provision that it could be subdivided at a later date, a transfer of New Mexican territory to the Lone Star State might have resulted in additional slave states—and that would mean increased southern political power in Washington, by virtue of sheer numbers. It only further complicated the territorial imbroglio that Mormons (or Latter-day Saints) occupying the land around the Great Salt Lake within New Mexico had drawn up their own constitution the previous March for a "State of Deseret" to be carved out of *both* California and New Mexico.

Quitman's pessimism that January, however, stemmed from the continuing deterioration of intersectional trust as well as from territorial developments. Southern politicians demanded better compliance by the northern states to the letter and spirit of the Fugitive Slave Law (1793). Northern antislavery interests were bound and determined to eradicate the unseemly slave trade, if not the institution of slavery itself, in the District of Columbia. Congress, meanwhile, showed no sign of being able to reconcile these conflicting demands, as sectional tension in Washington had reached unprecedented heights. The House of Representatives, after convening in December, had taken three weeks and sixty-three ballots just to choose a Speaker.[4]

Few Mississippians found more cause for alarm in these trends than John Quitman. An instinctive expansionist who had almost moved his own family to Texas at one time, he understood all too well the centrality of westward migration patterns to the stability of southern society. Western lands had always represented opportunity—a fresh start—for the region's slaveholders as well as nonslaveholders. When land became less fertile or obligations became too pressing in the East, southerners picked up stakes and sought cheap lands to the west.[5]

Quitman envisioned this process continuing to the Pacific Coast, and coveted a share of California's gold and "broad harbours" for his state. Ridiculing the supposition that plantation labor was unsuited for the desert terrain of the Mexican cession, he countered that no "sensible child" swallowed the notion that "God and nature" intended to keep slavery from California or that slavery would prove unprofitable there. Quitman even revealed that he would have committed some of his own blacks to the region had conditions for slavery been propitious, and he claimed knowledge that several Natchez neighbors would have done the same.

Quitman also conceptualized the crisis as one of strategy and power politics. If the South could not maintain the "balance of power" necessary for its "safety," southern influence in Washington might erode to a point where slavery might be abolished by legislation; antislavery spokesmen, Quitman reasoned, had already made Congress into a forum for "war" on the South. Conscious that free western states offered a haven for runaway slaves and a potential base for abolitionist attempts to incite servile rebellion, Quitman believed it "unmilitary" to tolerate any "cordon of *hostile* states" on the South's "only open border." [6]

Yet, for Quitman, and perhaps a majority of concerned Mississippians, far more lay at stake than even materialistic needs and power politics. The crux of the matter had a great deal to do with sectional psychology. When northerners tried to exclude slavery from the territories or the District of Columbia, opposed the admission of additional slave states, or interfered with slaves in transit or southern efforts to reclaim escaped bondsmen, they in effect stigmatized slavery—and thus the entire southern way of doing things—as inferior. By denying slaveowners the right to take their slave property where they wanted, northerners in effect branded southerners as second-class citizens: no parallel controls restricted the utilization of northern property. Southerners construed such restraints as limitations on their very freedoms as Americans, freedoms that their ancestors had fought for in the American Revolution. Deprived of freedom, southern whites would be reduced to a position tantamount to enslavement, and would no longer enjoy equality with other Americans. Such a finale could never be tolerated by a people intimately familiar with the catastrophe that slavery was for its victims. Southerners, for all their own monstrous infringement of American egalitarian ideals, had always commanded a peculiarly acute—if ironic—understanding of the fragile and precious character of personal liberty, and recent developments overseas had reinforced this awareness. When Hapsburg troops suppressed nationalistic revolution in Prague, when Russian troops returned Hungary to Austrian control, when throughout Europe the flame of republicanism which had burned so brightly in 1848 began to fade before the strength of counterrevolutionary determination, alarmed southerners vowed that they would not permit their own degradation into colonial dependencies. [7]

A close reading of Quitman's phraseology gives abundant proof that concern over this possibility of second-class citizenship influenced his outlook. Thus he did not deny that territorial inhabitants had the right to prohibit slavery in their state constitutions, but did insist that the "clear principle of equal justice" demanded that the people of all regions had the right to settle a territory with their property prior to that decision. He stressed that southerners, because of such restraints on their freedoms, felt "degraded" by their connection with the North and worried about being forced to forfeit their "positions of equals in the Union." He warned that the South might expect to emerge a tributary area, resembling Ireland's relationship to England, Poland's to Russia, and Hungary's subservience to Austria.[8]

Troubled by this reading of the American future, Quitman devoted more than three-quarters of his inaugural address to federal-state relations. He commenced with a dose of nullification orthodoxy, reviewing the status of the states as "equal co-ordinate sovereignties" with "reserved rights" under a federal constitution "compact" which only granted "delegated powers" to the government in Washington. Creeping centralism, fed by "national glory," however, had eroded this balanced relationship: Congress had already stretched the commerce, post office, and post roads clauses of the Constitution into authorizations of illicit internal improvements and national supervision of manufacturing and agriculture; it might proceed to create another national bank. Worst of all, the antislavery "crusade" being mounted in the northern states already inspired congressional tampering with slavery, an institution which half the states had retained as their means of controlling an "inferior race." Quitman branded such interference intolerable, on historic, legalistic, and pragmatic grounds: "[Slavery] has existed here since the cavaliers of Jamestown and the puritans of Plymouth Rock first built their pilgrim fires upon the shores of America. It was recognized in the formation of the Federal constitution, and to its existence among us, as much as to any other single cause, is attributable the rapid advance of our country in its career of prosperity, greatness and wealth." Quitman called on the legislature to map a course of resistance for the state, and pledged his intention to execute the lawmakers' will.

Quitman relegated his token pronouncements on internal state affairs to the end of his message. In what reads, retrospectively, almost like an addendum, he uttered liberal platitudes about the scientific "improvements" and "inventions in the arts" characterizing a "progressive age" and called on his listeners to utilize these new tools to increase the "wealth" and "happiness" of Mississippians. Specifically, he summoned the legislators to design a common school educational system, reform the judiciary and militia establishments, and commit funds to the "still open" realm of "internal improvements." Striving for perfection, he philosophized, merited "the highest exertion of the human intellect."[9]

If age brings circumspection, Quitman was probably fortunate to be addressing an unusually young political body—the most youthful legislators in the whole Deep South that year outside of Texas. Certainly they proved receptive to his calls for remedial state action against the federal threat. The day after Quitman's inaugural, the lawmakers referred his states' rights pronouncements to a special joint "Committee on Federal and State Relations." One week later, the committee reported back with a full endorsement of the proceedings of the October convention and recommendations that the legislature appropriate $250,000 for Quitman's use if he required funds to preserve "the constitutional and sovereign rights of the State" in the event that Congress implemented the Wilmot Proviso or interfered with slavery in the District of Columbia or with the interstate slave trade. The committee also recommended that Quitman arrange the election of a state convention if the June convention in Nashville advised action against federal aggression.[10]

While the legislators pondered their course of action, debate on federal questions filled the press. Democrats usually assumed an advance position, invoking southern aspirations to "dig gold with their negroes in California" and insisting that state resistance had become necessary for survival. Whigs tended toward more cautious policies, often suggesting that Quitman and other radicals had overreacted.[11]

On February 10, Mississippi's congressional delegation played into Quitman's hands. As their formal message explained, they anticipated that Congress would soon implement the Wilmot Proviso by admitting California as a free state, and requested that Quitman broach the calamity with the legislature. He did so, of course, two days later, suggesting that the lawmakers make "strong remonstrance" and call on the Nashville Convention to take up the matter. Quitman further inflamed the climate of crisis by chairing a public meeting on the nineteenth of Jackson citizens and "strangers" opposed to the admission of California "with its anti-slavery Constitution."[12]

While debate raged on federal relations, governor and legislators took up internal state affairs. Notwithstanding the progressive sentiments of his inaugural, Quitman displayed surprisingly cautious instincts about state activism. Taking his executive prerogatives quite seriously, Quitman became a veto governor, his most significant negative falling on a bill to incorporate the New Orleans and Jackson Railroad Company in Mississippi (a revival of the long-defunct project of connecting Mississippi's capital with New Orleans). Quitman justified his veto on constitutional grounds: provisions giving county boards of police the authority to tax to support the project became "a compulsion upon the minority of the citizens of such county to take stock against their will"; a provision exempting the company's capital stock and property from taxation for fifteen years discriminated against other corporations and was unfair to the state; a provision for a $2,000 state survey grant had not fulfilled the constitutional requirement that internal improvements surveys receive two-thirds approval of both houses. However, there is little reason to doubt that Quitman's opposition emanated at least partially from his longstanding hope of preserving Natchez's stake in the Jackson–New Orleans trade; certainly the party organ in Natchez appreciated his efforts, praising the veto as a "republican exercise" which would hinder the establishment of a "privileged class" of property holders. But the Jackson boosters got their way in the end. The legislature overrode "old Quitman's" veto, sparking celebrations among the "street politicians, outsiders, and lobby members" gathered in the capital.[13]

The governor also rejected initiatives bearing no relation at all to Natchez affairs, primarily along similar lines that they fostered privilege. Somehow, Quitman had contracted an advanced case of old-fashioned Jacksonian ideology, particularly its intolerance of anything which smacked of special interest legislation. Thus he negated the incorporation of a Wilkinson County Manufacturing Company because the bill promised it "perpetual" existence; "associated capital," he contended, posed hazards when not sufficiently restrained. A ferry company charter, similarly, evoked his disapproval because it offered "exclusive" control over the Tallahatchie River at Panola. Although it may be true, as one Whig newspaper suggested, that Quitman was trying to convince Democrats of his party regularity by demonstrating "extreme zeal," it seems more likely that Quitman's growing fear of federal abuses spilled over into a genuine, heightened sense of the dangers of corruption at the state level.[14]

Legislation promoting autonomy for minors also particularly troubled Quitman. He rejected private bills granting privileges of majority to youths under the age of twenty-one. He denied pardon to a boy sentenced to jail for striking his mother. He rejected a strongly supported clemency petition regarding a sixteen-year-old boy who had killed a schoolmate, despite the petitioners' explanation that the boy, an orphan suffering from a lung disease, had committed the crime only because provoked by "peculiarly aggravating circumstances."[15] Perhaps Quitman's emphasis on the preservation of authority reflected his own recent tribulations as a father.

Governor and legislature did find common ground on some issues. The lawmakers, for instance, took seriously Quitman's inaugural call for a common school system, and appropriated $200,000 for that purpose. Still, Quitman won few admirers, even among his own party, with his obstructionism. "Captious" was the way the Vicksburg *Sentinel* described his construction of executive power, and an Arkansas woman observing a legislative session noted how the senate had passed several bills over gubernatorial veto despite Quitman's presence at the debates, and concluded that Quitman was "not making himself at all popular."[16]

For all his sparring with the legislature, Quitman tried to uphold the social responsibilities of his station, though there was some criticism that he too often pardoned himself from entertaining with lame excuses such as the mansion's being inadequately furnished. He and Eliza received the public within two weeks of his inaugural, and their February levee proved quite a glittering—if crowded—affair. "I was luckless enough to find myself, about 9 on that night, jammed, crowded, pressed and squeezed by a mixed multitude of aristocrats and plebeians," noted one participant. The event drew some of the Natchez elite to Jackson, and Quitman's daughter Antonia reported that one woman was bedecked in a hat featuring a pretentious blue plume.

Eliza, meanwhile, welcomed to the mansion a veritable stream of Episcopal church leaders in town to celebrate the consecration of William M. Green, Mississippi's first resident Episcopal bishop—so many, in fact, that they began to grate on Quitman's more secular nerves. "We have had our house full of bishops," he moaned to Henry, now back at Princeton. "I like the society of some of the clergy—but most of them . . . assume so much superiority, that they become unpleasant. I sincerely respect a humble and devout minister, but can not tolerate an arrogant priest." [17]

Toward session's end, the lawmakers finally turned in earnest to the federal crisis. When they did so, they put earlier disagreements with the governor aside and fully measured up to Quitman's hopes. Despite considerable Whig opposition, the Democratic majority rammed through the radical recommendations of the joint Committee on Federal and State Relations, as well as an election of twelve delegates to the Nashville Convention by a joint legislative ballot. Whig unionists argued that it was unconstitutional to circumvent popular election, and warned that Democratic plans to interfere with the state-making process in California might establish precedent applicable against the admission of future slave states. But it was to little avail. On March 6, senators and representatives cast their ballots for the Nashville delegates. Four days later, the legislature adjourned. Mississippi seemingly had taken a giant step toward secession. [18]

The departure of the lawmakers removed what little glamor attached to gubernatorial stature in the "dreary," "two streeted" town. Quitman found himself with a wife and children who, once deprived of their rounds of parties, dinners, and social visits, took a jaded view of life in the capital. Eliza displayed a lower tolerance for Jackson's citizenry the more she became familiar with it. "Town boys," she discovered, had so little social grace that, at a town celebration, they raised a ruckus which would have "shamed the wildest set of Indians." The dinner guests Quitman now scrounged up seemed so "uncouth," compared to the outsiders they had entertained during the legislative session, that she would have willingly sacrificed their company.[19]

Quitman, though more tolerant of Jackson's shortcomings than was his wife, nonetheless found it difficult to concentrate on gubernatorial duties. "I do not like the drudgery of the office," he complained. The times seemed too exciting for paper shuffling, and the papers that he shuffled contained reminders of the growing precariousness of the slave system. Notification that a slave in Pike County had been sentenced to hang for killing his master, for instance, raised the specter of servile rebellion. Nor was it reassuring to hear from Henry that politics had consumed Princeton and that a faculty of "Northern Whigs" made life miserable for southern students by expressing offensive sectional views. As if this were not enough, a Presbyterian revival had also swept the campus and Henry's peers had occupied his room for a religious meeting and warned Henry that Hell awaited anyone resisting conversion. Quitman took a little solace in knowing that Henry was receiving the Jackson *Mississippian* for indoctrination in the true political faith, but considered transferring Henry to the University of Mississippi. Although Quitman told a nonpartisan meeting in nearby Raymond that southern pressure might yet force northern concessions on the California issue, privately he had reached the conclusion that the Union was nearing its end.[20]

Late in April, Quitman escorted Eliza and the girls back to Natchez. Ostensibly, his purpose was to accommodate his wife's wishes, and he alerted her that she should expect to return with him to Jackson in the fall to play hostess again. But Quitman's real intention was to free himself of family responsibilities for a while, so that he could go to New Orleans. He set out for the Crescent City almost immediately after returning to Monmouth. There he expected to make a much more dramatic contribution to southern welfare than he had been able to make from behind his desk at Jackson over the last several weeks. Quitman gave Eliza no idea of what he was up to; she was left with the most improbable illusion that he intended to pass a quiet summer with her at Monmouth after returning from his trip.[21]

18

The Pearl of the Antilles

PRIOR to 1850, John Quitman had shown little interest in the Spanish-owned island of Cuba, other than a taste for Havana cigars. Though the island—just ninety-two nautical miles from Key West—had long intrigued American expansionists, Quitman had been virtually oblivious to its potential. But when an adventurer named Narciso López called at the Executive Mansion that March with a plan to foment revolution in Cuba, Quitman's interest was immediately aroused.

Cuba, to all appearances, was ripe for revolution. Wealthy, native-born planters, the Creoles—or Criollos—resented mercantile constraints on their foreign trade, corrupt administrative practices by Peninsulares (Spanish-born bureaucrats) who monopolized island government, and high taxes which characterized metropolitan rule. They also feared that Spain might attempt to abolish slave labor, thus crippling the productive sugar industry which had made Cuba the Pearl of the Antilles. Britain, pressuring Spain to move in such a direction for decades, had extracted from Spain restrictions, only partially enforced, against the African slave trade. Finding outlet for their disenchantment in the Club de la Habana, a group consisting largely of sugar planters but including others such as John S. Thrasher, an American resident of Havana who edited a Cuban trade journal, many Creoles promoted annexation of their island to the United States as an alternative to Spanish rule. An auxiliary in exile, the Cuban Council, promoted the cause from its New York City headquarters. Other Cuban dissidents favored the creation of an independent Cuban republic.[1]

López, a swarthy Venezuelan native who married into a Cuban planter family, had once fought in the Spanish army against Latin American revolutionary forces and later served in the Spanish bureaucracy in Cuba. Following several reversals of fortune, he had turned against Spanish rule and plotted a revolution for June 29, 1848. Spanish officials, however, capitalizing on intelligence furnished by the Polk administration (then trying to purchase Cuba and under the erroneous impression that cooperation would win the Spanish good will necessary to effect the sale), were able to quash the revolt. After a narrow escape to the United States, López raised a private expeditionary army which he hoped would land on Cuban shores and ignite a popular revolution. Since he never clarified his ultimate objective, stressing independence to Cuban exiles and annexation after independence to American backers, he attracted support from both Cuban nationalists and American expansionists. But when, in September, 1849, he tried to launch his "filibuster" invasion, the United States government again proved his nemesis. President Taylor issued a proclamation warning Americans against participation, and federal officials took legal and military precautions to prevent the expedition's departure.[2]

One wing of the expedition was to have departed Round Island, off Mississippi's eastern coast. When U.S. Navy vessels blockaded the island and forced hundreds of assembled filibusters to disperse, Cuba became a cause célèbre in the state. Democrats construed the issue as a new Texas, hoping that Cuba, which, unlike California and New Mexico, already had a functioning slave system and thus promised advantage to the South "too apparent to require a detailed notice," might prove as beneficial to party fortunes as the Lone Star once had. Spanish rulers of Cuba, the *Mississippian* pointedly reminded its readers, belonged to the same race which slaughtered "Fannin, Crockett, Bowie and their companions in Texas." Quitman's Democratic predecessor as governor, Joseph W. Matthews, devoted a considerable share of his final address to the legislature to the Round Island incident, claiming that naval officials had infringed on Mississippi's sovereignty. Whigs, wary of repeating their 1844 Texas debacle, tried to maintain a stake in the issue. "DON'T STEAL OUR THUNDER," railed the Vicksburg *Whig*. "We are in favor of the *re*-annexation of Cuba to the United States. No Democratic paper has yet taken this position. It is solely and exclusively ours." But Whigs found themselves compromised by their president's antagonism to filibustering, and gradually forfeited the issue to their rivals.[3]

López called on Quitman in hopes that he could capitalize on this surge of interest in Cuba. Rebounding from the federal government's obstructionism, he had established a Junta Cubana in New York City and sought support in Washington, where John Henderson, Quitman's former ally in the Mississippi legislature and more recently a United States senator, suggested that the filibusters concentrate on the South for recruits and financing. Accepting the advice, López and second-in-command Ambrosio José González (a Cuban exile and onetime University of Havana professor) switched their headquarters to New Orleans. Setting out for the Crescent City via the northern river route, they raised support as they traveled and took a detour to Jackson to see if Quitman could be induced to lend his hand to the enterprise.

Plying Quitman with flattery about Chapultepec and Belén, and contending that Cubans would rally to his banner, López offered Quitman command of the filibuster army and rulership over a Cuban republic if the invasion force—which was scheduled to leave New Orleans on May 1—proved successful. Quitman, despite his obligations as governor, found himself sorely tempted to accept. "Your old commander is invited to become the Liberator of a beautiful and rich island in the Gulf," he informed his Mexican War aide Mansfield Lovell, still with the U.S. Fourth Artillery. Did Lovell want to join him? Perhaps he might serve as a prime minister or secretary of war in the new government. López, he prodded, had promised one million dollars and an army of four thousand for the invasion. "My spirit often reverts to the free air of the camp," Quitman explained. "I am by nature a soldier. No other life charms me." Quitman's martial spirit was again in the ascendant.[4]

Discretion, however, triumphed in the end. Quitman turned down the command. But that did not preclude his offering military advice or helping secure support after López departed Jackson. Working through Henderson, who maintained a New Orleans law practice and had become a leading investor in López bonds, Quitman put the filibuster in touch with some of his personal contacts in the Crescent City. Then, in April, when González implored Quitman to be on the scene, Quitman, as we have seen, made the trip downriver.[5]

Secrecy intrinsic to López's planning makes it difficult to decipher Quitman's doings on the filibusters' behalf during his stay in New Orleans. Newspapers adverted to Quitman's arrival at the St. Charles Hotel on April 26 and his attendance at a memorial meeting for John C. Calhoun, who had died on March 31. But the press maintained silence about any substantive assistance which Quitman might have furnished López. All that we know is that González in a letter alluded to how the filibusters depended on Quitman's "aid" in getting "out." If Quitman did provide material aid, he certainly did not mention it in family correspondence; Eliza remained as much in the dark as she had during her husband's Texas escapade.

What the filibusters do seem to have received from Quitman was a tentative commitment to command a reinforcement expedition to leave New Orleans between June 1 and 15, *if* López had by then effected a successful landing on the Cuban coast and rallied the people to the revolutionary standard. As Henderson put it, Quitman would drop his "civic pursuits" and come to Cuba when he received the "call." To this end, U.S. naval lieutenant Henry J. Hartstene, while in Havana, aboard the mail steamer *Falcon*, took extensive notes on Spanish troop movements and gun emplacements, and forwarded them to Quitman from New Orleans in a May 26 letter. Around the same time, prospective recruits began writing Quitman about securing a place in the expedition. Quitman's command responsibilities became such common knowledge that his sister in Philadelphia heard about it through the press (though she ridiculed the rumor on the grounds that Quitman surely had too much "standing and renown" to take on a "hairbrained" scheme). Eliza also heard the reports. Less naïve about her husband than was her sister-in-law, she asked McMurran as a personal favor to check out the rumors for her.[6]

Quitman returned to Jackson after the expeditionaries had departed from American shores, but before they actually landed in Cuba. López had concocted an elaborate plan to circumvent U.S. neutrality laws, which entailed separate departures by his filibuster groups, under the pretense that they were peaceful emigrants to California, and their later congregation at the island of Mujeres off the Yucatán coast where they would organize the actual invasion. López reached the rendezvous on May 9, days after Quitman reappeared at the capital.[7]

With time to spare before he could expect to hear anything, Quitman tended to his plantation interests. On May 13, he set out on the Yazoo River trip which resulted in the founding of his Belen plantation. For six days, he became a sojourner in the wilderness, and his time was spent surveying the region from river skiffs, cutting cane, wading through river backups, and even shooting a bear cub. Then, after resuming his gubernatorial station, Quitman learned that the Cuba filibuster had proven a fiasco. López's landing with some 520 men on May 19 at Cárdenas on the north coast of Cuba had been plagued by delays and unexpected resistance from the small garrison in the town. After absorbing some sixty casualties, López was forced to abandon all intentions of moving on Havana, and he hastily reembarked his men. He was lucky to escape. His steamer, the *Creole*, reached Key West just ahead of a Spanish warship. Thirty-nine deserters who had abandoned the expedition at Mujeres and at the island of Contoy, also off the Yucatán coast, were not even that fortunate. Spanish vessels captured them, their two ships, and fifteen crew members.[8]

López's precipitate return relieved Quitman of the responsibility of mustering reinforcements. About a week after the Cárdenas debacle broke in the press, he returned to Monmouth for the purpose of chaperoning Louisa to Jackson. Louisa had complained of boredom with the sewing, reading, and other "dull routine" of a "young lady's useless life" in Natchez. Eliza expressed reservations about Louisa's going to Jackson, but Quitman was always prepared to spoil his eldest daughter. She caused him a lot less grief than Henry, who had ranked only forty-ninth in his junior class at Princeton, and had been declared "deficient" in mathematics. (How could Henry achieve distinction at such a pace? Quitman wondered. Why did he give so much attention to "the other sex"?). Besides, Louisa was such a kindred spirit. Unlike her mother, who resented his political career and feared his adventurism, Louisa believed it deplorable that eligible Natchez males took the "important political questions of the day" too lightly, and even advised male acquaintances to participate in the Cuba filibuster.

So Quitman brought Louisa—and a friend—to Jackson and showed his daughter quite a time. He enjoyed her company at the Executive Mansion, and even turned up at the Cooper's Well resort "gallanting" the two girls around the premises. When the editor of the *Free Trader* dined with Quitman that July during a visit, he found "one of the most accomplished young ladies that I ever saw" presiding "at the head of the table." [9]

Quitman's ties with the filibusters, however, persisted. Some of the filibusters, disillusioned with López's capacity for command but still hopeful of liberating Cuba by force, turned to Quitman as their advisor. At Vicksburg, catching Quitman on his way back to Jackson with Louisa, John L. O'Sullivan beseeched him to assume command. Soon afterwards, Quitman heard from Henderson, now full of talk about how his prominence in the South would guarantee manpower and investment sufficient for a successful invasion. Henderson even believed that Quitman's Mexican War reputation would entice U.S. Army personnel to resign commissions so that they could serve Quitman as officers.

Quitman resisted the bait. López's ineffectual landing had shown that the Cuban people were nowhere near ready for mass revolution. Quitman wined, dined, and put up several of the filibusters at the Executive Mansion, as well as Judge Cotesworth P. Smith, his old nullifier ally, who was also one of López's organizers. Louisa, captivated by the aura of mystery surrounding the adventurers, wrote home that she enjoyed as many "beaux" as she might desire. But the last thing Quitman wanted to do was to risk his life in a hopeless cause. For the second time, he turned the command down. [10]

Quitman's new rejection of the filibusters' invitation, however, did not absolve him from legal liability for what had already transpired. López, who fully intended to initiate yet another invasion, had been arrested in New Orleans on June 7 for violating American neutrality laws. What began as hearings before a U.S. commissioner evolved into full-fledged proceedings in Judge Theodore H. McCaleb's U.S. District Court, with McCaleb instructing a grand jury to investigate whether the neutrality laws had been violated. The penalty for such infraction, he indicated, was a fine of up to $3,000 and up to three years in prison. López's counsel, which included Henderson, New Orleans *Delta* owner and López organizer Lawrence J.

Sigur, and S. S. Prentiss, hit upon the stratagem of having López incriminate so many prominent persons in his endeavor that it would become too embarrassing for the prosecution to go on. When the grand jury filed its true bills on June 21, therefore, the name of "John A. Quitman, Governor of the State of Mississippi" joined those of López, Henderson, Judge Smith, O'Sullivan, González, Sigur, and nine others on the list of filibusters to be tried in December. The defense lawyers had certainly achieved their objective.[11]

Lacking knowledge of the defense strategy which prompted the indictment, Quitman reacted angrily when he learned what had happened; the prosecution, he railed, was "founded in perjury, ignorance or malevolence," and he would "not readily let those off who have been instrumental in it." He simply bore no sense of guilt. There seemed nothing wrong with giving young men letters of introduction to López or loaning "personal friends of the expedition" "small sums of money." True, the command had been offered to him, but he had turned it down and made it abundantly clear that he would come to Cuba only if "invited" by its people "after they should have erected the standard of independence."[12]

Much of Quitman's fury derived from apprehensions that legal proceedings would sidetrack him from leadership of the southern resistance movement at precisely the moment that he was most needed. The Nashville Convention in June had proven less than the demonstration of southern unity its promoters had anticipated; six slave states had not been represented and the meeting had adopted relatively moderate resolutions. However, the U.S. Senate rejected a comprehensive compromise on July 31, and the Texas–New Mexico boundary crisis was approaching the explosion point. Prodded by U.S. military personnel, New Mexican settlers had held a state constitutional convention on May 15–25. Only a matter of weeks remained before Congress would be asked to admit New Mexico as a state with de facto control over the disputed area, and Governor Peter H. Bell of Texas had responded to this threat by taking steps to raise troops for an invasion of New Mexico. Back in the East, Hartford, Connecticut, gun manufacturer Samuel Colt promised to supply a thousand pistols for the invasion at a week's notice.[13]

Quitman believed it virtually certain that the moment of truth had come. Southerners, he assured his son, would "not submit to being robbed of the territory acquired from Mexico." Although there remained a faint hope that northern concessions might yet salvage the Union, he deemed it far more likely that the next Congress would prove America's last as a united country. Thus he planned to call a special legislative session to consider secession, once Congress actually passed the expected legislation denying southern rights. Meanwhile, he prepared organizationally and militarily for the confrontation ahead. On July 6, he chaired the resolutions committee of a Jackson meeting which called for "Southern States' Rights Associations" in every Mississippi county. Two days later, he ordered the adjutant general of the state militia to conduct an inventory of ordnance and handarms. When former governor of Texas and Mexican War hero James Pinckney Henderson inquired whether Mississippi stood prepared to aid Texas if it came to "drawn daggers" with federal troops at Santa Fe, Quitman pledged that, the moment the fighting erupted, Mississippi would act swiftly to aid her "sister state" in maintaining "sovereignty against federal usurpation." Quitman made this commitment public in a letter to the editor of the Vicksburg *Sentinel*, and presided over a meeting of the Jackson States' Rights Association which vowed that Mississippians would never tolerate an "abolition cordon" in the Southwest.[14]

Quitman feared that an extended court appearance, even if it did not result in a jail sentence, would preclude his leading an expedition into New Mexico. He knew that at the least it would greatly diminish his ability to influence the course of events in Mississippi. Perhaps government officials were even using the indictment in a premeditated scheme to demonstrate federal supremacy over the states at his expense. Horrified at this possibility, Quitman queried associates whether he might claim immunity from arrest by virtue of his gubernatorial position. Congressman Jacob Thompson thought so, as did Judge Smith. Smith contended that even if he could be held liable for appearance in court in another state, the reciprocal nature of the federal-state relationship mandated his exemption until his term expired.[15]

Encouraged by their advice, Quitman attempted to stall his court appearance. On September 28, U.S. District Attorney Horatio J. Harris, quite sensitive to the implications of arresting a governor, wrote Quitman from Vicksburg and gave him the option of proceeding voluntarily to New Orleans to give bail rather than suffer being served in Jackson. Quitman responded that although he was anxious to meet the "baseless charges" against him head on, he nonetheless owed a primary allegiance to his job and could not come to New Orleans until his duty as governor ended. Harris pressed a second time, which brought a contention from Quitman that the charge against him was "frivolous" as well as another plea for delay. Harris, however, rejoined that whether the charge was frivolous or not, it was incumbent upon him to enforce the indictment.[16] Quitman knew, from this point on, that his gubernatorial power depended on borrowed time.

Quitman managed to strike his new blow for southern rights before Harris forced him to decide whether he really would refuse to submit to arrest. Here he benefited from an unraveling of the impasse in Washington. President Taylor had died on July 9, an event which proved a watershed in the federal crisis. Though Old Rough and Ready's passing was mourned in the capital and throughout the country (Quitman even chaired a memorial meeting for his old commander),[17] his death removed an impediment to a legislative resolution of the controversies dividing the nation. Vice President Millard Fillmore, Taylor's successor, took a far less belligerent tack toward Texas than had his predecessor, and this paved the way to a break in the congressional stalemate. In August and September, Congress passed the series of measures which have become known, collectively, as the Compromise of 1850. The legislation awarded most of the disputed region to New Mexico, but compensated Texas with a $10 million payment, of which half would be allocated to paying off at par value the holders of heavily depreciated Texas securities. Although California was to enter the Union as a free state, New Mexico and Utah (the latter a second territory carved out of the cession area and inhabited primarily by Mormons) would decide the issue of slavery by popular sovereignty, thus providing southerners at least a technical chance of expanding slavery into the Southwest. The compromise abolished the slave trade in the District of Columbia; however, southerners could take some satisfaction that the measures did not tamper with slaveholding itself in the national capital and included a much stricter fugitive slave law.

Hundred-gun salutes, skyrockets, band renditions of patriotic tunes, and illuminations heralded the compromise in Washington. As word spread over the land, moderates everywhere breathed a collective sigh of relief. But to John Anthony Quitman and others of the "Quitman tribe of politicians," as the Vicksburg *Whig* denigrated them, the Compromise of 1850 was anything but a compromise. It created California as a free state, which Quitman regarded as practical implementation of the hated Wilmot Proviso, yet guaranteed nothing to slavery expansion. Aware that holders of the Texas bonds had lobbied for passage of the compromise because it was in their monetary interest to do so, he construed the sacrifice of slave territory in Texas to New Mexican sovereignty as evidence that fraud had captured the governmental process. "Money, influence, patronage and office, are freely used to bribe men from their integrity," he concluded. Stricter fugitive slave provisions, furthermore, hardly justified abolition of the District of Columbia slave trade.

Now an unabashed secessionist by every measure but formal declaration, Quitman drafted a message convening the state legislature so that it could consider withdrawal from the Union. He also followed up his earlier rapprochement with Jefferson Davis, sending the senator a letter explaining his

243

intended course of action—a gambit which worked, as Davis, who had been a vocal opponent of the congressional compromise anyway, responded with a promise of firm support. When Eliza (whose feelings about the Union had been vacillating considerably) advised caution, he brushed her off by saying that although "always happy" to hear her opinion, he believed that submission to the compromise would jeopardize their property, "liberties," and lives. Besides, it was "natural that woman should be timid and feel disposed to shrink from conflict and strife." [18]

Quitman issued his proclamation on September 26, calling upon the legislature to meet in special session on November 18 so that it could place Mississippi "in an attitude to assert her sovereignty." The compromise, the governor contended, had denied Mississippians their rights in the "vast and rich" Mexican cession; the abolition of the slave trade in the District of Columbia proved that there was no "reasonable hope" that the northern states would stop their aggression until they succeeded in destroying the South's "domestic institutions." [19]

The summons, combined with a similar call to the Georgia legislature by Governor George W. Towns of that state, rang like a firebell throughout the South. Secessionists experienced a sense of elation. Governor Seabrook of South Carolina, sending Quitman's document on to Towns, reported that the people of Charleston had become "clamorous" for a convocation of the South Carolina legislature once Quitman's pronouncement appeared in the press. Moderates, on the other hand, were disheartened. Way off in Baltimore, a Marylander expressed hope that Quitman would wind up in the penitentiary. Closer to home the Whig press stigmatized Quitman as a "monomaniac" and even jested that he had plagiarized his proclamation from an incident recounted in Washington Irving's satirical *History of New York*, when William Kieft, an ineffectual Dutch governor of colonial New Netherlands, tried to ward off English settlement by issuing a "well written, well sealed" proclamation that had everything going for it except that the Yankees treated it with "the most absolute contempt." Quitman, complained one critic, had put his state on a dangerous course. If moderates did not react effectively, "Genl. Cuba's Legislature" would "inflict a blow upon the peace and happiness of this country which it is horrible to think of." [20]

While argument raged over his bombshell Quitman joined a subsidiary debate within the secessionist camp as to how withdrawal from the Union was to be effected. The Nashville Convention had adjourned under a provision that it would reassemble if Congress did not meet its demands, and some radicals wanted it reconvened so that the southern states could make one last set of demands on the North, and then secede in unity when the demands were not met. Such a course, it was argued, would convince southern moderates that hope had passed of fair settlement within the Union, and provide strength in unity if the northern states tried to use force to contest southern withdrawal. Calhoun's replacement in the U.S. Senate, Robert W. Barnwell, urged this course on Quitman in a September 19 letter. Many extremists, however, believed that the southern states would never secede in union, and urged separate state action. The states could join together in a new government after the fact. But which state should take the step first? South Carolina was the most radical state; however, many of its leaders remained convinced that it would be self-defeating for their state to take the lead. Two days after issuing his proclamation, Quitman received a note from Governor Seabrook assuring him that the South Carolina legislature would be convened as soon as *two* other states took action.[21]

Quitman felt that a second Nashville Convention could do little more than present a plan for separate state action, and had serious doubts whether it would ever prove possible to get the delegates together again. William Sharkey, who, as president of the convention, had the authority to reconvene the meeting, strongly supported the compromise. By no means fixed in hostility to another convention and willing to grant that there remained a glimmer of possibility that the South could yet achieve "a radical cure of the evils" short of secession, Quitman nonetheless believed that Mississippi should start on the Calhounian path to secession. He would advise the legislature to call a state constitutional convention, which would "annul the Federal compact, establish new relations with other states, and adapt our organic laws to such new relations."

Quitman knew that his request would meet resistance and that the people might elect unionist convention delegates, who would refuse to secede. Merchants, brokers, and millionaires, he expected, would be particularly cautious, and they would exert considerable influence on the public mind. However, Quitman preferred to believe that the voters would see the flaws in the compromise: surely they knew the "difference between a loaf of bread and a stone, or a fish and a serpent." He shared his confidence with Seabrook, who was moved to respond that once Mississippi commenced its "patriotic work," the state could expect the "Palmetto banner" to "second" that effort.[22]

Hoping to woo the voters to the convention idea, Quitman took to the stump in October. The secessionists, he explained to John J. McRae, had to "challenge the submissionists to discussion, and agitate the question everywhere." Visiting Natchez early in the month, he addressed an Adams County meeting and again contended that slaves could have mined California gold; each slave, he estimated, would have produced $3,000 profit per year. Back in Jackson, he joined Congressman Albert G. Brown before a throng at the house of representatives, and reminded the audience that it was humiliating to watch slavery's exclusion from land that southerners had fought for. He also suggested that the northern people would probably not enforce the new fugitive slave law, one of the few benefits to the South in the compromise; the law, he reported with accuracy, had only passed because of northern abstentions during the voting. The very slaveholders whose cotton, rice, and tobacco made the North and Europe prosperous could only expect their position to deteriorate as their enemies grafted a consolidated government upon the country. Quitman's fervor affected Eliza, who took a moment off from packing jelly and sweetmeat jars for the family's upcoming return to Jackson to write Henry that the time had come for southerners to take a "decisive position." "We shall have an exciting time this winter," she predicted.[23]

That same October, Quitman experienced his first confrontation about secession with Senator Foote, who would become his nemesis in the months ahead. Foote had adopted an ambiguous course during congressional debates. Sometimes he appeared radical, as when he voted against the California bill. But more often he played the compromiser, and once the legislation was enacted he broke irrevocably with his radical colleagues by refusing to sign a protest against it. Returning to Mississippi following congressional adjournment, Foote boldly assumed leadership of the Union forces. Quitman encountered Foote in Vicksburg during his return to Natchez and, with his customary bluntness, announced his intent to recommend that the legislature convene a secession convention. Shocked at Quitman's extremism, Foote challenged him to a debate in Jackson prior to the gathering of the legislature. Quitman accepted, but fell seriously ill with what he called the "prevailing" "bone fever" (apparently a malarial attack), which confined him to bed and forced him to cancel the engagement.[24]

So enervated by his sickness that he gave up correspondence, Quitman languished in his room for weeks. At the end of the month when Eliza and the girls arrived—having left Monmouth entirely in the servants' hands— they found him just beginning to walk again. At this point, he pressed his luck and visited the capitol to hear a Jefferson Davis speech; the exertion proved too much and he experienced a severe relapse.

Eliza concluded that part of her husband's slow recovery was psychological, that he suffered "great anxiety" about his forthcoming message and could not "take things patiently." The diagnosis rings true. Quitman was acutely aware that Mississippi stood in a position to be the first state to secede, that other slave states awaited its signal, and that the nation realized that his message might trigger the event. "As this document will be the first of great official move[s] upon the chess board in events upon which perhaps the destiny of our country may hang," he wrote Henry, "I desire both for the success of the cause and my own fame, that it should be worthy the great occasion which calls it forth." "Abuse," undoubtedly, would follow his pronouncement. But his motives were purer than they had ever been before. He could take the blows.[25]

Quitman met his deadline. His message, signed November 18, was delivered to the legislature. It fell just short of being an outright secession document. Focusing as usual upon southern territorial grievances, Quitman submitted that the South would yet be satisfied if the northern states would agree to divide the remaining territories between slave and free at the 36°30' line and consent to constitutional amendments protecting slavery. However, Quitman argued that abolitionists controlled the federal government, that the equilibrium between the sections had been shattered, and that slavery would "perish" if nothing were done. He urged the legislature to call a convention which could then act alone or in coordination with other states, and expressed the opinion that barring last-minute northern concessions, secession presented the "only effectual remedy" to evils which would only worsen with time.[26]

The message, as Quitman had anticipated, sparked a barrage of criticism. All the worst motives were attached to his convention call: he wanted to be president of a southern confederacy; he hoped to supplant Foote in the U.S. Senate; he wanted secession to insulate himself from judicial procedures in New Orleans. Amite County unionists hanged him in effigy from a telegraph post, and a newspaper there urged readers to distrust his southern radicalism on the improbable logic that he was originally a "Yankee."[27]

Despite the outcry, Quitman expected success. He again contacted Governor Seabrook, now with only a few days left in his gubernatorial term, and told Seabrook that Mississippi verged on calling its convention. Seabrook returned a telegraph, assuring Quitman once again that South Carolina would follow if Mississippi would only lead, and requesting clarification as to whether the convention would attempt separate state secession or call a southern congress.[28]

The legislature referred the convention recommendation to a select joint committee. Though Quitman cultivated legislative good will at a "grand levee," he won only half a loaf. On November 30, the day the special session adjourned, he signed legislation calling on Mississippi's counties to elect delegates to a state convention. However, passage of congressional compromise had already diminished the sense of crisis in the state, and the convention call was hemmed in by important qualifications. To get their way, the radicals had to concede that the elections would not occur until the first Monday and Tuesday in September, 1851, and that the convention would not actually assemble until the second Monday in November, almost a full year away. The delay would tend to make the compromise a fait accompli; it certainly gave Foote and the unionists, heretofore poorly organized, an opportunity to mobilize opinion against secession. The simultaneous collapse of the Nashville movement, moreover, augured well for the procompromise forces. The convention had reconvened after all on November 11 and, though affirming the right of secession, had proven less effective than the June assemblage.[29]

Quitman would have preferred less time for debate. He explained to South Carolina radical Robert Barnwell Rhett that the concession on the September election had been necessitated by insistent opposition from a "respectable" minority in the legislature and by the "unsettled state of public opinion" in several counties. Still, he *had* persuaded the legislature to call the convention. So he sent a copy of the enactment on to Seabrook along with another optimistic assessment. (Seabrook wrote back of his "great satisfaction" with the news.) Knowing, moreover, that the issue would be decided by the public, whether or not the masses voted for radical delegates to the November convention, Quitman immediately took a new step to promote his views. On December 4, he helped found yet another extremist organization: the "Central Southern Rights Association of Mississippi." The first president? John Anthony Quitman, of course.[30]

It was at this juncture that the New Orleans prosecution finally closed in on Quitman. Henderson, who had "exhausted" his own financial resources on the Cárdenas expedition and had written Quitman as recently as November 6 soliciting "further pecuniary assistance" so that López might "move again," went on trial in McCaleb's court. Quitman's case would follow. District Attorney Harris, therefore, formally applied to Samuel J. Gholson, now federal judge for the district of Mississippi, for a warrant to arrest Quitman. Despite pressure from John Guion, Felix Huston, and Caswell R. Clifton (a former circuit court judge whom Quitman had appointed state penitentiary inspector) at the hearings, Gholson decided to issue the warrant. On January 25, U.S. Marshal for the Southern District of Mississippi Fielding Davis informed Quitman of the warrant, and gently asked "at what time it will best suit you to receive my official visit."[31]

Quitman thought the proceedings no less absurd in January, 1851, than he had the previous summer when he had first heard of his indictment. How ludicrous that so little as "furnishing a dinner" to López made him liable to prosecution under the neutrality laws. The whole affair merely demonstrated yet another facet of how centralized power could be abused. Federal district and circuit courts should be stripped of jurisdiction over all but revenue disputes; the whole federal court system needed revamping.[32]

He gave renewed thought to suggestions that he resist arrest, and sought additional opinions. Erasmus L. Acee, a former nullifier, put in a strong plea that he refuse to vacate his gubernatorial post. Acee rationalized that such duties as granting commissions and reprieves mandated his staying in Jackson, and warned that acquiescence to the indictment would reinforce the federal proclivity to usurp state power. Quitman should remember that his was a "sacred" duty to oppose "encroachments upon state rights." Compliance with arrest procedures would set a precedent detrimental to the cause.[33]

However, State Auditor of Public Accounts George T. Swann contended that neither the state nor the federal constitution exempted governors from prosecution for violation of criminal law. Quitman pondered Swann's findings. Could he really use the state militia as a personal shield? Would the masses support such a move? They might, if they were truly ready for secession and confrontation with federal authorities. But this would only be known after the September elections. If he asked the people to do so prematurely, he explained to Rhett, he might alienate public opinion and damage the southern rights cause. Quitman might have added that unionists were already charging that the whole Cuba movement represented a conspiracy to set up a southern empire after secession.[34]

Reluctantly, Quitman decided to submit. But how to avert the dilemma which Acee had posed? Quitman's answer was to resign the governorship. He had already established Mississippi's secession apparatus, thus fulfilling his main gubernatorial goal; and he could gladly sacrifice the rest of the job, which had never held more than marginal appeal for him. He knew, moreover, that the executive power would pass to trustworthy hands if he gave it up, for John Guion was serving as senate president. By resigning prior to arrest, he would go to New Orleans as a private citizen. National authorities would be foiled in their intention of using him as their tool to enhance central power.

Quitman took advantage of Marshal Davis' generosity about time of arrest, finished up a few matters, and resigned on February 3, protesting formally that he yielded only because of an unwillingness to cause possible "collision between the State and Federal Government in a case in which I am personally concerned." It was a brilliant coup. He attained the status of a martyr at little cost:

> Thou noble martyr to the petty hate
> And craven malice, which the vile and low,
> Who crawl to station, honored by the great,
> Forever on the patriot bestow;
> Well may the noblest envy thee thy fate,

Who thus in manly, proud obedience go,
The just acquittal of the law to wait,
Yet hurling scornful challenge to the foe.
Would that each Southern heart might emulate
Thy wisdom, virtue, courage, were it so,
No longer would Submission whine and prate
Of war and treason, but Resistance grow
More potent than Resolves and loud Debate,
And Mississippi stand a Free and Sovereign State.

In the U.S. Senate, Jefferson Davis exposed the hypocrisy of the federal rush to prosecute a man "grown old in honorable service, civil and military, and whose gray hairs had brought him accumulated honor," when the government showed far less legal assertiveness when it came to the recapture of fugitive slaves.[35]

Quitman's trip to New Orleans, however, almost brought tragedy. Marshal Davis served his warrant on the same day as Quitman's resignation, took him into custody, and escorted him downriver, allowing Quitman to drop off his family at Natchez on the way. A few days later, Henry—back from Princeton for his final winter break—and Louisa followed on another ship, intending to join their father in the Crescent City. Their steamer, a spanking new vessel with gas lighting and carpet from New York called the *Magnolia*, collided with another ship after leaving a wooding stop. The second ship sank, with the loss of thirty lives and considerable freight. The *Magnolia* survived, absorbing a hole in the bow, and continued to New Orleans. Louisa, rather shaken, felt that the ship would have gone down had it been moving faster at the time of impact. Eliza found herself thanking God for his "merciful preservation" of her children, and wrote Quitman that the accident proved that the family should strive more "to the honor and glory of God" and "live acceptably in His sight." Still resistant to his wife's religiosity, Quitman simply returned: "You truly say we should be thankful for the escape of our children. I hope they will continue to permit us to be proud of them."[36]

Quitman arrived in a strangely distracted city. Also in New Orleans was Jenny Lind, and the community, as had happened at her previous stops on the Atlantic coast and in Cuba, had gone into ecstasy over her. Her sponsor, entrepreneur P. T. Barnum, had done such a superb promotion job that tickets to her concerts—twelve were scheduled for the St. Charles Theater— brought auction prices as high as $240. People from as far away as Mobile were coming in to hear the Swedish Nightingale.[37]

The Lind craze could not help but touch Quitman's stay in New Orleans. He apparently attended one of the singer's concerts, and may have had a private audience with her. "Miss Lind has . . . expressed a wish that I should call on her," he noted on February 22. Later, when she headed upriver with plans to stop at Natchez, he wrote Eliza to be sure to take in her performance.[38]

Meanwhile, Quitman attracted his own share of public notice. From his first night in the city, when he was serenaded, he became public property. Mississippians flocked to his rooms by the hundreds. South Carolinians on hand sought him out. The "elite & most recherché gentlemen" in the city gave dinners for him. When he attended a masked ball, he found himself surrounded by a bevy of "*roguish* young ladies" who teased him about his alleged filibustering, leading him to quip that it had been easier to fight the Mexican War. Louisa reported home that she scarcely saw her father, and that "the only fear is that the good people of New Orleans will fete him to death." Quitman could not help but conclude that his message to the Mississippi legislature and his resignation as governor had given him even "more reputation" than he had commanded at the end of the war.[39]

The acclaim helped Quitman endure the irksome court business. Using McMurran as his attorney, he attended court on February 7, posted $1,000 bond, and, anxious to clear his name, requested Judge McCaleb to provide him a speedy trial. However, the Henderson case took precedence, and it wound up exhausting three hung juries. On February 13, the day the second hung jury was dismissed, Quitman rose in court and announced that he stood "ready to meet the charge," and that perhaps the court should put Henderson's retrial off, since it had proved so difficult, and consider his case instead. Henderson acknowledged that Quitman had a valid claim since he had come a long distance, but nonetheless insisted on his own "prior right." McCaleb upheld Henderson's request.

In the end, it all worked out. U.S. District Attorney Logan Hunton had been close to dismissing the Henderson case after the second hung jury, noting the difficulties of finding impartial jurors in a city which was a center for filibuster operations. He became even more discouraged when the third jury, which heard testimony from Quitman that López had not violated neutrality laws since he had no clear command structure and military organization when departing from American soil, also found it impossible to reach a consensus. When this jury announced its failure on March 6, Hunton gave up and entered a nolle prosequi against *all* the accused filibusters.[40]

Vindication! Quitman could not resist crowing to Eliza that "public sentiment" had forced the prosecution to end the "shameless farce." To Henry, back at Princeton, he described how "ingloriously" the federal government had failed in its attempt to "create prejudice" against him. His supporters, too, were overjoyed and held a big victory dinner at the St. Louis Hotel. Vowing to make a public "exposé" of the whole affair, Quitman returned to Mississippi, arriving at Monmouth on March 15. Two weeks later, in a message to the Central Southern Rights Association, Quitman suggested that the federal vendetta against him might have been intended to intimidate him so he would be less outspoken on southern rights.[41]

Relieved to be free of court restraint, Quitman put the López business behind him. Though there persisted a belief in some quarters that he maintained close ties with the filibusters,[42] Quitman did little, if anything, to abet López's plans to try another invasion of Cuba. This decision served him well, because the expedition, which occurred in August, came to a horrible end. López, misled by newspaper accounts of massive uprisings in central Cuba, launched his invasion before preparations were complete. Spanish authorities suppressed the Cuban insurgency—which had been vastly overplayed by initial American press accounts—even before the filibuster ship *Pampero* cleared American waters. Spotted before he debarked on the Cuban coast, López had insufficient time before Captain General José de la Concha's forces closed in on him. López, moreover, played into Concha's hands by dividing his command. He never had a chance. Of some 400 filibusters, about 250 suffered death in battle or execution after capture; thousands of spectators in Havana watched López die in a garrote. Most of the survivors (a few were freed) received stiff sentences to years of hard labor in the quicksilver mines at Cueta, a penal colony in Spanish Morocco.[43]

The denouement strengthened Quitman's conviction that filibustering was doomed without general, popular support. Yet, the events of that summer by no means removed Cuba from his consciousness. The island still beckoned the slave expansionist, and Quitman's interest must have been sharpened by a letter which Henry had posted after stopping in Havana on his way back to Princeton. Henry had found the island the "loveliest spot" he had ever seen, and gloried in its "undulating" hills and valleys which were "clothed with orange groves, cocoa nut, & every variety of strange tropical trees." "Oh! how dearly I would like to live in such a paradise," Henry had exclaimed, going on to declare that it was a "pity" that a "weak . . . imbecile people" controlled Cuba. However unprepared Quitman may have been in the winter of 1851 to fulfill his son's fantasies, he probably sensed that his destiny had already become inextricably linked to the fate of the Pearl of the Antilles.[44]

19

Southern Rights at Bay

SPRING at Monmouth played the siren. Returning from New Orleans, Quitman found his asparagus and lettuce doing well, his peas in blossom, and the trees budding forth in the anxious youth of the season. Soon, the family would be feasting on ripe strawberries. It was an alluring scene, a tempting contrast to the excitement and tension of the past few months. Fleeting visions danced before Quitman of how relaxing it might be to remain at his lovely residence "for a while in quiet." [1]

Too much, however, was expected of Quitman by other secessionists for him to play the fantasy out. This was especially true of South Carolina radicals, who not only found Quitman's politics congenial but also remembered his ties to the Palmetto Regiment in the war. Secession sentiment still controlled South Carolina, although some moderates now dared to praise the Union in public for the first time in years. Radical opinion, however, remained divided over whether the state dared to attempt unilateral withdrawal, and the December state legislature had followed an ambiguous course. The lawmakers endorsed "cooperationist" calls for southern unity before secession, by providing for an October, 1851, election of delegates to a southern congress expected to convene in Montgomery, Alabama, the following January. Yet, they also called for a February, 1851, election of delegates to a state convention which would have the authority to initiate separate secession. The ostensibly contradictory measures, moreover, were linked: the governor could not actually convene the state convention unless the southern congress was definitely going to meet. [2]

South Carolinians who believed in separate action looked to Quitman because of their legislature's conditional position. Quitman had intimated the previous fall that Mississippi would secede on its own. If this indeed happened, South Carolina cooperationists would no longer be able to prophesy that secession would mean the isolation of their state. Even though Quitman no longer held office in Mississippi, South Carolina disunionists counted on his formidable influence. "Genl," implored one Palmetto correspondent, "I believe that if there is a man in the whole South that has the nerve, and is capable of consummating the great object . . . you are the man." Similarly Quitman heard from Robert Barnwell Rhett, who had succeeded to John C. Calhoun's Senate seat, how South Carolina could be "released" peacefully if Mississippi and Georgia would act. Quitman could not resist such appeals. "I have become enlisted in the great struggle before us, and I must now see it out," he concluded.[3]

Fostering secessionist values among Mississippi's masses, however, presented no easy task. Moderates of both political persuasions who acquiesced in the 1850 Compromise had coalesced under the "Union Party" rubric and discovered, in the "Georgia Platform," an effective program to take to the voters. Georgia's state convention, held the previous December, had declared that though the Compromise of 1850 was less than ideal, Georgia would abide by it, provided the North faithfully execute the new fugitive slave law, refrain from congressional abolition of slavery in the District of Columbia, and prove willing to admit territories applying for admission to the Union as slave states. The conditional nature of Georgia's statement allowed Mississippi moderates to take an ostensibly tough stance against northern aggression while denying the radicals' position that acquiescence in the compromise was submission. It also put Mississippi radicals on the spot. Already some prominent secessionists, such as former governor Brown (now a congressman), were qualifying their endorsement of separate state resistance so as to protect their political flanks. Quitman found this trend troubling, and reported to Seabrook that he had observed "occasional indications of retrocession among office seekers."[4]

Still, antipathy to the compromise prevailed within the Democracy, which had been redesignated the "Democratic State Rights Party" to attract radical Whigs. Rather than capitulate to the unionist offensive, resistance advocates stressed that the sacrifice of political equilibrium in Congress, caused by the admission of California, far overshadowed superficial benefits derived from the new fugitive slave law. "Submission quacks," according to State Rights rhetoric, harked back to Toryism during the American Revolution. Two incidents in Boston, when mobs interfered with the recovery of fugitive slaves despite the new law, strengthened the radicals' hand. Radicals, moreover, claimed to have evidence that abolitionists were gaining control of both major political parties in the North. The ultimate horror lay ahead, when abolitionists would plunge the South into a horrifying race war:

> A war of brothers and of friends,
> Of color and of caste,

Of rapine, murder, butchery,
  While strength or life shall last,
With infant wail and midnight shriek
And deeds too horrible to speak.[5]

Quitman found that his own views and past actions occupied a central spot in this dialogue between moderates and radicals. Democratic State Rights men were promoting him for a new gubernatorial term, as a means of redeeming state honor from what was considered a federal usurpation. Unionists, on the other hand, stigmatized Quitman as a secessionist conspirator unwilling to consider any sectional accommodation no matter how reasonable the terms. James W. McDonald, Quitman's former gubernatorial private secretary, alerted Quitman that Henry Foote had been making such claims in public. Since Quitman had consistently maintained—even as recently as his New Orleans banquet—that meaningful northern concessions such as a division of the territories at 36°30′ would yet induce him to back away from his secession position, Foote's assertions amounted to a charge that Quitman was deceiving the people (or, as McDonald put it, holding "private opinions & designs" different from his "published sentiments"). Although Quitman had actually lost all genuine hope that southern pressure would extract from the North the concessions he advocated, he could ill afford to permit Foote and others to stain his reputation for integrity. Already proxies, such as Congressman Brown, were defending him from the unconditional-secession label in debates with unionists. Quitman knew that Foote's charge would damage both the resistance movement in the state and his own political prospects if he did not answer it more directly.[6]

Though hopeful that Mississippi public opinion was "daily" "more hostile" to the congressional settlement, Quitman nonetheless made an adjustment to the more conservative political ambience of the time as he entered the debate. He now realized that his earlier expectation that Mississippi would make history and secede first had been wishful thinking; as he informed South Carolina state senator John S. Preston, he could not even count on the "Southern-rights men"—much less the masses as a whole—to rally to separate secession. Mississippians simply could not be convinced that there were worse evils than unilateral withdrawal. Quitman knew he would have to make some concessions to cooperationists. So he spoke of the November convention offering new terms to the North, rather than declaring for immediate secession. When the North refused, the convention would propose to the other slave states a southern confederation.

Working from these lowered expectations, Quitman told a Democratic State Rights meeting in Natchez that though states had the constitutional right to secede, he would not "counsel" it for the present, even though recent U.S. senatorial elections in New York, Ohio, and Massachusetts indicated a growing antislavery influence in Congress. Similarly, Quitman used a public letter to review southern grievances against the North, yet argued in the same document that inflexible insistence on southern constitutional rights provided the "only mode of preserving the Union of the Constitution." [7]

What Quitman did not tell the voters was that he had so little faith that cooperation would work that he was taking steps to ensure that his own scenario for cooperation would never come to pass. Playing political hot potato, he now urged his South Carolina friends to do what they had begged of Mississippi, secede first. They should know, he wrote, that their scheme of a southern congress would come to nought; moderate upper South states like Virginia would control such a gathering and force "some new [useless] '*compromise*'" on the lower South. But if South Carolina seceded, his own state would follow suit. By winter, Mississippians would be antagonized by the latest northern refusal to make concessions, but would have no recourse to cooperation: "If . . . the people of South Carolina have made up their minds to withdraw . . . my advice would be to do so without waiting for the action of any other state, as I believe there would be more probability of favorable action . . . after her secession than before. So long as the several aggrieved states wait for one another, their action will be over-cautious and timid. Great political movements . . . must be bold." Quitman told Preston that if South Carolina risked secession, she could expect all the Gulf states to join her within two years. He further predicted that if federal authorities tried to interdict the movement with force, even the upper South would be moved to secede, which would enable South Carolina to create a "complete Southern confederacy." [8]

From late March to early May, Quitman threw himself into Natchez radical politics, including the organization of an "Adams County Southern Rights Association" (of which he became the first president). Then it was on to Jackson, for a giant barbecue called in his honor for the fourteenth by the Central Southern Rights Association. There, several thousand people, including "not a few of the sable race" who "listened attentively" while orators denounced abolitionism, turned out to honor their former governor. Quitman's speech—which ran some two to three hours—stressed his innocence in the Cuban affair.

The barbecue testified to Quitman's growing stature among radicals throughout the South. Its organizers had invited southern rights leaders from other states, which elicited letters praising Quitman and explaining why they could not make the trip. From Virginia, Nathaniel Beverley Tucker, who had shared his vision of a glorious southern confederacy with the 1850

Nashville Convention, called upon Mississippians to honor the man who had won an "empire" for the state, only to come "under the displeasure" of the same federal authorities who would usurp the lands for which Mississippians had fought and died. Tucker lauded Quitman for his efforts to "free *his* country [the South] from thraldom to a foreign power." The barbecue organizers also heard from Louisiana's Pierre Soulé, a French-born fire-brand who had opposed the Compromise of 1850 from his U.S. Senate seat and who designated Quitman one of the South's "most notorious champions and leaders." That night, a torchlit procession and ball provided a glittering finale to the celebration.[9]

Before leaving town, on May 16, Quitman took on Henry Foote in debate before a sizable audience in the house of representatives. Foote attacked the southern rights men as fanatic secessionists, excused Congress' refusal to declare null and void Mexican laws against slavery in New Mexico by say-ing that they did not work anyway, asserted that the land Texas had ceded to New Mexico was barren and thus worthless to the South, claimed that aboli-tionism was weakening in the North, reminded the audience how the state Democratic party had refuted nullification doctrine in the 1830s, and tried to discredit Quitman by referring to his "unpleasant" situation with regard to the popular Jefferson Davis. Quitman in rebuttal said that his dealings with Davis were not relevant to the crisis, that Democrats—including Foote—had previously supported the *theoretical* right of secession, and that Foote had obviously joined the camp of Daniel Webster of Massachusetts (a Whig who strongly supported the compromise) and other former Federalists who endorsed the settlement.[10]

Returning to Natchez, Quitman pressed his views on his neighbors again. At one meeting, he issued dire warnings of northern intentions to drive southerners into a "war of extermination with the servile race." Then it be-came central Mississippi's turn to hear from him. In early June he joined Jefferson Davis and other Democratic State Rights leaders for some radical agitation in Carroll, Attala, and Neshoba counties.[11]

Meanwhile, Quitman received encouraging news from South Carolina. In their February elections, South Carolinians chose a solidly secessionist dele-gation for their still unscheduled state convention. On May 12, John H. Means, Whitemarsh Seabrook's successor as governor, wrote Quitman that he should count on South Carolina's holding a convention in 1852 and that there was no longer "the slightest doubt" that South Carolina would then secede. Three days later Maxcy Gregg, an influential South Carolina lawyer-politician, dropped Quitman a line, promising South Carolina's readiness to take the initiative.

The gratifying news, however, also brought additional pressure to bear on

Quitman, for South Carolina's intended secession was based squarely on Quitman's past assurances that Mississippi would rally if South Carolina made the first move. "We will . . . lead off, even if we are to stand alone," avowed Means, "but trust that our sister states . . . will unite with us." Both Means and Gregg urged that Quitman fight unionist resurgence in Mississippi. Gregg, in fact, invoked the need for a "great leader" to carry on the struggle. "Be that leader and your place in history will remain conspicuous for the admiration of all ages to come," he prophesied. Quitman now had all the incentive necessary for doing everything possible to try to persuade Mississippians to elect a radical delegation to the November state convention. Quitman assured Means that he and his allies would probably carry the contest.[12]

On June 16, the Democratic State Rights convention met in Jackson to choose its state ticket and platform for the regular fall elections. Quitman, in attendance as one of five Adams County delegates, wanted the gubernatorial nomination. Running for high state office would give him a forum for presenting his views to the people.

The newspapers tell us that Quitman gained his nomination by acclamation at the June 17 morning session. What they do not reveal is what went on behind the "noise and confusion" to induce cooperationists and more moderate elements in the party to place their most radical spokesman at the head of their ticket. Many of the delegates surely realized that the selection of Quitman was bound to cost the Democrats some party votes at election time, since Quitman's secessionism had passed beyond the ideological limits of most of the party's rank and file. There was, however, considerable feeling that Quitman had been cheated by the federal government out of his rightful tenure as governor and that he deserved restitution if he desired another term. Quitman, moreover, apparently resorted to some arm twisting in order to capitalize on those sentiments. One delegate recalled later that Quitman and supporters intruded on the meeting of the nominations committee to press Quitman's case, and that several Quitman supporters even visited his main competitor Jefferson Davis—sick in his bed in a hotel room—and, taking advantage of Davis' physical weakness, induced Davis to write the nominating committee a note saying that he would decline the nomination.[13]

Driven by a sense of mission, Quitman had thrown himself on a somewhat reluctant party. "I have yielded to my destiny and accepted the nomination for governor," he wrote Seabrook. Jefferson Davis did Quitman a disservice when, having second thoughts a month later about making things so easy for his rival, he said Quitman's motives were based on mere "vanity." Committed to secession, Quitman was convinced that his candidacy was essential if Mississippians were to be persuaded to elect resistance men as delegates to the November convention.[14]

Unfortunately, Quitman could not fathom just what had transpired. The convention delegates had not exactly concealed the fact that Quitman's nomination derived more from a sense of obligation than concurrence in his radical doctrine; their platform reduced secession to a "last remedy" and deemed it "inexpedient" "under the existing circumstances." This was conservative stuff, and the implications were not lost on South Carolina radicals. Seabrook wrote Quitman that the platform had made an "unfavorable impression" in his state. Yet Quitman preferred to believe his nomination a more accurate indicator of Mississippi public opinion than was the platform. His selection, he insisted to Seabrook, proved the "firmness of the Southern rights party." Quitman had pinned his hopes so completely on secession that he just could not accept the truth.[15]

Some of Quitman's supporters, better attuned to the mood of the state than he was, sought to soften his image. "If we understand him aright," the *Free Trader* reassured its readers, "his views are, that circumstances render it unadvisable for separate state action." What a good time, too, to remind voters of the "deep reverence" Quitman had "always evinced for the Banner of the Stars and Stripes." Had not General Quitman insisted at Mexico City that his troops raise the "FLAG OF OUR UNION" first, before regimental colors? George Swann advised Quitman, along such lines, to model himself after Congressman Brown, who had already convinced audiences that he was no supporter of "immediate secession"; rather, he was simply practicing the more reputable kind of state resistance foreshadowed by the Virginia and Kentucky Resolutions of 1798 and 1799.[16]

Quitman accommodated such advice to a point. In a speech at Holly Springs, he professed a love of the Union and denied that he and his party were secessionist (though he reiterated that if the North did not rectify the deficiencies in the 1850 settlement, the South would have to take action). However, Quitman's secessionism had become too unqualified to permit him to maintain such a façade through a long summer. Occasionally, seduced by his own misguided instincts that the people at heart were with him, he relapsed into vitriolic extremist rhetoric. Alexander M. Clayton, justice of the Mississippi High Court of Errors and Appeals, joined Quitman during the later stages of the campaign. They traveled through a number of counties together by carriage, their servants following in a second vehicle. Clayton later recalled how Quitman could not entirely suppress his doctrinaire convictions: "I took the liberty of telling him on one occasion, that he went too far in his speeches, and that he was doing injury to us all. The next day he went farther than ever, and said, 'he would not be the Governor, of a submission State.'" [17]

Of course, even if Quitman had somehow managed to keep his secessionism under wraps, his unionist rivals would not have permitted people to forget his extremism. Throughout the summer, the Union press painted Quitman as a conspirator more than willing to transgress the legitimate bounds of political behavior to get his way. The Vicksburg *Whig* claimed to have incontrovertible evidence that Quitman had slipped away to Georgia in April to help the Cuba filibusters prepare their next expedition. A Madison County paper charged that Quitman, while governor, had hoarded in the state treasury $200,000 appropriated for common schools, because he wanted the funds handy for "war purposes." Unionists did not have to substantiate their accusations; they served the purpose of keeping Quitman and his supporters on the defensive. [18]

Quitman's position became infinitely more difficult when his antagonists came upon truly substantive material about his conspiratorial activities. The Union press, apparently benefiting from information furnished by a friend of Maxcy Gregg's father, exposed Quitman's ongoing correspondence with South Carolina radicals, particularly the notorious Robert Rhett. "Can it be true that Gen. Quitman has been privately writing letters to South Carolina, urging the madmen of that State to secede, and promising his official influence if elected Governor of Mississippi?" queried the *Whig*. Union papers reported that Rhett had even alluded publicly to Quitman's correspondence in a Fourth of July address intended to persuade a South Carolina audience to support secession. Given the republican values then current—the "people" were supposedly saints and majority decision was worshipped—both Quitman and Rhett were seriously compromised by the insinuation that they might be willing to thwart the public will to get disunion. Apparently without consulting each other, both men decided it would be better to lie rather than confess. "Gen. Quitman never, that I know of, wrote to me a letter in his life," proclaimed Rhett. Quitman issued a public letter saying that he had "no recollection of having ever written a letter to Carolina" after his nomination as governor (which was patently false) and that his letters before that time, though they encouraged South Carolina to resist federal oppression, gave no assurances about what Mississippi would do if South Carolina seceded (also untrue). Undecided voters may or may not have accepted Quitman's disavowals, but they were forced by the controversy to at least ponder whether their recent governor could be trusted again. [19]

Had Quitman faced an opponent such as Luke Lea, he might have survived the unionist attack. However, he had to deal with strong campaigner

Henry Foote as the Union nominee, and he made the mistake of agreeing to a grueling series of forty-eight scheduled debates, beginning at Yazoo City on July 7 and extending into the first week of September.[20]

Quitman's making this tactical miscalculation is a bit surprising, because he had in the past expressed sensitivity about his inadequacies as a speaker,[21] and he should have realized that he would be no match for his adversary. Never known for his wit or creativity, Quitman had always been prone to two- or three-hour ponderous addresses which seemed interminable and left audiences shifting in their seats. If he tried to infuse his orations with emotion, he wound up stammering and repeating himself. Rivals and friends who disagreed vehemently over the merits of Quitman's politics all concurred that it was painful to hear him out. "So subtle is his *collocation*," it was once said of Quitman, "that we defy the most astute critic to infer from a portion, amounting to seven-eighths of any one sentence, how it will most probable [*sic*] terminate. Indeed, it is not true, that he always terminates his sentences at all; but frequently, after one or two sublime *hems*, he leaps with most *elephantine* agility, from the bosom of one majestic period, *plump down* upon the bosom of a succeeding one, and rattles away . . . as if he had actually taken no leap whatever."[22] Even rare plaudits exposed his oratorical limitations. Eulogizers found themselves groping for such adjectives as "sensible," "plain," "earnest," and "masculine" to explain his style, and tended to couch their commendations in comparative terms. Quitman's speeches were never measured against standards of forensic excellence. Rather, they were judged against his own *prior* efforts or other speeches on the particular topic at issue.[23]

Perhaps Quitman had been carried away by managing to hold his own against Foote in Jackson. At any rate, if he anticipated gentlemanly, enlightened repartee, he was in for quick disillusionment. Occasionally he and Foote argued the acceptability of the 1850 Compromise, the true issue of the campaign. Foote continued to justify the legislation, now suggesting not only that Quitman's call for dividing California at 36°30′ offered little to the South since the rich gold mines were north of the line but also that Californians were on the verge of amending their state constitution to allow slavery after all. More often than not, however, the debate degenerated into personal acrimony and calumny. Foote, apparently hoping to reduce Quitman's heroic stature to human dimensions, summoned all the invective and wit he could muster—even mocking Quitman's sore throat, on one occasion—to get crowds laughing at Quitman. Foote also reported threats on his life before audiences, leaving the impression that Quitman had something to do with them. Quitman could not cope with Foote's methods. Within days, he heard from correspondents that Foote had been getting the better of him in the exchanges. "[W]ith the exception of a few *staunch State Rights men,*" his nephew Frederick reported about the debate at his own Yazoo City, "I have heard none who seemed disposed to do [your speech] . . . justice." [24]

Intimations of violence loomed over the debates from the start. At Lexington, in Holmes County, partisans of the candidates drew guns. On another occasion, Quitman suggested to Foote that they might have to work out their differences "at once in the woods." By the time they reached Panola County on July 17, both men had become too irritable to observe debate etiquette. Quitman had earlier contended that his indictment in New Orleans illuminated a federal conspiracy to suppress states' rights. Now Foote responded that Quitman had been known to consort openly with filibusters and that as governor he might have even allowed López's agents to draw arms from Mississippi militia supplies. When, on the next day, Foote repeated the charge despite Quitman's denial, Quitman could restrain his emotions no longer. He blasted Foote for making accusations which were "false and cowardly, scandalous and ungentlemanly." Foote interrupted, saying that he was willing to admit that the arms transfers might have occurred without Quitman's knowledge and that Quitman should retract his derogatory remarks. When Quitman refused, Foote charged Quitman and gave him a glancing blow. Onlookers tried to restrain Quitman, but he managed nonetheless to land a punch and kick Foote before they were separated. Foote took quite a shot. A full month later he still carried a "blue black place on his forehead" as a souvenir of the fracas. [25]

Though the unseemly brawl discredited both candidates ("I don't think now I can vote for either of them," concluded one Holmes County man in disgust), the incident worked most to Quitman's advantage because it provided a face-saving rationale for disengaging from the joint canvass. Shortly afterward, he announced that he had terminated the debates, releasing in their stead a schedule of his own appearances through the September convention elections. He would meet thirty-four speaking engagements, starting in De Soto County on July 24 and winding up at Brandon in Rankin County on September 4. The schedule would take him eastward across the northern part of the state and then straight down the tier of eastern Mississippi counties as far as Clarke County, before a westward visit to Rankin (which adjoined Hinds). He would miss only his home base, the old Natchez District, and the extreme southern part of the state. [26]

Quitman kept constantly on the move during the next few weeks to make his appointments. "I speak this morning here," he reported home from Oxford on July 28, "& must ride ten miles this afternoon." He found himself writing letters in rooms crowded with people, and with barely enough time to "sleep, wash & dress." Yet, how much more satisfying the campaign was than those exasperating encounters with Foote. Though he sacrificed the original schedule to Foote, which gave his opponent the advantage of addressing some people who turned out expecting a debate, Quitman found audiences receptive to his appeals, which now ran three to four hours. Even nonplanting counties seemed sympathetic. At Ripley, in Tippah County, Quitman was heard to comment favorably on his audience's size, in light of reports he had heard that the "County of the Hills" lacked even a "Corporal's guard" of State Rights people. Then, too, the romanticism of the campaign engendered hope. Supporters provided white chargers for him to make grand entrances into towns, and he was usually greeted by cannon salutes, banners, music, and women waving handkerchiefs from their windows. If Quitman found occasion to read his party's press, he might have noted that the Vicksburg *Sentinel* had predicted that he would triumph by 15,000 to 20,000 votes, and that the *Mississippian* had offered an open bet of $1,000 to $5,000 to anyone willing to wager on Foote. And, undoubtedly, some of the State Rights friends who put him up at night filled his ears with optimistic appraisals of his chances.[27]

Quitman never quite recognized just how quixotic his campaign had become—that, as Powhatan Ellis observed, he had "outstripped the views of the people in recommending secession." When Mississippi voters cast their ballots for convention delegates on September 1 and 2, they went overwhelmingly unionist, choosing more than two procompromise candidates for every southern rights man selected. Ironically, the State Rights ticket did best in relatively poor, Piney Woods counties; Quitman had failed to persuade Mississippi River planters, who had the most at stake in slavery, that northern aggressions posed an immediate threat to their survival. Finally Quitman saw the situation clearly: barring a dramatic, sudden shift in public opinion—which was hardly likely—he could expect the voters to choose Foote in November. More important, even if elected governor, he could not hope to persuade the state convention to support secession. Rather than challenge his state's republican mores, he decided that the gentlemanly thing to do would be to bow out of the race. From Monmouth, he sent a note dated September 6 to the *Free Trader* office announcing his "respectful submission" to the people's will. His party then replaced him on its ticket with Jefferson Davis. Though hampered by a severe case of pneumonia, Davis made a respectable effort, losing to Foote by only 999 votes. Nonetheless, it was still another State Rights reverse, and the Union party dominated the year's legislative elections (winning 63 of 98 lower house races and 7 of 16 senate contests). Unionists also defeated all of Mississippi's State Rights congressmen, with the exception of Albert G. Brown, who had softened his radical image enough to gain reelection.[28]

The September convention election in Mississippi proved a watershed in the crisis of the Union. Procompromise men throughout the South did not need to wait for the formality of the November convention's 72-to-17 vote that secession was "utterly unsanctioned by the Federal Constitution" to comprehend that they had successfully passed a crucial milestone in their efforts to preserve the Union. "The disunionists in South Carolina . . . may hang up their fiddles," celebrated a prominent South Carolina unionist upon hearing the news from Mississippi. With no hope that Mississippi would follow South Carolina's secession, the South Carolina state convention of 1852 became an embarrassment rather than the historic occasion its proponents had anticipated. The assemblage, though endorsing secession in principle, could only declare that it was an inexpedient time to put the principle into practice. The secession movement, at least for the present, had collapsed throughout the South.[29]

Over the next several months, Quitman observed his chastened State Rights party beat as precipitate a retreat as possible from the resistance position he had thrust upon it. Hopes of future elective office and patronage rested upon the ability of party leaders to align party doctrine with majoritarian sentiment before the Union party consolidated its gains and became the dominant political organization in the state. "[W]e yield to the opinion of the people," proclaimed the Jasper County party on October 6. Immediately following the September election, State Rights leaders announced that the State Rights–Union political division—which had proven so disadvantageous to them—had been rendered artificial by the conclusion of the sectional crisis, and demanded a return to the traditional Whig-Democratic rivalry and to issues associated with that competition such as state bonds, banking, and the tariff.

By 1852, Quitman's State Rights associates were prepared to take the next logical step: to formally rejoin the national Democracy. There was talk in the states' rights press about how northern Democrats could be trusted after all; voters need not be unduly concerned about discrepancies between the northern Democratic and State Rights positions on slavery in the territories because the issue would probably not rise again "during the present generation." When the party assembled in January for its first state convention since the September elections, it did so under the old Democratic designation. That May, delegates from the Mississippi party attended the Democratic National Convention in Baltimore, which nominated Franklin Pierce for president, and Mississippi Democrats supported the Mexican War general from New Hampshire afterwards in what had all the trappings of a political homecoming:

> Come Democrats enter together!
> We've started the New Hampshire Ball,
> And we'll roll it in fair and foul weather
> Till we stop it in Washington Hall;
> Old Tennessee Polk'ed 'em before,
> Young Granite shall sure Pierce 'em now,
> For we'll all be the same as of yore,
> United from city and plough.[30]

Quitman was appalled by the blatant political opportunism of the State Rights strategy. Too much an ideologue to be gracious about the repudiation of his policies, he had chided the electorate for capitulating to Congress' "late aggressive measures" in his letter of withdrawal from the gubernatorial race. Apostasy by fellow party leaders was even harder to take. Over the fall of 1851, he grumbled so much about Albert G. Brown's defection that Brown felt compelled to send Quitman reassurance that he "*never on any occasion attempted to throw you off*" during his successful congressional campaign. By December, 1851, Quitman had grown so frustrated that he decided to try to salvage something from the debris of the State Rights cause, no matter whom it alienated and no matter what its effect on his always shaky image as a consistent Democrat. Writing W. D. Chapman, editor of the Columbus *Standard*, Quitman urged that the state Democracy set a price on its reincorporation into the national party while it still had some leverage. Mississippi Democrats attending the May convention at Baltimore should insist upon the nomination for vice president of a southern rights man who had opposed the admission of California.[31]

Quitman made his point more forcefully the next month, when attending the state Democratic convention as an Adams County delegate. Upset that a resolution terming federal coercion of a seceded state unconstitutional was ruled out of order, Quitman gave an impassioned plea that the party rediscover its states' rights soul. Quitman warned his colleagues that they were falling victim to the lure of federal patronage: "The splendor of a government which dispenses fifty millions of revenue, and thirty thousand offices dazzles the eyes of most politicians." But Democrats could still redeem themselves if they at least championed abstract principles vital to southern survival; they had to renounce the November state convention and verify the *right* of secession. Any hesitation, he contended, would constitute "voluntary civil suicide." Again he stressed that southern demands need not hamper reunion with northern Democrats; northern presidential aspirants

265

required southern votes and would stifle their reservations. But the convention refused to go beyond a meaningless endorsement of the Virginia and Kentucky Resolutions. Quitman gave up hope that a "sound" northern Democrat (and he expressed an interest in New York's William Marcy—whom he considered safe on slavery—in private consultations during the convention) would garner the national Democracy's presidential nomination. The "noble and sublime" ideological struggle of the summer of 1851, he felt, had given way to scrambling for spoils. The best that faithful State Rights men could do now was form new associations to disseminate their views and wait for their position to achieve public acceptance again. After all, the "sacred fire" had been "preserved in the deep recesses of the temple for centuries by the vestal virgins."

Quitman's alienation reached yet another plateau after the May national Democratic convention. Quitman had known presidential nominee Pierce in the war and was fairly certain that Pierce was as reasonable a northerner on slavery as southerners could expect. But he was profoundly troubled by the Democratic platform which pledged party adherence to "the acts known as the Compromise measures" as well as by vice-presidential selection Senator William R. King of Alabama, who had become a notorious proponent of the compromise. To Quitman, the party had played into the hands of "political chameleons" like Foote and William Sharkey—the latter had fully joined the unionist camp–and had little value unless it could be persuaded to acknowledge southern rights. No party striding a "centaur hobby" with an "abolition head and Southern tail," he contended, was worth preserving. In July, he issued a public letter which lectured his state party on Jeffersonian and Calhounian principles and the benefits of slavery, and warned that congressional abrogation of the political "equilibrium" foreshadowed the North's ending slavery by constitutional amendment. Without slavery's expansion, the institution would die. If southern Democrats would only visualize national politics as akin to a military campaign, Quitman suggested, they too would comprehend how limited defeats like the compromise would ultimately destroy slavery: "As it is easier to defend a fortress against an open daylight attack than to guard against the secret approach of the sap and mine, so I have less fears of the open war of abolition and free-soilism than the more slow and insidious, but not less dangerous effects of compromises that take away, but never give." [32]

Mississippi Whigs quickly put Quitman's disapprobation of the Democracy to their own use. The Union party, in an attempt to reclaim states' rights Whigs who had defected to the Democratic State Rights party, had adopted the Whig label again, but party leaders were having trouble selling the national party's presidential nominee, General Scott, to the rank and file.

Scott, though a Virginian, was widely perceived as having ties to Free-Soil elements in the northern wing of the party. In addition, since Scott had side-stepped an explicit endorsement of the Compromise of 1850 in his acceptance letter, some potential Mississippi Whig voters feared that he would not enforce the pro-South clauses of the compromise, such as the fugitive slave law, if elected president. Mississippi Democrats were having a field day portraying Scott as a covert abolitionist, and when Quitman, who was universally accepted as a champion of slavery, made some offhand comments (while traveling on a river steamer) that his former commander had been misunderstood by southern Whigs and that if there was any Whig he might vote for, it was Scott, the Whig press could not resist plastering Quitman's statement on its pages and distorting it into an actual endorsement of the general.[33]

Quitman, however, eluded the trap. No one was going to manipulate him into supporting *anyone* running on a procompromise platform. Neither major party conformed to his standards, and, he informed Henry, he was indifferent whether Pierce or Scott won. So he had no choice but to issue yet another public letter, to clear the air. Yes, he had said that southern Whigs need not fear that Scott would repudiate the compromise. Yes, he had praised Scott's military achievements. But Scott, a supporter of a "strong national government," could not command his vote.[34]

Surprising developments in Alabama further complicated Quitman's position. In Mississippi, Quitman found himself virtually isolated by his insistence on preserving the southern rights movement; in Alabama, however, a considerable faction of the party leadership resisted reunion with the Democrats. On March 4, 1852, an Alabama Southern Rights party convention had resolved that the compromise was "unjust, unconstitutional, and dangerous to the South" and that the party remained prepared to resist it by any "effectual means." A standing committee was appointed to keep the organization functioning.

Quitman became involved when the Alabama party turned to the matter of endorsing the ticket for the presidential election. Although many party leaders, such as William Yancey, saw Pierce's nomination as a definite concession to the South by the northern Democracy and thought that supporting Pierce would encourage further concessions, majority sentiment in the party took a more cautious position. Another convention, held in July, resolved that the party would only endorse a major party candidate if Pierce or Scott satisfactorily answered questions posed to them by mail from the party committee. When Pierce refused a response and Scott simply referred Alabamians to his letter accepting the Whig nomination, the party felt it had little choice but to field a third-party ticket representing its own views. Yet another convention summons went out, this time for September 13, and meanwhile the committee asked Quitman and other potential candidates for their views. Quitman responded that the Alabamians should indeed preserve their party structure, realizing that by this encouragement he set himself up for a possible nomination: "Their convention meets . . . at Montgomery," he informed Henry, "& from numerous letters I have received, it may result in naming me." Unenthusiastic about running, he nonetheless felt a duty to support the "flag of states' rights." [35]

Quitman wound up unfurling the standard, because the September convention nominated him for vice president and George M. Troup of Georgia, a former governor, U.S. senator, and nullifier, for president. Although the nominations were primarily an ideological rallying point to keep the southern rights movement viable in Alabama, the Alabamians did undertake serious efforts after the convention to carry their state. At least three newspapers formally endorsed Troup and Quitman, an electoral ticket was fielded, and some of the electors and other party leaders began an active canvass. But only Montgomery and other slavery-oriented Black Belt counties had sent delegates to the state convention, and the ticket had limited appeal in the state as a whole. Elsewhere in the South the ticket drew only minuscule support, given the general Democratic satisfaction with Pierce's nomination. In Mississippi, in fact, Whigs gave the Southern Rights nominations more attention than did the Democrats, because they hoped to divide the Democratic vote and throw the state to Scott. The Natchez *Courier*, for instance, mischievously seized on the nominations as proof that the Baltimore Democratic platform and ticket had been "constructed to catch abolition," and challenged Mississippi Democrats to prove the sincerity of their proslavery stance by switching to Quitman and Troup. The ticket's chances, moreover, plummeted when Troup, in a highly irregular acceptance letter, reported his own intention of voting for Pierce. Troup explained that he lent his name to the ticket solely to foster states' rights principles. As if that were not bad enough, Troup also alluded to his advanced age of seventy-two and ill health, and pointed out that his physical condition would preclude his actually serving as president if elected. [36]

More swan song than a rejuvenation of the southern resistance spirit, the Troup-Quitman ticket fared miserably when election time arrived in November. Party officials fielded electoral slates in just two states, Georgia and Alabama, and even in those states the vote was pitiful. The ticket only drew some 2,000 votes in its Alabama stronghold (less than 5 percent of the votes cast in the state) and a truly paltry 126 votes (slightly over .2 percent) in Georgia. Pierce and King, the victors, swept the slave states except for Kentucky and Tennessee, which wound up in the Whig column. [37]

Quitman had written his son over the summer that he had begun taking political stands with an eye toward long-range developments, and it is doubtful that he thought his candidacy would make much of an impact on the election. Because he expected so little, he escaped the kind of acute discouragement which had plagued him after so many other political defeats. In fact, he began angling for the U.S. Senate seat of Walter Brooke (Foote's replacement) which was due to expire on March 4 the next year, and, though he made no headway in the Senate race, his newfound realism did help carry him through the final phases of Democratic reunification. Despite considerable intraparty strife, as State Rights and Union Democratic factions bickered over the terms of reconciliation, the party in 1853 elected its gubernatorial candidate John J. McRae by almost 5,000 votes and swept the legislative and congressional races.[38]

Quitman would learn to function within the emerging political order of Mississippi. He eventually regained much of his popularity. But he would ever afterward carry with him intellectual baggage from his lost crusade for southern rights—memories of how "even" "Southern politicians, and presses," instead of comprehending the reasonableness of his position, had convinced gullible voters that he and his allies were "secessionists and extremists whose opinions and actions are to be regarded as dangerous as those of the abolitionists." Years after Mississippi put its stamp of approval on the Compromise of 1850, John Quitman would still experience pangs of frustration as he recalled his futile war against the "California swindle."[39]

20

A Gentlemen's Expedition

TWELVE-YEAR-OLD Rose Quitman's diary was an unlikely source for political commentary. Her elder brother and sisters all imbibed their father's radical fervor, but Rose had yet to discover her political consciousness. Dolls held center stage in her vivid imaginary world, and her diary recounted doll pairings and marriages or everyday occurrences at her playhouse or around Monmouth. How curious, then, that Rose's entry of July 2, 1853, would indicate that her dolls had "a war at present with Mexico, Spain & Cuba so all the gentlemen have gone." [1]

Rose's remarks were so out of character, they raise the question of what prompted them. Although it may have been a fluke that her dolls abandoned nuptial affairs for martial combat for a day, it is probable that there was something going on at Monmouth which led her to mention Mexico, Spain, and Cuba. Most likely she had heard some talk about Cuba, for her father, after years of hedging, had become a filibuster.

Certainly Quitman had been around home enough for Rose to catch wind of something. On December 2, he had given Louisa in marriage to John S. Chadbourne, a Methodist minister from Maine who had been preaching in Baton Rouge. It was a joyous occasion. Gratified that his eldest daughter had finally made a match, Quitman approved of Chadbourne, despite his lack of standing and wealth, from the start. Days of feasting and socializing at Monmouth and Melrose followed the wedding. [2]

With the exception of a brief visit to New Orleans to purchase pork, plows, and other items required at Live Oaks, Quitman did not stray far from Monmouth's environs during the succeeding months. "Last Friday," Rose noted on one occasion, "Buddie Hennie [Henry] & Papa went to a fox hunt out at Col. [F. L.] Claibornes . . . they chased a fox but could not get him[.] Papa & Buddie Hennie came home in time for dinner & with fine appetites." Looking after Henry's well-being, Quitman made arrangements for his son to undertake a long-planned European tour. After completing his studies at Princeton in 1851, Henry had studied a little law and then spent most of 1852 at Live Oaks. Now the time had come for Henry to see the Old World—the capstone of his training as a cultured gentleman. Quitman sent him off in May on the steamer *Baltic* from New York, armed with the right references and advice that he make his tour "instructional & useful by close and active observation, reflection and reading." [3]

During this same period, as Rose may have inadvertently discovered, Cuba filibustering became Quitman's political opiate, his release from and antidote to Mississippi's emasculation of southern rights. Following the López disaster, some of the Louisiana filibuster element had fashioned a secret "Order of the Lone Star" to revive the Cuba annexation movement. Chapters sprang up quickly in Mississippi, New Orleans, New York City, and other parts of the country; and the order had an impact on the 1852 election, particularly in the Deep South, where Franklin Pierce was believed sympathetic and rumored a member. In October, 1852, moreover, a new Cuban Junta emerged in New York. [4]

Quitman could hardly stay aloof. Since December, 1851, when he played a prominent role at a Natchez meeting called to protest John S. Thrasher's arrest by Spanish officials during a crackdown following the last López expedition, Quitman had maintained intermittent contact with the filibusters by mail and apparently during business trips to New Orleans. In December, 1852, Quitman was visited at Monmouth by someone whom Rose identified as a "Hungarian," almost certainly Louis Schlessinger, an exile after the Revolution of 1848 who had been arrested at the time of López's Cárdenas expedition for trying to get a shipload of filibusters out of New York. [5]

By early 1853, encouraged by an apparent shift of official attitude in Washington toward filibustering, Quitman stood poised to take up arms. President Pierce included strident expansionist rhetoric in his inaugural address that March, and seemed to be stacking the deck for the filibusters with his appointments. Not only did he pack the U.S. diplomatic corps with Cuba enthusiasts like Pierre Soulé (minister to Spain), but he chose Jefferson Davis as secretary of war, and Davis had been empathic about filibustering in recent speeches—particularly at the Mississippi Democratic convention of 1852, when he had compared Narciso López's American soldiers to Lafayette and other Europeans who had helped Americans struggle for independence against England. Surely Pierce would show filibusters greater tolerance than had his immediate predecessors. [6]

On April 29, representatives of the New York Junta visiting Natchez offered Quitman appointment as "exclusive chief" of their planned revolutionary expedition, with supreme military and civil power until—in his judgment—it became possible to "constitute the island a sovereign and independent nation, and as such, form such a government as shall best fulfill its wishes." Responding the very next day with rhetoric about Spanish despotism on the island and how Cuban freedom would contribute to American prosperity, Quitman promised that he would indeed accept, provided the junta give him "adequate means" for the expedition and provided that all Cuban exiles in the United States rally behind him (he could not overlook how factionalism had plagued López). Assuming these conditions would be met, Quitman told his son that he had taken up the Cuban "enterprise." When President Pierce in May appointed Alexander M. Clayton—a Cuba annexationist and political associate of Quitman's—consul to Havana, Quitman's confidence was further enhanced.[7]

Quitman's emotional, if not yet contractual, tie to the filibusters explains his remarkable performance a few weeks later at the "Southern and Western Commercial Convention" in Memphis. Governor Foote had appointed him one of Mississippi's delegates to the June 6 gathering. While there, Quitman showed more interest in Cuba than in the issues for which the convention had been summoned.[8]

Heading Mississippi's large sixty-three-man delegation,[9] Quitman assumed a moderately obstructionist position regarding the significant commercial matters before the meeting. Thus, when a proposal for federal aid to a Pacific railroad came on the agenda, Quitman said that he favored the railroad in the abstract, but he could not endorse federal aid. He predicted that the project would drain the federal treasury of $300 million, produce an immense national debt, and accelerate the federal government's accumulation of power. Similarly, on the issue of federal aid for river improvements, Quitman refrained from outright opposition. However, he irritated some of the border state delegates by urging that the convention vote separately—and first—on improving the mouth of the Mississippi River, before turning to presumedly more controversial projects such as the improvement of the rapids on the upper Mississippi between the Des Moines and Rock rivers. Border state delegates feared that Quitman and some vocal Deep South followers would turn on projects benefiting the upper river, once their own interests were dealt with. Though Quitman hotly denied that he would stoop to such "sectional" tactics, he did wind up declining to vote for the Des Moines–Rock River project after improvements for Galveston were appended to the resolution. Both railroad and river measures passed, despite Quitman's objections.[10]

Quitman's remarks on Cuba, though brief, stood in stark contrast to his negativism regarding commercial measures. One item before the meeting concerned whether the federal government should exert pressure on Brazil to open the Amazon River to American navigation and trade. Quitman, after a resolution had been seconded to establish a committee to bring the matter before Congress, interjected that the delegates would be wise to consider that "little island"—Cuba—which they would pass on their "way" to the Amazon. In a thinly veiled allusion to the virtues of filibustering, Quitman noted how the "sabre and musket" had been used in the past to advance the "cause of civilization." Quitman's comment earned applause, but nothing more. John S. Thrasher, who had been released by Spanish officials and was now living in New Orleans, introduced a resolution endorsing American acquisition of Cuba. The delegates refused to even consider it, apparently for fear that it was too controversial and might destroy the consensus which had been achieved on commercial questions.[11]

A few weeks after the Memphis meeting adjourned, Quitman went north for the summer, leaving Chadbourne, who that April had been appointed temporary rector at Trinity Church, to watch over Louisa, Eliza, and the girls at Monmouth. For all Eliza knew, he merely intended to purchase a draining machine in Cincinnati for Live Oaks and visit his relations in upper New York. But what really inspired the trip was Quitman's hope of setting up the kind of organization he would require to effect a successful invasion of Cuba. His most important stop: the eastern filibuster capital, New York City, where Schlessinger—who had already written that he was anxious to settle the score against "Old Spain"—and other filibuster activists such as John L. O'Sullivan were waiting for his instructions.[12]

Low water and crowded boats on the Mississippi and Ohio made for a miserable trip to Cincinnati. Quitman's vessels ran aground on sandbars several times, and taverns along the way had so little room that he slept four nights in a row on a blanket on his steamer's hurricane deck. Tired and "jaded," he arrived in Cincinnati, only to discover anew how abolitionism was taking over the North. Major Henry Chotard and his family, fairly close Natchez acquaintances, had been staying in the city and almost lost all the servants they had taken along. Their "boy" ran off and could not be found; two servant girls came close to being liberated by habeas corpus procedures. Only the express desire of the girls to remain slaves allowed the Chotards to retain possession.[13]

Quitman spent a few days in Cincinnati visiting foundries and talking to contractors, and then traveled on to the Empire State. On July 16, after attending the grand opening of the Crystal Palace Exhibition in New York City, the closest thing to a world's fair held in the United States during Quitman's lifetime, he arrived at Red Hook (formerly a part of Rhinebeck) to pass some time with his sisters. He celebrated the beauty of the mountains he remembered from childhood, visited with his father's successor at the Old

Stone Church, and found that his soldier's reputation still had a magic charm in his native county. "[N]o sooner was his arrival known than every body flocked to see him," his sister Louisa reported to his family back home, "& nothing would do but a public reception." Quitman made the most of this chance to address a northern audience, and, after some platitudes about the valor of volunteer soldiers and how since the war even "John Bull" had become "polite to Young America," he launched into his recipe for preserving the "glorious Union." Surely the "stern freemen" of the area recognized that the South had "domestic institutions dissimilar from those in the North," and saw that southerners as a minority could not afford to permit their states' rights to be violated. If New Yorkers stuck by the "federative principle" shunning "consolidated government" and interference with slavery, they might yet keep the nation together.[14]

Leaving on July 19, Quitman spent the next several weeks at New York City, Philadelphia, Washington, D.C., and other eastern cities. He seems to have transacted most of his filibuster business from lodgings at New York's fashionable Astor House. But he may have tried to recruit his old Mexican War friend General George Cadwalader while in Philadelphia, and possibly tested President Pierce's position on filibustering during his visit to Washington. A reporter in the capital noted that he and the president had enjoyed some "cordial" discussions, and J. F. H. Claiborne later contended that when Quitman left the capital, he was convinced that federal authorities sympathized with his objectives and would not interfere by enforcing the neutrality laws.[15]

Quitman put his time in the East to good advantage. Rabble-rousing New York City congressman Mike Walsh, accepting Quitman's logic that the conquest of Cuba was essential to America's future, enlisted in the invasion force. An Irish native and controversial working-class spokesman, Walsh believed slavery the "mildest and most rational form" of employer-employee relations, and had no inhibitions about adding a slave state to the Union. Chatham Roberdeau Wheat also contacted Quitman during his New York stay. A volunteer in the Mexican War, Wheat had served with López and participated in several filibustering forays into Mexico. Disappointed in love, Wheat stood prepared to follow Quitman "wherever you may order," and introduced Quitman to his brother John, who expressed a similar interest in the plot. Kentuckians John T. Pickett and Theodore O'Hara, and New Yorker George Bolivar Hall (the son of a former mayor of Brooklyn), were all Mexican War veterans, López men, and professional adventurers willing to lend a hand. Mansfield Lovell, Quitman's former aide, also joined the invasion team at this time.[16]

While in the New York area, Quitman renewed contact with Schlessinger,

John S. Thrasher, and O'Sullivan. Pierce's selection as American minister to Portugal, O'Sullivan shared a cipher message from Havana. His contact reported that the Creole rebels were too disorganized to effect anything on their own, and depended on "an efficient cooperator to Ron"—code for Quitman—to "change the aspect of all." Quitman also learned from O'Sullivan that the Creoles hoped to ease his way by persuading a Spanish official on the island to issue a pro-Quitman pronouncement at the moment of landing.[17]

Seeing the pieces falling into place, Quitman was finally prepared to sign a formal contract with the junta. By a document dated New York, August 18, the junta conferred on Quitman "all the powers, rights and privileges" of "civil and military chief of the revolution," and all the powers of "dictatorship" necessary to overthrow Spanish rule in Cuba and make the island independent. The junta agreed to act only on Quitman's authorization and to transfer to Quitman control of its funds as well as authority to issue bonds, charter vessels, or take other action in its name. Quitman was even given the power to designate his second- and third-in-command, in case he should die before the revolution was complete. In return, Quitman pledged to invade Cuba "at as early a time as is possible" and to forfeit his total power as soon as he established a "free and liberal government" on the island.[18]

Expecting to handle the next planning phase from Monmouth and New Orleans, Quitman set out for home. After enduring another tedious journey on the low-water Ohio, he was soon reunited with his family. "This morning I got up practiced and eat [*sic*] my breakfast," Rose recorded on September 8, "just as we had got up from the table the children said that Papa was coming[.] [W]e went on the back gallery & saw Papa riding on Ellen Douglas through the gate . . . & just as he was getting off his horse we told him howdy do." Even for a family accustomed to an absent father, his appearance was a relief. "Papa has been away so long at the North," Rose reflected, "that I can hardly believe he is come home."[19]

By the time Quitman arrived, however, Natchez was in the throes of one of the worst yellow fever epidemics ever to strike the vulnerable river community. The place seemed besieged by the dread disease: stores and churches had closed, and many of the better off had fled northward or to country residences. Finding Eliza and the children in good health, Quitman dared hope that his own household would be spared (he attributed the six or so fatalities a day in Natchez to "unacclimated persons"). Still, to play it safe, Quitman kept his family out of town. A believer in preventive medicine, he also prescribed doses of mustard seed.[20]

Quitman's luck ran out in days. Chadbourne contracted the disease and died on September 27, leaving Louisa—who was pregnant—a widow after less than a year of marriage. Several of the children fell ill with the fever, and though the children recovered, other members of Quitman's extended family were not so fortunate. Quitman's brother-in-law Henry lost a son; nephew Frederick Quackenboss died; Eliza's mother and stepfather fell victims.

Sorrow weighed heavy upon Quitman and his household. Quitman could accept Mrs. Fyler's death; she had been ill for years. He had never been close, moreover, to Eliza's stepfather. But he worried about Frederick's leaving five children, anguished over the loss of several family servants, and watched in helpless frustration as Louisa so grieved for Chadbourne during the fall that she eventually fell seriously ill. Still-healthy members of the family were in dread of whom the fever would strike next, and the sense of gloom was heightened when word drifted in every now and then of the death of a Natchez or New Orleans acquaintance. Uncomfortable living conditions just added to the misery. Because the disease was believed communicable, whole rooms were given over to the sick. This forced the rest of the family to sleep three to a bed or on the floor.

Rarely had Quitman felt more isolated. Nabob visiting became a lost social art. Nursing at home and at Woodlands occupied so much time that he could not get away to Palmyra to check on the cotton crop, even though Turner had reported that it was poor. A trip to Live Oaks to see how Fuqua was managing was out of the question. Quitman could only wait anxiously for the killing frost, which he knew would bring relief.[21]

Liberation came on December 9. The family rose to find ice in the washhouse and tubs. Finally, normal living could be resumed. Eliza and some of the children took the carriage into town that very day for long-postponed shopping and visits. Quitman, too, ventured out more. Nights found him taking strolls around the grounds in the cool air, smoking his customary after-dinner cigars. When the circus came to the landing aboard a steamboat, Quitman descended the bluff with the children and took them to see the animals.[22]

Joy, however, reserved its genuine return for year's end. Quitman became a grandfather on December 31, when Louisa gave birth to a girl, named Eva Saub, at Monmouth. Soon afterward, word arrived that Henry, after a stormy voyage across the Atlantic, was back in the United States and staying at George and Annie Turner's house in New York City while he traced a missing trunk. Henry's letters over the last few months had been among Quitman's few satisfactions: with true filial loyalty, he had followed his father's advice on how to travel in Europe and sent home letters crammed with detail about all that he had learned on his trip. Now he announced that before coming home he planned to ask for the hand of an Alabama girl whom he had met while in Ireland. "Molly" (Mary L.) Gardner, the daughter of an extremely wealthy Selma area planter, won Quitman's instant approval. Delighted at the aristocratic match, father assured son that he would receive Molly as a "cherished daughter," a vow that he and Eliza did indeed keep.[23]

Once again, Quitman took up expedition preparations in earnest. Though Lovell had visited Monmouth in November about the enterprise, Quitman's hands had been tied by the epidemic. But from Christmas, which he passed in New Orleans rather than with his family, he devoted himself that winter to filibuster affairs, perhaps prodded by new evidence of his political impotence—the state legislature accorded him but a single vote when it selected Albert G. Brown for U.S. senator on January 7. Quitman put in several appearances in New Orleans, and tried some recruiting in Alabama. He also turned up at Jackson, where he established a Mississippi organization headed by James McDonald and pressed Reuben Davis, colonel of the Second Mississippi Regiment during the war (and a former judge), to participate.[24]

Recent disclosures from Cuba lent urgency to Quitman's movements. Spain, after years of hedging, seemed to be giving in to British pressure for emancipation. In September, Spain appointed a reputed abolitionist, Juan M. de la Pezuela, as captain general. Captains general held almost total political and military power in Cuba, and Pezuela, after taking office in December, appeared to be living up to that reputation. Not only did he issue a decree freeing slaves imported illegally from America (a substantial percentage of the island's bondsmen), he also instituted a policy of actively searching plantations for these emancipados, as well as of importing free black apprentices from Africa to supplant slave labor. New regulations facilitated the efforts of hired Cuban slaves to purchase their own freedom. Pezuela allowed racial intermarriage and black participation in the militia. All these developments, duly reported in the American press (which was accustomed to giving careful scrutiny to Cuban affairs), gave the impression that total emancipation was only a matter of time.[25]

Pezuela's policies not only threatened to shut the door upon one of the South's few potential outlets for slavery expansion; they also promised to bring the emancipation process dangerously close to the southern Gulf Coast. News from Cuba might spark unrest or rebellion among the South's own slave population. Could the South afford to watch passively while Cuba was transformed into another "hideous St. Domingo"? Quitman could not help but be appalled by this prospect. A "mongrel empire" on southern borders, he felt, would rend the "whole social fabric of the South. states." The *Free Trader* echoed his sentiments when it described the Africanization scenario as "too terrible to be contemplated without a shudder." [26]

To both Quitman and his supporters, filibustering offered the only quick, surgical means to avert Africanization and, as Quitman put it, guarantee "safety to the South & her institutions." They rejected calls for an American war with Spain to acquire Cuba, even though an incident in Havana harbor in February, when Spanish officials seized the cargo of the American coastal steamer *Black Warrior* (which had violated an obscure port regulation), had generated a lot of belligerent language in the press, halls of Congress, and administration circles. The filibusters believed that war against Spain would prove self-defeating, because Spanish authorities would then hurry the very emancipation process in Cuba that they (the filibusters) were out to stop, for reasons of defense—liberated blacks could be armed—and making the island less desirable to the United States. Similarly, the Quitman camp did not favor American purchase of Cuba, an idea gaining circulation among expansionists and particularly among the nation's diplomatic corps in Europe. Presumably the island, under such circumstances, would carry with it the hated edicts already promulgated by Pezuela. Quitman and his followers, moreover, feared that northerners might use their congressional power to hold Cuba in a territorial status until free-soil emigrants could shape the island into a nonslave state. The filibusters hoped to conquer Cuba so swiftly as to preempt Pezuela's final emancipation coup. Then, like Texas, Cuba could proclaim itself an independent republic, annul the offensive decrees, and insist on de facto slave state status as a condition of its annexation to the Union. [27]

Rumors of pending abolition in the South's "Gibraltar" generated a climate most conducive to Quitman's attempts to raise southern support. Southerners had considerable geopolitical motive to covet Cuba. McDonald, for instance, believed that Cuba would give his region "more power & influence than would a dozen wild deserts that may hereafter be formed into states" in the American West. That Cuba would provide the South additional congressional representation undoubtedly lay behind Pickett's allusion to how southerners, after annexation, would be released from debilitating dependence upon unreliable northern politicians for protection against abolitionists. Nevertheless, as one British consul in the United States noted, Africanization reports were doing far more than anything else to induce southerners to contemplate the filibusters' solution to the Cuba question; and even Whig newspapers which had previously been timid about expansion projects seemed to be shifting to the filibusters' viewpoint. Quitman's own Belen overseer typified the agitated southern mood. Upon hearing reports of his employer's plans, he informed Quitman of his desire to participate in the expedition so that the South would not wind up a "howling desert." Filibuster propaganda, of course, played upon such fears. John S. Thrasher, for instance, released a public letter warning Louisiana sugar planters that if Spain carried through on its African apprentice program, labor would become so cheap in Cuba that the island's sugar producers would easily undersell Louisiana planters in American markets.[28]

Since Africanization struck such a sensitive nerve throughout southern society, Quitman attracted manpower a distinct cut above the riffraff which usually characterized filibuster ranks. Quitman set out consciously to shape his movement into a southern gentlemen's expedition, with some northern and Cuban exile auxiliaries, and sought reliable men who shared his conviction that there was a compelling need to convert Cuba into a slave state. He conveyed this intent to his recruiters, and they in turn became somewhat selective about whom they approached. T. C. Hindman, a Mississippi state legislator from Jefferson County, revealed this process when he wrote Thrasher, "In my absence from home, a 'Private and Confidential' Circular, headed 'Cuba' and signed by you, as 'Secretary of the Corresponding Committee,' was sent me by Gen'l Quitman, with a note over his own signature assuring me of the reality of the rumored expedition and the worth and respectability of those engaged in it." McDonald, notifying Quitman that he had recruited several legislators as well as a judge's son, observed that the legislators were of the "right stripe" and that the son displayed a "high-toned chivalrous character."[29] Quitman drew inquiries from Mexican War veterans, U.S. Army personnel, volunteer militiamen, and college students anxious to participate, some for no better reason than mere adventurism. He also drew on an already available pool of experienced filibusters. His agent in Nashville, for instance, L. Norvell Walker, was the brother of the notorious William Walker who invaded Mexico's Lower California in 1853 with a band of men and proclaimed it a republic with himself as president before being driven out.[30] Nevertheless, Quitman succeeded to a remarkable degree in achieving his gentlemen's filibuster.

Throughout the Gulf and southwestern states, members of the political and social establishment recruited, raised funds, and purchased war goods on Quitman's behalf, some with the intention of participating personally in the actual invasion. In the New Orleans area, for instance, Quitman's agents included planter Samuel R. Walker (a former legal apprentice of Quitman's who had married one of Eliza's cousins); Duncan Kenner, an Ascension Parish sugar planter; Pierre Sauvé, a St. Charles Parish sugar planter; Emile La Sère, co-owner (with U.S. Senator John Slidell) of the *Louisiana Courier* and recently a member of Congress; New Orleans clothier Henry Forno; and

Samuel J. Peters, president of the Louisiana State Bank. Around Baton Rouge, Felix Huston solicited money on behalf of Quitman's New Orleans committee and made contact with "old and influential Whigs." [31]

In Georgia, C. A. L. Lamar, a young entrepreneur from one of the state's most prestigious families, raised funds for Quitman, and probate judge T. W. W. Sullivan planned to resign as soon as he was notified that the expedition was ready to depart. Quitman's Alabama agents included John A. Winston, Joseph White Lesesne, and F. B. Shepard. Winston, a Sumter County planter who operated a cotton commission business in Mobile, was serving his state as governor at the time. Lesesne and Shepard both hailed from Mobile; the former had just completed a term as chancellor of Alabama's southern division and the latter owned at least forty-five slaves. [32]

Out in Texas, Quitman's organizers included former governor James P. Henderson; Texas Ranger leader and onetime Texas Republic congressman John S. "Rip" Ford; former Texas Republic congressman and commander of the republic's 1841 Santa Fe expedition, Hugh McLeod; 1854 Whig gubernatorial candidate Judge William Beck Ochitree; and lawyer-politician Lemuel D. Evans (just a year away from serving in the U.S. Congress). In Arkansas, state supreme court associate judge Christopher Columbus Scott backed Quitman. In his own Mississippi, Quitman could count on former state legislator William M. Estelle, who recruited, in turn, yet another former legislator as well as a former mayor of Jackson. Around Natchez, wealthy planter Ferdinand L. Claiborne offered his twenty-year-old son for the enterprise. Newspaper editors and physicians in Arkansas, Texas, and Mississippi prepared to abandon their work for the expedition. Planter brother-in-law Henry Turner became so intrigued by Quitman's plan to visit "that large plantation spoken of in your letter to me" that he professed an interest in participating in the "excursion." [33]

Quitman's affiliates were unquestionably a violence-prone group. La Sère, Huston, and probably others had been involved in duels; Winston killed his second wife's lover with a shotgun blast; Hindman would soon shoot a man, in the very hall of the Mississippi House of Representatives. [34] However, Quitman's elite supporters worked for him primarily because they perceived southern security jeopardized by events in Cuba. Judge Scott, for instance, decried the "English and French policy of Africanization." Not a few of Quitman's recruiters had already gained notoriety as southern rights champions. Felix Huston had spoken out frequently against the 1850 Compromise, and was so obsessed in its aftermath with the gloomy prospects facing the South that he had talked of giving up and escaping to California. Estelle had denounced the compromise while in Mississippi's legislature. Winston had pronounced his disfavor at the Nashville Convention. To many

280

of these men, like Quitman, Cuba represented a new phase of the 1850 southern rights struggle.[35]

By mid-March, Quitman believed he was within two or three months of launching his expedition. He wrote Mike Walsh that his "financial department" had raised half the requisite funds, and that he had a "fair prospect of speedily procuring the residue." He made so many trips on filibuster business, in fact, that he could no longer fully hide his intent from Eliza. Convinced that her husband planned to invade Cuba "before a very great while," she beseeched Henry to avoid ensnarement in his father's "designs." Pleading that such involvement would break her heart, she reminded Henry, whose wedding was set for April 20, that he would soon have a wife to protect.[36]

On April 8, Quitman boarded his family on a steamer to begin the tedious journey to the Gardner plantation, where the wedding was to take place. Since there was no direct route, the Quitmans had to travel to New Orleans; take a train from New Orleans to Lake Pontchartrain; board a mail steamer for Mobile; transfer to an Alabama River steamer for Selma; and finally catch another steamer for the Gardner landing, which was located beyond Selma on the way to Montgomery. Rose's diary of the trip provides glimpses of Quitman the doting father. Thus Rose noted while aboard one of the river steamers how "Papa" had interrupted her reading to escort her (and the other children) to the pilot house to demonstrate how the boat was being steered. Nevertheless, Quitman managed to keep at his filibuster preparations, consulting with Governor Winston both in Mobile and at the wedding itself, and broaching the subject with one of Molly's cousins whom he met at Molly's grandmother's house on the way to the Gardner place.[37]

The wedding itself was a rather extravagant affair. The Gardners converted their back porch into a temporary ballroom, and the feasting and dancing after the ceremony lasted until at least two in the morning. Legend has it that so much wine was poured that day that the wedding became synonymous in Alabama with lavish entertainment. No wonder that Quitman and his family took the whole next day to recuperate, before setting out for home on April 22. By eliminating long layovers at Mobile and New Orleans, they were able to arrive back at Monmouth on April 27.[38]

Quitman alerted the junta in an April 16 note posted during the trip that he would move on Cuba once 3,000 men were recruited and after the junta provided him an expense fund of at least $220,000. During late April and the month of May, important strides were made. Quitman committees were activated in eight Texas counties. War matériel was stockpiled. Judge Lesesne, scouring the Mobile docks for troop transports, found that the New York and Alabama Steamship Company, owner of the U.S. mail steamer

Cahawba, might sell the ship at cost, and that three other vessels were available at a total purchase price of $65,000 to $70,000. U.S. naval lieutenant Robert Wilson Shufeldt, who had made many trips to Havana as commander of the sidewheeler, furnished political and military advice. He also negotiated for command of Quitman's navy, as did W. C. Flanders, commander of the steamer *Pampero* (which was engaged in the run from New Orleans to San Juan del Norte in Nicaragua). Bonds of the prospective Republic of Cuba were issued and distributed for sale.[39]

Hoping to wrap things up, Quitman returned to New Orleans in early June amid press speculation that Cuba verged on full-scale revolution. More needed to be done: one document shows that he still lacked 3,000 knapsacks, 20 wagons, 200 saddles, 1,500 percussion muskets, and 7,000 pairs of shoes. Some of his filibuster cohorts, moreover, had lost their trust in Jefferson Davis. Believing that the secretary of war perceived Quitman as a rival for Mississippi's next Senate seat, they suspected that Davis might influence President Pierce against the filibusters as a means of discrediting Quitman.[40]

Quitman, nonetheless, had cause sufficient to forge ahead. Samuel Walker shared news fresh from Havana Club contacts in Cuba that the island indeed was on the precipice of rebellion against Spain. Furthermore, Mike Walsh, at Quitman's instigation, had sounded out sentiment in Washington and reported assurances from Stephen Douglas and others on behalf of the administration that there would be "no active interference" by Pierce, provided filibuster activities were "conducted with decent caution." To ensure such a hands-off federal policy, Emile La Sère's newspaper partner, Senator John Slidell, had brought before Congress in May a proposal to suspend America's neutrality laws. Encouraged, Quitman continued his preparations. Word went out to recruits that he had neared "the point of leaving New Orleans for Cuba."[41]

What changed everything was the Kansas-Nebraska Act, a piece of legislation which President Pierce signed into law on May 20. The end product of over a year of congressional squabbling, the Kansas-Nebraska Act organized that part of the Louisiana Purchase west of Missouri and Iowa as the Kansas and Nebraska territories. Unfortunately for Quitman's intentions and, more important, the ultimate stability of the Union, the act included a provision on slavery which eventually restructured American politics. According to the Missouri Compromise (1820), which divided future territories carved out of the Louisiana Purchase at $36°30'$ as to whether they would be free or slave, Kansas and Nebraska should have been designated free territories since they lay north of that parallel. However, to secure the southern votes necessary to get the bill through, Stephen Douglas, its leading proponent in the Senate, agreed to include a provision repealing the applicability of the Missouri Compromise to the new territories and leaving the question of slavery up to territorial settlers.

The Kansas-Nebraska Act did not necessarily guarantee more slave *states* than if the Missouri Compromise had remained in effect. If more northern than southern settlers migrated into the new territories—a distinct possibility, given the North's larger population, the ease of transferring a northern farming establishment westward as compared to moving plantation operations, and the risk involved for those southerners bringing bondsmen into a region where the ultimate status of slavery was to be determined—the territories might well eventually apply for statehood under free constitutions. Nebraska, especially, given its location, presented an unlikely target for a slaveholders' migration. Nevertheless, the measure provoked a storm of protest in the North because it repealed what had become a consecrated sectional bargain to many northerners and allowed new slavery expansion without any concessions to northern free-soil convictions.

Kansas-Nebraska adversely affected Quitman's Cuba endeavor because, by the time it passed Congress, it had become identified as a Democratic party measure. Not only was Douglas a Democrat, but the legislation depended upon the support of the Pierce administration to pass. Pierce had used presidential patronage to muscle the measure through the Senate, and had, of course, signed it into law. Denounced throughout the North for having become a tool of the "Slave Power," Pierce could ill afford to furnish his critics with additional fodder for their charges. Thus, support for Quitman's invasion of Cuba became inconceivable. Pierce might attempt to purchase Cuba from Spain in the interests of national security, economic growth, and "manifest destiny"; but he could hardly condone a blatantly illegal expedition which was widely perceived as a southern plot to create a new slave state by force.

Just days after passage of the Kansas-Nebraska Act, Pierce signaled an apparent policy shift toward Quitman. He had heard from Senator James M. Mason of Virginia, chairman of the Senate Foreign Relations Committee, that the committee was planning to present a favorable report on John Slidell's proposal to suspend the neutrality laws. Pierce called Mason, Douglas, Slidell, and the other members of the Democratic majority of the committee to a White House meeting with himself and Jefferson Davis. There he informed the senators of his intention to issue a proclamation against filibustering. Slidell objected, arguing that it would be unfair to "our people in New Orleans" unless Pierce softened the blow, by first submitting to Congress a request for an appropriation for a special diplomatic mission to Spain to purchase Cuba. Pierce refused to delay his pronouncement. The next day he issued a proclamation declaring that filibustering against Cuba contradicted the letter and spirit of U.S.-Spanish treaties, violated "the obvious duties and obligations of faithful and patriotic citizens," and was "derogatory to the character" of the nation. Pierce warned his countrymen to stay clear of the enterprise, and stipulated that federal authorities would "not fail to prosecute with due energy" persons implicated in the scheme.[42]

Pierce apparently intended his proclamation more as a symbolic gesture to soothe northern opinion than as a signal of truly substantive change in administration intent. Shortly afterward, he intimated to Mobile congressman Philip Phillips that the administration would still refrain from enforcement measures, provided the filibusters not attract so much publicity that it would become embarrassing to remain inactive. The next month, Slidell informed Samuel Walker that both Pierce and Davis had assured him that "if the filibusters did go the government would not see them sacrificed."[43]

Eventually, this important information would be passed on to Quitman and would govern his course of action. But, for the time being, Quitman was put out with the administration. Perhaps because he harbored doubts that Kansas and Nebraska would ever actually become slave states,[44] Quitman had little empathy for the president's political dilemma which had induced the proclamation. Rather, Quitman could not help but surmise that Pierce had capitulated to what he believed was a congressional majority "averse to slavery." After all, the president had hardly been shy about bringing American fishing rights in Canadian waters—to Quitman a relatively inconsequential diplomatic question—before Congress, yet had not once asked for the nation's lawmakers to take up Africanization in Cuba, even though the whole future of the slave states seemed at stake.[45]

Pierce's position was particularly exasperating to Quitman and his coterie because they knew that the president wanted Cuba and that he was both aware of the Africanization trend and opposed to it. Obviously they had entirely failed to get across their message that filibustering offered the only feasible resolution of the problem. Judge Lesesne lamented that Pierce simply could not comprehend how many divisive judicial questions would arise over the emancipados if the United States did not allow Cuba to become independent prior to annexation. When Samuel Walker visited Washington in July, he found the administration bent on purchasing Cuba and virtually oblivious to why southerners believed that undesirable. When members of the administration complained that filibuster machinations impeded Pierce's strategy by alienating Spanish officials, Walker retorted that purchase was "the worst thing" for the South and that the filibusters would "make her [Cuba] independent in spite of the administration."[46]

Rather than give in to the president's fiat, Quitman held his ground. When Alfred G. Haley—a Mississippi lawyer-politician with ties to Jefferson Davis (whom many of Quitman's associates assumed was responsible for the proclamation) who was serving in the General Land Office in Washington—issued a well-intentioned public letter in the Washington *Union* denying Quitman's involvement "in any proposed descent upon Cuba," Quitman released a public denial of Haley's authority to speak on his behalf. Other filibuster leaders took out their frustration in print and through political channels. A pamphlet written by John Henderson, which argued that the Cuban people deserved the "assistance" of others in their bid for independence, rolled off the *Daily Delta* press just days after Pierce's decree. Henderson contended that the Constitution nowhere sanctioned presidential proclamations.[47]

Quitman and company, however, could not fully neutralize the impact of Pierce's initiative. The proclamation stripped the Cuba venture of its aura of quasi legitimacy, causing some prospective recruits and potential financial contributors to have second thoughts. Captain Shufeldt's plans to assume Quitman's naval command, for instance, were almost altered by the president's announcement. "I find that his mind has been unsettled by Pearce's [*sic*] ridiculous Proclamation," Lesesne reported to Quitman. Shufeldt eventually came around; he resigned his U.S. Navy commission rather than accept a transfer to the Pacific Coast (prompted, apparently, by rumors of his ties to the filibusters), which would have removed him from participation. Pierce's course also put Democratic newspapers, which had to choose whether to back their president or the general, on the spot. Quitman often came out on the short end of this competition with party regulars. Thus the *Mississippian*, which as recently as May had supported the effort in Congress to repeal the neutrality laws, now called upon Pierce to enforce that very legislation.[48]

The filibusters soon found themselves reeling from a second blow by federal authorities. Their scheme, by now, was attracting attention in newspapers across the country. "From what I see in the papers . . . I know that in all probability an effort will be made shortly to take the Island of Cuba," Quitman heard from Roberdeau Wheat's brother John. In New Orleans, the expedition had become such common knowledge that one theater ran a burlesque entitled "Those Fifteen Thousand Filibusters." It was all too much for antifilibustering Supreme Court justice John A. Campbell, presiding over the June session of the U.S. Circuit Court in the Crescent City. Though a southerner himself (from Alabama), Campbell charged a grand jury to investigate whether an expedition was in the works, and stacked the deck against Quitman by the wording of his instructions. Not only were the jurors to consider bringing indictments against actual expeditionaries, they were to consider the selling or purchasing of Cuban bonds, and even speechmaking at filibuster rallies, as evidence of guilt. Further, Campbell bluntly rejected filibusters' logic that no infraction of American laws occurred when participants were armed beyond America's territorial limits. *Intent*, Campbell insisted, was what was important.

Executing their charge promptly, the jurors summoned Henderson, Sauvé, Peters, Thrasher, and a Dr. A. L. Saunders (who had been involved in the López movement) to a hearing as witnesses. Several days later, the district attorney called Quitman to court. The filibusters, however, refused to testify on most questions, often invoking their right to avoid incriminating themselves. Saunders, for instance, admitted having discussed Spanish oppression in Cuba with Gaspar Betancourt Cisneros (a Cuban exile and one of Quitman's bond agents) and acknowledged that he had seen printed bonds, but refused to name persons attending meetings at 8 Rampart Street (apparently a headquarters established by Cuban exiles) or comment on the terms by which the Cuban bonds were to be redeemed. Faced with conspiratorial silence, the jurors, many of whom undoubtedly sympathized with the filibusters anyway, reported to Campbell on July 1 that although the rumors of an expedition were "not altogether without foundation," they felt that press reports had exaggerated the extent of the planning, that there existed no concrete evidence to justify indictments, and that it was "inexpedient" to continue the investigation.[49]

Chagrined that his charge to the jury had backfired, Campbell took upon himself the responsibility of thwarting the filibuster plot. Using the rather imprecise logic that there existed good probability of an invasion since Quitman, Thrasher, and Saunders had all been linked to Cuba filibustering by "public rumor," the judge announced that he would have to make the three men post bond as surety that they would abide by the neutrality laws. Stunned by Campbell's intent, defense attorney T. N. Waul requested and won an adjournment until 6:00 that night, so that his clients could prepare a response.

Quitman delivered the filibusters' answer when the court reassembled. Denouncing Campbell for misconstruing his silence as an admission of guilt and rebuking the judge for infringing individual freedom and punishing people for "imaginary offences," Quitman nonetheless proclaimed his readiness to "do anything" for the liberation of Cuba, which he deemed of the "highest importance" to the South. The statement was clearly meant more for public consumption than to sway the judge; Campbell proceeded to put Quitman, Thrasher, and Saunders each under $3,000 bond to abide by the neutrality laws for nine months. Hoping to embarrass the judge, the three refused payment and left court in a marshal's custody, intent on serving jail terms. Friends persuaded them to reconsider, and they returned to make payment, but Quitman filed a written protest with the court clerk, charging Campbell with an unconstitutional abuse of judicial power.[50]

Did more lie behind the prosecution than the ideological beliefs of one federal judge? Convinced that the Pierce administration had virtually allied itself with Spain to suppress Cuban independence, Quitman could not help but wonder whether pressure had been imposed on Campbell from Washington, perhaps from Campbell's fellow Supreme Court judges. Since the procedure's essence seemed political rather than judicial, Quitman decided that the only way to retaliate was through the mobilization of public opinion. In August, Quitman released a three-column public letter in the New Orleans *Daily Delta* which not only claimed that Campbell had distorted the court proceedings in his own explanation released previously in the *Delta* but also offered an implicit justification of filibustering. Quitman contended that there had been nothing wrong in his admiration for "American institutions" and his desire to see them extended to Cuba, especially in light of the "stupid and barbarous despotism" with which Spain controlled the island and the unwillingness of the federal government—which he linked to its distraction over the slavery controversy—to prevent the completion of the "cherished European policy of establishing a hostile negro or mongrel Empire on our borders." Quitman ended his piece with a ringing lesson in the meaning of his own surname: Quitman was Saxon for "freeman," and this name imposed a duty on him to always resist "political despotism."[51]

Posing in a not unfamiliar role as the victim of a federal vendetta, Quitman won his share of defenders. *Texas State Gazette* editor John Marshall urged him to keep in mind that he had committed an offense no greater than he had in 1836, when he became a hero for invading Texas. Robert J. Walker, encountering one of Quitman's Texas agents during a trip to Galveston, muttered that Campbell was "crazy" and that it had been "arbitrary" and "high handed" of the judge to require Quitman to post bond. The Vicksburg *Whig* thought Campbell's charge to the grand jury was based upon "monstrous" doctrine; a public meeting in that city passed resolutions in Quitman's support. From Washington, Slidell sent word that opinion was virtually unanimous that Campbell had gone too far. The outcry may have been strong enough to give Campbell at least some second thoughts. Traveling in the judge's company later in the year, Samuel Walker got the impression that Campbell was "conscious of having played the fool."[52]

Quitman continued to receive expressions of interest in the expedition. "I am determin[ed] to visit the lands of Cuby," insisted one anxious adventurer.

Nevertheless, Campbell's intervention, by dispelling lingering hope that federal authorities would countenance a Cuba filibuster, slowed recruitment and fund-raising. "The arrests in New Orleans had a very bad effect here," John Ford reported from Austin.[53]

Quitman returned to Monmouth from New Orleans, aware that it would prove more difficult than anticipated to launch his expedition. Needing time to reconsider tactics, Quitman allowed Cuban affairs to drift during July and August, though he became involved in the appearance of John Thrasher in Natchez for a public address on Cuba. As a result, the arrival of fall found him no closer to departure than he had been in June. When a Pennsylvanian announced that he had a sixty-one-man company ready to go and inquired about Quitman's intentions, Quitman responded vaguely that nothing was "certain." Similarly, he could express only a "hope" to Mike Walsh that he would soon be able to announce "a stirring event."[54]

Finally Quitman returned to New Orleans in September, resolved to put everything in motion. Rather than abide by Campbell's nine months' restriction, Quitman relied on tips that Pierce would yet let him attempt his invasion if he avoided public notice. Quitman enjoined the "greatest secrecy" upon cohorts and even used code in some of his correspondence. Meanwhile, his coconspirators continued their effort to educate the public. Samuel Walker even placed an explanation of the filibusters' rationale in the South's leading commercial journal, *De Bow's Review* (New Orleans). By mid-October, Quitman had hopes of an assault against Cuba around December 15. "Can I rely on your participation?" he queried Ford. "Inform me . . . how many associates you can bring to N. O. [New Orleans] or Galvn [Galveston]."[55]

When Quitman appeared in New Orleans, he needed approximately $200,000 more in his filibuster expense fund. Cuban bond sales during the next few weeks brought in several thousand dollars, but this was not nearly enough. Prospective investors hedged, saying that they first wanted a definite commitment from Quitman as to departure date or that they required evidence of an actual revolution in Cuba. Walker advised Quitman that it was unlikely that substantial "further sums" could be raised unless Quitman could manage something by his own "personal influence."[56]

Without sufficient funds, Quitman could purchase neither the armed steamers nor the military supplies he required. A December 14 memorandum shows that he still lacked 1,000 Sharps rifles, as well as heavy artillery, 1,500 percussion muskets, 3,000 pairs of shoes, 125 camp kettles, 3,500 blankets, and other equipment. Describing his "want of money" as a final "obstacle," Quitman pressured John Ford to raise "funds or promises." He had already shifted some of the burden to recruits, asking them to pay a $50 fee, supply their own arms, and provide their own transportation to a coastal rendezvous. But this undercut enlistment. Although Quitman promised that the $50 would be returned if the enterprise was never "consummated" and also offered in return for the fee a Cuban bond worth $150 after the conquest of the island, many men could not afford the gamble.[57]

Delay triggered a new crisis in confidence. "The uncertainty prevents persons from giving in their names," Ford reported from Texas. It also put less fortunate filibuster recruits into a financial bind. Quitman received a letter from one recruit who complained that he was virtually going broke waiting for Quitman to make up his mind. Some filibusters simply decided that their financial resources had already been strained to the limit. "I am very poor & worse than poor, in debt. I intend to get money enough to pay my debts to support me until you shall want me in Cuba," wrote Roberdeau Wheat from New Orleans. Wheat was going to Mexico, where he hoped to participate in a revolution and gain control over gold and silver mines.[58]

Junta leaders, moreover, had their doubts. Quitman learned that members of the New Orleans Junta were acting "queer" and becoming difficult to "deal with." In Savannah, the junta's anxieties were playing havoc with Quitman's operation. Quitman had left Manuel Macías in the Georgia city with administrative authority and $99,000 in republic bonds ($150 and $300 denominations) to market. Macías had established a command hierarchy and begun a search for armaments and seagoing vessels. Allison Nelson of Atlanta, captain of a Georgia volunteer company in the Mexican War and López activist, was handling a lot of Macías' recruitment. C. A. L. Lamar assumed responsibility for providing transportation for recruits needing to reach the coast. Unfortunately, junta treasurer Domingo de Goicouria, an antislavery Cuban exile and a fanatic republican, drove a wedge between Quitman and his Georgia organization. Troubled by Quitman's apparent indecision, he persuaded Macías to bypass Quitman, seized junta funds in Savannah, and capitalized on Nelson's insecurity. Nelson had a wife and three children, and had recently suffered reverses in some speculations; Goicouria promised that Nelson's family would be paid $10,000—an insurance bonanza—if their head-of-household did not return from Cuba.

Quitman heard of the Savannah situation from a greatly discouraged Louis Schlessinger, who thought that Quitman might as well write Georgia off. Ignoring this defeatism, Quitman dispatched Thrasher to Savannah and eventually rebuilt his Georgia organization. Nonetheless, considerable damage had been done. Applying those funds he had commandeered, Goicouria, working with junta vice secretary José Elias Hernandez, arranged his own expedition. An advance guard landed at Baracoa in eastern Cuba, only to be crushed. Precious funds had been wasted, and Spanish authorities were now on their guard.[59]

Cognizant that any further misuse of his limited resources would probably spell ruin, Quitman hastened preparations. From the last week of November through mid-February, Quitman made frequent trips to New Orleans. Personal affairs were put in order, so that he could take an extended absence in good conscience. Quitman was already in the process of turning Live Oaks over to Henry and Mary ("I hope Mary is well pleased with the rural scenes of Live Oaks," he wrote benevolently in one letter) and was having a house built there for them. Now he assigned Henry, whom he kept posted on his Cuba intentions, the task of clearing his financial obligations. "Try and settle up all outstanding claims, by giving drafts payable 1st March," he instructed. Perhaps the best indication of Quitman's resolve, however, was his truancy from a commercial convention which met in New Orleans that January. The convention had already chosen him for Mississippi's vice president, when Felix Huston arose to relay Quitman's "apologies" for not appearing. The general, Huston explained lamely, had been compelled to leave New Orleans because of "engagements of an imperious nature."[60]

Quitman also considered command structure during these months. Exact ranks and assignments within Quitman's invasion hierarchy remain unclear, but important spots went to Mansfield Lovell, Mexican War hero and West Point engineering professor Gustavus Woodson Smith, and Jones M. Withers of Mobile, a West Pointer who had served as a regular army colonel in the Mexican War but resigned his commission at its end. Lovell and Smith both resigned *their* commissions as of December 18, so that they would be free to go whenever Quitman gave the signal.[61]

Everything built toward the departure of the expedition. Thrasher dispatched word to McLeod in Texas to ready the transfer of three hundred "skilled rangers" to "some point on the Coast from which we can put them aboard our transports." Lovell urged Mike Walsh to prepare a force of one hundred to two hundred mechanics. Quitman, continually immersed in filibuster correspondence (he even wrote expedition letters on Christmas Day), alerted agents that enlistees should be put on ten days' notice and released word that those recruits coming to New Orleans could expect affiliated planters to put them up and provide living expenses pending departure. On February 4, Quitman told his agents in Shreveport to ready fifty men to assemble at his New Orleans rendezvous on "short notice," and entreated Alexander McClung—who was soliciting recommendations for a U.S. government appointment—to forgo federal patronage and join an enterprise destined to "decide the great question of American or European domination on this Continent." [62]

Sudden activity after months of indecision caught some of Quitman's men off guard. "The announcement . . . has somewhat taken me by surprise," said O'Hara in Kentucky. O'Hara recovered quickly and prepared his recruits to leave, but other agents discovered that men who had promised to enlist would not come through. L. Norvell Walker reported from Nashville that only one man was willing to join him in Quitman's ranks. Quitman's Selma, Alabama, agent met similar rebuff and could not negotiate a single bond sale. Excuses filled the mail. Walker attributed the problem to Quitman's insistence on silence. The "difficulty," he wrote, "is that we have to act *so secretly*, it requires a *drum* and *fife* to move Tennesseans." Quitman's man in Selma, on the other hand, believed that time had simply allowed too many doubts about military feasibility to fester. "I find among the young men . . . some difficulty in convincing them that the means provided will be competent to accomplish the object—All seem apprehensive on the question of being able to make a landing," he returned. Then there was John Thomas Wheat, who begged off because he feared that his departure would put his mother under such severe emotional strain that it would endanger her life.[63]

Nevertheless, Quitman received more than enough positive responses to forge onward. Saunders reported one thousand Kentuckians waiting their signal. Estelle wrote that he had drawn thirty-two men from a scattering of Mississippi towns. William H. Wood of Natchez had twelve men primed for action (seven more were available, he wrote, if the $50 fee were waived). Ford had already announced that there would be "no difficulty" in getting his Texans together, and that there would be "no scarcity" of "old-fashioned" rifles (but the men could come equipped with Sharps rifles and six-shooters if Quitman could send $1,500 to $2000). Other contingents could be expected from Alabama, Florida, Arkansas, Pennsylvania, and Virginia, and inquiries were still pouring in from men anxious to learn enrollment procedures for the "*Lone Star* Expedition." If Quitman had not fully achieved the three- to four-thousand-man "auxiliary force" he was now specifying in correspondence, he certainly had drawn close enough for action.[64]

Funding deficiencies also seemed to be resolving themselves. In January, Quitman claimed that $500,000 had been invested in his enterprise and that he only needed $50,000 more. Some recruits had paid the $50 fee, and bonds *were* selling in some areas. "Don't you want Cuban bonds. . . . I am in $1,000, Trow 1,000 and I want you in 1,000. It is a good egg," C. A. L. Lamar enthused to one correspondent. Emile La Sère collected $4,210.56 in cash in December and January. Walsh believed he could raise $5,000.

Quitman appeared in Mobile in mid-February and had some luck stimulating sales. Lesesne turned over $1203.61, and, after Quitman left, a Mobile trust committee was set up to coordinate future fund-raising in Alabama. Since the committee included such influential men as planter and state legislator Tristam B. Bethea and former legislator and commission merchant James E. Saunders, there seemed reason for optimism. In New Orleans, Quitman's factor R. W. Estlin busied himself paying out sums on Quitman's account to cover the expenses of Walker, Lovell, Thrasher, and other agents, and apparently the junta provided Quitman with a $50,000 fund in the city.[65]

Since Quitman never designated a specific date—at least in surviving correspondence—we cannot know his exact intentions. However, circumstantial evidence indicates that his objective was to leave around the first week of March. He wrote Lamar on January 5 that he stood to forfeit $500,000 already invested if he failed to "move" within sixty days. In addition, if information gathered by Spanish authorities can be credited, an early March invasion was timed to coincide with mass insurrection in Cuba: Spanish intelligence discovered that junta accomplices in Cuba planned to trigger a rebellion by assassinating the island's new captain general, José G. de la Concha, while Concha attended the opera on the night of February 12. Even more revealing is the behavior of Quitman's agents and some recruits who, by February, seem to have been proceeding on the assumption that just weeks or days remained. Walsh searched for vessels. Lamar recommended a point on the Savannah River eleven miles from Savannah as a troop rendezvous. Henry Forno arranged for a Louisiana rendezvous at a Gulf coast spot so inaccessible that it could be reached only by canal—a perfect place to gather four hundred to five hundred men without tipping off federal authorities. Some ninety filibusters jumped the gun and appeared in New Orleans, demanding that Quitman make good his promise to provide for them until expedition time. Fortunately, a sympathizer came through—his Magnolia plantation, on the Mexican Gulf Railroad some nine miles below the city, became a temporary residence for filibusters. The anxious adventurers, who had been passing much of their time loafing in New Orleans grogshops, were disguised as a party of "wood choppers" and taken to Magnolia. Around this time a Louisiana country store owner noted in his ledgers that Quitman had spent $1,300 on tobacco, whiskey, brandy, and gin "for the boys."[66]

What proved Quitman's undoing was his inability to maintain secrecy. Even in the early days of planning, some of his agents had been less than prudent. "Capt. Estelle . . . I fear . . . has spoken to one or two too easily on the subject," McDonald reported on one occasion. Many factors—the magnitude of the conspiracy, its having been drawn out for almost two years, the enlistment of thousands of men in operational or financial support, and Quitman's having approached many others—made expectations of preserving confidentiality unrealistic. By early 1855, talk of the expedition filled the air. It took no great insight for the commandant of West Point to surmise from a "long chain of circumstantial evidence" that Lovell and Smith's resignations related to Quitman's designs on Cuba, or for a press correspondent to track down the Louisiana filibuster encampment. This reporter exaggerated but slightly when he explained that "every man, woman and child" in New Orleans seemed knowledgeable about the expedition.[67]

Ever since the López escapades, Spanish officials in Cuba and the United States had been more than a little wary of the filibuster threat. "Filibusters seem to have frightened this functionary out of his proprieties," an English visitor to New Orleans observed of the Spanish consul there. Naturally Spanish officials went to considerable lengths to stay posted on filibusters' doings, and kept tabs on Quitman in particular. By early 1855, they knew that Quitman was prepared to move, knew his approximate troop strength and some of the vessels involved, and were close to the truth in believing New Orleans, Galveston, New York City, and Savannah to be Quitman's embarkation points. Determined to preclude any possibility of a successful landing or insurgent cooperation on the island, Concha put Cuba under martial law, mobilized new military companies, restricted private ownership of firearms, and made arrests. A siege mentality pervaded the island. A visiting British admiral observed: "I have had a very cordial reception from the Captain General . . . and he has given me to understand . . . he had reason . . . to expect the arrival of a filibustering expedition under Colonel Quitman, — and certainly since my arrival there have been some symptoms of activity with the Spanish squadron and troops. A frigate, two brigs and three steamers have gone to sea, taking the General second in command and some troops.[68]

Information leaks not only greatly lowered the odds that Quitman's invasion of Cuba could be coordinated with local insurrection; they also threatened the filibusters' rapprochement with the administration which had been grounded on the president's unofficial assurance of quiescence, provided the filibusters avoid publicity. Pierce had already suffered intolerable embarrassment in his Cuban policy. Soulé had proven an atrocious choice as minister to Spain—he crippled the French ambassador in a duel and ruined his diplomatic credibility by involvement in Spanish revolutionary politics. Further, a conference of American diplomats in Ostend, Belgium, called by the administration to devise a strategy for annexing Cuba, became such a farce that the House was in the process of demanding documents about it from Pierce (a resolution to this effect passed on February 23). Still reeling from the political aftereffects of the Kansas-Nebraska Act—Democrats had suffered striking defeats in the North in fall congressional races—Pierce could ill afford another mistake where Cuba was concerned. Besides, he could hardly feign ignorance about filibuster preparations when Spanish officials were feeding the administration their intelligence findings and demanding that the neutrality laws be enforced against Quitman.[69]

In late January, tipped off by the Spanish consul in New York City, U.S. revenue officers and marshals seized one of Quitman's ships—the steamer *Massachusetts*—which was at anchor off the Jersey shore, and put a second filibuster vessel under surveillance. Since ammunition, provisions, and thousands of flintlock muskets were confiscated aboard the *Massachusetts*, the operation virtually erased the expedition's important New York wing. Exasperated by this new setback, Quitman unloaded his frustration upon Congressman Alexander H. Stephens of Georgia. Pierce, he informed Stephens, had obviously joined an Anglo-French plot to suppress the Cuban revolution at precisely the time when the United States could help the Cuban people at little risk (since England and France had become involved in the Crimean War). In other correspondence, Quitman denounced the administration as a "humbug" which had "blundered frequently" and failed to show sensitivity to southern interests in Cuba.[70]

Rather than concede defeat, Quitman chose to take his case in person to Washington. "The course of our admn. in relation to our vessels leaves no hope for us," he explained to Henry, "but that of the influence I may exercise with government men . . . to force the admn. to change their course." Perhaps his prestige could sway Congress to repeal the neutrality laws. Perhaps something could be achieved at a personal interview with the president. Telling McDonald to keep everything on hold during his absence, he boarded an Alabama River steamer at Mobile on the night of February 20. Six days later, he arrived in Washington.[71]

Quitman was due for disappointment. He apparently persuaded his old southern rights cohort Albert G. Brown to replace Slidell—who had given up on Cuba—as filibuster champion in Congress. On March 3, Brown introduced in the Senate a bill to repeal certain sections of the neutrality laws. However, congressional interest in Cuba had waned over recent months. Even southerners had become less concerned about the island, because Captain General Concha moderated Pezuela's abolitionist policies. Several senators, not all of them northerners, objected to the introduction of Brown's bill, and it was dropped.[72]

Things went from bad to worse when Quitman tried to convert the president to his cause. They met accidentally on a Pennsylvania Avenue sidewalk and Pierce promised to pay Quitman "a visit previous to his departure for the neutral Island of Cuba." When Quitman persisted and secured an interview at the White House, he found himself closeted with the president and Secretary of State Marcy—who had reason to believe that Quitman's machinations had hurt his own diplomatic initiatives to acquire Cuba—as well as the Spanish minister to the United States, L. A. del Cueta. Pierce refused concessions and, as a deterrent, shared with Quitman what he had learned about the military buildup in Cuba.[73]

Pierce's intractability proved the last straw. Quitman finally capitulated—the odds against his effecting a successful invasion were astronomical. Throwing away two years of preparation, Quitman, sometime around March 15, released word to his agents that he had given up and that his army should be disbanded. A month later, he traveled to New Orleans. At a meeting on April 29, Quitman formally tendered his resignation to the junta.[74]

Cancelation, inevitably, brought recrimination. Bondholders, upset to learn that their investment had been squandered on supplies never utilized and that there would be no refunds despite earlier promises that funds would be returned in the event of cancelation, justifiably filed complaints. Junta members, sensing an obligation to tell the Cuban people why after so much planning their efforts had come to so little, issued a manifesto which put a large share of the blame upon the "chief." Quitman had "repeatedly" assured the junta that federal opposition would "never be an obstacle to detain him," yet used that very obstacle as a rationale for disengagement. Quitman also drew the junta's censure for unclear directives, inefficiencies in fund distribution, and unnecessary delays. Quitman, however, accepted no guilt. "On this subject," he assured Henry, "I am 'triply armed' for my cause is just."[75]

Quitman's imperial vision survived the disintegration of his conspiracy. In July he released a public letter which demanded Cuban independence and spoke of a need for the "Caucasian white race to carry humanity, civilization, and progress to the rich and fertile countries south of us, which now, in the occupation of inferior and mixed races, lie undeveloped and useless." Some of his true devotees hoped that he might yet act. Surely "there can be no such word as fail," suggested a Mobile ship captain involved in the cause, who decided to "advise my men to return to their avocations & 'bide the time.'" Rip Ford was full of talk of Quitman's participating in a republican revolution in northern Mexico under the assumption that Mexico could subsequently be used as a base for invading Cuba.[76] However, Quitman had finally closed the book on his military career. Still convinced that southern security depended on the annexation of Cuba and fascinated with the idea that southern slavery might be infused into free-labor regions of the tropics, Quitman would champion expansionist projects—but he would leave the actual conquests to others.

21

Immigrants' Son

THEY should have known where he would stand when nativism and anti-Catholicism became the issue. Far less sectarian than many Mississippians and the son of an immigrant couple, John Quitman was hardly a promising candidate for a crusade against foreigners and Catholics. Though Quitman was not one to talk much about his parents' origins, he had shown some empathy for Catholics and Catholic immigrants in the past. The *Free Trader*, after all, carried his 1844 Saint Patrick's Day letter to the local Hibernian Society which saluted local Irishmen for their emotional ties to their native land and their willingness to "defend the domestic institutions of their adopted country." Then, too, Quitman had participated in a dinner given by Charleston's Hibernian Society when he visited that city after the Mexican War. In an 1848 public letter, Quitman had praised Democratic party stoicism before nativist currents.[1] He contributed money to Catholic churches, and his Cuban endeavor, had it succeeded, would have made Americans of multitudes of Catholic foreigners.

Yet Mississippi nativists presumed Quitman's tacit cooperation, if not actual affiliation. Was not their American—or Know-Nothing—political party in the ascendant? Had not Quitman just exposed his utter exasperation with the Democratic administration in Washington? Surely Quitman could not resist their appeal; many far more committed Democrats had already executed a political leap into nativist ranks.

By all the logic of demographics, Quitman's Mississippi, and the greater South for that matter, should have been spared the Know-Nothings, a movement based upon secret meetings (the party had evolved from a fraternal society with northern origins known as the Order of the Star Spangled Banner, and members were instructed to respond "I know nothing" when queried about party affairs) and dedicated to stiffening naturalization requirements and excluding Catholics and immigrants from politics. Although immigrants had been flocking to the United States in great numbers since the Mexican War, hundreds of thousands arriving annually in the early 1850s, Mississippi's foreign-born as late as 1850 numbered only 4,788 among a total population which exceeded 200,000. The slave states had fewer foreigners, or Catholics, than did any region in the country.[2] Mississippi's Catholic immigrants lacked the visibility of their impoverished counterparts in the North, whose concentrated numbers in coastal cities such as New York and Boston aroused paranoic fears of their being papal agents bent upon subordinating the Republic to Rome's rule. There was little cause in Mississippi to blame immigrants, as northern nativists were prone to do, for crime, street violence, lower wage scales, unemployment, alcoholism, higher welfare costs, political corruption, and other indications of social malaise.

What prompted Mississippi Know-Nothingism was more an extant political party vacuum than any public perception that there existed urgent cause to purge immigrants from politics. A nationwide collapse of the Whig party during the early 1850s left masses of voters ripe for political realignment. In the North, many Democrats and former Whigs, outraged over the repeal of the Missouri Compromise, could labor together in an array of "anti-Nebraska" political coalitions, which gradually emerged as the Republican party. Campaigning primarily upon the theme that the Kansas-Nebraska Act exposed a "Slave Power" plot to force slavery on all territories, revive the African slave trade, and even legalize the institution in the North itself, the anti-Nebraska men won an impressive number of offices in free-state elections in 1854 and 1855. Since the Republican program naturally had no appeal in the slave states, former Whigs and defecting Democrats south of the Mason-Dixon Line often joined the Know-Nothings, sometimes because they were nativists but frequently because they saw the party as the only viable alternative to the Democracy.

Around the time Quitman resigned his filibuster command, Mississippi Know-Nothingism was nearing the peak of its popularity. Since the previous summer many influential Whig leaders and Whig newspapers had announced their affiliation with the new party, and nativist agitation was attracting sufficient support among the Democratic rank and file as to have that party's hierarchy running scared. In April, state Know-Nothings met in New Orleans and selected a slate of candidates for Mississippi's fall elections. For a while, the nominations were kept secret (though a platform was released which called for reforming naturalization laws and banning immigration of paupers and criminals to the United States). In other parts of the country, Know-Nothings had occasionally swept into office by concealing their nominations—thus inviting Democratic complacency—and then flooding the ballot boxes with votes for unannounced candidates on election day. However, Mississippi's Know-Nothings wanted the votes of Democrats and states' righters. Their gubernatorial candidate, Charles D. Fontaine, had Democratic states' rights, antibond credentials; one of their congressional nominees had been an elector for Pierce and editor of a Democratic newspaper. Only a "stump canvass," as Natchez *Courier* editor Giles M. Hillyer put it, would enable Know-Nothings to cash in on their appeal to Democrats and "show the people we are proud of our principles." So the American party press splashed the ticket on its editorial pages.[3]

Quitman, who correctly attributed the Know-Nothings' "mushroom" rise to party disorder and voter confusion, instinctively recoiled from political nativism. He held no great love for the Democracy, but saw less virtue in the Know-Nothing persuasion. Had Quitman had his way, the continued national discord over slavery would inspire purely sectional parties so that the South, no longer obliged to acquiesce in debilitating compromises to shield northern wings of cross-sectional parties from angry constituencies, would be able to directly defend its own interests. Could not the nation have a "Northern anti-slavery party" made up of "out & out consolidationists" and a "Southern slavery party" wholly committed to "strict construction"? "To this it is coming," he predicted to Benjamin Dill in hopeful expectation, "and the sooner the better."[4]

Quitman, however, delayed announcing his disapprobation, and his silence invited misconstruction, as did his strange behavior during the Democratic state convention in June. Selected an Adams County delegate, Quitman appeared in Jackson at convention time but refused his seat. When the delegates extended an invitation to address the assemblage, he declined and delivered instead a speech outside the convention which lashed out at the administration's course on Cuba. He then repeated his criticism in a discourse at Vicksburg on his way home.[5]

Probably Quitman's silence about Know-Nothingism can be explained by his preoccupation, until late April, with Cuba affairs. His conduct at Jackson should be attributed to his discovery, upon reaching the capital, that Jefferson Davis controlled the state Democracy. Not only did Quitman take this as a slap in the face, given Davis' contributions to administration antifilibustering policies, but he also realized that his ambitions for Mississippi's next U.S. Senate seat would likely have to give way before the secretary of war.

Nevertheless, his ambiguous course tempted Mississippi Know-Nothings to contemplate his affiliation. Quitman's denunciations of administration policy seemed to indicate that he was about to make a political shift, and Quitman did not exactly boast a history of party regularity. Know-Nothing managers relished Quitman's joining their party; his staunch southern rights reputation would go a long way toward undercutting Democratic propaganda that the American party was merely Whiggery in a new guise and that voters should thus beware Know-Nothing ties to antislavery northern Whigs. Hoping to widen the gap between Quitman and the state Democracy and prod him into the move, Know-Nothing papers played up his differences with Pierce, praised his Cuba endeavor, and plied him with unabashed flattery. In editorials released simultaneously on June 13, the Vicksburg *Whig* lauded Quitman as a "distinguished and gallant soldier," "able politician," and "friend without guile," and the Natchez *Courier* expressed its admiration for his "fearless independence" and "self-sacrificing" adherence to principle. The *Courier* even dared a cautious suggestion that Quitman had no quarrel with Know-Nothing principles and objectives.[6]

Quitman's political independence, however, cut two ways. His very refusal to play the partisan made him more appealing to the regular Democracy than he had been for some time. Many Democratic leaders saw the advantage of selecting candidates who could neutralize the Know-Nothings' influence on disillusioned Democrats. Quitman, who had been waging war on "spoilsmen" for years, fit the bill.[7] Then, too, Quitman's stubborn radicalism had become timely again. With the Kansas-Nebraska controversy driving northerners and southerners farther apart, his earlier warnings about northern intentions gained new relevance.

Quitman hankered to test political waters. As his popularity rose he found himself pulled by the old force of ambition. "My speeches at Jackson & Vicksburg . . . have attracted much & favourable notice," he reported happily to Henry. But he claimed an office commensurate with his former accomplishments and rejected a nomination to the state senate which was tendered to him on June 25 by a Democratic senate district meeting in Natchez. Quitman offered a flimsy excuse that he was too busy with private matters. Actually, he felt he deserved a higher station.[8]

Since Democrats needed Quitman more than he needed the party, he pulled it off, not only capturing a better nomination but also getting it on his own terms. When party managers soon after the state senate rejection sounded Quitman about a *congressional* race, they found him far more obliging. Quitman had long set his eyes on Washington, and genuinely felt that his presence there might make a difference in the slavery dispute. So he affirmed that the times had become too precarious for a "Southern man" to deny the "public voice." However, he imposed conditions. If Democrats wanted him, he stipulated in a letter released at the Fifth Congressional District nominating meeting on July 23, they would have to recognize that he would be under no obligation to follow party mandates in Congress when they controverted his states' rights credo. Anxious to have their southern rights maverick in the fold, the delegates not only tolerated this declaration of ideological independence but even put up with Quitman's criticizing their president. Pierce's Cuba policy, Quitman complained, had proven submissive to the "prevalent spirit of hostility to negro slavery"; the president should encourage rather than oppose the "diffusion of republican institutions" in areas south of the U.S. Democrats swallowed their medicine— partly because Senator Brown, locked in a feud with Jefferson Davis, was pulling strings for Quitman as a means of embarrassing Davis—and forged ahead with Quitman's nomination.[9]

The nomination and Quitman's subsequent acceptance brought the Know-Nothing courtship, of course, to an abrupt end. From a paragon of political virtue, Quitman found himself transformed, in Vicksburg *Whig* jargon, into something of a hypocritical knave. How could the state's most "bitter opponent" of the administration "place himself at the disposal of the wire-workers of that party, headed by his old 'friend,' Col. Jeff Davis"?[10]

Quitman was perturbed. The implication that he had deceived the people brought his honor into the forum again; the suggestion that he was a Democratic lackey threatened the very image of an independent which he had cultivated for so long and which underlay much of his appeal to voters. So he sent his complaints to *Whig* editor Rufus K. Arthur, a wartime friend. Quitman maintained that the *Whig* had no authority to make any of his private remarks about Pierce part of the public record, and that his relations with Davis were not germane to the campaign. Satisfaction came immediately, perhaps because the possibility of a duel always lay at the end of matters of honor in the South. Few of Quitman's rivals ever appeared anxious to push him that far. Arthur's brother Alexander assured Quitman that the offensive editorial had been written by a substitute editor, as Arthur was away on a trip. Arthur would never attribute Quitman's behavior to "improper motives," because he held "too high an opinion" of Quitman's "political honesty & integrity."[11] Thereafter, the paper toned down its criticism.

Electioneering hoopla, by now, was in full swing. Two nights after Quitman's nomination, a Democratic brass band conducted by the family's piano teacher came out to Monmouth to celebrate his candidacy. Lanterns swinging from nearby tree branches seemed to emphasize the shadows, giving Aunt Dicey occasion to frighten Quitman's younger children with declarations that the musicians "were soldiers come to take us all by storm."

Quitman gave his first campaign address at the local courthouse on August 4. Still the only candidate in the field—Fifth District Know-Nothings were encountering difficulty determining their nominee—Quitman then set out to tour the Mississippi Gulf coast. Shieldsboro, Pass Christian, Mississippi City, Biloxi, and East Pascagoula heard his views between August 10 and 15. These speeches earned a warm response, even though Giles Hillyer turned up to debate him. Back at Monmouth with a sore throat as souvenir of his tour, Quitman was prepared to predict an easy victory in the November election.[12]

Quitman saw quite a bit more of editor Hillyer over the following weeks. Shortly after their return from the coast, Hillyer became the Know-Nothing candidate. Quitman, despite the unfortunate occurrences during his last joint canvass, agreed to meet Hillyer in debate. Their schedule announced that they would match oratory in fourteen counties between September 5 and October 4.[13]

From the inception of his candidacy, in his political correspondence, and all the debates, Quitman took issue with Know-Nothingism primarily on the grounds that it pursued tangential matters and that southern rights remained the long-standing concern of his constituents and region. It was not that Quitman entirely ignored the immigration question—though he reportedly expressed the hope that nativism would die of its own accord, so that American party members would become so embarrassed about their affiliation that they would resemble the "point of being shipwrecked" woman who, queried by her husband about her fidelity, responded that "sink or swim, that secret shall never be told." Quitman praised immigrants for their contributions to the arts and sciences, and on one occasion asserted that he would rather vote a Catholic into office who shared his ideology than a native Protestant who did not. He also argued that immigrants were too small a percentage of the national voting population to cause concern. Rather, it was a case of Quitman's dwelling so much on abolitionism that his remarks about Know-Nothing doctrine could be overlooked by disaffected Democrats sympathetic to the nativist appeal. "His speech was almost entirely devoted to the Southern and Slavery questions; but two or three allusions being made to the American party or its principles," noted the *Courier* about one of his efforts.[14]

Quitman's main caveat against Know-Nothingism, thus, was pragmatic rather than moral. The American party, he contended, rode a false hobbyhorse; it distracted voters from the real issue facing southerners—the growing power of abolitionists in the North. Already the northern people had voted out of office some forty northern Democratic congressmen who supported the Fugitive Slave Law and the Kansas-Nebraska Act, he lamented. In rhetoric which contrasted starkly with his secessionism in 1850 and 1851, he insisted that northern Democrats had proved they could be trusted; they were the South's only reliable allies and the only hope for preserving the Union. Northern Americans, on the other hand, could not be trusted. That

June, most free-state delegations at the Know-Nothing national meeting had withdrawn because of a resolution implicitly endorsing the Kansas-Nebraska Act. Quitman suggested that all northern Know-Nothings were antislavery. Emphasizing his personal history of defending slavery against federal encroachments, Quitman rested his claims to a seat in Congress on his southern rights record.[15]

Quitman's strategy was well conceived. He had no desire, or need, to taint Hillyer—a Trinity Church vestryman and fellow Mason—personally with abolitionism. In a region paranoic about its peculiar institution, it was only necessary to establish abolitionist propensities in an opponent's party or political circle to secure advantage. However, the Democratic press felt less restraint. Late in the campaign, Democratic newspapers sought to smear Hillyer on account of his origins. Born in Connecticut and raised in New York, Hillyer proved vulnerable to the suggestion that he remained a Yankee. When Hillyer protested that Quitman, too, was a New Yorker, the *Free Trader* retorted that there was no comparison since Quitman had moved south before slavery had been abolished in the North, and therefore was safe. Hillyer, since he had migrated later, still needed to serve his "probation." [16]

If Quitman did not win the debates, he certainly held his own this time. Hillyer tried to establish nativism as the main issue, but could not evade Quitman's insinuations about antislavery elements in his party. Contending that American party abolitionism was a thing of the past, Hillyer reported that Free-Soilers had already "jumped off" the northern Know-Nothing "railway train." He also couched his calls for a twenty-one-year naturalization period within the context of sectional necessity. Recently the Wisconsin Supreme Court had set free an editor accused of violating the Fugitive Slave law on the grounds that the legislation was unconstitutional. Surely, Hillyer reasoned, Wisconsin had become the only state to flout the law openly because it had a large immigrant population. Similarly, Hillyer attributed the increased power of the free states in Congress to the tendency of immigrants to settle in the North. One day, if sectional differences brought civil war, he predicted with considerable foresight, foreigners would man northern armies.

Hillyer was waging the campaign on Quitman's level, which could only redound to Quitman's advantage, given his record of decades spent in advocacy of states' rights and southern rights principles. "In view of the crisis, which [the] next session [of Congress] may produce, on the slavery question," affirmed one constituent in a private letter written in the midst of the campaign, "it is important to have such a man as Quitman from this District. He understands the rights of the South, has the boldness to stand up to them, and the antecedents to give strength to whatever position he may assume." A dispute about schedules midway through the debates disturbed Quitman's equanimity enough to make him stigmatize Hillyer as a "slippery yankee." But, exulting that his speeches seemed to be creating an "unusual sensation," Quitman gained confidence as the canvass progressed.[17]

Quitman, in fact, encountered more difficulties managing his personal affairs that fall than he did in his campaign. On October 4, at the end of the canvass, he returned to Monmouth and a nearly empty household; yellow fever had imposed its rule upon Natchez again, and Eliza had sent Louisa and all the children except Antonia to Edward Turner's Franklin County place. Days later, word arrived from Henry and Mary, who had been staying at the Gardners', that Mary had given birth to a girl, Virginia ("Jenny"), of "striking resemblance" to Quitman. The news made it imperative that Quitman hasten the work on the new house at Live Oaks; Henry had already purchased silverware, rosewood furniture, and other items in New York City in expectation of occupancy the next year. But Quitman's desires for early completion were frustrated when James McClure, his architect, came down with fever and had to spend part of the month laid up at Monmouth. More serious difficulties presented themselves when McClure finally recovered, only to abscond with $300 in advances, leaving $15,000 in debts, the danger of a workers' lien, and Quitman fuming that his employee had proven himself a "real native American western Yankee." Meanwhile, Quitman had to deal with a family squabble about Louisa's servant, Sarah. Henry and Mary, anxious to visit Monmouth to show off their baby, planned a trip to Natchez and requested that Louisa lend Sarah to help with Jenny on the journey. Mary's own servant Frances, Henry explained, was "a perfect ninny & gawk" to whom he could not entrust the baby for five minutes. Sarah, however, was still nursing Louisa's baby, and Louisa did not want to part with her. Deciding that Henry's request was selfish, Quitman wrote back that "there should be no interruption in the relation of a nurse until the child requires it no more," and that if necessary he would help Henry finance the purchase of a new servant girl.[18]

The campaign rolled on through it all. October became Quitman's barbecue month. "Today I must again go to attend a political barbecue at Bell's Creek church," Quitman wrote on October 11. "I have just arrived home from attending two barbecues in Claiborne. . . . I am engaged to go to Wilkinson tomorrow," he noted on October 28. In a rare letter to his thirteen-year-old daughter Eliza, Quitman offered curt commentary not only about his barbecue obligations but also, in a sense, about his whole career. "There is no peace for public men," he summarized.[19]

Know-Nothing speakers and newspapers, hoping to offset Quitman's energetic campaign, dredged up whatever dirty linen they could find. Quitman was charged with putting Cuba funds to his own personal use, and Democratic voters were reminded of his Whiggish apostasy in the 1830s. The charges gave Quitman cause for concern, but made little difference in the end. Voters throughout the state were responsive to Democratic references to abolitionist influence in the American party and claims that Know-Nothingism was merely a rigged replacement for Whiggery. Watching his party lose momentum to Quitman and other Democratic orators, one Claiborne County Know-Nothing stalwart could only lament that there had been "but one speech on the American side" in his county "while the other party have never been more industrious, having had Quitman twice, [Wiley P.] Harris & others often, & I am sorry to say have made inroads into our circle." [20]

The election, which occurred on November 5–6, amply rewarded Quitman's effort. Fifth District voters gave the "Old Roman" their congressional seat by a majority of 6,558 to 4,543. Throughout the state, moreover, Democrats ran well. Governor McRae gained reelection with a margin of more than 5,000 votes, and Democrats emerged victorious in three of the four other congressional races. (Know-Nothings ran best in areas of former Whig strength such as Adams County—which Quitman lost—and the Vicksburg district where they achieved their only congressional success.) "Party organization" and "calm appeals to the good sense of the people" had overcome a "politically corrupt combination" manipulated by "cute Yankee genius," Quitman celebrated. Perhaps, he anticipated, Know-Nothingism would fade away as a political force in his region. Since so many Democrats had only joined the order "under a delusion," they would surely abandon it "the moment their eyes are open to its anti-Southern tendencies." Organize new Democratic State Rights Associations, he implored J. F. H. Claiborne, to rally the people to sound principles. [21]

Quitman would find occasion to declaim against nativist values again, since Know-Nothings would remain a force in Mississippi for a couple of years and on the national level would field a presidential ticket the next year. Just a few months after his election, in an address which Quitman gave to an audience which undoubtedly included Irishmen (it was delivered at Tammany Hall in New York), Quitman affirmed that the soul and intellect determined the man rather than his birthplace, and referred to his own background as the child of a "New-York Dutchman." [22]

Still, this immigrants' son sensed, even before leaving Natchez, that nativism would never be a primary concern of his again. For all his dislike of anti-immigrant and anti-Catholic prejudice, it was only the antislavery movement in the North which impressed Quitman as a significant threat to his way of life, and most of his campaign had been waged against the abolitionist danger from afar rather than the nativist conspiracy at hand. Quitman thought of his election as the southern rights mandate that had eluded him years earlier, and envisioned himself in the coming months as something of a sectional knight-errant, ready to joust in Congress with northern abolitionists over the future of states' rights and slavery in the Union. Quitman realized that his views remained in advance of many Mississippians, much less the South as a whole; he still cherished the Calhounian option of secession if "sound principles" of government could not be guaranteed. But this gave him little cause for constraint. One could never expect "unanimity," and he had, after all, been elected. There would surely be "Tories in '56" just as there had been "Tories in '76." But Congressman-elect Quitman would claim the status of "chosen representative" of the "heart and soul" of Mississippi. He had earned the right to play a bold hand. Duty allowed no evasion.[23]

22

Equal Rights or Dissolution

HAD it not been for the turmoil in Kansas, Quitman, his anxiety to take southern rights to Washington notwithstanding, would have turned up a bit late for the convening of Congress on December 3. He wanted to at least see his granddaughter before assuming the burdens of public office again. Besides, the McClure fiasco demanded his attention.

But it was already apparent that slavery's future in Kansas would be immediately at stake as soon as the nation's lawmakers began their deliberations. The previous March, slavery proponents had won the territory's first legislative elections, a victory which led to enactment of a series of territorial laws guaranteed to infuriate northern settlers (such as measures banning Free-Soilers from office, specifying jail terms for Kansans who criticized slavery, and setting the death penalty for persons aiding the escape of black fugitives). Free-Soilers considered these statutes not only intolerable but also illegal. Four to five thousand Missouri "border ruffians" had crossed into Kansas during the March elections and, though not residents of the new territory, cast ballots for proslavery legislative candidates. Convinced that the legislature had been fraudulently chosen, Free-Soilers held a convention in October and November which established an antislavery provisional government and drafted a constitution for Kansas' admission to the Union as a free state. Proslavery elements, seeing nothing amiss in the Missouri electioneering since antislavery groups like the New England Emigrant Aid Society had earlier interfered in Kansas by financing the in-migration of free-soil settlers, felt it imperative to suppress the free-state movement. By the time of Quitman's election, violence had erupted and many settlers believed full-scale civil war was at hand. One proslavery official, in fact, was so certain that "the battle of the independence of the South" lay ahead, he exhorted Quitman to bring filibusters into the territory.

Kansas affairs compelled Quitman's immediate attendance in Congress, and he had heard that anti-Nebraska congressmen, now increasingly using the Republican party label, would try to capture the House speakership. Quitman believed that his southern rights mission depended, to no small degree, upon keeping the speakership out of antislavery hands. Speakers decided who had the floor during debate, controlled committee assignments, and influenced legislation because they were arbiters of procedural controversies. He could hardly afford to be tardy for the very sectional showdown in Congress which he had been telling voters for months he was specially equipped to deal with. Thus, driven by the conviction that he had a new role to perform in the national drama over slavery, Quitman put private concerns aside. "I can not neglect a public duty which I have assumed," he wrote Henry in a letter explaining why he would have to postpone seeing Jenny. "The slavery contest may come on even in the organization of the House & I could not excuse myself if absent." [1]

Quitman left Natchez on November 21, arrived in Washington on December 1, and took quarters at John Guy's National Hotel on Pennsylvania Avenue at Sixth Street, an establishment popular with the Mississippi delegation. (Senator Brown and his wife took rooms at the National the same day Quitman arrived, as did two of Quitman's four Mississippi colleagues in the House.) When Congress assembled two days later, proceedings instantly confirmed Quitman's judgment in making a hasty trip. As expected, the speakership contest provided an immediate test of sectional and party strength. Republicans and other anti-Nebraska men composed the largest faction with some 108 members, but they fell short of the majority necessary to elect a speaker since there were also some 83 Democrats and 43 Know-Nothings. The anti-Nebraska forces put up Lewis D. Campbell of Ohio, a multiterm congressman well known for his opposition to the Kansas-Nebraska Act. Democrats, including Quitman, rallied behind caucus candidate William A. Richardson of Illinois, a Stephen Douglas supporter who had been instrumental in steering the Kansas-Nebraska Act through the House. Most Know-Nothings voted for Humphrey Marshall, an American party member from Kentucky. Several other congressmen drew votes, including Nathaniel P. Banks of Massachusetts, a former "Know-Nothing of Democratic roots" just turned Republican, who won a rather significant twenty-one endorsements on the initial ballot. Four times the House balloted, without success. Know-Nothings held the balance of power, and they refused to switch to either the Campbell or the Richardson column. Leaving the House at adjournment, Quitman realized that he had found the desired sectional battleground on his first day in Congress. [2]

Quitman's congressional baptism became a classic political impasse. The balloting went on for days, and then weeks, but nothing could be decided, though caucus candidates changed as the parties jockeyed for extra votes. Marshall backed out on December 6 following the fifteenth unsuccessful ballot, and was replaced by Henry M. Fuller of Pennsylvania; Campbell withdrew for Banks the next day. Other candidates, including Quitman, confused the picture by attracting a scattering of votes. Frequently Banks came within six or seven votes of election, but just could not gain those last few endorsements. With the House tied up over its speakership, all other business had to be deferred.[3]

At first, the House would convene, attempt four to six ballots, and simply adjourn early as members agreed that further efforts were futile. Inevitably, as the representatives grew exasperated with the standoff, speechmaking on Kansas, abolitionism, Know-Nothing secrecy, secession, vote buying, and other issues were injected into the proceedings. Quitman's party tried particularly to entice southern Americans to Richardson by amplifying on the theme that northern Know-Nothings were untrustworthy on slavery and that only the Democracy was both a national and a moderate party. Know-Nothings refused to budge, however, and retorted that either Republicans or Democrats should strike a deal with them. Christmas came and went, a new year began, over a hundred ballots were taken, and still the House remained unorganized. "Vote, vote, vote & then a gush of very poor thin blue & half sour stump oratory—& then vote & vote," observed a disgusted congressman from Maryland.[4]

Quitman remained subdued during the early skirmishing, but gradually warmed to the question. With his customary directness, he chided his colleagues for debating Kansas and the slavery issue under the pretense of deciding the speakership. The House, he felt, should organize and *then* confront national questions. On December 21 he rebuked other southern congressmen for claiming to speak for the South and announced that he expected to be heard on Kansas when it came up "properly for debate." The next day he proposed that speeches be limited to ten minutes until the House organized. Obviously other members, perhaps responding to criticism in the press, shared his views, for the resolution carried. Back home, the Vicksburg *Whig*, accustomed to Quitman's long-windedness, could only marvel that Quitman had limited his colleagues to less time than his own exordiums customarily consumed![5]

Anxious to get on with the business of defending southern interests, Quitman not only urged conclusion of the speakership contest but also demonstrated he was in earnest about putting southern rights before party dictates. On January 3, Percy Walker, an Alabama Know-Nothing, tried to break the deadlock with a resolution that the House select William W. Boyce of South

Carolina, a secessionist, as speaker. Walker reasoned that only a political independent could overcome rigid party lines and win a majority, and that Boyce, though a nominal Democrat, met that criterion since he had refused to participate in the Democratic caucus. Quitman supported Walker's motion, which got nowhere, earning a reprimand from fellow Mississippi Democrat William Barksdale, who pointedly instructed that "principles cannot be carried out except through the instrumentality of party." [6]

Eleven days later, Quitman diverged a second time from Democratic norms and in the process discussed Kansas despite his own intention to defer the issue. Irked by comments which Democratic candidate William Richardson had made about Kansas, Quitman abstained from voting at all on two roll calls. The next day, undoubtedly feeling heat from Democrats, Quitman returned to the fold and explained that his protest had been symbolic rather than substantive. Two days earlier, Richardson had claimed that Congress possessed constitutional power to prohibit slavery in territories, but it would be judicious to have the issue decided by popular sovereignty, which, he believed, would eventually make Kansas free. Quitman rejected Richardson's premise, and denied that Congress had any authority to shut slavery out of the territories. Richardson had also given implied endorsement to "squatter sovereignty," the doctrine which said that early settlers, through their territorial legislatures, could exclude slavery by failing to pass legislation protecting slave property. Quitman, well aware that it would be difficult to eradicate slavery once it became entrenched in Kansas, repeated a Calhounian exposition of territorial doctrine which he had invoked several times during the 1850 crisis. Territorial legislatures had *no* right to ban slavery, he argued. The first opportunity to do so would arise with the drafting of a state constitution, because it was only then, when the constitution met with Congress' approval, that territorial settlers truly assumed "sovereign powers." Until that moment Americans of all sections enjoyed the same right to use their property in the territories.

Had Quitman truly believed Richardson was antislavery, he would not have supported the Illinoisan at all. But Quitman knew that Richardson was only one of many northern Democrats espousing squatter sovereignty, and he had come to understand that such doctrines sometimes emanated from political necessity rather than conviction. Northern Democrats had to convince their constituents that the Kansas-Nebraska Act did not simply surrender the territories to the "Slave Power," and that there remained the possibility of a free Kansas, if they were ever to turn back their anti-Nebraska competition. Quitman's protest was designed to stake out an ideological position for the coming Kansas debates rather than to undermine Richardson's prospects or lead other southern Democrats away from the northern Democracy. In fact, though criticizing Richardson, Quitman also expressed confidence that Richardson would wind up doing "all that I could ask for the constitutional rights of all sections of the country." [7]

The weather turned exceedingly cold. Snows fell; Washingtonians took to sleighing. Quitman and his colleagues had to navigate pavement of sheer ice to make it to the capitol gate. And the contest went on. Richardson withdrew as Democratic candidate and was replaced by James L. Orr of South Carolina, to no avail. All the while, conditions worsened in Kansas, and a message arrived from President Pierce, who wanted an appropriation to uphold the proslavery legislature and maintain order in Kansas. Pierce cautioned that he might use army and militia forces in Kansas if Free-Soilers there pushed their protest to full insurrection.

Quitman spoke out again on Kansas before it was all over. He defended the Kansas-Nebraska Act because it had given "all portions of this country their equal rights in this Confederacy," and emphasized how southern "blood and treasure" had been expended in the acquisition of the national domain. Warming to the debate emotionally, he found himself silenced by the gavel, for violating his own ten-minute restriction, when he was in the process of repeating for the fourth time in one speech that the South "demanded" its rights. When Galusha A. Grow, a Pennsylvania Free-Soiler, attacked the repeal of the Missouri Compromise and blamed southern extremism for the rise of northern abolitionism, Quitman protested, "You robbed us of California." [8]

It took a Democratic miscalculation to bring the contest to a close on February 2, two months and 133 ballots after the stalemate began. Given some indications that southern Know-Nothings might support William Aiken, a South Carolina congressman who, like Boyce, had refused to participate in the Democratic caucus, the Democracy dropped Orr for Aiken, and a Tennessee Democrat proposed what Republicans had wanted all along—that decision be made by plurality. The resolution passed. When the next ballot was taken, most southern Know-Nothings did vote for Aiken; however, enough northern Know-Nothings deserted their party for Banks to give the Republicans a 103-to-100 victory. [9]

Quitman observed what followed with a sense of deep foreboding. Crowds of free-soil partisans rushed to the Hall to celebrate the antislavery triumph. With night falling on the capitol, the spectators, overcome with emotion, waved handkerchiefs, cried in joy, and cheered as Banks took his speaker's oath. Quitman could only wonder where it all would end. "How far they will dare to go is yet to be seen," he wrote Eliza. Surely the "abolitionists" would try to capitalize on their new power and bring antislavery measures before Congress. If the South and its northern Democratic allies could not stave off such measures by converting the abolitionists to "sound principles," it would become necessary to consider "dissolution." "This Congress," he believed, would "be decisive of the fate of the Union." [10]

Quitman would have been better able to cope with what had transpired had he been capable of distinguishing between free-soil and abolitionism. Banks and most Republicans were not true abolitionists, and certainly not racial egalitarians. That is to say, Republicans emphasized the need to curtail slavery expansion rather than end slavery in southern states themselves. The problem was that many Free-Soilers regarded containment of slavery as one of several means to establish conditions conducive to *eventual* abolition, and that southerners like Quitman—regarding slavery expansion as essential to the survival of the institution—defined containment as abolitionism in another garb. To many southerners, all Republicans seemed Negro-lovers, or "Black Republicans." In a sense, therefore, Quitman overdramatized the implications of Banks's election. Banks, moreover, announced upon taking his speaker's oath that he intended impartiality in his administration of House procedure, and gave immediate proof of his sincerity by his standing committee assignments. He appointed Quitman chairman of the Committee on Military Affairs, and selected southerners for many of the slots on other important committees. [11]

Yet Quitman was hardly fabricating a crisis. Republicans did have control of the House and could use their strength to promote the antislavery cause in Kansas. This became evident immediately. Two delegates from Kansas, one representing each of the major governmental factions, were on hand claiming Kansas' lone nonvoting seat. On March 19, after heated debate, Republicans succeeded in creating a three-man committee to resolve the delegate controversy and to collect evidence regarding election fraud in Kansas. The latter mission, since the president had upheld the legality of the proslavery government, appeared a step toward a free-soil Kansas. [12]

Quitman spoke sparingly during the delegate debates. Rather, he turned to learning the ropes of being a congressman. In a day prior to national political committees and civil service, though the federal bureaucracy was minuscule by modern standards, patronage requests nonetheless took a great deal of a representative's time. Quitman worked closely with Senator Brown—who had become something of a mentor about the ins and outs of Washington politics—on several cases. "The General agrees to Witters appointment and will have it made soon," Brown noted on one occasion, adding that he found Quitman somewhat "slow in his movements" on patronage but reliable in the long run. Special needs of constituents also compelled Quitman's attention. "You will ere this have observed that I have succeeded in giving your country a daily four hour mail coach . . . to Jackson," he responded to one request. Bogged down with busywork, composing ten to twenty letters on official business every day, Quitman found it difficult to steal a few moments to write his own family.[13]

Nothing demanded more of Quitman than his committee work. The Committee on Military Affairs had one of the fullest agendas in the House, and often gathered twice a week. With private military pensions, army appropriations, West Point, military road construction, weaponry, and a host of other matters within its purview, the committee was constantly deliberating issues and making recommendations to the House.[14]

Speaker Banks could not have done a better job matching a congressman and a committee. Quitman's reputation as a soldier had preceded him, and other congressmen—even Republican opponents—showed marked respect, sometimes bordering on the obsequious, for his expertise in military matters. When Thomas L. Clingman of North Carolina urged his colleagues that February to listen to Quitman on a military appropriations question because Quitman had "as much, if not more, experience in military matters than any other member upon this floor," he began a ritual which continued for the rest of Quitman's congressional career. Quitman, in turn, confident about his military competence, threw himself into his committee work. As Jefferson Davis later put it, Quitman's talent as a congressman related in considerable degree to his remarkable enthusiasm for the "labors of the committee-room."[15]

Had Quitman merely fulfilled the mechanical functions of his position, he would have made a mark as servant of the military establishment. As committee chair, he often assumed, or was assigned, the duty of presenting committee recommendations to the House. Thus, he appeared on the House floor sponsoring such measures as the purchase of new lands for government arsenals and a petition from West Point officers that they be granted a higher commutation price for rations.[16]

However, Quitman's dedication to army needs had a spiritual dimension. His Mexican War experience had given him a deep faith in the American military, and army officers soon learned that they had in Quitman a champion rather than a mere servant. When Ohio congressman Edward Ball introduced an amendment to curtail the use of army officers on government construction projects such as building post offices, Quitman rebuked Ball for what he interpreted as an implication of corruption. No "class of men" in the nation, Quitman argued, had demonstrated more "honor and integrity" than the army officer corps. Fascinated by innovations in military technology, Quitman urged appropriations for the conversion of government-owned smoothbore muskets and smoothbore coastal artillery to the far more accurate and long-range rifled muskets and rifled artillery, and pressed the principle upon Secretary of War Davis. On military appropriations, Quitman cast aside qualms about government spending and almost invariably voted yea, even when his committee colleagues did not and even though he objected to and voted against internal improvements bills and numerous other appropriations because they helped cause creeping federalism. The payoff came when a fellow southern Democrat, George W. Jones of Tennessee, protested a $10,000 appropriation recommended by Quitman's committee for a military road from Astoria to Salem in the Oregon Territory, and beseeched his "friends who claim to be strict Constructionists" to rally against the proposal on the grounds that, because the committee had not shown there was sufficient military purpose and the road was obviously intended for civilian use, it was thus unconstitutional. Quitman ignored the ideological bait. Military stores, he answered, could be transported on the road; federal road construction was necessary for the defense of the nation's "frontier Territories." [17]

Meanwhile, unrequited ambition made one last call upon Quitman. His Senate aspirations reached a dead end that January back in Jackson. Reportedly, twenty state legislators were set to promote Quitman in case of a deadlock between Jefferson Davis and Jacob Thompson in balloting for A. G. Brown's colleague, but Davis won so easily that Quitman's supporters never found an opportunity to bring his name forth. However, Quitman had other advancement in mind. The Democratic National Convention would meet in Cincinnati in June to choose a party ticket and platform for the November presidential election. Quitman believed that he would be nominated for vice president. Newspapers throughout the South were floating his name for the position, and talk circulated in Washington about his prospects. He had also heard from correspondents and family that he had supporters in the Louisiana legislature and Louisiana Democratic party hierarchy, and that several Mississippi delegates would go to the convention pledged to his candidacy. Excited, Quitman wrote Henry that he was in "high consideration" at the capital and that he had noticed a "wide disposition to place me on the ticket for V Prest." "I am regarded as the representative of progress, an element which most thinking men believe should be considered in the next canvass," he reported. [18]

By "progress," Quitman meant territorial expansion. Many Democrats, believing that the nation had yet to achieve its limits, favored new initiatives to get Cuba and more aggressive policies regarding other domains. Central America, where the United States and Great Britain were locked in a struggle for influence, if not hegemony, offered a particular focus for concern. The overland transit of passengers and freight across Central America had become a lucrative commercial enterprise involving American entrepreneurs, and canal projects to cross the region at either Nicaragua or Panama were already under serious consideration. To avoid a war for control of such a canal, the United States and England had initialed the Clayton-Bulwer Treaty in 1850, which stipulated that any canal would be neutral and under joint control of the two countries, and that neither country could establish colonies in Central America. However, the treaty had not really resolved the difficulty, because the British had earlier established colonial dependencies in the region and refused to evacuate them, claiming that the treaty was prospective in intent. The official American position, on the other hand, became that the British needed to pull out.

Democrats, far more than their Know-Nothing and Republican rivals, tended to favor aggressive policies to uphold the American interpretation of the treaty. Within the expansionist or "Young America" wing of the party, there was considerable feeling that the United States should aid the filibuster William Walker—who had led a group of adventurers to Nicaragua in 1855—as a means of strengthening the American hand in the region. Walker had gained virtual control of the country as commander in chief of the army in a regime headed by a native Nicaraguan. Viewing Walker as a pawn in the Anglo-American confrontation since England was supporting a coalition of Central American states out to overthrow him, many Democrats urged recognition of Walker's regime and a relaxation of American neutrality laws so that the filibuster would find it easy to draw reinforcements and supplies from the States.

Quitman's name surfaced in connection with the Democratic vice-presidential nomination for reasons transcending his imperialism. All three leading contenders for the party's *presidential* choice, Pierce, Douglas, and U.S. minister to England James Buchanan (who left his post that spring and returned home), were northerners. Their supporters, knowing that a sectionally balanced ticket would help carry the South in the fall, spoke of southerners for vice president to attract slave state delegate votes at the upcoming convention. Quitman, a war hero and undisputed symbol of his region's causes, naturally attracted consideration. Were Quitman still a secession advocate, he would have received little attention. But, believing that the Kansas-Nebraska Act—which he had come to regard as a demonstration of northern Democratic consideration for southern needs—might eventuate in a new slave state, he had mellowed over the last couple of years. His sectional diatribes were now tempered with intimations of unionism. Thus in his Tammany Hall speech he could urge strict construction of the Constitution and southern rights in Kansas, yet also enunciate a qualified vision of a perpetual nation. The "great Democratic Party of the North" had revealed an intention to defend the South; he hoped he would never see the day when

New Yorkers and Mississippians could not address each other as "fellow-citizens." Still, Quitman's popularity had a lot to do with his record as an expansionist, and he sharpened his imperialist image by his public pronouncements during the winter and spring. He raised cheers at Tammany Hall, in fact, by recalling how the Democracy had pushed through the annexation of Texas despite British resistance. Now, he suggested, the nation could "look John Bull in the teeth." [19]

Quitman reserved his most undiluted dose of imperialist dogma for an hour-long House address on April 29, his only full-length speech of the session. He described his country as having entered an age of "progress." The U.S. now needed to unleash the "free action and enterprising spirit" of its people. Quitman targeted Mexico as an appropriate object for American energy. Fertile lands and "jeweled mountains" made it worth seeking; moreover, that country had suffered so much from revolution and governmental instability that a European power might seize the "waif" if the United States did not take action. Cuba, an island so close to American shores that its "cliffs" echoed with Fourth of July cannon, already hailed America's Mississippi Valley trade. Did Americans really want to risk European possession of the rich island, which after a canal was built, would be the key to European trade with the Orient and communication between the Pacific Coast and the rest of the United States? Certainly Americans could not permit England, with its overall plan to establish a "barbaric black empire" throughout "insular America," to control Cuba; an abolitionized Cuba would give England a way to erode masters' control over slaves in the South itself. Besides, history had demonstrated that blacks were incapable of self-government. Perhaps influenced by some recent information he had received that William Walker intended to expand his base of control from Nicaragua into other Central American areas, Quitman told his colleagues that the filibuster had become that region's best hope. Merely a collection of petty states "pillaged by the avarice of rival chiefs," Central America too would fall to European intrigues unless Walker succeeded. Quitman disparaged the Clayton-Bulwer Treaty as an unconstitutional abridgment of Congress' right to admit new states to the Union.

For his "favored country" to "steadily ascend through all the grades of her glorious destiny," Quitman argued, America would have to finally revise its attitude toward filibustering. What had once, perhaps, been justifiable policy had now become morally wrong and "politically suicidal." Neutrality laws crippled the "spirit" of Americans anxious to help white Cuban descendants of "the best blood of the old Hidalgos" slake their unquenchable thirst for liberty; they also impaired efforts to give the benighted peoples of Mexico and Central America the blessing of American institutions. Willing to play any angle to make his case, Quitman resorted to some rather unlikely sources—for him—to prove that neutrality laws should go. Thus he cited Chancellor James Kent, the same jurist whose doctrines he had warned his son to avoid, for the theory that every nation had a right to protect itself, even against indefinite threats (*i.e.*, future British schemes). He also explained that Henry Clay, House speaker when the statutes were originally enacted, denounced them because they would impair American efforts to help Latin American colonies revolt against Spain. How could Americans embrace the memory of Lafayette, a French filibuster in the American Revolution, yet condemn the patriots of their own time? Contending that all Americans enjoyed the right of expatriation and that filibuster groups could only be prosecuted legally if they left American shores as fully organized military units, Quitman announced his intention to introduce a bill repealing the offensive sections of the 1818 act.[20]

Two days later, Quitman introduced his bill, which was immediately referred to the Committee on the Judiciary. However, such measures had been introduced in the past, without success. It was Quitman's speech, not his proposal, which made an impact. Antislavery and anti-imperialist factions, of course, despised his doctrines. A four-column article in one antislavery organ, for instance, denounced Quitman for employing Calhoun's old stratagem of throwing out the specter of British plots to justify slavery expansion. But the speech also pleased expansionists, and enhanced Quitman's prospects.[21]

Having given a major address, Quitman found the moment opportune for a trip home. ("My heart yearns to see my wife & children again," he had lamented to Eliza.) He would bring the family north for the summer. He considered asking his brother-in-law to escort them, so he would not have to leave while Congress was in session, but he concluded that he could afford to absent himself if he traveled quickly. So Quitman spent the next three weeks on a round trip to Monmouth. When he returned with Eliza, Louisa and her little girl, and his other daughters, he switched quarters, taking rooms at Willard's Hotel, an establishment near the White House.[22]

Quitman surely would have had Henry Turner handle his family's journey had he any inkling of what would occur during his absence. On May 19 and 20, Senator Charles Sumner of Massachusetts, one of the most caustic antislavery Republicans in Congress, delivered an incredibly mordacious speech about how the "Slave Power" had engaged in the "rape" of the "virgin territory" of Kansas. Not only did Sumner damn the South, its institutions, and southern political power, he also violated Senate codes of behavior by personally insulting his colleagues. He was especially hard on South Carolina Senator Andrew P. Butler, suggesting that Butler made vows to the "harlot, Slavery," and alluding to Butler's speech impediment. Representative Preston Brooks of South Carolina, Butler's nephew, then avenged his uncle's honor. The next day, after Senate adjournment, while Sumner sat at his desk writing letters. Brooks approached Sumner and, without giving him a chance to stand up, began clobbering him on the head with a gutta-percha cane, until Sumner, his head bloody, collapsed.

By the time Quitman returned on May 26, Congress was in an uproar. Sumner, who suffered such psychosomatic shock that he found it impossible to resume Senate duties even after recovering from the physical wounds, quickly became antislavery's newest martyr to what was depicted as the unrelenting aggression of a slavocracy bent on nationalizing slavery. Republicans wanted retribution. Southern congressmen, on the other hand, rallied behind Brooks on the rationale that the assault had been amply provoked.

Republican hands were tied in the Senate, where they lacked control; an investigative committee reported that the Senate lacked authority to arrest a House member. However, Republicans in the House on July 14 won a 121-to-95 vote to expel Brooks. Though the vote had no practical effect since expulsion required two-thirds assent, Brooks resigned his seat that day in a dramatic protest, saying that he preferred to let his own "fellow-citizens," rather than a *"packed jury"* (the Republican plurality in the House), pronounce judgment upon his course. Brooks had measured sentiment in his radical state well. He gained immediate reelection and, on August 1, reappeared in triumph before Speaker Banks to be sworn in once more as a House member.[23]

Quitman, who had once caned a newspaper editor over a perceived affront to his own honor, had little difficulty working out his feelings about the Brooks affair. To Quitman, Brooks was a hero. He had struck a physical blow, through Sumner, against abolitionism. It was something that Quitman, under the right circumstances, would like to have done himself. Quitman saw a lot of Brooks after the incident. ("Colnl. Brooks called to see us," Rose noted in her diary on June 4. "[H]e is a fine noble looking gentleman but with an air of firm determination impressed upon his lips.") He may have consulted with Brooks about the resignation. When Brooks had a birthday party later in the summer, Quitman was one of a select group of politicos who turned up for the occasion. Quitman brought along a new cane for Brooks, a present from the citizens of Holmes County to replace the one which Brooks had smashed while beating Sumner. Making an impromptu address, Quitman opined that his friend was "incapable of a dishonorable act."[24]

Congress took an informal adjournment on June 2 for the Democratic National Convention, which began at noon that day, leaving Kansas' status unresolved.[25] News had arrived in Washington of new violence in the territory. Proslavery militias had destroyed free-state presses, fired buildings (including the home of the free-state governor), and looted in the free-soil town of Lawrence, giving antislavery propagandists in the North new proof that the slavocracy was taking over the nation by force; an antislavery fanatic named John Brown and seven followers had murdered five proslavery settlers at Pottawatomie Creek, proving to countless southerners that abolitionists would stop at nothing in their ruthless conspiracy to destroy slavery. Stephen Douglas, blaming the territory's trouble on northern emigrant-aid groups, had presented the Senate a bill which, if enacted, would make Kansas a slave state; statehood would come when the territory achieved a population of 93,420 (the required total for a representative in Congress), and the statehood process would be under the slave faction's control because the legislature would establish the procedures for electing a constitutional convention. For the Republicans, Senator William Seward of New York had sponsored a measure which would have admitted Kansas immediately to the Union under the free-state constitution. But the lawmakers could not find an acceptable middle ground, and the language in both chambers had been heated.[26]

Quitman left for Cincinnati still confident that the vice-presidential nomination would be his, and full of ideas, which he was hardly reticent about sharing with others, concerning the other half of the ticket. Although he could "sustain" Pierce or be "contented" with Buchanan, he wanted Douglas. The whole South owed a great debt to Douglas, whose bill had repudiated "THE ABOMINABLE PRINCIPLE OF SQUATTER SOVEREIGNTY" by postponing Kansas' slavery decision until statehood, thus protecting southern property during the whole territorial period. In addition, Douglas had taken such a strong profilibuster stance that President Pierce, so as not to forfeit all expansionist support to his rival, officially recognized the Walker regime and became more militant against British influence in Central America. Quitman felt that Douglas, unlike Pierce, would remain independent of conservative "old fogies" when in office and would add territory to the national domain.[27]

Quitman's declarations for Douglas, however, only served to irritate many of his own supporters. Generally, Mississippi Democratic leaders favored the renomination of Franklin Pierce. This was partly because the influential Jefferson Davis was a close friend of the president, as well as his secretary of war, and in favor of Pierce's serving again. Pierce's Kansas policy had also won friends in Mississippi, as had his strict constructionist approach to congressional spending measures. To the dismay of many westerners, for instance, the president had vetoed an appropriations bill for federal improvements of rivers and harbors. Pierce, as one party stalwart put it, had "nationalized *state-rightism*." When the Mississippi delegation caucused in Cincinnati, it simply chose to disregard Quitman's preferences and decided on a Pierce-Quitman ticket. Quitman's out-of-state support, ironically, also came from Pierce delegations.[28]

Despite his miscalculation, Quitman's chances appeared promising. Mississippi, though entitled to only seven votes, flooded Cincinnati with over sixty delegates; and Quitman had several good friends, including Senator Brown, among the fourteen Mississippians who wound up sitting in the convention (each casting one-half of a vote). He also had acquaintances in other delegations. Thomas L. Harris, who had served under Quitman in the war as major of a regiment of Illinois volunteers, was on hand from Stephen Douglas' state. Emile La Sère and John Slidell of Louisiana, both of whom had worked with Quitman in the Cuba affair, were in Cincinnati and could be expected to use their influence for his candidacy. Quitman did not take a seat in the convention himself, but he knew that he could nonetheless count on a lot of votes when the vice-presidential balloting occurred.[29]

Unfortunately for Quitman, the convention offered a classic setting for political bargaining, and the group of men who pulled the right strings—a coterie of four U.S. senators—had no use for his vice-presidential plans. Slidell, his Louisiana senate colleague Judah P. Benjamin, Indiana's Jesse D. Bright, and James A. Bayard of Delaware were all in Cincinnati managing James Buchanan's presidential bid. The senators favored "Old Buck" for a variety of reasons, including his image as a seasoned statesman, his already having the support of a well-oiled political machine, his recent absence from the country, which had spared him the necessity of risking divisive pronouncements about Kansas, his role in the Ostend conference which, whatever its flaws, had taken a strong stand for American acquisition of Cuba, and their own personal ambitions. Deals were inevitable, given the two-thirds majority necessary for nomination and a field which included several presidential hopefuls in addition to Pierce, Douglas, and Buchanan. The senators made the right bargains, and gained Buchanan the nomination on the seventeenth ballot.[30]

When the convention turned to its vice-presidential selection, Quitman was one of eleven candidates nominated—Harris did him the honor with a brief speech dwelling on his Mexican War gallantry. On the first ballot, taking the entire delegations of Mississippi, South Carolina, Illinois, and Arkansas, and scattered votes from New Hampshire, Massachusetts, New York, Ohio, and Texas, Quitman emerged the leader, with 59 votes. However, his total fell far short of the 197 required to nominate, and he refused all deals, effectively sealing his fate. The Buchanan clique, throughout the convention, had shown an anxiety to appease the Douglas faction. Most of its overtures had been directed toward winning Douglas delegates over to Buchanan's candidacy; thus the party platform, which was adopted *before* the presidential balloting, included planks endorsing popular sovereignty and William Walker's regime. But the senators also deemed Douglas' support necessary for victory in November, and Slidell was more than happy to oblige Douglas' floor manager, William Richardson, who recommended that the two factions unite on Kentucky lawyer and recent congressman John C. Breckinridge for vice president. When the second ballot occurred, many delegations, having fulfilled their obligations to other candidates on the first ballot, by prearrangement went for Breckinridge in what became a land-slide.[31]

Quitman was stunned. After learning from some of his supporters why he had lost, he set off for Washington, his resentment smoldering. When he ran into Slidell—also traveling back to the capital—in a hotel reading room in Wheeling the morning after the convention, it was too much to bear. Confronting the senator, he asked whether his friends' accounts of the transaction at the convention were accurate. Sensing the direction of Quitman's inquiry, Slidell, though admitting that he and Richardson had manipulated Breckinridge's nomination, protested that Quitman had never asked for his aid. Quitman persisted. Knowing that several members of the Louisiana delegation had attended the convention pledged to his nomination but that the state had voted for Breckinridge from the start, he censured Slidell for persuading delegates to vote against their constituents' wishes—which he considered "wrong & immoral." Slidell remained passive until Quitman announced that he would make a public exposé of Slidell's course, regardless of how it hurt Slidell personally or politically. Then Slidell queried whether Quitman was threatening "war," and warned that he could "take care of himself." It may have finally dawned on Quitman at this point that he had gone too far. He offered an ineffectual remark about the need to think things out before making his next move, and terminated the conversation.[32]

Once back in Washington, Quitman, on the night of June 18, graciously endorsed Buchanan and the Democracy at a gaslit "Grand Ratification" meeting. He lauded Buchanan for having spent thirty years in public service, and praised Democrats for their fearless devotion to "eternal" constitutional principles. However, the turn of events at the convention still rankled, and he made a point of studiously ignoring Slidell whenever their paths crossed. "Slidell and Quitman have not spoken since the Cin. convention," Brown observed more than six months later.[33]

Congressional labor provided little solace. On June 25, when speaking about military roads in Oregon, Quitman said that construction was justified by Congress' power over the territories. Before the June 26 session, when reading the *Congressional Globe* reporter's transcription of the previous day's discussions, Quitman discovered that he had been quoted as arguing that "Where, in the Territories, the sovereignty is in the [Federal] Government, it may remove obstructions [from roads]." Realizing that Republicans could twist his words into an admission that Congress could abolish slavery in the territories, he took the House floor that day to explain that a cold and his poor seat location had caused him to be misquoted. He meant that sovereignty over the territories rested "in the United States, that is, the States jointly, not in the Government." But there was no getting off the hook. Implying that sovereignty became meaningless if it could not be utilized, Lewis Campbell, reasoning from Quitman's premise that the states—not Congress—controlled the territories, asked just how states could exercise their authority. Was not Congress the only political body in which states were represented? Quitman could only respond weakly that the "beautiful but somewhat complex system of government" created by the founding fathers had left states without any "constitutional channel" to exercise their sovereignty. Congress had only limited powers over the territories according to constitutional provisions, and these powers did not include domain over slavery.

Although it is unlikely that either Quitman or Campbell won any converts with their exchange, Campbell did get in the last word, pointing out that the same founding fathers extolled by Quitman had, in several cases, banned slavery in certain territories. Obviously they intended some legislative control over the slavery question. Quitman, Campbell argued, had misrepresented the "olden time."[34]

By the time the House adjourned on Thursday, July 3, for a long holiday weekend, Quitman coveted some relaxation. A week and a half earlier, Eliza and the children had escaped his "close, bad smelling" rooms at Willard's for the sea air at the Hygeia Hotel resort at Old Point Comfort on the Virginia coast. Quitman joined his family, which now included Henry, Mary, their baby, and the Gardners, all of whom were in the North for the summer and staying at the resort. Hearing of Quitman's arrival, the soldiers at nearby Fort Monroe invited the family over for their Fourth of July band performance and fireworks. Quitman's respite passed all too quickly.[35]

Anticipating that Congress would soon adjourn until December, Quitman began to plan a month's return to Monmouth to attend to plantation and business affairs.[36] But the session, bogged down in renewed controversy over Kansas, this time in the guise of an army appropriations dispute, dragged on well after the holiday break.

Back in January, by putting federal troops at Forts Leavenworth and Riley in the territory at the disposal of the proslavery faction's governor,

President Pierce had brought the army into the middle of the imbroglio. Perceiving the army a southern tool, antislavery congressmen sought restrictions on use of troops. When army appropriations came before the House, Republicans amended the bill to prohibit Pierce from using federal troops to enforce the proslavery legislature's laws until Congress verified the legislature's legitimacy, and called upon the president to disarm the militia in Kansas and prevent armed men (*i.e.*, Missouri border ruffians) from intruding into the territory. A stalemate occurred when the Democratic Senate refused to concur.

Quitman, with his abiding faith in the army and belief in the proslavery cause, naturally denounced the amendment. He argued that Republicans, in seeking to destroy the president's right to enforce the law, were tampering with the Constitution. If the laws of the Kansas legislature were indeed illegal, it fell to the courts, not Congress, to make that distinction. If Pierce's direction of the army in Kansas constituted an abuse of presidential powers, the appropriate corrective was impeachment proceedings.

Of course there was nothing that Quitman or anyone else could say to sway Republicans from their position. Since the Senate also held its ground, debate continued without result. One night, Quitman found himself listening to Lewis Campbell declaim upon the bill at three in the morning. Conference committees could not reach compromise. Yet, adjournment without a bill proved impossible. Congress attempted that tack on August 18, but Pierce immediately called a new session. Provision for the army, the president insisted, was essential for frontier security. Without funds, he would have to disband garrisons at western posts and halt arms manufacture—an open invitation to Indians to commit "rapine and murder" on settlers.[37]

Meanwhile, Quitman did what he could behind the scenes to promote the southward expansion of slavery. In a political coup, William Walker had seized the Nicaraguan presidency in a fixed election, a power play which had its price. President Pierce and Secretary of State Marcy had previously recognized the filibuster regime to pressure Great Britain into concessions on Central America and aid Pierce's renomination bid. By the time Walker's new minister to the United States—Maine native Appleton Oaksmith—arrived in Washington, Britain had begun diplomatic procedures to give up several of its Central American dependencies and Pierce was a lame duck. Marcy, never a friend of filibusters anyway, refused to receive Oaksmith. This brought Quitman into the picture, because Oaksmith expected Quitman, with his own filibuster record, to be sympathetic and to provide help. Quitman arranged a private audience for himself, Oaksmith, and Pierce at night on August 4. Then he pressed Oaksmith's credentials upon the president in a series of consultations over the course of a week. Gaining the impression at the last of these meetings that he had finally made a break-through, Quitman told Oaksmith, who had gone to New York, to hurry back. However, Quitman misunderstood administration intent, and Marcy still refused to receive the filibuster minister.[38]

In mid-July, Quitman was rejoined by Eliza, Louisa and child, and the rest of the family except for Henry and Mary, who left for weeks of travel in the mountains. Soon afterward, his sisters Eliza and Louisa, now living in Philadelphia, paid a visit. When not needed in the House, Quitman squired his relations around. Thus Rose's diary reports "Papa" taking the family into the ladies' gallery of the House, and then into the Senate chamber, which exposed them to that "rank abolitionist" Lyman Trumbull (really a relatively moderate Republican from Illinois). But this second stint in the capital did no one any good. Stifling heat and malaria plagued Washington summer residents. Louisa's baby became sick, as did Antonia, and the rest of the family experienced considerable discomfort. On August 8, Quitman sent Eliza and all the children off again, this time to Capon Springs, a mineral waters resort in the mountains of western Virginia. That same day, he made yet another change of quarters, taking lodging at the Kirkwood House at the corner of Twelfth Street and Pennsylvania Avenue, a move which brought him a couple of blocks closer to his congressional seat.[39]

Quitman's decision to send his family away proved wise, because it was not until August 30, and then only by a close vote, that the appropriations logjam broke. In a 101-to-98 vote, the House, after learning one more time that the Senate would absolutely not go along with the House rider, caved in and passed the army bill without the Kansas proviso. The president signed the bill immediately, and Congress adjourned until December 1.[40]

Following the dismissal of the House, Quitman traveled to Capon Springs for a few days with his family, which he found in restored health. (The resort was the "most delightful and pleasant mountain place" he had ever seen, he wrote Henry.) Then, leaving Eliza and some of the children at his sisters' boardinghouse in Philadelphia so that Eliza could shop for dresses, he went on to New York with Louisa and Antonia for a Montezuma Society gathering. Finally, he returned for Eliza and the rest of the brood, and journeyed to Monmouth for the month that he had promised himself.[41]

While home, Quitman kept himself posted on William Walker's situation, and was encouraged when word arrived in the United States that Walker had decreed slavery legal in Nicaragua. Quitman sent off assurance to his fellow filibuster that he wished to "be serviceable to your country." Quitman also kept a wary eye on the American presidential campaign. For the first time, the South confronted a major party antislavery candidate for president: at a June convention, Republicans had put up John C. Frémont for the office.

Quitman believed it imperative that this bid by a party dedicated to "war against the rights and social systems of 15 states" be turned back, and was convinced that Buchanan and the "stern old Democracy," which had been battling "treason at the North," rather than American party candidate and former president Millard Fillmore, offered slavery's best chance. Quitman suggested in a public letter that Know-Nothingism was in the sectional struggle a "half way house" for "timid and non committal men." Quitman had his wishes granted in November. Buchanan took all the slave states except Maryland, and won the election. However, the Republican ticket triumphed in all the northern states but five, hardly an auspicious omen for the South. Had Frémont taken Pennsylvania and either Indiana or Illinois, he would have become the next president. Quitman would return to Washington knowing that political antislavery had become a majority movement in much of the North.[42]

Late in November, leaving Eliza and the children behind, Quitman set off for the capital. He arrived on November 29, taking up lodgings again at the Kirkwood House. Perhaps feeling a twinge of guilt about abandoning his family once more, he sent a letter home a few weeks later which noted that two of Mississippi's other representatives *had* brought their wives. He assured Eliza that he had been so occupied with official duties that he had found time for only one party and that he had made few social calls.[43]

During his last months in the Thirty-fourth Congress, Quitman deviated little from the congressional role that he had set for himself. Again the military establishment became the beneficiary of his best legislative efforts. Although he constantly took the floor on measures relating to the army, his coup came when he steered through the House a bill to raise the pay of commissioned officers $20 a month and to provide a 50 percent increase in the commutation price of officers' rations (which under the measure rose from $.20 to $.30 per ration). Quitman's bill addressed a problem chronic in the army for decades, rapid turnover of personnel because of low pay; junior officers especially, having engineering expertise by virtue of the West Point curriculum, found it easy to locate lucrative employment in the civilian sector and often resigned their commissions soon after fulfilling their required four-year term of duty. Quitman steered the pay raise through with some rather alarmist rhetoric, exhorting his colleagues to save junior officers "from starvation" and cautioning that rejection would be tantamount to "the disbanding of the Army of the United States"; the bill passed 130 to 62 on January 26, subsequently gained Senate endorsement, and was signed into law by President Pierce. Crediting the legislation to Quitman's efforts, Commanding General Winfield Scott sent him thanks on behalf of all the officers for the "handsome" pay increase. Talk circulated in some officer circles of purchasing for Quitman a service of silver plate as a token of the army's gratitude.[44]

True to form, too, Quitman's main rhetorical efforts for southern rights concerned slavery expansion. His only major speech of the winter, delivered on December 18, concentrated on William Walker and Kansas. Quitman took the somewhat anomalous tack of applauding Pierce's position on Kansas (the president's final annual message to Congress disavowed any intention of investigating election irregularities in the territory) while condemning administration policy in Central America. Federal enforcement of the neutrality laws already left America's agent of "Providence" vulnerable to "annihilation" by "semi-savage foes."

On roll calls, Quitman continued to oppose measures which he perceived as enhancing federal powers and responsibilities. Thus he cast negatives against a $70,000 appropriation to aid private enterprise in the construction of an Atlantic Ocean telegraph cable between Newfoundland and Ireland, a measure to improve navigation on the Mississippi, and an amendment to the consular service appropriations bill which would have funded the training of consular clerks.[45]

Still, there appeared a new stridency in Quitman's oratory; influenced by the advance of Republicanism in the North, Quitman's words paved a return path to extreme southernism. Unlike many southern leaders who hoped the Democratic-controlled Supreme Court would be the ultimate arbiter of the right of territorial legislatures to ban slavery, Quitman rejected the authority of *any* national body to consider the issue. States, he reminded the House, had created the Constitution, and it was patently absurd, he believed, to think that they would have left their right to property in the hands of an institution which, because of presidential appointment and lifetime tenure, was of the three branches of federal government the "least responsible" to the people. Quitman imputed an abolitionist "soul" to Republicanism, and asserted that Republicans not only intended to destroy an institution beneficial to the whole nation but also to create, through their containment policies, conditions conducive to black overcrowding and servile rebellion. Demanding "elbow-room" for his region, he described the contest against the "Black Republican" party as a "war to the knife."[46]

Quitman's most startling pronouncements were about the African slave trade. Talk of reviving the trade, banned in the United States since 1808, had become fashionable in some parts of the Gulf states for both economic and philosophical reasons: high market prices for slaves in the South created demand for new sources of supply; many radicals believed that prohibition of the trade was an indirect assault on the southern way of life. In addition, some southern opinion leaders feared that nonslaveholders, aspiring to become masters themselves, might turn against the institution of slavery if the price of chattels became so high as to constrain class mobility in the region. In response to such agitation, resolutions were introduced and passed in the House which condemned revival talk as "shocking to the moral sentiment of the enlightened portion of mankind" and rejecting repeal of the ban as "inexpedient, unwise, and contrary to the settled policy of the United States."

Quitman not only voted against the resolutions (one of only ten to do so on one roll call) but also expounded on the virtues of trans-Atlantic human cargoes. Showing no patience for traditional humanitarian critiques of the trade, which had usually been based on the high proportion of blacks who died on slaving vessels from crowded and unhealthy conditions, Quitman defended the trade as an essentially moral process. Many African blacks, often captives in intertribal wars, were enslaved prior to sale to European slavers. Quitman believed, therefore, that the slave trade permitted transferral of "the negro" from a "cruel and despotic" African master to a "kind and humane white master" in the United States. He also suggested that before the House condemn the trade, it consider how northern employers destroyed the health and stunted the intellect of children by putting them to work in "unhealthy and fetid" factory rooms.[47]

When the Thirty-fourth Congress legally expired on March 4, 1857, Quitman could rest satisfied that he had fulfilled his pledge to Mississippi's voters. He had rendered vigorous defense of southern institutions and gained considerable recognition as a spokesman for his region's interests. Southern radicals once again looked to him for leadership. One correspondent, arguing that there could be no hope for a nation which tried to fuse descendants of "narrow minded, sanctimonious, biggots, who landed at Plymouth Rock" with successors to the "Cavaliers" who settled in colonial Virginia, suggested that Quitman be " 'the man of destiny' when the hour comes for the South to *be free and independent*."[48]

Quitman did not participate in the final session of the House, a frantic last-minute gathering on the morning of March 4 on the civil appropriations bill. (Kansas could be postponed for the Thirty-fifth Congress, but money matters were another story.) Rather, he became engrossed in an entirely different duty. March 4 also marked James Buchanan's inauguration as the nation's fifteenth president, and Quitman had been selected to serve as "Commander-in-Chief" of the "military cortege" of the inaugural parade, which was to accompany the presidential carriage along Pennsylvania Avenue to the capitol, where Buchanan would take his oath of office. Quitman, who took pride in his military capabilities, busied himself with parade preparations.[49]

That balmy afternoon, Quitman became a soldier again, and he did it in style. Before an unusually large crowd of spectators, Quitman conducted his marching column of regulars, state militia, and marines with such "military precision" that one Philadelphia reporter called the parade the grandest "display of military" he had ever witnessed. This same onlooker made special note of Quitman's rather conspicuous appearance: there the "chieftain" sat, noted the reporter, "on a fine gray horse, clothed in full military uniform, with all the trappings of a Major General, the most complete specimen of a general we ever beheld." [50] Little did this correspondent suspect that behind the impressive façade was a man suffering considerable pain.

23

Effects of the Poison

THE John Quitman who journeyed to Natchez immediately after James Buchanan's inauguration in March, 1857, was a greatly transformed man. He had been robustly healthy most of his life, and contemporaries were struck by his sturdy physique. He possessed, noted a newspaper correspondent during Quitman's fifty-fifth year, a "strongly built" frame, which rendered him "capable of enduring great fatigue. He is active in his movements and a good eater." All this changed, however, in February, 1857, when Quitman fell seriously sick in Washington, and he was unable to recover before returning home. "For the last month," he informed Henry while en route, "I have suffered severely from a neuralgic pain in my right leg, so much so as frequently to spend sleepless nights, and . . . I am sometimes almost unable to walk." The ailment had taken such a toll on his constitution that his family was quite taken aback when he arrived at Monmouth. "My dear Father reached us again . . . but we were grieved and shocked to see how worn out and suffering he looked," Antonia noted.[1]

Quitman had contracted a case of what became known in the Washington lexicon as the "National Hotel disease." During a siege of frigid weather that January, the plumbing at the hotel had frozen, causing the backup of sewer waste into the kitchen, where it apparently contaminated food (though there were also reports that rats seeking refuge from the cold had fallen into open vats in the attic where rainwater was collected, thus tainting the establishment's water system). Large numbers of hotel guests came down with dysentery.[2]

Sometime that winter, Quitman visited the National Hotel. It would have been logical for Quitman to call on James Buchanan at the hotel between January 27 and February 3, when the president-elect took quarters there for consultations with Democratic leaders about cabinet appointments, patronage, and Kansas policy; Quitman made no secret of his interest in being

Buchanan's secretary of war.[3] But all that is known for sure is that Quitman became ill after some time spent at the hotel, and that he blamed his ailment entirely upon what he stigmatized as the "National Hotel poison." Perhaps he gave credence to rumors circulating in Washington that abolitionists had tainted the hotel's food in a plot to eliminate Democratic leaders. Such would be a likely construction for his attributing the "effects of the poison" to arsenic.[4]

Once back at Monmouth, Quitman turned to laudanum (prescribed by a local physician) for a sleeping aid, and took to downing doses of lager beer in the belief that it was a restorative. Improvement followed, but full recovery proved elusive. Unaccustomed to physical limitations, Quitman lapsed into bouts of depression. "I scarce know why," he confessed to Henry, "but I am more than usually afflicted with melancholy.[5]

Quitman passed up public appearances, for once. Rather than attend a "jubilee" in Memphis to commemorate completion of the Memphis and Charleston Railroad, he sent regrets and congratulated Memphis for accomplishing an undertaking "fraught with advantage" to the South. Still, he recovered sufficiently to resume communication with his plantation world. "Gen. Quitman passed through our town on Tuesday last on his way to his sugar estate on Grand Caillou," noted the Houma *Ceres* on May 16. He also escorted his sisters, who had spent the winter with his family, to New Orleans so that they could board a ship for their return north, and visited the Belen place and apparently Palmyra. A late frost which killed several hundred acres of his cotton, measles among his house servants, legal matters, mules for Live Oaks, these became his concerns for a while.[6]

Political retirement, moreover, was out of question. Despite his debilities, Quitman resumed out-of-town appearances and speechmaking in the summer, and when his district's Democratic convention offered renomination to Congress he protested only in the family circle that "duty" would jeopardize his "business affairs." Never even considering the possibility of defeat ("I shall of course be a member of the next Congress"), Quitman began mapping strategy for new rounds of sectional confrontation in the House.[7]

From Quitman's perspective, prospects for slavery's survival looked increasingly unpromising, despite the controversial Dred Scott Supreme Court decision in March, which ruled that Congress' 1820 Missouri Compromise prohibition of slavery north of 36°30' in the Louisiana Territory had been unconstitutional. William Walker had been driven out of Nicaragua, and southern aspirations for Kansas had gone sour. Robert J. Walker, President Buchanan's appointee as Kansas territorial governor, had tilted federal policy toward the Free-Soilers. Determined to make majority rule work, Walker insisted to Buchanan before accepting the assignment that the "actual *bona fide* residents" be permitted to determine Kansas' "social institutions" by a "fair and regular vote." Once arrived in the territory, Walker hobnobbed with Free-Soil leaders at Topeka and encouraged free-staters, whom he discovered to hold a majority of better than two to one, to try to compete with the proslavery faction at the polls. His inaugural address, in which he defined Kansas as north of an "isothermal line" which excluded slavery because of climatic conditions, conveyed a presumption that Kansas would eventually become a free state.[8]

Quitman did not find anything particularly surprising about Walker's course. A northerner by upbringing, Walker had spent only nine years in Mississippi. Quitman even comprehended Walker's motives, which, rather than being antislavery, were calculated to make Kansas Democratic and win back for northern Democrats voters previously alienated by the Kansas-Nebraska Act. Nevertheless, Quitman could not help but see Walker's tactics as evidence that Buchanan and the northern Democracy had given up resisting abolitionist pressure.

Believing that the coming months would determine whether the South would "maintain" its "equality" or decline into "degrading subserviency to political masters," Quitman decided to muster southern rights forces *prior* to Congress' meeting, so that he would be better prepared for legislative battle than he had been in the past. "Our members will be so few in Congress, that to secure respect we must act with some concert," he wrote Lawrence Keitt, a radical South Carolina representative. "We must know one another and understand one another. . . . I am attempting to make up a list of the reliable state rights men of the House. Can you give me the names of those from your state?" Quitman expected Buchanan to fight back against any efforts by a southern rights caucus to influence policy. The president would surely manipulate patronage and make support of Robert Walker a test of party regularity. Quitman presumed that, as in 1850, some states' rights men would surrender to "seductive persuasions of power, place and salary." Once again he could anticipate denunciation as a secessionist. But, knowing that he only wanted to deter his region's politicians from trading off southern rights "under the pretext of preserving the Democratic party," he faced the future with what he described as a "good conscience."[9]

Appointed by Governor McRae a delegate to a new commercial convention, scheduled for Knoxville, Tennessee, on August 10, Quitman gave attendance serious consideration. Over the last few years, southern commercial conventions had evolved into radical forums, and Quitman saw the gathering as a good chance to get together with "many prominent southern men" at one sitting and advance his political program. At the last minute, however, he decided to pass it up, apparently because of his continuing ill health.[10]

Anxious to be well by the next Congress, Quitman went instead to the baths and waters at Hot Springs, Arkansas. He left Natchez on August 31 for what, because of a missed steamer connection at the mouth of the Arkansas River, became a rather disagreeable stage journey. Quitman's coach traversed swamplands for much of the route to Little Rock, and every time the coach stopped at a house Quitman encountered families down with chills and fever. Some of his fellow passengers became ill. Then the stage followed stony, bumpy roads for forty-seven hours, finally reaching Hot Springs.

Hot Springs, located some forty-five miles from Little Rock in a valley amid the Ouachita Mountains, had a pleasing appearance. Vapors rose from hills lush with cedar, elm, oak, dogwood, and hickory, where there were some eighty-three hot springs. But for Quitman, a usually healthy man, it was a bit disconcerting to be thrust into the company of "cripples, lame . . . and stiff jointed persons," some suffering from consuming too much whiskey or mercury, others from gout, rheumatism, and neuralgia—all of whom seemed to talk only about their ailments. Nevertheless, he began the Hot Springs regimen, which included "scalding" showers and baths (released from hot springwater collected in bathhouse rooftop reservoirs) and what was designated as the "*great renovator*"—a "vapor bath"—with enthusiasm. The latter offered a room excavated from mountain rock, which had flowing through it a hot spring. Guests took off their clothing, stood over a latticework floor built just over the water, drank large quantities of hot springwater, and presumably sweated their illnesses away. After spending one to eight minutes in the room (where the thermometer, Quitman noted, reached 130 degrees), guests emerged, dried off, donned flannels, and allowed their bodies to sweat for another half hour.

Quitman thought, at first, that he had found his miracle cure. After two days of the Hot Springs routine, he wrote home that though the baths weakened him somewhat, he felt that his health had been "entirely restored." A week later, however, he confessed that he had been unable to fully regain his appetite and he left Hot Springs improved rather than regenerated.[11]

Since no opponent had emerged to contest his congressional candidacy,[12] Quitman was free to concentrate again on his plantation interests following his return from Arkansas. A nationwide economic contraction had undercut credit markets and cotton prices. Quitman visited his factor, R. W. Estlin, in New Orleans in early October to discuss the best course for his year's crop, only to discover market conditions worse than he anticipated. "I have never yet seen the merchants more gloomy," he lamented to Eliza. "Cotton can not be sold for even five cents per pound less than it was two weeks since." Hoping that prices would turn around in the near future, Quitman withdrew his entire crop from the market.[13]

Problems at Live Oaks forced Quitman, in November, to pay the Crescent City a second visit. In August, 1856, a hurricane had devastated the plantation, damaging the sugar and corn crops, injuring the orange trees, killing mules, and knocking down a barn and chimneys. The crop had been short that winter, and prospects for 1857 seemed little better. Henry had overspent on improvements—despite being cautioned that retrenchment was necessary—and fallen $10,000 in debt to Estlin. Worse, he had failed to keep Quitman informed of what steps he was taking to meet the deficiency. Quitman rebuked his son for his neglect, and insisted on a New Orleans get-together in mid-November. There Henry promised that he would economize, and differences were patched up. "I feel now as if I can address you with the warmth & freedom of my former confidence," Quitman told Henry after the meeting. Since New Orleans banks had suspended making long-term loans to planters, Quitman solicited Henry Turner on his son's behalf for a $10,000 loan to cover the Estlin debt, promising to serve as his son's security. Quitman advised Henry to send Turner a "barrel of your best sugar for his table use," in the hope that it would dispose Turner to make the loan.[14]

Despite his persistent infirmities, Quitman traveled back to Washington during the first week of December. Accompanied by Antonia, Louisa and Eva, and Eva's nurse Sarah, he required assistance along the way, and did not help his condition with an unnecessary but characteristic display of gallantry. Forced to spend several hours in a hotel room without enough beds during a change of trains, he insisted on sleeping on the floor despite the protestations of his daughters, earning a sore throat for his gallantry. He arrived at Kirkwood House in a weakened state. "We are all pretty well except Father," Antonia reported back to her mother, "who has been complaining a good deal in the past few days: he has no appetite, and seems languid and feverish in the mornings."[15]

Quitman returned to Congress a reborn secessionist. His unionism over the past couple of years had been conditional, predicated upon the good faith and *political strength* of the northern Democracy. Now it appeared that his trust had been completely misplaced. Out in Kansas, Governor Walker had succeeded in persuading Free-Soilers to participate in the territory's third legislative elections, which occurred in October. By rejecting several precinct returns on the basis of blatant ballot-box fraud, Walker converted another proslavery triumph into Free-Soil control over both houses of the upcoming legislature. There remained a faint chance that Kansas would yet become a slave state; a constitutional convention arranged by the outgoing proslavery legislature met at the town of Lecompton and, following the territorial elections, drafted a document for Kansas' admission to the Union as a slave state. However, Quitman expected that congressional Republicans would do everything in their power to stymie the Lecompton movement and, more important, that President Buchanan would throw the power of the executive office behind Governor Walker's policy. Now Quitman claimed that he had always suspected that northern Democrats would "desert" the South when the moment came for them to "carry their professions into practice." Further, he believed the long-range prospects for slavery bleak even if by some miracle enough northern Democratic congressmen remained constant to win approval of the Lecompton document. Any northern Democrat supporting Lecompton would surely be voted out of Congress by antislavery constituents and be replaced by a Republican or an antislavery officeholder "under some other name." Republicans, too, would win the next presidential election. Abolitionist control of the entire federal government seemed inevitable.[16]

Reuben Davis' later reminiscences disclose Quitman's secessionist state of mind at the inception of the Thirty-fifth Congress. Davis, a fellow Mississippi Democrat elected to the House in the fall, recorded encountering Quitman near the capitol and asking him point blank whether he had reached any "definite policy." Quitman responded that sectional differences had passed "beyond compromise" and that his "aim" had become "disunion," but that secession would require time—the southern people needed preparation "for the wrench." When Davis suggested that secession should occur immediately or not at all, since the North's improving railroad network would soon give New York alone the capacity to invade the South with a hundred thousand men within ten days' time, Quitman retorted that Davis had "overestimated" the military advantages which railroads would give the North. "As he turned to leave me," Davis recalled, "he laughed, and added, 'It will be all right in the next four years. You must move up Davis, or you will be left behind.'"[17]

Given the unreliability of personal reminiscences, Davis' account would be suspect were it not confirmed by other evidence. Continuing his efforts to fashion a southern rights caucus in Congress, Quitman had written Roger A. Pryor, fire-eating editor of a Richmond, Virginia, paper, and Pryor's response is revealing. Pryor confirmed Quitman's opinion that Robert Walker's "treachery" had been damaging, but urged restraint as to secession until President Buchanan had fully played his "hand." Southern unity could only be achieved, Pryor contended, *after* it became clear that southern prospects within the Union had been destroyed. *"All we ask in Virginia is, that you gentlemen further South will not precipitate the catastrophe. Let things develop themselves in order, & we will be with you 'at the death.'"* [18]

Quitman found it necessary, in fact, to beat something of a strategic retreat after returning to Congress. The Lecompton convention in Kansas had scheduled a territorial referendum for December 21, asking voters to accept its document either with or without slavery. Pressured by southern members of his cabinet, cognizant that he owed his election to the slave states and that southerners now dominated his party (in the new House, southern Democrats outnumbered their northern cohorts 75 to 53), President Buchanan had swung in behind the Lecompton Constitution. His annual message to Congress, which Quitman listened to on December 8, described the Lecompton process as "in the main fair" and called upon Kansans to cooperate with the referendum. Since even the "Constitution with no slavery" option at the referendum would guarantee that slaves already in the territory—and their descendants—would remain their masters' property, Buchanan had, in effect, endorsed the creation of a slave Kansas. One week later, Walker resigned his governorship in protest. [19]

Buchanan's message actually promised nothing to the South. Free-Soilers in the territory and throughout the North attacked the referendum on the grounds that the Lecompton gathering did not truly represent territorial settlers, and that voters should have been given the option of complete rejection of the document. Many northern Democrats, aware that the Lecompton procedures controverted Stephen Douglas' promise that slavery in Kansas would be decided by majority will, broke with the president rather than risk repudiation by their constituents; Douglas himself came out bluntly against the president's position in a December 9 Senate speech. However, despite the outcry, no one could be sure that the president would not get his way. A solid faction of northern Democrats in Congress did support his stand, and he could employ patronage and other means of presidential persuasion to rally undecided Democratic congressmen behind administration policy. Since Democrats, in the past year's elections, had gained control of both houses of Congress, it seemed that Buchanan just might be able to steer the Lecompton Constitution through Congress. [20]

Given the uncertainty, Quitman had to reassess his tactics. Too many Deep South congressmen trusted Buchanan for Quitman to press his own views too strongly. "Mr B. is today the . . . soundest man in all the North," concluded Georgia's Augustus Wright. "I did not use to think so but do now. He will not flinch. He will 'make a spoon or spoil a horn'—I do hope we shall have no grumbling support from the South." Quitman, who was convinced that even Kansas' admission to the Union under Lecompton would prove a "barren victory" because Republicans would then overwhelm the Democrats in the next northern elections, saw little substantive benefit from Buchanan's conversion. Believing secession imperative, he had formulated a program to effect it in such a way as to dispel traditional fears in southern states that withdrawal would be followed by isolation. Apparently influenced by Pryor and other upper South politicians to believe border slave states victims of inertia, he wrote a Texan confidant that five Gulf states should hold conventions which would declare secession *intent* and announce that the act would be deferred pending consultations with other states "as to the proper time and manner of . . . withdrawal." Then, he explained, the five states should "appoint delegates . . . to consult with such of the slave-holding states as may *coincide* with her (not all the states, or we will perhaps be out-voted by the Submissionists). . . . After the act of secession, let delegates immediately assemble to form a Confederation or Constitution." Nevertheless, he could do little of immediate consequence to advance secession, because Buchanan's affiliation had put such "an entirely different phase upon the matter" that few Deep South congressmen could be convinced of his logic.[21]

His hands tied by Buchanan's policy, Quitman deferred radical advocacy. Prior to Christmas, his most significant comment in the House concerned minimal denominations for U.S. Treasury notes. In brief remarks, he contended that low-denomination notes would drive specie from circulation and undermine the independent treasury, and urged that minimum denominations be set at $1,000 rather than $100. His comments had sectional overtones; he sought to restrain growth within the federal bureaucracy—fewer notes would require the employment of fewer U.S. Treasury clerks. However, the issue crossed sectional and party lines, and Quitman's remarks drew only fleeting attention.[22]

Over the holiday season, however, the ongoing saga of William Walker released Quitman's repressed sectionalism. An incorrigible filibuster, Walker had returned to Nicaragua in November with some two hundred followers, and landed his forces at a couple of points on the Nicaraguan Caribbean coast. A small party of his men then captured a fortress up the San Juan River; but Walker could not capitalize on this initial success. Acting under vague antifilibustering orders from Secretary of the Navy Isaac Toucey, Commodore Hiram Paulding aboard the steam frigate *Wabash* (one of three U.S. war vessels in the region) intervened before Walker could move additional troops upriver and attempt pacification of Nicaragua's interior. Paulding surrounded the filibusters' coastal camp with marines, sailors, and naval artillery, and forced Walker's capitulation. Walker then returned to the United States under a voluntary surrender agreement, and turned himself in

335

to federal authorities after his arrival at New York City on December 27. Two days later, however, the administration freed Walker, on the grounds that he could only be arrested and held through judicial procedures. Walker, it turned out, would remain at large—later attempts at prosecution proved unsuccessful.

Quitman and his daughters were passing a Christmas week congressional recess in Philadelphia with his sisters when word broke in the press of Walker's capture and return. Returning to Washington, Quitman consulted at his rooms with Lawrence Keitt and Representative Thomas L. Clingman of North Carolina about the incident. The three southerners decided to make of the capture a new sectional rallying point. No one knew exactly where the administration stood. Buchanan had little sympathy for filibusters. However, there appeared no incontrovertible rule of international law which justified the use of American military force in a foreign country with which the United States was at peace, and there was some speculation that Buchanan would repudiate his commodore. It was decided that Clingman would force the president's hand by requesting him to supply the House with documents about the affair, including administration instructions to its naval officers, while Quitman would renew his call for modification of the neutrality laws. "I expect soon to be heard," he informed Henry on the last day of the year.[23]

Clingman and Quitman went to work at the very first postvacation House session, on January 4. Clingman won approval of a request for executive documents. However, his success was counterbalanced by the passage of several pro-Paulding resolutions. One, for instance, questioned whether Nicaragua had actually protested Paulding's intrusion into its domain. This was a suggestion that the legality of Paulding's act had become a moot point since the Nicaraguan government found Walker's removal desirable. Quitman tried to bring up a resolution repealing some sections of the 1818 Neutrality Act and modifying others, but found himself thwarted by a procedural objection.[24]

Quitman resumed his crusade the next day. President Buchanan's annual message had included substantial criticism of filibustering and a request that Congress put more teeth into America's neutrality legislation. Quitman used the message as a means to agitate for repeal, by moving that the president's suggestions be referred to a select five-member committee, and taking his own motion as the occasion for a full-length address. Quitman noted how the last Congress had given his proposals short shrift, and urged the House to reconsider now that repeal had received "vast attention" and approval throughout the nation. Thoughtful men who were not involved in the "scramble for office" and who shared his vision of "the future destiny of our country" (somewhat hypocritical rhetoric for a secessionist) also agreed with him about the necessity for change. The Constitution did not give the federal government any authority over one's personal choice of occupation, including filibustering. Paulding's action had been wrong, since it was not authorized by specific treaty stipulation with the Nicaraguan government. Claiming that thousands of Americans in the North as well as the South wanted the neutrality laws reformed and that he bore no "unkind feelings" toward Buchanan, Quitman called upon the lawmakers of "the most intelligent nation on earth" to at least vote on the issue this time and take a stand.[25]

Quitman's speech ignited heated debate. Keitt, of course, supported him as did Alexander Stephens of Georgia. Democrat Thomas S. Bocock of Virginia, however, condoned Paulding's act, citing wording in the 1818 Neutrality Act which authorized the use of military force to prevent filibustering. Stephens retorted that that provision applied only within one marine league from American shores, and that given the navy's error, the federal government was now responsible for getting Walker back to Nicaragua. Finally unmitigated sectionalism exploded into the debate. Republican Galusha Grow of Pennsylvania professed delight that Democrats had finally come to see the dangers posed to "citizens of the country" from "executive encroachments," and wondered why Democrats had not raised similar protest against Buchanan's use of army personnel to uphold despotism in Kansas. Tennessee Know-Nothing Horace Maynard, who supported Quitman's proposal, begged his colleagues to keep "*niggers*" out of the discussion. But a new sectional battle could not be averted. Republican Owen Lovejoy of Illinois contended that William Walker deserved no better than a "buccaneer" or "pirate," and that Paulding's only mistake had been not hanging the filibuster from the "yard-arm of his ship." Adjournment came without disposition of the question. Thus sectional divisions over slavery expansion were pushed by Quitman into a new phase.[26]

Quitman spoke out frequently during the next nine days, as the House debated President Buchanan's message until January 14, when the several parts of the document were separated and distributed to committees for consideration and recommendations. Other representatives acknowledged Quitman as the moving spirit behind the pro-Walker forces in the House and often addressed their remarks to him, prompting responses on his part. Thus Pennsylvanian William Montgomery alluded to Quitman's being "distinguished alike for his military glory and his ability as a statesman," but asserted that Quitman erred on the neutrality question. The federal government, Montgomery maintained, had the responsibility of seeing that every American citizen obeyed the neutrality laws. Quitman interrupted, quoting a passage from Vattel's *Law of Nations* which he believed authorized the right of individuals to "commit hostility against the individuals of another nation"

337

but not against that "nation itself." This earned Montgomery's rejoinder that Quitman should read Vattel more carefully, and he referred to an earlier passage in which Vattel emphasized the duty of nations to prevent their citizens from doing "an injury to the subjects of another State."

Quitman's efforts proved ineffectual. Although an obviously biased Pennsylvania correspondent overstated the case, reporting Quitman "overwhelmed" in his exchange with Montgomery, Quitman nonetheless did find it impossible to rally House sentiment behind filibustering. When the House finally acted on Buchanan's recommendations on January 14, it not only referred the matter to the Committee on the Judiciary but did so with a Republican amendment instructing the committee to consider legislation making the neutrality provisions more *rigorous.*

Nevertheless the debate served Quitman's radical intent, by revealing to other Deep South congressmen how little the northern Democracy could be trusted on slavery expansion. President Buchanan on January 7 issued a statement which, though criticizing Paulding for "exceeding his instructions," nonetheless praised the naval officer's "patriotic motives" and strongly condemned filibustering. When northern Democrats spoke to the issue, they sided with their president. Garnett B. Adrian of New York attacked Quitman for encouraging the "marauding spirit" and exciting the "bad passions of the youth of our country." "We northern Democrats," announced John B. Haskin, "believe . . . that this business of Walker was committing petty larceny." Resentful of such commentary and appalled by administration pressure to support Paulding, Augustus Wright decided that Buchanan no longer merited southern trust. The president, he concluded, has greatly wronged the South by holding out "*moonshine*" in Kansas while denying slave state interests in more important areas, such as "Central America, which was literally ours."

The debate also illuminated again how determined Republicans were to prevent any kind of slavery extension, stirring further resentment among many of Quitman's southern colleagues. When Republican Francis P. Blair lambasted those who supported "predator incursions against our neighbors" which would have those lands "planted with slavery" and annexed so slaveholders could "dominate this government," Georgia Democrat Lucius Gartrell was moved to answer with a ringing diatribe about how slavery had enabled an "idle, dissolute, improvident, lazy" race to contribute to the advancement of the Republic. When Republican Eli Thayer of Massachusetts announced that he would like to develop Quitman's idea of Americanizing Central America by forming a corporation to colonize it peacefully with *northern* emigrants, Reuben Davis responded angrily with a speech threatening secession. Davis predicted that efforts to circumscribe slavery's territorial limits would guarantee northern control of Congress and cause white southerners to live in "political bondage." [27]

Quitman, thus, did his part to aggravate sectional relations within the House prior to reconsideration of Kansas, which occurred in February. News had come from the territory of two elections. On December 21, because of free-state abstentions, proslavery men won overwhelming endorsement of the Lecompton Constitution with slavery in the scheduled referendum. On January 4, however, with proslavery men abstaining, free-staters rejected the entire Lecompton instrument in an election arranged by the new antislavery legislature. On February 2, discarding the results of the latter vote, President Buchanan submitted the Lecompton Constitution with slavery to Congress for approval, and denounced the free-state Kansas faction as a body of men bent on installing "revolutionary government" by "usurpation." The impasse required a spirit of measured compromise, but an ongoing deterioration of interregional trust within Congress guaranteed new sectional disharmonies. [28]

Quitman, fittingly, held the floor during the most blatant irruption of sectional feeling in the House that winter. On Friday, February 5, Thomas L. Harris of Illinois, Quitman's proponent at the 1856 convention but now head of the anti-Lecompton Democratic bloc in the House, moved that President Buchanan's message on Kansas be submitted to a select committee of fifteen which would be instructed to inquire whether the Lecompton Constitution truly reflected the wishes of the legal majority of voting Kansans. Harris, in explanation, read a letter from Frederick P. Stanton, whom Buchanan had recently removed as acting governor of Kansas, which adverted to fraud in elections arranged by Kansas' proslavery faction and justified free-state boycotts of the December 21 referendum. Debate raged over Harris' proposal into the early morning hours, with southern Democrats fighting unsuccessfully for adjournment as an alternative to a vote. At about 2:30, in what was meant as a compromise, Quitman offered something to each side: adjournment until noon on Monday, with a vote being fixed for 1:00 that day. Republican whip Galusha Grow, standing in a House aisle near the seat of Ohio Democrat Samuel S. Cox, called out "I object!" This provoked Keitt, a notorious hothead, to pronounce Grow a "black Republican puppy" who should make any objections from his own seat on the Republican side of the chamber. Grow yelled back that it was a free country and that he would not accept dictation from a "slave driver." Incensed, Keitt rushed at Grow, making a grab for his throat. Grow hit Keitt below the eye, and then some thirty representatives became involved in the melee. Finally, after the sergeant-at-arms confined Keitt to a cloakroom and after Elihu B. Washburne of Illinois caused laughter by knocking off William Barksdale's wig and exposing the obviously embarrassed Mississippian as bald, order was restored. A half hour after he had started, Quitman resumed his remarks saying that the "scene just before us" made his motion all the more necessary. But debate persisted until after 6:00 in the morning. Alexander Stephens could only wonder whether the fracas had been a harbinger of an eventual disruption of the Union; and it was perhaps symbolic that the next day Reuben Davis exhibited a dirk knife which some said he had actually brandished during the fighting.[29]

When Harris' proposal finally came to a vote on the eighth, it passed by a 114-to-111 margin. However, the triumph proved an empty one for the anti-Lecomptonites, since Democratic House Speaker James L. Orr of South Carolina subsequently appointed a pro-Lecompton majority, including Quitman, to the select committee. Instead of condemning rigged proslavery elections in Kansas, the committee presented an endorsement of Lecompton.[30]

Congress wrestled with Kansas through April. Administration men controlled the Senate and, on March 23, gained passage of Kansas' admission under the Lecompton instrument. In the House, however, a precarious anti-Lecompton coalition of Republicans and northern Democrats managed to hold on. On April 1 the lower house passed what became known as the Crittenden-Montgomery resolution which would have resubmitted the Lecompton Constitution for a new, and carefully supervised, vote by the settlers of Kansas.

Deadlock inspired agitated speechmaking, particularly in the House, where the swing of a few votes might make all the difference. Sometimes debate persisted into the early morning hours. Quitman played his part in the sectional accusations being exchanged when Republican Silas M. Burroughs of New York used the Kansas question as a forum for an attack on southern civilization in general. Burroughs attacked the slaveholding states as backward, and cited their lag in public schools, school libraries, and church property, mentioning that his congressional district boasted 285 school libraries as compared to one of the Mississippi congressional districts which had none. This was too much for Quitman, who interrupted with a defense of nabob culture. In "our section," Quitman explained, "we act individually." There were more books, he claimed, in the private collections within his district than within Burroughs' district. Quitman also fought Crittenden-Montgomery more directly, at one point forcing a vote on the original Senate proposition as a substitute. He lost this effort by a convincing 72-to-160 vote.[31]

Meanwhile, Quitman spoke out on numerous other issues, for Kansas never monopolized House proceedings. Having been reappointed chairman of the Committee on Military Affairs, he continued to actively enter debate regarding the military establishment. Of particular interest to him was House bill 313, proposing federal pacification of the Utah Territory and the Texas frontier, which he introduced on behalf of his committee on February 25.

Both Utah and Texas had become important areas of concern for the Buchanan administration. In 1857, determined to enforce federal authority in Utah, which condoned polygamy and remained semi-autonomous under the rule of Brigham Young despite its annexation to the United States, President Buchanan had appointed a governor to replace Young and dispatched some 2,500 federal troops to the territory under Colonel Albert Sidney Johnston. Panicked by Johnston's approach, Mormons had killed over one hundred California-bound travelers in what gained notoriety as the "Mountain Meadows Massacre." Johnston, moreover, encountered such stiff guerrilla resistance that he had been forced to assume winter quarters at Fort Bridger, well to the northeast of Salt Lake City and beyond territorial borders. During the same period, Comanche depredations had been on the rise in Texas, particularly against settlers on the northern frontier. White infringement of Indian hunting grounds provoked much of the raiding, but military reprisals against the tribes and confinement of Indians to reservations became the primary white responses in both Texas and Washington. A recommendation had reached the War Department from David E. Twiggs, U.S. Army commander in Texas, that Congress authorize Texas to enlist at federal expense a regiment of mounted volunteers, since the army lacked adequate manpower to effect pacification at that time. Buchanan's annual message had requested four new army regiments so that the government could march such an "imposing force" westward as to convince the "deluded people" in Utah to submit. On January 4, Lawrence Keitt introduced a bill calling for the authorization of a regiment of mounted Texas volunteers. Both requests were referred to Quitman's committee, and House bill 313 provided for all five regiments.[32]

Since Quitman's measure purposed an expansion of the military establishment during a pro-South, Democratic administration, it invited Republican opposition. Republicans attacked the proposal on a variety of grounds, but particularly with the politically loaded accusation that Buchanan had enough troops already to suppress the Mormon insurrection, and that he really intended to assign the new troops to Kansas, where they would be expected to uphold the Lecompton regime.[33]

Specific provisions within the bill, however, complicated debate. The bill provided that the four Utah-bound U.S. regiments would consist of volunteer troops serving eighteen-month enlistments. Quitman explained that

341

such terms would permit two summer campaigns. Many congressmen who favored the application of force in Utah found this volunteer designation troubling. Charles J. Faulkner of Virginia, particularly, fought Quitman's proposal in committee and on the House floor, where he presented a substitute minority report. Faulkner questioned whether volunteers would have the conditioning to accomplish a 1,200-mile march, and suggested that the Utah problem was too delicate for "raw and inexperienced troops." Volunteers, he argued, lacked restraint and discipline. They might provoke unnecessary violence; regulars might achieve a negotiated settlement.[34]

For Quitman, the bill evoked memories of the Mexican War, and he spoke out frequently in its behalf. He gave a full exposition of its provisions and rationale on March 4, and entered debate on several occasions between then and March 19, when it came up for a roll call vote. Careful to avoid any implication that his call for volunteers meant disapprobation of the regular establishment, he censured all "philosophers" who harbored "utopian" visions that government could exist without the support of a standing military establishment. Nevertheless, he maintained that volunteers were perfectly matched to temporary crises like the Utah troubles. Anxious to make as strong a case as possible, he forcefully responded to aspersions against volunteer troops as prone to disease, insubordination, and looting. To those who cited volunteer deaths from disease in the Mexican War as proof that volunteer soldiers were not cost-effective, Quitman answered that high volunteer death rates at the start of the Mexican War should be attributed to volunteer units being stationed in "miasmic" regions of the Rio Grande Valley while regulars were sent on to engage the enemy in the mountains. To those who cited volunteer desertion rates as proof of proclivity to insubordination, Quitman contended that volunteers rarely deserted and pointed out that the regular army had just lost some 3,000 men within a year to desertion. And he waxed particularly vehement against the insinuation that volunteers, being prone to violence and pillage, lacked the moderation and discipline necessary for the Mormon situation. Had not Texas volunteers, despite memories of the Alamo, taken prisoners at San Jacinto rather than committing atrocities? Quitman pointed also to the example of his own troops in the Mexican War; he claimed that his volunteers had done less than $100 total property damage in Mexico, and generally left behind them "smiling villages and a happy people."

Once again, as in the neutrality law debates, Quitman, whether consciously or inadvertently, resorted to brief but nonetheless surprising nationalistic rhetoric to support his case. Quitman based his suggestion that volunteers made superior short-term troops on the premise that most volunteers tended to be patriotic country boys imbued with a desire to win fame and honor for self and country in a short campaign; long-term army enlistees tended to be lower-class rabble from the nation's urban centers who saw remuneration as the main objective. This hypothesis produced Quitman's conclusion that any charge that volunteers lacked "moral restraint" constituted an "unjust imputation *upon the American people.*" [35]

On March 19, the House endorsed Quitman's bill 124-to-73, sending it on to the Senate. Voting adhered closely to party lines; every negative but two was cast by a Republican. The Senate returned the bill with several amendments, the most important of which cut the number of Utah-bound regiments from four to two. Quitman fought the alteration, but weakened his case by admitting that Secretary of War John B. Floyd had told him that the administration could manage the Utah expedition with only two more regiments. The House accepted the amendment 113-to-102, and on April 7, President Buchanan signed the measure into law. Later in the session, Quitman steered through the House appropriations to pay, clothe, and feed the new troops.

Ironically the volunteer bill wound up being one of the less consequential pieces of legislation of the Thirty-fifth Congress. Already, the Texas legislature, impatient for action, had funded its own volunteer force. On May 12, Rip Ford led a combined force of six-month volunteers, already enlisted Rangers, and reservation Indians against a major Comanche encampment on the Canadian River, and won a convincing victory. As for Utah, word reached Washington shortly after Quitman's appropriations bill cleared the House that Brigham Young had finally recognized the president's appointee as territorial governor, thus negating the need for new troops. The appropriations bill died in the Senate, rendering meaningless all Quitman's efforts. [36]

Quitman's other speechmaking tended toward strict constructionist advocacy. Thus he came out against a bill establishing an "auxiliary guard" to combat rising crime rates in Washington, partly on the rationale that the bill expanded federal authority. His comments against a military pension bill which he felt went too far, and put too heavy a burden on the federal treasury, offered a classic expression of distaste for the welfare state, and have a peculiarly modern relevancy: "Is it not the best policy to encourage the citizen to seek out his own livelihood, that the republican spirit may be preserved for the integrity of our institutions? Induce them to give up their enterprise; leave them with no care for their livelihood; let them be fed from the public crib, and how can we depend on them to maintain intact the independence and free spirit of our fathers?" [37]

Late sessions and frequent speechmaking jeopardized Quitman's already frail constitution. "Papa suffered . . . from sitting up all last Friday night," observed Antonia after a particularly grueling House gathering. Quitman's newest curative, a glass of "fine old Port" taken every day, did little to restore a diminished appetite, and he found that the rich food served at Washington social gatherings caused considerable digestive discomfort. "We were the first to leave after dinner," Antonia reported to her mother following one engagement, "as Papa had not been well." His weight plunged to 141 pounds.

Renewed pain in the extremities compounded Quitman's problems. One ankle became so swollen that he had to summon all his strength to remove his boots at night. Severe soreness of the wrist destroyed Quitman's usually firm hand, making correspondence discouraging and occasionally impossible. Physical pain and weakness, moreover, converted oratory into a personal trial of endurance. "I am too unwell to make any remarks on this question," Quitman admitted one day in the House. When he did take the floor, colleagues found that his voice had lost its resonance, and they adopted the custom of crowding around his desk so that they could understand his words. Quitman's almost pure white hair, beard, and moustache, combined with his diminishing frame, gave the impression of advanced age.[38]

Duty, however, carried Quitman on. He was strong enough still, as he noted in House debate, to walk Washington's streets alone (wondering, he admitted "whether anybody will attack me"). He had never been one to shirk responsibility, and rather than capitulate to his ailments, he followed a rather draining daily schedule. Customarily he rose before his daughters, taking breakfast and venturing out from Kirkwood House at so early an hour that neither Louisa nor Antonia saw him until his return at night. Mornings were devoted to committee meetings and related work such as visits to Secretary of War Floyd's office. House sessions began at noon, and Quitman was usually on hand from that moment until afternoon or evening adjournment, rarely missing a quorum or roll call and allowing himself few breaks. His disinclination to pace himself frustrated Louisa, who became convinced that her beloved father sacrificed his remaining stamina by working harder than his colleagues. "Whenever I have been up to the House, he is ever engaged in reading or writing, while the other members are sauntering about, lolling at their ease in their luxurious chairs or chatting with their neighbours," she complained. But there was little that she could do about it.[39]

Actually, Quitman did reserve moments for relaxation. His daughters' letters provide several vignettes of their father enjoying his family "[He] is somewhat relaxed today," Louisa reported on one occasion. "He is sitting near the table now & Dedie [Eva] is showing him her pennies." Quitman, moreover, had by this time developed a considerable social circle in Washington. He had a close relationship, for instance, with General Scott, and sometimes joined the commanding general for whist. "Gen. Scott . . . is the most enthusiastic friend and admirer of Papa's, and calls him Brother," Antonia observed. Old friends such as John Thrasher came to call at his rooms, and he received frequent visits from military acquaintances and younger congressmen. Mellowed by age, experience, and ailments, Quitman, in contrast to his militant political personality, had a kindly manner and became something of a father figure and ideological mentor for freshmen representatives from the South. "I called to see my good friend Gen Quitman—He is a very honest simple courteous gentleman, I do love the old man," Texas congressman Guy M. Bryan confided in a private letter to his fiancée. Well after his death, colleagues would recall his friendship with "young men" beginning their congressional careers as one of his most endearing traits.[40]

Quitman tackled several of the season's most important social events, taking care to guide his daughters through the web of polite society in Washington. They did the "rounds of visiting the cabinet" together. Decked out in a new suit, Quitman also escorted Louisa and Antonia to a most fashionable affair at Secretary of the Treasury Howell Cobb's mansion, where he made every effort to introduce them to as many dignitaries as possible. Then, too, there was the dinner they attended at the White House, where Louisa vented her southern nationalism by giving antislavery senator Jacob Collamer of Vermont some "good hard raps over the knuckles" when he broached the subject of slavery. Louisa preferred a dinner at Speaker Orr's, where she could mingle with a more southern crowd and avoid "cool stiff northerners."[41]

Whether Quitman hoped that his daughters' sojourn in Washington would lead to their finding husbands is unclear, but he did write to Henry to express his satisfaction that Louisa and Antonia had attained a "circle of society" which was "of the best." Antonia, in particular, attracted a stream of admirers, her most persistent "shadow"—as Quitman called him—being a naval officer who lacked estate and made but $1,500 a year. Lieutenant William Storrow Lovell, commander of the U.S. war steamer *Water Witch* based in Norfolk and brother of Quitman's Mexican War aide Mansfield Lovell, had met Antonia the previous year. A chance encounter at a party on February 1 ignited an intense courtship. On March 14, Lovell asked for Antonia's hand. Quitman undoubtedly would have preferred the kind of social match Henry had effected. "It seems to be the fate of our girls to be attracted by poor professional gentlemen," he wrote Eliza. However, he did find Lovell "noble, high toned and intelligent," as well as less subject to "simpering affectation" than many rich "fops" he had known, and gave "the lovers" his warm approval. The more he came to know Lovell that spring, the more certain he became that the lieutenant would make Antonia a fine husband.[42]

Soon after the engagement, Quitman sent his daughters home. His main reason for doing so seems to have been his apprehension that the Kansas issue would drag on for a long time, delaying adjournment, though he and his daughters could not remain indifferent to complaints of homesickness for Monmouth, "Missus & the young ladies" which Sarah announced with disturbing regularity. She "has the blues quite often," Louisa observed about her servant. Their departure left a considerable void in Quitman's routine, which frequent visits from Lovell could only partially fill. "Tears would come to my eyes when I took my solitary seat at the table, or saw around me only strangers," he admitted later to Louisa.[43]

Less than a month later, Quitman confronted the Kansas question one more time. A House-Senate conference committee had devised a compromise known as the English bill (for anti-Lecompton representative William H. English of Indiana), which returned the Lecompton Constitution to Kansas for another vote under carefully drafted provisions calculated to placate southerners yet attract votes from northern Democrats previously opposed to the Lecompton measure. The authors of the Lecompton Constitution had asked Congress for a 25,592,160-acre land grant, which would have exceeded that given any previous state upon admission to the Union. The English bill, reported to both congressional chambers on April 23, proposed to reduce the grant to 3,988,868 acres—a proportion of Kansas' domain equivalent to that awarded other recently admitted states. The bill's key provision asked Kansans to either accept Kansas' admission under Lecompton with the reduced land grant, or to forgo admission until the territory achieved a population—to be verified by a census—equivalent to that required for a U.S. representative in Congress (90,000), which would take at least two more years. The bill was designed to attract southern votes because it seemed to offer an incentive to wavering territorial settlers to endorse Lecompton: if they did not, they would have to forfeit the coveted benefits of statehood for the indefinite future. However, the bill also invited anti-Lecomptonite support, because it promised what northern Democrats had always claimed was the true intent behind the original Kansas-Nebraska Act—an impartial poll of Kansas' settlers and territorial decision-making on slavery. If the territory's free-soil majority cared enough about its cause, it could turn out to vote and reject statehood. Because the bill offered hope that the Democracy could be reunited, President Buchanan and other administration officials used exhortations, patronage, and even bribes to line up support for the measure.[44]

Quitman had waited since December for this moment. Given his conviction that compromise had always weakened the slave states, his belief that even if Kansans endorsed Lecompton slaveowners would suffer because Republicans would succeed to power in Washington, and his desire to further radicalize his southern colleagues and precipitate a spirit of secession, his opposition was predetermined. He preferred deadlock to renewed submission. In remarks on April 29, Quitman denounced the English bill as the resubmission of an already "binding act," and maintained that Congress had no right to bypass the "*quasi* sovereignty" (the Lecompton constitutional convention) which had originally enacted Kansas' instrument of admission. Quitman said that the only development justifying perpetuation of the Union would be a "final settlement" of the slavery question which would "forever recognize the full constitutional equality of the slaveholding States." Without guarantees for the South, it would behoove his region to "separate." [45]

Quitman's antipathy to the English measure, which remained firm despite administration pressure,[46] gave pause to some southern Democrats primed to vote for the compromise. John S. Millson of Virginia alluded to Quitman's reservations in debate. Guy Bryan felt compelled to explain why on this issue he could not, as had been his custom in the past, act with that "gentleman from Mississippi" whose hair had "silvered through long years of service . . . in behalf of the interests and rights of his sunny land." But when the vote came on April 30, Quitman found himself playing a lonely hand. Only one other Deep South representative, Milledge L. Bonham of South Carolina, joined him in opposition, and the English compromise passed, 112-to-103, despite a phalanx of Republican negatives. (Republicans believed that the measure conceded too *much* to slavery.) We will never know, though, how many southern Democrats shared Quitman's qualms but hesitantly capitulated to the administration's tactics. After the vote, Storrow Lovell encountered Democrat George S. Hawkins of Florida, and reported to Antonia that Hawkins had admitted his own lack of backbone: "Judge Hawkins said to me," Lovell recounted, " 'I wish *I* could have voted as the Genl. did, but there are *very few men*, who *could* take the *stand* he did, it needs a man of reputation to do it.' " [47] Lovell undoubtedly passed on the substance of this conversation to Quitman, but Quitman could have derived little satisfaction from the knowledge. The vote served as a review lesson that he remained well beyond the political consensus of his region.

Quitman escaped temporarily to more comfortable ideological surroundings following the House's disposition of Lecompton. Invited by his friends in South Carolina to give the main address at the annual assemblage of the Palmetto Association on May 4, Quitman took the trains to Columbia, arriving the day before the celebration. Excitement gripped South Carolina over his coming, not only because of lingering remembrances of his Mexican War ties to the Palmetto Regiment—the ostensible reason for the invitation—but also because of his established stature as a secessionist. Thus one South Carolina veteran who had fought under Quitman at the Belén Gate wrote him well in advance of his visit, "Excuse this Exhuberance [*sic*] of feelings towards one whose fate I know is linked with 'bonds of steel' to the destiny of the down-trodden South; [b]ut you may yet live to see the day when we of the South, shall have thrown off the yoke of bondage and assumed to ourselves the *seperate* [*sic*] *nationality* which we are obliged to do." When Quitman appeared at the Columbia depot, he was greeted by a considerable throng and salutes and speeches.

A colorful parade the next day brought Quitman to the banner-bedecked hall of South Carolina College, where his address was to be given. Preceding his remarks, which gave the audience what it wanted—reminiscences of that "prominent part" filled by the Palmettos during the "brilliant victories which conquered an empire"—Quitman was greeted with "flowery wreaths" and the choir's rendition of an ode written in his honor by the noted South Carolina author William Gilmore Simms. "Welcome to the Chief" called on Quitman to remember his "brethren" who followed him "with bended spears," when at Chapultepec the Palmettos "crushed" Mexico's "powers" and "storm'd, through all her gates, our way to Aztec towers." After Quitman's address, enthusiastic cheers rang out. Later Quitman attended a ball and supper given in his honor. Chivalry again reigned supreme.[48]

Quitman returned to Washington psychologically revived. His reception at Columbia, he enthused to Louisa, had been "very triumphant." Reminders that kindred militaristic and secessionist spirits persisted in his region helped mitigate Quitman's ideological isolation in Washington. More positive about his stature in the southern political universe, Quitman was prepared for physical rejuvenation. Following the visit, he regained much of the weight he had recently lost, and felt fit enough to accept an invitation to command a "Grand Military Encampment" (units were expected from all over Mississippi and Louisiana, as well as from Mobile) scheduled for the Pharsalia Race Course outside Natchez on July 1–3.[49]

Dramatic sectional issues in the House, however, had been mostly played out by the time Quitman returned from Columbia. He spoke often during the remaining days of the session, but his more lengthy remarks dealt with matters of minimal sectional import, such as whether Congress should establish a board of land commissioners to examine private land titles in New Mexico and a measure giving army sutlers the right to a lien upon the pay of soldiers for unpaid charges at their stores. If Quitman expressed his checked radicalism, it seems to have been in the form of votes which he regularly registered against federal expenditures. Quitman opposed appropriations for such purposes as completing the Washington aqueduct, building customhouses, publishing the American State Papers, compensating Maine and Massachusetts for claims arising from land ceded to Britain in the Webster-Ashburton treaty (1842), and subsidies for the transport of U.S. mails in privately owned ocean steamers. By no means an unrelenting obstructionist, Quitman supported appropriations which he believed in, such as his own amendment to the army appropriations bill to spend $100,000 to convert old muskets to breechloaders. But he tended toward restricting federal spending. Concerning a bill to construct fortifications and military barracks, Quitman strongly urged that the House avoid block grants and asked that the measure be sent to the Committee of Ways and Means for revision, so that the House could learn just "how much money is needed for the repair and preservation of each particular work." [50]

In early June, Quitman became ill again. He stuck to his House duties right up to the end of the session, but was failing rapidly by the time he boarded the train for home following adjournment sine die on June 14. He slept virtually the entire trip to Memphis, needed assistance when it became necessary to move, and was thoroughly exhausted when he arrived at Natchez on June 21. He took to bed immediately, and hardly stirred for the next week, sleeping almost all the time. Beset by fever as well as weakness, he sent his regrets to the organizers of the military encampment. Only Antonia's wedding, which occurred on June 29, roused him for any length of time. [51]

Alarmed by his lassitude and unwillingness to eat, his family telegraphed an appeal for help to his old friend Samuel Cartwright, now one of the most renowned physicians in the entire South. Cartwright hurried to Quitman's side, but could effect little improvement. When he persuaded Quitman to try some light food—it was, he said, a "duty," a word calculated to agitate the honor-conscious patient—Quitman cooperated but immediately threw up. By July 14, newspapers were carrying Cartwright's dispatch that Quitman had developed a "very low typhoid condition." By July 17, death had become a matter of hours. Louisa, aware that the end was nearing, leaned over his bed that afternoon, and begged, "Father, put your trust in Jesus, he alone can help you now." "I *do*, my Child," Quitman answered. A few hours later, at 5:00 P.M., he died. [52]

Quitman, like Calhoun with whom he was sometimes linked in subsequent eulogies, died without seeing accomplished the driving purpose behind his political career, permanent security for slavery and the southern way of life within the Union or a separate nationality without. Because he was a prominent military hero and political personage, his death was mourned throughout the Deep South. But only companion radicals fully comprehended the essence of his passing. "Genl. Quitman's death is truly a serious blow to our cause," lamented a South Carolina secessionist in a private letter. "He was indeed a noble spirit." [53]

Epilogue

It took only a decade to prove Henry Foote wrong. In July, 1851, taking the measure of secession's receding appeal in his state, Foote predicted that "Quitman and Quitmanism" were "*dead*" in Mississippi forever." On January 9, 1861, Mississippi became the second state to secede from the Union, and John Quitman's legacy presided over that momentous event. Quitman had done more than any other public man to familiarize Mississippi voters with states' rights constitutional theories and the secession option; and no Mississippi politico better articulated to the state's citizenry the fears which compelled Mississippi's eventual decision. Abolitionist control of the federal government, the degrading context of second-class citizenship, free-soil antagonism toward slavery expansion west and south, northern defiance of the Fugitive Slave Law, and abolitionist instigation of slave revolt—concerns which Quitman had brought before Mississippi's political forum over and over again—remained imprinted upon Mississippi's collective consciousness at the time of secession.[1]

Given Quitman's instrumental role in Mississippi secessionism, his July, 1858, death seems preclimactic. He deserved to live at least a few weeks longer; Kansas' conclusive rejection of the Lecompton Constitution that August legitimized Quitman's lonely stance against the English compromise and might have made him something of a prophet in his region. But his life story would have only achieved genuine symmetry had he shared in the Confederate experience, the true product of his political advocacy. Longevity, however, would have come at a steep price. Barring the unlikely possibility that his contribution to the Confederacy—say as secretary of war—would have made a significant difference in the Civil War's outcome, we can presume that he would have become a very disillusioned man by the time of Appomattox.

Quitman would have been proud of how his heirs faced the crucible of the Civil War. Eliza died on August 22, 1859, little more than a year after being widowed. However, Quitman had other survivors to confront the Union menace, and all proved spiritually prepared to do their part. Louisa

351

embraced secession so that she could escape "Black republicans" and their hostility to the South's "great and main institution." Antonia championed her "beloved Confederacy" in its "struggle for independance [*sic*]." Henry described the cause as a fight against "Yankee thralldom." True to Quitman's martial spirit, the family contributed its entire manpower to the Confederate war effort. Louisa remarried in January, 1859, and her husband Joe Lovell (brother of Storrow and Mansfield) joined the Fencibles and spent the whole war fighting for the Confederacy. Henry served in Confederate field forces and then as a captain in the army's quartermaster department (collecting taxes and impressing farm produce). Storrow Lovell, who achieved the rank of lieutenant colonel, filled a variety of posts ranging from chief of the harbor police at Pensacola to acting inspector general in the Mississippi River valley to head of a conscript training center. In June, 1861, Rose married William P. (Pat) Duncan. Duncan served as a major in the Confederate army. When Fredericka married in the midst of the war, she appropriately accepted the hand of Francis Eugene Ogden, a wounded Confederate officer.[2]

Yet, pride in kin might have provided scant comfort to a man forced to see his family endure tragedy, deprivation, and humiliation because of a war engendered, in part, by his values and actions. Quitman probably could have accepted Pat Duncan's wartime death from typhoid fever—he had survived many such tragedies in his own life, including the deaths of some of his own children. He could have coped with Frank Ogden's being taken captive at the Battle of the Wilderness and his imprisonment at Fort Delaware on Pea Patch Island in the Delaware River for the balance of the War.[3] But he would have found insufferable the desecration of Monmouth and his plantations wrought by Union armies, and would have been repulsed by some psychologically degrading behavior forced upon his heirs by Federal troops.

Vulnerable to Union military power because of their locations on or near important waterways at the Confederacy's periphery, Quitman's holdings felt Federal wrath early in the war. In May, 1862, threatened by an enemy squadron on the Mississippi and backed by only nine armed men, the mayor of Natchez discreetly surrendered his city to Yankee forces. Permanent Federal occupation waited until the capture of Vicksburg in July, 1863, but then Yankee troops took over Quitman's hometown. Monmouth's occupants within days were watching the movements, as Rose put it, of "blue coats moving about" on a hill opposite their residence. Subsequently Monmouth became the headquarters of a Union brigade. Soldiers camped on the front lawn, and brigade officers took over the mansion's lower story, forcing the Quitmans to crowd together upstairs.[4]

Meanwhile, Union power intruded on Palmyra. As early as May, 1862, threatened by a Union fleet approaching Vicksburg, Palmyra's overseer burned 413 bales of cotton rather than permit them to fall into Union hands. The next month a Confederate officer visited the plantation, and destroyed seed cotton sufficient to gin 60 bales, for the same purpose. Federal troops took over the entire peninsula following Vicksburg's conquest and initiated the famous "Davis Bend Experiment," in which the land of planters was expropriated and distributed among former slaves to farm in the hope of converting them into an independent black yeomanry. Rose and her sister Eliza retrieved the Quitman holdings temporarily from the experiment by traveling to Vicksburg, taking a loyalty oath to the Union, and arranging to lease the family property to a northern speculator; however, in November that year a Union general by special order returned Palmyra to the experiment and warned all whites to vacate the peninsula by January 1, 1865.[5]

Live Oaks met a similar fate. Union conquest of New Orleans in April, 1862, opened up Louisiana's cane country to Federal penetration. Fighting erupted in the Houma area, and Thibodaux became a Union army headquarters. By fall, Henry was engaged in plans to evacuate his plantation slaves. Ultimately Federal troops did occupy the Caillou place, confiscating household items and crops. Neighbor John Pelton, who collaborated with the enemy, was selling off Live Oaks' silver as the war ground to its close.[6]

Quitman would have been profoundly disturbed by Yankee rule, because enemy occupation entailed far worse effects than the mere curtailing of plantation revenues. The family, Rose later recalled, had particularly "bad names" among Union soldiers because of Quitman's notorious secessionism, and during the early stages of Monmouth's occupation Federal troops took delight in destroying family furnishings, confiscating horses and poultry, cutting down the estate's magnificent front lawn oaks for firewood, and pillaging Quitman's beloved gardens. "The Quitmans, like most southern people of their rank who lived out of town," a veteran of the Twelfth Wisconsin Volunteer Infantry Regiment would recall after the war, "kept up a garden of several acres. It contained all sorts of things from onions and potatoes to pineapples, pomegranates, figs and large pecan-nut trees. . . . We used to like to walk in that garden. Its close proximity to our camp enabled us now and then to get a taste of something delicious." Yankee depredations and confiscations reduced Quitman's survivors quickly to near-penury. Louisa took to selling family carriages and carpets for spending money, and peddling old clothing to afford milk for Alice, her baby by Joe Lovell.[7]

Federal rule, more important, exposed Quitman's most cherished values and beliefs as based upon fallacious assumptions. As late as July, 1861, noting how Monmouth's servants greeted her with inquiries about how "Master" (in this case, Joe Lovell) was faring as a Confederate soldier in Virginia,

Louisa remained convinced that the "abolitionists" understood "nothing of the bond that unites the master & servant of its tenderness and care on the one side, and its pride fidelity and attachment on the other." She reassured Joe, in fact, that the household's "good creatures" had "*all* behaved extremely well," and were concerned about their master's safety. "They are . . . very sympathizing with us all," she reported. "They often speak to me about the war and there was great rejoicing in the kitchen at the news of our recent glorious victory in Virginia [the First Battle of Bull Run]." [8]

Disillusionment began as slaves discerned that absent household males could hardly exert discipline at plantation and home, and reached profound proportions after the arrival of Yankee troops. By September, 1861, fear stalked Monmouth over a slave insurrection panic in the neighborhood. The next month, Louisa wrote Joe that slave "carelessness" had caused a fire at Palmyra which destroyed the gin, all its appurtenances, all bagging, all unginned cotton, and 300 pressed bales, and that quite a few of the blacks had "run off." Later some of the Live Oaks slaves ran away. One former servant at the sugar plantation, Mary's maid, infuriated the Quitmans by accepting Mary's wardrobe from Union authorities and wearing the clothes around without shame. [9]

The ultimate shock attended the Union occupation of Monmouth, when even the family's most trusted servants expressed their individuality, exposing starkly how little the Quitmans really understood their slaves. Egged on by Union officials and soldiers who preached to them that they were "just as good as their Mistresses sitting up in that fine house," the household blacks became disrespectful and "flaunting" at first, and then left the fold. Isaac took to driving a dray in Natchez for fares. Harry left for a while, came back demanding wages, and then talked about joining the Davis Bend community. Maria, the cook, took "her departure," forcing the Quitmans to hire a replacement at $15 per month. By February, 1865, Louisa was reporting that only Harry, his wife, and "Fred's family" remained of the Quitman's once sizable household retinue. Before the war's end, the Quitmans even had to face the stationing of armed black Union troops on Monmouth's premises, surely the most provoking manifestation of a world turned upside down. [10]

John Quitman's heirs survived the Civil War. Eventually befriended by a sympathetic Union general, Henry W. Slocum, they managed to preserve Monmouth from total destruction and to salvage many of the family's furnishings and belongings. Their property restored after the war, the Lovell brothers immediately, and Henry somewhat later, resumed planting operations using hired blacks at bare subsistence wages. The family recovered sufficiently that decades later Storrow Lovell attracted press recognition as a "planting magnate." [11]

However, to reach that point the Quitmans suffered a most exacting trauma of humiliation and hurt pride. Louisa, for instance, felt intense degradation when compelled to take an oath of loyalty to the Union in order to preserve title to her property, and her bitter reactions to revelations of black alienation show how much the Civil War experience contravened an entire upbringing and heritage. "Oh! deliver me from the 'citizens of African descent,'" she raged. "I am disgusted with the whole race. . . . They are all alike ungrateful and treacherous." Anticipations of living indefinitely as an "enslaved" people under conquering Yankee "fiends" and "demons" evoked thoughts of permanent exile within the family circle, and Henry could not help but become upset when Mary, because of poor health, suggested a move to New York once the war ended. Henry said that he would take her anywhere "upon the face of the globe" rather than the North, and mentioned England, Scotland, and Hawaii as possibilities. The Civil War tested the faith of the Quitman family to its limits before it reached a merciful end, and it is no wonder that the righteous Louisa, who in 1861 had avowed that God would deliver the Confederacy from its enemies, came by 1865 to ponder whether there was "justice in Heaven." [12]

Even had Quitman somehow reconciled himself to the disillusionment, shame, and despair imposed upon his once proud family by Union armies, he still would have had to face the ideological implications of Confederate defeat. He would, above all, have had to at least confront the possibility that the "submissionists" had been right all along. Secession, after all, ended rather than preserved the South's peculiar institution. Perhaps it was best that this stubborn, dedicated southern radical died satisfied, as his gravestone inscription so aptly put it, that he had "kept the faith." [13]

Bibliographical Essay

The following essay represents a very selective guide to those primary and secondary sources which proved most essential to the completion of this study. An enumeration of *all* primary and secondary sources cited would entail reference to numerous materials of only tangential value in understanding Quitman, and necessitate many superfluous pages. Rather, this essay is intended to aid scholars and other readers desiring to identify those sources which I found most helpful about Quitman and his social, political, economic, and military milieu.

Manuscripts

Quitman manuscripts, except about his childhood (for which little material of any kind is available), are plentiful but divided among several repositories. I found the Quitman Family Papers at the Southern Historical Collection, University of North Carolina, the most valuable collection of Quitman manuscripts, because the papers focus more than any other one group of Quitman papers upon his early manhood. They contain a wealth of information about family and plantation affairs. Several other Quitman collections, however, are also indispensable. For Quitman's career in Mississippi politics and the Mexican War, the John Quitman Papers and the J. F. H. Claiborne Papers at the Mississippi Department of Archives and History in Jackson are a must. The latter collection includes a large number of letters addressed to Quitman. The John Quitman Papers at the Houghton Library, Harvard University, concentrate on Cuba filibustering, and the John Quitman Papers at the Historical Society of Pennsylvania reveal Quitman's relationship with his son and many of his social attitudes. Sizable collections of Quitman materials are also available at the University of Virginia, the University of the South (Lovell Family Papers), and Louisiana State University. Ron Riches, owner of Monmouth, Quitman's mansion, provided me with copies of his own collection of Quitman letters. These manuscripts, which provided fascinating insights into Eliza Quitman's personality during the latter stages of their marriage, have since been reproduced for the benefit of scholars visiting the Mississippi Department of Archives and History. Other Quitman letters, as the footnotes indicate, are scattered at libraries and archives throughout the country, both under Quitman's name and within the collected papers of his contemporaries. The most valuable of these minor collections is the Mansfield Lovell Papers, Huntington Library.

The Powhatan Ellis Papers at the Barker Texas History Center Archives (University of Texas) are rich in materials relating to the politics of early Jacksonian Mississippi. The Reuben Ross Papers and the Thomas J. Rusk Papers at the same repository illuminated several aspects of Quitman's intervention in the Texas Revolution. The J. F. H. Claiborne and Whitemarsh B. Seabrook collections at the Library of Congress provided useful information, the former on Mississippi politics, the latter on Quitman's secessionist advocacy and movements during the crisis of 1850. At the William R. Perkins Library (Duke University), the Samuel Smith Downey Papers include correspondence dealing with Quitman's connection with the Mississippi Railroad Company. The Campbell Family Papers at Duke have a large number of items pertaining to Quitman's role in Zachary Taylor's campaign in northern Mexico.

A trip to the Mississippi Department of Archives and History is essential to serious study of Quitman. Deed records, chancery court records, census records, the Jefferson College papers, Quitman's gubernatorial papers, and legislative and militia records collected there provide a virtual gold mine of data about Quitman. Records at the National Archives, similarly, proved invaluable to this study, particularly about Quitman's Mexican War experience but also in relationship to several other aspects of Quitman's life including his service in the United States House of Representatives.

Printed Primary Sources

Printed public documents offer considerable data about Quitman, because he held such a variety of official stations. The *Congressional Globe*, December, 1855–June, 1858, for instance, offers by far the single best source of information about Quitman's career in Washington. *House Executive Documents* and *Senate Executive Documents* for the Twenty-ninth through the Thirty-first Congress contain a body of correspondence and reports pertaining to Quitman's Mexican War service. A superb guide to U.S. government documents from the Mexican War is contained in Norman E. Tutorow (comp. and ed.), *The Mexican-American War: An Annotated Bibliography* (Westport, 1981). The journals of the Mississippi House of Representatives and the Mississippi Senate are the main resource for Quitman's career in the state legislature, and an important reference for Quitman's two terms as governor. *The Journal of the Convention of the State of Mississippi Held in the Town of Jackson* (Jackson, 1832) stands alone as a collection of data covering Quitman's participation in Mississippi's constitutional convention.

J. F. H. Claiborne's *Life and Correspondence of John A. Quitman* (2 vols.; New York, 1860) is packed with Quitman letters, most of which are unavailable at any archive and presumably lost to the public. Claiborne's collection of documents not only includes much of Quitman's most important political correspondence, such as several letters pertaining to his efforts to get Mississippi to secede from the Union while he was governor of the state, but also provides the only letters available relating to his adolescent and early manhood years at Hartwick Academy and Mount Airy College as well as some of the few materials about his residence in Ohio from 1819 to 1821. Claiborne deserves consultation, moreover, for important documents about Quitman's filibuster arrangements, some speeches, and several diary fragments (one of which covers part of his intervention in the Texas Revolution). Quitman's career crossed that of Jefferson Davis on innumerable occasions; *The Papers of Jefferson Davis* (four volumes to date) contain frequent mentions of Quitman and some Quitman correspondence. The exhaustive footnoting undertaken by the editors of these papers provided some of the most accurate and useful biographical material which I have been able to locate about many of Quitman's Mississippi political contemporaries. William R. Hogan and Edwin A. Davis' edition of *William Johnson's Natchez: The Ante-Bellum Diary of a Free Negro* (Baton Rouge, 1951), Henry S. Foote, *Casket of Reminiscences* (Washington, D.C., 1874), and [G. L. Prentiss (ed.)], *Memoir of S. S. Prentiss* (2 vols.; New York, 1856) contain information pertaining to Quitman's personality and his career in Natchez public life and Mississippi politics. [William Wood], *Autobiography of William Wood* (2 vols.; New York, 1895), provided a surprising source of information about Quitman, his partner (and brother-in-law) Henry Turner, and their planting operations from the perspective of a New Orleans factor. Rosalie Quitman Duncan's "Life of General John A. Quitman," *Publications of the Mississippi Historical Society*, IV (1901), 415–24, is a reminiscence about Quitman by one of his daughters.

Newspapers

Virtually every Mississippi newspaper consulted contained some material about John Quitman's career, because he held such a variety of public offices in the state and because he was such a formidable political personality. The Democratic organ in the state capital, the Jackson *Mississippian*, was particularly useful concerning Quitman's political activities. Quitman's role as a

Natchez civic leader and his planting interests near Vicksburg combined with his political and military behavior to attract constant coverage in his hometown press, particularly the *Mississippi Free Trader* (Natchez) and the politically opposed Vicksburg papers, the *Whig* and the *Sentinel.* The New Orleans *Daily Picayune* had some very useful material about Quitman's Mexican War career, because it had correspondents covering the conflict. The Mexico City *Daily American Star* and the *North American* (Mexico City) offered a good body of material about Quitman's tenure as civil and military governor. Quitman's Cuba filibustering activities, because they centered upon New Orleans, attracted considerable attention in the Crescent City's press; I utilized the *Picayune*, New Orleans *Bee*, and New Orleans *Courier* for this facet of his life.

Books

For reasons unclear to this writer, Quitman's career has not attracted the biographical attention it merits. James H. McLendon wrote a competent dissertation about Quitman entitled "John A. Quitman" (University of Texas, 1949), but it never found its way into print. The only full-length study about Quitman available in book form is Claiborne's two-volume treatment, cited above. As explained in the preface, this book has severe limitations as a secondary work. William L. Barney has grappled with the implications of Quitman's political career at some length in his provocative *The Road to Secession: A New Perspective on the Old South* (New York, 1972). John Hope Franklin's *The Militant South, 1800–1861* (Cambridge, Mass., 1956) considers Quitman as one of the prime examples of the martial temperament of his region.

Several books proved so essential to my understanding of the milieu in which Quitman functioned, they deserve particular mention. I found myself constantly picking up D. Clayton James's *Antebellum Natchez* (Baton Rouge, 1968) and Edwin A. Miles's *Jacksonian Democracy in Mississippi* (Chapel Hill, 1960), the former to obtain information about the historical, political, social, and economic context of Quitman's home community, the latter for the setting and chronology of Mississippi politics in the 1820s and 1830s. Richard Aubrey McLemore (ed.), *A History of Mississippi* (Jackson, 1973), Volume I, also provided reliable data about antebellum Mississippi. An enlightening overview of Quitman's social class in Natchez is Morton Rothstein, "The Natchez Nabobs: Kinship and Friendship in an Economic Elite," in Hans L. Trefousse (ed.), *Toward a New View of America: Essays in Honor of Arthur C. Cole* (New York, 1977), 97–112. Fletcher Melvin Green's *The Role of the Yankee in the Old South* (Athens, 1972) helped me to perceive that there was little unique about Quitman's conversion from the son of a New York Lutheran minister to a southern radical.

Although there is now a considerable body of substantial studies about slavery, none has done more to inform my understanding of Quitman's relationships with his field hands and house servants than Eugene D. Genovese, *Roll, Jordan, Roll: The World the Slaves Made* (New York, 1974). K. Jack Bauer's *The Mexican War, 1846–1848* (New York, 1974) and Charles H. Brown's *Agents of Manifest Destiny: The Lives and Times of the Filibusters* (Chapel Hill, 1980) are exceptionally fine syntheses about two important facets of Quitman's life. For Quitman's career in Congress, I relied heavily on Roy F. Nichols' *The Disruption of American Democracy* (New York, 1948) and Allan Nevins' *Ordeal of the Union* (2 vols.; New York, 1947) and *The Emergence of Lincoln* (2 vols.; New York, 1950). Richard H. Sewell, *Ballots for Freedom: Antislavery Politics in the United States, 1837–1860* (New York, 1976), provided crucial insights into why Quitman and other southern radicals lived in such mortal fear of the free-soil movement. David M. Potter, *The Impending Crisis, 1848–1861* (New York, 1976), not only became my Bible for the sectional controversy but also, more than any other single book, molded my interpretation of Quitman as both American nationalist and southern secessionist. Finally, J. Mills Thornton, *Politics and Power in a Slave Society: Alabama, 1800–1860* (Baton Rouge, 1978), William James Cooper, *The South and the Politics of Slavery, 1828–1856* (Baton Rouge, 1978), John McCardell, *The Idea of a Southern Nation: Southern Nationalists and Southern Nationalism, 1830–1860* (New York, 1979), and Stephen A. Channing, *Crisis of Fear: Secession in South Carolina* (New York, 1970), have affected my perceptions of southern ideology, politics, and society, and the meaning of Quitman's career, to a far greater degree than my footnotes could ever acknowledge.

Journal Articles

A substantial number of periodical pieces have focused upon aspects of Quitman's career. These include: James H. McLendon, "Ancestry, Early Life, and Education of John A. Quitman," *Journal of Mississippi History*, X (1948), 271–89; McLendon, "John A. Quitman in the Texas Revolution," *Southwestern Historical Quarterly*, LII (1948), 163–83; McLendon, "John A. Quitman, Fire-Eating Governor," *Journal of Mississippi History*, XV (1953), 73–89; John McCardell, "John A. Quitman and the Compromise of 1850 in Mississippi," *Journal of Mississippi History*, XXXVII (1975), 239–66; Ray Broussard, "Governor John A. Quitman and the López Expeditions of 1851–1852," *Journal of Mississippi History*, XXVIII (1966),

103–120; C. Stanley Urban, "The Abortive Quitman Filibustering Expedition to Cuba, 1853–1855," *Journal of Mississippi History*, XVIII (1956), 175–96; and John Edmond Gonzales, "John Anthony Quitman in the United States House of Representatives, 1855–1858," *Southern Quarterly*, IV (1966), 276–88. Michael de L. Landon, "The Mississippi State Bar Association, 1821–1825: The First in the Nation," *Journal of Mississippi History*, XLII (1980), 222–42, includes considerable data pertaining to Quitman's stature in Mississippi's legal profession. Quitman's role as a territorial imperialist opposed to commercial development schemes is traced in Jere W. Roberson, "The Memphis Commercial Convention of 1853: Southern Dreams and 'Young America,'" *Tennessee Historical Quarterly*, XXXIII (1974), 279–96. Quitman's actions while a radical Mississippian during the nullification and Compromise of 1850 controversies can be followed in lengthy treatments of those events by Cleo Hearon, "Nullification in Mississippi," *Publications of the Mississippi Historical Society*, XII (1912), 37–71, and "Mississippi and the Compromise of 1850," *Publications of the Mississippi Historical Society*, XIV (1914), 7–229.

Published Lecture

Robert W. Johannsen's *A New Era for the United States: Americans and the War with Mexico* (Urbana, 1975) conforms to none of the above categories, but should nonetheless be mentioned. In a historiographical era when it became the fashion to write about dissent during America's wars, Johannsen was perceptive enough to see that the Mexican War also unleashed patriotic pride throughout the American body politic. His interpretation helped me make sense of war veteran Quitman's unabashed nationalism just two years before he advised Mississippi's secession from the Union.

Notes

CHAPTER 1

1. [Richard Penn Smith (?)], *Col. Crockett's Exploits and Adventures in Texas . . . Written by Himself* (Philadelphia, 1836), 59.

2. Vicksburg *Whig*, January 12, 1856; Undated scrapbook newspaper clipping, William Clark Breckinridge Papers, Western Historical Manuscript Collection, State Historical Society of Missouri, Columbia.

3. William Gwin to J. F. H. Claiborne, November 5, 1878, J. F. H. Claiborne Papers, SHC; William Gwin to Charles D. Fontaine, January 30, 1849, Charles D. Fontaine Papers, MDA. For similar contemporary assessments of Quitman's ambition, see Henry S. Foote, *Casket of Reminiscences* (Washington, D.C., 1874), 356; Zachary Taylor to Joseph P. Taylor, January 19, 1848, Zachary Taylor Papers, LC; John Elliott to William N. Mercer, December 6, 1836, William Newton Mercer Papers, Howard Tilton Memorial Library, Tulane University, New Orleans; J. F. H. Claiborne, *Life and Correspondence of John A. Quitman* (2 vols.; New York, 1860), II, 294.

4. Timothy Dwight, *Travels in New England and New York*, ed. Barbara Miller Solomon (4 vols., 1821–22; rpr. Cambridge, Mass., 1969), III, 298; Louisa S. Quitman to JAQ, August 4, 1849, Quitman Family Papers, SHC; Louisa S. Quitman to F. Henry Quitman, October 24, 1849, JAQ Papers, HSP.

5. James H. McLendon, "Ancestry, Early Life, and Education of John A. Quitman," *JMH*, X (1948), 272–73; Claiborne, *Quitman*, I, 16.

6. A. B. Gregg, "Schoharie's Other Two Governors," *Schoharie County Historical Review*, XXIV (Fall, 1960), 4; Edmund Belfour to Mrs. William Lovell, April 2, 1897, Lovell Family Papers, UnS; Minutes of the Evangelical Lutheran Ministerium of the State of New York and Adjacent Parts, 1786–1806 (Microfilm copy, courtesy of the Graduate Theological Union, Berkeley); "Historical discourse delivered by Rev. J. A. Earnest, pastor at the Reopening of the Old St. Peter's Lutheran Church of Rhinebeck, New York, November 2, 1881," *Lutheran Observer*, January 20, 1882, in Scrapbook, Dutchess County Historical Society, Poughkeepsie.

7. Reverend William Hull, *History of the Lutheran Church in Dutchess County, N.Y.* (Gettysburg, 1881), 11; Louisa S. Quitman to JAQ, August 4, 1849, Quitman Family Papers, SHC; Mrs. Jacob H. Strong, "The Old Stone Church," *Dutchess County Historical Society Yearbook*, XL (1955), 30; Church and Corporation Records, 1802, p. 39 (record of witness of the certification of elected trustees for St. Peter's Church), typewritten copy in County Clerk's Office, Dutchess County, Poughkeepsie.

8. Hull, *History of the Lutheran Church*, 3, 7; "Biography of Rev. Dr. Quitman,"

in Minutes, Ministerium of New York, 19–20, Lutheran Theological Seminary, Philadelphia; Edward M. Smith, *Documentary History of Rhinebeck* (Rhinebeck, 1881), 104–105; Henry Hardin Heins, *Throughout All the Years: The Bicentennial Story of Hartwick in America, 1746–1946* (Blair, Neb., 1946), 34–36; Paul H. Mattingly, *The Classless Profession: American Schoolmen in the Nineteenth Century* (New York, 1975), 21–22; Harry Julius Kreider (ed.), "Minutes of the Evangelical Lutheran Ministerium of the State of New York and Adjacent States and Countries for the Years 1807 to 1818 Inclusive," Transcribed for the Editorial Committee for the Documentary History of the United Lutheran Synod of New York (Microfilm copy, courtesy of the Graduate Theological Union, Berkeley), 47 (page numbers refer to the actual numbers in the synod records). Reverend Quitman gave up all his ministerial duties in 1815 except Rhinebeck and the church in Wurtemburg.

9. "Extracts from a diary in the possession of James A. Bourne, Rhinebeck," in Mrs. Theodore de Laporte (comp.), Rhinebeck Records, III, 179, Starr Library, Rhinebeck; Kreider (ed.), "Minutes of the Evangelical Lutheran Ministerium," 1797, 1807, and *passim*; Harry J. Kreider, *History of the United Lutheran Synod of New York and New England, 1786–1860* (Philadelphia, 1954), 42, 45–47; Friedrich Paulsen, *German Education, Past and Present*, trans. T. Lorenz (London, 1908), 116–20; Sydney E. Ahlstrom, *A Religious History of the American People* (New Haven, 1972), 236–38, 378; Frederick Henry Quitman, *Evangelical Catechism: or, A Short Exposition of the principal doctrines and precepts of the Christian Religion* . . . (Hudson, N.Y., 1814); Frederick Henry Quitman, *A Treatise on Magic, or, On the Intercourse Between Spirits and Men* (Albany, 1810).

10. "Baptism Record, St. Paul's Lutheran Church, Schoharie, New York, 1728–1899," p. 116, Schoharie County Historical Society, Old Stone Fort Museum, Schoharie, N.Y.; "Baptismal Record of St. Peter's Lutheran Church, Rhinebeck, New York," 109, 114, Starr Library; Memorial plaque to Anna Elizabeth Hueck in Old Stone Church, quoted in Rollin Howard Masten, "Dutchess County Churches," VI, 48, typescript in Adriance Memorial Library, Poughkeepsie; Rosalie Quitman Duncan, "Life of General John A. Quitman," *PMHS*, IV (1901), 416.

11. JAQ to his brother, Febraury 23, 1821, February 1, 1823, in Claiborne, *Quitman*, I, 56, 77; Louisa S. Quitman to JAQ, August 4, 1849, JAQ Diary, December 2, 24, 1819, Quitman Family Papers, SHC; Louisa S. Quitman to JAQ, August 25, 1851, Lovell Family Papers, UnS; friend quoted in Claiborne, *Quitman*, I, 25.

12. William F. Quitman to Frederick Henry Quitman, November 18, 1819, F. H. Quitman Papers, Lutheran Archives Center, Krauth Memorial Library, Philadelphia; friend quoted in Claiborne, *Quitman*, I, 25. Frederica married Peter Quackenboss of Schoharie, on February 9, 1807. They had at least four children: Walter Henry (born in 1808), Frederick William (born in 1809), Augustus (born in 1811), and Cathrine Eliza (born in 1815). "Marriage Record of Two Early Schoharie, New York Churches," 67, and "Baptism Record, St. Paul's Lutheran Church," 134, 139, 148, 154, Schoharie County Historical Society.

13. Minutes of the Evangelical Lutheran Ministerium, 1803–1819; Hull, *History of the Lutheran Church*, 8; Duncan, "Life of General John A. Quitman," 415. Reverend Quitman had presided over Augustus Wackerhagen's marriage at Rhinebeck on September 9, 1806. Helen Wilkinson Reynolds (comp.), *Notices of Marriages and Deaths . . . Published in Newspapers Printed at Poughkeepsie, New York, 1778–1825* (Poughkeepsie, 1930), 113.

14. Gregg, "Schoharie's Other Two Governors," 4; McLendon, "Ancestry of

John A. Quitman," 280; Claiborne, *Quitman*, I, 27; Walter C. Livingston to JAQ, October 18, 1857, Quitman Family Papers, SHC.

15. Heins, *Throughout All the Years*, 1–36; G. F. Krotel, "The Beginnings of the Seminary," *Lutheran Church Review* (July, 1896), 255–67; "Historical Address by Rev. Henry N. Pohlman" and "Biography of Rev. E. L. Hazelius, S. C.," in *Memorial Volume of the Semi-Centennial Anniversary of Hartwick Seminary Held August 21, 1866* (Albany, 1867), 37–38, 57–58; Kreider (ed.), "Minutes of the Evangelical Lutheran Ministerium," 1815, p. 61; JAQ Account, Archives of Hartwick Seminary, Hartwick College Archives, Oneonta, N.Y.; Otsego *Herald*, October 3, 1816. Most accounts place John at Hartwick for its opening in December, 1815, but he was not hired until the summer of 1816. Since there are separate accounts of his traveling there in the fall of 1816, it is likely that this was his initial trip. For his hiring, see John W. Schmitthenner, "The Origin and Educational Contribution of Hartwick Seminary" (Ph.D. dissertation, New York University, 1934), 40.

16. JAQ to his brother, June 28, 1816, Frederick Henry Quitman to JAQ, October 17, 1817, in Claiborne, *Quitman*, I, 29, 30. John was paid $300 for his labors from September 1, 1817, to May 1, 1818. His salary for the rest of his stay is unknown. See JAQ Account.

17. JAQ to Miss [?], February 18, 1818, Quitman Family Papers, SHC; Frederick Henry Quitman to JAQ, October 17, 1817, JAQ to his brother, December 10, 1820, in Claiborne, *Quitman*, I, 30, 54; Claiborne, *Quitman*, I, 28; *Hartwick Seminary Monthly* (May, 1886); Heins, *Throughout All the Years*, 38; Louisa S. Quitman to Henry Pohlman, March 7, 1859, JAQ Papers, HSP.

18. JAQ to J. R. Simms, May 5, 1854, in *Historical Magazine* (January, 1867), 41–42; Claiborne, *Quitman*, I, 26; Gregg, "Schoharie's Other Two Governors," 5; Frederick Henry Quitman to JAQ, October 17, 1817, in Claiborne, *Quitman*, I, 30.

19. Henry N. Pohlman to Henry Newman, February 1, 1818, Henry N. Pohlman Papers, New York State Library, Albany; Letter of recommendation, in Quitman Family Papers, SHC; JAQ to Frederick Henry Quitman, August 13, 1818, in Claiborne, *Quitman*, I, 30.

20. Samuel Fitch Hotchkin, *Ancient and Modern Germantown, Mt. Airy, and Chestnut Hill* (Philadelphia, 1889), 349, 364–76, 385–86; Edward W. Hocker, *Germantown, 1683–1933* (Germantown, 1933), 139–40; Lisabeth M. Holloway, "The Mount Airy Schooldays of Charles Fleury Bien-Aimé Guillou," *Germantown Crier*, XXIX (Fall, 1977), 87–91, XXX (Winter, 1978), 13–17, XXX (Summer, 1978), 57–62; Saul Sack, *History of Higher Education in Pennsylvania* (2 vols.; Harrisburg, 1963), I, 210.

21. Holloway, "Mount Airy Schooldays," 60, 61; JAQ to Frederick Henry Quitman, August 13, 1818, JAQ to his brother, November 8, 1818, March 21, 1819, Frederick Henry Quitman to JAQ, November 23, 1818, in Claiborne, *Quitman*, I, 30, 31, 33.

22. Louisa S. Quitman to JAQ, February 3, 1833, Quitman Family Papers, SHC; JAQ to his brother, March 21, 1819, March 11, 1823, in Claiborne, *Quitman*, I, 32–33, 78.

23. Claiborne, *Quitman*, I, 33n; JAQ to his brother, March 21, 1819, Platt Brush to JAQ, n.d., Frederick Henry Quitman to JAQ, June 22, 1819, in Claiborne, *Quitman*, I, 32–33, 34. McLendon, "Ancestry of John A. Quitman," 283, suggests that John's initial contact must have been with Henry Brush rather than Platt Brush, since Claiborne mistakenly identified Platt Brush as a congressman. I am inclined to be-

lieve, however, that the contact from the beginning was with Platt Brush. For one thing, Henry Brush's congressional term did not commence until a full half year after Quitman left Hartwick. Second, Quitman's engagement to tutor Platt Brush's children—he had seven boys under twenty-five (four of them under ten)—would explain why an arrangement was made in the first place. Third, Quitman's legal and business arrangements in Ohio were primarily with Platt Brush. Quitman, moreover, did not like Henry Brush. JAQ Diary, 1820–1821, particularly June 3, 1820, Quitman Family Papers, SHC; *Fourth Census, 1820: Population*, Ohio, Delaware County, 91; *Scioto Gazette and Fredonian Chronicle* (Chillicothe), March 30, 1820.

24. Affidavit, November 2, 1820, about Albert Quitman "American Seaman," in JAQ Papers, MDA; Helen R. de Laporte (comp.), "Sketches of the Rhinebeck Precinct," Rhinebeck Records, V, 155; Wurtemburg Church History and Records, I, 1760–1855, pp.10–11, Dutchess County Historical Society; Minutes, Ministerium of New York, 1811, 1819, 1824, *passim*; Photograph of portrait in Quitman Family Papers, SHC; Frederick Henry Quitman to JAQ, September 15, 1821, in Claiborne, *Quitman*, I, 66; Kreider, *History of the United Lutheran Synod*, 40–47, 70–71.

25. Frederick Henry Quitman to JAQ, June 22, 1819, JAQ to his father, November 12, 1820, JAQ to his brother, September 2, 1821, in Claiborne, *Quitman*, I, 34, 53, 65.

26. Quoted in Louisa S. Quitman to JAQ, August 4, 1849, Quitman Family Papers, SHC.

27. JAQ Diary, October 21, 1819, in Quitman Family Papers, SHC. See R. Carlyle Buley, *The Old Northwest: Pioneer Period, 1815–1840* (2 vols.; Indianapolis, 1950); Malcolm J. Rohrbough, *The Land Office Business: The Settlement and Administration of American Public Lands, 1789–1837* (New York, 1968).

28. JAQ Diary, October 21–November 16, 1819, Quitman Family Papers, SHC. For William Griffith, who had served briefly as one of President John Adams' ill-fated "midnight judges," see *The Biographical Encyclopaedia of New Jersey of the Nineteenth Century* (Philadelphia, 1877), 47–48; Lucius Q. C. Elmer, *The Constitution and Government of the Province and State of New Jersey . . .* (Newark, 1872).

29. JAQ Diary, November 19–22, 1819, in Claiborne, *Quitman*, I, 42. Quitman was quoting Virgil's *Aeneid*, Book 3, line 714. Roughly: "This was my hardest ordeal, this is my goal." Claiborne apparently misread one word in Quitman's diary or Quitman's Latin was a bit deficient. "Extremis" should have been "extremus."

30. Thomas Hulme, *A Journal Made During a Tour in the Western Countries of America: September 30, 1818–August 7, 1819*, extracted from William Cobbett's *A Year's Residence in the United States of America* (London, 1828), in Reuben Gold Thwaites (ed.), *Early Western Travels, 1748–1846* (30 vols.; Cleveland, 1905–1906), X, 70, 71; James Flint, *Letters from America, Containing Observations on the Climate and Agriculture of the Western States, the Manners of the People, the Prospects of Emigrants, &c. &c.* (Edinburgh, 1822), in Thwaites (ed.), *Early Western Travels*, IX, 118–19; Chillicothe *Supporter*, November 10, December 1, 1819; *Scioto Gazette and Fredonian Chronicle* (Chillicothe), November 12, December 2, 1819, May 18, 1820; Morris Birbeck, *Notes on a Journey in America from the Coast of Virginia to the Territory of Illinois* (London, 1818), 52.

31. Federal Writers' Project of Ohio, *Chillicothe and Ross County* (N.p., 1938), 10, 13–14, 25, 32, 33, 46; Flint, *Letters from America*, 118–19; James M. Miller, *The Genesis of Western Culture: The Upper Ohio Valley, 1800–1825* (Columbus,

1938), 29–30; Hulme, *Journal*, 70, 71; *Narrative of Richard Lee Mason in the Pioneer West, 1819* (New York, n.d.), 25; John D. Barnhart, *Valley of Democracy: The Frontier versus the Plantation in the Ohio Valley, 1775–1818* (Bloomington, 1953), 122–23, 140; Marie Dickoré (ed.), *General Joseph Kerr of Chillicothe, Ohio* (Oxford, Ohio, 1941), 8; Randolph Chandler Downes, *Frontier Ohio, 1788–1803* (Columbus, Ohio, 1935), 81, 83, 155, 201, 203.

32. JAQ Diary, date uncertain, in Claiborne, *Quitman*, I, 42.

33. JAQ Diary, December 2, 8, 11, 14, 19, 1819, January 3, 4, 6, 7, 9, 11, 24, February 1, 2, 13, March 9, 17, 19, May 9, 13, 1820, Quitman Family Papers, SHC; JAQ to Louisa Quitman, June 26, 1820, in Claiborne, *Quitman*, I, 49. John wrote to his brother on May 1 that Brush had given him "the credit of having suggested some very pertinent hints to him in conducting his cases" at the Court of Common Pleas of Ross County (Claiborne, *Quitman*, I, 46).

34. JAQ Diary, January 3, February 2, April 5, May 8, 1820, Quitman Family Papers, SHC; Miller, *Genesis of Western Culture*, 58–61; Clement L. Martzolff (ed.), "The Autobiography of Thomas Ewing," *Ohio Archaeological and Historical Publications*, XXII (Columbus, 1913), 170; JAQ to his brother, May 1, 1820, in Claiborne, *Quitman*, I, 46. The Ohio Supreme Court was required by the state constitution to have a term once a year in each county. The state, in addition, was divided into three common pleas circuits, each with a court of common pleas. F. R. Aumann, "The Development of the Judicial System of Ohio," *Ohio Archaeological and Historical Quarterly*, XLI (1932), 202–203.

35. JAQ to his brother, March 29, 1820, in Claiborne, *Quitman*, I, 45; JAQ Diary, December 3, 10, 23, 1819, March 18, 25, April 7, 9, June 2, 20, 22, 1820, Quitman Family Papers, SHC. The fracas occurred when John rescued Brush from two assailants. John was called into court as a witness in the case.

36. JAQ Diary, November 29, December 4, 7, 11, 1819, January 2, 6, 9, 16, 26, February 13, 20, March 12, 1820, Quitman Family Papers, SHC. John's blasé approach to religion was nowhere better revealed than in the following: "The day closed in a beautiful evening. From seeing the sublime works of God, I felt an inclination to see also the beautiful; accordingly I visited the beauties of Chillicothe." JAQ Diary, February 3, 1820.

37. JAQ Diary, December 20, 26, 1819, January 2, 14–16, 18, 26, 28, 30, February 7, 16, 19, 22, 25, 26, March 1, 6, 31, April 11, May 30, June 4, 7, 8, 10, 11, 14, 16, 17, July 12, 1820, Quitman Family Papers, SHC.

38. JAQ Diary, May 23, 27, 1820, Quitman Family Papers, SHC; JAQ to William Quitman, June 24, 1820, in Claiborne, *Quitman*, I, 48; Rohrbough, *Land Office Business*, 130, 141.

39. JAQ Diary, June 17, July 13–16, 1820, Quitman Family Papers, SHC; JAQ to William Quitman, June 24, 1820, in Claiborne, *Quitman*, I, 48–49.

40. *Fourth Census, 1820: Population*, Ohio, Delaware Town, 126A; JAQ to his brother, August 16, 1820, in Claiborne, *Quitman*, I, 51; Ray E. Buckingham, *Delaware County Then and Now: An Informal History* (Delaware, Ohio, 1976), 1, 3, 228, 259, 261; W. H. Perrin and J. H. Battle, *History of Delaware County and Ohio* (Chicago, 1880), 185, 191, 329; JAQ Diary, February 18, March 18, November 18, 1820, Quitman Family Papers, SHC.

41. JAQ to his brother, December 10, 1820, February 23, September 2, 1821, in Claiborne, *Quitman*, I, 55, 58, 64; JAQ Diary, August 7, 8, 10–12, September 17,

26, 1820, Quitman Family Papers, SHC. John received $54 in fees for his services at the October, 1820, sales, and presumably earned money at other sales also. JAQ Diary, November 6, 1820.

42. JAQ Diary, July 25–31, August 10, 13, 23, September 12, October 13, 23, November 9, 25, December 12, 1820, March 6, 7, June 22, 24, 1821, Quitman Family Papers, SHC.

43. The main evidence for Quitman's pedagogical career in Delaware derives from Perrin and Battle's undocumented *History of Delaware County*, 246: "Quitman's Academic Grove was an institution that received its name from the proprietor, preceptor, etc., all in the person of John A. Quitman . . . and also from its being in the actual grove, with its fallen log seats, its tree columns, festooned with their wild grape hangings, and having the clear canopy of heaven above. The exact location . . . was on the promontory of high ground running south of the present [Ohio Wesleyan University] library building. Here was a cozy little opening in the dense woods around. . . . It was here that young Quitman took his pupils, the sons of a queer, eccentric old gentleman, whenever they could stealthily get there, for they were closely housed in town by the old gentleman." Buckingham later repeated this legend and embellished it: John's school now included other children in addition to Brush's. Buckingham, *Delaware County*, 181–82.

44. JAQ to his brother, February 23, 1821, in Claiborne, *Quitman*, I, 58; JAQ Diary, August 3, 9, 10, 18, 24, 30, 31, September 1, 8, 13, 14, October 16, 25, November 1, 8, 15, 29, December 13, 20, 25, 27, 1820, January 1, 5, March 13, July 4, August 4, 14, October 1, 1821, Quitman Family Papers SHC; JAQ to Frederick R. Backus, September 18, 1820, in Claiborne, *Quitman*, I, 52. An 1815 Ohio law mandated that all white males eighteen to forty-five had to serve in the militia. However, the law probably was not enforced in Delaware. John clearly indicated that he volunteered for the militia, and his company's title seems to indicate that it was of a volunteer nature. For the 1815 law, see Salmon P. Chase (ed.), *The Statutes of Ohio and of the Northwestern Territory, Adopted or Enacted from 1788 to 1833 Inclusive* . . . (3 vols.; Cincinnati, 1834), II, 871–91. Ohio militia records identified John's unit as the Second Rifle Company in the Third Regiment of the Second Brigade in the Seventh Division of the state militia system. Document dated July 27, 1821, in Series 9, Certificates of Election, Adjutant General, Ohio Militia, Ohio Historical Society, Columbus. John Hope Franklin, in *The Militant South, 1800–1861* (Cambridge, Mass., 1956), 38, 103, 105–106, 110–14, 209, has interpreted Quitman as a prime example of the militaristic impulse of the Old South; but it seems that Quitman's military career began in Ohio.

45. JAQ Diary, July 26–28, 1821, Quitman Family Papers, SHC.

46. JAQ Diary, May 23, 1820, Quitman Family Papers, SHC; JAQ to Frederick R. Backus, February 28, 1821, JAQ to Frederick Henry Quitman, May 7, 1821, JAQ to his brother, June 10, 1821, in Claiborne, *Quitman*, I, 59–63. John may have believed that a move to Natchez would bring him back into contact with Mary Griffith, with whom he had corresponded for a while after the keelboat trip. JAQ Diary, December 21, 22, 1819, January 9, February 21, 1820, Quitman Family Papers, SHC. Mary was still living after John's removal to Natchez, because she is mentioned in her father's 1823 will. However, she apparently returned to New Jersey with her mother, and John may never have seen her again. Will of William Griffith, September 3, 1823, Book C, Wills, 652ff, Surrogate's Office, Burlington County, New Jersey (copy provided by the State Library of New Jersey, Trenton).

47. JAQ to his brother, August 16, 1820, JAQ to Frederick R. Backus, September 18, 1820, in Claiborne, *Quitman*, I, 51, 52. John conveyed the land back to Brush, rather than pay the debt. Deed dated October 6, 1821, JAQ to Platt Brush, in Delaware County Deed Records, V, Delaware County Courthouse, Delaware, Ohio.

48. Francis S. Philbrick, *The Rise of the West, 1754–1830* (New York, 1965), 340–42; Rohrbough, *Land Office Business*, 137–40; Charles Hammond to John Wright, July 1, 1821, Charles Hammond Collection, Charles Hammond Microfilm Edition, Roll 1, Ohio Historical Society.

49. JAQ to Frederick R. Backus, February 26, 1821, JAQ to Frederick Henry Quitman, May 7, 1821, JAQ to his brother, June 10, 1821, in Claiborne, *Quitman*, I, 59–63; JAQ Diary, October 5, 1820, January 30, February 25, 1821, Quitman Family Papers, SHC.

50. JAQ to his brother, September 2, 1821, in Claiborne, *Quitman*, I, 65. Although John had no contract with Brush, he expected a bonus for all his work and he hoped Brush would give him the colt John had broken. Claiborne states that Quitman's total income in Ohio amounted to only $150 per year, and that Brush did provide "some aid" before John left town. JAQ to his brother, June 10, 1821, in Claiborne, *Quitman*, I, 64; Claiborne, *Quitman*, I, 67. John may have asked his father for funds, for his father wrote that he could "add nothing" to the payment from Hartwick. Frederick Henry Quitman to JAQ, September 15, 1821, in Claiborne, *Quitman*, I, 66.

51. JAQ Diary, November 5, 1821, Quitman Family Papers, SHC.

52. JAQ Diary, December 30, 1819, January 12, 15, 28, February 19, 25, April 18, 27, May 6, 16, 22, July 14, 19, August 3, October 13, November 16, 1820, March 13, 1821, Quitman Family Papers, SHC.

53. Portrait in JAQ Papers, MDA; Jackson *Mississippian*, April 21, 1848; Charles J. Peterson, *The Military Heroes of the War with Mexico: With a Narrative of the War* (Philadelphia, 1848), 261–62; JAQ Diary, February 9, 11, 24, March 1, 22, 1820, January 5, 1821, Scott's "The Violet," in Quitman's hand, dated Chillicothe, January 21, 1820, Quitman Family Papers, SHC; JAQ to William Quitman, March 29, 1820, JAQ to Anna Quitman, June 26, 1820, in Claiborne, *Quitman*, I, 45, 49. He also read the poetry of Robert Burns (JAQ Diary, November 25, 1820).

54. JAQ Diary, January 1, February 14, June 23, 30, October 8, November 27, 1820, Quitman Family Papers, SHC; Buckingham, *Delaware County*, 154; JAQ to William Quitman, June 24, 1820, JAQ to Anna Quitman, June 26, 1820, JAQ to his brother, December 10, 1820, JAQ to Frederick Henry Quitman, May 7, 1821, JAQ to his brother, June 10, 1821, in Claiborne, *Quitman*, I, 49, 54–56, 60, 64.

CHAPTER 2

1. JAQ Diary, November 25–December 3, 1821, Quitman Family Papers, SHC; JAQ to Ernest L. Hazelius, December 20, 1821, photostatic copy in Freiberger Library, Case Western Reserve University, Cleveland.

2. JAQ Diary, December 3, 1821, Quitman Family Papers, SHC; W. B. Dewees, *Letters from an Early Settler of Texas*, comp. Cara Cardelle (Louisville, 1852), 10; Estwick Evans, *A Pedestrious Tour . . . Through the Western States . . .* (Concord, 1819), in Reuben Gold Thwaites (ed.), *Early Western Travels, 1748–1846* (30 vols.; Cleveland, 1905–1906), VIII, 319; Virginia Park Matthias, "Natchez-Under-the-Hill as It Developed Under the Influence of the Mississippi River and the Natchez

Trace," *JMH*, VII (1945), 201–221; JAQ to Frederick Henry Quitman, January 16, 1822, in J. F. H. Claiborne, *Life and Correspondence of John A. Quitman* (2 vols.; New York, 1860), I, 71–72.

3. JAQ to Ernest L. Hazelius, December 20, 1821 (copy), Case Western Reserve Library; D. Clayton James, *Antebellum Natchez* (Baton Rouge, 1968), 3–76, 81.

4. James, *Antebellum Natchez*, 85, 114; Charles S. Sydnor, *A Gentleman of the Old Natchez Region: Benjamin L. C. Wailes* (Durham, 1938), 125; Joseph Miller Free, "The Ante-Bellum Theatre of the Old Natchez Region," *JMH*, V (1943), 14–27.

5. Morton Rothstein, "The Natchez Nabobs: Kinship and Friendship in an Economic Elite," in Hans L. Trefousse (ed.), *Toward a New View of America: Essays in Honor of Arthur C. Cole* (New York, 1977), 97–112; James, *Antebellum Natchez*, 51–52, 112, 136–61; *Fifth Census, 1830: Population*, Mississippi, Adams County, 19, 20; Lucianne Wood, "William Dunbar, Early Scientist," in Joan Warren McRaney and Carolyn Vance Smith (eds.), *Silhouettes of Settlers* (Natchez, 1974), 11–21; Laura D. S. Harrell, "Jockey Clubs and Race Tracks in Antebellum Mississippi, 1795–1861," *JMH*, XXVIII (1966), 304–318. James, *Antebellum Natchez*, 93–97, shows that beginning lawyers and "rising entrepreneurs" of modest incomes tended to dominate city politics.

6. JAQ to his brother, December 4, 1821, in Claiborne, *Quitman*, I, 70.

7. JAQ to Ernest L. Hazelius, December 20, 1821 (copy), Case Western Reserve Library; JAQ Diary, December 4–6, 1821, Quitman Family Papers, SHC; JAQ to his brother, December 4, 1821, February 1, 1823, in Claiborne, *Quitman*, I, 70, 77.

8. JAQ Diary, January 8, 18, February 22, March 25, 29, 31, April 3, 10, 13, May 20, 27, June 10, 1822, Quitman Family Papers, SHC; *Mississippi Republican* (Natchez), January 16, 1823; Partnership agreement, January 1, 1823, in JAQ Papers, UV; William B. Griffith to JAQ, n.d., in Claiborne, *Quitman*, I, 75. James McLendon, noting that the Griffith-Quitman practice was probably enhanced by Griffith's prestige as United States district attorney and justice of the Mississippi Supreme Court (starting in February, 1827), found that Griffith and Quitman handled a disproportionate number of cases in the Adams County Circuit Court. For instance, they handled 78 of 227 cases in the January, 1824, court term and 58 of 148 cases in the May, 1824, term. In addition, they each served as sole attorney in other cases. James H. McLendon, "John A. Quitman" (Ph.D. dissertation, University of Texas, 1949), 60.

9. JAQ to Frederick Henry Quitman, January 16, 1822, Platt Brush to JAQ, n.d., in Claiborne, *Quitman*, I, 71, 77; John T. McMurran to JAQ, February 24, 1823, J. F. H. Claiborne Papers, MDA; *Mississippi Free Trader* (Natchez), June 5, 1843.

10. JAQ to Frederick Henry Quitman, January 16, 1822, in Claiborne, *Quitman*, I, 72; JAQ Diary, January 23, 24, February 23, 25, March 7, 9, 10, 1822, Quitman Family Papers, SHC.

11. JAQ to Frederick Henry Quitman, January 16, August 12, 1822, JAQ to Platt Brush, August 23, 1823, in Claiborne, *Quitman*, I, 72, 73, 83–84; JAQ to Ernest L. Hazelius, December 20, 1821 (copy), Case Western Reserve Library.

12. JAQ Diary, December 24, 1821, Quitman Family Papers, SHC; JAQ to Frederick Henry Quitman, January 16, 1822, JAQ to Platt Brush, August 23, 1823, in Claiborne, *Quitman*, I, 72, 86.

13. JAQ to Platt Brush, August 23, 1823, in Claiborne, *Quitman*, I, 83–85.

14. Arthur Zilversmit, *The First Emancipation: The Abolition of Slavery in the North* (Chicago, 1967), 4, 13, 14–16, 19–20, 139, 146–47, 151, 180–84, 208–

213; "Record of Children Born of Slaves After the Fourth day of July One Thousand Seven Hundred and Ninety Nine," Rhinebeck Records, New York State Library, Albany; Poughkeepsie *Journal and Constitutional Republican*, June 10, 1807; Claiborne, *Quitman*, I, 28; Chauncey Rickard, "A Glimpse of Schoharie County in 1813," *Schoharie County Historical Review*, XVIII (May, 1954), 30.

15. Massive black revolt had struck the French West Indies colony of Saint Domingue in 1791, and Curaçao was also a slave society. J. F. H. Claiborne, who may have discussed the matter with John Quitman, asserted that Reverend Quitman had been distressed by French Revolutionary ideas and their implications of racial egalitarianism. Lutheran church documents, similarly, note that Reverend Quitman "on account of war disturbances had come to our states." Johannes Postma, "The Origins of African Slaves: The Dutch Activities on the Guinea Coast, 1695–1795," in Stanley L. Engerman and Eugene D. Genovese (eds.), *Race and Slavery in the Western Hemisphere* (Princeton, 1975), 35; Frances P. Karner, *The Sephardics of Curaçao: A Study of Socio-Cultural Patterns in Flux* (Assen, [The Netherlands], 1969), 10; Claiborne, *Quitman*, I, 17–19; Minutes of the Evangelical Lutheran Ministerium of the State of New York and Adjacent Parts, 1796 (Microfilm copy, courtesy of the Graduate Theological Union, Berkeley), 24.

16. *Second Census, 1800:* New York, Dutchess County, Rhynbeck [*sic*]; *Third Census, 1810:* New York, Dutchess County, Rhinebeck; "Record of Children," entry dated November 26, 1802; "Unbound diary fragments," n.d., Quitman Family Papers, SHC; Frederick Henry Quitman to JAQ, November 23, 1818, in Claiborne, *Quitman*, I, 31. As late as 1830, the Quitman household in Rhinebeck still had a black (a woman between the ages of twenty-four and thirty-five) who presumably did servants' tasks. *Fifth Census, 1830: Population*, New York, Dutchess County, Rhinebeck.

17. W[illiam] Faux, *Memorable Days in America: Being a Journal of a Tour to the United States . . .* (London, 1823), in Thwaites (ed.), *Early Western Travels*, XI, 167; Chillicothe *Supporter*, October 6, 1819, February 2, 9, March 8, May 3, November 10, 1820; *Scioto Gazette and Fredonian Chronicle* (Chillicothe), November 12, December 24, 31, 1819, January 14, June 15, 1820; *Fourth Census, 1820: Population*, Ohio, Delaware Town, 126A, Delaware County, 91.

18. Fletcher Melvin Green, *The Role of the Yankee in the Old South* (Athens, 1972), 5, 24–26, 131–32; Joseph A. Farnsworth to I. D. Farnsworth, December 14, 1828, Isaac T. Farnsworth Papers, DU; John Black to JAQ, January 2, 1834, Claiborne Papers, MDA; Frances Anne Kemble, *Journal of a Residence on a Georgian Plantation in 1838–1839*, ed. John A. Scott (Paper ed.; New York, 1975), 46.

19. JAQ Diary, January 22, 1822, Quitman Family Papers, SHC.

20. JAQ to Frederick Henry Quitman, August 12, 1822, in Claiborne, *Quitman*, I, 73; "Table of the Payne & Turner families made by Henry Fielding Turner, May 29, 1893," in JAQ Papers, MDA; Clarence Edwin Carter (comp. and ed.), *The Territorial Papers of the United States* (25 vols.; Washington, D.C., 1934–62), V, 116, 139, 263, 265; Dunbar Rowland, *Mississippi: Comprising Sketches of Counties, Towns, Events, Institutions, and Persons, Arranged in Cyclopedic Form* (3 vols.; Atlanta, 1907), II, 830–32; Woodville *Republican*, November 22, 1834; James, *Antebellum Natchez*, 95; Deeds dated April 11, June 6, 1810, January 14, 28, February 23, 1811, January 13, 1812, March 7, 1818, in Deed Records, Warren County, 1811–1826, Vol. ABC, Microfilm Roll 107, MDA; Personal Tax Rolls, Mississippi, Adams County, 1823, MDA; Edward Turner to Gideon Fitz, April 20, 1833 (copy),

"Family Record," and genealogy, Lovell Family Papers, UnS. Tax records listed the Henry Turner estate in Adams County in 1824 as consisting of fifty acres, two town lots, two carriages, and five slaves. Personal Tax Rolls, Mississippi, Adams County, 1824, MDA. Henry Turner died in 1821, and his will designated his wife Sarah (Baker) Turner, her brother Love Baker, and his brother Fielding Turner as executors. Sarah subsequently married Jared D. Fyler. Will of Henry Turner, November 26, 1821, Order of Probate Judge Robert Ogden of Concordia Parish, Louisiana, April 25, 1827, making Sarah and Jared Fyler executors of Fielding Turner's property in Concordia Parish, JAQ Papers, MDA; Legal document, November 23, 1821, Quitman Family Papers, SHC. Fielding Turner practiced law for a while in New Orleans, and in 1828 moved back to Kentucky, where he died, a large landowner, in 1843. Theodosia Turner was Edward Turner's daughter by his first marriage. His wife had died in 1811, and in 1812 he had married Elizabeth Baker.

21. JAQ Diary, January 25, February 28, 1822, Quitman Family Papers, SHC; Carl Bridenbaugh, *Myths and Realities: Societies of the Colonial South* (Baton Rouge, 1952), 11–12. Surviving volumes from Edward Turner's library show his diverse scholarly interests. They include *The Congressional Record*, *The Works of Benjamin Franklin*, a run of the *North British Review*, John Bunyan's *Pilgrim's Progress*, issues of the *Edinburgh Review*, and Adolph Ludvig Koeppen's *The World in the Middle Ages* (New York, 1854), and are now in the library of Dr. Thomas Gandy, Natchez.

22. JAQ to his brother, February 1, 1823, in Claiborne, *Quitman*, I, 78; JAQ to Eliza Turner, September 20, 1824, Quitman Family Papers, SHC.

23. JAQ to Eliza Turner, September 20, November 17, 26, 1824, [?] to Sarah Turner, November 23, 1824, Quitman Family Papers, SHC.

24. Contract, December 20, 1824, JAQ Papers, UV. John and Eliza apparently maintained separate accounts throughout their marriage. See JAQ to Eliza Quitman, April 11, 1856, Lovell Family Papers, UnS.

25. Frederick Henry Quitman to JAQ, February 12, 1825, Quitman Family Papers, SHC.

26. Statement of expenses for a journey to the northern states in 1825, "Notes" on northern trip in "Unbound diary fragments," in Quitman Family Papers, SHC; *British Poets* (inscribed by John A. Quitman) in library of Dr. Thomas Gandy, Natchez. Apparently Eliza's mother, Sarah Turner, left Natchez with John and Eliza, and later went her own way in the North, visiting her family and putting Eliza's brothers in a Trenton, New Jersey, school operated by J.D. Fyler, whom she would later marry. See Richard Stockton to Robert Stockton, May 17, 1825, Claiborne Papers, MDA; Sarah Turner to Eliza Quitman, July 4, 1825, Quitman Family Papers, SHC.

27. JAQ to Frederick Henry Quitman, January 29, 1826, Quitman Family Papers, SHC.

28. *Mississippi Republican* (Natchez), March 3, December 15, 1824; Deed Records, Adams County, Vol. P, pp. 61–63, microfilm copy, MDA; JAQ to Frederick Henry Quitman, January 29, 1826, Quitman Family Papers, SHC; Jackson *Mississippian*, December 10, 1847, May 10, 1850; Caroline C. Lovell, "Natchez Notes" (Typescript in Quitman Family Papers, SHC); Inventory-Nomination Form for Monmouth, National Register of Historic Places; Mary Wallace Crocker, *Historic Architecture in Mississippi* (Jackson, 1973), xi. John later purchased 8.15 additional acres in March, 1827. Deed Records, Adams County, Vol. P, p. 413, microfilm copy, MDA.

29. Annie Rosalie Quitman to Louisa T. Chadbourne, December 8, 1857, JAQ Papers, LSU.

CHAPTER 3

1. JAQ to William Quitman, March 29, 1820, in J. F. H. Claiborne, *Life and Correspondence of John A. Quitman* (2 vols.; New York, 1860), I, 44.

2. Quitman had not been politically active in Ohio, though one of his letters home from Chillicothe suggests that he may have pretended to be a Republican—which was vastly more popular at the time than the dying Federalist party—in order to enhance his social acceptability: "They think me a clever fellow and a *good Republican*, because I turn out to musters and wear a straw hat cocked up behind!" Quitman's father held elitist, and apparently Federalist, political views; it is unclear how much Quitman was influenced by his father's political ideology. JAQ to William Quitman, March 29, 1820, Frederick Henry Quitman to JAQ, May 20, 1820, September 15, 1821, in Claiborne, *Quitman*, I, 44, 47–48, 66.

3. John Nevitt, Clermont Journal, January 1, 1827, SHC; JAQ to Eliza Quitman, March 21 [31], 1825, JAQ Memoranda Book, August 31, September 2, 1827, Quitman Family Papers, SHC; JAQ to Eliza Quitman, June 27, 1826, Bills of sale, May 26, November 22, December 2, 1828, Lovell Family Papers, UnS; W[illiam] C. Harris to JAQ, August 2, 1828, J. F. H. Claiborne Papers, MDA. One contemporary said that he heard Quitman claim several times that the partnership with Griffith had a $54,000 profit in less than six years. Henry S. Foote, *Casket of Reminiscences* (Washington, D.C., 1874), 345.

4. JAQ to William Quitman, March 29, 1820, in Claiborne, *Quitman*, I, 44.

5. JAQ to his brother, February 1, 1823, in Claiborne, *Quitman*, I, 78; Commission, January 10, 1823, in JAQ Papers, UV.

6. Arrell M. Gibson, "The Indians of Mississippi," in Richard Aubrey McLemore (ed.), *A History of Mississippi* (2 vols.; Jackson, 1973), I, 69–89.

7. *Mississippi Free Trader* (Natchez), April 26, 1845; *Mississippi Republican* (Natchez), October 20, 1824; Natchez *Ariel*, February 20, 1826; Fountain Winston to JAQ, June 30, 1827, Claiborne Papers, MDA; *Godspeed's Biographical and Historical Memoirs of Mississippi* (2 vols.; Chicago, 1891), I, 96.

8. *Mississippi Republican* (Natchez), October 20, 1824; Natchez *Ariel*, July 7, 1826.

9. Natchez *Ariel*, March 31, November 24, 1826, March 29, 1828; R. Somerby to JAQ, February 8, 1827, Isaac Caldwell to JAQ, April 11, 1828, Claiborne Papers, MDA; JAQ Diary, November 7, 1821, Quitman Family Papers, SHC; Emmett N. Thomas (ed.), *Proceedings of the Grand Lodge, F & A.M. of the State of Mississippi (1818–1914)* (Atlanta, 1914), 12–16; Natchez *Gazette*, January 7, 1826; *Mississippi Free Trader* (Natchez), April 27, 1845; Michael de L. Landon, "The Mississippi State Bar Association, 1821–1825: The First in the Nation," *JMH*, XLII (1980), 222–42; Charles Stietenroth, *One Hundred Years with "Old Trinity" Church, Natchez, Miss.* (Natchez, 1922), 55, 67. Quitman was Masonic Grand Master from 1826 to 1836 and again in 1845–1846; he served on the Trinity Church vestry from 1829 to 1831 and was active in church affairs even earlier. Whether the antiduelling society actually prevented duels is unclear. But Quitman seems to have adhered somewhat to its code later in his life. See Robert E. May, "John A. Quitman and the Southern Martial Spirit," *JMH*, XLI (1979), 174.

10. William L. Barney, *The Road to Secession: A New Perspective on the Old South* (New York, 1972), 85–100.

11. *Mississippi Republican* (Natchez), April 21, 1824; JAQ Memoranda Book, August 19, 1827, Quitman Family Papers, SHC; James D. Richardson (comp.), *Messages and Papers of the Presidents, 1789–1904* (10 vols.; Washington, D.C., 1899–1904), II, 299–317; Edwin A. Miles, *Jacksonian Democracy in Mississippi* (Chapel Hill, 1960), 8. Quitman continued his support of the Bank the following year while serving in the state legislature. *Laws of the State of Mississippi*, 1828, p. 137; *Mississippi House Journal*, 1828, pp. 257–58.

12. D. Clayton James, *Antebellum Natchez* (Baton Rouge, 1968), 131–32; Charles Gyles to Powhatan Ellis, August 13, 1827, Powhatan Ellis Papers, UT; Claiborne, *Quitman*, I, 91–92; M. Philip Lucas, "Beyond McCormick and Miles: The Pre-Partisan Political Culture of Mississippi," *JMH*, XLIV (1982), 329–48. It is possible, however, that some votes were determined by public knowledge that Quitman and Bingaman had supported John Quincy Adams for president, and that Green was a proponent of Andrew Jackson.

13. JAQ to his brother, December 6, 1827, in Claiborne, *Quitman*, I, 88–89; JAQ to Eliza Quitman, November 1, 1826, JAQ Memoranda Book, October 19, 27, 1827, Quitman Family Papers, SHC; John T. McMurran to Powhatan Ellis, October 31, 1827, Ellis Papers; "Table of the Payne & Turner families made by Henry Fielding Turner, May 29, 1893," JAQ Papers, MDA; Claiborne, *Quitman*, II, 287. McMurran married Mary Louisa Turner, Turner's first child by his second wife. The marriage made Quitman and McMurran cousins-in-law.

14. JAQ to Eliza Quitman, January 4, 7, 12, 15, 1828, Quitman Family Papers, SHC; John I. Guion to JAQ, July 13, 1833, Claiborne Papers, MDA; Deed of purchase, February 5, 1827, in Lovell Family Papers, UnS.

15. JAQ to Eliza Quitman, January 7, 8, 12, 26, 1828, Quitman Family Papers, SHC.

16. Robert V. Haynes, "The Road to Statehood," in McLemore (ed.), *History of Mississippi*, I, 249–50; Miles, *Jacksonian Democracy*, 23, 33; Robert C. Weems, Jr., "Mississippi's First Banking System," *JMH*, XXIX (1967), 386–408. The bank's charter mandated that the state would not establish any rival institution prior to 1841.

17. Miles, *Jacksonian Democracy*, 18–19, 27; Griffin H. Holliman to JAQ, August 12, 1830, Claiborne Papers, MDA. The "New Purchase" represented the most recent of the Choctaw cessions.

18. Miles, *Jacksonian Democracy*, 16, 28.

19. Robert J. Walker to Powhatan Ellis, March 20, 1828, Hiram G. Runnels to Powhatan Ellis, September 13, 1827, Ellis Papers; George Dangerfield, *The Era of Good Feelings* (New York, 1952), 119–20, 399; Richardson (comp.), *Messages and Papers of the Presidents*, II, 315–16.

20. William Haile to Powhatan Ellis, July 30, 1827, Ellis Papers; John C. Calhoun to William Haile, September 28, 1828, in Clyde N. Wilson and W. Edwin Hemphill (eds.), *The Papers of John C. Calhoun* (12 vols.; Columbia, S.C., 1959–79), X, 424; William W. Freehling, *Prelude to Civil War: The Nullification Controversy in South Carolina, 1816–1836* (New York, 1965), 154–59.

21. William Haile to Powhatan Ellis, July 30, 1827, Hiram G. Runnels to the Mississippi Congressional Delegation, January 23, 1828, Ellis Papers; Mary E. Young, *Redskins, Ruffleshirts, and Rednecks: Indian Allotments in Alabama and*

Mississippi, 1830–1860 (Norman, 1961), 5–10, 13–14, 23–26, 39–40; Danger-field, *Era of Good Feelings*, 390–91; Marie B. Hecht, *John Quincy Adams: A Personal History of an Independent Man* (New York, 1972), 449–50; *Laws of the State of Mississippi*, 1828, approved February 11, 1828; *Mississippi House Journal*, 1828, pp. 182, 220; Mississippi Legislative Records, 1828, RG 47, No. 326, MDA.

22. *Mississippi House Journal*, 1828, pp. 6, 13, 36, 51; JAQ to Eliza Quitman, January 17, 1828, Lovell Family Papers, UnS.

23. A. Sprague to JAQ, January 28, 1828, Claiborne Papers, MDA; *Mississippi House Journal*, 1828, pp. 32, 117, 207; Mississippi Legislative Records, 1828, RG 47, No. 326, MDA.

24. *Mississippi House Journal*, 1828, p. 66; JAQ to Eliza Quitman, January 12, 1828, Quitman Family Papers, SHC; JAQ to John T. McMurran, February 9, 1828, Claiborne Papers, MDA.

25. *Mississippi House Journal*, 1828, pp. 14–15, 101–102, 111, 130, 167, 174, 243–44, 247, 268, 269, 332, 347; JAQ to John T. McMurran, February 9, 1828, Claiborne Papers, MDA; John Ray Skates, Jr., *A History of the Mississippi Supreme Court* (Jackson, 1973), 9. The bill giving Natchez a supreme court session did pass the state senate and was signed into law.

26. *Mississippi House Journal*, 1828, pp. 305, 319–21, 352, 353; Mississippi Legislative Records, 1828, RG 47, No. 326, *MDA; Laws of the State of Mississippi*, 1828, pp. 72–75.

27. JAQ to Frederick Henry Quitman, January 29, 1826, JAQ to Eliza Quitman, January 15, February 2, 9, April 22, 1828, Quitman Family Papers, SHC; "Family Record," Lovell Family Papers, UnS; Natchez *Statesman & Gazette*, July 24, 1828; Natchez *Ariel*, July 26, 1828.

28. *Laws of the State of Mississippi*, 1827, pp. 131, 144; George Adams to JAQ, September 20, 1828, Claiborne Papers, MDA. Quitman was Mississippi's second chancellor. His appointment was confirmed by the legislature early in 1829. *Mississippi House Journal*, 1829, p. 153; Commission, February 3, 1829, JAQ Papers, UV.

29. JAQ to Eliza Quitman, December 1, 1828, Quitman Family Papers, SHC; *James C. Dickson* v. *Andrew E. Beaty, Thomas Farrar* v. *Paris A. Hickman & Joseph Andrews, Silas Brown* v. *William A. Old and John R. Bedford*, Supreme Court of Chancery, Record Book, 1827–1829, RG 8, Vol. 46, *John Hayes* v. *Asa Carman, Peter Brewer* v. *Sarah Brewer*, Superior Court of Chancery, Record Book, 1833–1834, RG 68, Vol. 66, MDA; Franklin Plummer to JAQ, December 19, 1828, Claiborne Papers, MDA; JAQ to Franklin Plummer, January 12, 1829, in Claiborne, *Quitman*, I, 93–94; Foote, *Casket of Reminiscences*, 346.

30. Stephen Duncan to Powhatan Ellis, January 23, 1828, White Turpin to Powhatan Ellis, January 13, 1829, Ellis Papers; John I. Guion to JAQ, August 5, 1830, Claiborne Papers, MDA; Richardson (comp.), *Messages and Papers of the Presidents*, II, 456–59; Ronald N. Satz, *American Indian Policy in the Jacksonian Era* (Lincoln, 1975), 31, 66–79; Young, *Redskins*, 31–32. Technically the Dancing Rabbit Creek Treaty included provisions allowing individual Choctaws to remain in Mississippi on individual plots of land. Thousands chose to take advantage of these provisions, but most Choctaws were cheated out of their allotted lands through various means. Some of these dispossessed Choctaws, rather than move west, remained in the state as impoverished migrant agricultural workers. See Satz, *American Indian Policy*, 82–87.

31. JAQ to Franklin Plummer, January 12, 1829, in Claiborne, *Quitman*, I, 94; Miles, *Jacksonian Democracy*, 56.

32. Edward Turner to JAQ, July 4, 1830, JAQ to Henry Clay, April 3, 1830, Claiborne Papers, MDA; JAQ to J. F. H. Claiborne, October 25, 1830, in Claiborne, *Quitman*, I, 96–97; J. F. H. Claiborne to Richard Abbey, July 12, 1879, in C. E. Cain (ed.), "Letter from J. F. H. Claiborne to Richard Abbey," *JMH*, VI (1944), 50.

CHAPTER 4

1. Jackson *Mississippian*, June 23, 1854.

2. John I. Guion to JAQ, December 10, 1827, J. F. H. Claiborne Papers, MDA; Deed Records, Adams County, Vol. R, pp. 572–75, 684, copies in MDA; James P. Shenton, *Robert John Walker: A Politician from Jackson to Lincoln* (New York, 1961), 13–14; Jefferson College Papers, "Archives," Boxes 4, 13, 14, MDA. John G. Rowan was Quitman's partner in the sheriff's sale speculation.

3. Deeds of sale, October 16, 1828, April 24, 1829, Conveyance Book E, pp. 27, 79, Office of the Clerk of Court, Terrebonne Parish, Houma, La.; [William Wood], *Autobiography of William Wood* (2 vols.; New York, 1895), I, 460–62; Leonidas Polk to Susan S. Prentiss, April 7, 1841, Leonidas Polk Papers, UnS; Seargent Smith Prentiss to William Prentiss, April 9, 1829, in [G. L. Prentiss (ed.)], *Memoir of S. S. Prentiss* (2 vols.; New York, 1856), I, 94–95; Thomas R. Shields to Powhatan Ellis, March 16, 1832, Powhatan Ellis Papers, UT; Thibodaux *Minerva*, October 8, 1853; F. Henry Quitman to JAQ, February 16, 1845, F. Henry Quitman to Mary Quitman, June 11, 1864, M-N. Quitman also joined Duncan and Robert Walker in spending $1,600 to gain title to 600 acres of Terrebonne Parish land on Bayou Petit Terrebonne, and spent $3,000 on his own to purchase a 320-acre tract from Henry C. McNeil on Grand Caillou near the tracts he purchased with Bell. Deeds of sale, October 9, 1828, Conveyance Book D, pp. 414–16, and April 16, 1829, Conveyance Book G, p. 494.

4. JAQ to Eliza Quitman, March 20, 25, 1829, Quitman Family Papers, SHC.

5. JAQ to Eliza Quitman, March 25, 1831, JAQ to Albert Quitman, February 4, 1832, August 31, November 19, 1833, Albert Quitman to JAQ, April 3, 1832, Quitman Family Papers, SHC; Deed of probate sale, April 28, 1831, Conveyance Book F, p. 216; Deeds of sale, April 22, 1833, September 5, 1834, Conveyance Book G, pp. 116, 176, August 9, 1837, Conveyance Book H, p. 79; Albert Quitman to JAQ, March 25, October 9, 1833, Henry Quitman to JAQ, August 16, 1833, Lovell Family Papers, UnS; Philip F. Mayer to JAQ, June 24, 1833, Claiborne Papers, MDA. The September, 1834, purchase cost Quitman $2,000. Terms for the purchase from Walker were $2,000 down, and two separate $1,728 payments (due on April 12, 1839, and April 12, 1840).

6. Deed Records, Adams County, Vol. U, pp. 414–16, Vol. W, p. 109, Vol. X, pp. 54–55, copies in MDA; JAQ to Henry Quitman, April 30, 1835, Springfield Plantation Book, December 25, 27, 28, 30, 1833, February 11, August 14, 1834, Quitman Family Papers, SHC. By 1838, according to his Springfield Plantation Book, a recent purchase had brought the total acreage up to 2,000.

7. JAQ to Henry Quitman, April 30, 1835, Quitman Family Papers, SHC.

8. Stephen B. Oates, *The Fires of Jubilee: Nat Turner's Fierce Rebellion* (New York, 1975), 129–35.

9. William K. Scarborough, "Heartland of the Cotton Kingdom," in Richard Aubrey McLemore (ed.), *A History of Mississippi* (2 vols.; Jackson, 1973), I, 326–27; Woodville *Republican*, October 19, 1833; *Mississippi Democrat* (Woodville), May 28, July 9, August 31, September 17, November 26, 1831.

10. Norwood Allen Kerr, "The Mississippi Colonization Society (1831–1860)," *JMH*, XLIII (1981), 1–30.

11. William W. Freehling, *Prelude to Civil War: The Nullification Controversy in South Carolina, 1816–1836* (New York, 1965), 11, 27–32, 49–63, 82, 125, and *passim*.

12. JAQ Memoranda Book, undated 1830 entries, Quitman Family Papers, SHC; JAQ to Gerard C. Brandon, December 31, 1829, quoted in *Southern Galaxy* (Natchez), April 1, 1830; JAQ to J. F. H. Claiborne, January 8, 1830, in J. F. H. Claiborne, *Life and Correspondence of John A. Quitman* (2 vols.; New York, 1860), I, 103–104; Lewis Cecil Gray, *History of Agriculture in the Southern United States* (2 vols., 1933; rpr. Gloucester, 1958), I, 531.

13. JAQ to J. F. H. Claiborne, July 31, August 6, 1831, in Claiborne, *Quitman*, I, 105–110.

14. Powhatan Ellis to JAQ, January 9, 1831, Claiborne Papers, MDA; J. F. H. Claiborne to JAQ, October 20, 1830, in Claiborne, *Quitman*, I, 95–96.

15. JAQ to J. F. H. Claiborne, August 6, 1831, in Claiborne, *Quitman*, I, 107–108. Actually, Clay was a Mason, and in 1832 the Anti-Masons formed their own political party and nominated William Wirt for president.

16. B. B. French to his sister, May 12, 1834, B. B. French Papers, LC; Mack Swearingen, *The Early Life of George Poindexter: A Story of the First Southwest* (New Orleans, 1934); Edwin A. Miles, *Jacksonian Democracy in Mississippi* (Chapel Hill, 1960), 48–49; Samuel Hathorn to Powhatan Ellis, March 31, 1832, Ellis Papers. Poindexter, like Quitman, had originally been a supporter of John Quincy Adams.

17. JAQ to J. F. H. Claiborne, August 6, 1831, JAQ to James K. Cook, August 28, 1832, in Claiborne, *Quitman*, I, 107, 131; Cleo Hearon, "Nullification in Mississippi," *PMHS*, XII (1912), 43; John Nevitt, Clermont Journal, January 1, 1827, July 14, 1832, SHC. In 1831, Quitman had been offered the directorship of the Natchez branch of the Bank of the United States. Samuel A. [?], Cashier (Natchez Branch), to JAQ, February 7, 1831, Claiborne Papers, MDA.

The ticket Quitman declined to serve on would have been pledged specifically to the Bank rather than to Henry Clay. The ticket never actually materialized. Years later, Quitman said that in 1832 he had voted for Jackson, but on a ticket with Philip P. Barbour of Virginia, not Van Buren, as vice-presidential candidate. Claiborne, *Quitman*, I, 212–13; Miles, *Jacksonian Democracy*, 72.

18. JAQ to [?], March 19, 1842, in Claiborne, *Quitman*, I, 192–93; *Mississippi Democrat* (Woodville), May 28, 1831; JAQ to Eliza Quitman, January 14, 1843, Quitman Family Papers, SHC.

CHAPTER 5

1. JAQ to Eliza Quitman, September 12, 16, October 2, 12, 1832, Quitman Family Papers, SHC; Jackson *State Rights Banner*, June 13, 1833; Vicksburg *Whig*, November 3, 1843; John D. Freeman to JAQ, January 5, 1855, JAQ Papers, HU.

Wilbourne Magruder Drake characterized Quitman as the convention's "outstanding and most useful member." Drake, "The Mississippi Constitutional Convention of 1832," *Journal of Southern History*, XXIII (1957), 360.

2. Drake, "Mississippi Constitutional Convention," 354–56; Edwin A. Miles, *Jacksonian Democracy in Mississippi* (Chapel Hill, 1960), 35; Peter L. Fortune, Jr., "The Formative Period," in Richard Aubrey McLemore (ed.), *A History of Mississippi* (2 vols.; Jackson, 1973), I, 279.

3. JAQ to Albert Quitman, February 4, 1832, JAQ to Eliza Quitman, August 19, 1832, Louisa Quitman to JAQ, November 18, 1832, Quitman Family Papers, SHC; JAQ to his brother, July 23, 1832, in J. F. H. Claiborne, *Life and Correspondence of John A. Quitman* (2 vols.; New York, 1860), I, 131–32; "Table of the Payne & Turner families made by Henry Fielding Turner, May 29, 1893," JAQ Papers, MDA.

4. *"Public Meeting"* call by "MANY CITIZENS," *"To the Citizens of Adams County,"* by JAQ (July 17, 1832), in Claiborne, *Quitman*, I, 112–14. Calhoun's response to secession charges was remarkably similar to Quitman's. See John C. Calhoun to David Franklin Caldwell, May 1, 1831, John Caldwell Calhoun Papers, DU.

5. Proceedings of the July 19, 1832, meeting, in Claiborne, *Quitman*, I, 114–15; John Nevitt, Clermont Journal, July 14, 1832, SHC.

6. JAQ, "To the Electors of Adams County," in Claiborne, *Quitman*, I, 116–26; *Natchez*, August 10, 1832; JAQ to Eliza Quitman, August 19, 1832, Quitman Family Papers, SHC. Quitman disregarded one correspondent's advice that Quitman focus on nullification and prove that the doctrine was not an "outlandish beast with horns and a long tail and saucer eyes." See Christopher Adams Parker to JAQ, July [?], 1832, J. F. H. Claiborne Papers, MDA.

7. *Journal of the Convention of the State of Mississippi Held in the Town of Jackson* (Jackson, 1832) 3–4, 14–16; JAQ to Eliza Quitman, September 12, 16, 23, 1832, Quitman Family Papers, SHC. Judge Black represented the district including Jones, Perry, Greene, Hancock, Jackson, and Wayne counties.

8. *Journal of the Convention*, 52–55, 66–68. Quitman's report recommended two high courts for the state: a supreme court and a superior court of equity (the latter to have original jurisdiction in equity matters involving sums over $500). At the convention, "Whole hogs" favored election of all judges, while "half hogs" wanted the popular election of county and circuit judges. The terminology was used by delegate Stephen Duncan. Drake, "Mississippi Constitutional Convention," 359, 360n.

9. JAQ to Eliza Quitman, October 2, 1832, Quitman Family Papers, SHC; *Journal of the Convention*, 121, 128, 149–50, 151–52.

10. *Journal of the Convention*, 28, 79, 81, 190–91, 192, 194, 259, 260; JAQ to Eliza Quitman, September 23, 1832, Quitman Family Papers, SHC. Other democratic reforms encompassed the outlawing of property qualifications for officeholding and voting, and changing the basis of senatorial representation from free white taxable inhabitants to free white inhabitants. Democratization included opening up politics more to the young. The convention adopted twenty-one as the minimum age for a state representative, despite an effort—supported by Quitman—to set the minimum age at twenty-five. *Journal of the Convention*, 76.

11. JAQ to Eliza Quitman, October 2, 1832, Quitman Family Papers, SHC, *Journal of the Convention*, 28–29, 49, 50, 57, 173–74.

12. JAQ to Eliza Quitman, September 23, October 2, 8, 12, 18 [28?], 1832, Quitman Family Papers, SHC; *Journal of the Convention*, 289–90, 299, 302–304. The nine other delegates against the constitution's adoption all came from the Mississippi River counties and the Piney Woods counties.

13. Woodville *Republican*, January 5, 1833; John T. Black to JAQ, January 23, 1833, Frederick Quackenboss to JAQ, May 1, 1833, Claiborne Papers, MDA. Quackenboss, having moved to Mississippi to become a lawyer, stayed at Monmouth and helped Eliza while Quitman was at the convention. Quitman, subsequently, gave him a loan so that he could set up a law practice at Manchester in Yazoo County.

Quitman claimed on two separate occasions during the winter that he would have preferred retiring from the judiciary, but that he was bowing to the public will in consenting to run. Woodville *Republican*, January 5, 1833; JAQ to Nathan G. Howard *et al.*, February 28, 1833, Nathan G. Howard Papers, MDA.

14. John Ray Skates, Jr., *A History of the Mississippi Supreme Court* (Jackson, 1973), 15; Miles, *Jacksonian Democracy*, 42–43; JAQ to J. Fenwick Brent, March 22, 1845, in Claiborne, *Quitman*, I, 128. Quitman's new commission as chancellor was dated June 10, 1833. He took his oath of office on June 14. Legal documents, in JAQ Papers, UV.

CHAPTER 6

1. JAQ to Eliza Quitman, March 7, 11, 1833, Louisa Quitman to JAQ, May 19, 1833, Quitman Family Papers, SHC; Natchez *Courier*, May 3, 1833.

2. JAQ to his sister, May 21, 1833, Felix Huston to JAQ, June 16, 1833, in J. F. H. Claiborne, *Life and Correspondence of John A. Quitman* (2 vols.; New York, 1860), I, 132–33, 133n–134n; "Table of the Payne & Turner families made by Henry Fielding Turner, May 29, 1893," JAQ Papers, MDA; JAQ to Henry Quitman, August 31, 1833, Louisa Quitman to JAQ, August 16, 1833, "Family Record," Lovell Family Papers, UnS; Philip F. Mayer to JAQ, June 24, 1833, J. F. H. Claiborne Papers, MDA.

3. Lucie Robertson Bridgforth, "Mississippi's Response to Nullification, 1833," *JMH*, XLV (1983), 1–21; Jackson *State Rights Banner*, June 13, 1833; *Congressional Globe*, 35th Cong., 2nd Sess., 225. For Quitman's admiration of Calhoun as an ideologically pure conservative who refused to appease mass democracy, see JAQ to J. F. H. Claiborne, January 27, 1840, in Claiborne, *Quitman*, I, 188.

4. Jackson *State Rights Banner*, January 24, 1834; Isaac Caldwell to George Poindexter, January 29, 1834, Claiborne Papers, MDA; Jackson *Mississippian*, January 24, 31, May 2, 30, 1834; Edwin A. Miles, *Jacksonian Democracy in Mississippi* (Chapel Hill, 1960), 68.

5. Jackson *Mississippian*, May 23, 1834; Woodville *Republican*, June 7, 1834; Cleo Hearon, "Nullification in Mississippi," *PMHS*, XII (1912), 59. Hearon, pp. 60–61, portrays Mississippi nullifiers as politicians who, having already broken with President Jackson, were trying to preserve their political fortunes. But some nullifiers fell out with the administration precisely because they became nullifiers. See, for instance, John Black to JAQ, March 2, 1833, Claiborne Papers, MDA.

6. Thomas Brown, "Southern Whigs and the Politics of Statesmanship, 1833–1841," *Journal of Southern History*, XLVI (1980), 363–64; Arthur Charles Cole, *The Whig Party in the South* (1913; rpr. Gloucester, 1962), 1–38; James E. Winston,

"The Mississippi Whigs and the Tariff, 1834–1844," *Mississippi Valley Historical Review*, XXII (1936), 570–508. Calhoun never considered himself a Whig in the technical sense of party membership, but he worked with the Whigs against Jackson.

7. John Black to JAQ, June 3, 1834, Claiborne Papers, MDA; Jackson *Mississippian*, April 19, 1834; Miles, *Jacksonian Democracy*, 72, 77–78, 84. Miles explains that Poindexter's pro-Bank stance may have been influenced by loans which the Bank provided him under very favorable—if not illegal—conditions.

8. Miles, *Jacksonian Democracy*, 83.

9. Jackson *Mississippian*, June 20, 27, July 25, 1834. The *Mississippian*, August 8, 1834, also claimed to have learned from intimate acquaintances of Quitman that Quitman had favored protective tariffs during the period when he had supported John Quincy Adams.

10. JAQ to F. L. Claiborne, September 5, 1834 (copy in the hand of Quitman's secretary, transcribed on September 1, 1855), Quitman Family Papers, SHC; JAQ to James K. Cook, August 28, 1832, in Claiborne, *Quitman*, I, 131. Later in his career, Quitman again suggested that he had never really become a Whig. See Claiborne, *Quitman*, I, 213.

11. Supreme Court of Chancery, Northern District, 1831–1834, RG 8, Vol. 47, MDA; JAQ to Eliza Quitman, July 7, 16, 22, 1834, Eliza Quitman to JAQ, July 12, 1834, Quitman Family Papers, SHC; JAQ to Hiram G. Runnels, September 27, 1834, Mississippi Papers, New York Public Library, New York City. Quitman's explanation, issued several weeks later, declared that his resignation was virtually mandatory because of conflict of interest: some thirty cases in which he was involved as a lawyer had recently been transferred from the High Court of Errors and Appeals to the docket of the superior court of chancery. Columbus (Miss.) *Democrat*, November 1, 1834.

12. JAQ to Henry Quitman, September 25, 1834, Quitman Family Papers, SHC; JAQ to "Judge," February 5, 1835, Claiborne Papers, MDA; James H. McLendon, "John A. Quitman" (Ph.D. dissertation, University of Texas, 1949), 87–88; Samuel Gwin to Martin Van Buren, October 27, 1836, Martin Van Buren Papers, LC.

13. John Edmond Gonzales, "Flush Times, Depression, War, and Compromise," in Richard Aubrey McLemore (ed.), *A History of Mississippi* (2 vols.; Jackson, 1973), I, 284–85; Miles, *Jacksonian Democracy*, 99–101; Governor's Message, January 21, 1835, in *Mississippi Senate Journal*, 1835, p. 19. The Whig state convention of December, 1834, did not put forth any one candidate to oppose Walker. Poindexter had announced his retirement, and Franklin Plummer hoped to attract Whig support. Miles, *Jacksonian Democracy*, 104–105. Apparently Quitman had some support for the U.S. Senate. See Henry Foote's statement in the Jackson *Mississippian*, September 11, 1835.

14. Jackson *Mississippian*, May 9, 1834.

15. *Mississippi Senate Journal*, 1835, pp. 6–8, 15–23, 39–40, 41–42, 45, 51–52.

16. *Ibid.*, 41, 73, 74, 95; JAQ to Eliza Quitman, January 27, 1835, Lovell Family Papers, UnS; JAQ to "Judge," February 5, 1835, Claiborne Papers, MDA; Columbus (Miss.) *Democrat*, February 27, 1835.

17. JAQ to Henry Quitman, April 30, 1835, Quitman Family Papers, SHC; JAQ to Henry Quitman, October 17, 1835, in Claiborne, *Quitman*, I, 138.

18. Morton Rothstein, "The Natchez Nabobs: Kinship and Friendship in an Eco-

nomic Elite," in Hans L. Trefousse (ed.), *Toward a New View of America: Essays in Honor of Arthur C. Cole* (New York, 1977), 97–112; William K. Scarborough, "Slavery—The White Man's Burden," in Harry P. Owens (ed.), *Perspectives and Irony in American Slavery* (Jackson, 1976), 106–107.

19. J. J. H. Morris to JAQ, March 19, 1834, T. B. J. Hadley to JAQ, March 19, 1834, Claiborne Papers, MDA; Jackson *Mississippian*, October 31, December 12, 1834, January 16, March 20, November 6, 1835; *Mississippi Senate Journal*, 1835, p. 44; John Hebron Moore, "Railroads of Antebellum Mississippi," *JMH*, XLI (1979), 57–58. Quitman seems initially to have envisioned that the railroad would be built on already existing roads rather than on specially constructed railbeds. See John T. Griffith to JAQ, October 25, 1834, Claiborne Papers, MDA.

20. Minutes of the Board of Trustees, Jefferson College, April 11, May 28, 1831, June 6, 1835–July 23, 1842, Security document, dated June 18, 1833, Jefferson College Papers, MDA; *Mississippi Free Trader* (Natchez), August 12, 1837. On March 29, 1836, the board elected Quitman vice president, a position he would hold until his resignation in April, 1839. Minutes, March 29, 1836; JAQ to Levin Wailes, April 22, 1839, Jefferson College Papers, MDA. Attendance at meetings by trustees was spotty; often there was no quorum. Quitman absented himself from sixty-eight board meetings. But many of these absences were unavoidable, several occurring in early 1836 when he was attending the state legislature.

Founded in 1802, Jefferson College had experienced its share of growing pains, and, during its early history, was closer to an academy in character than to a true college. William T. Blain, *Education in the Old Southwest: A History of Jefferson College, Washington, Mississippi* (Washington, Miss., 1976).

21. JAQ to Henry Quitman, October 17, 1835, in Claiborne, *Quitman*, I, 138; Joseph Holt Ingraham, *The South-West by a Yankee* (2 vols.; New York, 1835).

22. James Lal Penick, Jr., *The Great Western Land Pirate: John A. Murrell in Legend and History* (Columbia, Mo., 1981).

23. William Johnson Diary, November 8, 9, 13, 1835, William R. Hogan and Edwin A. Davis (eds.), *William Johnson's Natchez: The Ante-Bellum Diary of a Free Negro* (Baton Rouge, 1951), 74–76; [William F. Gray], *From Virginia to Texas, 1835: Diary of Col. Wm. F. Gray* . . . (1909; rpr. Houston, 1965), 31–32; Eliza Quitman to JAQ, January 3, 1836, JAQ to Eliza Quitman, January 15, 1836, Quitman Family Papers, SHC; McLendon, "Quitman," 80; D. Clayton James, *Antebellum Natchez* (Baton Rouge, 1968), 259.

24. JAQ to Henry Quitman, October 17, 1835, in Claiborne, *Quitman*, I, 138–39.

25. Vicksburg *Whig*, November 12, 1851; *Mississippi Senate Journal*, Called Session, 1835, pp. 3–4; Jackson *Mississippian*, November 27, 1835.

26. *Mississippi Senate Journal*, Called Session, 1835, pp. 5–7; JAQ to Eliza Quitman, December 3, 1835 [with December 5 postscript], Quitman Family Papers, SHC.

27. JAQ to Eliza Quitman, December 5 [postscript to December 3 letter], 9, 1835, January 10, 1836, Quitman Family Papers, SHC; JAQ to Eliza Quitman, December 6, 1835, "Family Record," Lovell Family Papers, UnS. Surviving state records offer scant insight into just what duties Quitman performed while governor. His file in "Governors' Papers" (RG 29, MDA), contains two resignations, a resolution of the Jackson branch of the Planters' Bank concerning an appropriate notary-public appointment, and a request by the governor of Georgia for Mississippi's cooperation in

the return of a fugitive slave. Quitman issued a December 8 proclamation calling upon state officers to deliver the fugitive to two Georgia agents after these agents paid "all costs and expenses incurred in apprehending & securing said fugitive."

28. JAQ to Eliza Quitman, December 9, 1835, January 6, 1836, Quitman Family Papers, SHC; *Mississippi Senate Journal*, 1836, p. 34.

29. *Mississippi Senate Journal*, 1836, pp. 34–38. Predictably, the *Mississippian*, January 22, 1836, attacked the radical implications of Quitman's speech, mocking Quitman's pretentiousness in even giving the speech and arguing that the American system of "self-government will stand strong as the hills of our country."

30. *Mississippi Senate Journal*, 1836, pp. 38–47. Quitman wrote home that his message had received "very high compliments." JAQ to Eliza Quitman, January 10, 1836, Quitman Family Papers, SHC.

31. *Mississippi Senate Journal*, 1836, pp. 62–69; JAQ to Eliza Quitman, January 10, 1836, Quitman Family Papers, SHC. Later Quitman would be accused of voting for himself to break the deadlock. See Warner Moss, "Governor Alexander G. McNutt (1802–1848)," *JMH*, XLII (1980), 248n.

32. *Mississippi Senate Journal*, 1836, pp. 71–76; JAQ to Eliza Quitman, January 6, 10, 14–16, 1836, Quitman Family Papers, SHC; Miles, *Jacksonian Democracy*, 112; William Johnson Diary, January 27, 1836, Hogan and Davis (eds.), *William Johnson's Natchez*, 97. At a party honoring Governor Lynch, George Poindexter had mounted a table and delivered a searing anti-Jacksonian tirade. When Gwin had hissed Poindexter in response, Caldwell came to his law partner's rescue and challenged Gwin. The duel was fought at Clinton on January 12, witnessed by a considerable crowd. Gwin received a serious wound in the duel and, never fully recovering, died less than three years later.

33. JAQ to Eliza Quitman, January 15, 1836, Quitman Family Papers, SHC; George Adams to Robert J. Walker, January 24, 1836, Robert J. Walker Papers, NYHS; *Mississippi Senate Journal*, 1836, pp. 180, 181, 192–93; *Laws of the State of Mississippi*, 1836, pp. 173–95.

34. *Mississippi Senate Journal*, 1836, pp. 248–53, 267, 272, 336, 345–46; JAQ to Eliza Quitman, January 26, February 3, 1836, Quitman Family Papers, SHC. The New Orleans and Nashville Railroad Company did win Mississippi legislative endorsement a year later. *Laws of the State of Mississippi*, 1837, pp. 25–33. However, the panic of 1837 would destroy the project. Moore, "Railroads," 59. Quitman not only supported amendments restricting the New Orleans line but was one of six senators voting against the whole project on February 18. *Mississippi Senate Journal*, 1836, p. 267.

35. *Laws of the State of Mississippi*, 1836, pp. 20–24; *Mississippi Senate Journal*, 1836, pp. 144–54. The 1836 legislature also amended an 1805 law so that the trustees of the Natchez hospital were now given authority to aid indigent boatmen and paupers passing through town. The amendment appointed eleven additional trustees for the institution—Quitman was one of these. *Laws of the State of Mississippi*, 1836, pp. 260–63. Overhaul of the militia awaited the 1837 legislative meeting. *Laws of the State of Mississippi*, 1837, pp. 46–107.

36. JAQ to Eliza Quitman, January 15, 1836, Quitman Family Papers, SHC. Quitman, however, did occasionally advise her on plantation matters. See JAQ to Eliza Quitman, February 5, 1836.

37. Eliza Quitman to [?], January 31, 1836, Eliza Quitman to JAQ, January 20,

February 21, 1836, JAQ to Eliza Quitman, January 16, 1836, Quitman Family Papers, SHC.

38. JAQ to Eliza Quitman, January 16, February 8, 1836, Quitman Family Papers, SHC.

39. JAQ to Eliza Quitman, January 10, 16, February 5, 18, 1836, Eliza Quitman to JAQ, January 20, February 14, 1836, Quitman Family Papers, SHC. Quitman pledged, as part of his program to raise Eliza's spirits, that they would entertain more at Monmouth after his return. Irregular mails exacerbated Quitman's misunderstanding with his wife. See, for instance, Quitman's January 16 letter.

CHAPTER 7

1. *Mississippi Free Trader*, (Natchez), September 9, 1858. Reuben Davis recalled Quitman as a "man of heroic military instincts." Reuben Davis, *Recollections of Mississippi and Mississippians* (Rev. ed., Hattiesburg, 1972), 79.

2. JAQ to J. R. Simms, May 5, 1854, in *Historical Magazine* (January, 1867), 41–42; JAQ Diary, November 25, 28, 1821, Quitman Family Papers, SHC.

3. JAQ Memoranda Book, September 21, 1827, Quitman Family Papers, SHC; *Mississippi House Journal*, 1829, pp. 15–16, 33; Resolution, February 5, 1829, in *Laws of the State of Mississippi*, 1829; JAQ to Gerard C. Brandon, December 31, 1829, in *Southern Galaxy* (Natchez), April 1, 1830; Act, February 12, 1830, in *Laws of the State of Mississippi*, 1830; *Journal of the Convention of the State of Mississippi Held in the Town of Jackson* (Jackson, 1832), 259. At least one volunteer militia unit in Mississippi was named after Quitman, the (Port Gibson) "Quitman Riflemen." *Mississippi Free Trader* (Natchez), May 24, 1845.

4. *Mississippi Free Trader* (Natchez), June 26, 1843; New York *Times*, July 19, 1858; JAQ to Eliza Quitman, February 18, 1836, Quitman Family Papers, SHC. The Jackson *Mississippian*, May 21, 1847, claimed that Quitman was "peculiarly fitted for military life and military *command*—with *physical* strength, possessed by few."

5. JAQ to his brother, October 17, 1835, in J. F. H. Claiborne, *Life and Correspondence of John A. Quitman* (2 vols.; New York, 1860), I, 139; JAQ to Eliza Quitman, January 16, 1836, Quitman Family Papers, SHC; Sam Houston to JAQ, February 12, 1836, Oversized Documents Collection, Map Room, UT.

6. John Ross to Randolph Ross, February 12, 1836, Reuben Ross to Randolph Ross, March 28, 1836, Reuben Ross Papers, UT; [William F. Gray], *From Virginia to Texas, 1835: Diary of Col. Wm. F. Gray* . . . (1909; rpr. Houston, 1965), 112; Undated statement in Quitman's hand of his reasons for going to Texas, filed 1837, Quitman Family Papers, SHC; Harris Gaylord Warren, *The Sword Was Their Passport: A History of American Filibustering in the Texas Revolution* (Baton Rouge, 1943), 233–47; Antonio López de Santa Anna to General José María Tornel, February 16, 1836, in John H. Jenkins (ed.), *The Papers of the Texas Revolution, 1835–1836* (10 vols.; Austin, 1973), IV 358. John Ross apparently was a close friend of Quitman's. See JAQ to S. S. Prentiss, September 17, 1837, in [G. L. Prentiss (ed.)], *Memoir of S. S. Prentiss* (2 vols.; New York, 1856), I, 234n.

7. Thomas J. Green to Jessee Benton, April 4, 1836, J. F. H. Claiborne Papers, MDA; Claiborne, *Quitman*, I, 140–41; *Mississippi Free Trader* (Natchez), April 8, 1836.

8. *Mississippi Free Trader* (Natchez), April 8, 1836; Claiborne, *Quitman*, I,

142–44; Thomas J. Green to Jessee Benton, April 4, 1836, Claiborne Papers, MDA. Exactly how many men accompanied Quitman is unclear. Reuben Ross, a member of the expedition, said there were sixteen, other than Quitman and himself. He did not say whether Quitman's servant was included in this total. The local newspaper claimed that about thirty accompanied Quitman, including about fifteen Fencibles. Natchez black barber William Johnson, writing in his diary the day the expedition departed, could recall the names of only nine individuals (including Quitman). Quitman's muster roll of April 12 listed twenty-three in his company, specifying that three had joined after the company was organized. Probably Ross's total is the most reliable for April 5. Reuben Ross to Randolph Ross, May 28, 1836, Ross Papers; *Mississippi Free Trader* (Natchez), April 8, 1836; William Johnson Diary, April 5, 1836, in William R. Hogan and Edwin A. Davis (eds.), *William Johnson's Natchez: The Ante-Bellum Diary of a Free Negro* (Baton Rouge, 1951), 113; Muster Roll, April 12, 1836 [from Nacogdoches, Texas], General Land Office, Austin. See Claiborne, I, 142, for the Fencibles' banner song.

9. The *Mississippi Free Trader* (Natchez), April 8, 1836, said that Huston intended to go with Quitman, but that some of the men had been unable to assemble their provisions in time, so he had postponed his departure until April 21. Huston, according to the paper, intended to have mounted men exclusively, some 150 in number. Reuben Ross, however, claimed that Huston had stayed behind because of his wife's poor health. See Randolph Ross [reporting on a letter from Reuben] to Randolph Ross, May 6, 1836, Ross Papers.

10. *Mississippi Free Trader* (Natchez), April 8, 1836; Receipt, March 29, 1836, JAQ Papers, MDA; Eliza Quitman to JAQ, April 11, 1836, JAQ to Eliza Quitman, April 13, 1836, Quitman Family Papers, SHC.

11. Thomas J. Green to David G. Burnet, April 13, 1836, Thomas Jefferson Green Papers, SHC; JAQ to Felix Huston, April 8, 1836, in Claiborne, *Quitman*, I, 144–45.

12. JAQ to Felix Huston, April 8, 1836, quoted in Claiborne, *Quitman*, I, 144–45; JAQ to Henry Quitman, July 31, 1836, Quitman Family Papers, SHC; Francis Paul Prucha, *The Sword of the Republic: The United States Army on the Frontier, 1783–1846* (London, 1969), 306–307; A. A. Parker, *Trip to the West and Texas . . .* (1836; rpr. Austin, 1968), 143, 145.

13. Claiborne, *Quitman*, I, 145; JAQ Journal, April 10, 1836, *ibid.*, 145–46.

14. H. M. Henderson, "A Critical Analysis of the San Jacinto Campaign," *Southwestern Historical Quarterly*, LIX (1956), 344–48; Thomas J. Green to Jessee Benton, March 30, 1836 (copy), Green Papers, SHC; A. Somerville to James F. Perry, March 16, 1836, James Franklin Perry Papers, UT; Ray Allen Billington, *The Far Western Frontier, 1830–1860* (New York, 1956), 129–30; Antonio López de Santa Anna, "Manifiesto Que De Sus Operaciones en la Campaña de Tejas . . . ," in Carlos E. Castañeda (trans.), *The Mexican Side of the Texan Revolution* (Dallas, 1928), 15–16, 22.

15. JAQ to Felix Huston, April 15, 1836, in Claiborne, *Quitman*, I, 148. The Mexican force reported threatening Nacogdoches was probably a detached part of Santa Anna's army of 725 men operating under General Gaona. Santa Anna, after the Alamo, had concluded that Texan resistance was at an end, and had dispersed his own forces for purposes of occupation. See Henderson, "Critical Analysis," 354–55.

16. Reuben Ross to Randolph Ross, May 28, 1836, Ross Papers; JAQ to Henry Quitman, July 31, 1836, Quitman Family Papers, SHC; JAQ Journal, April 12, 1836, in Claiborne, *Quitman*, I, 146–47; [Gray], *From Virginia to Texas*, 89.

17. JAQ Journal, April 12, 1836, JAQ to Felix Huston, April 15, 1836, in Claiborne, *Quitman*, I, 146–47, 149; Muster Roll, April 12, 1836, General Land Office, Austin.

18. JAQ Journal, April 14, 1836, JAQ to Felix Huston, April 15, 1836, in Claiborne, *Quitman*, I, 147, 150; JAQ to Henry Quitman, July 31, 1836, Quitman Family Papers, SHC; Henry Raguet to Mrs. M. A. Raguet, April 17, 1836, in Carolyn Reeves Ericson, "Prelude to San Jacinto: Nacogdoches 1836," *East Texas Historical Journal*, XI (Fall, 1973), 36–40.

19. John T. Mason to Edmund P. Gaines, April 13, 1836, John T. Mason to [?], April 16, 1836, Edmund P. Gaines to Secretary of War Lewis Cass, April 20, 1836, in Jenkins (ed.), *Papers of the Texas Revolution*, V, 459–60, 489, 510–12; Edmund P. Gaines to Sam Houston, April 25, 1836, Thomas J. Rusk Papers, UT; JAQ to Eliza Quitman, April 14, 1836, Quitman Family Papers, SHC; James W. Silver, *Edmund Pendleton Gaines: Frontier General* (Baton Rouge, 1949), 191–98.

20. JAQ to Eliza Quitman, April 14, 15, 1836, Quitman Family Papers, SHC. Some of Quitman's men, apparently, did not share Quitman's luck with his health, and suffered from bowel problems. See JAQ to Thomas J. Rusk, June 13, 1836, Rusk Papers.

21. JAQ to Felix Huston, August [April] 15, 1836, in Claiborne, *Quitman*, I, 150.

22. JAQ Journal, April 17, 1836 [and later, unspecified dates], in Claiborne, *Quitman*, I, 151, 153; Reuben Ross to Randolph Ross, May 28, 1836, Ross Papers; JAQ to Eliza Quitman, April 29, 1836, Quitman Family Papers, SHC. Quitman said in his April 29 letter that about one hundred other soldiers had left Naeogdoches with him besides his own men. He probably got his information at Robin's Ferry from Captain Wylie Martin of the Texas army, who had been sent there by Houston with two hundred troops to protect the fleeing families. See Henderson, "Critical Analysis," 348.

23. JAQ Journal, April 17, 1836 [and later, unspecified dates], in Claiborne, *Quitman*, I, 151; JAQ to Sam Houston, April 7, 1842, A. J. Houston Papers, Texas State Library and Archives, Austin; JAQ to Henry Quitman, July 31, 1836, Quitman Family Papers, SHC; D. Ramón Martínez Caro, "Verdadera Idea de la Primera Campaña de Tejas y Sucesos Ocurridos Después de la Accion de San Jacinto," in Castañeda (trans.), *Mexican Side*, 128.

24. JAQ Journal, April 17, 1836 [and later, unspecified dates], in Claiborne, *Quitman*, I, 152; Mary Whatley Clark, *Thomas J. Rusk: Soldier, Statesman, Jurist* (Austin, 1971), 75; JAQ to Eliza Quitman, May 5, 1836, Quitman Family Papers, SHC; Document, May 5, 1836, at Camp Jacinto, JAQ Papers, UV, by which twenty-three men enrolled in the Texas army as volunteers. Thus Quitman's men qualified for land grants. See Mark E. Nackman, *A Nation Within a Nation: The Rise of Texas Nationalism* (Port Washington, 1975), 34.

25. JAQ to Eliza Quitman, May 5, 7, 1836, JAQ to Henry Quitman, July 31, 1836, Quitman Family Papers, SHC.

26. William Johnson Diary, May 27, 1836, Hogan and Davis (eds.), *William Johnson's Natchez*, 122; JAQ to Henry Quitman, July 31, 1836, Quitman Family Papers, SHC; JAQ Journal, April 17, 1836 [and later, unspecified dates], in Clai-

borne, *Quitman*, I, 152. Claiborne claimed that Quitman years later returned the gambler's favor by providing $500 so he could pay a fine for being caught in a faro game. Claiborne, *Quitman*, I, 152n–53n.

27. JAQ to Eliza Quitman, April 29, 1836, JAQ to Henry Quitman, May 28, July 31, Quitman Family Papers, SHC; Nackman, *Nation Within a Nation*, 34. Most of Quitman's holdings were located on the Sabine, but he may have purchased some lands on or near Galveston Bay. It is virtually impossible to trace Quitman's exact holdings, as, by Texas law, lands could not be held in his own name since he was not a citizen of the republic. What is clear is that he purchased some, or all, of his lands from a Manuel Elisardo, and that most, or all, of his lands were held for him by his former law student David Kaufman, who moved to Texas and eventually became a congressman from that state. Quitman reimbursed Kaufman for taxes on the holdings. Quitman did try to sell some of his claim as early as 1838, but encountered difficulties because of hard economic times and the uncertainty of land claims based upon Spanish title. JAQ to Eliza Quitman, May 7, 1836, Emile La Sère to JAQ, July 17, 1856, Quitman Family Papers, SHC; T.B.J. Hadley to JAQ, June 28, 1838, Claiborne Papers, MDA; JAQ Daybook, November 3, 1840, JAQ Papers, LSU; Jackson *Mississippian*, December 17, 1847.

Quitman's economic stake in Texas went beyond his own holdings. He talked his brother Henry into investing in Texas lands, and also handled legal transactions involving Texas lands for others, including Felix Huston and Samuel Williams. See Henry Quitman to JAQ, March 15, 1846, JAQ to A. Alderson, December 1, 1852, Lovell Family Papers, UnS; *Mississippi Free Trader* (Natchez), September 15, 1836; Felix Huston to JAQ, March 4, 1854, JAQ Papers, HU.

28. JAQ to Henry Quitman, July 31, December 7, 1836, Quitman Family Papers, SHC; JAQ to Thomas J. Rusk, June 13, 1836, February 27, 1837, Rusk Papers. Exactly how much Quitman laid out for the Texas expedition is unclear. He commented on paying steamboat passage for his men and a few others in a letter to Felix Huston, April 8, 1836, in Claiborne, *Quitman*, I, 144–45. In 1843, Quitman categorically denied that he had equipped his men at his own expense, except in two cases. They accompanied him "as friends, not as mercenaries." Vicksburg *Whig*, February 10, 1843. Later he claimed that the trip cost him about $6,000. See memorandum in Quitman's hand, filed with affidavit of Charles Baldwin, February 26, 1861, Court of Claims File No. 6734, General Land Office, Austin.

29. JAQ to Thomas J. Rusk, June 13, 1836, February 27, 1837, Rusk Papers; JAQ to Sam Houston, November 25, 1836, A. J. Houston Papers; Felix Huston to JAQ, January 4, 1839, Claiborne Papers, MDA; William Campbell Binkley, *The Expansionist Movement in Texas, 1836–1850* (Berkeley, 1925), 18–19. Huston's 1839 letter to Quitman shows that Quitman handled many of his affairs, including the sale of slaves, while he served in Texas.

30. JAQ to [?], in Claiborne, *Quitman*, I, 192–93; *Mississippi Free Trader* (Natchez), April 4, 1842, May 30, 1849; P. Edmunds to Sam Houston, April 5, 7, 1842, A. J. Houston Papers; Binkley, *Expansionist Movement*, 68–102.

31. JAQ to Henry Quitman, July 31, 1836, Quitman Family Papers, SHC; Woodville *Republican*, May 14, 1836.

CHAPTER 8

1. James D. Davidson Diary, November 1, 1836, Herbert A. Kellar (ed.), "A Journey Through the South in 1836: Diary of James D. Davidson," *Journal of Southern History,* I (1935), 355; McKay W. Campbell to James K. Polk, November 23, 1833, Herbert Weaver (ed.), *Correspondence of James K. Polk* (5 vols.; Nashville, 1969–), II, 137; Edwin A. Miles, *Jacksonian Democracy in Mississippi* (Chapel Hill, 1960), 117–20, 122; Jackson *Mississippian,* January 18, September 2, 1836; William Johnson Diary, March 13, 14, 1836, William R. Hogan and Edwin A. Davis (eds.), *William Johnson's Natchez: The Ante-Bellum Diary of a Free Negro* (Baton Rouge, 1951), 107, 108; Joseph Hicks to Samuel Smith Downey, October 29, 1836, Samuel Smith Downey Papers, DU.

2. William James Cooper, *The South and the Politics of Slavery, 1828–1856* (Baton Rouge, 1978), 74–97.

3. JAQ to Henry Quitman, May 28, December 7, 1836, Henry Quitman to JAQ, April 10, June 26, July 24, October 30, 1836, August [?], 1837, June 20, 1841, Quitman Family Papers, SHC; Henry Quitman to JAQ, September 11, 1836, Louisa Quitman to Albert Quitman, April 2, 1837, Lovell Family Papers, UnS; Deed Records, Leflore County, Vol. AA, pp. 26–28, Rankin County, Vol. II, p. 319, copies in MDA; Partnership agreement, October, 1835, JAQ Papers, MDA; Deed Records, Book 61, pp. 537–39, in County Clerk's Office, Dutchess County, Poughkeepsie. The land consortium involved Quitman, James C. Wilkins, John McMurran, and Jacob B. Womack (with a provision that Henry Turner—Eliza's brother who was studying medicine in Philadelphia—could join at a later date). Womack was to purchase all lands in Quitman's name. Profits were to be divided in proportion to amounts invested in the consortium.

4. "Address of the Committee of the Democratic Convention of Mississippi," in *Mississippi Free Trader* (Natchez), October 20, 1836; Jackson *Mississippian,* September 23, 30, October 21, 1836; James H. McLendon, "John A. Quitman" (Ph.D. dissertation, University of Texas, 1949), 137.

5. Woodville *Republican,* October 8, 15, 1836; JAQ to Eliza Quitman, October 17, November 1, 1836, Quitman Family Papers, SHC; Hanson Alsbury to JAQ, January 5, 1837, J. F. H. Claiborne Papers, MDA; *Mississippi Free Trader* (Natchez), October 25, 1836.

6. William Johnson Diary, November 5, 7, 1836, Hogan and Davis (eds.), *William Johnson's Natchez,* 144; *Mississippi Free Trader* (Natchez), November 8, 12, 1836.

7. J. F. H. Claiborne, *Life and Correspondence of John A. Quitman* (2 vols.; New York, 1860), I, 162; JAQ to Henry Quitman, December 7, 1836, Quitman Family Papers, SHC; Jackson *Mississippian,* December 9, 1836; William Johnson Diary, November 16, 18, 1836, Hogan and Davis (eds.), *William Johnson's Natchez,* 122. Johnson wagered twenty dollars on Quitman's defeat, developed second thoughts, and canceled the bet at the last minute.

8. William Johnson Diary, December 8, 15, 1836, Hogan and Davis (eds.), *William Johnson's Natchez,* 152–53, 154.

9. Robert V. Remini, *Andrew Jackson* (New York, 1966), 181, 185; John Edmond Gonzales, "Flush Times, Depression, War, and Compromise," in Richard Aubrey McLemore (ed.), *A History of Mississippi* (2 vols.; Jackson, 1973), I, 292; Reginald C. McGrane, *Foreign Bondholders and American State Debts* (New York, 1935), 14–15.

10. Henry A. Garrett, MSS Reminiscences, J. F. H. Claiborne Papers, LC; John P. Stewart to Duncan McLaurin, July 30, 1840, Duncan McLaurin Papers, DU; Jackson *Mississippian*, March 17, June 23, July 7, August 4, September 7, November 17, 1837, June 20, 1838; Vicksburg *Sentinel*, October 16, 1838; S. S. Prentiss to his youngest brother, October 6, 1837, in [G. L. Prentiss (ed.)], *Memoir of S. S. Prentiss* (2 vols.; New York, 1856), I, 242; Vicksburg *Register*, May 25, 29, June 8, 1838.

11. Document of slave hire, January 21, 1836, Joseph Hicks to Samuel Smith Downey, February 27, 1836, January 23, 1837, Samuel Smith Downey to Joseph Amis, May 28, 30, 1837, Joseph Amis to Samuel Smith Downey, December 9, 1837, all in Downey Papers; *Mississippi Free Trader* (Natchez), December 22, 1836.

12. In 1837, for instance, Quitman presided over a Natchez meeting about the *Ben Sherod* steamboat disaster; the meeting petitioned the legislature to do something about the kind of reckless steamboat racing which caused the accident. See *Mississippi Free Trader* (Natchez), May 19, 1837.

13. JAQ to Nicholas Biddle, February 7, 1837, Henry Turner to Eliza Quitman, July 26, 1838, Quitman Family Papers, SHC; Joseph Hicks to Samuel Smith Downey, March 28, May 14, July 14, 1836, Downey Papers; William Johnson Diary, July 8–10, 1837, Hogan and Davis (eds.), *William Johnson's Natchez*, 183–84; JAQ to the Trustees of the Town of Washington, August 14, 1838, Adams County (Town of Washington) Papers, Municipal Archives, MDA; Vicksburg *Sentinel*, June 12, 1838; John T. McMurran to JAQ, April 29, 1837, Claiborne Papers, MDA.

14. *Mississippi Free Trader* (Natchez), April 27, August 17, 1837; Jackson *Mississippian*, June 16, 1837; Undated, unsigned manuscript, JAQ Papers, MDA; T. B. J. Hadley to JAQ, June 13, 1837, Claiborne Papers, MDA. Quitman's support of Whig S. S. Prentiss' claim to a disputed seat in the House is a further indication of his Whiggish inclinations at that time. JAQ to S. S. Prentiss, September 17, 1837, January 17, 1838, in [G. L. Prentiss (ed.)], *Memoir of S. S. Prentiss*, I, 234n, 251.

15. *Mississippi Free Trader* (Natchez), August 12, September 9, 1837. A third candidate was Gustavus H. Wilcox of Jefferson County. *Mississippi Free Trader* (Natchez), August 31, 1837.

16. *Mississippi Free Trader* (Natchez), September 7, 12, 21, 1837; William Johnson Diary, September 9, 1837, Hogan and Davis (eds.), *William Johnson's Natchez*, 191; Natchez *Courier*, October 31, 1837. Besançon, a Cooperstown, New York, native and journeyman printer, had come to Natchez in 1834 when twenty-two. Edwin A. Miles, "The Mississippi Press in the Jackson Era, 1824–1841," *JMH*, XIX (1957), 12.

17. William Johnson Diary, September 12, 1837, Hogan and Davis (eds.), *William Johnson's Natchez*, 192; *Mississippi Free Trader* (Natchez), September 21, 1837; Natchez *Courier*, October 31, 1837; Adjutant General's Records, Register, Military Appointments, Series K, Vol. A, p. 4, MDA. Quitman was recommissioned major general of the Second Division on November 15, 1841. His division included Claiborne, Jefferson, Adams, Franklin, Lawrence, Covington, Jones, Lauderdale, Clarke, Jasper, and Wayne counties.

18. Margaret L. Coit, *John C. Calhoun: American Patriot* (Boston, 1950), 326–41; JAQ to J. Bole and S. Shackleford, December 13, 1838, quoted in Vicksburg *Sentinel*, December 28, 1838; Vicksburg *Sentinel*, January 21, March 30, 1839; Vicksburg *Whig*, March 10, 1840; Grenada (Miss.) *Grenadian*, January 4,

1839; Woodville *Republican*, January 12, 29, 1839; Jackson *Mississippian*, April 12, 1839. The Mississippi Whigs and Democrats openly competed for the nullifier vote in 1839, by incorporating the term *state rights* into their respective party titles: the press reported the meetings of the "Democratic State Rights Party" and the "State Rights Whig Convention." The Whig convention combined traditional Whig planks, such as the national bank, with endorsement of such things as Jefferson's resolutions of 1798, etc. Woodville *Republican*, February 9, March 2, 1839.

19. *Mississippi Free Trader* (Natchez), November 27, 1839; Edward Turner to JAQ, October 18, 1837, in Claiborne, *Quitman*, I, 164; Claiborne, *Quitman*, I, 163; "Family Record," Lovell Family Papers, UnS.

20. William Johnson Diary, December 17, 1837, Hogan and Davis (eds.), *William Johnson's Natchez*, 211; Natchez *Courier*, January 15, 1838; *Mississippi Free Trader* (Natchez), January 22, 1838; Vicksburg *Sentinel*, June 12, 1838; "Railroads," Subject File, MDA.

21. *Mississippi Free Trader* (Natchez), December 25, 1838. In January, 1839, Quitman paid up $500 on his own stock. JAQ Daybook, January 25, 1839, JAQ Papers, LSU.

22. Natchez *Courier*, February 22, 1838; Edward Turner to JAQ, August 18, 1838, George Winchester to JAQ, December 17, 1838, Claiborne Papers, MDA; *Mississippi Free Trader* (Natchez), August 20, 1838, February 18, August 19, 1839; JAQ to Eliza Quitman, February 6, 14, 1839, Quitman Family Papers, SHC; *Laws of the State of Mississippi*, 1839, pp. 61–66; McLendon, "Quitman," 147–48.

23. *Laws of the State of Mississippi*, 1838, pp. 191–94; JAQ to J. Bole and S. Schackleford, December 13, 1838, quoted in Vicksburg *Sentinel*, December 28, 1838; D. Clayton James, *Antebellum Natchez* (Baton Rouge, 1968), 196; *Mississippi Free Trader* (Natchez), February 7, 13, 18, 22, 26, 1839; Vicksburg *Sentinel*, February 7, March 7, 1839; Henry S. Foote, *Casket of Reminiscences* (Washington, D.C., 1874), 32–33.

24. *Mississippi Free Trader* (Natchez), February 25, March 21, 1839; Vicksburg *Sentinel*, June 12, 1838. Quitman later heard from people with links to the convention that he would have been strongly supported for president of the meeting had he attended. JAQ to Eliza Quitman, May 19, 1839, Quitman Family Papers, SHC.

25. JAQ to Levin Wailes, April 22, 1839, Jefferson College Papers, MDA; JAQ to Eliza Quitman, May 19, 1839, Eliza Quitman to JAQ, June 16, 1839, Quitman Family Papers, SHC; JAQ to Eliza Quitman, May 24, 1839, December 18, 1840, Lovell Family Papers, UnS.

26. JAQ to Eliza Quitman, July 5, 1839, JAQ to Henry Quitman, July 5, 1839, Quitman Family Papers, SHC; J. B. Thacher to JAQ, May 16, 1839, Claiborne Papers, MDA. Thacher, at the time, was also judge of the criminal court for Adams, Claiborne, Jefferson, Warren, and Wilkinson counties.

27. JAQ to Henry Quitman, July 5, 1839, Quitman Family Papers, SHC.

28. JAQ to Eliza Quitman, June 26, July 5, 8, 1839, JAQ to Henry Quitman, July 5, 1839, Quitman Family Papers, SHC; JAQ to Eliza Quitman, June 18, 1839, Lovell Family Papers, UnS.

29. William Brune to JAQ, July 12, 1839, J. F. H. Claiborne Papers, SHC; JAQ to Eliza Quitman, August 19, 1839, Quitman Family Papers, SHC; JAQ to Eliza Quitman, July 9, 1839, Lovell Family Papers, UnS; JAQ to Henry Quitman, August 11, 1839, in Claiborne, *Quitman*, I, 183–84; Claiborne, *Quitman*, I, 177–81.

30. McGrane, *Foreign Bondholders*, 8, 9, 16, 18; JAQ to Eliza Quitman, August

19, 1839, Quitman Family Papers, SHC; JAQ to Henry Quitman, August 11, 1839, in Claiborne, *Quitman*, I, 183–84.

31. JAQ to Henry Quitman, September 29, 1839, Eliza Quitman to JAQ, June 16, July 26, 1839, Quitman Family Papers, SHC; *Mississippi Free Trader* (Natchez), November 13, 14, 1839; Carl C. Cutler, *Queens of the Western Ocean: The Story of America's Mail and Passenger Sailing Lines* (Annapolis, 1961), 230, 236. Thacher went his own way after he and Quitman landed in the United States.

32. *Mississippi Free Trader* (Natchez), November 13, 1839, January 10, 31, February 17, 1840; Thomas S. Munce to JAQ, July 23, 1839, in Claiborne, *Quitman*, 182n; Joseph R. Hicks to the President and Directors of the Mississippi Railroad Company, March 2, 1840, Downey Papers. The company apparently continued to suffer from slave runaways and other problems. A fire in November, 1839, destroyed sixty-five to seventy cotton bales and partially burned two baggage cars. Jackson *Mississippian*, November 29, 1839; *Mississippi Free Trader* (Natchez), November 15, 1839. According to the Vicksburg *Sentinel*, September 25, 1839, the bank paid specie on its notes at least through September 24.

33. *Mississippi Free Trader* (Natchez), January 11, 1840; Vicksburg *Sentinel*, February 21, 1840.

34. *Mississippi Free Trader* (Natchez), March 4, June 15, 26, 1840; Legal documents, in Downey Papers, DU.

35. *Mississippi Free Trader* (Natchez), May 11, October 13, 30, 1840; JAQ to Eliza Quitman, May 10, 1840, Eliza Quitman to JAQ, May 10, 1840, Quitman Family Papers, SHC; John F. Stover, *The Railroads of the South, 1865–1900: A Study in Finance and Control* (Chapel Hill, 1955), 192. The farthest the Mississippi Railroad Company reached was Hamburg in northwestern Franklin County. In January, 1842, the legislature ruled that the state should take the company's assets and apply them to the interest on the Planters' Bank bonds. In January, 1844, the legislature put the company into liquidation. "Railroads," "Mississippi Railroad Company," Subject Files, MDA.

CHAPTER 9

1. *Mississippi Free Trader* (Natchez), December 31, 1839, January 6, 7, 11, 16, 21, 1840; JAQ Daybook, January 11, 15, 1840, JAQ Papers, LSU.

2. JAQ to J. F. H. Claiborne, February 26, 1840, in J. F. H. Claiborne, *Life and Correspondence of John A. Quitman* (2 vols.; New York, 1860), I, 187–89.

3. Jackson *Mississippian*, February 28, September 11, October 16, 1840; *Mississippi Free Trader* (Natchez), April 8, 1840.

4. Democratic governor Alexander G. McNutt offered Quitman the judicial appointment in January, to fill a vacancy caused by the death of P. Rutilius R. Pray, judge of Mississippi's second judicial district. Offer of appointment, January 8, 1840, JAQ Papers, UV. In the fall, Quitman even stayed aloof from a new "Democratic States Rights Association" in his home county. *Mississippi Free Trader* (Natchez), September 13, 17, 18, 1840. Quitman had made $3 a day as state legislator and $2,000 a year as chancellor. Woodville *Republican*, January 25, 1834, May 2, 1835.

5. JAQ petition to the state legislature, RG 47, Vol. 20, MDA; "AN ACT for the relief of John Stone and Samuel Matthews, executors of the last will and testament of Perry Cohea, deceased, and John A. Quitman," *Laws of the State of Mississippi*,

1852, pp. 259–60; JAQ to the President and Directors of the Planters['] Bank of the State of Mississippi, 1840 [no exact date], Claiborne Papers, MDA; Judgments, Circuit Court of Adams County, November, 1841, Court House, Natchez.

6. JAQ Daybook, January [?], 1839, June 28, 1841, October 1, 1842, February 6, April 17, 1843, July 1, 1844, JAQ Papers, LSU. Quitman's adult theological outlook encompassed a belief in church-state separation. See JAQ to Eliza Quitman, October 2, 1832, Quitman Family Papers, SHC.

7. JAQ to J. F. H. Claiborne, January 27, February 26, 1840, in Claiborne, *Quitman*, I, 186–89.

8. JAQ to J. F. H. Claiborne, January 27, 1840, in Claiborne, *Quitman*, I, 187; *Mississippi Free Trader* (Natchez), May 18, 1840, February 15, 1842; JAQ to Eliza Quitman, May 6, 1840, April 22, November 18, 1842, January 18, 1843, Quitman Family Papers, SHC; JAQ to Eliza Quitman, December 18, 1840, Lovell Family Papers, UnS; *J. & L. Brewster* v. *Robert Patterson*, *S. H. Belsinger* v. *William Taylor*, Judgments, Circuit Court of Adams County, November, 1841, Court House, Natchez; Peter Hagner, Third Auditor, to JAQ, November 4, 1842, RG 217, Third Auditor, Letters Sent, NA; Vicksburg *Whig*, March 25, 27, 28, 1843. Graves fled to Canada following his escape.

9. Louisa Quitman to JAQ, January 10, 1843, JAQ to Eliza Quitman, January 18, 1843, Eliza Quitman to JAQ, January 19, 1843, Quitman Family Papers, SHC.

10. JAQ to Eliza Quitman, May 12, 1843, January 18, 1844, Quitman Family Papers, SHC.

11. Eliza Quitman to JAQ, November 7, 14, 1841, JAQ to Eliza Quitman, May 16, 1840, November 18, 1841, Quitman Family Papers, SHC. Eliza was furious in 1840, for instance, when Quitman's sisters did not visit her at Monmouth on a trip south. On another occasion, Eliza called John McMurran her "only friend." Eliza Quitman to JAQ, November 18, 1846, Quitman Family Papers, SHC.

12. Eliza Quitman to JAQ, January 8, 1842, January 22, 1844, July 8, 1845, JAQ to Eliza Quitman, February 11, 1846, Quitman Family Papers, SHC.

13. JAQ to Eliza Quitman, May 19, 1839, Eliza Quitman to JAQ, February 16, 1845, April 13, 1846, Quitman Family Papers, SHC; F. Henry Quitman to JAQ, February 16, 1845, Quitman Family Papers, M-N.

14. "Family Record," in Lovell Family Papers, UnS; JAQ to Louisa Quitman, January 27, 1844, Quitman Family Papers, SHC. See Eliza Quitman to JAQ, June 14, 1845, Quitman Family Papers, SHC, for an illustration of how the death and sicknesses of children put her under tension.

15. Deed Records, Warren County, Vol. I, pp. 283–84, Vol. R, pp. 242–44, MDA; Tax receipt, 1842, signed by P. Stafford, Tax Collector of Warren County, JAQ Papers, MDA; Henry Turner to Eliza Quitman, November 23, 1836, Quitman Family Papers, SHC. According to the deed by which George Turner sold Palmyra to Quitman and Henry Turner, the slaves at Palmyra were almost entirely of prime age. Only two of the slaves were above sixty in age, and only eight were between the ages of fifty and fifty-nine.

16. JAQ to George W. Turner, December 20, 1841, Norris & Co. to JAQ, June 9, 1842, JAQ Papers, MDA; Summons, March 29, 1841, Deposition, October 11, 1841 (copy), Settlement signed November 1, 1842, by Ballard's attorneys and signed November 21, 1842, by Quitman and McMurran for Turner, Quitman and McMurran to John M. Pelton, October 2, December 28, 1841, Henry Turner to JAQ, April 9, 1841, June 7, 11, December 8, 1842, Final settlement, November 6, 1857 (copy),

and other documents, in Quitman Family Papers, SHC. The slaves were returned to Ballard in December, 1842. Henry Turner to JAQ, December 8, 1842, Receipt of John R. George in behalf of Rice Ballard, December 10, 1842, Quitman Family Papers, SHC.

17. JAQ to Eliza Quitman, January 3, 1841[?], A. & J. Dennistoun & Co. to JAQ, April 10, 1842, Henry Turner to JAQ, January 29, 1843, Quitman Family Papers, SHC; *Mississippi Free Trader* (Natchez), January 28, 1842. Quitman's advertisement described Springfield as about 2,000 acres in all, of which about 900 were being cultivated. Springfield was partly hill and partly bottomland. Quitman did manage to rent part of Springfield for $300 to a James Lum. JAQ Daybook, April 5, 1842, JAQ Papers, LSU.

18. JAQ to Eliza Quitman, May 17, 1842, Quitman Family Papers, SHC; Deed Records, Yalobusha County, Vol. H, pp. 410–11, Lafayette County, Vol. D, pp. 1–2, Rankin County, Vol. 8, p. 109, Adams County, Vol. DD, p. 561, Vol. EE, pp. 181–82, MDA. Grant must have shown up in court. In 1845, Quitman again became security for a $600 bond that Grant would appear in court on charges of receiving stolen goods.

19. William Johnson Diary, October 19, 1843, William R. Hogan and Edwin A. Davis (eds.), *William Johnson's Natchez: The Ante-Bellum Diary of a Free Negro* (Baton Rouge, 1951), 456; *Mississippi Free Trader* (Natchez), December 23, 1843; *Historical Catalogue of the University of Mississippi* (Nashville, 1910), 81; Vicksburg *Whig*, January 31, 1845. These are only some of Quitman's civic activities which received notice in the press. Quitman attended the first meeting of the board of trustees of the University of Mississippi, chaired the meeting, and received appointment to the executive committee. Vicksburg *Sentinel*, January 25, 1845.

20. Louisa Quitman to JAQ, May 8, 1844, Quitman Family Papers, SHC.

CHAPTER 10

1. Eliza Quitman to JAQ, December 6, 1832, Louisa Quitman to JAQ, December 27, 1840, Quitman Family Papers, SHC; JAQ Daybook, May 26, November 6, 1841, April 5, 1842, June 1, 1843, Louisa Quitman Penmanship Book, 1839–40, JAQ Papers, LSU; O. H. Waldo to JAQ, September 26, 1847, J. F. H. Claiborne Papers, MDA.

2. Eliza Quitman to JAQ, January 13, 1842, JAQ to Eliza Quitman, May 3, 1843, Quitman Family Papers, SHC; JAQ Daybook, January 26, September 28, 1841, November 19, 29, 1842, April 12, 1843, JAQ Papers, LSU. Some of Quitman's children returned to the Marcilly school years later. Eliza Quitman to F. Henry Quitman, August 9, 1849 (Copy courtesy of the editors of *The Papers of Jefferson Davis*; original in private hands).

3. J. B. Matthews to JAQ, August 12, 1857, Louisa Quitman to JAQ, January 2, February [?], 1847, Antonia Quitman to JAQ, March 19, 1856, Mary L. McMurran to Eliza Quitman, June 15, 1846, Quitman Family Papers, SHC; JAQ Daybook, April 12, 1843, April 23, 1844, March 5, 29, 1845, January 13, 1849, JAQ Papers, LSU; Lida [Eliza Theodosia] Quitman to F. Henry Quitman, April 3, 1850, F. Henry Quitman to Eliza Quitman, March 15, 1849, JAQ Papers, MDA; Eliza Quitman to F. Henry Quitman, April 5, 1851, Quitman Family Papers, M-N; O. H. Waldo to JAQ, September 26, 1847, Claiborne Papers, MDA.

4. JAQ to Louisa Quitman, August 14, 1850, Quitman Family Papers, SHC; Louisa S. Quitman to Louisa T. Quitman, November 19, 1843, JAQ Papers, LSU.

5. JAQ to F. Henry Quitman, January 19, 1843, January 28, 1844, May 9, 1845, March 2, May 25, 1847, JAQ Papers, HSP; JAQ to Eliza Quitman, May 3, 1843, Quitman Family Papers, SHC. For the aristocratic fear of unchecked passion, see Dickson D. Bruce, *Violence and Culture in the Antebellum South* (Austin, 1979), 8–12, 39–41, and *passim*.

6. Louisa Quitman to JAQ, January 9, 1843, JAQ Papers, LSU.

7. Jackson *Mississippian*, August 11, 1837, February 23, 1838; Woodville *Republican*, May 28, 1838; Charles Hillman Brough, "The History of Banking in Mississippi," *PMHS*, III (1900), 329–30.

8. Edwin A. Miles, *Jacksonian Democracy in Mississippi* (Chapel Hill, 1960), 150, 155; James Rogers Sharp, *The Jacksonians versus the Banks: Politics in the States After the Panic of 1837* (New York, 1970), 64–71, 73–79; Brough, "History of Banking," 331, 332–35; William L. Coker, *Repudiation and Reaction: Tilghman M. Tucker and the Mississippi Bond Question* (Floral Park, N.Y., 1969), 23–25; Jackson *Mississippian*, January 10, February 7, 1840; Vicksburg *Sentinel*, March 7, 1840.

9. Vicksburg *Sentinel*, April 5, November 4, 1841; Jackson *Mississippian*, July 17, 1840, January 15, 1841; Vicksburg *Whig*, January 12, 29, March 17, 27, July 3, 1841; Jackson *Southron*, July 13, August 12, 1841; John P. Stewart to Duncan McLaurin, July 30, 1840, Duncan McLaurin Papers, DU.

10. JAQ to Robert J. Walker, February 14, 1842, Robert J. Walker Papers, MDA.

11. *Mississippi Free Trader* (Natchez), October 26, 29, 30, 1841.

12. Vicksburg *Whig*, February 1, 1842; Woodville *Republican*, February 19, 1842; JAQ to Robert J. Walker, February 14, 1842, Walker Papers, MDA.

13. Jackson *Mississippian*, June 3, 22, 1843; Brough, "History of Banking," 336–37; Reginald C. McGrane, *Foreign Bondholders and American State Debts* (New York, 1935), 204; Sharp, *Jacksonians versus the Banks*, 84–88; Albert G. Brown to J. F. H. Claiborne, February 6, 1843, J. F. H. Claiborne Papers, LC. Although the legislature never formally repudiated the Planters' Bank bonds, no tax revenues were pledged to retire them; Mississippi never did redeem the bonds, despite complex legal battles which continued until a 1934 U.S. Supreme Court decision. See McGrane, *Foreign Bondholders*, 205–221.

14. S. S. Prentiss to Felix Huston, May 15, 1842, S. S. Prentiss Papers, MDA; Virginia Quitman McNealus (ed.), *Code Duello: Letters Concerning the Prentiss-Tucker Duel of 1842* (Dallas, 1931); JAQ to Eliza Quitman, June 10, 1843, Quitman Family Papers, SHC. In 1843, Hagan had attacked Jackson lawyer and federal judge George Adams, a man whom Eliza called one of Quitman's "intimate" friends, over Adams' handling of the Richard Graves embezzlement case. Daniel Adams, George's son, shot Hagan in Vicksburg in response. See James T. McIntosh (ed.), *The Papers of Jefferson Davis* (4 vols.; Baton Rouge, 1971–), II, 318n–19n; Eliza Quitman to JAQ, June 10, 1843, Quitman Family Papers, SHC; Edwin A. Miles, "The Mississippi Press in the Jackson Era, 1824–1841," *JMH*, XIX (1957), 15–16.

Quitman apparently served as a second in another affair of honor around this time, on behalf of Democratic bond-paying ally B. D. Howard; and in 1845 he acted as second on behalf of Congressman Jacob Thompson. See Howard to JAQ, September 27, October 18, 1843, Claiborne Papers, MDA; William Johnson Diary, October 17,

1843, William R. Hogan and Edwin A. Davis (eds.), *William Johnson's Natchez: The Ante-Bellum Diary of a Free Negro* (Baton Rouge, 1951), 456; Jacob Thompson to J. F. H. Claiborne, June 3, 1878, J. F. H. Claiborne Papers, SHC.

15. Vicksburg *Whig*, February 25, March 7, July 13, 15, November 3, 1843; Volney E. Howard to JAQ, March 1, 1843, JAQ to B. D. Howard, August 23, 1843, Claiborne Papers, MDA; Sharp, *Jacksonians versus the Banks*, 60, 78, 82; *Mississippi Free Trader* (Natchez), May 31, June 2, 1843; Jackson *Mississippian*, January 12, 1843; JAQ to Gary A. Chandler, President, and Charles R. Crusoe, Secretary, Anti-Repudiating Club of Lowndes County, September 22, 1843, quoted in Vicksburg *Whig*, July 12, 1849.

16. Vicksburg *Whig*, February 1, March 1, March 23 [citing Yazoo *Whig*], July 15, November 3, 1843; Samuel J. Gholson to S. S. Prentiss, March 25, 1843, J. M. Duffield to S. S. Prentiss, April 18, 1843, Henry Clay to S. S. Prentiss, April 27, 1843, in [G. L. Prentiss (ed.)], *Memoir of S. S. Prentiss* (2 vols.; New York, 1856), II, 224, 225–26, 230–31.

17. Ferdinand L. Claiborne to JAQ, October 11, 1843, Claiborne Papers, MDA; JAQ to Eliza Quitman, November 17, 1843, Quitman Family Papers, SHC; Lorenzo A. Besançon to Robert J. Walker, December 18, 1843, Robert J. Walker Papers, LC; *Mississippi Free Trader* (Natchez), December 20, 1843. Nevitt had sided with Quitman in the call for bond payment at the February, 1843, Democratic state convention.

18. Jackson *Southron*, January 17, 1844; Jackson *Southern Reformer*, May 11, 1844; *Mississippi Free Trader* (Natchez), July 3, 1844.

19. Vicksburg *Sentinel*, May 8, 1844; *Mississippi Free Trader* (Natchez), April 10, September 9, 1844.

20. *Mississippi Free Trader* (Natchez), August 3, 10, 17, September 13, October 25, 30, 1844.

21. JAQ to Samuel A. Cartwright, September 9, 1844, Samuel A. Cartwright and Family Papers, LSU. Cartwright ignored Quitman's request and endorsed the protective tariff anyway. Vicksburg *Whig*, September 30, October 7, 1844.

22. *Mississippi Free Trader* (Natchez), April 10, November 26, 1844.

23. JAQ to Eliza Quitman, February 7, 11, 1845, Quitman Family Papers, SHC; [William Wood], *Autobiography of William Wood* (2 vols.; New York, 1895), I, 460.

24. JAQ to Eliza Quitman, February 11, 1845, Quitman Family Papers, SHC; *Mississippi Free Trader* (Natchez), March 11, 18, 1845.

25. *Mississippi Free Trader* (Natchez), March 18, 1845; Coffeeville *Dollar Democrat*, March 7, 1845.

26. John J. McRae to JAQ, June 19, 1845, Volney E. Howard to JAQ, May 26, 1845, Milton P. Smyth to JAQ, June 10, 1845, Claiborne Papers, MDA; Jackson *Mississippian*, June 11, 1845; Joseph E. Davis to the Editor of the *Southern Reformer*, April 15, 1845, in McIntosh (ed.), *Papers of Jefferson Davis*, II, 239–40.

27. Jackson *Mississippian*, June 18, 1845; *Mississippi Free Trader* (Natchez), July 24, 1845.

28. Vicksburg *Whig*, March 28, May 29, 31, 1845; Holly Springs *Guard*, July 31, 1845; Woodville *Republican*, July 19, 1845; Volney E. Howard to JAQ, May 26, 1845, Claiborne Papers, MDA; Miles, *Jacksonian Democracy*, 127, 128; Miles, "Mississippi Press," 10–11; Jacob Thompson to J. F. H. Claiborne, June 3, 1878, Claiborne Papers, SHC; J. F. H. Claiborne, *Life and Correspondence of John A.*

Quitman (2 vols.; New York, 1860), I, 218–19; Jackson *Mississippian*, June 11, 1845.

29. Jackson *Southron*, January 17, 1844; Reuben Davis, *Recollections of Mississippi and Mississippians* (Rev. ed.; Hattiesburg, 1972), 83–84, 101; Henry Stuart Foote, *Texas and the Texans, or, Advance of the Anglo-Americans to the Southwest* (2 vols.; Philadelphia, 1841), II, 340; Vicksburg *Whig*, September 11, 1849.

30. Jackson *Southern Reformer*, March 29, May 24, June 7, 1845.

31. A. G. McNutt address on Texas, May 19, 1845, quoted in Coffeeville *Dollar Democrat*, August 13, 1845; Jackson *Southern Reformer*, May 24, 1845; Vicksburg *Sentinel*, April 12, June 9, 11, 1845.

32. "HUME" letter, quoted in Vicksburg *Whig*, August 18, 1849. The Jackson *Southern Reformer* and the Port Gibson *Correspondent* both accused McNutt of authorship. A Whig in Vicksburg, P. W. Thompson, blamed McNutt in a letter to Quitman. When asked about authorship later in the summer, McNutt sidestepped the question. The *Sentinel*, however, issued a categorical denial of McNutt's authorship. Jackson *Southern Reformer*, August 9, 23, September 20, 1845; P. W. Tompkins to JAQ, September 15, 1845, Claiborne Papers, MDA; Vicksburg *Sentinel*, August 8, 1845. Quitman obviously was not convinced of McNutt's authorship. He wrote Franklin Plummer on September 6, asking whether Plummer was "Hume," and received a denial. Franklin E. Plummer to JAQ, September 17, 1845, Claiborne Papers, MDA.

33. Jackson *Southern Reformer*, June 28, 1845; *Mississippi Free Trader* (Natchez), July 3, 1845; Jackson *Mississippian*, October 8, 1845; Hernando *Phenix*, July 12, 1845.

34. Vicksburg *Sentinel*, August 8, 1845.

35. Henry S. Foote to JAQ, August 9, 1845, in Claiborne, *Quitman*, I, 220 (see also Claiborne's discussion on p. 219); Henry S. Foote, *Casket of Reminiscences* (Washington, D.C., 1874), 211–13; Vicksburg *Sentinel*, September 5, 1845.

36. Henry S. Foote to JAQ, August 9, 1845, in Claiborne, *Quitman*, I, 220; Port Gibson *Correspondent*, October 1, 1845; *Mississippi Free Trader* (Natchez), October 11, 1845; Albert G. Brown to Jesse Speight, October 1, 1845, Alexander Gallatin McNutt Papers, DU.

37. Davis, *Recollections of Mississippi*, 84–85; Port Gibson *Correspondent*, October 1, 1845; Jackson *Mississippian*, August 6, October 29, 1845; Vicksburg *Sentinel*, October 17, 1845; Benjamin F. Dill to JAQ, September 18, October 9, 1845, Lehilia[?] Dickson to JAQ, October 12, 1845, Claiborne Papers, MDA; Vicksburg *Whig*, September 25, 1845.

38. *Mississippi Free Trader* (Natchez), October 28, November 18, 1845; Jackson *Mississippian*, April 30, 1845; JAQ to R. H. Boone, October 29, 1845, in Claiborne, *Quitman*, I, 214–15; F. Henry Quitman to JAQ, November 6, 1845, JAQ Papers, MDA; Jackson *Southern Reformer*, December 27, 1845; Newspaper clipping and formal invitation to the burial, in Quitman Family Papers, SHC.

39. Eliza Quitman to JAQ, January 7, 10, 1846, Quitman Family Papers, SHC; Grenada *Dollar Democrat*, January 2, 1846.

40. Jackson *Mississippian*, January 14, 1846; Fayette (Miss.) *Southern Watch Tower*, January 15, 1846. In the actual vote in the legislature on January 10, Foote received ninety-three votes, the Whig candidate George Winchester won thirty-five votes, and one legislator supported Quitman. Joseph M. Chalmers then was elected to the balance of Walker's unexpired term.

41. Claiborne, *Quitman*, I, 222; John I. Guion to Jefferson Davis, January 16, 1846, McIntosh (ed.), *Papers of Jefferson Davis*, II, 413; Foote, *Casket of Reminiscences*, 211–12.

CHAPTER 11

1. F. Henry Quitman to JAQ, July 7, 1847, JAQ Papers, MDA; Vicksburg *Sentinel*, July 8, 1847; Vicksburg *Whig*, July 21, 1847; Houston *Democratic Telegraph and Texas Register*, August 9, 1847; Jackson *Mississippian*, May 10, 1850; Vidalia (La.) *Intelligencer*, October 28, 1843.

2. Tax receipt, 1842, signed by P. Stafford, Tax Collector of Warren County, JAQ Papers, MDA; JAQ to Eliza Quitman, April 16, 1842, Henry Turner to JAQ, June 11, October [?], 1842, January 29, June 27, October 6, 1843, September 5, 1845, April 28, 1848, December 17, 1852, Eliza Quitman to JAQ, October 29, 1846, Louisa Quitman to JAQ, December 4, 1846, Quitman Family Papers, SHC; JAQ to F. Henry Quitman, May 12, 1850, September 13, 1852, December 10, 1853, JAQ Papers, HSP; Janet Sharp Hermann, *The Pursuit of a Dream* (New York, 1981), 21–25.

3. Personal Tax Rolls, Mississippi, Warren County, 1848, MDA; JAQ Memoranda Book, September 13, 1827, Henry Turner to JAQ, November 21, 1841, June 11, July 25, 1842, January 28, November 5, 18, 1853, Quitman Family Papers, SHC. The 1850 census credited Palmyra with producing 2,000 pounds of butter that year. *Seventh Census, 1850*: Agricultural Statistics, Mississippi, Warren County.

4. F. Henry Quitman to JAQ, November 17, 1846, Lovell Family Papers, UnS; Annie Rosalie Quitman Diary, December 25, 1856, Albert Quitman to JAQ, November 25, December 28, 1844, Eliza Quitman to JAQ, January 30, 1847, JAQ to Eliza Quitman, December 15, 1849, Louisa Chadbourne to JAQ, January 6, 1857, Robert O. Love to JAQ, January 15, 1858, Quitman Family Papers, SHC; F. Henry Quitman to JAQ, January 30, 1852, November 20, 1857, N. D. Fuqua to JAQ, October 16, 1856, JAQ Papers, MDA; J. B. Dunn to F. Henry Quitman, September 11, 1856, Quitman Family Papers, M-N; JAQ to F. Henry Quitman, July 30, 1852, December 10, 1853, December 31, 1857, JAQ Papers, HSP.

5. JAQ Daybook, January 30, 1840, April 14, 1841, JAQ Papers, LSU; JAQ to Eliza Quitman, February 6, 1836, January 25, 1842, Eliza Quitman to JAQ, February 5, 1836, Quitman Family Papers, SHC; JAQ to F. Henry Quitman, February 13, 1857, Eliza Quitman to Mary Quitman, January 5, 1858, Quitman Family Papers, M-N.

6. Springfield Plantation Account Book, P. M. Alley to JAQ, August 12, 1848, Tax receipt, 1850, Adams County, filed 1851, JAQ Papers, MDA; Antonia Lovell, "The Story of Isaac" [dated April 26, 1897], handwritten pamphlet, Quitman Family Papers, SHC; JAQ Daybook, December 12, 30, 1842, JAQ Papers, LSU; Eliza Quitman to JAQ, January 10, 1844, Quitman Family Papers, SHC. Antonia mentioned that one of Moses' arms "had been injured by a falling tree" and hung limp at his side.

Eliza notified Quitman in October, 1846, that Springfield's cotton crop was expected to be about eleven or twelve bales. Eliza Quitman to JAQ, October 29, 1846, Quitman Family Papers, SHC.

7. Springfield Plantation Account Book, S. Chamberlain ferriage account, 1852,

JAQ Papers, MDA. Profits from the ferriage and wood operations fluctuated considerably by month. Ferriage operations in 1845, for instance, ranged from a low of $6.50 in September to a high of $46.50 in October. Although some users paid as they went, many kept outstanding accounts.

8. Henry Turner to JAQ, February 11, 1846, December 17, 1852, Henry Quitman to JAQ, November 20, 1838, JAQ to Eliza Quitman, January 3, 1841, Quitman Family Papers, SHC.

9. JAQ to F. Henry Quitman, May 12, 1850, JAQ Papers, HSP; Eliza Quitman to F. Henry Quitman, June 15, September 23, 1850, Quitman Family Papers, M-N; Eliza Quitman to JAQ, April 2, 1847, Quitman Family Papers, SHC; Personal Tax Rolls, Mississippi, Holmes County, 1855, Deed Records, Holmes County, Vol. P, pp. 473–74, MDA.

10. Sarah Fyler to Eliza Quitman, August 13, 1837, August 7, 1838, George W. Turner to JAQ, Novmber 25, 1852, William Q. Morris to JAQ, December 11, 1852, James A. Grubbs to JAQ, January 14, October 28, 1853, Louisa Chadbourne to JAQ, February 8, 1857, Quitman Family Papers, SHC; [William Wood], *Autobiography of William Wood* (2 vols.; New York, 1895), I, 445, II, 41; JAQ to Lemuel P. Conner, April 3, 1854, Lemuel Parker Conner Papers, LSU.

11. Henry Turner to JAQ, October 23, 1855, April 15, 1842, JAQ to Eliza Quitman, December 15, 1849, A. & J. Dennistoun & Co. to JAQ, December 8, 1843, Quitman Family Papers, SHC; JAQ Daybook, January 1 [?], February 1, 1845, JAQ Papers, LSU; Hermann, *Pursuit of a Dream*, 24.

12. Memorandum of Quitman's liabilities at his death, Quitman Family Papers, M-N; Louisa Chadbourne to Eliza Quitman, February 8, 1857, Quitman Family Papers, SHC; JAQ to F. Henry Quitman, December 10, 1853, JAQ Papers, HSP; Harold Woodman, *King Cotton & His Retainers: Financing & Marketing the Cotton Crop of the South, 1800–1925* (Lexington, Ky., 1968). Quitman's factors also performed many personal services. For instance, in January, 1856, while Quitman was in Washington, D.C., Estlin agreed to escort Eliza on the difficult journey from Monmouth to Live Oaks. See Mary Quitman to Eliza Quitman, January 11, 1856, Quitman Family Papers, M-N.

13. JAQ to F. Henry Quitman, September 14, 1853, September 6, 1856, JAQ Papers, HSP; John Hope Franklin, *A Southern Odyssey: Travelers in the Antebellum North* (Baton Rouge, 1976), 81–112. The Richmond *Enquirer*, January 24, 1851, attacked Quitman for keeping his son in Princeton while Virginia and other slave states had good institutions.

14. Mention of plantation visits in family corresondence, and occasional notices in the press, constitute the only guides to how often Quitman visited his holdings. He seems to have visited Live Oaks about once a year, and to have made more frequent inspections of Springfield and Palmyra. There is little surviving material about the Belen plantation.

15. JAQ to Elias Jenkins, January 18, 1839, JAQ Papers, MDA.

16. [Wood], *Autobiography*, I, 457–58; JAQ to Eliza Quitman, June 17, 1842, Quitman Family Papers, SHC; Mary Quitman to Mrs. Virgil Gardner, February 17, 1856, Quitman Family Papers, M-N.

17. JAQ to F. Henry Quitman, September 13, 1852, October 28, 1855, JAQ Papers, HSP; Houma (La.) *Ceres*, October 11, 1855; Travis M. Brooks (overseer at Belen) to JAQ, October 14, 1857, JAQ Papers, MDA.

18. JAQ Daybook, June 26, 1842, JAQ Papers, LSU; W. R. Smither statement, December 16, 1852, Henry Turner to JAQ, March 16, 1853, Quitman Family Papers, SHC; [Wood], *Autobiography*, I, 459.

19. JAQ to F. Henry Quitman, July 30, 1852, July 6, 1855, January 26, 1856, July 29, August 5, December 31, 1857, JAQ to [N. D. Fuqua], May 2, 1852, JAQ Papers, HSP; N. D. Fuqua to JAQ, October 16, 1856, JAQ Papers, MDA; JAQ to Eliza Quitman, June 17, 1842, Henry Turner to JAQ, January 29, 1843, Louisa Chadbourne to JAQ, February 8, 1857, Antonia Quitman to JAQ, January 5, May 19, 1857, Quitman Family Papers, SHC. Love had claimed, following his dismissal from Belen, that he had been a good overseer and that Quitman had given too much consideration to unverified reports from Bee Lake neighbors. Love asserted that he had not played up to these neighbors because he was too busy concentrating on Quitman's affairs. Apparently Quitman reconsidered the dismissal in the months following Love's protest. Springfield Plantation Account Book, Robert O. Love to JAQ, May 24, 1855, JAQ Papers, MDA.

20. Eliza Quitman to F. Henry Quitman, April 5, 1851, September 17, 1849, Quitman Family Papers, M-N; Annie Rosalie Quitman Diary, December 11, 1853, JAQ Papers, LSU; "Monmouth Fruits & c," Springfield Plantation Account Book, F. Henry Quitman to JAQ, June 7, 1843, JAQ Papers, MDA; JAQ to Eliza Quitman, February 11, 1833, Lovell Family Papers, UnS; JAQ to Eliza Quitman, September 5, 1857, March 28, 1858, Quitman Family Papers, SHC. Quitman sold some of the celery from his gardens during his hard times in the early 1840s. See JAQ to Eliza Quitman, January 3, 1841, Eliza Quitman to JAQ, April 17, 1842, Quitman Family Papers, SHC.

21. JAQ to F. Henry Quitman, September 24, 1849, JAQ Papers, HSP; F. Henry Quitman to Eliza Quitman, November 5, 1854, JAQ Papers, MDA; Eliza Quitman to F. Henry Quitman, February 19, 1849, Quitman Family Papers, M-N; [Wood], *Autobiography*, II, 41; Daniel Barringer to his wife, April 11, 1855, Daniel Moreau Barringer Papers, SHC; [Hosea W. Rood], *Story of the Service of Company E, and of the Twelfth Wisconsin Regiment of Veteran Volunteer Infantry, in the War of the Rebellion* (Milwaukee, 1893), 220.

22. *Sixth Census, 1840: Population*, Louisiana, Terrebonne Parish; *Seventh Census, 1850: Slave Population*, Mississippi, Adams County; Personal Property Tax Rolls, Warren County, 1848, Holmes County, 1855, 1858, MDA; "Slaves on Springfield March 1, 1842," Springfield Plantation Account Book, JAQ Papers, MDA. Since the 1850 census credited only twenty-seven slaveholders in Mississippi with over two hundred slaves, Quitman merits recognition as being in his state's slaveowning elite (but not its very upper crust). J. D. B. De Bow, *Statistical View of the United States . . . Being a Compendium of the Seventh Census . . .* (Washington, D.C., 1854), 95.

23. JAQ to Albert Quitman, May 9, 1839, in J. F. H. Claiborne, *Life and Correspondence of John A. Quitman* (2 vols.; New York, 1860), I, 190; Henry Turner to JAQ, October 12, 1843, October 20, 1844, Quitman Family Papers, SHC; John M. Pelton to Eliza Quitman, December 19, 1846, Lovell Family Papers, UnS.

24. Henry Turner to JAQ, March 16, 1853, Quitman Family Papers, SHC. A year earlier, Turner had encountered similar problems with another overseer. See Turner to Quitman, March 30, 1852, Quitman Family Papers, SHC. Smither resolved Turner's dilemma by resigning later in the year. Henry Turner to JAQ, October 27, 1853, Quitman Family Papers, SHC.

25. Eliza Quitman to JAQ, November 15, 1842, JAQ to Eliza Quitman, November 18, 1842, September 7, 1843, Quitman Family Papers, SHC; JAQ to F. Henry Quitman, June 28, 1856, JAQ Papers, HSP.

26. Henry Turner to JAQ, June 7, 1842, February 16, 1844, November 18, 1853, Mary L. McMurran to Eliza Quitman, August 11, 1856, Antonia Quitman to JAQ, January 13, 1857, Louisa Chadbourne to JAQ, January 6, 12, 1857, Annie Rosalie Quitman Diary, December 27, 29, 1856, January 10, 1857, Quitman Family Papers, SHC.

27. Henry Rowntree to "Esteemed Friends," April 13, 1864, RG 105, Records of the Bureau of Refugees, Freedmen and Abandoned Lands, Mississippi, NA; JAQ to F. Henry Quitman, May 24, 1849, February 6, 1852, JAQ Papers, HSP; F. Henry Quitman to JAQ, January 30, 1832, Leggett bill, 1846 folder, JAQ Papers, MDA; Jackson *Mississippian*, June 22, 1849; JAQ Daybook, December 12, 1849, JAQ Papers, LSU; Eliza Quitman to JAQ, June 28, 1847, Quitman Family Papers, SHC. Little is known about the location of the slave quarters on Quitman's holdings, but William Wood mentioned "a sort of street called 'The Quarter'" behind the overseer's house at Palmyra. [Wood], *Autobiography*, I, 459.

28. JAQ to F. Henry Quitman, September 14, 1853, JAQ Papers, HSP; Henry Turner to JAQ, October 26, November 18, 1853, Quitman Family Papers, SHC; JAQ to N. D. Fuqua, February 9, 1852, Springfield Plantation Account Book, 1842, July 16, 1851, P. M. Alley to JAQ, August 12, 1848, JAQ Papers, MDA; [Wood], *Autobiography*, I, 457.

29. JAQ to Antonia Quitman, March 24, 1856, Quitman Family Papers, SHC.

30. Henry Quitman to JAQ, August 16, 1833, Lovell Family Papers, UnS; Annie Rosalie Quitman Diary, May 22, August 2, 1853, JAQ Papers, LSU; Eliza Quitman to Annie Rosalie Quitman, January 18, 1848, Annie Rosalie Quitman Diary, December 25, 1858, Louisa [Quitman] Chadbourne to JAQ, September 14, 1855, Quitman Family Papers, SHC.

31. *Mississippi Free Trader* (Natchez), December 19, 1848; JAQ to F. Henry Quitman, September 14, 1853, JAQ Papers, HSP; JAQ to F. Henry Quitman, January 11, 1847, F. Henry Quitman to Eliza Quitman, March 10, 1856, JAQ Papers, MDA; Annie Rosalie Quitman Diary, December 25, 1853, JAQ Daybook, December 12, 1849, JAQ Papers, LSU; Annie Rosalie Quitman to Louisa Quitman, February 4, 1853, Eliza Quitman to JAQ, January 14, 1856, Antonia Quitman to JAQ, September 24, 1856, Annie Rosalie Quitman Diary, December 25, 1857, Quitman Family Papers, SHC. Quitman, however, does not seem to have been so paternalistic as to voluntarily free household servants, a practice not unknown in Mississippi. See Terry L. Alford, "Some Manumissions Recorded in the Adams County Deed Books in Chancery Clerk's Office, Natchez, Mississippi, 1795–1835 [1855]," *JMH*, XXXIII (1971), 39–50.

32. Mary L. McMurran to Eliza Quitman, January 25, 1848, JAQ to Eliza Quitman, February 7, 1845, Annie Rosalie Quitman Diary, December 29, 1858, Quitman Family Papers, SHC; F. Henry Quitman to Eliza Quitman, December 20, 1847, JAQ Papers, HSP.

33. *Congressional Globe*, 34th Cong., 3rd Sess., Appendix, 118, 119 (December 18, 1856); JAQ to Eliza Quitman, January 18, 1843, Quitman Family papers, SHC; JAQ to J. F. H. Claiborne, January 27, 1840, in Claiborne, *Quitman*, I, 186.

34. Henry Turner to JAQ, September 26, 1842, August 2, October 12, 19, 26, 1843, September 5, 12, 1845, February 2, 1852, Eliza Quitman to JAQ, November

15, 1842, May 19, 1847, Quitman Family Papers, SHC; Springfield Plantation Account Book, January 15, 1853, JAQ Papers, MDA. The Davis slaves on the Palmyra peninsula, in contrast, do *not* seem to have run away. Hermann, *Pursuit of a Dream*, 29.

35. JAQ to Albert Quitman, May 9, 1839, in Claiborne, *Quitman*, I, 190; Henry Turner to JAQ, May 29, 1843, April 20, 1849, Quitman Family Papers, SHC.

36. JAQ to Henry Clay, April 3, 1830, Claiborne Papers, MDA; Eliza Quitman to JAQ, July [?], 1842, February 5, 1845, May 19, 1847, January 14, 1856, Louisa Chadbourne to JAQ, January 5, 1856, Quitman Family Papers, SHC.

37. Louisa Quitman to Eliza Quitman, March 6, 1849, Quitman Family Papers, SHC.

38. William Johnson Diary, November 18, 1836, William R. Hogan and Edwin A. Davis (eds.), *William Johnson's Natchez: The Ante-Bellum Diary of a Free Negro* (Baton Rouge, 1951), 147; Louisa Quitman to JAQ, May 2, 1843, Quitman Family Papers, SHC; Annie Rosalie Quitman Diary, December 25, 1858, Quitman Family Papers, SHC. Later, when in Congress, Quitman advocated the compensation of a free black who had illegally served in American forces during the Mexican War, on the grounds that the black was an "honest man" and gainfully employed. *Congressional Globe*, 34th Cong., 1st Sess., 913.

39. Annie Rosalie Quitman Diary, May 15, 1856, JAQ to Eliza Quitman, January 6, 1856 [1857], Quitman Family Papers, SHC. See also Eliza Quitman to JAQ, January 20, 1836, Louisa Quitman to JAQ, May 2, 1843, Louisa Chadbourne to JAQ, January 6, 1857, Antonia Quitman to Rosalie Quitman, December 6, 1857, Louisa Chadbourne to Rosalie Quitman, March 3, 1858, Quitman Family Papers, SHC.

40. JAQ to Eliza Quitman, September 14, 1846, Eliza Quitman to JAQ, April 2, 1847, January 14, 1856, Louisa Chadbourne to JAQ, January 5, 1856, Quitman Family Papers, SHC; F. Henry Quitman to JAQ, August 16, 1846, JAQ Papers, MDA. The Jackson *Mississippian*, September 2, 1846, presented an unverified report that "the slave [John] recently captured from Mrs. Quitman, is already in Canada."

41. Eliza Quitman to JAQ, May 27, 1850, December 23, 1855, Louisa Chadbourne to JAQ, January 5, 1856, Quitman Family Papers, SHC. One of Quitman's daughters later recalled that Isaac had once run away after being unfairly accused of stealing silver and had been found years later in a New Orleans jail. Antonia Lovell, "The Story of Isaac," handwritten pamphlet in Quitman Family Papers, SHC. Since Isaac left no account of his motives for returning, any interpretation is mere conjecture. But it should be noted that Isaac had a wife back in Mississippi. The marriage, to a maid in a nearby household, is mentioned in Annie Rosalie Quitman to Louisa Quitman, January 27, 1853, Quitman Family Papers, SHC.

42. JAQ to Eliza Quitman, May 12, 1840, January 29, June 17, 1842, Eliza Quitman to JAQ, October 21, 1850, Annie Rosalie Quitman Diary, September 13, 1851, February 23, 1852, Quitman Family Papers, SHC; JAQ to F. Henry Quitman, January 28, 1844, JAQ Papers, HSP; Annie Rosalie Quitman Diary, April 9, August 2, 1853, JAQ Papers, LSU.

43. Annie Rosalie Quitman Diary, August 11, 1855, JAQ Papers, LSU; Louisa Quitman to JAQ, August 2, 1846, Louisa Chadbourne to JAQ, January 5, 1856, May 16, 1858, Annie Rosalie Quitman to JAQ, March 19, 1856, Annie Rosalie

Quitman Diary, December 25, 1857, JAQ to Eliza Quitman, October 27, 1847, Quitman Family Papers, SHC.

CHAPTER 12

1. JAQ to Albert G. Brown, September 6, 1845, Albert G. Brown to JAQ, September 17, 1845, in J. F. H. Claiborne, *Life and Correspondence of John A. Quitman* (2 vols.; New York, 1860), I, 223, 224; Henry Turner to JAQ, May 1, 1846, Quitman Family Papers, SHC; William H. Goetzmann, *Army Exploration in the American West, 1803–1863* (New Haven, 1959), 65–108. For the August-September, 1845, war scare, see K. Jack Bauer, *The Mexican War, 1846–1848* (New York, 1974), 19–21.

2. Henry Turner to JAQ, May 1, 1846, Quitman Family Papers, SHC; "Family Record," Lovell Family Papers, UnS; JAQ to James K. Polk, May 21, 1846, RG 107, Records of the Secretary of War, NA; JAQ to the Mississippi delegation in Congress, May 22, 1846, in Claiborne, *Quitman*, I, 225–26; Albert K. Weinberg, *Manifest Destiny: A Study of Nationalist Expansionism in American History* (Baltimore, 1935), 111.

3. Eliza Quitman to JAQ, July 12, October 7, 1846. Quitman Family Papers, SHC; James B. Ranck, *Albert Gallatin Brown, Radical Southern Nationalist* (New York, 1937), 43; Henry S. Foote to James K. Polk, May 30, 1846, Powhatan Ellis to James K. Polk, May 25, 1846, John B. Nevitt and J. M. Thacher to James K. Polk, May 26, 1846, R. W. Gaines to James K. Polk, May 22, 1846, RG 107, NA; Joseph W. Chalmers *et al.* to James K. Polk, June 3, 1846, U.S.-Mexican War Papers, San Jacinto Museum of History Association, Deer Park, Tex.; James K. Polk Diary, June 29, 1846, Milo Milton Quaife (ed.), *The Diary of James K. Polk* (4 vols., 1910; rpr. New York, 1970), I, 492. Governor Brown apparently consulted militia units around the state before forwarding Quitman's name to the president. J. A. Wilcox to JAQ, May 25, 1846, J. F. H. Claiborne Papers, MDA.

4. Edward Turner to JAQ, March 22, 1846, Mary L. McMurran to Eliza Quitman, June 15, 1846, Fanny [?] to Louisa Quitman, July 4, 1846, Quitman Family Papers, SHC; James H. McLendon, "John A. Quitman" (Ph.D. dissertation, University of Texas, 1949), 200n; Jefferson Davis to Varina Howell Davis, June 22, 1846 (Original owned by Robert E. Canon and Newton Wilds, Houston; copy courtesy of Lynda L. Crist, Editor, *The Papers of Jefferson Davis*).

5. Jackson *Mississippian*, May 13, 1846; Vicksburg *Whig*, May 6, 13, 26, 1846; Ranck, *Brown*, 45; Francis B. Heitman, *Historical Register and Dictionary of the U.S. Army, 1789–1903* (Washington, D.C., 1903), 812. Quitman's appointment was applauded in the Mississippi press. Vicksburg *Whig*, July 14, 1846; Jackson *Mississippian*, July 15, 1846.

6. JAQ to William Marcy, July 2, 1846, RG 107, JAQ to the Adjutant General of the United States Army, July 8, 1846, RG 94, Records of the Adjutant General, Letters Received, NA; JAQ to J. & A. Dennistoun & Co., July 5, 1846 (copy), Eliza Quitman to JAQ, July 12, 1846, Quitman Family Papers, SHC; Bauer, *Mexican War*, 74–75; JAQ Diary, July 6, 7, 1846, in Claiborne, *Quitman*, I, 235–36. The actual rankings of the brigadier generals can be found in a document dated July 7, 1846, signed by Marcy and Jones, in RG 94, NA.

7. JAQ Diary, July 9–30, 1846, in Claiborne, *Quitman*, I, 237–39; Annie Turner

to Eliza Quitman, July 27, 1846, Quitman Family Papers, SHC; Claiborne, *Quitman*, I, 238n.

8. JAQ Diary, July 30 [entry covered several days], 1846, in Claiborne, *Quitman*, I, 238; Ivor Debenham Spencer, *The Victor and the Spoils: A Life of William L. Marcy* (Providence, 1959), 153–54; Otis A. Singletary, *The Mexican War* (Chicago, 1960), 35.

9. JAQ Diary, July 30, 1846, in Claiborne, *Quitman*, I, 238–39; Winfield Scott to William Marcy, January 16, 1847, William Marcy Papers, LC. Taylor did, in fact, put most of his emphasis in July on getting his regulars to the front. See Bauer, *Mexican War*, 88.

10. JAQ to Eliza Quitman, August 14, 1846, JAQ to Louisa and F. Henry Quitman, August 18, 1846, Quitman Family Papers, SHC; JAQ Diary, August 10, 11, 17, 18, 20, 1846, in Claiborne, *Quitman*, I, 239–40; Mansfield Lovell Diary, n.d., Mansfield Lovell Papers, Huntington Library, San Marino, Ca.; Zachary Taylor to the Adjutant General, August 19, 1846, RG 94, NA; Special Orders No. 124 (copy), signed by W. W. S. Bliss, Assistant Adjutant General, August 19, 1846, JAQ Papers, MDA.

11. JAQ Diary, August 11, 1846, in Claiborne, *Quitman*, I, 239; JAQ to Louisa and F. Henry Quitman, August 18, 1846, Quitman Family Papers, SHC. In his August 18 letter, Quitman mentioned that most of the "better" Mexican families had fled Camargo for the interior, revealing that his mind was open to making class distinctions among the Mexican people.

12. JAQ Diary, August 20, 1846, in Claiborne, *Quitman*, I, 240.

13. JAQ to the Adjutant General, August 20, 1846, Zachary Taylor to the Adjutant General, September 3, 1846, RG 94, NA; "Military Papers," September 1–6, 1846, JAQ Papers, MDA; JAQ to Eliza Quitman, August 28, 1846, Quitman Family Papers, SHC; JAQ to Felix Huston, August 24, 1846, JAQ to J. F. H. Claiborne, September 5, 1846, in Claiborne, *Quitman*, I, 241n–42n, 240.

14. Zachary Taylor to the Adjutant General, September 3, 1846, RG 94, JAQ to G. H. Grossman [Assistant Quartermaster, Camargo], September 8, 1846, RG 92, Quartermaster General's Office, Consolidated Correspondence File, NA; William A. Nichols to William B. Campbell, September 6, 1846 ("Orders No. 3"), William B. Campbell to his wife, September 5, 14, 1846, Campbell Family Papers, DU.

15. Mansfield Lovell Diary, n.d., Mansfield Lovell Papers, Huntington Library; William B. Campbell to his wife, September 14, 1846, Campbell Family Papers, DU; Zachary Taylor to William O. Butler, September 12, 1846, RG 94, NA; William A. Nichols to William B. Campbell, September 13, 1846 [Quitman's orders], Campbell Family Papers, DU; New Orleans *Daily Picayune*, October 6, 1846.

16. Zachary Taylor to the Adjutant General, September 17, 1846, RG 94, NA; New Orleans *Daily Picayune*, October 4, 22, 1846; Captain William P. Rogers Diary, September 18, 1846 (Photocopy; original in private hands), UT; Seymour V. Connor and Odie B. Faulk, *North America Divided: The Mexican War, 1846–1848* (New York, 1971), 46; Mansfield Lovell Diary, n.d., Mansfield Lovell Papers, Huntington Library; Captain John Sanders to Robert J. Walker, September 25, 1846, Robert J. Walker Papers, LC; Samuel G. French, *Two Wars: An Autobiography of Gen. Samuel G. French* (Nashville, 1901), 59. The grove had been used during peacetime as a picnic grounds. New Orleans *Daily Picayune*, September 29, 1846.

17. JAQ Proclamation, September 19, 1846, Campbell Family papers, DU.

18. Bauer, *Mexican War*, 92–93; Singletary, *Mexican War*, 35–36; Connor and Faulk, *North America Divided*, 47; Cadmus M. Wilcox, *History of the Mexican War* (Washington, D.C., 1892), 119; William B. Campbell to his wife, October 10, 1846, Campbell Family Papers, DU; Major Luther Giddings to "Messrs. Comly," November 14, 1846, in George Winston Smith and Charles Judah, *Chronicles of the Gringos: The U.S. Army in the Mexican War, 1846–1848* (Albuquerque, 1968), 78.

19. Zachary Taylor to the Adjutant General, September 22, 1846, RG 94, NA; John Garland to General David Twiggs, September 29, 1846, RG 107, NA; Electus Backus, "A Brief Sketch of the Battle of Monterrey . . . ," *Historical Magazine*, X (1866), 207–213; B. F. Cheatham to William B. Campbell, September 27, 1846, William B. Campbell to JAQ, September 27, 1846, William B. Campbell to [?], February 5, 1848, Campbell Family Papers, DU; Vicksburg *Sentinel*, November 21, 1846; Vicksburg *Whig*, November 26, 1846; McLendon, "Quitman," 213–14; Bauer, *Mexican War*, 95–97; [Major Luther Giddings], *Sketches of the Campaign in Northern Mexico in Eighteen Hundred Forty-Six and Seven by an Officer of the First Regiment of Ohio Volunteers* (New York, 1853), 159–60; JAQ to Eliza Quitman, September 25, 1846, Quitman Family Papers, SHC; Justin H. Smith, *The War with Mexico* (2 vols.; New York, 1919), I, 253–55; John S. Holt Journal, n.d., in Claiborne, *Quitman*, I, 277.

20. *House Executive Documents*, 30th Cong., 1st Sess., No. 17, pp. 14–17 [Quitman's report]; James T. McIntosh (ed.), *The Papers of Jefferson Davis* (4 vols.; Baton Rouge, 1971–), III, 25–27, 30n–31n, 42n–43n, 44–45, 47–52, 52n–53n, 67–68, 86–88, 101–105, 109n, 402–406; "Field Return of the United States Forces, Commanded by General Z. Taylor, U.S.A. before Monterey, Mexico, Sept. 21, 1846," Thomas L. Hamer to L. Thomas, September 25, 1846, RG 94, NA; James K. Holland Diary, September 21, 1846, in James K. Holland, "Diary of a Texan Volunteer in the Mexican War," *Southwestern Historical Quarterly*, XXX (July, 1926), 25.

21. Bauer, *Mexican War*, 98; Smith, *War with Mexico*, I, 223–24; JAQ to Eliza Quitman, September 25, 1846, Quitman Family Papers, SHC; JAQ to Thomas L. Hamer, September 28, 1846, *House Executive Documents*, 29th Cong., 2nd Sess., No. 4, p. 94.

22. "Terms of Capitulation of the City of Monterrey, the Capital of Nuevo León, agreed upon by the undersigned commissioners . . . ," RG 94, NA; Bauer, *Mexican War*, 99–101; Edward J. Nichols, *Zach Taylor's Little Army* (Garden City, 1963), 154–57; Smith, *War with Mexico*, I, 255–60; R. S. Ripley, *The War with Mexico* (2 vols., 1849; rpr. New York, 1970), I, 230–37; JAQ to Eliza Quitman, September 25, 1846, Quitman Family Papers, SHC; French, *Two Wars*, 65–67; JAQ to Thomas L. Hamer, September 28, 1846, *House Executive Documents*, 29th Cong., 2nd Sess., No. 4, pp. 95–96; Jefferson Davis to JAQ, September 26, 1846, Stephen A. D. Greaves to Jefferson Davis, October 18, 1846, William H. H. Patterson to Jefferson Davis, October 18, 1846, McIntosh (ed.), *Papers of Jefferson Davis*, III, 35–36, 64–66, 69.

23. Zachary Taylor to the Adjutant General, September 25, 1846, RG 94, NA; Dr. [Seymour] Halsey to [?], quoted in Vicksburg *Sentinel*, October 9, 1846; JAQ to Robert J. Walker, November 12, 1846, in Claiborne, *Quitman*, I, 272; JAQ to F. Henry Quitman, October 14, 1846, JAQ Papers, HSP; JAQ to Eliza Quitman, September 25, October 7, November 22, 1846, Quitman Family Papers, SHC.

24. JAQ to Louisa Quitman, November 28, 1846, Eliza Quitman to JAQ, November 10, 1846, Quitman Family Papers, SHC; JAQ to Robert J. Walker, November 12, 1846, in Claiborne, *Quitman*, I, 272–74.

25. JAQ to Eliza Quitman, September 25, October 7, 19, 1846, Quitman Family Papers, SHC; New Orleans *Daily Picayune*, November 14, 1846; JAQ to F. Henry Quitman, October 14, 1846, JAQ Papers, HSP. Quitman named the encampment "Camp Allen" in honor of Captain William B. Allen, of the Tennessee volunteers, who had fallen in battle. Quitman's Orders No. 11, October 1, 1846, Campbell Family Papers, DU.

26. JAQ to Eliza Quitman, October 19, November 22, December 10, 1846, JAQ to Louisa Quitman, November 28, 1846, Quitman Family Papers, SHC.

27. Captain William P. Rogers Diary (photocopy), October 8, 1846, UT; Zachary Taylor to the Adjutant General, October 26, 1846, JAQ to W. W. S. Bliss, November 27, 1846, Zachary Taylor to D. Francis de P. Morales, October 1, 1846 (copy), RG 94, NA; JAQ to Eliza Quitman, November 22, 1846, Quitman Family Papers, SHC; Daniel Harvey Hill Diary, n.d., 39, SHC; William B. Campbell to his wife, October 14, 20, November 15, 1846, Campbell Family Papers, DU; W. W. Bishop, *A Journal of the Twelve Months Campaign of Gen. Shields' Brigade in Mexico: In the Years 1846–7* (St. Louis, 1847), 15; JAQ to William B. Campbell, November 28, 1847, MS at Morristown National Historical Park, Morristown, N.J.; Nichols, *Zach Taylor's Little Army*, 170–75. Some soldiers found diversion at the Mexican dances, or "fandangoes." In November, the arrival of a circus helped relieve some of the boredom. William B. Campbell to his wife, November 23, 1846, Campbell Family Papers, DU; New Orleans *Daily Picayune*, November 14, 1846. It should be noted that occasionally Mexicans, rather than soldiers, were responsible for the incidents. Bauer, *Mexican War*, 102.

28. Mansfield Lovell Diary, n.d., Mansfield Lovell Papers, Huntington Library; JAQ to Roger Jones, October 10, 1846, RG 94, NA; JAQ to Eliza Quitman, June 3, 1847, Quitman Family Papers, SHC; [Quitman's] Orders No. 12, October 1, 1846, Campbell Family Papers, DU.

29. Ripley, *War with Mexico*, I, 189; Bauer, *Mexican War*, 201; Oakah L. Jones, *Santa Anna* (New York, 1968), 109.

30. Zachary Taylor to the Adjutant General, October 15, 1846, RG 94, "William Marcy to Zachary Taylor, October 13, 1846, RG 107, NA.

31. Zachary Taylor to the Adjutant General, November 8, 12, December 8, 1846, Zachary Taylor to General D. Antonio López de Santa Anna, November 5, 1846, RG 94, William Marcy to Zachary Taylor, October 22, 1846, RG 107, NA; Bauer, *Mexican War*, 201–204; Ripley, *War with Mexico*, I, 324–26, 329.

32. Smith, *War with Mexico*, I, 356–57; JAQ to Eliza Quitman, December 10, 1846, Quitman Family Papers, SHC; [Quitman's] Orders No. 26, December 18, 1846, Campbell Family Papers, DU.

CHAPTER 13

1. James K. Polk Diary, November 20, 1846, Milo Milton Quaife (ed.), *The Diary of James K. Polk* (4 vols., 1910; rpr. New York, 1970), II, 246–48; Winfield Scott to William Marcy, January 16, 1847, William Marcy Papers, LC; Russell F. Weigley, *The American Way of War: A History of United States Military Strategy and*

Policy (New York, 1973), 65–66; K. Jack Bauer, *The Mexican War, 1846–1848* (New York, 1974), 75, 142n, 147, 161n, 235–36.

2. Winfield Scott to Zachary Taylor, November 25, 1846 (copy), Marcy Papers, LC; Justin H. Smith, *The War with Mexico* (2 vols.; New York, 1919), I, 358.

3. John S. Holt Journal, December 18, 1846, in J. F. H. Claiborne, *Life and Correspondence of John A. Quitman* (2 vols.; New York, 1860), I, 278–79; Vicksburg *Whig*, July 14, 1846; *Mississippi Free Trader* (Natchez), November 11, 1858. Less than twenty years old, Holt was the son of a prosperous Wilkinson County physician. *Seventh Census, 1850: Population*, Mississippi, Wilkinson County.

4. W.W.S. Bliss to JAQ, December 17, 1846, W. W. S. Bliss to Robert Patterson, December 17, 1846, Zachary Taylor to the Adjutant General, December 17, 1846, RG 94, Records of the Adjutant General, Mexican War, Army of Occupation, Letters Sent, NA.

5. Quitman's Orders No. 26, December 18, 1846, William B. Campbell to his wife, January 2, 1847, Campbell Family Papers, DU; John S. Holt Journal, December 19–30, 1846, in Claiborne, *Quitman*, I, 283–88; John R. Kenly, *Memoirs of a Maryland Volunteer, War with Mexico, in the Years 1846–7–8* (Philadelphia, 1873), 185–86, 188; JAQ to Louisa Quitman, January 6, 1847, JAQ to Eliza Quitman, December 30, 1846, Quitman Family Papers, SHC; Vicksburg *Whig*, January 28, 1847; JAQ to W. W. S. Bliss, December 30, 1846, RG 94, NA; Samuel G. French, *Two Wars: An Autobiography of Gen. Samuel G. French* (Nashville, 1901), 59.

6. JAQ to W.W. S. Bliss, December 30, 1846, January 4, 1847, RG 94, NA; William B. Campbell to his wife, January 2, 1847, Campbell Family Papers, DU; George Gordon Meade (ed.), *The Life and Letters of George Gordon Meade* (2 vols.; New York, 1913), I, 170, 172. Patterson had been instructed to make a "demonstration" against Tula, if possible, after his arrival at Victoria. W. W. S. Bliss to Robert Patterson, December 17, 1846, RG 94, NA.

7. JAQ to F. Henry Quitman, January 11, 1847, JAQ Papers, MDA; Captain William P. Rogers Diary, January 1, 1847 (Photocopy; original in private hands), UT; W. W. Bishop, *A Journal of the Twelve Months Campaign of Gen. Shields' Brigade in Mexico: In the Years 1846–7* (St. Louis, 1847), 23–24; George C. Furber, *The Twelve Months Volunteer; or, Journal of a Private in the Tennessee Regiment of Cavalry in the Campaign, in Mexico, 1846–7* (Cincinnati, 1848), 324; William B. Campbell to his wife, January 2, 14, 1847, Campbell Family Papers, DU; Thomas Tennery Diary, January 4, 7, 10, 1847, D. E. Livingston-Little (ed.), *The Mexican War Diary of Thomas D. Tennery* (Norman, 1970), 53–55; Vicksburg *Whig*, January 28, 1847.

8. R. S. Ripley, *The War with Mexico* (2 vols., 1849; rpr. New York, 1970), I, 337. Santa Anna temporarily suspended his attack when he learned about Wool's reinforcement of Worth. Bauer, *Mexican War*, 205.

9. George B. McClellan Diary, January 4, 1847, William Starr Myers (ed.), *The Mexican War Diary of George B. McClellan* (Princeton, 1917), 43–44; JAQ to F. Henry Quitman, January 11, 1847, JAQ Papers, MDA.

10. Smith, *War with Mexico*, I, 362; Ripley, *War with Mexico*, I, 340–46.

11. Ripley, *War with Mexico*, I, 346; Zachary Taylor to Joseph [P. Taylor], January 14, 1847, Zachary Taylor Papers, Presidential Papers, LC; Zachary Taylor to H. L. Scott, January 15, 1847, RG 94, NA; Furber, *Twelve Months Volunteer*, 337, 339.

12. Eliza Quitman to JAQ, November 10, 1846, JAQ to Louisa Quitman, January 11, 1847, JAQ to Eliza Quitman, January 27, 1847, Quitman Family Papers, SHC; JAQ to F. Henry Quitman, January 11, 1847, JAQ Papers, MDA; Jefferson Davis to JAQ, January 13, 1847, Jefferson Davis to Joseph E. Davis, January 26, 1847, James T. McIntosh (ed.), *The Papers of Jefferson Davis* (4 vols.; Baton Rouge, 1971–), III, 113, 114–16. Quitman tried to keep private his disillusionment with Davis. See JAQ to Louisa Quitman, January 11, 1847, Quitman Family Papers, SHC.

13. Furber, *Twelve Months Volunteer*, 342–85; Vicksburg *Whig*, February 27, 1847; Bishop, *Journal*, 25–27; JAQ to Eliza Quitman, January 27, 1847, Quitman Family Papers, SHC; Thomas Tennery Diary, January 16–28, 1847, Livingston-Little (ed.), *Mexican War Diary*, 57–62; William B. Campbell to David Campbell, January 26, 1847, Campbell Family Papers, DU; Kenley, *Memoirs*, 227–29; William H. T. Walker to his wife, January 23, 1847, William Henry Talbot Walker Papers, DU; Robert Anderson to his wife, January 25, 1847, Eba Anderson Lawton (comp.), *An Artillery Officer in the Mexican War: Letters of Robert Anderson* (New York, 1911), 14–15; New Orleans *Daily Picayune*, January 11, 1847.

14. Ivor Debenham Spencer, *The Victor and the Spoils: A Life of William L. Marcy* (Providence, 1959), 163–64; JAQ to Louisa Quitman, February 15, 1847, Quitman Family Papers, SHC.

15. Eliza Quitman to JAQ, January 30, 1847, JAQ to Eliza Quitman, February 20, 1847, Quitman Family Papers, SHC. Developments following Davis' return to Mississippi after Buena Vista further strained the Davis-Quitman relationship. Quitman learned that in Natchez ceremonies celebrating Davis' return, Davis had been puffed into a god for his Monterrey heroism while his own name had been strangely absent from the speeches and the toasts. William Mellen to JAQ, June 15, 1847, J. F. H. Claiborne Papers, MDA; Louisa Quitman to JAQ, July 7, 1847, Quitman Family Papers, SHC; F. Henry Quitman to JAQ, July 7, 1847, JAQ Papers, MDA. Davis, however, seems to have wanted a reconciliation with Quitman; or Davis may have been unaware of the depth of Quitman's resentment. After returning to Mississippi, Davis made a special effort to send his respects to Eliza and promised a visit. Eliza Quitman to JAQ, June 28, 1847, Quitman Family Papers, SHC.

16. Winfield Scott General Order, January 30, 1847, RG 94, NA; Charles Winslow Elliott, *Winfield Scott: The Soldier and the Man* (New York, 1937), 450–51; Richard Beldon Screven to Louise P. Screven, February 16, 1847, Richard Beldon Screven Papers, Georgia Historical Society, Savannah; Ulysses S. Grant to Julia Dent, February 25, 1847, John Y. Simon (ed.), *The Papers of Ulysses S. Grant* (8 vols.; Carbondale, 1967–), I, 125–26; George Gordon Meade to his wife, February 24, 1847, Meade (ed.), *Life and Letters*, I, 184; George T. M. Davis, *Autobiography of the Late Col. Geo. T. M. Davis: Captain and Aide-de-Camp, Scott's Army of Invasion (Mexico), from Posthumous Papers* (New York, 1891), 119; JAQ to Eliza Quitman, February 20, 1847, Quitman Family Papers, SHC; Winfield Scott to William Marcy, February 28, 1847, *House Executive Documents*, 30th Cong., 1st Ses., No. 56, p. 86.

17. Davis, *Autobiography*, 121–23; Theodore O'Hara to John M. McCalla, March 3, 1847, John M. McCalla Papers, DU; Mansfield Lovell Diary, n.d., Mansfield Lovell Papers, Huntington Library, San Marino, Ca.; JAQ to Eliza Quitman, April 10, 1847, Quitman Family Papers, SHC; JAQ to Thomas Jesup, March 3,

1847, RG 92, Quartermaster General's Office, Consolidated Correspondence File, NA; Vicksburg *Whig*, April 3, 1847.

18. Bauer, *Mexican War*, 107, 241–45; JAQ to Eliza Quitman, April 10, 1847, Quitman Family Papers, SHC; Ernest M. Lander, Jr., *Reluctant Imperialists: Calhoun, the South Carolinians, and the Mexican War* (Baton Rouge, 1980), 81; J. Jacob Oswandel, *Notes of the Mexican War 1846–47–48* (Philadelphia, 1885), 68, 70; Seymour V. Connor and Odie B. Faulk, *North America Divided: The Mexican War, 1846–1848* (New York, 1971), 108–109.

19. Weigley, *American Way of War*, 71–72; JAQ to Eliza Quitman, April 10, 1847, Quitman Family Papers, SHC; H. Judge Moore, *Scott's Campaign in Mexico from the Rendezvous on the Island of Lobos to the Taking of the City . . .* (Charleston, 1849), 7–8; Vicksburg *Whig*, April 3, 1847; Bauer, *Mexican War*, 245–53; Ripley, *War with Mexico*, II, 42. Quitman experienced supply difficulties to the end of the siege. His camp was five miles from his assigned provision depot, necessitating excruciating walks by his men with provisions on their backs, since horses could not successfully carry men and goods across the sandhills. He requested that a depot be established on a beach closer to his brigade's position along the siege line. JAQ to George A. McCall, March 24, 1847, RG 94, NA.

20. New Orleans *Daily Picayune*, April 9, 1847; James Mason to JAQ, April 6, 1847, RG 94, NA; JAQ to Eliza Quitman, March 30, 1847, Quitman Family Papers, SHC; Bauer, *Mexican War*, 112–15.

21. JAQ to H. L. Scott, April 7, 1847, RG 94, NA; Moore, *Scott's Campaign*, 44–48.

22. Samuel Eliot Morison, *"Old Bruin": Commodore Matthew C. Perry, 1794–1858* (Boston, 1967), 223–24; Raphael Semmes, *Service Afloat and Ashore During the Mexican War* (Cincinnati, 1851), 147–48; Caspar F. Goodrich, "Alvarado Hunter," *United States Naval Institute Proceedings*, XLIV (1918), 495–514; Poem from New York *Sun*, May 7, 1847, quoted in James H. McLendon, "John A. Quitman" (P.D. dissertation, University of Texas, 1949), 239; JAQ to H. L. Scott, April 7, 1847, RG 94, NA; Captain William Harwar Parker, *Recollections of a Naval Officer, 1841–1865* (New York, 1883), 103–104. Quitman struck a positive note in his report, claiming that the "exemplary conduct" of his troops had "conciliated" the Mexican people south of Veracruz and reporting that negotiations were in progress for the purchase of horses and beef cattle.

23. William S. Johnson Diary, April 6, 18–22, 1847, John Hammond Moore (ed.), "Private Johnson Fights the Mexicans, 1847–1848," *South Carolina Historical Magazine*, LXVII (1966), 210–13; Oswandel, *Notes*, 105; Moore, *Scott's Campaign*, 50, 53, 61; General Orders No. 105, RG 94, NA; H. L. Scott to JAQ, April 11, 1847, P. M. Butler to JAQ, April 13, 1847, JAQ Papers, MDA; JAQ to Louisa Quitman, April 23, 1847, JAQ to Eliza Quitman, April 29, 1847, Quitman Family Papers, SHC; *Congressional Globe*, 35th Cong., 2d Sess., p. 226; Bauer, *Mexican War*, 263–68.

24. JAQ to Louisa Quitman, April 23, 1847, Quitman Family Papers, SHC; H. G. Wilson to JAQ, April 16, 1847, Orders No. 7, Robert Patterson to JAQ, April 25, 1847, JAQ Papers, MDA; JAQ to W. H. French, April 26, 1847 (and accompanying reports), RG 94, NA. For General Scott's strict policies against depredations, see General Orders No. 20, February 19, 1847, RG 94, NA.

25. Robert Patterson to JAQ, May 3, 1847, Orders No. 15, signed by William H.

French, May 3, 1847, JAQ Papers, MDA; Lander, *Reluctant Imperialists*, 38, 93; Bauer, *Mexican War*, 268–70.

26. R. H. Allen to [Captain J. R. Irwin], May 9, 1847, RG 92, NA; Oswandel, *Notes*, 161; JAQ to Louisa Quitman, May 8, 1847, Quitman Family Papers, SHC; William S. Johnson Diary, April 23–24, 1847, Moore (ed.), "Private Johnson," 214; Jackson *Mississippian*, June 25, 1847.

27. Ripley, *War with Mexico*, II, 108–112; Moore, *Scott's Campaign*, 90–93; Lander, *Reluctant Imperialists*, 94; William Henry Talbot Walker to Molly Walker, May 19, 1847, William Henry Talbot Walker Papers, DU; Mansfield Lovell Diary, n.d., Mansfield Lovell Papers, Huntington Library; Bauer, *Mexican War*, 271; JAQ to Eliza Quitman, May 21, 1847, Quitman Family Papers, SHC.

28. Bauer, *Mexican War*, 271–73.

29. JAQ to F. Henry Quitman, May 25, 1847, JAQ Papers, HSP; JAQ to Louisa Quitman, January 6, 1847, JAQ to Eliza Quitman, December 30, 1846, June 3, 1847, Quitman Family Papers, SHC; JAQ to John McMurran, June 14, 1847, JAQ Papers, LSU; JAQ to Robert J. Walker, May 3, 1847, Quitman Biographical File, Texas State Library and Archives, Austin.

30. JAQ to John McMurran, June 14, 1847, JAQ Papers, LSU; JAQ to F. Henry Quitman, May 25, 1847, JAQ Papers, HSP; JAQ to Eliza Quitman, May 21, 1847, Quitman Family Papers, SHC.

31. *Statutes at Large, 1847* (29th Cong., 1st Sess.), Ch. 61, pp. 184–86; James K. Polk to JAQ, April 15, May 12, 1847 (copies), James K. Polk Papers, Presidential Papers, LC; William L. Marcy to JAQ, April 14, 1847, RG 107, NA. Polk commissioned Quitman on April 14, three days after receiving a laudatory report about him from Colonel Joseph G. Totten, chief engineer during the siege of Veracruz. James K. Polk Diary, April 11, 1847, Quaife (ed.), *Diary*, II, 469–70. Brigadier Gideon Pillow of Tennessee received the other major-general appointment.

32. JAQ to Eliza Quitman, May 6, 1847, Quitman Family Papers, SHC; William Henry Talbot Walker to Molly Walker, February 1, March 30, 1847, W. H. T. Walker Papers, DU; Semmes, *Service Afloat*, 283; Vicksburg *Whig*, February 18, 1847; Bishop, *Journal*, 28; Oswandel, *Notes*, 246; Charles J. Peterson, *The Military Heroes of the War with Mexico: With a Narrative of the War* (Philadelphia, 1848), 261–62; Robert Anderson to his wife, August 27, 1847, Lawton (comp.), *Artillery Officer*, 297; Isaac Ingalls Stevens Diary, November 1, 1847, in Hazard Stevens, *The Life of Isaac Ingalls Stevens* (2 vols.; Boston, 1900), I, 220–21.

33. JAQ to Eliza Quitman, May 6, 1847, Quitman Family Papers, SHC. Quitman wrote that he had learned of the appointment on May 5.

34. JAQ to H.L. Scott, May 30, June 3, 1847, Winfield Scott to JAQ, May 31, 1847, filed with JAQ to H. L. Scott, October 25, 1847, Orders dated July 9, 1847, RG 94, NA; JAQ to John McMurran, June 14, 1847, JAQ Papers, LSU; Semmes, *Service Afloat*, 280–81. The Worth-Scott dispute emanated from Scott's repudiation of some of the arrangements Worth had made with city authorities concerning terms of the American occupation, and from Scott's anger over an order from Worth to his division warning his men against poisoned Mexican food. Scott particularly objected to Worth's attributing poisoning techniques to Spanish tutelage. Robert Anderson to his wife, June 25, 26, July 3, Lawton (comp.), *Artillery Officer*, 226–28, 236; Elliott, *Scott*, 486–87. One account suggests that Worth, unlike Quitman, initially aroused Scott's ire by not paying attention at meals. Uncompleted MS, Ethan A. Hitchcock Papers, United States Military Academy Library, West Point, N.Y.

35. Claiborne, *Quitman*, I, 307n; William Marcy to JAQ, December 24, 1847, March 2, 1848, JAQ to William Marcy, January 10, 1847 [1848], March 9, 1848, quoted in New York *Times*, November 10, 1857; *Congressional Globe*, 30th Cong., 1st Sess., 50. For details of the attempt to bribe Santa Anna, see Vicksburg *Whig*, December 21, 1847; Bauer, *Mexican War*, 284–86; Oakah L. Jones, *Santa Anna* (New York, 1968), 114–15.

36. Oswandel, *Notes*, 246; Moore, *Scott's Campaign*, 125; William S. Johnson Diary, August 4, 1847, Moore (ed.), "Private Johnson," 219.

37. William S. Johnson Diary, August 9, 10, 12, 15, Moore (ed.), "Private Johnson," 219–21; Daniel Harvey Hill Diary, August 15, 1847, SHC.

38. Bauer, *Mexican War*, 288–92; Smith, *War with Mexico*, II, 99–119.

39. JAQ memorandum, August 20, 1847, in Claiborne, *Quitman*, I, 347n–48n; JAQ to Eliza Quitman, August 23, 1847, Quitman Family Papers, SHC; Lander, *Reluctant Imperialists*, 117–18; JAQ to H. L. Scott, August 26, 1847, James Shields to Mansfield Lovell, August 24, 1847, RG 94, NA; Cadmus M. Wilcox, *History of the Mexican War* (Washington, D.C., 1892), 397–99; JAQ letter, January 6, 1848, in Washington *Union*, January 15, 1848; Otis A. Singletary, *The Mexican War* (Chicago, 1960), 91.

40. Elliott, *Scott*, 518–22; Robert Hagan Diary, August 23, 1847, UT; Bauer, *Mexican War*, 306–307; Smith, *War with Mexico*, II, 133.

41. JAQ to Eliza Quitman, August 23, 1847, Quitman Family Papers, SHC; Robert Anderson to his wife, August 27, 1847, Lawton (comp.), *Artillery Officer*, 297; Claiborne, *Quitman*, I, 348–49; Ripley, *War with Mexico*, II, 320–26; Elliott, *Scott*, 522–26. Quitman's new aide, George T. M. Davis, appointed at San Agustín, later confirmed that Quitman considered resigning. Quitman, Davis remembered, did not want to be a party to any "disreputable" peace which might be patched up, and expected to be kept in a support role if hostilities happened to resume. Davis, *Autobiography*, 215–16.

CHAPTER 14

1. JAQ to Louisa Quitman, October 5, 1847, Quitman Family Papers, SHC.

2. K. Jack Bauer, *The Mexican War, 1846–1848* (New York, 1974), 307; Oakah L. Jones, *Santa Anna* (New York, 1968), 116; Justin H. Smith, *The War with Mexico* (2 vols.; New York, 1919), II, 142–47; Cadmus M. Wilcox, *History of the Mexican War* (Washington, D.C., 1892), 429.

3. JAQ to Eliza Quitman, September 19, 1847, Quitman Family Papers, SHC; William S. Johnson Diary, September 8, 1847, John Hammond Moore (ed.), "Private Johnson Fights the Mexicans, 1847–1848," *South Carolina Historical Magazine*, LXVII (1966), 223; C. M. Wilcox to JAQ, May 8, 1854, J. F. H. Claiborne Papers, MDA.

4. Charles Winslow Elliott, *Winfield Scott: The Soldier and the Man* (New York, 1937), 530–31; Bauer, *Mexican War*, 311; Vicksburg *Whig*, January 21, 1848; Smith, *War with Mexico*, II, 147–48; R. S. Ripley, *The War with Mexico* (2 vols., 1849; rpr. New York, 1970), II, 390.

5. J. F. H. Claiborne, *Life and Correspondence of John A. Quitman* (2 vols.; New York, 1860), I, 353–56; P. G. T. Beauregard Diary, September 11, 1847, LC.

6. Winfield Scott to William Marcy, September 18, 1847, RG 94, Records of the Adjutant General, Letters Received, NA; P. G. T. Beauregard Diary, September 11,

1847, LC; JAQ to Eliza Quitman, September 19, 1847, Quitman Family Papers, SHC; Smith, *War with Mexico*, II, 152; C. M. Wilcox to JAQ, May 8, 1854, Claiborne Papers, MDA.

7. P. G. T. Beauregard Diary, September 12, 1847, LC; Wilcox, *History of the Mexican War*, 452–56; New Orleans *Daily Picayune*, October 14, 1848; JAQ to H. L. Scott, September 29, 1847, *House Executive Documents*, 30th Cong., 1st Sess., No. 8, pp. 410–11.

8. Ripley, *War with Mexico*, II, 490; Wilcox, *History of the Mexican War*, 456; Daniel Harvey Hill Diary, September 12, 1847, SHC. Promises of special brevets, commissions, and bonuses helped encourage the men to volunteer.

9. Bauer, *Mexican War*, 313, 316–18; Wilcox, *History of the Mexican War*, 457–61; Smith, *War with Mexico*, II, 156; Daniel Harvey Hill Diary, September 13, 1847, SHC; Charles B. Brower to Mansfield Lovell, September 15, 1847, Claiborne Papers, MDA; William S. Walker to his uncle, October 27, 1847, clipping in Robert J. Walker scrapbook, Robert J. Walker Papers, LC; Philip Gadsden to his sister, June 20, 1854, Gadsden-Trapier Papers, South Carolina Historical Society, Charleston; Robert Hagan Diary, September 22, 1847, UT.

10. JAQ to Captain H. L. Scott, September 29, 1847, *House Executive Documents*, 30th Cong., 1st Sess., No. 8, pp. 411–14; JAQ to Eliza Quitman, September 19, 1847, Quitman Family Papers, SHC; Testimony of Roswell S. Ripley, April 14, 1848, in Mexico City *Daily American Star*, April 15, 1848; D. D. Baker to JAQ, May 5, 1851, C. M. Wilcox to JAQ, May 8, 1854, Claiborne Papers, MDA; Gideon Pillow to Winfield Scott, October 3, 1847, RG 94, NA; Allan R. Millett, *Semper Fidelis: The History of the United States Marine Corps* (1980; paper ed. New York, 1982), 78–79.

11. Winfield Scott to William Marcy, September 18, 1847, RG 94, NA; Testimony of Roswell S. Ripley, April 14, 1848, in Mexico City *Daily American Star*, April 15, 1848; Charles J. Peterson, *The Military Heroes of the War with Mexico: With a Narrative of the War* (Philadelphia, 1848), 125.

12. Winfield Scott to William Marcy, September 18, 1847, RG 94, NA; P. G. T. Beauregard Diary, September 13, 1847, LC; John P. Gaines to JAQ, October 27, 1847, Claiborne Papers, MDA; New Orleans *Daily Picayune*, October 14, 1847; JAQ to Captain H. L. Scott, September 29, 1847, *House Executive Documents*, 30th Cong., 1st Sess., No. 8, pp. 414–15; Richmond *Enquirer*, January 25, 1848; Bauer, *Mexican War*, 318–19; Ernest M. Lander, Jr., *Reluctant Imperialists: Calhoun, the South Carolinians, and the Mexican War* (Baton Rouge, 1980), 126.

13. Winfield Scott to William Marcy, September 18, 1847, RG 94, NA. Historians have been, perhaps, less charitable than Scott. See, for instance, Peterson, *Military Heroes*, 125; Bauer, *Mexican War*, 319; Lander, *Reluctant Imperialists*, 126–27.

14. JAQ to Captain H. L. Scott, September 29, 1847, *House Executive Documents*, 30th Cong., 1st Sess., No. 8, pp. 415–18; A. H. Gladden to David Johnson, November 20, 1848 [copy], Adley Hogan Gladden Papers, Caroliniana Library, University of South Carolina, Columbia; Peterson, *Military Heroes*, 125; Winfield Scott to William Marcy, September 18, 1847, RG 94, NA; Raphael Semmes, *Service Afloat and Ashore During the Mexican War* (Cincinnati, 1851), 462–63; Ripley, *War with Mexico*, II, 434–35, 441; Lander, *Reluctant Imperialists*, 126–27; P. G. T. Beauregard Diary, September 13, 1847, LC; Edmund Hardcastle to JAQ, October 26, 1847, JAQ Papers, HU. James H. McLendon, "John A. Quitman" (Ph.D. dis-

sertation, University of Texas, 1949), 271. Quitman's daughter later recounted, as Mansfield Lovell had said, that during the afternoon's fighting, amid all the smoke of battle, Harry came forward with a bowl of chicken broth for his master, who had not eaten since the previous day. She added that "as a reward . . . the 13th of September never returned that '*Harry*' did not receive a five dollar gold piece." Rosalie Quitman Duncan, "Life of General John A. Quitman," *PMHS*, IV (1901), 421.

15. JAQ to Eliza Quitman, September 19, 1847, Quitman Family Papers, SHC; P. G. T. Beauregard Diary, September 13, 14, 1847, LC; Winfield Scott to William Marcy, September 18, 1847, RG 94, NA; Mexico City *Daily American Star*, February 26, 1848; Mansfield Lovell to the Chairman of the Senate Committee on Military Affairs, January 21, 1856, Mansfield Lovell Papers, Huntington Library, San Marino, Ca. Worth could have easily moved on the plaza with or before Quitman; Scott's decision to give Quitman the honor of taking the palace caused some disappointment in Worth's command. See Semmes, *Service Afloat*, 461–63.

16. General Orders of Winfield Scott, September 17, 18, 20, 1847, RG 94, NA; JAQ to Louisa Quitman, October 5, 1847, Quitman Family Papers, SHC.

17. JAQ to Eliza Quitman, September 19, October 11, 13, Quitman Family Papers, SHC; P. G. T. Beauregard Diary, September 15, 1847, LC; New Orleans *Daily Picayune*, October 14, 1847; Bauer, *Mexican War*, 322; Henry O. Whiteside, "Winfield Scott and the Mexican Occupation: Policy and Practice," *Mid-America*, LII (April, 1970), 111.

18. George T. M. Davis, *Autobiography of the Late Col. Geo. T. M. Davis: Captain and Aide-de-Camp, Scott's Army of Invasion (Mexico), from Posthumous Papers* (New York, 1891), 258–61; New Orleans *Daily Picayune*, October 14, 15, 1847; Edward H. Moseley, "The Religious Impact of the American Occupation of Mexico City, 1847–1848," Eugene R. Huck and Edward H. Moseley (eds.), *Militarists, Merchants and Missionaries: United States Expansion in Middle America* (University, Ala., 1970), 41–42.

19. Lieutenant Colonel Ethan Allen Hitchcock to JAQ, September 24, October 4, 1847, JAQ Papers, HU; Quitman Orders, September 27, 1847, RG 94, NA; Mexico City *Daily American Star*, September 25, 28, October 10, 15, 1847; Davis, *Autobiography*, 247–49. The specifics of the ayuntamiento's working with Quitman to restore order are traced in Dennis E. Berge, "A Mexican Dilemma: The Mexico City Ayuntamiento and the Question of Loyalty, 1846–1848," *Hispanic American Historical Review*, L (1970), 229–56. Berge shows that, later in the occupation, friction did arise between the Americans and the ayuntamiento.

20. Daniel Harvey Hill Diary, September 17, 18, 1847, SHC; P. G. T. Beauregard Diary, October 1, 1847, LC; Vicksburg *Sentinel*, November 9, 1847; Mexico City *Daily American Star*, September 30, October 2, 28, 1847; New Orleans *Daily Picayune*, October 15, November 10, 1847; *North American* (Mexico City), October 15, 1847.

21. Daniel Murphy to JAQ, October 22, 1847, and other papers, "Military Papers," JAQ Papers, MDA; Juan Palacios to JAQ, September 24, 1847, Ethan Allen Hitchcock to JAQ, October 2, 1847, Charles Naylor to JAQ, October 2, 1847, JAQ Papers, HU; Recommendation for discharge of Captain James Murray, October 24, 1847, Application for leave of Robert Porter, October 24, 1847, William J. Healy to JAQ, October 16, 1847, A. H. Hamilton to JAQ, October 18, 1847, RG 94, NA; R. O. Ledyard Case, Various documents, in Franklin Pierce Papers, Presidential Papers, LC; Mexico City *Daily American Star*, September 28, 30, 1847; Bauer, *Mexi-*

can War, 329–51, 378–82. Daniel Harvey Hill, a regular soldier who questioned Quitman's command skill because Quitman lacked military training, nonetheless acknowledged Quitman's evenhandedness as an occupation governor. Daniel Harvey Hill Diary, September 18, 1847, February 1, 1848, SHC.

22. JAQ to Eliza Quitman, October 11, 13, 1847, JAQ to Henry S. Foote, October 15, 1847 (copy), Quitman Family Papers, SHC.

23. JAQ to Eliza Quitman, October 11, 13, 1847, JAQ to Henry S. Foote, October 15, 1847 (copy), Quitman Family Papers, SHC; JAQ to H. L. Scott, September 17, October 25, 1847, Winfield Scott Orders, October 22, 1847, RG 94, NA. On the earthquake, which was severe, yet barely mentioned by Quitman in letters home, see Mexico City *Daily American Star*, October 5, 1847; P. G. T. Beauregard Diary, October 2, 1847, LC; JAQ to Louisa Quitman, October 5, 1847, Quitman Family Papers, SHC. Quitman shared the palace with other officers and several regiments. The *Star* (September 20) listed Quitman's staff and noted that Colonel Francis Belton of the Third Artillery was lieutenant governor.

24. Winfield Scott, October 27 endorsement on Quitman's October 25 letter, RG 94, NA.

25. JAQ to Eliza Quitman, October 27, 1847, Eliza Quitman to JAQ, February 19, April 2, 1847, Quitman Family Papers, SHC; Mexico City *Daily American Star*, October 28, 1847; *North American* (Mexico City), October 29, November 3, 1847. According to one anecdote related after Quitman's return, Eliza had so adjusted to her husband's militarism that she shocked visiting ladies trying to console her over her husband's life being in jeopardy. Supposedly Eliza said she would rather be the widow of a soldier killed in battle than the wife of a coward. Jackson *Mississippian*, December 10, 1847.

26. Bauer, *Mexican War*, 224, 332; William S. Johnson Diary, November 1, 1847, Moore (ed.), "Private Johnson," 224; Mexico City *Daily American Star*, October 28, 1847; Vicksburg *Sentinel*, November 17, December 1, 1847; New Orleans *Daily Picayune*, November 7, 24, 1847.

27. JAQ to Eliza Quitman, October 27, 1847, September 13, 1856, Antonia Quitman to Annie Rosalie Quitman, September 14, 1856, Quitman Family Papers, SHC; Jackson *Mississippian*, January 9, 1852; Vicksburg *Whig*, September 27, 1854; "ANNUAL CIRCULAR OF THE MONTEZUMA SOCIETY," December [?], 1855, Letterbooks, Claiborne Papers, MDA. The circular shows that the society collected a $1 initiation fee and $3 annual dues. Commodore Perry served as its president and Mansfield Lovell was its secretary. The organization was a social group intended to perpetuate national feelings of "chivalry" and "military propriety."

28. JAQ to F. Henry Quitman, September 13, 1852, JAQ Papers, HSP; JAQ Daybook, March 14, 1849, JAQ Papers, LSU; Receipt from William W. Yerby, dated Washington, D.C., March 4, 1848, JAQ Papers, MDA; Jackson *Mississippian*, September 20, 1850; Vicksburg *Sentinel*, September 21, 1850. Quitman also subscribed to five copies of a play about Mexico called "Cortez the Conqueror: A Tragedy." He gave one copy to P. G. T. Beauregard. See the bound play and Quitman's notebook, in JAQ Papers, LSU.

29. Jackson *Mississippian*, September 5, 1851, September 2, 1853; William A. Stone to JAQ, December 27, 1855, JAQ Papers, MDA.

CHAPTER 15

1. Eliza Quitman to JAQ, October 17, 1847, Quitman Family Papers, SHC; Philip Hone Diary, October 25, 1847, Allan Nevins (ed.), *The Diary of Philip Hone, 1828–1851* (1927; rpr. New York, 1970), 822; Robert W. Johannsen, *A New Era for the United States: Americans and the War with Mexico* (Urbana, 1975), 25; Jackson *Mississippian*, November 12, 1847.

2. New Orleans *Daily Picayune*, November 25, 1847; Mexico City *Daily American Star*, December 23, 1847; JAQ to Eliza Quitman, November 24, 1847, Quitman Family Papers, SHC. Either during this stay in New Orleans, or during his December return, Quitman apparently startled one later chronicler with the extremity of his imperialistic views. William H. Sparks claimed that Quitman told him that General Scott erred by not establishing an empire in Mexico with himself (Scott) emperor, which could have been accomplished had Scott induced American and British immigration by appointing "dukes, marquises, lords, and barons" and offering "principalities." William H. Sparks, *The Memories of Fifty Years* . . . (Philadelphia, 1870), 347–48. Surely Sparks embellished whatever remarks Quitman made. Such monarchical language would have been out of character for Quitman, a professed republican despite his aristocratic self-consciousness.

3. *Mississippi Free Trader* (Natchez), October 23, November 30, December 2, 4, 9, 1847; Jackson *Mississippian*, December 10, 1847; Vicksburg *Sentinel*, May 17, 1848. The sword was completed by a local gunsmith in March, 1848, and put on display at his shop pending the arrival of Quitman, who was then in the East. It was quite a work of art, with a pure gold hilt inlaid with mother-of-pearl, rubies, other gems, inscriptions of "Try Us!" (the Fencibles' motto) and a long testimony to Quitman's wartime feats. It had a steel blade, and a scabbard with gold plate and "elegant designs." See Natchez *Courier*, March 17, 1848.

Quitman could not keep the Alvarado cannon permanently; Army regulations did not allow officers to keep the spoils of war. In May, 1848, he donated the cannon to the state of Mississippi during a visit to Jackson. *Mississippi Free Trader* (Natchez), May 16, 1848; Vicksburg *Sentinel*, May 17, 1848.

4. Montgomery *Tri-Weekly Flag and Advertiser*, December 18, 1847; *Alabama Senate Journal*, 1847, p. 73; [?] to Armistead Burt, January 15, 1848, John Caldwell Calhoun Papers, DU; "Masonic Honors Paid in Charleston, S.C., To Generals Quitman and Shields, U. S. A.," *Freemason's Monthly Magazine* (February, 1848), in MDA; Robert Rowand Diary, December 20, 23, 24, 1847, DU. While in Charleston, Quitman met a childhood friend, John Bachman, and received a copy of John James Audubon and Bachman's *The Viviparous Quadrupeds of North America* (3 vols.; New York, 1845–48). Bachman, who had been influenced into the ministry by Quitman's father (who had been his teacher), presented Quitman the copy in memory of their friendship rather than for "what you are now." John Bachman to JAQ, December 23, 1847, American Philosophical Society Library, Philadelphia.

5. *Mississippi Free Trader* (Natchez), January 11, 22, 1848; New Orleans *Daily Picayune*, January 13, 1848; Washington *Daily National Intelligencer*, January 3, 1848. Mayor W. W. Seaton and Senator Douglas had called at the White House in committee to invite President Polk. Polk, however, doubted the propriety of a president attending such a dinner, emphasizing a lack of precedent for his so doing; Andrew Jackson's famous dinner toast to the Union had been made on a more official occasion—Thomas Jefferson's birthday. Polk authorized Douglas to "express to the

company the personal gratification it would have afforded me to be present" had not precedent precluded his attendance. James K. Polk Diary, December 30, 1847, Milo Milton Quaife (ed.), *The Diary of James K. Polk* (4 vols., 1910; rpr. New York, 1970), III, 267–68.

6. *National Era* (Washington), January 6, 1848; Washington *Daily National Intelligencer*, January 3, 1848.

7. Eliza Quitman to F. Henry Quitman, February 19, 1848, Quitman Family Papers, M-N; JAQ to Mansfield Lovell, n.d., in J. F. H. Claiborne, *Life and Correspondence of John A. Quitman* (2 vols.; New York, 1860), II, 10.

8. JAQ to Mansfield Lovell, n.d., in Claiborne, *Quitman*, II, 10; Richmond *Enquirer*, January 18, 25, 1848; New Orleans *Daily Picayune*, February 17, 1848; Poughkeepsie *Telegraph*, February 9, 1848; Mexico City *Daily American Star*, March 14, 1848; Eliza Quitman to F. Henry Quitman, February 19, 1848. The proceedings in Richmond were for Shields also, and involved some lower-ranking officers in addition.

There is no way of knowing how many gifts were bestowed on Quitman. For a thank-you for a volume of original poetry, see JAQ to David Woodweak [?], February 16, 1848, Morristown National Historical Park.

9. Richmond *Enquirer*, January 25, 1848; Poughkeepsie *Telegraph*, February 9, 1848; *New York Assembly Journal*, 71st Sess., 1848, pp. 158, 307, 320–25.

10. F. R. Backus to JAQ, November 20, 1847, J. F. H. Claiborne Papers, MDA; Louisa S. Quitman to JAQ, October 27, 1847, Quitman Family Papers, SHC; Tombstone, Old Stone Church graveyard, Rhinebeck, N.Y. Quitman's sisters moved to Philadelphia, staying initially in a boardinghouse next to the Mayers, later in a rooming house on Chesnut Street. Quitman did arrange a regular schedule of support payments. Auction notice, n.d., Louisa Quitman to JAQ, March 29, April 24, October 3, 1848, October 18, 1849, Quitman Family Papers, SHC; Louisa S. Quitman to F. Henry Quitman, April 4, 28, 1849, Quitman Family Papers, M-N.

11. Eliza Quitman to F. Henry Quitman, February 19, 1848, Quitman Family Papers, M-N; Jackson *Mississippian*, March 10, 1848; [William Wood], *Autobiography of William Wood* (2 vols.; New York, 1895), II, 41; Edward Turner to Eliza Quitman, March 22, 1846, Louisa Quitman to JAQ, January 31, February [?], March 31, May 2, 1847, Louisa Quitman to Eliza Quitman, March 27, 1847, Quitman Family Papers, M-N; Patty Dahlgren to Louisa Quitman, November 18, 1848, JAQ Papers, LSU.

12. Louisa Quitman to JAQ, July 9, 1848, JAQ to Louisa Quitman, June 6, 1848, Quitman Family Papers, SHC; Eliza Quitman to F. Henry Quitman, Febraury 19, 1848, Quitman Family Papers, M-N. Louisa's frustration was compounded when rumors subsequently circulated that she and Shields were engaged. Such reports hampered prospects elsewhere. See Louisa Quitman to Eliza Quitman, [no exact date], 1849, Quitman Family Papers, M-N.

Quitman harbored no hostility toward Shields as a result of the misunderstanding. See JAQ to James Shields, September 9, 1848 (in Claiborne, *Quitman*, II, 15), which, though political in content, has nonetheless a cordial tone. A year later, Quitman joined Stephen A. Douglas in rebutting charges that Shields favored a congressional prohibition against the expansion of slavery. See Robert W. Johannsen (ed.), *The Letters of Stephen A. Douglas* (Urbana, 1961), 182–83.

13. Vicksburg *Sentinel*, December 8, 18, 1847; Jackson *Mississippian*, January 14, April 14, 1848; *Mississippi Free Trader* (Natchez), January 15, 1848.

14. Jackson *Mississippian*, December 17, 1847, January 11, 1848; Mexico City *Daily American Star*, January 13, 1848; Vicksburg *Sentinel*, December 22, 1847; New York *Sun*, quoted in Poughkeepsie *Telegraph*, February 23, 1848; *New York Assembly Journal*, 71st Sess., 1848, p. 323. Quitman amplified his strategic views in a memorandum prepared for presidential perusal. Quitman stressed that American forces should occupy "a limited number" of key points in Mexico which could be easily secured and which would produce revenues through import duties, direct taxes, and taxes on the assaying, coining, and export of precious metals. He advocated the holding of positions "commanding the internal trade of the great sea ports" such as San Luis Potosí, which commanded trade passing through Tampico. He felt that Monterrey and Saltillo could be given up. His plan now required a 27,000-man occupation force. JAQ to [President Polk?], January 17, 1848, RG 94, Office of the Adjutant General, Mexican War, Army of Occupation, Miscellaneous Papers, NA.

15. New Orleans *Daily Picayune*, January 13, 1848; Jackson *Mississippian*, January 11, 1848; James M. Howry to James K. Polk, January 17, 1848, James K. Polk Papers, Presidential Papers, LC; Henry Gourdin to John C. Calhoun, February 4, 1848, J. Franklin Jameson (ed.), "Correspondence of John C. Calhoun," *Annual Report of the American Historical Association, 1899* (Washington, D.C., 1900), II, 1160–61; Willie P. Mangum to William A. Graham, January 23, 1848, Henry Thomas Shanks (ed.), *The Papers of Willie Person Mangum* (5 vols.; Raleigh, 1950–56), I, xxxv, V, 95. See also D. B. Hancock to Dixon H. Lewis, March 3, 1848, Dixon H. Lewis Papers, UT.

16. JAQ to Mansfield Lovell, n.d., in Claiborne, *Quitman*, II, 10; Kenneth M. Johnson, "Nicholas P. Trist: Treaty-Maker," in Odie B. Faulk and Joseph A. Stout, Jr. (eds.), *The Mexican War: Changing Interpretations* (Chicago, 1973), 173–91; Jackson *Mississippian*, March 31, 1848; Frederick Merk, *Manifest Destiny and Mission in American History: A Reinterpretation* (New York, 1963), 107–143, 180–201. The ten-regiment bill passed the Senate but met defeat in the House.

17. Quitman probably arrived home on March 30. He had traveled the northern route, passing through Cincinnati and Memphis. Vicksburg *Whig*, March 31, 1848; C. M. Wilcox to JAQ, April 5, 1848, Claiborne Papers, MDA.

18. *Mississippi Free Trader* (Natchez), April 13, May 16, 1848; New Orleans *Daily Picayune*, April 16, 1848 (Sunday supplement); Lewis Sanders, Jr., to JAQ, December 4, 1847, Claiborne Papers, MDA; Vicksburg *Whig*, May 9, 11, 1848; Jackson *Mississippian*, May 12, 1848. Late in May, a Natchez artist offered a portrait of Quitman for sale. It showed Quitman standing, his hand on the hilt of his sword. *Mississippi Free Trader* (Natchez), May 25, 1848. Quitman continued receiving war-related honors for some time afterward. In December, 1848, a special presentation ceremony was held in Natchez so that he could receive the sword Congress had awarded him for his role at Monterrey. In March, 1849, he received a special medal from New York City. *Mississippi Free Trader* (Natchez), December 5, 1848, March 31, 1849.

19. JAQ to Mansfield Lovell, n.d., JAQ to John O. Knox, March 18, 1848, in Claiborne, *Quitman*, II, 10, 13–14; New Orleans *Daily Picayune*, April 16, 1848 (Sunday supplement); Jackson *Mississippian*, May 12, 1848; JAQ to Peter G. Washington, April 29, 1848, JAQ Papers, LSU; C. M. Wilcox to JAQ, April 5, 1848, Claiborne Papers, MDA. A report from the *Mississippian's* Washington correspondent, dated May 2, claimed that Democrats in Congress preferred Quitman as their vice-presidential candidate. Jackson *Mississippian*, May 19, 1848.

The biography was published that year. See [Peter G. Washington?], *A Brief Sketch of the Life, Civil and Military, of John A. Quitman, Major General in the Army of the U. S.* (Washington, D.C., 1848).

20. S. C. Ridgely to JAQ, May 8, 1848, JAQ Papers, MDA; *Mississippi Free Trader* (Natchez), May 16, 1848.

21. Edward S. Wallace, *General William Jenkins Worth: Monterey's Forgotten Hero* (Dallas, 1953), 172–84; Justin H. Smith, *The War with Mexico* (2 vols.; New York, 1919), II, 185–88; K. Jack Bauer, *The Mexican War, 1846–1848* (New York, 1974), 371–74; Otis A. Singletary, *The Mexican War* (Chicago, 1960), 124–25, 134–36; James K. Polk Diary, December 18, 1847, April 25, 1848, Quaife (ed.), *Diary*, III, 251–52, IV, 434; *Senate Executive Documents*, 30th Cong., 1st Sess., No. 65, pp. 1–3, 317–28. The court had met in Mexico in March and April, then met briefly in New Orleans and Louisville in May.

22. *Mississippi Free Trader* (Natchez), May 16, 1848; JAQ to Eliza Quitman, May 27 [?], 1848, Quitman Family Papers, SHC; Vicksburg *Sentinel*, May 31, 1848; JAQ to Eliza Quitman, May 24, 1848, Lovell Family Papers, UnS; *Proceedings of the Democratic National Convention Held in Baltimore, May 22[–26], 1848* (Washington, D.C., 1848); Joseph G. Rayback, *Free Soil: The Election of 1848* (Lexington, Ky., 1970), 174–75, 191; John H. Martin, "William R. King and the Vice Presidency," *Alabama Review*, XVI (January, 1963), 46–48. Butler had considerable support among the New York "Barnburners," a faction of the New York Democracy which had withdrawn from the convention in protest over a seating matter. Apparently Butler's nomination was intended, at least in part, as a sop to the Barnburners to entice them to rejoin the party and support Cass. Chaplain W. Morrison, *Democratic Politics and Sectionalism: The Wilmot Proviso Controversy* (Chapel Hill, 1967), 128–40.

23. JAQ to Eliza Quitman, May 27 [?], 1848, JAQ to Louisa Quitman, June 6, 1848, Quitman Family Papers, SHC; JAQ to John B. Nevitt, June 9, 1848, in Claiborne, *Quitman*, II, 15; George W. Kendall to JAQ, May 19, 1848, Claiborne Papers, MDA. The *Mississippian* later felt compelled to publish a denial that McNutt had sabotaged Quitman's candidacy. Jackson *Mississippian*, June 16, 1848.

24. JAQ to Louisa Quitman, June 6, 1848, Quitman Family Papers, SHC; JAQ to William L. Marcy, June 4, 1848, in Claiborne, *Quitman*, II, 12; Washington *Daily National Intelligencer*, May 26, 1848.

25. *Senate Executive Documents*, 30th Cong., 1st Sess., No. 65, pp. 254–66, 316–35; William J. Worth to JAQ, November 3, 1847, JAQ Papers, UV; James Duncan to JAQ, November 27, 1847, Claiborne Papers, MDA.

26. JAQ to James K. Polk, June 27, 1848 (rough draft), Quitman Family Papers, SHC; James K. Polk Diary, July 6, 7, 1848, Quaife (ed.), *Diary*, IV, 5–9; Henry S. Foote, *Casket of Reminiscences* (Washington, D.C., 1874), 349–52; JAQ to Eliza Quitman, June 9, 1848, Lovell Family Papers, UnS; Francis B. Heitman, *Historical Register and Dictionary of the U.S. Army, 1789–1903* (Washington, D.C., 1903), 812; Vicksburg *Whig*, July 20, 1848. Foote had already experienced a confrontation with Davis over Quitman in the Senate. On July 1, Foote had lambasted Davis for having a report read about the raising of the American flag on the palace in Mexico City which totally ignored Quitman's role. *Congressional Globe*, 30th Cong., 1st Sess., 890.

27. Sarah Turner to Eliza Quitman, July 4, 1825, JAQ to Charles H. Parker, July 20, 1840, JAQ to Louisa Quitman, June 6, 1848, Louisa Quitman to JAQ, July 9,

1848, Quitman Family Papers, SHC; JAQ to Eliza Quitman, June 9, 1848, Lovell Family Papers, UnS; John B. Nevitt to Powhatan Ellis, February 26, 1832, Powhatan Ellis Papers, UT; F. Henry Quitman to Eliza Quitman, March 15, 1849, JAQ Papers, MDA; Thomas Jefferson Wertenbaker, *Princeton, 1746–1896* (Princeton, 1946), 115; John Hope Franklin, *A Southern Odyssey: Travelers in the Antebellum North* (Baton Rouge, 1976), 62.

28. Vicksburg *Sentinel*, July 26, 1848; George Cavallor Graham to William A. Graham, July 27, 1848, J. G. de Roulhac Hamilton (ed.), *The Papers of William Alexander Graham* (6 vols.; Raleigh, 1957–76), III, 240; Eliza Quitman to JAQ, June 6, 1848, Quitman Family Papers, SHC.

29. JAQ to John B. Nevitt, June 9, 1848, in Claiborne, *Quitman*, II, 15; JAQ to the Democrats of Philadelphia, June 30, 1848, quoted in Vicksburg *Sentinel*, August 9, 1848; Vicksburg *Sentinel*, July 26, 1848. Quitman returned to his antimilitaristic political theme later in the year, when he warned a Democratic meeting, with Taylor in mind, that giving way to "military extremism" would destroy the Republic, as it once had France. *Mississippi Free Trader* (Natchez), October 24, 1848.

30. JAQ to James Shields, September 9, 1848, in Claiborne, *Quitman*, II, 15; *Mississippi Free Trader* (Natchez), September 12, October 24, November 7, 9, 1848; JAQ Daybook, September 9, 1848, JAQ Papers, LSU.

31. Jackson *Mississippian*, November 3, 24, December 8, 1848; *Mississippi Free Trader* (Natchez), November 2, 4, 1848; Document signed by the Mississippi Secretary of State, dated December 4, 1848, JAQ Papers, UV.

32. Jackson *Mississippian*, March 10, 1848; *Mississippi Free Trader* (Natchez), September 12, 1848.

33. JAQ to the Democrats of Philadelphia, June 30, 1848, quoted in Vicksburg *Sentinel*, August 9, 1848; *Mississippi Free Trader* (Natchez), October 24, 1848.

CHAPTER 16

1. JAQ to Eliza Quitman, January 25, 1849, Quitman Family Papers, SHC. Henry's departure ended Waldo's responsibilities at Monmouth. Waldo gave thought to becoming a California "Forty-Niner," but in August moved to Milwaukee, where he became a lawyer. F. Henry Quitman to Eliza Quitman, March 15, 1849, JAQ to F. Henry Quitman, April 21, 1849, JAQ Papers, MDA; Eliza Quitman to F. Henry Quitman, August 9, 1849 (Copy courtesy of the editors of *The Papers of Jefferson Davis*; original in private hands); JAQ to F. Henry Quitman, August 5, 1849, JAQ Papers, HSP; O. H. Waldo to Louisa Quitman Lovell, February 15, 1864, Quitman Family Papers, SHC.

2. JAQ to George Cadwalader, January 21, 1849, George Cadwalader Papers, HSP; F. Henry Quitman to George Cadwalader, February 18, 1849, John Cadwalader to F. Henry Quitman, August 9, 1849, JAQ to F. Henry Quitman, May 24, July 2, JAQ Papers, HSP; F. Henry Quitman to JAQ, April 15, 1849, JAQ to F. Henry Quitman, April 21, 1849, JAQ Papers, MDA.

3. JAQ to F. Henry Quitman, August 5, 25, September 7, 20, 24, November 11, 1849, Louisa S. Quitman to F. Henry Quitman, October 24, 1849, JAQ Papers, HSP; F. Henry Quitman to Eliza Quitman, September 17, 1849, Louisa Quitman to JAQ, August 4, 1849, Quitman Family Papers, SHC; F. Henry Quitman to JAQ, September 17, 1849, JAQ Papers, MDA; Eliza Quitman to JAQ, September 17, 1849, Quitman Family Papers, M-N.

4. JAQ to F. Henry Quitman, May 24, and n.d., 1849, April 6, 1850, JAQ Papers, HSP.

5. JAQ to Eliza Quitman, January 25, February 3, 1849, Quitman Family Papers, SHC; JAQ petition to the state legislature, RG 47, Vol. 20, MDA; Jackson *Mississippian*, February 23, 1849; JAQ to Robert J. Walker, December 28, 1849, Robert J. Walker Papers, DU; JAQ to F. Henry Quitman, July 2, n.d., November 17, 1849, JAQ Papers, HSP. Quitman's financial obligations may explain why he chose this time to sell some of his landholdings, including Jefferson College lots in Natchez. Deed Records, Adams County, Vol. GG, pp. 509, 510, MDA; Agreement of sale, JAQ to B. A. Crawford, December 18, 1849, Quitman Family Papers, SHC.

6. Louisa Quitman to Eliza Quitman, March 6, 1849, Eliza Quitman to JAQ, October 9, 1849, Quitman Family Papers, SHC; Louisa Quitman to Eliza Quitman, March [?], 1849, Eliza Quitman to F. Henry Quitman, February 19, September 8, 17, October 9, 1849, Quitman Family Papers, M-N.

7. JAQ to Eliza Quitman, March 8, 9, 1851, Lovell Family Papers, UnS; Eliza Quitman to Sarah Fyler, December 8, 1850, Eliza Quitman to JAQ, June 10, 1850, March 4, 1851, Quitman Family Papers, SHC; Eliza Quitman to F. Henry Quitman, March 6, 1849, May 1, July 1, 1850, Quitman Family Papers, M-N; Antonia Quitman to Louisa Quitman, February 19, 1851, Edward Turner to Eliza Quitman, January 1, 1851, JAQ Papers, LSU. Eliza was appalled when the Minors, a Catholic family, gave a polka party during Lent and disrupted its sanctity. Eliza Quitman to F. Henry Quitman, March 15, 1851, Quitman Family Papers, M-N.

Eliza's bouts of depression were more periodic than chronic. Her spirits revived when friends did call, and occasionally her letters were very cheerful. See Eliza Quitman to F. Henry Quitman, September 13, 1851, Quitman Family Papers, M-N.

8. Eliza Quitman to JAQ, June 10, 1850, Quitman Family Papers, SHC; Eliza Quitman to F. Henry Quitman, June 9, 1849, Quitman Family Papers, M-N; *Journal of the Proceedings of the Twenty-second Annual Convention, of the Protestant Episcopal Church, of the Diocese of Mississippi, Held at Christ's Church, Jefferson County, Wednesday, May 10, 1848* (New York, 1848), 20–21; *Journal of the Proceedings of the Twenty-third Annual Convention, of the Protestant Episcopal Church, of the Diocese of Mississippi, Held at Trinity Church, Natchez, May 17th, 18th, 19th, 1849* (New York, 1849), *passim*; *Journal of the Proceedings of the Twenty-fourth Annual Convention of the Protestant Episcopal Church, of the Diocese of Mississippi, Held at St. Andrews Church, Jackson, May 8th, 9th, 10th, and 11th, 1850* (Natchez, 1850), 22–25.

9. Jackson *Mississippian*, April 20, May 4, 18, June 1, 1849; Oxford *Organizer*, March 31, 1849; *Mississippi Free Trader* (Natchez), February 17, June 9, 1849; JAQ to Louisa Quitman, February 2, 1849, JAQ to Eliza Quitman, February 3, 1849, Quitman Family Papers, SHC; Vicksburg *Whig*, January 11, February 3, April 12, 1849. Quitman's reaction to Taylor should be contrasted with his inviting the retiring Democratic president James K. Polk and his wife to stay at Monmouth for an extended visit on their way to Tennessee from Washington. JAQ to James K. Polk, March 17, 1849, James K. Polk Papers, Presidential Papers, Series 2, LC. Polk, however, took sick on his trip and bypassed Natchez. James K. Polk to Robert J. Walker, May 9, 1849, Robert J. Walker Papers, NYHS.

10. Jackson *Mississippian*, June 22, 1849; Vicksburg *Whig*, August 9, 1849; *Mississippi Free Trader* (Natchez), June 23, 1849.

11. Vicksburg *Whig*, June 19, July 12, 1849; *Mississippi Free Trader* (Natchez),

July 25, August 19, 1849. The Whig press, however, occasionally issued sporadic attacks on Quitman. See, for instance, the Jackson *Southron*, quoted in the *Free Trader*, June 27, 1849, which reminded voters of Quitman's onetime support for John Quincy Adams and revived the "aristocrat" stigma against Quitman.

12. Vicksburg *Whig*, August 2, 7, October 16, 1849; Oxford *Organizer*, September 29, 1849; Jackson *Mississippian*, December 20, 1843, August 17, September 14, 1849; "Luke Lea," Subject File, MDA; *Mississippi Free Trader* (Natchez), October 3, 1849; "Madison" correspondent for Jackson *Southron*, dated Canton, September 10, 1849, clipping in Claiborne Papers, SHC.

13. JAQ to F. Henry Quitman, April 21, 1849, JAQ Papers, MDA; Vicksburg *Whig*, August 21, 1849; JAQ to F. Henry Quitman, July 2, September 7, 1849, JAQ Papers, HSP.

14. John Marshall to JAQ, September 11, 1849, J. F. H. Claiborne Papers, MDA; JAQ to F. Henry Quitman, September 24, 1849, JAQ Papers, HSP; Oxford *Organizer*, August 18, September 29, 1849.

15. Michael F. Holt, *The Political Crisis of the 1850s* (New York, 1978), 62, 72–76; Arthur Charles Cole, *The Whig Party in the South* (1913; rpr. Gloucester, 1962), 134; Jackson *Mississippian*, May 18, June 1, 8, 1849.

16. David M. Potter, *The Impending Crisis, 1848–1861* (New York, 1976), 72–76, 84, 86–87; Chaplain W. Morrison, *Democratic Politics and Sectionalism: The Wilmot Proviso Controversy* (Chapel Hill, 1967), 162–63; Holt, *Political Crisis*, 76–78; Paul Finkelman, *An Imperfect Union: Slavery, Federalism, and Comity* (Chapel Hill, 1981); John Hope Franklin, *A Southern Odyssey: Travelers in the Antebellum North* (Baton Rouge, 1976), 132–44. Mississippians also feared that the upper South was in the process of ending slavery, and that these states would then pressure Mississippi to follow suit. Cleo Hearon, "Mississippi and the Compromise of 1850," *PMHS*, XIV (1914), 36–37.

17. Vicksburg *Whig*, June 26, 1849; Jackson *Mississippian*, May 4, 11, 18, June 1, 8, July 20, August 10, 24, 31, October 5, 1849. Temperance agitation and demands for the expulsion of free blacks from the state may also have reflected the surge of uneasiness. Jackson *Mississippian*, April 20, August 31, 1849.

18. John McCardell, *The Idea of a Southern Nation: Southern Nationalists and Southern Nationalism, 1830–1860* (New York, 1979), 284, 289–92; Potter, *Impending Crisis*, 83–85; Holt, *Political Crisis*, 69–71; Vicksburg *Whig*, June 23, 1849. The Whig state convention in July had approved the call for the October convention. Vicksburg *Whig*, July 21, 1849.

19. Potter, *Impending Crisis*, 88; Daniel H. Wallace to Whitemarsh B. Seabrook, October 20, 1849, Whitemarsh B. Seabrook Papers, LC; Thelma Jennings, *The Nashville Convention: Southern Movement for Unity, 1848–1851* (Memphis, 1980), 24–25. For the specific origins of the October convention in Jackson, see Jennings, *Nashville Convention*, 25–26.

20. JAQ to David Hayden, July 12, 1849, in J. F. H. Claiborne, *Life and Correspondence of John A. Quitman* (2 vols.; New York, 1860), II, 20. Quitman apparently learned sometime after the war that John was living in Boston, and even discovered John's exact address, but concluded that the impediments Massachusetts had established to recovering slave property made any effort to recapture John prohibitively expensive in time and money. See speech by Jefferson Davis, July 11, 1851, at Fayette, Miss., in Lynda Lasswell Crist (ed.), *The Papers of Jefferson Davis* (4 vols.; Baton Rouge, 1971–), IV, 198–99.

21. "Minutes of the Convention of Delegates . . . in . . . Jackson, on Monday, October 1, 1849," "Address of the Committee of the Mississippi Convention to the Southern States," *Mississippi Senate Journal*, 1850, pp. 277–90, 291–310. The previous month, Quitman had participated in Adams County meetings which drew up resolutions about the crisis and chose delegates to the convention. *Mississippi Free Trader* (Natchez), September 12, 19, 1849.

22. Daniel H. Wallace to Whitemarsh B. Seabrook, October 20, November 7, 1849, Seabrook Papers, LC; Jackson *Mississippian*, May 18, September 7, 21, 1849.

23. Election returns, *Mississippi Senate Journal*, 1850, pp. 314–15; JAQ to F. Henry Quitman, November 17, 1849, JAQ Papers, HSP. For more on Quitman's canvass, including his declining debates with Lea, see Jackson *Mississippian*, October 12, 26, 1849; Eliza Quitman to JAQ, October 9, 30, 1849, Quitman Family Papers, SHC; *Mississippi Free Trader* (Natchez), October 3, 13, 1849.

24. JAQ to Eliza Quitman, December 15, 1849, Quitman Family Papers, SHC; JAQ to Robert J. Walker, December 28, 1849, Robert J. Walker Papers, DU; Jackson *Mississippian*, December 28, 1849; F. Henry Quitman to Eliza Quitman, March 15, November 21, 1849, JAQ to F. Henry Quitman, November 11, 1849, JAQ Papers, HSP; Louisa S. Quitman to F. Henry Quitman, November 25, 1849, Quitman Family Papers, M-N; Martha Bowman, "A City of the Old South: Jackson, Mississippi, 1850–1860," *JMH*, XV (1953), 1–32. Quitman's political defenders still felt compelled to establish his credentials as a man of the people. See, for instance, *Mississippi Free Trader* (Natchez), October 13, 1849. Eliza's reluctance to move to Jackson, moreover, apparently became a source of political gossip that winter. F. Henry Quitman to Eliza Quitman, January 6, 1850, Quitman Family Papers, SHC.

25. F. Henry Quitman to Eliza Quitman, November 21, 1849, JAQ to F. Henry Quitman, November 11, 17, 1849, JAQ Papers, HSP; F. Henry Quitman to Eliza Quitman, January 6, 1850, JAQ to Eliza Quitman, January 11, 1850, Quitman Family Papers, SHC; David G. Sansing and Carroll Waller, *A History of the Mississippi Governor's Mansion* (Jackson, 1977), 10–26. An 1850 inventory of the furnishings of the mansion further illustrates its inadequacies. The list includes such notations as two "worn out" mahogany sofas, a piano with no stool and out of repair, four "worthless" side lamps, and two mahogany tables "in a dilapidated condition." Inventory, filed 1850, JAQ Papers, MDA. The legislature did, in fact, appropriate $3,500 during its 1850 session for the mansion. *Laws of the State of Mississippi*, 1850, p. 113.

26. JAQ to F. Henry Quitman, September 24, November 11, 1849, JAQ Papers, HSP.

CHAPTER 17

1. Rosalie Quitman Duncan, "Life of General John A. Quitman," *PMHS*, IV (1901), 423.

2. John McCardell, *The Idea of a Southern Nation: Southern Nationalists and Southern Nationalism, 1830–1860* (New York, 1979), 6.

3. JAQ to F. Henry Quitman, March 2, 1850, JAQ Papers, HSP; JAQ to Robert J. Walker, February 13, 1850, Robert J. Walker Papers, NYHS.

4. Holman Hamilton, *Prologue to Conflict: The Crisis and Compromise of 1850* (Lexington, Ky., 1966), 17–18, 21, 23; David M. Potter, *The Impending Crisis,*

1848–1861 (New York, 1976), 90–91; Michael F. Holt, *The Political Crisis of the 1850s* (New York, 1978), 80, 82–83.

5. James P. Oakes, *The Ruling Race: A History of American Slaveholders* (New York, 1982), *passim*.

6. JAQ to Samuel A. Cartwright, October 2, 1850, Samuel A. Cartwright and Family Papers, LSU; Jackson *Mississippian*, October 18, 1850; *Mississippi Senate Journal*, 1850, p. 324; JAQ to Robert J. Walker, February 13, 1850, Robert J. Walker Papers, NYHS.

7. J. Mills Thornton, *Politics and Power in a Slave Society: Alabama, 1800–1860* (Baton Rouge, 1978), 25, 213, 214–15, 218, 221, 437, 449, 451, 458; Holt, *Political Crisis*, 4–6; Eugene D. Genovese, *The Political Economy of Slavery: Studies in the Economy and Society of the Slave South* (New York, 1965), 250.

8. *Mississippi Senate Journal*, 1850, pp. 495–96; JAQ to Robert J. Walker, February 13, 1850, Robert J. Walker Papers, NYHS; Jackson *Mississippian*, October 18, 1850, April 9, 1852.

9. *Mississippi Senate Journal*, 1850, pp. 322–25. Quitman also called for correction of "abuses" by petty corporations, the creation of a more equitable taxation system, and a system of gradual elimination of the state debt.

10. *Ibid.*, 327, 355–59; Ralph Wooster, *The People in Power: Courthouse and Statehouse in the Lower South, 1850–1860* (Knoxville, 1969), 29.

11. Jefferson Davis *et al.* to JAQ, January 21, 1850, quoted in *Laws of the State of Mississippi*, 1850, pp. 42–44; *Mississippi Senate Journal*, 1850, pp. 495–96.

12. *Mississippi Senate Journal*, 1850, pp. 495–96; *Mississippi Free Trader* (Natchez), February 27, 1850; Vicksburg *Sentinel*, February 26, 1850.

13. *Mississippi Senate Journal*, 1850, pp. 540–43, 553; *Mississippi Free Trader* (Natchez), February 27, 1850; Vicksburg *Sentinel*, February 26, 1850; *Laws of the State of Mississippi*, 1850, p. 70.

14. *Mississippi House Journal*, 1850, pp. 393–94; *Mississippi Senate Journal*, 1850, pp. 621–22; Vicksburg *Whig*, February 20, 1850.

15. *Mississippi Senate Journal*, 1850, pp. 550–51; JAQ to H. F. Johnson, May 29, 1850, JAQ to Joseph McAfee, June 3, 1850, Executive Journal, 1850, RG 27, Vol. 42, MDA; Allen Wardsworth petition, Governors' Papers, RG 27, MDA.

16. *Laws of the State of Mississippi*, 1850, 67–69; Vicksburg *Sentinel*, February 21, 26, March 2, April 13, 1850; Mrs. Isaac H. Hilliard Diary, February 19, 1850, LSU. The school legislation specified that the funds would be distributed only to counties which had levied their own tax for common schools (based on 25 percent of the 1849 state tax for schools), and that starting May 1, 1851, $50,000 would be allocated by the state per year to maintain the schools.

17. Vicksburg *Sentinel*, January 26, February 26, 1850; Mrs. Isaac H. Hilliard Diary, February 19, 1850, LSU; Antonia Quitman to F. Henry Quitman, February 25, 1850, Quitman Family Papers, M-N; JAQ to F. Henry Quitman, March 2, 1850, JAQ Papers, HSP. Besides church leaders, the Quitmans also put up several guests of the family during the period of the February levee, including Henry Turner and the daughters of the influential Haller Nutt of Natchez. Antonia Quitman to F. Henry Quitman, February 25, 1850, Quitman Family Papers, M-N.

18. *Laws of the State of Mississippi*, 1850, pp. 521–28; *Mississippi Senate Journal*, 1850, pp. 595, 609–613, 667–68, 680, 692–93; Thelma Jennings, *The Nashville Convention: Southern Movement for Unity, 1848–1851* (Memphis, 1980), 65; Vicksburg *Sentinel*, March 7, 12, 1850; Vicksburg *Whig*, February 13, March 13,

1850. Democrats justified legislative selection of the Nashville delegates on the basis that farmers would be too involved in spring planting to find time to vote on short notice.

19. Eliza Quitman to F. Henry Quitman, March 4, 13, 20, April 10, 1850, Antonia Quitman to F. Henry Quitman, April 27, 1850, Quitman Family Papers, M-N; JAQ to F. Henry Quitman, March 2, 1850, JAQ Papers, HSP.

20. JAQ to Mansfield Lovell, March 15, 1850, Mansfield Lovell Papers, Huntington Library, San Marino, Ca.; Eliza Quitman to F. Henry Quitman, April 10, 1850, Quitman Family Papers, M-N; D. C. Glenn to JAQ, April 18, 1850, Governors' Papers, RG 27, MDA; F. Henry Quitman to Eliza Quitman, March 4, 1850, Quitman Family Papers, SHC; JAQ to F. Henry Quitman, March 2, April 12, 1850, JAQ Papers, HSP. Late in April, the governor of Arkansas requested that Quitman extradite a slave wanted in an Arkansas murder case. See document dated April 30, 1850, Governors' Papers, RG 27, MDA.

21. Eliza Quitman to F. Henry Quitman, May 1, 1850 (Copy courtesy of the editors of *The Papers of Jefferson Davis*); JAQ to F. Henry Quitman, May 12, 1850, JAQ Papers, HSP; Jackson *Mississippian*, May 10, 1850.

CHAPTER 18

1. Franklin W. Knight, *Slave Society in Cuba During the Nineteenth Century* (Madison, 1970), 25–26, 88–90, 102; Philip Foner, *A History of Cuba and Its Relations with the United States* (2 vols.; New York, 1962–63), I, 5, 10, 14, 53–55, 177; Arthur F. Corwin, *Spain and the Abolition of Slavery in Cuba, 1817–1886* (Austin, 1967), 22–28, 69–70, 96.

2. Charles H. Brown, *Agents of Manifest Destiny: The Lives and Times of the Filibusters* (Chapel Hill, 1980), 39–51; Louis N. Feipel, "The Navy and Filibustering in the Fifties," *United States Naval Institute Proceedings*, XLIV (April-July, 1918), 770–79; Basil Rauch, *American Interest in Cuba, 1848–1855* (New York, 1948), 42–44, 73–100, 108, 114–18.

3. Jackson *Mississippian*, March 24, 1848, April 6, June 15, August 24, September 14, November 9, December 21, 1849; Vicksburg *Sentinel*, April 30, June 4, 1850; Vicksburg *Whig*, March 22, December 12, 1848, September 4, 6, December 6, 1849; *Mississippi Senate Journal*, 1850, pp. 28–29.

4. JAQ to Mansfield Lovell, March 15, 1850, Mansfield Lovell Papers, Huntington Library, San Marino, Ca.; Brown, *Agents of Manifest Destiny*, 47, 52–53; Foner, *History of Cuba*, II, 47–48; Ambrosio J. González to JAQ, April 5, 1850, JAQ Papers, MDA.

5. J. F. H. Claiborne, *Life and Correspondence of John A. Quitman* (2 vols.; New York, 1860), II, 55–58; Ambrosio J. González to JAQ, April 5, 1850, JAQ Papers, MDA; Antonia Quitman to F. Henry Quitman, April 27, 1850, Quitman Family Papers, M-N. Ray Broussard suggests that Quitman's consideration of López's offer was influenced by recent information from the Cuban Council in New York that "López was acting on his own initiative and did not have the backing of their organization." Ray Broussard, "Governor John A. Quitman and the López Expeditions of 1851–1852," *JMH*, XXVIII (1966), 110. Actually this January, 1850, document (now in JAQ Papers, MDA) is a translation for Quitman's benefit of a letter the Cuban Council had sent López, telling him that he was too impulsive and that he

would have to make more cautious and long-range plans if he wanted their support. It is most likely that the document was sent to Quitman *after* the Jackson meeting, when the council learned that López had enrolled Quitman among his supporters.

6. New Orleans *Daily Picayune*, April 27, 1850; New Orleans *Bee*, April 29, 1850; Eliza Quitman to F. Henry Quitman, June 15, 1850, Quitman Family Papers, M-N; John Henderson to JAQ, May 9, 16, 1850, Henry J. Hartstene to JAQ, May 26, 1850, George Marcy to JAQ, May 24, 1850, A. B. Bannon to JAQ, May 25, 1850, JAQ Papers, MDA; Thomas R. Wolfe to Rev. John Thomas Wheat, May 9, 1850, John Thomas Wheat Papers, SHC; Louisa S. Quitman to JAQ, May 17, 1850, John McMurran to Eliza Quitman, June 13, 1850, Quitman Family Papers, SHC; Jackson *Mississippian*, June 7, 1850; Vicksburg *Whig*, May 21, 1851; [F. C. M. Boggess], *A Veteran of Four Wars: The Autobiography of F. C. M. Boggess* (Arcadia, Fla., 1900), 11, 21.

7. Brown, *Agents of Manifest Destiny*, 58–60; JAQ to F. Henry Quitman, May 7, 1850, JAQ Papers, HSP.

8. JAQ to F. Henry Quitman, May 7, 12, 1850, JAQ Papers, HSP; Account of the Yazoo exploration, filed April-May, 1850, Quitman Family Papers, SHC; Jackson *Mississippian*, June 7, 1850; John Henderson to JAQ, May 25, 1850, JAQ Papers, MDA; Brown, *Agents of Manifest Destiny*, 61–67.

9. Louisa Quitman to JAQ, May 30, July 12, 1850, JAQ to Louisa Quitman, May 25, August 14, 1850, Eliza Quitman to JAQ, June 10, 1850, Quitman Family Papers, SHC; JAQ to F. Henry Quitman, July 7, 21, August 1, 1850, JAQ Papers, HSP; Eliza Quitman to F. Henry Quitman, July 1, 1850, Quitman Family Papers, M-N; JAQ to Eliza Quitman, March 8, 1851, Lovell Family Papers, UnS; *Mississippi Free Trader* (Natchez), July 27, 1850; JAQ to W. E. T. Griffith, July 22, 1850, JAQ Papers, MDA.

10. John L. O'Sullivan to JAQ, June 26, 1850, John Henderson to JAQ, July 2, 1850, JAQ Papers, MDA; Louisa Quitman to Eliza Quitman, July 15, 18, 1850, Quitman Family Papers, SHC; Robert G. Caldwell, *The Lopez Expeditions to Cuba, 1848–1851* (Princeton, 1915), 69–71.

11. New Orleans *Bee*, June 8, 10–12, 14, 15, 17, 18, 20, 22, 1850; Copy of indictment and James Dunlap to JAQ, July 3, 1850, JAQ Papers, MDA. On June 28, Angel Calderón de la Barca, Spanish minister to the United States, forwarded documents to the State Department which incriminated Quitman. The documents had been confiscated from the captured filibuster vessels. Angel Calderón de la Barca to John M. Clayton, June 28, 1850, *Senate Executive Documents*, 31st Cong., 1st Sess., No. 41, pp. 56–57.

12. JAQ to F. Henry Quitman, July 7, 1850, JAQ Papers, HSP; JAQ to W. E. T. Griffith, July 22, 1850, JAQ Papers, MDA.

13. David M. Potter, *The Impending Crisis, 1848–1861* (New York, 1976), 104–105, 110n–11n; Vicksburg *Sentinel*, June 20, 1850; Peter H. Bell to Zachary Taylor, June 15, 1850 (copy), Samuel Colt to Thomas J. Rusk, July 26, 1850, W. P. Miller to Thomas J. Rusk, August 16, 1850, Thomas J. Rusk Papers, UT; Robert S. Neighbors to Colonel J. Munson, April 14, 1850 (copy), Eli Chandler to Peter H. Bell, August 15, 1850, Proceedings and Resolutions of Matagorda County Meeting, July 1, 1850, Governors' Papers, Archives Division, Texas State Library, Austin; William Fitzhugh to Peter H. Bell, August 16, 1850, Peter Hansbrough Bell Papers, UT. The most significant of the Nashville Convention resolutions announced that

though the southern states claimed a right to unlimited slavery expansion in the territories, they would accept a division of the territories all the way to the Pacific along the old Missouri Compromise line of 36°30′.

14. JAQ to F. Henry Quitman, August 25, 1850, JAQ Papers, HSP; *Mississippi Free Trader* (Natchez), July 27, 1850; Jackson *Mississippian*, September 13, 1850; J. Pinckney Henderson to JAQ, July 22, 1850, JAQ to J. Pinckney Henderson, August 18, 1850, in Claiborne, *Quitman*, II, 41–42; JAQ to the editor of Vicksburg *Sentinel*, August 18, 1850, quoted in Vicksburg *Whig*, August 8, 1850. Earlier in the year, Quitman had persuaded the legislature to fund an arsenal on the capital green (weapons had been decaying in storage in various rooms of the capitol) and to create the position of state armorer so that the arms would be cared for. However, the salary was only $250, and his choice for the job, James Riddell (a member of the Mississippi Rifles during the war), turned it down after first soliciting the position. *Mississippi Senate Journal*, 1850, pp. 717–18; Architects' estimate, March 28, 1850, James Riddell to JAQ, March 25, April 4, 1850, Governors' Papers, RG 27, MDA; JAQ to James Riddle [*sic*], March 29, 1850, Executive Journal, RG 27, Vol. 42, MDA; Jackson *Mississippian*, March 28, 1851. Quitman's instructions for an arms inventory were dated July 8, and the report was made in November. See Charles B. Green to JAQ, November 20, 1850, Governors' Papers, RG 27, MDA.

15. JAQ to W. E. T. Griffith, July 22, 1850, Cotesworth P. Smith to JAQ, August 4, 1850, JAQ Papers, MDA; JAQ to Jacob Thompson, August 15, 1850, Jacob Thompson to JAQ, September 2, 1850, in Claiborne, *Quitman*, II, 62–65.

16. Horatio J. Harris to JAQ, September 28, November 4, 13, 1850, JAQ to Horatio J. Harris, October 2, November 9, 1850, JAQ Papers, MDA.

17. Jackson *Mississippian*, July 26, 1850.

18. Holman Hamilton, *Prologue to Conflict: The Crisis and Compromise of 1850* (Lexington, Ky., 1966), 160, 166; David Herbert Donald, *Liberty and Union* (Lexington, Mass., 1978), 46–47; Robert W. Barnwell to James H. Hammond, August 14, September 26, 1850, in John Barnwell (ed.), " 'In The Hands Of The Compromisers': Letters of Robert W. Barnwell to James H. Hammond," *Civil War History*, XXIX (1983), 164, 168; JAQ to Eliza Quitman, September 21, 1850, Quitman Family Papers, SHC; D. W. Haley to Peter H. Bell, October 4, 9, 1850, Governors' Papers, Archives Division, Texas State Library; Vicksburg *Whig*, September 14, 1850; Eliza Quitman to F. Henry Quitman, August 9, 1849, March 13, 1850, Quitman Family Papers, M-N.

19. JAQ proclamation, September 26, 1850, Governors' Papers, RG 27, MDA. Quitman's proclamation may have been influenced by his good friend Felix Huston, who wrote him on September 19 that Mississippi or Georgia should secede immediately. Huston downplayed the dangers of separate state secession, arguing that all the slave states would join together if the federal government used force against a state that had seceded. Felix Huston to JAQ, September 19, 1850, J. F. H. Claiborne Papers, MDA.

20. Whitemarsh B. Seabrook to George W. Towns, October 8, 1850, Whitemarsh B. Seabrook Papers, LC; V. S. Wallis [?] to Daniel Barringer, October 7, 1850, Daniel M. Barringer Papers, SHC; Vicksburg *Whig*, October 9, November 6, 1850; Natchez *Courier*, October 15, 1850; Rufus K. Arthur to A. K. Farrar, October 19, 1850, Alexander K. Farrar Papers, LSU; Diedrich Knickerbocker [Washington Irving], *A History of New York* (New York, 1848), Book IV, Chs. 2–3.

21. Robert W. Barnwell to JAQ, September 19, 1850, Whitemarsh B. Seabrook

to JAQ, September 20, 1850, Claiborne Papers, MDA; JAQ to Whitemarsh B. Seabrook, September 29, 1850, Seabrook Papers, LC; John Tyler, Jr., to Henry A. Wise, November 18, 1850, in Philip Gerald Auchampaugh, *Robert Tyler: Southern Rights Champion, 1847–1866* (Duluth, 1934), 20–21. Seabrook feared that unionist Whigs in Georgia would sidetrack that state from secession at the last moment. His reservations were confirmed in a letter from Governor Towns announcing that most former nullifiers had gone over to the Union camp, and that the "odds" were against Georgia's taking the first step. Whitemarsh B. Seabrook to John Leland, September 18, 1850, George W. Towns to Whitemarsh B. Seabrook, September 25, 1850, Seabrook Papers, LC.

22. JAQ to John J. McRae, September 28, 1850, Whitemarsh B. Seabrook to JAQ, October 23, 1850, in Claiborne, *Quitman*, II, 44–46, 37–38; JAQ to Whitemarsh B. Seabrook, September 29, 1850, Seabrook Papers, LC; JAQ to Samuel A. Cartwright, October 2, 1850, Samuel A. Cartwright and Family Papers, LSU; Jackson *Mississippian*, November 15, 1850.

23. Natchez *Courier*, October 11, 18, 1850; Jackson *Mississippian*, October 18, 1850; Vicksburg *Sentinel*, October 5, 1850; JAQ to John J. McRae, September 28, 1850, in Claiborne, *Quitman*, II, 45; Potter, *Impending Crisis*, 112–13; Eliza Quitman to F. Henry Quitman, October 9, November 4, 1850, Quitman Family Papers, M-N.

24. Vicksburg *Whig*, November 13, 1850, January 11, 1854; Henry Foote to JAQ, October 16, 1850, JAQ to Henry Foote, n.d. and October 18, 1850, quoted in Jackson *Mississippian*, November 1, 1850; JAQ to F. Henry Quitman, November 16, 1850, JAQ Papers, HSP; Mary L. McMurran to Louisa Quitman, November 19, 1850, JAQ Papers, LSU. Foote's tortuous course during the summer can be traced in John McCardell, "John A. Quitman and the Compromise of 1850 in Mississippi," *JMH*, XXXVII (1975), 246–48. Foote was one of only two southern Democrats failing to sign the protest.

25. Eliza Quitman to F. Henry Quitman, November 4, 1850, Quitman Family Papers, M-N; JAQ to F. Henry Quitman, November 16, 1850, JAQ Papers, HSP.

26. Jackson *Mississippian*, November 22, 1850.

27. Natchez *Courier*, November 19, 1850; Liberty (Amite County) *Advocate*, quoted in Vicksburg *Whig*, January 15, 1851; Vicksburg *Whig*, November 27, 1850. Foote also made charges, around this time, that Quitman's old friend, U.S. Senator Thomas Rusk, had recently commented that Quitman had proven to be an unreliable ally for Texas. Quitman asked Rusk for a clarification, and Rusk denied the substance of Foote's charges. See correspondence in Jackson *Mississippian*, January 17, 1851.

28. Whitemarsh B. Seabrook to JAQ, telegraph dated December 3, 1850, Claiborne Papers, MDA.

29. William Sharkey to Luke Lea, December 24, 1850, quoted in Vicksburg *Whig*, January 29, 1851; James Alcorn to Amelia Walton Glover, November 26, 1850, James Alcorn Papers, MDA; Vicksburg *Whig*, December 4, 1850; Jackson *Mississippian*, January 10, 1851; Thelma Jennings, *The Nashville Convention: Southern Movement for Unity, 1848–1851* (Memphis, 1980), 191–93; Potter, *Impending Crisis*, 126. Fewer delegates were on hand in November than in June (Arkansas and Texas were not even represented) and their selection was more irregular. Quitman was criticized for selecting some of Mississippi's delegates. Natchez *Courier*, November 22, 1850.

30. JAQ to Robert Barnwell Rhett, November 30, 1850, Seabrook Papers, LC; Whitemarsh B. Seabrook to JAQ, December 17, 1850, in Claiborne, *Quitman*, II, 39–40; Jackson *Mississippian*, December 6, 1850; Oxford *Organizer*, December 14, 1850. Rhett had attended the Nashville Convention. Quitman's letter was a response to one from Rhett dated November 18.

Seabrook's letter encouraged Mississippi to accede to a call being issued by South Carolina for a southern congress to be held in Montgomery, Alabama, in January, 1852. There a new nation of seceded states could be formed. Since 1852 was a presidential year, Seabrook suggested, the northern states would be too distracted "for a season" to resist. Meanwhile, the southern states could effect a military buildup.

31. John Henderson to JAQ, November 6, 1850, in Claiborne, *Quitman*, II, 69–71; New Orleans *Bee*, January 7, 1851; Jackson *Mississippian*, January 3, 1851; Fielding Davis to JAQ, January 25, 1851, JAQ Papers, MDA. Henderson told Quitman that the funds would be applied to the purchase of a $25,000 steamer, which would take the new expedition to Cuba from the coast of Georgia. Henderson was obviously working in concert with L. J. Sigur, who wrote Quitman a day later saying that just $4,000 would put López in Cuba within a fortnight. Lawrence J. Sigur to JAQ, November 7, 1850, JAQ Papers, MDA.

32. JAQ to Robert Barnwell Rhett, January 24, 1851, in Claiborne, *Quitman*, II, 72–73.

33. E. L. Acee to JAQ, January 13, 1851, Samuel S. Boyd to JAQ, January 13, 1851, JAQ Papers, MDA; William S. Lyles *et al.* to JAQ, January 27, 1851, Claiborne Papers, MDA; Vicksburg *Sentinel*, January 22, 1851.

34. George T. Swann to JAQ, January 13, 1851, JAQ Papers, MDA; JAQ to Robert Barnwell Rhett, January 24, 1851, in Claiborne, *Quitman*, II, 72–73; Vicksburg *Whig*, May 22, 1850. Some Mississippi imperialists did envision Cuba as part of a superior southern nation *after* secession. A. G. Haley to Peter H. Bell, October 9, 1850, Governors' Papers, Archives Division, Texas State Library; Jackson *Mississippian*, February 21, 1851.

35. JAQ to Fielding Davis, January 27, 1851, JAQ Papers, MDA; Vicksburg *Whig*, February 5, 1851; Poem in Jackson *Mississippian*, February 14, 1851; *Congressional Globe*, 31st Cong., 2nd Sess., 598–99; Vicksburg *Sentinel*, February 4, 1851. Quitman, of course, was no martyr to Whig unionists. See, for instance, Vicksburg *Whig*, January 12, April 30, 1851. The April 30 issue compared him to Aaron Burr.

36. Vicksburg *Sentinel*, February 12, 1851; Louisa Quitman to Eliza Quitman, February 14, 1851, Eliza Quitman to JAQ, February 19, 1851, JAQ to Eliza Quitman, February 22, 1851, Quitman Family Papers, SHC; Louis C. Hunter, *Steamboats on the Western Rivers: An Economic and Technological History* (Cambridge, Mass., 1949), 143. Quitman took the *Belle Creole*, which he boarded on February 5, to New Orleans. For details of his trip, which included a certain amount of fanfare along the way, see *Mississippi Free Trader* (Natchez), February 15, 1851; William Johnson Diary, February 5, 1851, William R. Hogan and Edwin A. Davis (eds.), *William Johnson's Natchez: The Ante-Bellum Diary of a Free Negro* (Baton Rouge, 1951), 775.

37. W. Porter Ware and Thaddeus C. Lockard, Jr., *P. T. Barnum Presents Jenny Lind: The American Tour of the Swedish Nightingale* (Baton Rouge, 1980), 65–70, and *passim*; *Mississippi Free Trader* (Natchez), February 18, 1851; Claiborne, *Quitman*, II, 75.

38. Antonia Quitman to Louisa Quitman, February 19, 1851, JAQ Papers, LSU; JAQ to Eliza Quitman, February 22, 1851, Quitman Family Papers, SHC; JAQ to Eliza Quitman, March 8, 1851, Lovell Family Papers, UnS. Eliza followed instructions, saw Jenny Lind, and was unimpressed. Eliza Quitman to F. Henry Quitman, March 15, 1851, Quitman Family Papers, M-N.

39. Louisa Quitman to Eliza Quitman, February 22, 1851, Quitman Family Papers, SHC; Vicksburg *Sentinel*, February 20, 1851; *Mississippi Free Trader* (Natchez), March 5, 1851.

40. New Orleans *Bee*, January 22, February 8, March 7, 1851; *Mississippi Free Trader* (Natchez), February 19, 1851; Jackson *Mississippian*, March 14, 1851.

41. JAQ to F. Henry Quitman, March 15, 1851, JAQ Papers, HSP; JAQ to Eliza Quitman, March 8, 1851, Lovell Family Papers, UnS; Vicksburg *Sentinel*, March 25, 1851; Jackson *Mississippian*, May 2, 1851. Quitman made his main exposé at a Jackson barbecue two months later. See *Mississippi Free Trader* (Natchez), May 21, 1851; Vicksburg *Whig*, May 21, 1851.

42. See, for instance, J. H. Sims to JAQ, February 19, 1851, and M. J. Bunch to JAQ, August 18, 1851, JAQ Papers, MDA.

43. Brown, *Agents of Manifest Destiny*, 70–88; Edward Seccomb Wallace, *Destiny and Glory* (New York, 1957), 81–97; D. C. Corbitt, "The Junta De Fomento of Havana and the López Expeditions," *Hispanic American Historical Review*, XVII (1937), 340–41.

44. F. Henry Quitman to Eliza Quitman, February 24, 1851, JAQ Papers, MDA.

CHAPTER 19

1. Eliza Quitman to F. Henry Quitman, March 15, 1851, Quitman Family Papers, M-N; JAQ to F. Henry Quitman, March 15, April 21, 1851, JAQ Papers, HSP.

2. Philip May Hamer, *The Secession Movement in South Carolina, 1847–1852* (Allentown, 1918), 74–75, 78–83.

3. James Brewer to JAQ, January 18, 1851, JAQ Papers, MDA; Robert Barnwell Rhett to JAQ, February 22, 1851, John S. Preston to JAQ, March 4, 1851, J. F. H. Claiborne Papers, MDA; JAQ to F. Henry Quitman, March 15, 1851, JAQ Papers, HSP; Charleston *Courier*, August 23, 1851.

4. Vicksburg *Whig*, November 20, December 4, 1850, January 29, 1851; Natchez *Courier*, October 4, 1850; James B. Ranck, *Albert Gallatin Brown, Radical Southern Nationalist* (New York, 1937), 86–92; JAQ to Whitemarsh B. Seabrook, June 26, 1851, Whitemarsh B. Seabrook Papers, LC.

5. Jackson *Mississippian*, September 13, December 13, 1850, January 3, 24, 31, February 28, March 7, 28, April 4, 25, May 8, 1851; *Mississippi Free Trader* (Natchez), December 11, 1850. Radical Democrats kept "Democratic" in their party title for fear that the unionists might preempt it if they did not utilize it. A. Hutchinson *et al.* to Charles D. Fontaine, April 5, 1851, Charles D. Fontaine Papers, MDA.

6. Oxford *Constitution*, March 22, 1851; *Mississippi Palladium* (Holly Springs), May 16, 23, 1851; Vicksburg *Sentinel*, February 4, 20, March 25, 1851; James W. McDonald to JAQ, March 9, April 3, 1851, Claiborne Papers, MDA; Jackson *Mississippian*, April 18, 25, 1851; Vicksburg *Whig*, November 13, 1850; John McCardell, "John A. Quitman and the Compromise of 1850 in Mississippi," *JMH*, XXXVII (1975), 252.

7. JAQ to C. S. Tarpley *et al.*, Committee of the Central Southern Rights Associ-

ation, in J. F. H. Claiborne, *Life and Correspondence of John A. Quitman* (2 vols.; New York, 1860), II, 127–32; *Mississippi Free Trader* (Natchez), May 7, 1851.

8. JAQ to John S. Preston, March 29, 1851, in Claiborne, *Quitman*, II, 123–27.

9. JAQ to F. Henry Quitman, April 21, 1851, JAQ Papers, HSP; Eliza Quitman to F. Henry Quitman, April 5, 1851, Quitman Family Papers, M-N; Vicksburg *Sentinel*, March 18, 1851; *Mississippi Free Trader* (Natchez), May 7, 14, 21, 1851; Vicksburg *Whig*, May 21, 1851; Jackson *Mississippian*, May 2, 16, 23, 30, 1851.

10. Vicksburg *Whig*, May 28, 1851; Vicksburg *Sentinel*, May 20, 1851; Jackson *Mississippian*, May 23, 1851.

11. *Mississippi Free Trader* (Natchez), May 23, 28, 1851; Jason Niles Diary, June 9, 1851, SHC; J. C. Bates to JAQ, July 28, 1854, JAQ Papers, MDA; Vicksburg *Sentinel*, June 8, 1851.

12. Hamer, *Secession Movement*, 85–88; John H. Means to JAQ, May 12, 1851, Maxcy Gregg to JAQ, May 15, 1851, JAQ to John H. Means, May 25, 1851, in Claiborne, *Quitman*, II, 133–36.

13. *Mississippi Free Trader* (Natchez), June 21, 25, 1851; Jackson *Mississippian*, June 16, 1851; JAQ to Eliza Quitman, May [June] 17, 1851, Quitman Family Papers, SHC; Jefferson Davis to David L. Yulee, July 18, 1851, James T. McIntosh (ed.), *The Papers of Jefferson Davis* (4 vols.; Baton Rouge, 1971–), II, 108n; Reuben Davis, *Recollections of Mississippi and Mississippians* (Rev. ed.; Hattiesburg, 1972), 315–17. Jefferson Davis' wife later claimed that Quitman turned down a deal by which Davis would have resigned his Senate seat to run, and Governor Guion would have appointed Quitman to the balance of Davis' term. Varina Davis, *Jefferson Davis . . . A Memoir by his Wife* (2 vols.; New York, 1890), I, 465–67.

14. JAQ to Whitemarsh B. Seabrook, June 26, 1851, Seabrook Papers, LC; Jefferson Davis to David L. Yulee, July 18, 1851, McIntosh (ed.), *Papers of Jefferson Davis*, II, 108n.

15. Jackson *Mississippian*, June 20, 1851; JAQ to Whitemarsh B. Seabrook, June 26, 1851, Whitemarsh B. Seabrook to JAQ, July 15, 1851, Seabrook Papers, LC.

16. *Mississippi Free Trader* (Natchez), June 25, 1851; Jackson *Mississippian*, July 11, 1851; George T. Swann to JAQ, July 18, 1851, Claiborne Papers, MDA. Quitman's reputation as a "dissolver" was used by the Union press to tarnish other politicians who had connections with him. See Woodville *Republican*, July 29, 1851.

17. *Mississippi Palladium* (Holly Springs), August 1, 1851; Alexander M. Clayton to J. F. H. Claiborne, February 23, 1878, July 18, 1879, J. F. H. Claiborne Papers, SHC.

18. Vicksburg *Whig*, June 4, 1851; *Mississippi Palladium* (Holly Springs), August 1, 1851; Jackson *Mississippian*, July 25, 1851. Quitman claimed that the school money had not been spent because of procedural technicalities. In some counties, for instance, assessors did not comply with legislative provisions that the number of children be determined. Jackson *Mississippian*, April 29, 1851.

19. Maxcy Gregg to JAQ, November 15, 1851, Claiborne Papers, MDA; *Mississippi Palladium* (Holly Springs), August 15, 1851; Vicksburg *Whig*, September 3, 1851; Vicksburg *Sentinel*, September 18, 1851 (includes Rhett's denial); JAQ to W. Q. Poindexter, August 23, 1851, quoted in Jackson *Mississippian*, September 5, 1851; William James Cooper, *The South and the Politics of Slavery, 1828–1856* (Baton Rouge, 1978), 23–29. I have been unable to locate Rhett's supposed public allusion to corresponding with Quitman. However, Rhett did say at the June 28

Charleston Celebration of the Revolutionary War Battle of Fort Moultrie that Quit-man had been "blowing a bugle" that would be "heard to the extremities of Yankee-dom." There was considerable talk, moreover, at the Fort Moultrie occasion and at Fourth of July celebrations throughout the state, of Quitman and Jefferson Davis for president and general in chief of a southern republic (both names were promoted for both positions). When Henry Foote alluded to such intentions in a Senate speech in December, Jefferson Davis was moved to issue an angry denial that personal ambi-tion lay behind his, and Quitman's, ideological commitment to southern rights. Charleston *Mercury*, July 2, 7, August 7, 1851; *Congressional Globe*, 32nd Cong., 1st Sess., Appendix, 49–54; Vicksburg *Sentinel*, January 31, 1852.

20. JAQ to Whitemarsh B. Seabrook, June 26, 1851, Seabrook Papers, LC; John Edmond Gonzales, "Flush Times, Depression, War, and Compromise," in Richard Aubrey McLemore (ed.), *A History of Mississippi* (2 vols.; Jackson, 1973), I, 305.

21. See *Mississippi Free Trader* (Natchez), October 24, 1848.

22. Jackson *Mississippian*, May 23, 1834; Henry S. Foote, *Casket of Reminis-cences* (Washington, D.C., 1874), 356; Claiborne, *Quitman*, II, 292, 294–95; Davis, *Recollections of Mississippi*, 317; Edward R. Welles Diary, June [?], 1855, Old Courthouse Museum, Vicksburg (Typescript copy courtesy of the editors of *The Papers of Jefferson Davis*); Vicksburg *Whig*, August 14, 1849, January 12, 1856; Vicksburg *Sentinel*, October 16, 1849; *Mississippi Free Trader* (Natchez), Sep-tember 9, 1837.

23. Vicksburg *Sentinel*, May 8, 1844; Jackson *Mississippian*, July 11, 18, August 1, 1851; Vicksburg *Whig*, February 1, 1842, November 3, 1843, May 9, 1848.

24. *Mississippi Free Trader* (Natchez), July 26, 1851; Jackson *Mississippian*, July 18, August 1, 1851; T. J. Wharton to JAQ, July 9, 1851, Lewis Sanders, Jr., to JAQ, July 13, 1851, Frederick W. Quackenboss to JAQ, July 23, 1851, Claiborne Papers, MDA. Foote's predictions about slavery in California were not entirely far-fetched. California did have some slaves after the compromise of 1850. See Rudolph M. Lapp, *Blacks in Gold Rush California* (New Haven, 1977), 130–34.

25. A. G. Haley to F. Henry Quitman, July 17, 1851, M. J. Bunch to JAQ, Au-gust 18, 1851, JAQ Papers, MDA; *Mississippi Palladium* (Holly Springs), August 1, 1851; Vicksburg *Whig*, July 30, 1851.

26. Richard C. Glenn to Henry St. George Harris, August 1, 1851, Henry St. George Harris Papers, DU; *Mississippi Palladium* (Holly Springs), August 1, 1851.

27. JAQ to F. Henry Quitman, July 28, 1851, JAQ Papers, HSP; JAQ to Eliza Quitman, August 13, 1851, Quitman Family Papers, SHC; *Mississippi Palladium* (Holly Springs), August 8, 1851; *Mississippi Free Trader* (Natchez), August 6, 13, 1851; Jackson *Mississippian*, August 1, 8, 15, 23, September 5, 1851; Vicks-burg *Sentinel*, August 6, 1851; McCardell, "Quitman and the Compromise," 259; William R. Cannon to JAQ, August 11, 1851, Claiborne Papers, MDA. Quitman timed his appearances to follow Foote's by two days. Jackson *Mississippian*, August 1, 15, 1851.

28. Powhatan Ellis to his sister, October 8, 1851, Munford-Ellis Family Papers, DU; Jackson *Mississippian*, September 19, 1851; JAQ to the Democratic State Rights Party of Mississippi, September 6, 1851, quoted in *Mississippi Free Trader* (Natchez), September 10, 21, 1851; Vicksburg *Sentinel*, September 16, 1851; McCardell, "Quitman and the Compromise," 262.

29. Vicksburg *Whig*, November 26, 1851; Lillian Adele Kibler, *Benjamin F. Perry: South Carolina Unionist* (Durham, 1946), 263; Harold S. Schultz, *Nation-*

alism and Sectionalism in South Carolina, 1852–1860: A Study of the Movement for Southern Independence (Durham, 1950), 36–42. The Mississippi convention, while not entirely approving of the congressional legislation, held that it would abide by the compromise as a "permanent adjustment" of the sectional controversy. It also rebuked Mississippi's legislature for calling the convention without a public referendum. Jackson *Mississippian*, November 21, 1851.

30. Jackson *Mississippian*, September 19, 26, October 3, 17, 24, November 8, December 5, 12, 26, 1851, January 2, 25, April 9, June 11, 25, 1852; *Mississippi Free Trader* (Natchez), December 10, 1851; Vicksburg *Whig*, April 7, 14, 28, 1852.

31. *Mississippi Free Trader* (Natchez), September 10, 1851; Albert Gallatin Brown to JAQ, November 13, 1851, Claiborne Papers, MDA; JAQ to W. D. Chapman, December 29, 1851, in Claiborne, *Quitman*, II, 152–55. Several months later, Brown defended Quitman in a speech in Congress. *Congressional Globe*, 32nd Cong., 1st Sess., Appendix, 355–59.

Quitman's public endorsement of a new—and extreme—defense of slavery (published the next year) further testified to his continuing radicalism. JAQ to Jackson Warner, October 14, 1851, *Mississippi Free Trader* (Natchez), October 18, 1851; John Fletcher, *Studies on Slavery, in Easy Lessons* (Natchez, 1852).

32. *Mississippi Free Trader* (Natchez), January 17, April 7, 1852; J. A. Thomas to William Marcy, [January 12], February 9, 1852, William Marcy Papers, LC; JAQ to B. F. Dill, February 20, 1852, JAQ to W. D. Chapman, June 9, 1852, JAQ to J. C. Carpenter *et al.*, July 17, 1852, in Claiborne, *Quitman*, II, 165–72.

33. Arthur Charles Cole, *The Whig Party in the South* (1913; rpr. Gloucester, 1962), 255–60; Jackson *Mississippian*, July 23, 1852; Natchez *Courier*, July 20, 1852; Vicksburg *Whig*, July 28, 1852; New York *Times*, August 5, 1852.

34. JAQ to F. Henry Quitman, September 13, 1852, JAQ Papers, HSP; JAQ to the editor of the *Mississippi Free Trader* (Natchez), July 23, 1852, in Claiborne, *Quitman*, II, 173–76.

35. Thaddeus Sanford to John Bragg, March 13, 1852, John Bragg Papers, SHC; Sydenham D. Moore to John M. Berrien, August 23, 1852, John M. Berrien to Sydenham D. Moore, September 9, 1852 (draft), John Berrien Papers, SHC; Lewy Dorman, *Party Politics in Alabama from 1850 through 1860* (Wetumpka, Ala., 1935), 46–79; J. Mills Thornton, *Politics and Power in a Slave Society: Alabama, 1800–1860* (Baton Rouge, 1978), 247–50, 262–64; Elwood Fisher to JAQ, August 17, 1852, JAQ to Thomas Williams, September 5, 1852, in Claiborne, *Quitman*, II, 177–79, 182–85; JAQ to F. Henry Quitman, September 13, 1852, JAQ Papers, HSP.

36. Jackson *Mississippian*, October 1, 15, November 12, 1852; Vicksburg *Whig*, September 22, October 6, 13, 20, 27, 1852; Natchez *Courier*, September 21, 24, October 10, 15, 22, 1852; George M. Troup to Thomas Williams, J. A. Elmore, and G. B. DuVal, September 27, 1852, in Edward J. Harden, *The Life of George M. Troup* (Savannah, 1859), 530–31.

37. Thornton, *Politics and Power*, 156–58, 265; Svend Petersen, *A Statistical History of the American Presidential Elections* (New York, 1963), 31.

38. JAQ to F. Henry Quitman, July 30, 1852, JAQ Papers, HSP; Giles M. Hillyer to JAQ, January 4, 1853, Quitman Family Papers, SHC; Jackson *Mississippian*, November 18, 1853; Donald M. Rawson, "Democratic Resurgence in Mississippi, 1852–1853," *JMH*, XXVI (1964), 1–27.

39. JAQ to F. Henry Quitman, August 5, 1857, JAQ Papers, HSP.

CHAPTER 20

1. Louisa Quitman to JAQ, July 25, September 1, 1851, Antonia Quitman to JAQ, August 14, 1851, F. Henry Quitman to JAQ, June 18, 1853, Quitman Family Papers, M-N; Louisa Quitman to JAQ, November 17, 1846, Quitman Family Papers, SHC; Annie Rosalie Quitman Diary, July 2, 1853, JAQ Papers, LSU.

2. "Family Record," JAQ to John S. Chadbourne, December 5, 1851, Lovell Family Papers, UnS; Annie Rosalie Quitman Diary, December 2–7, 1852, JAQ Papers, LSU.

3. Annie Rosalie Quitman to Louisa Quitman, January 27, February 4, 1853, F. Henry Quitman to Eliza Quitman, October 28, 1850, Louisa Quitman to JAQ, July 17, 1851, Quitman Family Papers, SHC; JAQ to F. Henry Quitman, February 6, 1852, May 7, 1853, JAQ Papers, HSP; Eliza Quitman to F. Henry Quitman, July 25, September 4, 1852, Quitman Family Papers, M-N. Quitman asked Stephen A. Douglas and Robert J. Walker to help his son gain entrée to the right European circles. Henry had John McMurran's nephew, Thomas M. Jordan, as a traveling companion. JAQ to Stephen A. Douglas, May 4, 1853, Quitman Family Papers, SHC; Robert J. Walker to Francis C. Corbin, May 22, 1853, Quitman Family Papers, M-N.

4. John V. Wren to the editors of the New York *Sachem*, September 1, 1852, quoted in *Mississippi Free Trader* (Natchez), December 29, 1852; Henry Hughes Diary, October 24, 1852 (typewritten copy), Henry Hughes Papers, MDA; *Congressional Globe*, 34th Cong., 1st Sess., Appendix, 1294; Richard Elward to J. F. H. Claiborne, November 14, 1852, J. F. H. Claiborne Papers, MDA; George Parr to Daniel M. Barringer, August 17, 1852, Daniel M. Barringer Papers, SHC; Vicksburg *Whig*, September 29, 1852; Cuban Junta to JAQ, April 29, 1853, in J. F. H. Claiborne, *Life and Correspondence of John A. Quitman* (2 vols.; New York, 1860), II, 387.

5. *Mississippi Free Trader* (Natchez), December 24, 1851; Francis V. R. Mace to JAQ, October 14, 1852, JAQ Papers, HU; Annie Rosalie Quitman Diary, December 15, 1852, JAQ Papers, LSU.

6. Jackson *Mississippian*, January 16, June 18, 1852. Basil Rauch, analyzing the wording of the Pierce administration's instructions to Soulé, gives circumstantial evidence that Pierce initially favored Cuban filibustering. Rauch, *American Interest in Cuba, 1848–1855* (New York, 1948), 262–64, 272.

7. Cuban Junta to JAQ, April 29, 1853, JAQ to the Cuban Junta, April 30, 1853, in Claiborne, *Quitman*, II, 386–88; JAQ to F. Henry Quitman, September 14, 1853, JAQ Papers, HSP; Alexander M. Clayton, commission, May 24, 1853, RG 59, General Records of the Department of State, Temporary Consular Commissions, Vol. 2, p. 74, NA; Alexander M. Clayton to JAQ, November 10, 1853, JAQ Papers, HU.

8. Jackson *Mississippian*, March 11, 1853. Quitman and Foote effected something of a rapprochement after their 1851 campaign. Foote praised Quitman for standing up for principle while other politicians only did what was popular. At the Memphis convention Quitman nominated Foote, who attended, as head of Mississippi's delegation. Foote declined because he could not remain for the whole meeting. Vicksburg *Whig*, January 13, 1852, June 11, 1853.

9. Jackson *Mississippian*, June 17, 1853; Vicksburg *Whig*, June 14, 1853. An estimated 499 delegates attended the convention, representing fourteen states. Mississippi's delegation was easily the second largest after Tennessee's. The convention

became a southern affair, though Indiana and Illinois each supplied one delegate. Jere W. Roberson, "The Memphis Commercial Convention of 1853: Southern Dreams and 'Young America,'" *Tennessee Historical Quarterly*, XXXIII (1974), 283–84, 284n.

10. Jackson *Mississippian*, June 17, 1853; Vicksburg *Whig*, June 18, 1853.

11. Jackson *Mississippian*, June 17, 24, 1853; Vicksburg *Whig*, June 18, 1853; C. Y. Baylor to JAQ, August 1, 1854, JAQ Papers, MDA. Much of the delegates' reticence upon Cuba reflected the high proportion of Whigs at the convention. Powhatan Ellis to Charles Ellis, Jr., June 28, 1853, Munford-Ellis Family Papers, DU; Roberson, "Memphis Commercial Convention," 284. Former president Fillmore had committed his party to oppose filibustering; commercially minded Whigs feared war with Spain for Cuba would disrupt trade; and the Whig party, having generally fewer Catholic immigrants within its ranks than did the Democratic party, tended to be more hesitant about annexing Cuba's Catholic population to the United States.

12. Brevoort Butler *et al.* to John S. Chadbourne, April 8, 1853, Quitman Family Papers, SHC; Annie Rosalie Quitman Diary, July 2, 1853, JAQ Papers, LSU; JAQ to F. Henry Quitman, September 14, 1853; JAQ Papers, HSP; JAQ to Eliza Quitman, July 6, 1853, Lovell Family Papers, UnS; Jackson *Mississippian*, September 2, 1853; Louis Schlessinger to JAQ, May 18, 1853, JAQ Papers, HU.

13. JAQ to Eliza Quitman, July 6, 1853, Lovell Family Papers, UnS; *Daily Cincinnati Gazette*, July 6, 1853.

14. JAQ to Eliza Quitman, July 6, 1853, Lovell Family Papers, UnS; Louisa S. Quitman to Louisa T. Chadbourne, July 20, 1853, Quitman Family Papers, SHC; New York *Herald*, quoted in Claiborne, *Quitman*, II, 189–91; Richmond *Enquirer*, July 20, 1853. Quitman shared the speaker's platform at the exhibition opening with the president and many other dignitaries.

15. Louisa S. Quitman to Louisa T. Chadbourne, July 20, 1853, Quitman Family Papers, SHC; JAQ to George Cadwalader, August 11, 1853, George Cadwalader Papers, HSP; Claiborne, *Quitman*, II, 195; Jackson *Mississippian*, September 2, 1853.

16. Mike Walsh to JAQ, October 3, 1853, May 25, September 6, 1854, G. Bolivar Hall to JAQ, August 2, 1853, JAQ Papers, HU; Chatham Roberdeau Wheat to JAQ, November 9, 1853, J. Thomas Wheat to JAQ, June 13, 1854, John T. Pickett to JAQ, August 18, 1853, JAQ Papers, MDA; "Funny Wonders" section, Annie Rosalie Quitman Diary, 1853, JAQ Papers, LSU.

17. Louis Schlessinger to JAQ, July 12, September 3, 1853, John T. Pickett to JAQ, August 18, 1853, JAQ Papers, MDA; John L. O'Sullivan to JAQ, August 29, 1853, JAQ Papers, HU.

18. "Articles entered into between the Cuban Junta and General Quitman, and signed by them respectively," August 18, 1853, in Claiborne, *Quitman*, II, 389–90.

19. Annie Rosalie Quitman Diary, September 8, 1853, JAQ Papers, LSU.

20. D. Clayton James, *Antebellum Natchez* (Baton Rouge, 1968), 267–69; Annie Rosalie Quitman Diary, August 28, October 29, 1853, JAQ Papers, LSU; JAQ to F. Henry Quitman, September 14, 1853, JAQ Papers, HSP. Quitman's September 14 letter mentioned that several of his servants, and John McMurran's, had been seriously ill, and that one of his own servants—Flora—had died; however, he attributed these cases to typhoid or bilious fever rather than yellow fever.

21. JAQ to F. Henry Quitman, September 29, October 26, December 10, 1853, JAQ Papers, HSP; "Table of the Payne & Turner families made by Henry Fielding

Turner, May 29, 1893," JAQ Papers, MDA; Annie Rosalie Quitman Diary, October 29, December 13, 1853, JAQ Papers, LSU; *Mississippi Free Trader* (Natchez), June 30, 1852; Eliza Quitman to Sarah Fyler, April 24, 1852, Henry Turner to Eliza Turner, April 24, 1852, Quitman Family Papers, SHC. Quitman and Eliza inherited a share of the Fylers' Woodlands place. The following April, they apparently made $4,000 by selling their share to Edward Turner, who bought out the claims of the Quitmans, George and Annie Turner, and Henry Turner for a total of $12,000. That same month, Quitman borrowed $2,000 from his wife at 8 percent interest, the money coming from her "distributive share of her late mother's estate." Deed Records, Adams County, Vol. KK, pp. 273–74, MDA; Promissory note, April 8, 1854, JAQ Papers, HSP.

22. Annie Rosalie Quitman Diary, December 9, 11, 16, 1853, JAQ Papers, LSU.

23. Annie Rosalie Quitman Diary, December 31, 1853, April 8, 1854, JAQ Papers, LSU; F. Henry Quitman to JAQ, June 8, 18, 26, October 28, 1853, January 7, 1853 [1854], F. Henry Quitman to Molly Gardner, January 15, 1853 [1854], Quitman Family Papers, M-N; JAQ to F. Henry Quitman, March 17, 1854, JAQ Papers, HSP. Molly's father, Colonel Virgil H. Gardner, kept his residence at Riverdale, a plantation on the Alabama River above Selma in Dallas County, and owned a plantation in Shelby County. He held title to sixty slaves at Riverdale and nineteen slaves in Shelby County. Mary's grandmother, also Mary, held title to an additional forty-three slaves. Virgil's brother, Garland T., had a plantation in Dallas County, with eighty-one slaves. Selma *Times Journal*, October 6, 1929; *Seventh Census, 1850*: Population and Slave Schedules, Alabama, Dallas and Shelby Counties. Quitman's positive attitude toward the match was reflected in his writing a note to President Pierce regarding a patronage request of one of Molly's brothers before he even met his prospective daughter-in-law. After the wedding, Eliza gave the couple a generous supply of household goods. See JAQ to F. Henry Quitman, March 17, 1854, JAQ Papers, HSP; Mary Quitman to her mother, December 8, [1854], Quitman Family Papers, M-N.

24. Annie Rosalie Quitman Diary, November 5, December 26, 1853, JAQ Papers, LSU; *National Intelligencer* (Washington), December 17, 1853; Vicksburg *Whig*, January 11, 1854; Mike Walsh to JAQ, October 3, 1853, JAQ to J.M.N., December 28, 1853 (draft), Reuben Davis to JAQ, March 6, 1854, JAQ Papers, HU; JAQ to Mike Walsh, March 14, 1854, Mike Walsh Papers, NYHS.

25. C. Stanley Urban, "The Africanization of Cuba Scare, 1853–1855," *Hispanic American Historical Review*, XXXVII (1957), 29–37; Rauch, *American Interest*, 276–78; Philip Foner, *A History of Cuba and Its Relations with the United States* (2 vols.; New York, 1962–63), I, 104–105.

26. Jackson *Mississippian*, March 24, 1854; JAQ to B. F. Dill, June 18, 1854 (draft), Felix Huston to JAQ, September 13, 1854, JAQ Papers, HU; JAQ to B. F. Dill, February 9, 1854 [1855], F. L. Claiborne to JAQ, June 15, 1854, JAQ Papers, MDA; *Mississippi Free Trader* (Natchez), May 27, 1854.

27. JAQ to F. R. Witter, February 11, 1855, JAQ Misc. MSS, LC; JAQ to B. F. Dill, June 18, 1854 (draft), Alexander M. Clayton to JAQ, November 10, 1853, JAQ Papers, HU; James W. McDonald to JAQ, March 10, 1854, John T. Pickett to JAQ, March 20, 1854, JAQ Papers, MDA; Samuel R. Walker, "Cuba and the South," *De Bow's Review*, XVIII (November, 1854), 519–25; Alexander Walker to A. G. Haley, June 15, 1854, Jefferson Davis Papers, LC; Robert E. May, *The Southern Dream of a Caribbean Empire, 1854–1861* (Baton Rouge, 1973), 33–36; Henry L. Janes,

"The *Black Warrior* Affair," *American Historical Review*, XII (1907), 280–98.

28. E. L. Acee to JAQ, June 8, 1855, JAQ Papers, HU; *Arkansas State Gazette and Democrat* (Little Rock), May 26, 1854; Vicksburg *Whig*, June 28, 1854; Natchez *Courier*, May 18, 1854; Laura A. White, "The United States in the 1850's as Seen by British Consuls," *Mississippi Valley Historical Review*, XIX (1933), 528n–29n; Robert O. Love to JAQ, May 24, 1854, JAQ Papers, MDA; John S. Thrasher, *Cuba and Louisiana: Letter to Samuel J. Peters, Esq.* (New Orleans, 1854), 8.

29. T. C. Hindman to John S. Thrasher, June 12, 1854, JAQ Papers, MDA; James W. McDonald to JAQ, March 26, 1854, JAQ Papers, HU. Recruiting able personnel also promised military dividends. There was a conviction in filibuster circles that López had failed because of his dependence—as Felix Huston put it—upon "loafers and city vagabonds" who were unwilling to submit to their officers' commands and could not maintain secrecy because they drank too much and talked too freely. Jackson *Mississippian*, September 27, 1854; Theodore O'Hara to William Nelson, March 18, 1854, JAQ Papers, MDA.

30. A. J. McNeil to JAQ, June 10, 1854, L. Norvell Walker to JAQ, August 19, 1854, JAQ to L. Norvell Walker, August 24, 1854, "X & Y" to JAQ, June 17, 1854, JAQ Papers, MDA; Isaac H. Trahue to JAQ, July 1, 1854, William Mason to JAQ, July 15, 1854, JAQ Papers, HU; Cadmus M. Wilcox to JAQ, May 8, 1854, J. F. H. Claiborne Papers, MDA.

31. Cincinnati *Daily Enquirer*, June 27, 1854; Samuel R. Walker, "The Diary of a Louisiana Planter," December 19, 1859 (Typescript copy, Purdue University Library, Lafayette, Ind.); Samuel R. Walker to JAQ, February 7, 1854, Felix Huston to JAQ, March 4, 1854, Henry W. Forno to JAQ, January 23, 1855, JAQ Papers, HU; Eliza Quitman to F. Henry Quitman, September 17, 1849, Quitman Family Papers, M-N.

32. JAQ to C. A. L. Lamar, January 5, 1855, J. W. Lesesne to JAQ, May 29, June 10, 1854, JAQ Papers, HU; T. W. W. Sullivan to JAQ, April 10, 1854, John A. Winston to JAQ, June 3, 1854, JAQ Papers, MDA; *Seventh Census, 1850*: Slave Schedules, Alabama, Mobile County.

33. John Marshall to JAQ, June 14, 1854, James P. Henderson to JAQ, October 6, 1854, JAQ Papers, HU; W. D. Ron to JAQ, June 7, 1854, C. C. Danley to JAQ, June 27, 1854, John S. Ford to JAQ, June 5, 1854, F. L. Claiborne to JAQ, June 15, 1854, William M. Estelle to JAQ, May 25, 1854, Edward Latham to JAQ, January 26, 1855, JAQ Papers, MDA; Henry Turner to JAQ, May 22, 1854, Quitman Family Papers, SHC; John S. Ford to Hugh McLeod, January 14, 1855, Hugh McLeod Papers, Texas State Library and Archives, Austin.

34. A. L. Diket, "Slidell's Right Hand: Emile La Sère," *Louisiana History*, IV (1963), 180–82; J. Mills Thornton, *Politics and Power in a Slave Society: Alabama, 1800–1860* (Baton Rouge, 1978), 322; T. C. Hindman to JAQ, January 31, 1855, JAQ Papers, MDA.

35. C. C. Danley to JAQ, June 27, 1854, JAQ Papers, MDA; *Mississippi Free Trader* (Natchez), November 24, 1851; Louisa Chadbourne to JAQ, November 24, 1851, Quitman Family Papers, SHC; Jackson *Mississippian*, September 13, 1850; Thelma Jennnings, *The Nashville Convention: Southern Movement for Unity, 1848–1851* (Memphis, 1980), 151; John Tyler, Jr., to JAQ, July 31, 1851, JAQ Papers, HU.

36. JAQ to Mike Walsh, March 14, 1854, Mike Walsh Papers, NYHS; Eliza Quitman to F. Henry Quitman, March 21, 1854, Quitman Family Papers, M-N.

37. Antonia Quitman to F. Henry Quitman, March 21, 1854, Quitman Family Papers, M-N; Annie Rosalie Quitman Diary, April 8–19, 1854, JAQ Papers, LSU; JAQ to the Cuban Junta, April 16, 1854, in Claiborne, *Quitman*, II, 391–92; W. M. Brantly to JAQ, June 29, 1854, JAQ Papers, MDA.

38. Annie Rosalie Quitman Diary, April 20–27, 1854, JAQ Papers, LSU; Selma *Times Journal*, October 6, 1929.

39. JAQ to the Cuban Junta, April 16, 1854, in Claiborne, *Quitman*, II, 391; John S. Ford to JAQ, June 5, 1854, J. W. Lesesne to JAQ, June 6, 1854, Robert W. Shufeldt to JAQ, June 7, 1854, JAQ Papers, MDA; Samuel R. Walker to JAQ, May 30, 1854, J. W. Lesesne to JAQ, May 29, June 10, 1854, JAQ Papers, HU; Edward W. Callahan (comp.), *List of Officers of the Navy of the United States and of the Marine Corps from 1775 to 1900* (New York, 1901), 496; New Orleans *Daily Picayune*, May 25, 1854. Circumstantial evidence indicates that another U.S. naval officer, William Nelson, may have furnished Quitman strategic advice around this time. Henry Waller Diary, June 22, 1854, Filson Club, Louisville.

40. Cincinnati *Daily Enquirer*, June 27, 1854; New Orleans *Daily Picayune*, May 26, 1854; Memphis *Appeal*, June 6, 1854; Estimate of invasion costs, June, 1854, JAQ Papers, MDA. The new Davis-Quitman political rivalry was reflected, the next year, in a fight for editorial control of the *Free Trader*, which Quitman won. James W. McDonald to JAQ, January 6, December 20, 1855, JAQ Papers, HU; JAQ to Edward Pickett, November 19, 1855, JAQ Papers, MDA; James W. McDonald to J. F. H. Claiborne, December 27, 1855, February 16, 1856, Claiborne Papers, MDA.

41. Samuel R. Walker to JAQ, May 30, 1854, Mike Walsh to JAQ, May 25, 1854, JAQ Papers, HU; Louis Schlessinger to JAQ, September 9, 1854, JAQ Papers, MDA; May, *Southern Dream*, 53. Walsh's account was confirmed by a report that cabinet members had told "Southern gentlemen" that Pierce would "wink" at attempts to invade Cuba. New York *Herald*, June 3, 1854.

42. John Slidell to James Buchanan, June 17, 1854, James Buchanan Papers, HSP; May, *Southern Dream*, 59; James D. Richardson (comp.), *Messages and Papers of the Presidents, 1789–1904* (10 vols.; Washington, D.C., 1899–1904), V, 272–73. This interpretation of Pierce's motivation is reinforced by a letter in which Secretary of State William Marcy informed American minister to France John Y. Mason that the Kansas-Nebraska uproar had "shattered" the northern Democracy and "deprived it of the strength which was needed and could have been much more profitably used for the acquisition of Cuba." William L. Marcy to John Y. Mason, May 25, 1854, William Marcy Papers, LC. Other circumstances, however, certainly contributed to Pierce's decision, including Spanish pressure, antifilibustering attitudes among cabinet members, and a genuine trust that Cuba could be acquired—without filibustering—by means of purchase.

43. J. W. Lesesne to JAQ, June 8, 1854, Samuel R. Walker to JAQ, July 31, 1854, JAQ Papers, HU.

44. Quitman was aware that some northern congressmen supporting the Kansas-Nebraska Act had publicly expressed a conviction that the legislation would, in Quitman's words, "limit, not extend slave area." JAQ to B. F. Dill, February 9, 1854 [1855], JAQ Papers, MDA.

45. JAQ to B. F. Dill, June 18, 1854, JAQ Papers, HU.

46. *Ibid.*; J. W. Lesesne to JAQ, June 6, 1854, Samuel R. Walker to JAQ, July 7, 1854, JAQ Papers, MDA. Pierce and Marcy had sent agents to Cuba to investigate

Africanization reports, and had cautioned Spain through diplomatic channels against the policy. May, *Southern Dream*, 54–55.

47. Alexander Walker to A. G. Haley, June 15, 1854, Jefferson Davis Papers, LC; Washington *Union*, June 4, 17, 1854; John Henderson, *Considerations on the Constitutionality of [the] President's Proclamations*, Southern Filibusters Collection, LSU. Davis never clarified his role concerning the proclamation. After its issuance, he continued to proclaim himself a friend of Cuba's liberation. However, he later conceded that he and Quitman had differed about the neutrality laws. Jefferson Davis to Ambrosio José González, October 28, 1854 (copy), Jefferson Davis Papers, DU; New York *Herald*, June 23, 1855; *Congressional Globe*, 35th Cong., 2nd Sess., 225.

48. J. W. Lesesne to JAQ, June 6, 10, 1854, Samuel R. Walker to JAQ, July 7, 1854, JAQ Papers, MDA; Columbus (Miss.) *Democrat*, June 10, July 1, 1854; Jackson *Mississippian*, May 5, 12, June 23, 1854; G. Chandler to JAQ, May 8, 1854, JAQ Papers, HU.

49. J. Thomas Wheat to JAQ, June 13, 1854, JAQ Papers, MDA; New Orleans *Daily Picayune*, June 15, 20, 22–24, July 2, 1854; Buffalo *Express*, June 26, 1854, quoted in New York *Herald*, July 4, 1854; Richmond *Whig*, June 21, 1854; Cincinnati *Daily Enquirer*, June 27, 1854; Memphis *Appeal*, May 26, 1854; New Orleans *Daily Picayune*, June 15, 1854.

50. New Orleans *Daily Picayune*, July 2, 1854; JAQ to F. Henry Quitman, July 1, 1854, JAQ Papers, HSP; *Louisiana Courier* (New Orleans), July 2, 1854; Quitman's protest, July 3, 1854, JAQ Papers, MDA; Claiborne, *Quitman*, II, 197.

51. JAQ to F. Henry Quitman, July 1, 1854, JAQ Papers, HSP; JAQ to H. T. Ellet, September 11, 1854, in Claiborne, *Quitman*, II, 208–209; JAQ letter, dated August 15, 1854, in New Orleans *Daily Delta*, August 25, 1854.

52. John Marshall to JAQ, July 12, 18, 1854, Samuel R. Walker to JAQ, December 21, 1854, JAQ Papers, HU; Vicksburg *Whig*, June 28, 1854; Clarksville (Tenn.) *Jeffersonian*, August 2, 1854; JAQ to Thomas Reed, August 24, 1854, in Claiborne, *Quitman*, II, 206–208.

53. John W. Fleener to JAQ, August 17, 1854, John S. Ford to JAQ, August 12, 1854, JAQ Papers, MDA; Samuel R. Walker to JAQ, December 21, 1854, William Langley to JAQ, January 13, 1855, JAQ Papers, HU. Years later, Campbell denied having second thoughts and claimed to have seen circulars of the Cuban Junta which established Quitman's guilt even by Quitman's "own interpretation of the neutrality laws." John A. Campbell to [?], November 5, 1859, John A. Campbell Misc. MSS, NYHS.

54. James Madison Miller to JAQ, September 17, 1854 [a notation of Quitman's response is on the envelope], JAQ Papers, HU; JAQ to Mike Walsh, October 10, 1854, Mike Walsh Papers, NYHS; *Mississippi Free Trader* (Natchez), August 22, 23, 1854.

55. Samuel R. Walker to JAQ, September 21, 1854, JAQ Papers, HU; Walker, "Cuba and the South," 519–25; Felix Huston, public letter, in Jackson *Mississippian*, September 27, 1854; [Gaspar Betancourt and John S. Thrasher], *Addresses Delivered at the Celebration of the Third Anniversary in Honor of the Martyrs for Cuban Freedom at the Mechanics' Institute Hall, New Orleans, Sept. 1, 1854* (New Orleans, 1854); JAQ to John C. Walker, cipher note filed November, 1854, JAQ to John S. Ford, October 16, 1854, [JAQ] to Mansfield Lovell, October 6, 1854, JAQ Papers, MDA.

56. John Marshall to JAQ, September 18, 1854, J. D. Rush McHenry to JAQ, December 12, 1854, Samuel R. Walker to JAQ, October 8, 1854, JAQ Papers, HU; Thomas P. Farrar to John S. Thrasher, July 6, 1854, Lucius Lusk to JAQ, October 14, 1854, JAQ Papers, MDA.

57. JAQ to John S. Ford, October 16, 1854, Memorandum, December 14, 1854, JAQ to L. Norvell Walker, August 24, 1854, George Bolivar Hall to JAQ, January 14, 1855, Theodore O'Hara to William Nelson, March 18, 1854, Hugh McLeod to JAQ, May 31, 1854, JAQ Papers, MDA; Quitman notation on envelope of James Madison Miller to JAQ, September 17, 1854, JAQ Papers, HU.

58. John S. Ford to JAQ, August 12, 1854, Theodore O'Hara to JAQ, September 28, 1854, Chatham Roberdeau Wheat to JAQ, October 13, 29, 1854, JAQ Papers, MDA; Charles Cummings to JAQ, November 14, 1854, JAQ Papers, HU.

59. Samuel R. Walker to JAQ, October 11, 1854, JAQ to C. A. L. Lamar, January 5, 1855, JAQ Papers, HU; Bond contract, signed by J. S. Thrasher, dated May 19, 1854, T. W. W. Sullivan to JAQ, April 10, 1854, A. Nelson to JAQ, June 4, 1854, JAQ Papers, MDA; Walker, "Diary of a Louisiana Planter," December 19, 1859; "Manifesto of the Junta to the People of Cuba," New York *Times*, September 12, 1855; Robert Benson Leard, "Bonds of Destiny: The United States and Cuba, 1848–1861" (Ph.D. dissertation, University of California, 1953), 138–39. Nelson signed his name A. Nelson, and is occasionally listed as Allen rather than Allison. See, for instance, Lucian Lamar Knight, *Georgia's Landmarks, Memorials and Legends* (2 vols.; Atlanta, 1913–14), II, 679.

60. New Orleans *Daily Picayune*, January 10, 11, 22, 1855; William M. Estelle to JAQ, December 19, 1854, William H. Wood to JAQ, February 1, 1855, William Langley to JAQ, January 13, 1855, JAQ Papers, HU; Powhatan Jordan to JAQ, January 3, 1855, Theodore O'Hara to JAQ, December 22, 1854, JAQ Papers, MDA; JAQ to F. Henry Quitman, October 26, 1853, January 8, 1855, JAQ Papers, HSP; Vicksburg *Whig*, January 3, 1855.

61. William H. Powell (comp.), *List of Officers of the Army of the United States from 1799 to 1900* (New York, 1900), 441, 594–95, 684; Jones M. Withers to JAQ, December 11, 1854, Gustavus W. Smith to C. A. L. Lamar, February 21, 1855 (copy), JAQ Papers, MDA; New Orleans *Daily Picayune*, February 17, 1855.

62. John S. Thrasher to Hugh McLeod, January 24, 1855, Hugh McLeod Papers, Texas State Library and Archives; Mike Walsh to JAQ, January 25, 1855, JAQ Papers, MDA; Henry W. Forno to JAQ, January 23, 1855, William Langley to JAQ, January 13, 1855, W. A. Lacy to JAQ, February 19, 1855, JAQ to Alexander K. McClung, February 4, 1855, JAQ Papers, HU.

63. Theodore O'Hara to JAQ, December 22, 1854, John Thomas Wheat to JAQ, March 1, 1855, JAQ Papers, MDA; William Brantly to JAQ, January 17, 1855, William Langley to JAQ, January 13, 1855, L. Norvell Walker to JAQ, March 20, 1855, JAQ Papers, HU. Quitman's hopes of an Indiana contingent had apparently fallen through in December. See John C. Walker to JAQ, November 26, December 13, 1854, JAQ Papers, MDA.

64. A. L. Saunders to JAQ, February 4, 1855, William M. Estelle to JAQ, December 19, 1854, William H. Wood to JAQ, February 1, 1855, Samuel Mitchell to JAQ, February 6, 1855, F. J. Mitchell to JAQ, February 10, 1855, Henry Gillespey to JAQ, February 9, 1855, R. Harris to JAQ, January 3, 1855, Howard Tillotson to JAQ, March 3, 1855, W. M. Weaver to JAQ, February 7, 1855, W. A. Lacy to JAQ, February 19, 1855, J. McRagh to JAQ, March 2, 1855, JAQ Papers, HU;

J. M. Withers to JAQ, December 11, 1854, W. C. Capers to JAQ, January 11, 22, 1855, JAQ Papers, MDA; John S. Ford to Hugh McLeod, January 14, 1855, Hugh McLeod Papers, Texas State Library and Archives.

65. JAQ to C. A. L. Lamar, January 5, 1855, R. W. Estlin to JAQ, December 21, 1854, Samuel R. Walker to JAQ, September 21, 1854, JAQ Papers, HU; Edward Latham to JAQ, January 26, 1855, Mike Walsh to JAQ, January 25, 1855, Julius Hessee to JAQ, February 22, 1855, Estlin ledger (in May-June, 1855, file), Emile La Sère memorandum, dated January 3, 1855, JAQ Papers, MDA; C. A. L. Lamar to John M. Dow, February 12, 1855, in "A Slave-Trader's Letter Book," *North American Review*, CXLIII (1886), 448, 451; JAQ to F. Henry Quitman, February 3, 1855, JAQ Papers, HSP; JAQ to F. R. Witter, February 11, 1855, JAQ Misc. MSS, LC.

66. JAQ to C. A. L. Lamar, January 5, 1855, Henry W. Forno to JAQ, January 23, February 6, 1855, JAQ Papers, HU; Leard, "Bonds of Destiny," 139–40; D. Clayton James, "Tribulations of a Bayou Boeuf Store Owner, 1853–1857," *Louisiana History*, IV (Summer, 1963), 255; C. A. L. Lamar to John S. Thrasher, February 25, 1855, in "Slave-Trader's Letter Book," 448; Charles H. Brown, *Agents of Manifest Destiny: The Lives and Times of the Filibusters* (Chapel Hill, 1980), 255. Magnolia was owned by one H. C. Story. The plantation was later renamed Repose. Collin B. Hamer, Jr. (Head, Louisiana Division, City of New Orleans Public Library), to Robert E. May, August 11, 1982.

67. James W. McDonald to JAQ, March 26, 1854, JAQ Papers, HU; William Henry Talbot Walker to Adam[?], January 4 [1855], William Henry Talbot Walker Papers, DU; New York *Times* reporter, quoted in Brown, *Agents of Manifest Destiny*, 255.

68. Henry A. Murray, *Lands of the Slave and the Free: Or, Cuba, the United States, and Canada* (London, 1855), 271; *National Era* (Washington), April 12, 1855; New York *Times*, January 26, 1855; New Orleans *Daily Picayune*, February 14, 1855; Arthur Fanshawe to John F. Crampton, February 6, 1855, in Gavin B. Henderson, "Southern Designs on Cuba, 1854–1857 and Some European Opinions," *Journal of Southern History*, V (1939), 380–81; Leard, "Bonds of Destiny," 139–40; Foner, *History of Cuba*, II, 92.

69. May, *Southern Dream*, 58–59, 67–76; Brown, *Agents of Manifest Destiny*, 255; David M. Potter, *The Impending Crisis, 1848–1861* (New York, 1976), 175.

70. New York *Times*, January 26, 1855; Alexander H. Stephens to JAQ, February 24, 1855, JAQ to Alexander K. McClung, February 4, 1855, JAQ Papers, HU. According to Samuel Walker, the *Massachusetts* had been purchased by Goicouria, who had sought and won a pardon from Quitman since the Savannah escapade. Walker claimed that $45,000 had been spent by the filibusters to make the vessel seaworthy. Walker, "Diary of a Louisiana Planter," December 19, 1859.

71. JAQ to F. Henry Quitman, February 19, 20, 1855, JAQ Papers, HSP; James W. McDonald to G. W. Smith, March 13, 1855, JAQ Papers, MDA; Natchez *Courier*, March 9, 1855. Some of Quitman's agents, meanwhile, tried to legitimize the enterprise by using Henry L. Kinney's Central American Colonization Company as a foil. Kinney's project, though a filibustering scheme too, operated under the pretense of peacefully settling Americans in Nicaragua (Kinney had obtained a disputed land grant on Nicaragua's eastern coast). It was widely believed in the press and some filibuster circles that President Pierce favored Kinney's scheme because some close associates were involved in it. Walsh in New York sought to board Quitman's men on Kinney's ships; Mobile recruitment for Quitman was effected under the cover of

Kinney's office in that city. However, Kinney's track record with federal authorities was similar to Quitman's. Kinney was indicted by a federal grand jury in April, and though he did get to Nicaragua, his scheme was so weakened by federal interference that the enterprise failed. James T. Wall, "Henry L. Kinney and the Mosquito Colony," James T. Wall (ed.), *The Landscape of American History: Essays in Memoriam to Richard W. Griffin* (Washington, D.C., 1979), 21–40; Brown, *Agents of Manifest Destiny*, 271–73; Powhatan Jordan to JAQ, January 3, 1855, [?] to Mansfield Lovell, January 9, 1855, Mike Walsh to JAQ, January 25, 1855, JAQ Papers, MDA; William Brantly to JAQ, January 17, 1855, JAQ Papers, HU; Henry L. Kinney to Mike Walsh, February 23, 1855, Mike Walsh Papers, NYHS; New Orleans *Daily Picayune*, February 25, 1855.

72. *Congressional Globe*, 33rd Cong., 2nd Sess., 1148; Vicksburg *Whig*, April 4, 1855; John Slidell to James Buchanan, October 18, 1854, James Buchanan Papers, HSP.

73. *Mississippi Free Trader* (Natchez), March 10, 1855; C. Stanley Urban, "The Abortive Quitman Filibustering Expedition to Cuba, 1853–1855," *JMH*, XVIII (1956), 192; Rauch, *American Interest*, 300; Horatio G. Perry to William L. Marcy, September 6, 1854, William L. Marcy to Augustus Dodge, May 12, 1855, William Marcy Papers, LC. Quitman may have had difficulty arranging an interview with Pierce. See Sidney Webster to JAQ, March 9, 1855, JAQ Papers, MDA.

74. Harry Maury to G. W. Smith, March 23, 1855, JAQ Papers, MDA; JAQ to F. Henry Quitman, April 26, 1855, JAQ Papers, HSP; Vicksburg *Whig*, May 23, 1855.

75. John S. Thrasher to C. A. L. Lamar, May 29, 1855, JAQ Papers, MDA; "Manifesto of the Junta to the People of Cuba," New York *Times*, September 12, 1855; E. L. Acee to JAQ, June 8, 1855, James W. McDonald to JAQ, December 20, 1855, JAQ Papers, HU; Jane Cazneau to Moses S. Beach, June 25, 1855, Jane McManus Cazneau Papers, NYHS; JAQ to F. Henry Quitman, June 26, 1855, JAQ Papers, HSP. Later, according to one account, Quitman came to see Goicouria's miscalculation as the cause of his failure. Appleton Oaksmith to Domingo de Goicouria, January 22, 1859, Appleton Oaksmith Papers, DU.

76. JAQ to W. A. Stone, June 19, 1855, in Claiborne, *Quitman*, II, 210–12; *Mississippi Free Trader* (Natchez), September 14, 1855; Harry Maury to G. W. Smith, March 23, 1855, JAQ Papers, MDA; John S. Ford to JAQ, July 2, 1855, JAQ Papers, UV; Edward M. Taylor and Leo Black to JAQ, April 15, 1855, Richard S. Graves to JAQ, July 31, 1855, JAQ Papers, HU.

CHAPTER 21

1. *Mississippi Free Trader* (Natchez), March 20, 1844; Robert Rowand Diary, December 23, 1847, DU; Vicksburg *Sentinel*, August 9, 1848.

2. William Darrell Overdyke, *The Know-Nothing Party in the South* (Baton Rouge, 1950), 7–11, 15, 31.

3. William Sharkey to Charles D. Fontaine, May 3, 1855, D. W. Owen to Charles D. Fontaine, May 14, 1855, Giles M. Hillyer to Charles D. Fontaine, 1855 [no exact date], Charles D. Fontaine to Giles M. Hillyer and James H. R. Taylor, April 25, 1855, James H. R. Taylor to Charles D. Fontaine, June 11, 1855, Charles D. Fontaine Papers, MDA; Vicksburg *Whig*, August 23, December 6, 20, 1854, July 18, 1855; Natchez *Courier*, May 3, 15, June 12, 20, 1855; John J. McRae to J. F. H.

Claiborne, December 17, 1854, Albert G. Brown to J. F. H. Claiborne, December 17, 1854, J. F. H. Claiborne Papers, MDA.

4. JAQ to B. F. Dill, February 9, 1854 [1855], JAQ Papers, MDA.

5. *Mississippi Free Trader* (Natchez), May 8, June 12, 1855; Vicksburg *Whig*, June 13, 1855; Jackson *Mississippian*, June 13, 1855; Edward R. Welles Diary, June [?], 1855, Old Courthouse Museum, Vicksburg (Typescript copy courtesy of the editors of *The Papers of Jefferson Davis*).

6. John Duncan to JAQ, May 25, 1855, E. L. Acee to JAQ, June 8, 1855, JAQ Papers, HU; Albert G. Brown to J. F. H. Claiborne, June 7, 1855, Claiborne Papers, MDA; Natchez *Courier*, June 1, 13, 1855; Vicksburg *Whig*, May 23, June 13, 1855.

7. Richard Elward to J. F. H. Claiborne, August 3, 1855, Claiborne Papers, MDA.

8. JAQ to F. Henry Quitman, June 26, 1855, JAQ Papers, HSP; *Mississippi Free Trader* (Natchez), June 29, 1855.

9. William A. Stone to JAQ, June 25, 1855, JAQ Papers, MDA; JAQ to W. A. Stone, July 19, 1855, in J. F. H. Claiborne, *Life and Correspondence of John A. Quitman* (2 vols.; New York, 1860), II, 210–12; *Mississippi Free Trader* (Natchez), July 31, August 1, 1855; Albert G. Brown to JAQ, August 2, 1855, JAQ Papers, HU; Albert G. Brown to J. F. H. Claiborne, August 14, 1855, Claiborne Papers, MDA.

10. Vicksburg *Whig*, August 1, 1855; Natchez *Courier*, July 28, 1855.

11. JAQ to Rufus K. Arthur, August 3, 1855, Alexander H. Arthur to JAQ, August 11, 1855, JAQ Papers, HU.

12. *Mississippi Free Trader* (Natchez), August 8, 10, 24, 1855; JAQ to F. Henry Quitman, August 17, 26, 1855, JAQ Papers, HSP; Annie Rosalie Quitman Diary, July 24, 1855, JAQ Papers, LSU.

13. Natchez *Courier*, August 11, 22, 1855; *Mississippi Free Trader* (Natchez), September 4, 1855; Eliza Quitman to JAQ, September 26, 1855, Quitman Family Papers, SHC.

14. Richard Elward to J. F. H. Claiborne, August 3, 1855, Claiborne Papers, MDA; *Mississippi Free Trader* (Natchez), August 8, 24, 1855; Claiborne, *Quitman*, II, 215; Natchez *Courier*, August 7, 1855; JAQ to M. G. Wilkinson, September 2, 1855 (draft), JAQ Papers, HU.

15. *Mississippi Free Trader* (Natchez), August 24, September 26, October 2, 23, 1855; Natchez *Courier*, September 18, 1855.

16. William James Cooper, *The South and the Politics of Slavery, 1828–1856* (Baton Rouge, 1978), *passim*; *Mississippi Free Trader* (Natchez), October 16, 19, 23, 1855; Natchez *Courier*, October 18, 1855.

17. *Mississippi Free Trader* (Natchez), August 24, September 26, October 23, 1855; Natchez *Courier*, September 18, October 2, 1855; Jackson *Mississippian*, September 26, 1855; Hiram Cassedy to J. F. H. Claiborne, August 24, 1855, Claiborne Papers, MDA; JAQ to F. Henry Quitman, October 4, 16, 1855, JAQ Papers, HSP; JAQ to Louisa Chadbourne, September 7, 1855, JAQ to Eliza Quitman, September 9, 1855, Quitman Family Papers, SHC. For the scheduling dispute, see Natchez *Courier*, October 9, 12, 19, 1855; *Mississippi Free Trader* (Natchez), October 10, 16, 31, 1855.

18. Eliza Quitman to JAQ, September 26, 1855, F. Henry Quitman to Eliza Quitman, October 12, 1855, JAQ to Louisa Chadbourne, October 28, 1855, Quitman

Family Papers, SHC; JAQ to F. Henry Quitman, October 4, 28, 1855, JAQ Papers, HSP; Antonia Quitman to Mary Quitman, October 7, 1855, F. Henry Quitman to Mary Quitman, July 6, 1855, Receipts dated July 16, 17, 1855, Quitman Family Papers, M-N; F. Henry Quitman to Eliza Quitman, October 1, 1855, F. Henry Quitman to Louisa Quitman, October 23, 1855, JAQ Papers, MDA; Thibodaux *Minerva*, September 8, 1855. Quitman also opposed sending Sarah to Alabama because, he said, she was too timid and simple to undergo a long, solo trip away from "her protectors."

19. JAQ to Eliza Theodosia Quitman, October 11, 1855, Quitman Family Papers, SHC; JAQ to F. Henry Quitman, October 28, 1855, JAQ Papers, HSP; Henry Hughes to JAQ, October 22, 1855, JAQ Papers, MDA.

20. T. J. Humphreys to JAQ, November 16, 1855, JAQ Papers, HU; Natchez *Courier*, October 18, 1855; JAQ to F. Henry Quitman, October 28, 1855, JAQ Papers, HSP; James W. McDonald's September 1, 1855, copy of JAQ to F. L. Claiborne, September 5, 1834, Quitman Family Papers, SHC; Joseph Regard to Charles D. Fontaine, October 30, 1855, Charles D. Fontaine Papers, MDA.

21. H. H. Worthington to Richard Griffith, November 13, 1855, Richard Griffith Papers, MDA; D. Clayton James, *Antebellum Natchez* (Baton Rouge, 1968), 127; Overdyke, *Know-Nothing Party*, 277–78; JAQ to J. F. H. Claiborne, November 18, 1855, in Claiborne, *Quitman*, II, 216.

22. New York *Times*, February 23, 1856. Quitman's speech also attacked Know-Nothing values for their antidemocratic tendencies. Withdrawing immigrant voting privileges would set a precedent for the return of property requirements, so that eventually only the man with "$1000 in his pocket" could cast a ballot. See also *Congressional Globe*, 34th Cong., 1st Sess., 730.

23. *Mississippi Free Trader* (Natchez), November 23, 1855 (report of Quitman's farewell speech at the Natchez courthouse); JAQ to Eliza Quitman, February 11, 1856, Quitman Family Papers, SHC; JAQ to J. F. H. Claiborne, November 18, 1855, in Claiborne, *Quitman*, II, 215–16.

CHAPTER 22

1. George W. Clarke to JAQ, January 29, 1856, JAQ Papers, MDA; T. J. Humphreys to JAQ, November 16, 1855, JAQ Papers, HU; JAQ to F. Henry Quitman, November 18, 1855, JAQ Papers, HSP.

2. Washington *Evening Star*, December 3, 1855; *Congressional Globe*, 34th Cong., 1st Sess., 2–4; Louisa Chadbourne to JAQ, June 24, 1856, Quitman Family Papers, SHC; William E. Van Horne, "Lewis D. Campbell and the Know-Nothing Party in Ohio," *Ohio History*, LXXV (1967), 204–207; Allan Nevins, *Ordeal of the Union* (2 vols.; New York, 1947), II, 414; Richard H. Sewell, *Ballots for Freedom: Antislavery Politics in the United States, 1837–1860* (New York, 1976), 275. The 108–83–43 breakdown is an approximation. Actual party affiliation, because of the nationwide political flux, was so unclear that the editor of the *Congressional Globe* refrained from the usual custom of designating party membership. Too many congressmen were in the process of changing parties for an accurate count. Gerald R. Lientz, "House Speaker Elections and Congressional Parties, 1789–1860," *Capitol Studies*, VI (1978), 83–84, 84n; David M. Potter, *The Impending Crisis, 1848–1861* (New York, 1976), 255.

3. *Congressional Globe*, 34th Cong., 1st Sess., 8, 10–12, 17, 139–42, 229–35; Roy F. Nichols, *Franklin Pierce, Young Hickory of the Granite Hills* (Rev. ed.; Philadelphia, 1958), 436.

4. *Congressional Globe*, 34th Cong., 1st Sess., 31–144; Henry Winter Davis to S. F. Du Pont, [January 4, 1856], in Gerald S. Henig, *Henry Winter Davis: Antebellum and Civil War Congressman from Maryland* (New York, 1973), 82.

5. *Congressional Globe*, 34th Cong., 1st Sess., 69, Appendix, 38; Vicksburg *Whig*, January 12, 1856; Washington *Daily National Intelligencer*, December 10, 1855, January 7, 1856.

6. *Congressional Globe*, 34th Cong., 1st Sess., 139–43.

7. *Congressional Globe*, 34th Cong., 1st Sess., 222–23, 229–35. Richardson's remarks had been made in response to interrogation by Tennessee Know-Nothing Felix Zollicoffer, who hoped to demonstrate that northern Democrats were unreliable on slavery so that southern Democrats would join the Know-Nothings.

8. Joshua Giddings to J. A. Giddings, January 25, 1856, Joshua Giddings Papers, Ohio Historical Society, Columbus; *Congressional Globe*, 34th Cong., 1st Sess., 261–70, 294–98; B. B. French to his brother, February 24, 1856, B. B. French Papers, LC.

9. *Congressional Globe*, 34th Cong., 1st Sess., 325, 335–37; Nichols, *Pierce*, 443. All southern Know-Nothings—including Mississippi's lone American congressman, William A. Lake—except two, voted for Aiken. However, only four free state Know-Nothings stayed with their party. Albert G. Brown to J. F. H. Claiborne, February 4, 1856, J. F. H. Claiborne Papers, MDA; *Congressional Globe*, 34th Cong., 1st Sess., 337.

10. Joshua Giddings to his daughter, February 3, 1856, Giddings-Julian Papers, LC; JAQ to Eliza Quitman, February 11, 1856, Lovell Family Papers, UnS.

11. Sewell, *Ballots for Freedom*, 170–202, 292–342; Fred Harvey Harrington, *Fighting Politician: Major General N.P. Banks* (Philadelphia, 1948), 8, 20, 31–32; *Congressional Globe*, 34th Cong., 1st Sess., 342–43, 409–412; *National Era* (Washington), February 21, 1856.

12. *Congressional Globe*, 34th Cong., 1st Sess., 690–92; Nevins, *Ordeal*, II, 416; Potter, *Impending Crisis*, 204–205; Harrington, *Fighting Politician*, 32.

13. JAQ to F. Henry Quitman, January 26, 1856, JAQ Papers, HSP; Roy Franklin Nichols, *The Disruption of American Democracy* (New York, 1948), 86; A. G. Brown to JAQ, November 19, 1855, John M. Brewer to JAQ, February 14, 1856, Franklin Love to JAQ, May 6, 1856, JAQ Papers, MDA; A. G. Brown to J. F. H. Claiborne, December 19, 1855, February 4, 1856, Claiborne Papers, MDA; JAQ to R. G. W. Jewell, January 26, 1856, Wakefield Autograph Collection, Bancroft Library, University of California, Berkeley; Richard M. Gaines to JAQ February 5, 1856, JAQ Papers, HU; *Congressional Globe*, 34th Cong., 1st Sess., Appendix, 178. Quitman's busywork included looking to his own interests. On December 26 he applied to the Department of the Interior for a bounty land grant of 160 acres for his service in the Mexican War. Two days later he received the grant. Affidavit, December 26, 1855, Warrant No. 27301, Land Grant No. 3917, RG 15, Bounty Land Files, NA.

14. Minutes, Committee on Military Affairs, 34th Cong., 1st Sess., NA. Quitman cited his committee's heavy work load when requesting in the House that his committee be given a clerk. *Congressional Globe*, 34th Cong., 1st Sess., 477–78.

15. *Congressional Globe*, 34th Cong., 1st Sess., 509, 34th Cong., 2nd Sess., 225.

16. *Congressional Globe*, 34th Cong., 1st Sess., 641, 673, 764, 913; Minutes, April 10, 1856, Committee on Military Affairs, 34th Cong., 1st Sess., NA.

17. *Congressional Globe*, 34th Cong., 1st Sess., 522–23, 814, 984–85, 997, 1038, 2036; JAQ to Jefferson Davis, April 29, September 1, 2, 1856, Jefferson Davis to JAQ, May 6, 1856, RG 156, Records of the Chief of Ordnance, NA; Jane M. Cazneau to JAQ, March 12, 1856, JAQ Papers, MDA; Elmer Townsend to JAQ March 21, 1856, Claiborne Papers, MDA. For examples of Quitman's correspondence from army officers, see Joseph G. Totten to JAQ, February 23, 1856, Claiborne Papers, MDA; John Titcomb Sprague to JAQ, April 14, 1856, JAQ Papers, HU.

18. Reuben Davis to JAQ, January 12, 1856, Edward Pickett to JAQ, February 7, 1856, William A. Stone to JAQ, December 27, 1855, M. D. Haynes to JAQ, March 5, 1856, W. Grandin to JAQ, April 6, 1856, JAQ Papers, MDA; *Mississippi Senate Journal*, 1856, 342–43; James W. McDonald to JAQ, December 20, 1855, B. F. Dill to JAQ, December 5, 1855, JAQ Papers, HU; W. W. Wood to JAQ, December 27, 1855, James W. McDonald to J. F. H. Claiborne, February 16, 1856, Claiborne Papers, MDA; Louisa Quitman to JAQ, March 29, 1856, Quitman Family Papers, SHC; *Mississippi Free Trader* (Natchez), January 23, April 9, May 14, 1856; JAQ to F. Henry Quitman, January 26, April 10, 1856, JAQ Papers, HSP.

19. New York *Times*, February 23, 1856.

20. *Congressional Globe*, 34th Cong., 1st Sess., 1061, Appendix, 668–72; Thomas Harney to JAQ, March 7, 1856, JAQ Papers, MDA. Quitman was cut off by a time limit. The last part of his speech as printed was not actually given on the House floor.

21. *Congressional Globe*, 34th Cong., 1st Sess., 1081; *National Era* (Washington), June 19, 1856; James K. Paulding to JAQ, May 23, 1856, newspaper clipping, John Heiss MSS Scrapbook, Tennessee State Library and Archives, Nashville; Israel B. Bigelow to JAQ, April 26, 1856, JAQ Papers, MDA.

22. JAQ to Eliza Quitman, April 11, 1856, Lovell Family Papers, UnS; Vicksburg *Whig*, May 16, 17, 1856; Washington *Evening Star*, May 24, 1856; Annie Rosalie Quitman Diary, May 15, 21, 1856, Quitman Family Papers, SHC. Quitman was greeted at Natchez by homecoming ceremonies and apparently a group of rather inebriated well-wishers. Benjamin L. C. Wailes Diary, May 15, 1856 (Microfilm of typescript copy), DU.

23. *Congressional Globe*, 34th Cong., 1st Sess., 1628, Appendix, 529–44, 831–33; Potter, *Impending Crisis*, 209–211; David Donald, *Charles Sumner and the Coming of the Civil War* (New York, 1960), 278–311; Avery O. Craven, *The Coming of the Civil War* (New York, 1942), 374–77. Sumner did not return to his Senate duties on a regular basis for over three years.

24. Annie Rosalie Quitman Diary, June 4, August 6, 18, 1856, Quitman Family Papers, SHC; New York *Times*, August 23, 1856. Quitman had known Brooks during the Mexican War, when Brooks had served as captain of one of the companies in the Palmetto Regiment for part of the Mexico City campaign. After the caning incident, Quitman was reported acting as Brooks's second in duel negotiations with the editor of the New York *Courier and Enquirer* concerning remarks in the *Enquirer* about the assault. Baltimore *Sun*, May 27, 1856.

25. *Congressional Globe*, 34th Cong., 1st Sess., 1367–68. The House convened, took note of the lack of a quorum, and immediately adjourned.

26. Nevins, *Ordeal*, II, 424–28, 431–37, 472–76; James A. Rawley, *Race and Politics: "Bleeding Kansas" and the Coming of the Civil War* (Philadelphia, 1969), 122–23, 129–34.

27. JAQ to [?], March 24, 1856, quoted in *Mississippi Free Trader* (Natchez), October 29, 1860; Ethelbert Barksdale to William R. Cannon, May 9, 1856, William R. Cannon Papers, LC; Benjamin L. C. Wailes Diary, May 15, 1856, DU; Robert W. Johannsen, *Stephen A. Douglas* (New York, 1973), 530–32; Ivor Debenham Spencer, *The Victor and the Spoils: A Life of William L. Marcy* (Providence, 1959), 372. Quitman may have had a proprietary interest in Douglas' bill, as well as an ideological commitment to its principles. Prior to its introduction, he and Senator Brown had been reported as influencing Douglas behind the scenes. Johannsen, *Douglas*, 492.

28. Benjamin L. C. Wailes Diary, May 15, 1856, DU; Ethelbert Barksdale to William R. Cannon, May 9, 1856, William R. Cannon Papers, LC; C. R. Dickson to D. W. Haley, May 21, 1856, David W. Haley and Family Papers, MDA; Cincinnati *Daily Enquirer*, June 1, 1856; Nichols, *Disruption*, 27.

29. Cincinnati *Daily Enquirer*, June 1, 3, 1856; New York *Evening Post*, quoted in *National Era* (Washington), February 14, 1856; *Official Proceedings of the National Democratic Convention Held in Cincinnati, June 2–6, 1856* (Cincinnati, 1856), 3–9.

30. Nichols, *Disruption*, 25–28.

31. *Official Proceedings*, 61–67; JAQ to [?], June 8, 1856, William A. Richardson to JAQ, February 16, 1857, Quitman Family Papers, SHC; Washington *Evening Star*, June 6, 1856; William C. Davis, *Breckinridge: Statesman, Soldier, Symbol* (Baton Rouge, 1974), 139–46.

32. JAQ to [?], June 8, 1856, John D. McConnell to JAQ, June 13, 1856, Quitman Family Papers, SHC; Vicksburg *Whig*, September 30, 1856.

33. Washington *Evening Star*, June 19, 1856; Albert G. Brown to J. F. H. Claiborne, January 4, 1857, Claiborne Papers, MDA.

34. *Congressional Globe*, 34th Cong., 1st Sess., 1495–96.

35. *Ibid.*, 1539–41; Louisa Chadbourne to JAQ, June 24, 1856, Antonia Quitman to Eliza Quitman, June 24, 1856, Annie Rosalie Quitman Diary, June 24, July 4, 1856, Quitman Family Papers, SHC.

36. Annie Rosalie Quitman Diary, July 16, 1856, Quitman Family Papers, SHC; JAQ to F. Henry Quitman, August 10, 18, 1856, JAQ Papers, HSP.

37. John Brown to Joshua Giddings, February 20, 1856, Joshua Giddings Papers, Ohio Historical Society; *Congressional Globe*, 34th Cong., 1st Sess., 1749–58, 1788–96, 1811–14, 1873, 2037–38, 2198–99, 2239–40, 2nd Sess., 5–8. Quitman served on one of the House conference committees. He would, of course, have gone along with the Senate. But the other two members of the committee, to reflect the composition and sentiment of the House, were Republicans. *Congressional Globe*, 34th Cong., 1st Sess., 2182.

38. Robert E. May, *The Southern Dream of a Caribbean Empire, 1854–1861* (Baton Rouge, 1973), 104–106; Charles H. Brown, *Agents of Manifest Destiny: The Lives and Times of the Filibusters* (Chapel Hill, 1980), 343–47; Appleton Oaksmith to William Walker, September 9, 1856, Official Records of the Legation of Nicaragua (July-September, 1856, folder), Appleton Oaksmith Papers, DU.

39. Louisa Chadbourne to JAQ, July 13, 1856, Annie Rosalie Quitman Diary, July 19, 21, 25, 30, August 6, 7, 8, 1856, Quitman Family Papers, SHC; Nichols, *Disruption*, 147; Washington *Evening Star*, August 9, 1856; Margaret Leech, *Reveille in Washington, 1860–1865* (New York, 1941), 8.

40. *Congressional Globe*, 34th Cong., 2nd Ses., 81–85.

41. Annie Rosalie Quitman Diary, October 6, 18, 1856, JAQ to Eliza Quitman, September 13, 1856, Quitman Family Papers, SHC; "ANNUAL CIRCULAR OF THE MONTEZUMA SOCIETY," December [?], 1855, Letterbooks, Claiborne Papers, MDA.

42. New York *Times*, October 20, 1856; JAQ to William Walker, November 22, 1856, in T. Harry Williams (ed.), *With Beauregard in Mexico: The Mexican War Reminiscences of P. G. T. Beauregard* (Baton Rouge, 1956), 107–108; Appleton Oaksmith to JAQ, September 4, 1856; JAQ to G. W. Mimms *et al.*, October 21, 1856, JAQ Papers, HU; Potter, *Impending Crisis*, 261, 265. Quitman's comments to Walker were in a letter recommending P. G. T. Beauregard for a commission in Walker's army. Quitman posted his letter from New Orleans, where he apparently had run into Beauregard, who was frustrated with a dull army assignment as superintending engineer of the New Orleans customhouse. See J. Preston Moore, "Pierre Soulé: Southern Expansionist and Promoter," *Journal of Southern History*, XXI (1955), 207–217; T. Harry Williams, *P. G. T. Beauregard, Napoleon in Gray* (Baton Rouge, 1955), 39–43.

43. JAQ to Louisa Chadbourne, November 29, 1856, JAQ to Eliza Quitman, January 6, 1856 [1857], Quitman Family Papers, SHC; J. H. Gibbs to JAQ, August 27, 1857, Michael V. Cluskey to JAQ, October 5, 1857, JAQ Papers, MDA.

44. *Congressional Globe*, 34th Cong., 1st Sess., 178–79, 194, 232, 477, 604; *Senate Journal*, 34th Cong., 3rd Sess., 217, 294; Russell F. Weigley, *History of the United States Army* (New York, 1967), 169; Robert M. Utley, *Frontiersmen in Blue: The United States Army and the Indian, 1848–1865* (New York, 1967), 28–33; Winfield Scott to JAQ, February 24, 1857, Tampa *Peninsular*, n.d., quoted in *Mississippi Free Trader* (Natchez), April 17, 1856; [Major] D. H. Vinton to JAQ, June 27, 1857, JAQ Papers, HU.

45. *Congressional Globe*, 34th Cong., 3rd Sess., 56, 101, 173, 212–13, 232, 730, 740, 841, 842, Appendix, 118–22; James D. Richardson (comp.), *Messages and Papers of the Presidents, 1789–1904* (10 vols.; Washington, D.C., 1899–1904), V, 406–407. Quitman seems to have continued working behind the scenes in Walker's behalf. A press report in December noted his intervening with Secretary of State Marcy to allow one of Walker's reinforcement vessels, the *Tennessee*, to clear New York harbor. Federal officials subsequently did permit the ship to leave, but it suffered a broken shaft, put in at Norfolk, and never got to Nicaragua. Cincinnati *Daily Enquirer*, December 24, 1856; William O. Scroggs, *Filibusters and Financiers: The Story of William Walker and His Associates* (New York, 1916), 238–39.

46. *Congressional Globe*, 34th Cong., 3rd Sess., Appendix, 118–22.

47. Ronald T. Takaki, *A Pro-Slavery Crusade: The Agitation to Reopen the African Slave Trade* (New York, 1971), 1–85; *Congressional Globe*, 34th Cong., 3rd Sess., 123–26, Appendix, 120. Quitman emphasized that he did not personally desire the trade revived, but that his complaint was with "lectures" upon its morality which were intrinsic to the resolutions. He explained that renewal of the trade would actually hurt the "interests" of his "section." Presumably he meant either that new Africans would drive down the value of slave property of established planters like

himself, or that trade revival would increase the Deep South's black population to the point of creating demographic conditions favorable to servile revolt.

48. R. Barlow to JAQ, January 10, 1857, J. Foster Marshall to JAQ, February 24, 1858, JAQ Papers, HU; R. J. Fitz to JAQ, January 3, 1857, JAQ Papers, MDA. Quitman also contributed to the proslavery defense during the Thirty-fourth Congress by circulating a treatise which contended that blacks constituted an inferior race. John H. Van Evrie to JAQ, November 6, 1853, Claiborne Papers, MDA; F. R. Witter to JAQ, March 5, 1856, JAQ Papers, MDA; John H. Van Evrie, *Negroes and Negro "Slavery": The First an Inferior Race: The Latter Its Normal Condition* (New York, 1861).

49. *Congressional Globe*, 34th Cong., 3rd Sess., 995–96.

50. Philadelphia *Argus*, quoted in Memphis *Daily Appeal*, March 17, 1857; Nichols, *Disruption*, 83; Allan Nevins, *The Emergence of Lincoln* (2 vols.; New York, 1950), I, 87.

CHAPTER 23

1. New York *Herald*, July 2, 1854; Edward R. Welles Diary, June [?], 1855, Old Courthouse Museum, Vicksburg (Typescript copy courtesy of the editors of *The Papers of Jefferson Davis*); JAQ to F. Henry Quitman, March 14, 1857, JAQ Papers, HSP; Antonia Lovell Diary, March 18, 1857, Lovell Family Papers, UnS.

2. Washington *Evening Star*, January 20, 1857; Roy F. Nichols, *Franklin Pierce, Young Hickory of the Granite Hills* (Rev. ed.; Philadelphia, 1958), 497; Roy Franklin Nichols, *The Disruption of American Democracy* (New York, 1948), 75–76; Philip S. Klein, *President James Buchanan: A Biography* (University Park, Pa., 1962), 267–69.

3. Nichols, *Disruption*, 74–76; Albert G. Brown to J. F. H. Claiborne, January 4, 1857, J. F. H. Claiborne Papers, MDA; J. R. Harris to JAQ, January 5, 1857, JAQ Papers, MDA; New Orleans *Daily Delta*, January 7, 1857.

4. JAQ to F. Henry Quitman, February 27, 1858, JAQ Papers, HSP; JAQ to Louisa Chadbourne, September 8, 1857, Quitman Family Papers, SHC; Vicksburg *Whig*, July 31, 1858. Quitman may have suffered from an ailment apart from the "National Hotel disease." His emphasis upon leg pain rather than diarrhea suggests such a likelihood. However, he wrote in an August letter about being confined to bed for thirty hours by a "sudden disarrangement" of his bowels, indicating that all was not well with his digestive system. Quitman's self-diagnosis must have been based upon the timing of his visit and the similarity of his symptoms to those of other hotel visitors. Without countervailing evidence, it seems best to accept his evaluation. JAQ to F. Henry Quitman, March 14, August 5, 1857, March 14, 1858, JAQ Papers, HSP.

5. Annie Rosalie Quitman to F. Henry Quitman, March 22, 1857, Quitman Family Papers, M-N; JAQ to F. Henry Quitman, April 15, 1857, JAQ Papers, MDA; JAQ to F. Henry Quitman, July 29, 1857, JAQ Papers, HSP.

6. JAQ to Robertson Topp *et al.*, April 23, 1857, quoted in Memphis *Daily Appeal*, May 2, 1857; Caleb G. Forshey to JAQ, May 20, 1857, JAQ Papers, HU; Houma (La.) *Ceres*, May 16, 1857; JAQ to F. Henry Quitman, March 28, July 29, August 5, 1857, JAQ Papers, HSP; Annie Rosalie Quitman to F. Henry Quitman, May 3, 1857, JAQ Papers, MDA; JAQ to Eliza Quitman, May 19, 1857, Quitman Family Papers, SHC.

7. *Mississippi Free Trader* (Natchez), June 30, July 3, 14, 1857; David G. Sansing and Carroll Waller, *A History of the Mississippi Governor's Mansion* (Jackson, 1977), 43; Columbus (Miss.) *Democrat*, June 13, 1857; JAQ to Lawrence Keitt, July 23, 1857 (copy), Quitman Family Papers, SHC; JAQ to F. Henry Quitman, July 29, 1857, JAQ Papers, HSP.

8. David M. Potter, *The Impending Crisis, 1848–1861* (New York, 1976), 267–96, 298–301.

9. JAQ to Lawrence Keitt, July 23, 1857 (copy), Quitman Family Papers, SHC; JAQ to F. Henry Quitman, July 29, 1857, JAQ Papers, HSP.

10. *Mississippi Free Trader* (Natchez), July 24, September 4, 1857; JAQ to F. Henry Quitman, August 5, 1857, JAQ Papers, HSP. Despite his absence from the convention, the meeting assigned Quitman to a committee appointed to make recommendations to the *next* commercial convention regarding the reopening of the African slave trade. *Official Record of the Debates and Proceedings at the Southern Commercial Convention Assembled at Knoxville, Tennessee, August 10th, 1857* (Knoxville, 1857), Appendix.

11. Vicksburg *Whig*, May 16, 1855; *Mississippi Free Trader* (Natchez), September 4, 1857; JAQ to Eliza Quitman, September 5, 1857, JAQ to Louisa Chadbourne, September 8, 1857, JAQ to Annie Rosalie Quitman, September 16, 1857, Quitman Family Papers, SHC.

12. Quitman's reelection, which occurred in October, was not unanimous. Fifteen votes were cast for F. W. Adams in Jones County; eighteen were registered against Quitman in Adams County. There may have been a scattering of non-Quitman ballots elsewhere in the district. Election returns, Jones County, October 13, 1857, Secretary of State Records, RG 28, MDA; *Mississippi Free Trader* (Natchez), October 9, 1857; Michelle Hudson (Historian, Mississippi Department of Archives and History), to Robert E. May, October 27, 1982.

13. JAQ to Eliza Quitman, October 10, 1857, Quitman Family Papers, SHC.

14. JAQ to F. Henry Quitman, August 26, 27, 1856, July 27, November 17, 1857, JAQ Papers, HSP; JAQ to Eliza Quitman, November 11, 1857, Quitman Family Papers, SHC.

15. Louisa Chadbourne to Eliza Quitman, December 5, 1857, Antonia Quitman to Annie Rosalie Quitman, December 6, 1857, Antonia Quitman to Eliza Quitman, December 21, 1857, Lovell Family Papers, UnS. The Quitmans traveled almost entirely by rail, taking trains from Memphis to Portsmouth, Virginia, before catching a steamer for the capital.

16. James A. Rawley, *Race and Politics: "Bleeding Kansas" and the Coming of the Civil War* (Philadelphia, 1969), 214–15; JAQ to Eliza Quitman, December 21, 1857, Lovell Family Papers, UnS; JAQ to John Marshall, February 1, 1858, in J.F.H. Claiborne, *Life and Correspondence of John A. Quitman* (2 vols.; New York, 1860), II, 250–54.

17. Reuben Davis, *Recollections of Mississippi and Mississippians* (Rev. ed.; Hattiesburg, 1972), 369–71.

18. Roger A. Pryor to JAQ, November 2, 1857, JAQ to Reuben Davis, October 21, 1857, JAQ Papers, HU; Michael W. Cluskey to JAQ, August 24, 1857, JAQ Papers, MDA.

19. Allan Nevins, *The Emergence of Lincoln* (2 vols.; New York, 1950), I, 234–49; James D. Richardson (comp.), *Messages and Papers of the Presidents, 1789–1904* (10 vols.; Washington, D.C., 1899–1904), V, 449–54; Bruce W. Col-

lins, "The Democrats' Electoral Fortunes During the Lecompton Crisis," *Civil War History*, XXIV (1978), 318; Nichols, *Disruption*, 160.

20. *Congressional Globe*, 34th Cong., 1st Sess., 14–18, 53–56; Nevins, *Emergence of Lincoln*, I, 255.

21. Augustus R. Wright to Frank [?], December 18, 1857 (copy), Augustus Wright Papers, LC; JAQ to F. Henry Quitman, February 27, March 14, 1858, JAQ Papers, HSP; JAQ to John Marshall, February 1, 1858, in Claiborne, *Quitman*, II, 250–53; James Henry Hammond to Harry Hammond, January 14, 1858, James Henry Hammond Papers, South Caroliniana Library, University of South Carolina, Columbia.

22. *Congressional Globe*, 35th Cong., 1st Sess., 151–52.

23. JAQ to F. Henry Quitman, December 31, 1857, JAQ Papers, HSP; Antonia Quitman to Annie Rosalie Quitman, December 27, 31, 1857, Quitman Family Papers, SHC; New York *Times*, December 28, 1857; Cincinnati *Daily Enquirer*, January 1, 1858.

24. *Congressional Globe*, 35th Cong., 1st Sess., 178–82.

25. Richardson (comp.), *Messages and Papers of the Presidents*, V, 447–48; *Congressional Globe*, 35th Cong., 1st Sess., 194–96.

26. *Congressional Globe*, 35th Cong., 1st Sess., 197–202.

27. *Ibid.*, 207–301; Pittsburgh *Post*, January 18, 1858; Richardson (comp.), *Messages and Papers of the Presidents*, V, 471–81; Augustus Wright to Frank [?], March 4, and n.d., Augustus R. Wright Papers, LC; Emerich de Vattel, *The Law of Nations or the Principles of Natural Law, Applied to the Conduct and to the Affairs of Nations and of Sovereigns*, trans. Charles G. Fenwick (1758; rpr. New York, 1964), 137, 270. For a moderate southerner's dismay at Quitman's success in using the Paulding issue to radicalize southern opinion, see David Campbell to William B. Campbell, January 13, 1857 [1858], David Campbell Papers, Tennessee State Library and Archives, Nashville.

28. Potter, *Impending Crisis*, 318–19; *Congressional Globe*, 35th Cong., 1st Sess., 533–34.

29. *Congressional Globe*, 35th Cong., 1st Sess., 596–606; Cincinnati *Daily Enquirer*, February 10, 1858; James T. DuBois and Gertrude S. Mathews, *Galusha A. Grow: Father of the Homestead Law* (Boston, 1917), 173–76; Rawley, *Race and Politics*, 239–40; Nichols, *Disruption*, 161–65.

30. *Congressional Globe*, 35th Cong., 1st Sess., 622, 679; Nevins, *Emergence of Lincoln*, I, 288.

31. *Congressional Globe*, 35th Cong., 1st Sess., 814–15, 1423, 1435–38; Potter, Impending Crisis, 322–23; Nichols, *Disruption*, 167–70.

32. *Congressional Globe*, 35th Cong., 1st Sess., 182, 878; Ray Allen Billington, *The Far Western Frontier, 1830–1860* (New York, 1956), 212–16; Robert M. Utley, *Frontiersmen in Blue: The United States Army and the Indian, 1848–1865* (New York, 1967), 70–77, 125–28; Richardson (comp.), *Messages and Papers of the Presidents*, V, 456.

33. *Congressional Globe*, 35th Cong., 1st Sess., 1040, 1073, 1180.

34. *Ibid.*, 1007–1009, 1166–68, 1180–82.

35. *Ibid.*, 970–72, 1009, 1042, 1130, 1165, 1180, 1183–87. Quitman's passionate provolunteer oratory led one opponent, Sherrard Clemens of Virginia, to suggest that Quitman was out to glorify his own Mexican War reputation. Quitman immediately rejoined that he had commanded regulars as well as volunteers in that war. *Ibid.*, 1172.

36. *Ibid.*, 1188–89, 1474–76, 1564, 2560–62, 2591; W. J. Hughes, *Rebellious Ranger: Rip Ford and the Old Southwest* (Norman, 1964), 129–51; Nevins, *Emergence of Lincoln*, I, 323–24; Nichols, *Disruption*, 184–85.

37. *Congressional Globe*, 35th Cong., 1st Sess., 1573, 1595, 1839–40. Quitman also voted against Representative Justin S. Morrill's bill providing federal land grants to states for agricultural colleges. The bill passed the House, but failed to come to a vote in the Senate. *Ibid.*, 32, 1739–40, 2229. The pension bill offered federal support for veterans of the War of 1812 and the Indian conflicts of that period. Quitman admitted the logic of pensions for *needy* veterans, such as Revolutionary War soldiers who had been paid in worthless, inflated currency. But War of 1812 soldiers, he felt, had been better treated. In addition, he argued that the bill would subsidize soldiers who would not fight, such as New York militiamen in the War of 1812 who had refused to fight in Canada.

38. Antonia Quitman to Eliza Quitman, February 5, March 3, 1858, Louisa Chadbourne to Eliza Quitman, March 16, 1858, JAQ to Louisa Chadbourne, May 29, 1858, Quitman Family Papers, SHC; *Congressional Globe*, 35th Cong., 1st Sess., 714, 970, 2nd Sess., 229; Cincinnati *Daily Enquirer*, January 9, 1858.

39. *Congressional Globe*, 35th Cong., 1st Sess., 1573; Louisa Chadbourne to Eliza Quitman, January 26, February 23, 1858, Antonia Quitman to Eliza Quitman, March 3, 1858, Quitman Family Papers, SHC; Minutes, January-April, 1858, Committee on Military Affairs, 35th Cong., 1st Sess., NA; JAQ to John B. Floyd, January 20, 1858, RG 156, Records of the Chief of Ordnance, NA.

40. Louisa Chadbourne to Eliza Quitman, February 23, March 3, 7, 1858, Louisa Chadbourne to Annie Rosalie Quitman, January 8, 1858, Antonia Quitman to Eliza Quitman, January 23, March 3, 1858, Winfield Scott to JAQ, May 14, 1858, Quitman Family Papers, SHC; Guy M. Bryan to Laura Jack, May 8, 1858, Guy M. Bryan Papers, UT; *Congressional Globe*, 35th Cong., 2nd Sess., 228, 231. Jacob Thompson later attributed Quitman's charm to his being easy to approach, affable, and committed to his beliefs. Mansfield Lovell, more to the point, remembered that Quitman had been firm, not harsh, and understanding of the failings of others, and that he inspired "especially in his younger friends a confiding reliance and affectionate regard, much akin to the holy feeling that should exist between child and parent." *Mississippi Free Trader* (Natchez), August 27, 1858; Mansfield Lovell to Eliza Quitman, July 20, 1858, Quitman Family Papers, SHC.

41. Antonia Quitman to Annie Rosalie Quitman, December 31, 1857, Antonia Quitman to Eliza Quitman, January 23, 1858, Louisa Chadbourne to Annie Rosalie Quitman, January 8, 1858, Louisa Chadbourne to Eliza Quitman, January 26, 1858, Quitman Family Papers, SHC.

42. JAQ to F. Henry Quitman, March 14, 1858, JAQ Papers, HSP; Antonia Quitman to Annie Rosalie Quitman, December 19, 1858, Louisa Chadbourne to Annie Rosalie Quitman, March 3, 1858, Antonia Quitman to Eliza Quitman, February 5, 1858, Quitman Family Papers, SHC; Louisa S. Quitman to Louisa Chadbourne, January 30, 1858, JAQ Papers, LSU; Edward W. Callahan (comp.), *List of Officers of the Navy of the United States and of the Marine Corps from 1775 to 1900* (New York, 1901), 339.

43. Louisa Chadbourne to Eliza Quitman, March 7, 14, 1858, JAQ to Eliza Quitman, March 28, 1858, Louisa Chadbourne to JAQ, May 16, 1858, JAQ to Louisa Chadbourne, May 29, 1858, Quitman Family Papers, SHC.

44. *Congressional Globe*, 35th Cong., 1st Sess., 1627, 1765–66; Potter, *Impending Crisis*, 323–24; Nevins, *Emergence of Lincoln*, I, 297–98.

45. *Congressional Globe*, 35th Cong., 1st Sess., 1889–90.

46. Nichols, *Disruption*, 179; Memphis *Daily Appeal*, July 20, 1858. According to the *Appeal*, Buchanan asked Quitman to an interview and tried to alter Quitman's position, but Quitman proved so resolute that Buchanan finally declared, "You are right Gen. Quitman, both of us are now too old to sacrifice what we regard as our sense of duty."

47. *Congressional Globe*, 35th Cong., 1st Sess., 1900, 1905–1906; William Storrow Lovell to Antonia Quitman, May 8, 1858, Lovell Family Papers, UnS. Joining Quitman in opposition, in addition to Republicans, were four border state Know-Nothings and eleven anti-Lecompton northern Democrats. David E. Meerse, "The Northern Democratic Party and the Congressional Elections of 1858," *Civil War History*, XIX (1973), 125n.

48. J. Foster Marshall to JAQ, February 24, 1858, JAQ Papers, HU; *Mississippi Free Trader* (Natchez), May 21, 1858; Claiborne, *Quitman*, II, 277, 280–84, 366–79. Originally the celebration was scheduled for May 14, but the committee of arrangements altered the date to May 4 to accommodate Quitman. William B. Stanley to Milledge L. Bonham, March 29, 1858, Milledge L. Bonham Papers, South Caroliniana Library.

49. JAQ to Louisa Chadbourne, May 29, 1858, Quitman Family Papers, SHC; William Cannon and W. W. W. Wood to JAQ, May 19, 1858, JAQ to William Cannon and W. W. W. Wood, May 30, 1858, JAQ Papers, MDA.

50. *Congressional Globe*, 35th Cong., 1st Sess., 2094–95, 2274, 2394, 2395, 2440–41, 2472, 2814–15, 2906–2907, 2975. Appalled by the way the whole Lecompton business had been handled, Quitman did on May 17 introduce a resolution that henceforth *no* territory should be considered for statehood until it contained a population adequate to justify one representative in Congress. However, enough of his colleagues wanted to prevent a revival of the Kansas imbroglio that the House refused to suspend the rules so that his motion could be considered. *Ibid.*, 2187, 2196; *National Era* (Washington), April 29, 1858.

51. Claiborne, *Quitman*, II, 285; JAQ to W. W. W. Wood, June 30, 1858, Samuel A. Cartwright to J. F. H. Claiborne, April 20, 1859, Claiborne Papers, MDA; Antonia Lovell to Louisa Lovell, June 29, 1859, Quitman Family Papers, SHC. It is impossible to pinpoint exactly when Quitman fell ill again, but it may have occurred around June 11. On that date, for reasons left unexplained, his committee voted that he step down as chairman. Minutes, June 11, 1858, Committee on Military Affairs, 35th Cong., 1st Sess., NA.

52. Samuel A. Cartwright to J. F. H. Claiborne, April 20, 1859, Claiborne Papers, MDA; Vicksburg *Whig*, July 15, 1858; Louisa Chadbourne to Joseph Lovell, November 24, 1858, Quitman Family Papers, SHC; Claiborne, *Quitman*, II, 287–91.

53. *Mississippi Free Trader* (Natchez), July 20, 23, 24, 31, August 27, 30, September 9, 1858; Vicksburg *Whig*, July 15, 1858; William Porcher Miles to B. F. DeBow, August 18, 1858, William P. Miles Misc. MSS, South Carolina Historical Society, Charleston.

EPILOGUE

1. Henry S. Foote to Howell Cobb, July 9, 1851, Ulrich Bonnell Phillips (ed.), "The Correspondence of Robert Toombs, Alexander H. Stephens, and Howell Cobb," *Annual Report of the American Historical Association for the Year 1911* (2 vols.; Washington, 1913), II, 242; William L. Barney, *The Secessionist Impulse: Alabama and Mississippi in 1860* (Princeton, 1974), 15–26, 163–88.

2. "Table of the Payne & Turner families made by Henry Fielding Turner, May 29, 1893," JAQ Papers, MDA; Louisa Lovell to Joseph Lovell, January 27, 1861, Joseph Lovell to Louisa Lovell, September 9, 1861, August 19, 1864, Annie Rosalie Quitman to Louisa Lovell, April 4, 1861, Antonia Lovell to Annie Rosalie Duncan, June 24, 1861, Antonia Lovell to Louisa Lovell, July 2, 1861, Special Orders No. 20 (January 28, 1862) and 86 (March 14, 1862), Confederate War Department orders, dated March 18, 1862, Antonia Lovell, "The Story of Isaac" [dated April 26, 1897], handwritten pamphlet, Quitman Family Papers, SHC; Antonia Lovell Diary, June 21, 1863, "Family Record," Lovell Family Papers, UnS; Edward Turner to F. Henry Quitman, August 23, 1859, Mary Quitman to her mother, May 24, [1861], F. Henry Quitman to Mary Quitman, October 1, 1862, October 7, 1863, Quitman Family Papers, M-N; *Journal of the Congress of the Confederate States of America, 1861–1865* (1904–1905; rpr. 7 vols., Washington, D.C., 1968), III, 664, IV, 238, 248–49; William S. Lovell to J. R. Waddy, November 2, 1862, *The War of the Rebellion: A Compilation of the Official Records of the Union and Confederate Armies* (130 vols.; Washington, D.C., 1880–1901), Ser. I, Vol. XV, pp. 852–53; Edwin C. Bearss, *Decision in Mississippi* (Jackson, 1962), 399; Rosalie Quitman Duncan, "Life of General John A. Quitman," *PMHS*, IV (1901), 423.

3. Duncan, "Life of General John A. Quitman," 423; Antonia Lovell, "The Story of Isaac," Quitman Family Papers, SHC.

4. James S. Palmer to John Hunter, May 12, 1862, John Hunter to James S. Palmer, May 13, 1862, C. G. Dahlgren to Thomas Jordan, May 17, 1862, *Official Records of the Union and Confederate Navies in the Civil War* (31 vols.; Washington, D.C., 1894–1922), Ser. I, Vol. XVIII, pp. 490–91, 494–96; Annie Rosalie Quitman Diary, August 8, 1863, Quitman Family Papers, SHC; Duncan, "Life of General John A. Quitman," 415n.

5. John L. Adams deposition, March 27, 1863, Louisa Lovell to Joseph Lovell, March 8, 1864, Quitman Family Papers, SHC; Stephen Joseph Ross, "Freed Soil, Freed Labor, Freed Men: John Eaton and the Davis Bend Experiment," *Journal of Southern History*, XLIV (1978), 212–32; Special Orders No. 15 of Adjutant General Lorenzo Thomas, March 28, 1864, James T. Currie, *Enclave: Vicksburg and Her Plantations, 1863–1870* (Jackson, 1980), 92; Henry Rowntree to "Esteemed Friends," April 13, 1864, RG 105, Records of the Bureau of Refugees, Freedmen and Abandoned Lands, Mississippi, NA; Janet Sharp Hermann, *The Pursuit of a Dream* (New York, 1981), 49–50.

6. John A. Keith to Benjamin F. Butler, May 22, 1862, R. A. Cameron to George B. Drake, July 22, 1864, B. B. Campbell to C. L. Harris, July 22, 1864, *Official Records of the Union and Confederate Armies*, Ser. I, Vol. XV, pp. 450–51, Vol. XVI, Pt. 2, p. 328; Inventory of Live Oaks, October 7, 1864, Louisa S. Quitman to F. Henry Quitman, March 8, 1866, Quitman Family Papers, M-N; Louisa Lovell to Joseph Lovell, April 9, 1865, Quitman Family Papers, SHC; Richard Taylor, *De-*

struction and Reconstruction: Personal Experiences of the Late War, ed. Richard B. Harwell (New York, 1955), 133–34; A. J. H. Duganne, *Twenty Months in the Department of the Gulf* (New York, 1865), 54–56, 124–37; Charles P. Roland, *Louisiana Sugar Plantations During the American Civil War* (Leiden, 1957), 49.

7. Duncan, "Life of General John A. Quitman," 423; Annie Rosalie Quitman Diary, August 8, 1863, Louisa Quitman to Joseph Lovell, February 7, 1864, Quitman Family Papers, SHC; [Hosea W. Rood], *Story of the Service of Company E, and of the Twelfth Wisconsin Regiment of Veteran Volunteer Infantry, in the War of the Rebellion* (Milwaukee, 1893), 220.

8. Louisa Quitman to Joseph Lovell, July 28, 1861, Quitman Family Papers, SHC. Similarly, Rosalie commented that February on the obvious "sincerity" of Palmyra's blacks. Annie Rosalie Quitman to William P. Duncan, February 11, 1861, Quitman Family Papers, SHC.

9. Louisa Lovell to Joseph Lovell, September 21, October 9, 1861, April 9, 1865, Quitman Family Papers, SHC; F. Henry Quitman to Mary Quitman, July 6, 1863, Quitman Family Papers, M-N.

10. Antonia Lovell, "Story of Isaac," Louisa Lovell to Joseph Lovell, August 17, 1863, February 7, August 29, 1864, February 4, 1865, Quitman Family Papers, SHC; Edwin L. Hobart, "History of the 58th U.S.C. Infantry," in Hobart, *Semi-History of a Boy-Veteran of the Twenty-eighth Regiment Illinois Infantry Volunteers* . . . (Denver [?], 1909), 1–16.

11. Louisa Lovell to Joseph Lovell, June 12, 1864, Clipping, dated July, 1903, "H. Turner Memorandum Book," Quitman Family Papers, SHC; Joseph Lovell to Louisa Lovell, October 16, 1866, JAQ Papers, LSU; William Storrow Lovell to Eliza Quitman, December 7, 1879, Lovell Family Papers; William Storrow Lovell gravestone, Natchez City Cemetery; Michael Stuart Wayne, "Ante-Bellum Planters in the Post-Bellum South: The Natchez District, 1860–1880" (Ph.D. dissertation, Yale University, 1979), 195–97; Chicago *Tribune*, May 7, 1879.

12. Louisa Lovell to Joseph Lovell, June 29, 1861, February 7, March 8, 1864, April 9, 1865, Quitman Family Papers, SHC; F. Henry Quitman to Mary Quitman, September 1, 1864, Quitman Family Papers, M-N; Antonia Lovell Diary, March 20, April 11, October 27, 1865, Lovell Family Papers, UnS.

13. JAQ gravestone, Natchez City Cemetery.

Index

Index

Johannsen, Robert W., 200
Johnson, Reverdy, 202
Johnson, William: and JAQ and Mississippi
  Railroad Company, 94; relations with
  JAQ, 144; anticipates JAQ's defeat, 387;
  mentioned, 86, 94, 97, 384
Johnston, Albert Sidney, 341
Jones, George W., 313
Jones, Roger, 149
Jordan, Thomas M., 431
Junta Cubana, 237

Kansas: difficulties in, 306, 321–22, 329–
  30, 351; as congressional issue, 307–11,
  322, 323, 330, 334–35, 337–40 passim,
  346–47
Kansas-Nebraska Act: provisions of, 282–
  83; impact on JAQ's Cuba filibuster, 283,
  293–94; and political realignment, 297,
  299, 301–302; JAQ's possible influ-
  ence upon, 444; mentioned, 309, 314,
  330, 435
Kaufman, David, 79, 148, 386
Kearny, Stephen W., 150
Keitt, Lawrence: and JAQ and Walker-
  Paulding affair, 336; brawl with Galusha
  Grow, 339; mentioned, 330, 341
Kendall, Amos, 96
Kenner, Duncan, 279
Kent, James, 217, 316
Ker, John, 114
King, William R., 266, 268
Kinney, Henry L, 154–55, 438–39
Knight, John, 134
Know-Nothing party, 296–304 passim,
  441. See also Quitman, John Anthony:
  congressman

Lafayette, Marquis de, 30, 316
Lake, William A., 442
Lamar, C. A. L., 280, 289, 291
La Sère, Emile, 279, 282, 291, 319
Lea, Luke, 221, 225, 260
Lecompton Constitution, 331–51 passim
Lee, Robert E., 183, 189
Lesesne, Joseph White, 280, 281–82,
  284, 285
Lind, Jenny, 250–51, 427
Live Oaks plantation: JAQ purchases, 42–
  43; JAQ develops, 43–44; black popula-
  tion density in vicinity of, 47; economy
  of, 131–32, 135; management of, 136–
  37, 138, 140, 397; slavery at, 138, 140;
  Quitman family visits, 144; JAQ turns

over to son, 290; new house constructed
  at, 303; hurricane damage at, 332; in
  Civil War, 353, 354; mentioned, 128,
  133, 134, 273, 329, 397
Lone Star, Order of the, 271
López, Narciso: invites JAQ to join filibuster, 236, 237–38; failure of first filibuster, 236–37; JAQ's involvement with,
  238–39, 248, 252, 262; arrest of, 240–
  41; death of, 252; mentioned, 271, 272,
  274
Loring, William W., 192
Love, Robert O., 137, 142, 398
Lovejoy, Owen, 337
Lovell, Alice, 353
Lovell, Joe, 352, 353, 354
Lovell, Mansfield: becomes JAQ's aide,
  164; at Mexico City, 189, 194; in Montezuma Society, 199; and JAQ and Cuba
  filibusters, 238, 274, 277, 290, 292, 293;
  on JAQ's personality, 449; mentioned,
  207, 345, 411
Lovell, William Storrow: marries JAQ's
  daughter, 345–46, 349; in Civil War,
  352, 354; mentioned, 347
Lynch, Charles, 68, 69, 382

McCaleb, Theodore H., 240, 248, 251
McClung, Alexander K., 158, 290
McClure, James, 303, 306
McDonald, James W., 255, 277, 278, 279,
  292
Macías, Manuel, 289
McLendon, James H., 370
McLeod, Hugh, 280, 290
McMurran, John, Jr., 150
McMurran, John T.: and JAQ in Ohio, 12;
  moves to Mississippi, 22; partnership
  with JAQ, 33, 78, 109; marriage, 33,
  374; and JAQ's plantation school, 114;
  visits JAQ, 150; defends JAQ at filibuster
  trial, 251; land consortium with JAQ,
  387; close friendship with Eliza Quitman,
  391; mentioned, 38, 115, 180, 431, 432
McMurran, Mary, 141
McNeil, Henry C., 376
McNutt, Alexander G.: revokes Mississippi
  Railroad Company's banking privileges,
  105; as governor and repudiator, 116–17;
  JAQ throws influence against, 119; com-
  petes with JAQ for Senate seat, 123–28,
  395; and JAQ's vice-presidential aspirations, 209; offers JAQ judicial vacancy,
  390; mentioned, 212

457

459